D0081153

LESBIAN SOURCES

GARLAND GAY AND LESBIAN STUDIES
(VOL. 9)

GARLAND REFERENCE LIBRARY
OF THE HUMANITIES
(VOL. 1557)

GARLAND
GAY AND LESBIAN STUDIES

General Editor: Wayne R. Dynes

LESBIAN SOURCES
A Bibliography
of Periodical Articles
1970 - 1990

Linda Garber

GARLAND PUBLISHING, INC. • NEW YORK & LONDON
1993

Library of Congress Cataloging-in-Publication Data

Garber, Linda.
  Lesbian sources : a bibliography of periodical articles, 1970–1990 / Linda
Garber.
      p.   cm. — (Garland reference library of the humanities ; vol. 1557)
(Garland gay and lesbian studies ; vol. 9)
    ISBN 0-8153-0782-9 (alk. paper)
    1. Lesbianism—Bibliography. 2. Lesbianism—Periodicals—
Bibliography. 3. Lesbians—Bibliography. I. Title. II. Series. III. Series:
Garland gay and lesbian studies ; vol. 9.
Z5866.L44G37   1993
[HQ75.5]
016.30548'9664—dc20   92-21941
                                                                            CIP

Printed on acid-free, 250-year-life paper
Manufactured in the United States of America

This book is dedicated to Barbara Blinick
because it led to our first date

Contents

BIBLIOGRAPHY AND CROSS-REFERENCES

Abortion
    See Reproduction

Abuse
    See Child Abuse; Incest; Sexual Harassment; Substance Abuse
    and Recovery; Violence Against Lesbians and Gay Men;
    Violence Against Women; Violence Among Lesbians

    See Also: Child Custody; Foster Care; Parenting

Foreword

In a half century our understanding of homosexual behavior has been transformed. During the 1940s psychiatric and medical approaches dominated the subject. When not simply characterized as social pathology, same-sex behavior still ranked as an aberration, something to be overcome. Hence the emphasis on therapy or "cures." Even then, though, change was in the air. The two Kinsey Reports of 1948 and 1953 not only revealed that the incidence of homosexual activity was much greater than previously thought but, by adopting neutral, nonjudgmental terminology, suggested that it lay within the normal range of human experience. This implicit assumption found confirmation in the research of a psychologist, Dr. Evelyn Hooker, who showed that using a random sample chosen from the general population—instead of the clinical sample routinely employed at that time—the performance of homosexual subjects on objective tests was indistinguishable from that of heterosexual ones. In retrospect, the most startling innovation was the founding of the homophile movement by Henry Hay and others in Los Angeles in 1950. Bedeviled by growing pains and the hostile climate engendered by the McCarthyite trend, the movement evolved slowly. In 1969, however, in a climate of social ferment conditioned by the Civil Rights movement and opposition to the Vietnam War, the homophile movement turned a corner, a development symbolized by the Stonewall Riots in New York City.

The ensuing decades saw not only a torrent of publications but also a decisive shift in the center of gravity. Major works that could not be ignored now appeared under the authorship of open, proud gay men and lesbians. No longer was gay life described as a remote, exotic phenomenon, but directly by those who had actually experienced it and who had no hesitation in saying so. "They" yielded to "we." In an effort to correct previous distortions, some of these writings erred on the side of advocacy. Today, however, thanks to the mingling of many voices, a balance is being struck that is moving rapidly toward consensus. Another shift was away from present-minded social science toward a new emphasis on cultural themes. Gay men and lesbians, it was increasingly recognized, had made immense contributions to the worlds of literature and drama, art and music, film and photography. Scholars could chart the role of the sexuality of many creative figures. Moreover, scrutiny of records from other societies—Islam, China, and Japan, as well as a host of tribal cultures known from the field work of ethnographers—signaled the need for an understanding of same-sex behavior as a worldwide phenomenon. The new climate of acceptance revitalized the older approaches of sociology and psychology. Even those in the natural sciences, which insofar as they had addressed the subject at all were hostile, reentered the arena with interesting though often still speculative contributions in the realms of sociobiology and constitutional biology.

Although the new research rightly seeks to overcome older negative approaches, questions of value persist. A survey of the history of the subject shows that in addition to ascertaining the facts of same-sex behavior and its cultural expression, it is essential to scrutinize attitudes toward it. All too often these have been disparaging—they have reflected facets of homophobia, the irrational dislike of sexual attraction between members of the same sex. While some scholars have contented them-selves with tracing and recording the influence of these adversarial views, others have felt compelled to refute them. As in women's studies and black studies, this sense of a need to correct the record leads to a perceived departure from older ideals of dispassionate objectivity. Yet now that the more vehement expressions of outrage have passed, it is possible to see that a passion for justice is not incompatible with an objective search for truth.

Today the panorama of studies in the field is a rich one, and it is becoming richer still. In all likelihood, however, the subject of sexuality, linked as it is to so many other spheres of human aspiration, is inexhaustible.

The conception of this series is deliberately pluralistic. Some volumes collect representative papers or articles together with critical commentary by the editor to bring a current issue into focus. Other books are substantial monographs reconsidering major aspects of the field. Intersecting with these two categories are research manuals, sometimes overtly bibliographic and sometimes more discursive, which serve as critical tools for advancing work in the field.

Linda Garber is a lesbian scholar and feminist bookseller living in the Bay Area. The rich material she has gathered for her book is a stunning proof of the research progress that has been achieved.

Wayne R. Dynes

Preface

Linda Garber

Lesbian Sources is a cross-referenced bibliography of articles
written by and/or about lesbians and published in nationally- or
internationally-distributed periodicals between 1970 and 1990.
Comprehensive as it sounds, and weighty as the final volume is, the
bibliography is not exhaustive. Rather, it is intended only as a guide to
materials readily available in major library collections, or through standard
inter-library loan services.

On the other hand, "only" understates the case. Standard reference
guides, from the *Readers' Guide* to newer computer databases, have never
facilitated lesbian studies research. While it is possible to find "lesbian" as
a subject heading in some indexes and bibliographies, it is often difficult
to proceed with more detailed research. The researcher usually must look
up each reference to "lesbian" in order to discern the specific topic of an
article. *Lesbian Sources* illustrates that "lesbian" is not a single topic, but
an entire field of study.

Subject categories in *Lesbian Sources* include standard academic
topics such as history, literature, and anthropology, but also incorporate
and in some instances favor topics of specific interest to lesbian culture.
For example, the researcher consulting "Eating Disorders" is referred to
"Body Image," and from there to "Fat Liberation." The sociologist
certainly should consult "Sociology," but also is advised to seek
information under specific categories, from "Fashion" and "Music
Festivals" to "Parenting" and "Work."

Major subject categories are further divided into pertinent sub-
topics, usually by a person's name or by geographical region. After six
pages of general citations under "Literature: Prose" come 24 pages of
listings about authors from "Alcott, Louisa May" to "Yuasa, Yoshiko."
Articles about individuals are included only if they specifically address
lesbian identity or concerns. The article about Louisa May Alcott, titled

"The Borders of Ethical, Erotic, and Artistic Possibilities in *Little Women,*" qualifies; an essay about a lesbian writer that ignores her lesbianism or fails to address lesbian themes in her writing does not. Inclusion of one's name in this bibliography does not always indicate that she is or was a lesbian; it only means that she has been written about from a lesbian studies perspective, or that she did or wrote something of significance to lesbians, as defined by the author of a journal article.

Subject categories with geographical subdivisions are either geographical themselves (e.g., "Lesbians Around the World"), or are concerned with legal issues (e.g., "Domestic Partnership"; "Foster Care") and the progress of court cases or legislation in particular countries, regions, or states. Each article is listed in as many subject categories as apply; for example, an entry that is an interview with an African-American poet appearing at a benefit in London would be listed under four categories: "African-American Lesbians" (poet's name), "Interview" (poet's name), "Lesbians Around the World" (England), and "Poetry" (poet's name).

Subject categories posed the most difficult problems in compiling *Lesbian Sources.* For example, during the four years it took to research the bibliography, "Black" lesbians began using the term "African-American," and the "USSR" dissolved on the evening news. In the first instance, the solution was simple: researchers looking for "Black Lesbians" are instructed to "See African-American Lesbians." Geographical shifts were not so easily redirected. Articles published before 1991 about lesbians in the former Soviet Union are in fact talking about the "USSR," and the same goes for East Germany, West Germany, etc. Thus, sub-topics under the main category "Lesbians Around the World" reflect national boundaries that existed from 1970 to 1990.

Several lesbians, experts in their own ways about academic and/or political concerns, helped name and rename subject categories as they evolved from 1987 to 1991; in addition, terms used in journal articles helped determine subject headings. The intent is always to use the label currently in most widespread use among the lesbians who are defined by that label, while correctly directing researchers who search for an older or lesser-used term.

After the ongoing problem of language, the scope of the bibliography was the most difficult decision in shaping *Lesbian Sources.* This bibliography consciously does not repeat the work done by Clare Potter's *Lesbian Periodicals Index* (Naiad Press, 1986), which includes citations for 42 lesbian periodicals published in the 1970s, from *Amazon Quarterly* to *Wicce.* Potter's index includes material that is most easily found in feminist or lesbian archives, which also hold many of the periodicals included in *Lesbian Sources*. (See page xlv for a list of archives.) Some of the feminist and lesbian periodicals collected by community archives are available in major libraries in the "Women's Herstory Microfilm Collection" -- an invaluable source with an unfortunately difficult indexing system. Researchers also will find useful J.R. Roberts' *Black Lesbians: an Annotated Bibliography* (Naiad Press, 1981), and Barbara Grier's *The Lesbian in Literature* (Naiad Press, 1981), in addition to the bibliographies of varying length that accompany most major books of lesbian studies research.

Because *Lesbian Sources* does not attempt to cover archival material, it may be only a starting place for some in-depth lesbian studies projects. Would that our lesbian communities and cultures were more fully represented in major library collections! Nevertheless, this volume is a testament to the surprisingly large number of lesbian and feminist periodicals available to researchers who do not have easy access to archives.

Lesbian Sources begins with 1970, when lesbian culture, fueled by the Women's Liberation Movement and the Stonewall Uprising, exploded in a burst of publishing. Prior to 1970, much of the widely-distributed literature about lesbians was hostile and misinformed. An exception is *The Ladder,* the magazine of the lesbian homophile organization The Daughters of Bilitis. Available in the Women's Herstory Microfilm Collection, *The Ladder* was published from 1956-1972 and is a gold mine for research into a particular political history of an otherwise virtually silent time.

For both practical and political reasons, the only newspapers included in *Lesbian Sources* are the feminist publications *New Directions for Women* and *off our backs*. These two newspapers cover lesbian news from a feminist perspective, unlike mainstream newspapers. (To find mainstream newspapers' coverage of lesbian issues, researchers can consult traditional reference guides, where they will encounter the lack of specificity discussed above.) *New Directions* and *off our backs* are available in major libraries; unfortunately, Boston-based *Sojourner* currently is not as easily available.

Two important publications whose weekly publication schedules made them impossible to index here are *The Advocate* and *Gay Community News*. *Lesbian Sources* leaves it to future bibliographers to undertake the monumental job of mining gay/lesbian periodicals -- usually predominantly focused on gay men -- for the wealth of information by and about lesbians that may exist there. (The exception is *Out/Look,* a 3-year-old, quarterly gay/lesbian magazine, which is indexed in *Lesbian Sources*.)

A list of periodicals indexed in *Lesbian Sources* (non-fiction articles only) can be found on page xxxiii. In addition, this bibliography relies on and adds information to citations listed under "Lesbian" in traditional and feminist reference sources, including the *Alternative Press Index, Arts and Humanities Citation Index,* Dialog computer database, *Feminist Periodicals: a Current Listing of Contents, MLA Bibliography, Studies on Women Abstracts,* and *Women's Studies Abstracts.*

Sample Citation

Citations take the following form:
Author of article. "Title of Article" (brief annotation, if necessary). *Title of Periodical* (Country of Publication if other than United States), "Special Issue Title, if applicable" Vol:Issue # (Date):page number.

Sample Citation:
Amana, Rue. "Becoming a 'Real' Dyke: Employment and Housing" (moving out of cities as the lesbian dream; returning to cities to work with People With AIDS). *Canadian Woman Studies* (Canada), "Women & Housing" 11:2 (Fall 1990):43+.

Acknowledgments

It would have been impossible to create *Lesbian Sources* without the support of talented and patient librarians. I would especially like to thank the reference, inter-library loan, and current periodicals librarians of Stanford University's Green Library; Diane Hamer of the Schlesinger Library at Radcliffe College; Bill Walker of the Gay and Lesbian Historical Society of Northern California; and Judith Schwarz of the Lesbian Herstory Archives in New York.

Others deserve thanks for moral and emotional support: Peg Cruikshank, who blazed the path, personally pointed the way, and has become a dear friend; Lillian Faderman, who provided encouragement at a crucial point and a gracious introductory essay in the end; Terry Castle and Diane Middlebrook, who continue to advise me through a lesbian graduate career at Stanford; and Leonard and Sylvia Garber, the best folks a dyke could hope for, who have always offered love, encouragement, and material support.

I have not completed a project in the last decade without my Friend Elizabeth Hutchison propping me up, generally commiserating, and telling me what I was thinking all along. And finally, thanks to my lover Barbara Blinick, who endured the final year of this sometimes enervating, sometimes exhilarating project, and who has brought new joy to my life.

Introduction

Lillian Faderman

The emergence of both a gay liberation movement and a feminist movement in the late 1960s soon led to the burgeoning of a unique lesbian culture that was reflected in scores of periodicals devoted to feminism, women, and gay and lesbian life. Over a period of twenty years (1970-1990) the written material dealing with lesbianism proliferated tremendously, reflecting every aspect of life as it affects lesbians: ageing, art, body image, class, economics, fashion, health, language, legal systems, media, parenting, spirituality, etc. Where does the researcher who is interested in working on such lesbian topics begin? This volume is an excellent place.

The scholar interested in lesbian studies has had to do double duty in pursuing her research. Unlike scholars in most other areas, she could not go to a generalized bibliography such as *The Reader's Guide to Periodical Literature,* nor to a specialized resource such as the *MLA Bibliography,* and look up her topic with much hope of reward. "Lesbian" is seldom a subject heading in most bibliographies, and when it is the listings are generally few and very limited. The most useful journals for the lesbian researcher's purpose, those that focus exclusively on lesbians and/or feminists -- such as *Conditions: A Magazine of Writing by Women with an Emphasis on Writing by Lesbians, Lesbian Ethics* or *Refractory Girl* -- seldom find their way into those bibliographies.

To be thorough in her research, the lesbian scholar of the past, at a great disadvantage compared to those who were doing more traditional research, would laboriously go through the table of contents of each issue of as many lesbian and feminist journals as she could locate, to see if by some chance they contained anything pertinent to her topic. Unless she lived in the vicinity of lesbian archives which house large collections of lesbian periodicals, such as the New York Lesbian Herstory Archives or the Los Angeles June Mazer Lesbian Collection, what she could discover was undoubtedly sparse. And unlike researchers in other areas, she had little opportunity to utilize efficiently the wonderful national inter-library loan service in order to obtain periodicals not available in her vicinity, because she could not know what to request, in which particular journal issues she would find the material pertinent to her subject.

But this publication of Linda Garber's *Lesbian Sources: A Bibliography of Periodical Articles, 1970-1990* promises the alleviation of such major difficulties. It will guarantee the lesbian studies researcher that her preliminary detective work in locating crucial sources will be far less time-consuming and frustrating. It will help her achieve a thoroughness in researching lesbian subject matter that has been extremely difficult earlier, since bibliographic aids have been scarce and inadequate. Its 162 subject headings will facilitate the exploration of specific topics and also will help the student of lesbian studies discover which topics lend themselves to research because of availability of material and which do not.

Lesbian Sources will be the most useful volume in the lesbian researcher's library. It will change the way all scholars of lesbian studies do research.

List of Periodicals Indexed

Affilia: Journal of Women and Social Work   Quarterly
Vol. 1, no. 1 - vol. 5, no. 4 (Spring 1986-Winter 1990)
Prof. Betty Sancier
School of Social Welfare
Box 786
University of Wisconsin - Milwaukee
Milwaukee, WI 53201

Atlantis: a Women's Studies Journal/Journal d'Études Sur la Femme 2x/yr
Vol. 1, no. 1 - vol. 16, no. 1 (Fall 1975-Fall 1990)
 Mount Saint Vincent University
166 Bedford Highway
Halifax, Nova Scotia
B3M 2J6
Canada

Belles Lettres   Quarterly
Vol. 1, no. 1 - vol. 6, no. 1
(September/October 1985-Fall 1990)
11151 Captain's Walk Court
North Potomac, MD 20878-0441

Black/Out   Quarterly
Vol. 1, no. 1 - vol. 2, no. 2 (Summer 1986-Summer 1989)
National Coalition of Black Lesbians and Gays (NCBLG)
19641 West Seven Mile
Detroit, MI 48219

Camera Obscura: a Journal of Feminism and Film Theory　　3x/yr
Number 1 - 23 (Fall 1976-May 1990)
Rush Rhees Library
University of Rochester
Rochester, NY 14627

Canadian Woman Studies/Les Cahiers de la Femme　　Quarterly
Vol. 1, no. 1 - vol. 11, no. 2 (1978-Fall 1990)
Inanna Publications and Education, Inc.
212 Founders College, York University
4700 Keele Street
Downsview, Ontario
M3J 1P3
Canada

Chrysalis, a Magazine of Women's Culture　　(defunct)
Number 1 - 10 (1977-c.Winter 1980)
Los Angeles, CA

Common Lives/Lesbian Lives　　Quarterly
Number one - thirty-six (1981-Fall 1990)
P.O. Box 1553
Iowa City, IA 52244

Conditions: a Feminist Magazine of Writing by Women　　(defunct)
with an Emphasis on Writing by Lesbians
Number one - seventeen (1977-1990)
P.O Box 150056
Van Brunt Station
Brooklyn, NY 11215-0001

Connexions　　Quarterly
Number 0 - 34 (1981-1990)
People's Translation Service
4228 Telegraph Avenue
Oakland, CA 94609

Differences　　3x/yr
Vol. 1, no. 1 - vol. 2, no. 3 (Winter 1989-Fall 1990)
Box 1958
Brown University
Providence, RI 02912

Feminisms 6x/yr
Vol. 1, no. 1 - vol. 3, no. 6 (Winter 1988-November/December 1990)
Center for Women's Studies, Ohio State University
207 Dulles Hall
230 W. 17th Ave.
Columbus, OH 43210

Feminist Issues 2x/yr
Vol. 1, no. 1 - vol. 10, no. 2 (Summer 1980-Fall 1990)
2948 Hillegass
Berkeley, CA 94705

Feminist Review 3x/yr
Number 1 - 36 (1979-Autumn 1990)
11 Carleton Gardens
Brecknock Road
London, England N19 5AQ

Feminist Studies 3x/yr
Vol. 1, no. 1 - vol. 16, no. 3 (1975-Fall 1990)
c/o Women's Studies Program
University of Maryland
College Park, MD 20742

Fireweed: a Feminist Quarterly Quarterly
Number 1 - 31 (Autumn 1978-Fall 1990)
P.O. Box 279, Station B
Toronto, Ontario M5T 2W2
Canada

Frontiers: a Journal of Women's Studies 3x/yr
Vol. 1, no. 1 - vol. 11, no. 2 & 3 (Fall 1975-1990)
Mesa Vista Hall 2142
University of New Mexico
Albuquerque, New Mexico 87131

Gender & History   3x/yr
Vol. 1, no. 1 - vol. 2, no. 3 (Spring 1989-Autumn 1990)
Leonore Davidoff, Editor
Dept. of Sociology
University of Essex
Colchester CO4 3SQ
England
or
Nancy Hewitt
Dept. of History
University of South Florida
Tampa, FL 33620

Gender & Society   Quarterly
Vol. 1, no. 1 - vol. 4, no. 4 (March 1987-December 1990)
Prof. Margaret Andersen
Dept. of Sociology
University of Delaware
Newark, DE 19716

Genders   3x/yr
Numbers 1 - 9 (March 1988-Fall 1990)
Ann Kibbey, Editor
Dept. of English
Campus Box 226
University of Colorado at Boulder
Boulder, CO 80309

Gossip   (defunct)
Number 1 - 6 (1986-c.1987)
Onlywomen Press
London, England

Hecate: a Women's Interdisciplinary Journal   2x/yr
Vol. 1, no. 1 - vol. 16, no. 1/2 (January 1975-1990)
P.O. Box 99
St Lucia
Brisbane, Queensland 4067
Australia

Helicon Nine: the Journal of Women's Arts and Letters   (defunct)
Number 1 - 20 (Spring/Summer 1979-1989)
P.O. Box 22412
Kansas City, MO 64113

Heresies: a Feminist Publication on Art and Politics   2x/yr
Issue #1, vol. 1, no. 1 - issue #25, vol. 7, no. 1
(January 1977-1990)
P.O. Box 1306
Canal Street Station
New York, NY 10013

Hot Wire: a Journal of Women's Music and Culture   3x/yr
Vol. 1, no. 1 - vol. 6, no.3 (November 1984-September 1990)
c/o Empty Closet Enterprises
5210 N. Wayne
Chicago, IL 60640

Hypatia: a Journal of Feminist Philosophy   3x/yr
(originally published as Special Issue of
Women's Studies International Forum in 1983;
first three issues of *Hypatia* were *WSIF* vol. 6, no. 6;
vol. 7, no. 5; and vol. 8, no. 3)
Vol. 1, no. 1 - vol. 5, no. 3 (Spring 1986-Fall 1990)
Editor, Hypatia
Southern Illinois University at Edwardsville
Edwardsville, IL 62026-1437

International Journal of Women's Studies   (defunct)
Vol. 1, no. 1 - vol. 8, no. 5
(January/February 1978-November/December 1985)

Journal of Feminist Family Therapy   Quarterly
Vol. 1, no. 1 - vol. 2, nos. 3/4 (1989-1990)
The Haworth Press
10 Alice Street
Binghamton, NY 13904

Journal of Feminist Studies in Religion   2x/yr
Vol. 1, no. 1 - vol. 6, no. 2 (Spring 1985-Fall 1990)
Elizabeth Lemons
Harvard Divinity School
45 Francis Avenue
Cambridge, MA 02138

Journal of Homosexuality   Quarterly
Vol. 1, no. 1 - vol. 19, no. 4 (1974-1990)
John P. DeCecco
Center for Research and Education in Sexuality
San Francisco State University
San Francisco, CA 94132

Journal of the History of Sexuality   Quarterly
Vol. 1, no. 1 - 2 (July 1990-April 1990)
Bard College
Annandale-on-Hudson, NY 12504

Journal of Women & Aging   Quarterly
Vol. 1, no. 1/2/3 - vol. 2, no. 4 (1989-1990)
J. Dianne Garner, editor
Dept. of Social Work
Washburn University
Topeka, KS 66621

Journal of Women's History   3x/yr
Vol. 1, no. 1 - vol. 2, no. 2 (Spring 1989-Fall 1990)
History Dept., Ballantine Hall
Indiana University
Bloomington, IN 47405

Kalliope: a Journal of Women's Art   3x/yr
Vol. 1, no. 1 - Vol. 12, no. 3 (Winter 1979-1990)
Florida Community College
3939 Roosevelt Blvd.
Jacksonville, FL 32205

Lesbian Ethics   2x/yr
Vol. 1, no. 1 - vol. 4, no.1 (Fall 1984-Spring 1990)
LE Publications
P.O Box 4723
Albuquerque, NM 87196

Lilith: the Jewish Women's Magazine   Quarterly
Vol. 1, no. 1 - vol. 15, no. 1 (Fall 1976-Winter 1990/5750)
250 W. 57th Street
New York, NY 10107

Moving Out: Feminist Literary & Arts Journal   (defunct)
Vol. 1, no. 1 - vol. 14, nos. 1&2 (1971-1989)
P.O. Box 21249
Detroit, MI 48221

Ms. Magazine   (defunct)
Vol. 1, no. 1 - vol. 18, no. 5 (July 1972-November 1989)

Ms. Magazine: The World of Women   6x/yr
Vol. 1, no. 1 ("Premier Issue 1990") - vol. 1, no. 3
(July 1990-November/December 1990)
Lang Communications, Inc.
One Times Square
New York, NY 10036

New Directions for Women   6x/yr
Vol. 1, no. 1 - vol. 19, no. 6
(January 1972-November/December 1990)
108 West Palisade Avenue
Englewood, NJ 07631

NWSA Journal: Quarterly
a Publication of the National Women's Studies Association
Vol. 1, no. 1 - vol. 2, no. 4 (Autumn 1988-Autumn 1990)
1070 Carmack Road
038 Pressey Hall
The Ohio State University
Columbus, OH 43210-1002

off our backs   Monthly, except September
Vol. 1, no. 1- vol. 20, no. 11
(February 27, 1970-December 1990)
2423 18th St., NW
Washington, D.C. 20009-2003

Out/Look   Quarterly
Vol. 1, no. 1 - Number 10, vol. 3, no. 2
(Spring 1988-Fall 1990)
2940 - 16th Street, Suite 319
San Francisco, CA 94103

Phoebe: an Interdisciplinary Journal of Feminist Scholarship,   2x/yr
Theory and Aesthetics
Vol. 1, no. 1 - vol. 2, no. 2 (February 1989-Fall 1990)
c/o Women's Studies Program
SUNY Oneonta
Oneonta, NY 13820-4015

Psychology of Women Quarterly   Quarterly
Vol. 1, no. 1 - vol. 14, no. 4 (Fall 1976-December 1990)
237 Dickey Hall
University of Kentucky
Lexington, KY 40506-0017

Quest: a Feminist Quarterly   (defunct)
Vol. 1, no. 1 - vol. 5, no. 4 (Summer 1974-1982)
Washington, DC

Radical Teacher: a Socialist and Feminist Journal   3x/yr
on the Theory and Practice of Teaching
Number 1 - 38 (December 1975-Summer 1990)
Boston Women's Teachers' Group
P.O. Box 102
Cambridge, MA 02142

Refractory Girl   (defunct)
No. 1 - 22 (Summer 1972/73-May 1981)
Women's Studies Group
25 Alberta St.
Sydney, NSW 2000
Australia

Resources for Feminist Research/Documentation Sur   Quarterly
la Recherche Féministe
(formerly *Canadian Newsletter of Research on Women*)
Vol. 8, no. 1 - vol. 19, no. 3&4
(March 1979-September/December 1990)
Ontario Institute for Studies in Education
252 Bloor Street West
Toronto, Ontario M5S 1V6
Canada

Sage: a Scholarly Journal on Black Women   2x/yr
Vol. 1, no. 1 - vol. 6, no. 2 (Spring 1984-Fall 1989)
P.O. Box 42741
Atlanta, GA 30311

Signs: Journal of Women in Culture and Society   Quarterly
Vol. 1, no. 1 - vol. 16, no. 1 (Autumn 1975-Autumn 1990)
Center for Advanced Feminist Studies
495 Ford Hall
University of Minnesota
Minneapolis, MN 55455

Sinister Wisdom   Quarterly
Number 1 - 42 (July 1976-Winter 1990/91)
P.O. Box 3252
Berkeley, CA 94703

Spare Rib   Monthly
Numbers 1 - 219 (July 1972-December/January 1990/91)
27 Clerkenwell Close
London, England EC1R 0AT

Trivia   3x/yr
Number 1 - 16/17 (Fall 1982-1990)
P.O. Box 606
N. Amherst, MA 01059

Tulsa Studies in Women's Literature   2x/yr
Vol. 1, no. 1 - vol. 9, no. 2 (Spring 1982-Fall 1990)
600 South College
Tulsa, OK 74104

Visibilities   6x/yr
Vol. 1, no. 1 - vol. 4, no. 6
(January/February 1987-November/December 1990)
P.O. Box 1169
Olney, MD 29830-1169

Woman of Power: Quarterly
a Magazine of Feminism, Spirituality, and Politics
Issue one - eighteen (1984-Fall 1990)
P.O. Box 827
Cambridge, MA 02238-9990

Women & Language   2x/yr
(formerly *Women & Language News,*
from vol. 1, no. 1 - vol. 8, no. 23)
Vol. 1, no. 1 - vol. 13, no. 2 (January 1978-Winter 1990)
Anita Taylor, Executive Editor
Communication Dept.
George Mason University
Fairfax, VA 22030

Women & Therapy: a Feminist Quarterly   Quarterly
Vol. 1, no. 1 - vol. 10, no. 4 (Spring 1982-1990)
Esther D. Rothblum, Ph.D.
Co-Editor, Women & Therapy
Dept. of Psychology, John Dewey Hall
University of Vermont
Burlington, VT 05405

Women's Studies: an Interdisciplinary Journal   Quarterly
Number 1 - vol. 18, no. 2-3 (1973-1990)
Wendy Martin, Editor
Women's Studies
Dept. of English
Queens College, CUNY
Flushing, NY 11367

Women's Studies International Forum   6x/year
(formerly *Women's Studies International Quarterly*)
Vol. 5, no. 1 - vol. 13, no. 6 (1982-1990)
Sue V. Rossen and Charlotte Hogsett
Women's Studies
University of South Carolina
1710 College Street
Columbia, SC 29208
or
Christine Zmroczek, Managing Editor
8 St. Martin's Street
Brighton
East Sussex, BN2 3HJ
England

Women's Studies Newsletter
(becomes *Women's Studies Quarterly*)
Vol. 1, no. 1 - vol. 8, no. 4 (Fall 1972-Fall/Winter 1980)
The Feminist Press at the City University of New York
311 East 94 St.
New York, NY 10128

Women's Studies Quarterly   Quarterly
(formerly *Women's Studies Newsletter*)
Vol. 9, no. 1 - vol. 18, no. 3&4 (1981-Fall/Winter 1990)
The Feminist Press at the City University of New York
311 East 94 St.
New York, NY 10128-5603

13th Moon   (defunct)
Vol. 1 - 8 (1973-1984)
New York, NY

List of Archives

The articles listed in *Lesbian Sources* are published in journals that are available in major U.S. university and municipal libraries, and through those libraries' inter-library loan services. Special lesbian and gay collections exist at the City University of New York, Cornell University, Duke University, and at Harvard/Radcliffe in the Schlesinger Library at Radcliffe College, as well as in the New York Public Library. The San Francisco Public Library is expected to open its lesbian and gay collection in 1995 or 1996.

Many of the journals indexed in *Lesbian Sources* are also available at the regional archives listed below. In addition, archives are an invaluable source for material that is not collected by mainstream libraries. This list is by no means exhaustive; it focuses on U.S. archives that contain substantial holdings of lesbian and feminist periodicals and includes archives around the world that may not hold periodicals published in English.

United States

California
Gay and Lesbian Historical Society of Northern California Archives
(GLHS/NC Archives)
Box 42126
San Francisco, CA 94142

International Gay and Lesbian Archives (IGLA)
Box 38100
Los Angeles, CA 90038

June Mazer Lesbian Collection
626 North Robertson Blvd.
W. Hollywood, CA 90069

Lesbian/Gay Archives of San Diego
Box 4186
San Diego, CA 92104

Florida
Lesbian and Gay Archives of Naiad Press
Box 10543
Tallahassee, FL 32302

Stonewall Library and Archives
c/o Holy Spirit MCC
330 SW 27 Street
Fort Lauderdale, FL 33315

Georgia
Atlanta Lesbian Feminist Alliance (ALFA)
Library Committee
Box 5502
Atlanta, GA 30307

Illinois
Gerber/Hart Library and Archives
3352 North Paulina Street
Chicago, IL 60657

Kentucky
Kentucky Collection of Lesbian Herstory
Box 1701
Louisville, KY 40203

Massachusetts
New Alexandria Lesbian Library
Box 402, Florence Station
Northampton, MA 01060-0402

Women's Movement Archives and Library
46 Pleasant Street
Cambridge, MA 02139

Minnesota
Quatrefoil Library
1619 Dayton Ave.
St. Paul, MN 55104

New York
Herizon Archives
Box 1082
Binghamton, NY 13902

Lesbian Herstory Archives
Box 1258
New York, NY 10116

National Museum of Lesbian and Gay History
208 - 13th Street
New York, NY 10011

Oregon
Douglas County Gay Archives
Box 942
Dillard, OR 97432

Pennsylvania
Lesbian and Gay Library and Archives
Box 15748
Philadelphia, PA 19103

Texas
Dallas Gay/Lesbian Historic Archives
6146 St. Moritz
Dallas, TX 75214

Metropolitan Community Church Library
1919 Decatur
Houston, TX 77007

Tennessee
TLA
c/o Teresa Hornsby
303 Kennon Road
Knoxville, TN 37909

Virginia
Gay and Lesbian Archives of Washington DC
Box 4218
Falls Church, VA 22044

International

Australia
Australian Gay Archives
Box 124
Parkville, 3052

Queensland Gay Archives
GPO Box 2030
Brisbane, 4001

Belgium
Federatie Werkgroepen Homofilie
Dambruggestraat 204
B-2008 Antwerpen

Canada
Canadian Gay Archives
Box 639, Station A
Toronto, Ontario
M5W 1G2

Gay Archives Collective
P.O. Box 3130 MPO
Vancouver, BC
U6B 3X6

Denmark
Archiv for bosser og lesbiske
Forbundet af 1948
Postboks 1023
DK-1007 Kobenhavn K

England
Hall-Carpenter Memorial Archives
67-69 Cowcross St.
London EC1M 6BP

Lesbian Archive and Information Centre (LAIC)
BCM Box 7005
London WC1N 3XX

France
Archives, Recherches et Cultures Lesbiennes
Boite Postale 622
75531 Paris Cedex 11

Germany
Spinnboden - Lesbenarchiv
Burgsdorfstr. 1
1000 Berlin 65

Ireland
Gay Community Archives
c/o Hirschfeld Centre
10 Fownes St.
Dublin 2, Ireland

Women's News
185 Donegall St.
Belfast, BT1 2FJ
N. Ireland

Italy
ALI (Archivi Lesbici Italiani)
Via San Francesco di Sales 1A
I - 00165 Rome

Il Centro Cassero
CP 691
40100 Bologna

Japan
Regumi Studio
Nakazawa Building 3F
32 Araki-cho
Shinjuku-ku
Tokyo, 161

The Netherlands
Dokumentatiecentrum Homostudies (Homodok)
Oudezijds Achterburgwal 185
NL - 1012 DK Amsterdam

International Informatiecentrum en Archief voor de Vrouwenbeweging
Keizersgracht 10
1015 CN Amsterdam

Lesbisch Archief Amsterdam
Eerste Helmersstr. 17 I
1054 CX Amsterdam

New Zealand
Lesbian and Gay Archives of New Zealand
c/o Phil Parkinson
Box 11-695, Manners St P.O.
Wellington

New Zealand Lesbian Archives
c/o Windeler
Taylor Rd., R.D. 1
Hamilton

Spain
Pilar Lopez Diez
"La Mujer Feminista"
Calle Almagro 28
Madrid 28010

Yugoslavia
Lezbiska Sekcija
c/o SKUC SKUC-Forum
Kersnikova 4
61000 Ljubljana

Lesbian Sources

<u>Abortion</u> (see Reproduction)

<u>Abuse</u> (see Child Abuse; Incest; Sexual Harassment; Substance Abuse
   and Recovery; Violence Against Lesbians and Gay Men;
   Violence Against Women; Violence Among Lesbians)

Acquired Immune Deficiency Syndrome (AIDS)

Amana, Rue. "Becoming a 'Real' Dyke: Employment and Housing"
   (moving out of cities as the lesbian dream; returning to cities to
   work with People With AIDS). *Canadian Woman Studies*
   (Canada), "Women & Housing" 11:2 (Fall 1990):43+.

". . . and Lesbian Transmission?" *Science News* 131 (January 3, 1987):8.

Appleman, Rose and Linda Kahn. "Lesbians Face AIDS on Several
   Fronts." *New Directions for Women* 18:3 (May/June 1989):12.

Apuzzo, Virginia M. "Brand X: Why We Need to Be More Generic" ("Is
   this a movement for social change, or is it a movement to make
   it okay to be gay or lesbian?" -- part of "Messages to the
   Movement . . . Where We Are Twenty Years After Stonewall").
   Out/Look #5, 2:1 (Summer 1980):60-1.

"Australia: Gay Immigration Curb." *off our backs* 20:4 (April 1990):6.

Biller, Ray and Susan Rice. "Experiencing Multiple Loss of Persons with
   AIDS: Grief and Bereavement Issues." *Health and Social Work*
   15:4 (November 1990):283-90.

"Britain: a New Intimacy" (bisexual women write about AIDS and sexual
   practices, from *Bisexual Lives* (England) (1988)). *Connexions,*
   "Women and AIDS" 33 (1990):26.

"Britain: 'Pass the Clingfilm, Dear!'" (plastic wrap as safe sex
   paraphernalia; from *Square Peg,* England, 1987). *Connexions,*
   "Women and AIDS" 33(1990):28.

Chiaramonte, Lee. "Lesbian Safety and AIDS: the Very Last Fairy Tale." *Visibilities* 2:1 (January/February 1988):4-9.

DAR. "Lesbians & AIDS" (survey in Minnesota/St. Paul area about how informed lesbians feel they are). *off our backs* 18:8 (August-September 1988):5.

Einhorn, Lena. "New Data on Lesbians and AIDS." *off our backs* 19:4 (April 1989):10.

Eskenazi, B., C. Pies, A. Newstetter, C. Shepard, and K. Pearson. "HIV Serology in Artificially Inseminated Lesbians." *Journal of Acquired Immune Deficiency Syndromes* 2:2 (1989):187-93.

Foty, Caroline. "Orange County Cancels Lesbian Blood Drive." *off our backs* 15:4 (April 1985):2.

Gessen, Masha. "We Have No Sex: Soviet Gays and AIDS in the Era of Glasnost." *Out/Look #9,* 3:1 (Summer 1990):42-54.

Green, Frankie and Vicky Ryder. "Some Thoughts on AIDS" (response to Vada Hart, "Lesbians and AIDS," *Gossip* (Great Britain) 2 (1986):90-6). *Gossip* 4 (no date):40-3.

Hart, Vada. "Lesbians and AIDS." *Gossip* (Great Britain) 2 (1986):90-6.

Hutchins, Loraine. "Colevia Carter -- Women and AIDS" (interview with activist, member of AIDS outreach program of the National Coalition of Black Lesbians and Gays). *off our backs* 17:1 (January 1987):20-1.

Johnson, Lynell. "Women of Color and AIDS." *Black/Out,* "Tenth Anniversary Edition: NCBLG Celebrates Homecoming" (National Coalition of Black Lesbians and Gays) 2:1 (Fall 1988):27-8.

Juhasz, Alexandra. "The Contained Threat: Women in Mainstream AIDS Documentary." *Journal of Sex Research* 27:1 (February 1990):25-46.

Kaspar, Barbara. "Women and AIDS: a Psycho-Social Perspective." *Affilia* 4:4 (Winter 1989):7-22.

Kelly, Janis. "The Global Impact of AIDS on Women" (includes section on "lesbians and AIDS"). *off our backs* 18:8 (August-September 1988):20-1.

Kulp, Denise. "On Working with My Brothers: Why a Lesbian Does AIDS Work." *off our backs* 18:8 (August-September 1988):22.

Kvaleng, Inger Marie, Elizabeth Bjørk, and Berit Rossvold. "When Penis Equals Sexuality" (trans. from Norwegian lesbian quarterly, *Kvinnejournalen*, 1987). *Connexions*, "Women and AIDS" 33 (1990):11-12.

Laws, Sophie. (letter responding to Vada Hart, "Lesbians and AIDS," *Gossip* (Great Britain) 2 (1986):90-6). *Gossip* 5 (no date):7-11.

"Lesbian Blood Victory" (Nottingham Lesbian Line and others succeed in overturning refusal of lesbian blood donors at the National Blood Transfusion Service in England). *Spare Rib* (Great Britain) 170 (September 1986):47.

Marx, Sabine. "Desire Cannot Be Fragmented" (trans. and excerpted from West German feminist quarterly, *Tarantel*, 1988). *Connexions*, "Women and AIDS" 33 (1990):6-9.

Miller, Barbara. "AIDS -- Should We Care?" *Spare Rib* (Great Britain) 141 (April 1984):28.

Morganthau, Tom, et al. "Gay America in Transition; a Turning Point Has Been Reached, and AIDS May Mean the Party Is Over" (mostly about gay men). *Newsweek* 102 (August 8, 1983):30-8.

Murray, Marea. "AIDS Update: Lesbians." *off our backs* 17:5 (May 1987):15.

"Nicaragua: Moving Forward Together" (interview with Sandinista activist Rita Arauz about AIDS activism and education in Nicaragua). *Connexions,* "Women and AIDS" 33 (1990):13.

Oikawa, Mona. "Safer Sex in Santa Cruz" (workshop at the First National Asian/Pacifica Lesbian Network Retreat, Santa Cruz, California, 1989). *Fireweed* (Canada), "Awakening Thunder: Asian Canadian Women" 30 (February 1990):31-4.

O'Sullivan, Sue. "Mapping: Lesbians, AIDS and Sexuality -- an Interview with Cindy Patton" (author of *Sex and Germs: The Politics of AIDS*). *Feminist Review* (Great Britain), "Perverse Politics: Lesbian Issues" 34 (Spring 1990):120-33.

Parker, Jan. "Lesbians -- Laying Down the Law" (how present laws affect lesbians; why lesbian/gay rights legislation is important for everyone). *Spare Rib* (Great Britain) 175 (February 1987):15-19.

Pearson, Hunter. "'Why Aren't You Out Dancing?'" (caring for people with AIDS, written by a 23-year-old lesbian volunteer support worker). *Out/Look* 1:1 (Spring 1988):75-7.

Richardson, Diane. "Lesbians and AIDS." *Women's World* 18 (1982):21.

Robinson, Bryan E., Lynda Henley Walters, and Patsy Skeen. "Response of Parents to Learning That Their Child Is Homosexual and Concern Over AIDS: a National Study" (of 402 parents of lesbians and gay men). *Journal of Homosexuality,* "Homosexuality and the Family" 18:1/2 (1989):59-80.

Russell, Tanya G. "AIDS Education, Homosexuality, and the Counselor's Role." *School Counselor* 36:5 (May 1989):333-7.

Schwanberg, Sandra L. "Attitudes Towards Homosexuality in American Health Care Literature 1983-1987." *Journal of Homosexuality* 19:3 (1990):117-36.

Segrest, Mab. "Southern Reflections: Nothing Can Stop Us Now! But From What?" (keynote address to 12th annual Southeastern Lesbian and Gay Conference, Atlanta, Georgia, 1988). *Out/Look* 1:4 (Winter 1989):10-15.

Sorella, Naja. "A/part of the Community" (environmental illness, and the fact that "Lesbians put their . . . energy into AIDS" and not into other chronic illness as well). *Sinister Wisdom*, "On Disability" 39 (Winter 1989-90):104-7.

Stato, Joanne. "I Am Your Sister Celeconference: Tribute to Audre Lorde" (Boston, Massachusetts, October 1990). *off our backs* 20:11 (December 1990):1-5+.

Stowe, Ayofemi. "Black Women and AIDS." *Black/Out*, "Tenth Anniversary Edition: NCBLG Celebrates Homecoming" (National Coalition of Black Lesbians and Gays) 2:1 (Fall 1988):33+.

Watstein, Sarah Barbara. "Because AIDS Is: a Report on a 'Women and AIDS' Conference." *Visibilities* 4:2 (March/April 1990):10-11.

------. "Documenting the Undocumented -- Films and Videos on Women and AIDS." *Visibilities* 4:5 (September/October 1990):20-1.

Winnow, Jackie. "Lesbians Working on AIDS: Assessing the Impact on Health Care for Women." *Out/Look #5*, 2:1 (Summer 1989):10-18.

AIDS Coalition to Unleash Power (ACT-UP):
"ACT-UP" (plans for London chapter of the the AIDS Coalition to Unleash Power, U.S. activist organization; includes discussion of women's participation). *Spare Rib* (Great Britain) 197 (December 1988/January 1989):18-19.

"New York: Cathedral Demo" (St. Patrick's Cathedral, New York City, December 1989). *off our backs* 20:3 (March 1990):13.

The Women's Caucus of ACT-UP. "ACT UP on AIDS" (letter
debunking misconceptions about women/lesbians and AIDS by
members of the AIDS Coalition to Unleash Power). *off our
backs* 18:9 (October 1988):22-3.

OUTRAGE (Great Britain):
"OUTRAGE: New Lesbian and Gay Direct Action Group" (modeled
after U.S. AIDS Coalition to Unleash Power (ACT-UP)). *Spare
Rib* (Great Britain) 214 (July 1990):43.

Adolescent Lesbians

Andrews, Jane. "Don't Pass Us By: Keeping Lesbian and Gay Issues on
the Agenda." *Gender and Education* 2:3 (1990):351-5.

Bird, Jenny. "Young People and Sex." *Healthright: a Journal of Women's
Health, Family Planning, and Sexuality* 2 (February 1983):45-
6+.

Borhek, Mary V. "Helping Gay and Lesbian Adolescents and Their
Families" (with psychotherapy). *Journal of Adolescent Health
Care* 9:2 (March 1988):123-8.

Boxer, Andrew M. and Bertram J. Cohler. "The Life Course of Gay and
Lesbian Youth: an Immodest Proposal for the Study of Lives."
Journal of Homosexuality, "Gay and Lesbian Youth: Part II"
17:3/4 (1989):315-44.

Bronwen. "Life Is Just a Phase I'm Going Through" (coming out as a
lesbian at school). *Spare Rib* (Great Britain) 115 (February
1982):54-5.

Browning, Christine. "Therapeutic Issues and Intervention Strategies with
Young Adult Lesbian Clients: a Developmental Approach."
Journal of Homosexuality, "Psychotherapy with Homosexual
Men and Women: Integrated Identity Approaches for Clinical
Practice" 14:1/2 (1987):45-52.

CAD. "Passages: Aging Lesbians Meet" (keynote speech by Charlotte
Bunch; Washington, D.C., March 1990). *off our backs* 20:5
(May 1990):8.

Ching, C.L. "Adolescent Homosexual Behavior and the Health Educator."
Journal of School Health 50 (November 1980):517-21.

Coleman, E. and G. Remafedi. "Gay, Lesbian, and Bisexual Adolescents
-- a Critical Challenge to Counselors." *Journal of Counseling
and Development* 68:1 (1989):36-40.

Cooper, Margaret. "Rejecting 'Femininity': Some Research Notes on
Gender Identity Development in Lesbians." *Deviant Behavior*
11:4 (October-December 1990):371-80.

"Dancing Forward" (two young women attend high school prom together
in Carnation, Washington). *off our backs* 20:8
(August/September 1990):6.

Devlin, Diane. "The Plight of the Gay Student" (confrontations with high
school and college officials). *off our backs* 1:6 (May 30,
1970):11.

Garden, Nancy. "Annie on My Mind" (article by author of this book
about two teenage lesbians). *Hotwire* 4:3 (July 1988):46-7.

Gerstel, Camille J., Andrew J. Feraios, and Gilbert Herdt. "Widening
Circles: an Ethnographic Profile of a Youth Group" (Chicago
Gay and Lesbian Youth Project). *Journal of Homosexuality,*
"Gay and Lesbian Youth: Part I" 17:1/2 (1989):75-92.

Goddemaer, Nicky. "The 'She Wolf'" (personal account of incarceration in
Belgian juvenile hall). *Connexions,* "Women Inside and Out" 14
(Fall 1984):18-19.

Gonsiorek, John C. "Mental Health Issues of Gay and Lesbian
Adolescents." *Journal of Adolescent Health Care* 9:2 (March
1988):114-22.

Hetrick, Emery S. and A. Damien Martin. "Developmental Issues and Their Resolution for Gay and Lesbian Adolescents." *Journal of Homosexuality*, "Psychotherapy with Homosexual Men and Women: Integrated Identity Approaches for Clinical Practice" 14:1/2 (1987):25-44.

"High School Dyketactics" (Philadelphia lesbian group, Dyketactics, demonstrate at high school where lesbian students and alumni were harassed). *off our backs* 6:5 (July-August 1976):13.

Hunter, Joyce. "Violence Against Lesbian and Gay Male Youths" (especially people of color, and related suicide attempts). *Journal of Interpersonal Violence* 5:3 (1990):295-300.

Journal of Homosexuality, "Gay and Lesbian Youth: Part I," vol. 17, nos. 1/2, 1989.

------, "Gay and Lesbian Youth: Part II," vol. 17, nos. 3/4, 1989.

Kourany, Ronald F.C. "Suicide Among Homosexual Adolescents." *Journal of Homosexuality* 13:4 (Summer 1987):111-8.

Krysiak, Gloria J. "A Very Silent and Gay Minority." *School Counselor* 34:4 (March 1987):304-7.

LeBitoux, Jean. "To Be Twenty and Homosexual in France Today." *Journal of Homosexuality*, "Gay and Lesbian Youth: Part II" 17:3/4 (1989):291-8.

Lenskyj, Helen. "Beyond Plumbing and Prevention: Feminist Approaches to Sex Education." *Gender and Education* 2:2 (1990):217-30.

------. "Often Invisible: Conference on Counselling Gay and Lesbian Youth" (Toronto, Ontario, Canada, March 29, 1989). *Resources for Feminist Research* (Canada) 18:2 (June 1989):37-8.

Martin, A. Damien and Emery S. Hetrick. "The Stigmatization of the Gay and Lesbian Adolescent." *Journal of Homosexuality,* "Psychopathology and Psychotherapy in Homosexuality" 15:1/2 (1988):163-84.

Mercier, Lucy R. and Raymond M. Berger. "Social Service Needs of Lesbian and Gay Adolescents: Telling It Their Way." *Journal of Social Work and Human Sexuality* 8:1 (1989):75-95.

Nava, Mica. "'Everybody's Views Were Just Broadened': a Girls Project and Some Responses to Lesbianism." *Feminist Review* (Great Britain) 10 (Spring 1982):37-59.

"Nobody Listens to Me" (interview with Claudet and Charlotte, 14- and 15-year-old Dutch lesbians). *Connexions,* "Young and Old Women" 7 (Winter 1983):10-11.

Parker, Richard. "Youth, Identity, and Homosexuality: the Changing Shape of Sexual Life in Contemporary Brazil." *Journal of Homosexuality,* "Gay and Lesbian Youth: Part II" 17:3/4 (1989):269-90.

Pierce, Dean. "Who Speaks for Lesbian/Gay Adolescents: Voices to be Silenced, Voices to be Heard" (speech delivered at the annual meeting of the Organization for the Study of Communication, Language, and Gender, 1990). *Women and Language* 13:2 (Winter 1990):37-41.

Plummer, Ken. "Lesbian and Gay Youth in England." *Journal of Homosexuality,* "Gay and Lesbian Youth: Part II" 17:3/4 (1989):195-224.

Robinson, Dawn R. "'I Found My Thrill . . . '" (autobiographical narrative of adolescent lesbianism). *Common Lives/Lesbian Lives* 3 (Spring 1982):15-21.

Rofes, Eric. "Opening Up the Classroom Closet: Responding to the Educational Needs of Gay and Lesbian Youth." *Harvard Educational Review* 59:4 (November 1989):444-53.

11

Sang, Barbara. "Reflections of Midlife Lesbians on Their Adolescence." *Journal of Women & Aging,* "Women, Aging and Ageism" 2:2 (1990):111-17.

Savin-Williams, Ritch. "Coming Out to Parents and Self-Esteem Among Gay and Lesbian Youths." *Journal of Homosexuality,* "Homosexuality and the Family" 18:1/2 (1989):1-36.

------. "Gay and Lesbian Adolescents." *Marriage and Family Review* 14:3-4 (1989):197-216.

------. "Parental Influences on the Self-Esteem of Gay and Lesbian Youths: a Reflected Appraisals Model." *Journal of Homosexuality,* "Gay and Lesbian Youth: Part I" 17:1/2 (1989):93-110.

Schneider, Margaret. "Sappho Was a Right-On Adolescent: Growing Up Lesbian" (study of 25 lesbians, age 15-20; many are members of Lesbian and Gay Youth Toronto, Canada). *Journal of Homosexuality,* "Gay and Lesbian Youth: Part I" 17:1/2 (1989):111-30.

Schneider, Margaret and Bob Tremble. "Training Service Providers to Work with Gay or Lesbian Adolescents: a Workshop." *Journal of Counseling and Development* 65:2 (October 1986):98-9.

Sears, James T. "The Impact of Gender and Race on Growing Up Lesbian and Gay in the South." *NWSA Journal* 1:3 (Spring 1989):422-57.

"SF - Counseling Ok'd" (Board of Education in San Francisco, California approves program for lesbian and gay youth). *off our backs* 20:8 (August/September 1990):6.

Slater, B.R. "Essential Issues in Working with Lesbian and Gay Male Youths." *Professional Psychology -- Research and Practice* 19:2 (1988):226-35.

Smart, Corinna. "Counselling Practice: Counselling Homosexual/ Bisexual People with Particular Reference to Young Lesbian Women." *International Journal of Adolescence and Youth* 1:4 (1989):379-93.

Sobocinski, M.R. "Ethical Principles in the Counseling of Gay and Lesbian Adolescents: Issues of Autonomy, Competence, and Confidentiality." *Professional Psychology - Research and Practice* 21:4 (1990):240-7.

Steinhorn, Audrey I. "Lesbian Adolescents in Residential Treatment." *Social Casework* 60 (October 1979):494-504.

"Sweden: Speaking the Truth in Schools" (Eva Hansson tours Sweden with one-woman play about teenage lesbian love; trans. and excerpted from Swedish feminist bimonthly *Kvinnobulletinen* (January/February 1988)). *Connexions,* "Girls Speak Out!" 27 (1988):23.

Tremble, Bob, Margaret Schneider, and Carol Appathurai. "Growing Up Gay or Lesbian in a Multicultural Context" (study based on Toronto, Ontario, Canada). *Journal of Homosexuality,* "Gay and Lesbian Youth: Part II" 17:3/4 (1989):253-68.

Williams, Dennis A. and Susan Agrest. "A School for Homosexuals" (Harvey Milk School, New York City). *Newsweek* 105 (June 17, 1985):93.

"Young Lesbians in India: Bury Us Together" (lesbians today and in ancient history). *Connexions,* "Global Lesbianism" 3 (January 1982):7.

"Young Lesbians in Indonesia: Trial and a Marriage" (trans. from mainstream Indonesian news magazine *Tempo,* May 23 and 30, 1981). *Connexions,* "Global Lesbianism" 3 (January 1982):6.

"Young Lesbians in West Berlin: Be a Sweetie . . . Don't Tell Anyone." *Connexions,* "Global Lesbianism" 3 (January 1982):4-5.

<u>Adoption</u> (see also: Child Custody; Foster Care; Parenting)

Butke, Maryellen. "A Child's Right to Know" (about her/his birth
    parents). *Sojourner* 13:12 (August 1988):7-8.

FPE. "Lesbians Adopt" (in San Francisco, California). *off our backs* 20:1
    (January 1990):5.

"Gay Adoption: in Britain" (promoted by Newcastle City Council,
    opposed by British Home Secretary). *off our backs* 20:11
    (December 1990):6.

"Gay Adoption: in Netherlands" (legalization considered by federal
    government, which legalized same-sex marriage in 1989). *off our
    backs* 20:11 (December 1990):6.

Monagle, Katie. "Court Backs Two-Mom Family" (lesbian adopts two-
    year-old her lover conceived through artificial insemination). *Ms.*
    18:4 (October 1989):69.

Ricketts, Wendell and Roberta Achtenberg. "Adoption and Foster
    Parenting for Lesbians and Gay Men: Creating New Traditions in
    Family." *Marriage and Family Review* 14:3-4 (1989):83-118.

Sutton, Stuart A. "The Lesbian Family: Rights in Conflict Under the
    Uniform Parentage Act." *Golden Gate University Law Review*
    10:1 (1980):1007-41.

Thomas, June. "Reagan Task Force: Gays Shouldn't Adopt." *off our
    backs* 18:1 (January 1988):8.

Zuckerman, Elizabeth. "Second Parent Adoption for Lesbian-Parented
    Families: Legal Recognition of the Other Mother." *U.C. Davis
    Law Review* 19:3 (Spring 1986):729-59.

African-American Lesbians (see also: Lesbians of Color; Racism)

Abdullahad, Tania and Leigh H. Mosley. "Third World Lesbian & Gay Conference" (second annual national conference, Chicago, Illinois, November 1981; includes workshop reports on "mature lesbians," "urban black lesbians," "media," "grassroots," "racism & sexism"). *off our backs* 12:2 (February 1982):4.

Anderson, Jacqueline. "Separation in Black: a Personal Journey." *Lesbian Ethics* 3:2 (Fall 1988):78-81.

"Australia: Uma" (native black lesbian feminist and her political affiliations as a Third World woman). *Connexions* 10 (1983):5-7.

Banks, Johnette E. "A House Divided" (factionalization of the African-American lesbian community). *Black/Out* 1:3/4 (1987):40.

Berry, Delores. "Come Out, Come Out . . . " (African-American lesbian minister). *Women: a Journal of Liberation* 5:2 (1977):47-9.

Black Scholar, "Black Women and Feminism," vol. 16, no. 2, March/April 1985.

Black/Out, "Tenth Anniversary Edition: NCBLG Celebrates Homecoming" (National Coalition of Black Lesbians and Gays), vol. 2, no. 1, Fall 1988.

Bowen, Angela. "From the Editor" (about African-American lesbians and gay men as "family"). *Black/Out,* "We Are Family" 2:2 (Summer 1989):2+.

Brooke. "A Feminist Future?" ("The Women's Movement: Forum," The Matriarchists, New York City, September 1978; speakers Robin Morgan, Gloria Steinem, Dianne Feeley, Willamette Brown, Elizabeth Shanklin, Jean O'Leary, Judith Levy, Kate Millett, Arlie Scott, Midge Costanza, Marisa de Los Angeles, Flo Kennedy, and Ti-Grace Atkinson; accused of token inclusion of women of color). *off our backs* 8:10 (November 1978):10-12.

CAD. "D.C. -- Barry Listens" (Washington, D.C. mayor Marion Barry supports community efforts on behalf of African-American lesbians and gays, gay clinic, and enforcement of anti-discrimination laws). *off our backs* 9:3 (March 1979):8.

------. "Lesbian Plenary: Combatting Heterosexism" (at 10th annual National Women's Studies Association convention, University of Minnesota in Minneapolis, June 1988; panel members Beth Brant, Michelle Parkerson, Joan Nestle, Gloria Anzaldúa). *off our backs* 18:8 (August-September 1988):3+.

Carmen, Gail, Sheila, and Pratibha. "Becoming Visible: Black Lesbian Discussions." *Feminist Review* (Great Britain), "Many Voices, One Chant: Black Feminist Perspectives" 17 (Autumn 1984):53-72.

Cauthern, Cynthia R. "Nine Hundred Black Lesbians Speak." *off our backs* 9:6 (June 1979):112.

Clark, Jil. "Becoming Visible: Black Lesbian Conference in New York City" (First Annual Black Lesbian Conference for the Eastern Regional States, January 1981). *off our backs* 11:3 (March 1981):14-15.

Clarke, Cheryl. "Coming Out" (speech delivered by poet at Gay Pride Day, New York City, June 29, 1986). *Black/Out* 1:2 (Fall 1986):11+.

Clarke, Cheryl, Jewelle Gomez, Evelyn Hammonds, Bonnie Johnson, and Linda Powell. "Black Women on Black Women Writers: Conversations and Questions." *Conditions: nine* 3:3 (Spring 1983):88-137.

Cochran, S.D. and V.M. Mays. "Disclosure of Sexual Preference to Physicians by Black Lesbian and Bisexual Women." *Western Journal of Medicine* 149:5 (1988):616-19.

Daniels, Gabrielle. "First Black Lesbian Conference" (of the Western Regional States, San Francisco, California, October 1980). *off our backs* 10:11 (December 1980):4-5+.

De Veaux, Alexis. "Sister Love." *Essence* 14 (October 1983):82-4+.

Dirzhud-Rashid, Shani. "New Age Rage: Spiritual Path a Choice" (response to Angela Johnson, "Pre-packaged Spiritualism," *off our backs* 19:1 (January 1989):10; note: cover reads 18:11 (December 1988)). *off our backs* 19:2 (February 1989):19.

Folayan, Ayofemi. "National Black Gay and Lesbian Leadership Forum: a Conference Report" (Atlanta, Georgia, February 1990). *off our backs* 20:4 (April 1990):2-3.

Frechette, D. "A New Movement of Black Lesbians and Gays." *Advocate* 440 (February 18, 1986):39.

Goldsby, Jackie. "What It Means to Be Colored Me." *Out/Look #9,* 3:1 (Summer 1990):9-17.

Gomez, Jewelle. "Black Women's Humour." *Black/Out,* "We Are Family" 2:2 (Summer 1989):14+.

------. "Imagine a Lesbian . . . a Black Lesbian . . . " *Trivia* 12 (Spring 1988):45-60.

------. "Re-Casting the Mythology: Writing Vampire Fiction." *Hot Wire* 4:1 (November 1987):42-3+.

------. "Repeat After Me: We Are Different, We Are the Same." *New York University Review of Law & Social Change* 14:4 (Fall 1986):935-41.

------. "We Haven't Come Such a Long Way, Baby" (part of "Messages to the Movement . . . Where We Are Twenty Years After Stonewall"). *Out/Look #5,* 2:1 (Summer 1989):55-6.

Gomez, Jewelle and Barbara Smith. "Talking About It: Homophobia in the Black Community." *Feminist Review* (Great Britain), "Perverse Politics: Lesbian Issues" 34 (Spring 1990):47-55.

Greene, Beverly A. "When the Therapist Is White and the Patient Is Black: Considerations for Psychotherapy in the Feminist Heterosexual and Lesbian Communities." *Women & Therapy* 5 (Summer/Fall 1986):41-65.

Grosvenor, T.G. "Midwest Lesbian Conference" (Michigan State University, May 1974). *off our backs* 4:7 (June 1974):6-7.

Harris, Craig. "Black Lesbians and Gays: Empirically Speaking" (report on "The Black Women's Relationship Project: a National Survey of Black Lesbians" (Mays, Cochran, Peplau, 1986) and "Influence of Assimilation on the Psychosocial Adjustment of Black Homosexual Men" (Johnson, 1981)). *Black/Out*, "Tenth Anniversary Edition: NCBLG Celebrates Homecoming" (National Coalition of Black Lesbians and Gays) 2:1 (Fall 1988):9-11+.

Hernton, Calvin. "Sexual Mountain and Black Women Writers" (lesbian and heterosexual writers). *Black Scholar* 16:4 (July 1985):2-11.

Hooks, Bell. "Reflections on Homophobia and Black Communities." *Out/Look* 1:2 (Summer 1988):22-5.

Hull, Gloria T. and Barbara Smith. "'Keep Black Women at the Center': a Conversation Between Gloria T. Hull and Barbara Smith" (co-editors, with Patricia Bell Scott, of *But Some of Us Are Brave: Black Women's Studies*). *off our backs*, "education issue" 12:5 (May 1982):22-3.

Jewell, Terri L. "A Call to Black Lesbian Sisters" (racism and skin-color prejudice among African-American lesbians). *Sinister Wisdom*, "Passing" 35 (Summer/Fall 1988):12-4; and *Black/Out*, "Tenth Anniversary Edition: NCBLG Celebrates Homecoming" (National Coalition of Black Lesbians and Gays) 2:1 (Fall 1988):53.

18

------. "A Conversation With Stephanie Byrd" (poet). *Visibilities* 3:2 (March/April 1989):7-10.

Johnson, Lynell. "Women of Color and AIDS." *Black/Out,* "Tenth Anniversary Edition: NCBLG Celebrates Homecoming" (National Coalition of Black Lesbians and Gays) 2:1 (Fall 1988):27-8.

Joseph, Gloria I. "Black Mothers and Daughters: Traditional and New Perspectives" (includes discussion of lesbian mothers). *Sage,* "Mothers and Daughters" 1:2 (Fall 1984):17-21.

Krige, Eileen Jensen. "Woman-Marriage, with Special Reference to the Lovendu -- Its Significance for the Definition of Marriage." *Africa* 44:1 (1974):11-37.

Kris. "Another Kind of Coming Out" (child sexual abuse in the British black community). *Gossip* (Great Britain) 2 (1986):80-9.

Lee, Anna. "For the Love of Separatism" (African-American lesbian separatism). *Lesbian Ethics* 3:2 (Fall 1988):54-63.

------. "Interstices of Race and Class: Creating Intimacy" (building community). *Lesbian Ethics* 4:1 (Spring 1990):77-83.

Loiacano, Darryl K. "Gay Identity Issues among Black Americans: Racism, Homophobia, and the Need for Validation." *Journal of Counseling and Development,* "Lesbian, Gay and Bisexual Issues in Counseling" 68:1 (September-October 1989):21-5.

Lorde, Audre. "I Am Your Sister: Black Women Organizing Across Sexualities." *Women & Therapy* 6 (Winter 1987):25-30.

Lorde, Audre. "Manchild: a Black Lesbian Feminist's Response." *Conditions: four* 1:4 (Winter 1979):30-6; also, *Conditions: sixteen,* "Retrospective" (1989):28-35.

------. "No, We Never Go Out of Fashion . . . for Each Other" (discussion among three black feminists and Audre Lorde at International Feminist Bookfair, June 1984, England). *Spare Rib* (Great Britain) 149 (December 1984):26-9.

------. "Other Voices, Other Moods: African Co-Wives." *Ms.* 7:8 (February 1979):52+.

------. "Poems Are Not Luxuries." *Chrysalis* 3 (1977):7-9.

------. "Turning the Beat Around" (speech delivered at the Hunter College Lesbian and Gay Community Center's Forum on Lesbian and Gay Parents of Color, October 1986). *Black/Out* 1:3/4 (1987):13-16.

Louise, Vivienne. "Defining Ourselves: Black Lesbian Gathering" (November 1988, Sausalito, California). *off our backs* 19:2 (February 1989):3.

------. "Genuine Desire" (letter to "A Readers' Forum -- Separatism: Beyond the Debate," asking "Why don't white lesbians have a genuine desire to learn from lesbians of African descent?"). *Lesbian Ethics* 3:2 (Fall 1988):5-8.

McCoy, Renée. "Church for a Different Community" (African-American lesbian/gay alternative churches, and homophobia of the traditional African-American Church). *Black/Out,* "We Are Family" 2:2 (Summer 1989):60-1.

------. "NCBLG Is a Family" (National Coalition of Black Lesbians and Gays). *Black/Out,* "We Are Family" 2:2 (Summer 1989):3-4.

------. "Ten Years Ago: Ten Years Ahead" (tenth anniversary of the National Coalition for Black Lesbians and Gays). *Black/Out,* "Tenth Anniversary Edition: NCBLG Celebrates Homecoming" 2:1 (Fall 1988):3-4.

------. "The Truth of the Matter" (written by new executive director of the National Coalition for Black Lesbians and Gays, about the organization). *Black/Out* 1:3/4 (1987):3.

McCray, Chirlane. "I Am a Lesbian" (personal narrative in the self-proclaimed "magazine for today's black women"). *Essence* 10:5 (September 1979):90-1+.

Martin, Annette. "My Own Story" (growing up African-American and lesbian). *Common Lives/Lesbian Lives* 1 (Fall 1981):15-19.

Mays, Vickie M. "Black Women Working Together: Diversity in Same Sex Relationships." *Women's Studies International Forum* 8:1 (1985):67-71.

------. "I Hear Voices But See No Faces: Reflections on Racism and Women-Identified Relationships of Afro-American Women." *Heresies #12,* "The Sex Issue" 3:4 (1981):74-6.

Members of the Coalition of Black Gay Women and Men. "Gay Pride Day -- a Community Affair?" (controversy over lack of political protest message in Washington, D.C. Gay Pride Day, June 1978). *off our backs* 8:7 (July 1978):12+.

Obbo, Christine. "Dominant Male Ideology and Female Options: Three East African Case Studies" (woman-marriage in Africa). *Africa* 46:4 (1976):371-89.

Parker, Pat. "1987 March on Washington: the Morning Rally." *Hot Wire* 5:1 (January 1989):16-17.

Parkerson, Michelle. "Lesbian Alliances: Heterosexism in the Eighties -- Challenging Otherness" (speech at the National Women's Studies Association conference, Minneapolis, Minnesota, June 1988). *Sojourner* 14:3 (November 1988):14.

------. "No More Mammy Stories: an Overview of Black Women Filmmakers" (not exclusively lesbian). *Gallerie: Women's Art* (1989 annual):12-15.

Radical Teacher, on black women, no. 17, November 1980.

Rushin, Kate. "What's In a Name?" (discusses the following labels: African-American, Afro-American, Colored, Black, People of Color, Negro). *Black/Out,* "We Are Family" 2:2 (Summer 1989):15.

Shabazz, Naeemah. "Homophobia: Myths and Realities." *Heresies #8,* "Third World Women: the Politics of Being Other" 2:4 (1979):34-6.

Shockley, Ann Allen. "Black Lesbian Biography: Lifting the Veil." *Other Black Woman* 1 (1982):5-9.

---------. "The Black Lesbian in American literature: An Overview." *Conditions: five* 2:2 (Autumn 1979):133-42.

Smartt, Dorothea and Val Mason-John. "Black Feminists Organising on Both Sides of the Atlantic." *Spare Rib* (Great Britain) 171 (October 1986):20-4.

Smith, Barbara. "Just Between Us: a Black Gay Dialogue" (keynote address to the Second National Third World Lesbian and Gay Conference, Chicago, Illinois, November 1981). *off our backs* 12:2(February 1982):5.

------. "Some Home Truths on the Contemporary Black Feminist Movement." *Black Scholar,* "Black Women and Feminism" 16:2 (March/April 1985):4-13.

------. "The NEA Is the Least of It" (silencing through overt censorship, as the National Endowment for the Arts, and through internalized oppression). *Ms.: The World of Women* 1:3 (November/December 1990):65-7.

------. "Toward a Black Feminist Criticism." *Conditions: two* 1:2 (October 1977):25-44; also *Radical Teacher* 7 (March 1978):20-7; also *Women's Studies International Quarterly* 2:2 (1979):183-94; also *Conditions: sixteen,* "Retrospective" (1989):6-25.

------. "Visions and Revisions: Women and Power to Change" (part of final panel at First National Women's Studies Association Conference, Lawrence, Kansas, May 30-June 3, 1979). *Women's Studies Newsletter* 7:3 (Summer 1979):19-20.

------. "Working for Liberation and Having a Damn Good Time." *Black/Out* 1:1 (Summer 1986):13-14+.

Smith, Barbara and Gloria T. Hull. "'Keep Black Women at the Center': a Conversation Between Gloria T. Hull and Barbara Smith" (co-editors, with Patricia Bell Scott, of *But Some of Us Are Brave: Black Women's Studies*). *off our backs,* "education issue" 12:5 (May 1982):22-3.

Smith, Barbara and Beverly Smith. "'I am not Meant to be Alone Without You Who Understand': Letters from Black Feminists, 1972-8." *Conditions: four* 1:4 (Winter 1979):62-77.

Smith, Beverly, with Judith Stein and Priscilla Golding. "'The Possibility of Life Between Us': A Dialogue Between Black and Jewish Women." *Conditions: seven* 3:1 (Spring 1981):25-46.

"Statement by Blacklesbians of African Descent." *off our backs* 17:8 (August-September 1986):2.

Stowe, Ayofemi. "Black Women and AIDS." *Black/Out,* "Tenth Anniversary Edition: NCBLG Celebrates Homecoming" 2:1 (Fall 1988):33+.

Sulter, Maud. "Black Codes: the Misrepresentation of Blacklesbians in Film" (considers "Born in Flames," "The Color Purple," "Mark of Lilith," "Mona Lisa," "Passion of Remembrance," and "She's Gotta Have It"). *Gossip* (Great Britain) 5 (no date):29-36.

"Surge of Lesbian Moms to Present Legal Problems." *Jet* 75 (March 20, 1989):37.

"Three Black Women Talk About Sexuality and Racism." *Spare Rib* (Great Britain) 135 (October 1983):6-8.

Vitale, Sylvia Witts. "A Herstorical Look at Some Aspects of Black Sexuality." *Heresies: 12,* "The Sex Issue" 3:4 (1981):63-5.

Weems, Renita J. "Just Friends" (written by a woman who is friends with a lesbian, about homophobia and the black community). *Essence* 20 (May 1989):60+.

West, Cheryl. "Lesbian Daughter" (of a lesbian mother). *Sage,* "Mothers and Daughters II" 4:2 (Fall 1987):42-4.

White, Evelyn C. "Comprehensive Oppression: Lesbians and Race in the Work of Ann Allen Shockley." *Backbone* 3 (1981):38-40.

Williams, Natalie. "Lesbian and Gay People of Colour Gather in London" (Sixth International Lesbian and Gay People of Colour Conference, London, England, November 1990). *Spare Rib* (Great Britain) 219 (December/January 1990/91):66-7.

Armatrading, Joan (pop musician):
Fudger, Marion. "Joan Armatrading" (deals in part with African-Americans, feminists, and gays/lesbians wanting musician to support their politics explicitly). *Spare Rib* (Great Britain) 53 (December 1976):6-8.

Arobateau, Red Jordan (writer):
Shockley, Ann Allen. "Red Jordan Arobateau: A Different Kind of Black Lesbian Writer." *Sinister Wisdom* 21 (Fall 1982):35-9.

Bentley, Gladys (blues musician of the Harlem Renaissance):
Garber, Eric. "Gladys Bentley: the Bulldagger Who Sang the Blues." *Out/Look* 1:1 (Spring 1988):52-61.

Bogus, SDiane (writer):
Birtha, Becky. "Celebrating Themselves: Four Self-Published Black Lesbian Authors" (part 2: III. Doris Davenport; IV. SDiane Bogus). *off our backs* 15:8 (August-September 1985):19-21.

Brown, Linda (writer):

Birtha, Becky. "Celebrating Themselves: Four Self-Published Black Lesbian Authors" (part 3: V. Linda Brown, and "Books by Self-Identified Black Lesbians"). *off our backs* 15:9 (October 1985):16-17.

Byrd, Stephanie (writer):

Birtha, Becky. "Celebrating Themselves: Four Self-Published Black Lesbian Authors" (part 1: I. Introduction; II. Stephanie Byrd). *off our backs* 15:7 (July 1985):22.

Carter, Colevia (AIDS activist):

Hutchins, Loraine. "Colevia Carter -- Women and AIDS" (interview). *off our backs* 17:1 (January 1987):20-1.

Clarke, Cheryl (poet):

Clarke, Cheryl, Jewelle Gomez, Evelyn Hammonds, Bonnie Johnson, and Linda Powell. "Black Women on Black Women Writers: Conversations and Questions." *Conditions: nine* 3:3 (Spring 1983):88-137.

Ruby, Jennie. "The Black Diaspora" (report on Michelle Parkerson, Audre Lorde, and Cheryl Clarke speaking on diversity of self-expression among African-American women, in a session at the 10th annual National Women's Studies Association conference, University of Minnesota in Minneapolis, June 1988, "African American Women and the Black Diaspora"). *off our backs* 18:8 (August-September 1988):10.

Cliff, Michelle (writer):

Dejanikus, Tacie and Loie Hayes. "Claiming an Identity: an Interview with Michelle Cliff" (poet and novelist). *off our backs* 11:6 (June 1981):18-20.

The Color Purple (novel by Alice Walker, and film):

Henderson, Mae G. "*The Color Purple:* Revisions and Redefinitions" (deals in part with Shug and Celie's lesbian relationship). *Sage,* "Women as Writers" 2:1 (Spring 1985):14-18.

Craft, Ellen (escaped slave):
Archer, Koree. "This Great Drama" (Ellen Craft, escaped slave from
    Georgia, and Sarah Edmonds, Canadian passing woman who
    spied for the Union Army). *Sinister Wisdom,* "Passing" 35
    (Summer/Fall 1988):86-94.

Davenport, Doris (poet):
Birtha, Becky. "Celebrating Themselves: Four Self-Published Black
    Lesbian Authors" (part 2: III. Doris Davenport; IV. SDiane
    Bogus). *off our backs* 15:8 (August-September 1985):19-21.

DeLarvie, Miss Stormé (entertainer and male impersonator):
Parkerson, Michelle. "Beyond Chiffon" (1950s drag show at The
    Jewel Box, including male impersonator Miss Stormé DeLarvie,
    about whom Parkerson made the film "Stormé"). *Black/Out*
    1:3/4 (1987):21-2.

Eyega, Zeinab (Sudanese feminist living in exile):
Salomyn, Shay. "Black Women in Sudan" (interview). *off our backs*
    20:3 (March 1990):8.

Gomez, Jewelle (writer):
Clarke, Cheryl, Jewelle Gomez, Evelyn Hammonds, Bonnie
    Johnson, and Linda Powell. "Black Women on Black Women
    Writers: Conversations and Questions." *Conditions: nine* 3:3
    (Spring 1983):88-137.

Hammonds, Evelyn (writer):
Clarke, Cheryl, Jewelle Gomez, Evelyn Hammonds, Bonnie
    Johnson, and Linda Powell. "Black Women on Black Women
    Writers: Conversations and Questions." *Conditions: nine* 3:3
    (Spring 1983):88-137.

Hampton, Mabel (born 1903; co-founder of the Lesbian Herstory
    Archives)
Nestle, Joan. "Surviving and More: Interview with Mabel Hampton."
    Sinister Wisdom, "On Being Old and Age" 10 (Summer
    1979):19+.

Rushin, Kate. "Mabel Hampton: 'Cracking Open the Door.'" *Sojourner* 13:12 (August 1988):21.

Hopkins, Lea (activist, mother, former Playboy bunny):
Ebert, Alan. "Lea Hopkins: Just Different." *Essence* 10:12 (April 1980):88-9+.

Hull, Gloria (literary critic and poet):
Thomas, June. "Public-Private Diary: Finding Black Women's History" (interview). *off our backs* 15:5 (May 1985):20-2.

Ifateyo, Ajowa (co-founder of *Upfront* and former editor of *The Running Spear*, African People's Socialist Party newspaper):
Douglas, Carol Anne. "Ajowa Ifateyo: Speaking Up Front" (interview). *off our backs* 14:10 (November 1984):10-12.

Jewell, Terri L. (poet):
Jewell, Terri L. "Crawling Around Inside One Black Writer." *off our backs* 13:6 (June 1983):18.

Johnson, Bonnie (writer):
Clarke, Cheryl, Jewelle Gomez, Evelyn Hammonds, Bonnie Johnson, and Linda Powell. "Black Women on Black Women Writers: Conversations and Questions." *Conditions: nine* 3:3 (Spring 1983):88-137.

Johnson, Eva (Aboriginal playwright):
Poggi, Stephanie, Jennifer Abod, Jacqui Alexander, and Evelyn Hammonds. "Claiming My Mothers, Exposing Aboriginal Consciousness to the World: an Interview with Aboriginal, Black Lesbian Playwright Eva Johnson." *Black/Out,* "We Are Family" 2:2 (Summer 1989):48-53.

Kennedy, Flo (activist lawyer):
Kennedy, Flo. "Color Me Flo" (excerpt from 1976 autobiography). *Woman of Power,* "Humor" 17 (Summer 1990):16-19.

Kitchen Table: Women of Color Press:

Jewell, Terri L. "Barbara Smith and Kitchen Table Women of Color Press." *Hot Wire* 6:2 (May 1990):20-2+.

Lorde, Audre (writer):

Alexander-Fleurant, Maimouna Pausa. "'Audre Lorde Is Very Special To Me.'" *Sojourner* 13:1 (September 1987):18.

Chiaramonte, Lee. "Letter From Berlin: Audre Lorde Answers Questions on Writing, Voice and Being a Woman Warrior." *Visibilities* 2:5 (September/October 1988):4-7.

Christian, Barbara. "No More Buried Lives -- the Theme of Lesbianism in Lorde, Naylor, Shange, Walker." *Feminist Issues* 5:1 (Spring 1985):3-20.

Cornwell, Anita. "'So Who's Giving Guarantees?' An Interview with Audre Lorde." *Sinister Wisdom* 4 (Fall 1977):15-21.

Culpepper, Emily Erwin. "New Tools for Theology: Writings by Women of Color" (draws on works of Audre Lorde, Pat Parker, Beverly Smith, Gloria Anzaldúa, but never explicitly discusses lesbianism). *Journal of Feminist Studies in Religion* 4:2 (Fall 1988):39-50.

Folayan, Ayofemi. "I Am Your Sister: a Tale of Two Conferences" (celebrating African-American writer/activist Audre Lorde, Boston, Massachusetts, October 1990; disabled women's access limited). *off our backs* 20:11 (December 1990):1-2.

Greene, Laureen A. "Breaking the Barriers of Silence: an Interview with Audre Lorde" (discusses surviving as an African-American woman in the United States, and living with cancer). *Woman of Power,* "Life Cycles: Conscious Birthing, Living, and Dying" 14 (Summer 1989):39-41.

Harper, Jorjet and Toni L. Armstrong. "Audre Lorde" (interview). *Hot Wire* 5:1 (January 1989):2-6.

"An Interview: Audre Lorde and Adrienne Rich." *Signs* 6:4 (Summer 1981):713-36.

Lewis, Gail. "Audre Lorde: Vignettes and Mental Conversations" (about Lorde's poetry). *Feminist Review* (Great Britain), "Perverse Politics: Lesbian Issues" 34 (Spring 1990):100-114.

Lorde, Audre. "Breast Cancer: a Black Lesbian Feminist Experience." *Sinister Wisdom,* "On Being Old and Age" 10 (Summer 1979):44-61.

------. "A Burst of Light" (selection from book of same title, about living with cancer). *Spare Rib* (Great Britain) 198 (February 1989):6-10.

Moira, Fran and Lorraine Sorrel. "Audre Lorde: Lit from Within" (interview). *off our backs* 12:4 (April 1982):2-3.

Parmer, Pratibha and Jackie Kay. "Frontiers: Interview [with] Black Author and Activist, Audre Lorde." *Spare Rib* (Great Britain) 188 (March 1988):37-41.

Ruby, Jennie. "The Black Diaspora" (report on Michelle Parkerson, Audre Lorde, and Cheryl Clarke speaking on diversity of self-expression among African-American women, in a session at the 10th annual National Women's Studies Association conference, University of Minnesota in Minneapolis, June 1988, "African American Women and the Black Diaspora"). *off our backs* 18:8 (August-September 1988):10.

Stato, Joanne. "I Am Your Sister Celeconference: Tribute to Audre Lorde" (Boston, Massachusetts, October 1990). *off our backs* 20:11 (December 1990):1-5+.

Sturgis, Susanna J. "Audre Lorde: a Radio Profile." *Sojourner* 14:5 (January 1989):33.

<u>Lunden, Doris</u> (born 1936, came out 1953):

Bulkin, Elly. "An Old Dyke's Tale: an Interview with Doris Lunden." *Conditions: six* 2:3 (Summer 1980):26-44; also *Conditions: sixteen,* "Retrospective" (1989):63-82.

<u>McKenzie, Michelle</u> (publisher):

Ross, Becki. "Black Women of Letters" (excerpt of interview with Michelle McKenzie and Araba Mercer of Sheba Publishers, England, from Canadian monthly *Rites* (November 1988)). *Connexions,* "Women on Work" 30 (1989):24-5.

<u>Mercer, Araba</u> (publisher):

Ross, Becki. "Black Women of Letters" (excerpt of interview with Michelle McKenzie and Araba Mercer of Sheba Publishers, England, from Canadian monthly *Rites* (November 1988)). *Connexions,* "Women on Work" 30 (1989):24-5.

<u>Naylor, Gloria</u> (novelist):

Christian, Barbara. "No More Buried Lives -- the Theme of Lesbianism in Lorde, Naylor, Shange, Walker." *Feminist Issues* 5:1 (Spring 1985):3-20.

Mills, Bronwyn. "Gloria Naylor: Dreaming the Dream" (author of *The Women of Brewster Place,* lesbian-themed novel). *Sojourner* 13:9 (May 1988):17.

<u>Nelson, Alice Dunbar</u>:

Hart, Betty. "A Cry in the Wilderness: The Diary of Alice Dunbar Nelson." *Women's Studies Quarterly* 17:3&4 (Fall/Winter 1989):74-8.

Thomas, June. "Public-Private Diary: Finding Black Women's History" (interview with Gloria T. Hull, editor of *Give Us Each Day: the Diary of Alice Dunbar Nelson* (1873-1935)). *off our backs* 15:5 (May 1985):20-2.

<u>Nolan, Faith</u> (musician):

Brand, Dionne. "Faith Nolan: 'I'm a working class, Black lesbian. In everything I do I have to fight for that voice to be heard.'" *Hot Wire* 5:1 (January 1989):39+.

<u>Norman, Pat</u> (activist):

Bowen, Angela. "Pat Norman, the Y.E.S. Woman: an Interview" (director of the Youth Environment Studies Training Center and coordinator of the People of Color Caucus for the 1987 March on Washington for Lesbian and Gay Rights). *Black/Out*, "We Are Family" 2:2 (Summer 1989):41+.

<u>Parker, Pat</u> (poet):

Beemyn, Brett. "Bibliography of Works By and About Pat Parker (1944-1989)." *Sage* 6:1 (Summer 1989):81-2.

Brimstone, Lyndie. "Pat Parker: a Tribute" (1944-1989). *Feminist Review* (Great Britain), "Perverse Politics: Lesbian Issues" 34 (Spring 1990):4-7.

"Coming Together: the Benefit for Pat Parker" (fundraiser for poet to attend seminar at the Cancer Support and Education Center). *Hot Wire* 5:1 (January 1989):38.

Culpepper, Emily Erwin. "New Tools for Theology: Writings by Women of Color" (draws on works of Audre Lorde, Pat Parker, Beverly Smith, Gloria Anzaldúa, but never explicitly discusses lesbianism). *Journal of Feminist Studies in Religion* 4:2 (Fall 1988):39-50.

Stato, Joanne. "Pat Parker, 1944-1989." *off our backs* 19:8 (August-September 1989):1+.

Stevens, Wendy. "Pat Parker: Reading Her Work" (touring the U.S.). *off our backs* 5:5 (May-June 1975):16.

Parkerson, Michelle (filmmaker):

Leveritt, Annie and Toni L. Armstrong. "Filmmaker, Activist, Writer: Michelle Parkerson" (co-chair, National Coalition of Black Lesbians and Gays). *Hot Wire* 3:3 (July 1987):26-8.

Parkerson, Michelle: "Beyond Chiffon" (1950s drag show at The Jewel Box, including male impersonator Miss Stormé DeLarvie, about whom Parkerson made the film "Stormé"). *Black/Out* 1:3/4 (1987):21-2.

Ruby, Jennie. "The Black Diaspora" (report on Michelle Parkerson, Audre Lorde, and Cheryl Clarke speaking on diversity of self-expression among African-American women, in a session at the 10th annual National Women's Studies Association conference, University of Minnesota in Minneapolis, June 1988, "African American Women and the Black Diaspora"). *off our backs* 18:8 (August-September 1988):10.

Powell, Linda (writer):

Clarke, Cheryl, Jewelle Gomez, Evelyn Hammonds, Bonnie Johnson, and Linda Powell. "Black Women on Black Women Writers: Conversations and Questions." *Conditions: nine* 3:3 (Spring 1983):88-137.

Reagon, Bernice Johnson (musician):

Yount, Rena. "Each in Her Own Generation: Bernice & Toshi Reagon" (African-American singer/songwriters who are mother and daughter). *Hot Wire* 5:2 (May 1989):34-5+.

Reagon, Toshi (musician):

Yount, Rena. "Each in Her Own Generation: Bernice & Toshi Reagon" (African-American singer/songwriters who are mother and daughter). *Hot Wire* 5:2 (May 1989):34-5+.

Roberts, Roxanne E.B. (writer):

Ottey, Shan. "Black Lesbian: Alienation and Aloneness" (interview; includes discussion of being African-American in a lesbian bar). *off our backs* 5:5 (May-June 1975):15.

<u>Shange, Ntozake</u> (writer):

Christian, Barbara. "No More Buried Lives -- the Theme of Lesbianism in Lorde, Naylor, Shange, Walker." *Feminist Issues* 5:1 (Spring 1985):3-20.

<u>Smith, Barbara</u> (activist, publisher, and writer):

Jewell, Terri L. "Barbara Smith and Kitchen Table Women of Color Press." *Hot Wire* 6:2 (May 1990):20-2+.

Parkerson, Michelle. "Some Place That's Our Own -- an Interview with Barbara Smith." *off our backs* 14:4 (April 1984):10-12.

<u>Smith, Beverly</u> (activist and writer):

Bellos, Linda. "Beverly Smith in Conversation" (about African-American women's literature, and needlework). *Spare Rib* (Great Britain) 121 (August 1982):8.

Culpepper, Emily Erwin. "New Tools for Theology: Writings by Women of Color" (draws on works of Audre Lorde, Pat Parker, Beverly Smith, Gloria Anzaldúa, but never explicitly discusses lesbianism). *Journal of Feminist Studies in Religion* 4:2 (Fall 1988):39-50.

Walker-Crawford, Vivienne. "Interview with Beverly Smith." *Common Lives/ Lesbian Lives* 11 (Spring 1984):10-16.

<u>Tillery, Linda</u> (musician):

Feld, Sarie and Sheri Maeda. "Linda Tillery and Adrienne Torf: Looking at Issues" (interview). *off our backs* 13:10 (November 1983):22-3.

Gautreaux, Michele. "Sweet Linda Divine: an Interview with Linda Tillery." *Hot Wire* 1:2 (March 1985):2-5.

Pollock, Mary S. "The Politics of Women's Music: a Conversation with Linda Tillery and Mary Watkins." *Frontiers* 10:1 (1988):14-19.

<u>Walker, Alice</u> (see also: *The Color Purple,* this subject category)

Christian, Barbara. "No More Buried Lives -- the Theme of Lesbianism in Lorde, Naylor, Shange, Walker." *Feminist Issues* 5:1 (Spring 1985):3-20.

<u>The Washington Sisters</u> (musicians Sondra and Sharon Washington):

Armstrong, Toni L. "The Washington Sisters." *Hotwire* 4:1 (November 1987):2-4+.

JAG. "A Dialogue: The Washington Twins." *Hot Wire* 1:1 (November 1984):20.

<u>Watkins, Mary</u> (musician):

Pollock, Mary S. "The Politics of Women's Music: a Conversation with Linda Tillery and Mary Watkins." *Frontiers* 10:1 (1988):14-19.

Ageing (see Ageism; Old Lesbians and Ageing)

Ageism (see also: Old Lesbians and Ageing)

Adelman, Marcy. "Quieting Our Fears: Lesbians and Aging." *Out/Look* 1:3 (Fall 1988):78-81.

CAD. "Passages: Aging Lesbians Meet" (keynote speech by Charlotte Bunch; Washington, D.C., March 1990). *off our backs* 20:5 (May 1990):8.

Copper, Baba. "The View from Over the Hill: Notes on Ageism Between Lesbians." *Trivia* 7 (Summer 1985):48-63.

Dykewomon, Elana. "Notes for a Magazine: On Passing." *Sinister Wisdom,* "Passing" 35 (Summer/Fall 1988):3-6.

Henry, Alice. "Workshop Reports" (from the second national Women in Print Conference, Washington, D.C., October 1981; includes reports on "Creating a Lesbian Literature: How Conscious Are We?" of race, class, age, and disability; "Lesbian/Feminism and Radical Feminism in the 1980s"; and "Lesbian Feminists and Heterosexual Feminists"). *off our backs* 11:11 (December 1981):3+.

Jennings, Cheryl. "Aging and Ageism Focus of Third Passages Conference" (Passages III -- a Conference on Aging and Ageism for Lesbians of All Ages, Silver Spring, Maryland, January 1987). *off our backs* 16:11 (December 1986):17.

Journal of Homosexuality, "Lesbians Over 60 Speak for Themselves," vol. 16, nos. 3/4, 1988.

Koolish, Lynda. "Choosing Ourselves, Each Other, and This Life: Feminist Poetry and Transgenerational Affiliations." *Sinister Wisdom* 10 (Summer 1979):94-102.

MacDonald, Barbara. "A Call for an End to Ageism in Lesbian and Gay Services." *Lesbian Ethics* 1:1 (Fall 1984):57-63.

"Questionnaire: What Misunderstandings or Cross-Purposes Have Arisen in Your Group Due to Racial, Sexual, Class, Religious, or Age Differences?" *Heresies #20,* "Activists" 5:4 (1985):82-5.

Ruby, Jennie. "Passages V: A Multiracial Conference on Aging and Ageism for All Lesbians" (Washington, D.C., March 1989). *off our backs* 19:5 (May 1989):8-9.

Sinister Wisdom, "On Being Old & Age," no. 10, Summer 1979.

AIDS (see Acquired Immune Deficiency Syndrome)

Alcoholism (see Substance Abuse and Recovery)

<u>Androgyny</u> (see also: Transsexualism; Transvestism)

Carlson, Helena M. and Leslie A. Baxter. "Androgyny, Depression and Self-Esteem in Irish Homosexual and Heterosexual Males and Females." *Sex Roles* 10 (March 1984):457-67.

Fassler, Barbara. "Theories of Homosexuality as Sources of Bloomsbury's Androgyny" (Virginia Woolf's circle of literary/artist friends). *Signs* 5:2 (Winter 1979):237-51.

Kweskin, Sally L. and Alicia S. Cook. "Heterosexual and Homosexual Mothers' Self-Described Sex Role Behavior and Ideal Sex-Role Behavior in Children." *Sex Roles* 8:9 (September 1982):967-75.

Law, Sylvia A. "Homosexuality and the Social Meaning of Gender" (homophobia as related to disapprobation of violation of gender norms). *Wisconsin Law Review* 2 (1988):187-235.

Shapiro, Susan C. "Amazons, Hermaphrodites, and Plain Monsters: the 'Masculine' Woman in English Satire and Social Criticism from 1580-1640." *Atlantis* (Canada) 13 (Fall 1987):65-76.

Stimpson, Catherine. "The Androgyne and the Homosexual." *Women's Studies,* "The Androgyny Papers" 2:2 (1974):237-48.

Zeig, Sande. "The Actor as Activator: Deconstructing Gender Through Gesture" (lesbians in political theater). *Feminist Issues* 5:1 (1985):21-5.

<u>Baudelaire, Charles</u> (poet):
Shaw, Annette. "Baudelaire's *'Femmes Damnées':* the Androgynous Space." *Centerpoint #11,* 3:3/4 (Fall-Spring 1980):57-65.

<u>Hall, Radclyffe</u> (writer):
Newton, Esther. "The Mythic Mannish Lesbian: Radclyffe Hall and the New Woman." *Signs,* "The Lesbian Issue" 9:4 (Summer 1984):557-75.

<u>Anthropology</u> (see also: Lesbians Around the World)

Blackwood, Evelyn. "Breaking the Mirror: the Construction of
    Lesbianism and the Anthropological Discourse on
    Homosexuality." *Journal of Homosexuality,* "Anthropology and
    Homosexual Behavior" 11:3/4 (Summer 1985):1-18.

di Leonardo, Micaela. "Warrior Virgins and Boston Marriages:
    Spinsterhood in History and Culture" (implications of
    spinsterhood cross culturally in Boston marriages, Kwantung
    marriage resistance, Nuer Woman-Marriage, Hausa Housewives
    and Prostitutes). *Feminist Issues* 5:2 (Fall 1985):47-68.

Gay, Judith. "'Mummies and Babies' and Friends and Lovers in Lesotho."
    Journal of Homosexuality, "Anthropology and Homosexual
    Behavior" 11:3/4 (Summer 1985):97-116.

Jeter, Kris. "The Shaman: the Gay and Lesbian Ancestor of Humankind."
    Marriage and Family Review 14:3-4 (1989):317-34.

Journal of Homosexuality, "Anthropology and Homosexual Behavior,"
    vol. 11, nos. 3/4, Summer 1985.

Lockard, Denyse. "The Lesbian Community: an Anthropological
    Approach." *Journal of Homosexuality,* "Anthropology and
    Homosexual Behavior" 11:3/4 (Summer 1985):83-96.

Riley, Claire. "American Kinship: a Lesbian Account." *Feminist Issues*
    8:2 (Fall 1988):75-94.

Sankar, Andrea. "Sisters and Brothers, Lovers and Enemies: Marriage
    Resistance in Southern Kwangtung" (Hong Kong). *Journal of
    Homosexuality,* "Anthropology and Homosexual Behavior"
    11:3/4 (Summer 1985):69-81.

Wieringa, Saskia. "An Inverted Parthenogenesis: Anthropology and
    Female Homosexuality" (in Dutch, titled "Een omgekeerde
    parthenogenese: antropologie en vrouwelijke homoseksualiteit").
    Antropologische Verkenningen 9:1 (Spring 1990):1-10.

Anti-Feminism (see Lesbians and the Right; Pornography)

Anti-Nuclear Activism (see Nonviolence; Peace Activism)

Anti-Racism (see Racism)

Anti-Semitism (see also: The Holocaust; Jewish Lesbians)

Brown, Fern. "As a Jewish Lesbian: Questions of Race and Anti-Racism." *Common Lives/Lesbian Lives* 3 (Spring 1982):42-6.

Cohen, Sherrie. "White Wimmin Have Got to Educate Themselves" (about racism; response to Burning Cloud (Consuelo Sison), Nisqually Nation. "Open Letter from Filipina/Indian Dyke," *off our backs* 8:11 (December 1978):8-9). *off our backs* 9:2 (February 1979):2.

Dykewomon, Elana. "Notes for a Magazine: On Passing." *Sinister Wisdom,* "Passing" 35 (Summer/Fall 1988):3-6.

Kaye/Kantrowitz, Melanie. "Anti-Semitism, Homophobia, and the Good White Knight." *off our backs* 12:5 (May 1982):30.

------. "The Issue is Power: Some Notes on Jewish Women in Therapy." *Women & Therapy,* "Jewish Women in Therapy: Seen But Not Heard" 10:4 (1990):7-18.

Miriam, Selma. "Anti-Semitism in the Lesbian Community: A Collage of Mostly Bad News by One Jewish Dyke." *Sinister Wisdom* 19 (1982):50-60.

Moirai, Catherine Risingflame, with Merril Mushroom. "White Lies and Common Language: Notes for Lesbian Writers and Readers." *Common Lives/Lesbian Lives* 5 (Fall 1982):46-58.

Morris, Bonnie. "Anti-Semitism in the Women's Movement: a Jewish Lesbian Speaks." *off our backs* 20:11 (December 1990):12-13.

Mushroom, Merril. "Merril Mushroom Is a Jew." *Common Lives/Lesbian Lives* 7 (Spring 1983):78-85.

Architecture

Lew, Margaret. "Relocating the Hedge Transforms the House: Monique Wittig and Pueblo Architecture." *Trivia* 12 (Spring 1988):6-35.

Archives (see also: History)

Europe:

Lesselier, Claudie. "Dykuments" (trans. from *Archives Recherches Lesbiennes,* French lesbian quarterly, no.1, June 1984, with list of lesbian archives in Belgium, France, The Netherlands, Switzerland, and West Germany). *Connexions,* "Media: Getting to Women" 16 (Spring 1985):19.

The Lesbian Herstory Archives, New York City:

CAD. "Herstorians Harassed" (threats to founders of the Lesbian Herstory Archives). *off our backs* 11:11 (December 1981):9.

Day, Susie. "Joan Nestle: 'Taking Pride in Lesbian Herstory'" (co-founder). *Sojourner* 14:10 (June 1989):17-19.

Edel, Deborah. "The Lesbian Herstory Archives: a Statement of Cultural Self-Definition." *Woman of Power,* "ReVisioning History" 16 (Spring 1990):22-3.

Hodges, Beth. "An Interview with Joan [Nestle] and Deb [Edel] of the Lesbian Herstory Archives (Part 1)." *Sinister Wisdom* 11 (Fall 1979):3-13.

------. "Preserving Our Words and Pictures" (part two of interview with Joan Nestle and Deb Edel). *Sinister Wisdom*, "Lesbian Writing and Publishing" 13 (Summer 1980):101-5.

"Lesbian Archives" (announces the establishment of the Lesbian Herstory Archives in New York City). *off our backs* 8:2 (February 1978):3.

Nestle, Joan. "The Will to Remember: the Lesbian Herstory Archives of New York." *Feminist Review*, "Perverse Politics: Lesbian Issues" 34 (Spring 1990):86-99.

Schwarz, Judith. "Living Herstory." *off our backs* 8:5 (May 1978):20.

------. "Researching Lesbian History." *Sinister Wisdom* 5 (Winter 1978):55-9.

The Netherlands:

"Keeping Everything" (formation of Dutch lesbian archives). *Connexions*, "Global Lesbianism 2" 10 (Fall 1983):11.

The Women's Music Archives:

Kimber, Kim. "The Women's Music Archives: Preserving Our Musical Heritage." *Hot Wire* 2:1 (November 1985):44-5.

Art (see also: Photography)

Anderson, Eileen. "Compulsory Performance: Rescuing My Lesbian Self from the Shell of the Prodigy" (art and artists under patriarchy; written by a trained classical musician). *Lesbian Ethics* 3:3 (Summer 1989):7-29.

Brown, Rita Mae. "Gay Arts" (letter responding to Frances Lang, "Gay Arts Festival," *off our backs* 3:1 (September 1972):22; reply by Lang follows Brown's letter). *off our backs* 3:2 (October 1972):21.

Chapman, Frances and Bernice. "A Conference Is Bringing Together" (Midwest Gay Pride Conference, Iowa City, Iowa, and Lesbian Extravaganza, East Lansing, Michigan; topics covered include building community, athletics, parenting, publications, gay art and politics (talk by Rita Mae Brown), music, and theater). *off our backs* 5:5 (May-June 1975):4-5+.

Collins, Beth. "Iowa City Lesbian Artists: a Collection of Work" (text and photos). *Common Lives/Lesbian Lives* 8 (Summer 1983):17-50.

Durkin, Jean. "Visiting with the Michigan [Womyn's Music Festival] Craftswomyn." *Hotwire* 4:1 (November 1987):34-6.

Elliot, Marguerite Tupper. "Lesbian Art and Community." *Heresies #3*, "Lesbian Art and Artists" 1:3 (Fall 1977):106-7.

Fishman, Louise, ed. "The Tapes" (edited comments of 10 visual artists who met as a group in New York City, Winter 1977). *Heresies #3*, "Lesbian Art and Artists" 1:3 (Fall 1977):15-21.

Gidlow, Elsa. "Lesbianism as a Liberating Force." *Heresies #3*, "Lesbian Art and Artists" 1:3 (Fall 1977):94-5.

Hammond, Harmony. "Class Notes" (assumptions of class and heterosexuality in art). *Heresies #3*, "Lesbian Art and Artists" 1:3 (Fall 1977):34-6.

------. "A Sense of Touch" (difference between lesbian imagery and sexuality in art) *Heresies #12*, 3:4 (1981):43-7 and *New Art Examiner* 6:10 (Summer 1979):4+.

Heresies: a Feminist Publication on Art and Politics #3, "Lesbian Art and Artists," vol. 1, no. 3, Fall 1977.

------ *#12*, "The Sex Issue," vol. 3, no. 4, 1981.

Lang, Frances. "Gay Arts Festival" (Catholic University, August 1972; festival included reading and lecture by Rita Mae Brown and reading by Lee Lally; Brown responds to article in *off our backs* 3:2 (October 1972):21). *off our backs* 3:1 (September 1972):22.

Meigs, Mary. "Lesbians in the Visual Arts." *Resources for Feminist Research* (Canada), "The Lesbian Issue/Etre Lesbienne" 12:1 (March 1983):28-30.

Michaele. "Notes on an Artist in Search of an Erotic Image." *Sinister Wisdom* 15 (Fall 1980):51-5.

Nappi, Maureen. "Clit Tapes" (video installation of women masturbating, with transcript of dialog between artist and one of her models). *Heresies #16,* "Film and Video" 4:4 (1983):24-5.

Nelson, Dona. "Growing Up a Painter." *Heresies #3,* "Lesbian Art and Artists" 1:3 (Fall 1977):80-1.

"A New York City Collective" (of lesbian artists, meeting and showing together in the mid-1970s). *Heresies #3,* "Lesbian Art and Artists" 1:3 (Fall 1977):102-5.

Orenstein, Gloria F. "Creation and Healing: an Empowering Relationship for Women Artists." *Women's Studies International Forum* 8:5 (1985):439-58.

"Racism: Lesbian Artists Have Their Say" (the Dynamics of Color Art Exhibition, part of the Dynamics of Color Conference, San Francisco, California, October 1989). *Out/Look #8,* 2:4 (Spring 1990):38-43.

Raven, Arlene and Ruth Iskin. "Through the Peephole: Toward a Lesbian Sensibility in Art." *Chrysalis* 4 (1977):19-31.

Rising, Senecarol. "Ourstory in Fabric" ("Women and Nature" quilting project). *Common Lives/Lesbian Lives* 20 (Summer 1986):75-80.

Seajay, Carol. "Visual Conceptions: a Review of Two Slide Shows" (JEB's "Lesbian Images in Photography: 1850-1980" and Tee Corinne's "Erotic Images of Lesbians in the Fine Arts"). *off our backs* 10:3 (March 1980):18-19+.

Springer, Judy. "Goddesses Unite: the Making of a Mural." *Canadian Woman Studies* (Canada), "Feminism & Visual Art/Le féminisme et l'art visuel" 11:1 (Spring 1990):97-8.

Anstruther-Thomson, Clementina (Kit):

Mannocchi, Phyllis F. "Vernon Lee and Kit Anstruther-Thomson: a Study of Love and Collaboration Between Romantic Friends" (Vernon Lee, writer, critic, and historian (1856-1935); Clementina (Kit) Anstruther-Thomson, artist (1857-1921)). *Women's Studies* 12:2 (1986):129-48.

Barney, Natalie Clifford:

Orenstein, Gloria F. "Natalie Barney's Parisian Salon: the *Joie de Vivre* and *Savoir Faire* of a Life of Love and Letters." *13th Moon* 5:1/2 (1980):76-94.

------. "The Salon of Natalie Clifford Barney: an interview with Berthe Cleyrerque" (Barney's cook). *Signs* 4:3 (Spring 1979):484-96.

Bladebridge, Persimmon (sculptor):

Mintz, Chavah. "Persimmon Bladebridge" (interview). *Fireweed* (Canada) "Lesbiantics" 13 (1982):135-40.

Rooney, F. "Interview: Persimmon." *Resources for Feminist Research* (Canada) 13:4 (1984):30-2.

Brooks, Romaine (painter):

Langer, S.L. "Fashion, Character, and Sexual Politics in Some of Romaine Brooks' Lesbian Portraits." *Art Criticism* 1:3 (1981):25-40.

Raven, Arlene. "The Eye of the Beholder: The Lesbian Vision of Romaine Brooks." *Sinister Wisdom* 16 (1981):35-42.

Wickes, George (editor). "A Natalie Barney Garland" (recollections of
Barney's life and work as gathered from interviews, memoirs, and
books of Sylvia Beach, Romaine Brooks, Madame Gaston
Bergery, Elizabeth Eyre, Virgil Thomsen, Truman Capote, and
Janet Flanner). *Paris Review* (New York) 61 (Spring 1975):84-
134.

Courbet, Gustave (painter):

Kuthy, S. "Courbet und die Zwei Freudinnen" ("Courbet and the Two
Friends"; controversial depiction of lesbians by 19th century
French painter). *Berner Kunstmitteilungen* (Switzerland) 222-223
(June-July 1983):1-9.

De Sando, Sandra:

Gleason, Kathryn. "Art -- Sandra De Sando." *Visibilities* 2:3
(May/June 1988):14-15.

Heresies #3 Collective. "Lesbianartists" (individual statements by
Jane Stedman, Maryann King, Ellen Ledley, Joan Nestle, Sandra
DeSando, Melanie Kaye (/Kantrowitz), Janice Hellelord, Monica
Sjoo, Debbie Jones, Kathryn Kendall, Olga Broumas, Sandy
Boucher, Amy Sillman, and Phylane Norman). *Heresies #3,*
"Lesbian Art and Artists" 1:3 (Fall 1977):38-49.

Field, Rachael (painter):

Field, Rachael. "Lesbian Tradition." *Feminist Review* (Great Britain),
"Perverse Politics: Lesbian Issues" 34 (Spring 1990):115-19.

Fishman, Louise (painter):

Fishman, Louise. "How I Do It: Cautionary Advice from a Lesbian
Painter." *Heresies #3,* "Lesbian Art and Artists" 1:3 (Fall
1977):74-5.

Gilliland, Elizabeth. "An Interview with Louise Fishman." *Kalliope*
11:1 (1989):29-42.

Fried, Nancy:

Levin, Jenifer. "An Interview with Artists Nancy Fried and Christina
Schlesinger." *Visibilities* 1:1 (Summer 1987):8+.

Fuseli, Henry:

Bertelli, C. "I Disegni Che Non Sono Stati Esposti al Poldi Pezzoli: L'Incubo Erotico di Fusseli" ("The Drawings Which Were Not Exhibited at the Poldi Pezzoli Museum: Fuseli's Erotic Nightmare"; includes lesbian themes in Henry Fuseli's art). *Bolaffiarte* (Italy) 75:8 (December 1977):9-11.

Graney, Pat (choreographer):

Mills, Bronwyn. "Pat Graney: Lesbian-Feminist-Formalist-Choreographer." *Sojourner* 15:3 (November 1989):35.

The Great American Lesbian Art Show:

The GALAS Collective. "The GALAS Dinner Party" (part of nation-wide lesbian artists' network, 1981; text and photos). *Common Lives/Lesbian Lives* 3 (Spring 1982):49-64.

Hammond, Harmony (sculptor):

Lippard, Lucy R. "Binding/Bonding." *Art in America* 70:4 (April 1982):112-18.

Hellelord, Janice:

Heresies #3 Collective. "Lesbianartists" (individual statements by Jane Stedman, Maryann King, Ellen Ledley, Joan Nestle, Sandra DeSando, Melanie Kaye (/Kantrowitz), Janice Hellelord, Monica Sjoo, Debbie Jones, Kathryn Kendall, Olga Broumas, Sandy Boucher, Amy Sillman, and Phylane Norman). *Heresies #3,* "Lesbian Art and Artists" 1:3 (Fall 1977):38-49.

Jones, Debbie:

Heresies #3 Collective. "Lesbianartists" (individual statements by Jane Stedman, Maryann King, Ellen Ledley, Joan Nestle, Sandra DeSando, Melanie Kaye (/Kantrowitz), Janice Hellelord, Monica Sjoo, Debbie Jones, Kathryn Kendall, Olga Broumas, Sandy Boucher, Amy Sillman, and Phylane Norman). *Heresies #3,* "Lesbian Art and Artists" 1:3 (Fall 1977):38-49.

Kendall, Kathryn:

Heresies #3 Collective. "Lesbianartists" (individual statements by
Jane Stedman, Maryann King, Ellen Ledley, Joan Nestle, Sandra
DeSando, Melanie Kaye (/Kantrowitz), Janice Hellelord, Monica
Sjoo, Debbie Jones, Kathryn Kendall, Olga Broumas, Sandy
Boucher, Amy Sillman, and Phylane Norman). *Heresies #3*,
"Lesbian Art and Artists" 1:3 (Fall 1977):38-49.

King, Maryann:

Heresies #3 Collective. "Lesbianartists" (individual statements by
Jane Stedman, Maryann King, Ellen Ledley, Joan Nestle, Sandra
DeSando, Melanie Kaye (/Kantrowitz), Janice Hellelord, Monica
Sjoo, Debbie Jones, Kathryn Kendall, Olga Broumas, Sandy
Boucher, Amy Sillman, and Phylane Norman). *Heresies #3*,
"Lesbian Art and Artists" 1:3 (Fall 1977):38-49.

Ledley, Ellen:

Heresies #3 Collective. "Lesbianartists" (individual statements by
Jane Stedman, Maryann King, Ellen Ledley, Joan Nestle, Sandra
De Sando, Melanie Kaye (/Kantrowitz), Janice Hellelord, Monica
Sjoo, Debbie Jones, Kathryn Kendall, Olga Broumas, Sandy
Boucher, Amy Sillman, and Phylane Norman). *Heresies #3*,
"Lesbian Art and Artists" 1:3 (Fall 1977):38-49.

Meigs, Mary (painter):

Meigs, Mary. "Lily Briscoe: a Self Portrait -- an excerpt from the
memoirs of Mary Meigs." *Fireweed* (Canada) "Writing" 10
(Spring 1981):31-45.

------. "Mary Meigs: a Self-Portrait" (excerpt from *Lily Briscoe: a
Self-Portrait*). *Broadside* (Canada) 3:1 (1981):10-11.

Natalie Barney Art Collective:

Wolverton, Terry. "Lesbian Art Project" (Natalie Barney Art
Collective, Los Angeles, California). *Heresies #7*, "Women
Working Together" 2:3 (Spring 1979):14-19.

Norman, Phylane:

Heresies #3 Collective. "Lesbianartists" (individual statements by
Jane Stedman, Maryann King, Ellen Ledley, Joan Nestle, Sandra
DeSando, Melanie Kaye (/Kantrowitz), Janice Hellelord, Monica
Sjoo, Debbie Jones, Kathryn Kendall, Olga Broumas, Sandy
Boucher, Amy Sillman, and Phylane Norman). *Heresies #3,*
"Lesbian Art and Artists" 1:3 (Fall 1977):38-49.

Schlesinger, Christina:

Levin, Jenifer. "An Interview with Artists Nancy Fried and Christina
Schlesinger." *Visibilities* 1:1 (Summer 1987):8+.

Sillman, Amy:

Heresies #3 Collective. "Lesbianartists" (individual statements by
Jane Stedman, Maryann King, Ellen Ledley, Joan Nestle, Sandra
DeSando, Melanie Kaye (/Kantrowitz), Janice Hellelord, Monica
Sjoo, Debbie Jones, Kathryn Kendall, Olga Broumas, Sandy
Boucher, Amy Sillman, and Phylane Norman). *Heresies #3,*
"Lesbian Art and Artists" 1:3 (Fall 1977):38-49.

Smith, Beverly:

Bellos, Linda. "Beverly Smith in Conversation" (about African-
American women's literature, and needlework). *Spare Rib* (Great
Britain) 121 (August 1982):8.

Stedman, Jane:

Heresies #3 Collective. "Lesbianartists" (individual statements by
Jane Stedman, Maryann King, Ellen Ledley, Joan Nestle, Sandra
DeSando, Melanie Kaye (/Kantrowitz), Janice Hellelord, Monica
Sjoo, Debbie Jones, Kathryn Kendall, Olga Broumas, Sandy
Boucher, Amy Sillman, and Phylane Norman). *Heresies #3,*
"Lesbian Art and Artists" 1:3 (Fall 1977):38-49.

Artificial Insemination (see Reproduction)

Asian-American Lesbians (see Asian/Pacifica Lesbians)

<u>Asian/Pacifica Lesbians</u> (see also: Lesbians of Color; Lesbians Around the World; Racism)

Bennett, Linda. "Asian/Pacifica Lesbian Network" (plans to meet in Hawaii, March 1990). *off our backs,* "20th Anniversary" 20:2 (February 1990):8.

Burning Cloud (Consuelo Sison), Nisqually Nation. "Open Letter from Filipina/Indian Dyke." *off our backs* 8:11 (December 1978):8-9.

Chan, C.S. "Issues of Identity Development Among Asian-American Lesbians and Gay Men." *Journal of Counseling and Development,* "Gay, Lesbian, and Bisexual Issues in Counseling" 68:1 (September-October 1989):16-20.

Fukaya, Michiyo. "Will the Real Me Please Stand Up?" *Common Lives/Lesbian Lives* 10 (Winter 1983):89-98.

Islam, Sharmem. "Asian Lesbian Refused Entry to U.S." (on her way to Asian Pacific Lesbian Conference, September 1989, University of California, Santa Cruz). *Sojourner* 15:4 (December 1989):11.

Islam, Sharmem and Sarah Devi. "Asian Lesbian Conference" (sponsored by Asian Pacific Lesbian Network, University of California, Santa Cruz, September 1989). *Sojourner* 15:4 (December 1989):11.

"Lesbian Refused Admission to U.S." (Dutch woman of South Asian descent stopped on her way to the Asian Pacific Lesbian Conference in San Francisco, California). *off our backs* 20:3 (March 1990):17.

Oey, Susan. "Asian-American Lesbian Visibility." *Sojourner* 13:10 (June 1988):7.

Oikawa, Mona. "Safer Sex in Santa Cruz" (workshop at the First National Asian/Pacifica Lesbian Network Retreat, Santa Cruz, California, 1989). *Fireweed* (Canada), "Awakening Thunder: Asian Canadian Women" 30 (February 1990):31-4.

------. "Some Thoughts on Being a Sansei Lesbian Feminist." *Fireweed* (Canada) "Lesbiantics" 28 (Spring 1989):95-104.

Patel, Madhu. "The Struggle to Be Accepted as a Person" (coming out as an Asian lesbian). *Spare Rib* (Great Britain) 136 (November 1983):26.

Sam, Canyon. "Untitled." *Common Lives/Lesbian Lives* 11 (Spring 1984):67-71.

Stato, Joanne. "14th Michigan Womyn's Music Festival" (the politics of the event -- who attended, what was discussed, including lesbians of color, racism, S/M, disability, and music). *off our backs* 19:9 (October 1989):20-1.

Millington, Jean (musician):
Bull, Barbara. "Sisters." *Hot Wire* 1:3 (July 1985):22-3+.

Millington, June (musician):
Bull, Barbara. "Sisters." *Hot Wire* 1:3 (July 1985):22-3+.

Millington, June. "Music, Life, and Politics." *Hot Wire* 3:1 (November 1986):48-50.

Woo, Merle (activist and educator):
Sorrel, Lorraine. "Perb Orders Woo Rehired" (Asian/Pacifica socialist lesbian professor ordered rehired by U.C. Berkeley; her contract had been terminated in 1982). *off our backs* 13:2 (February 1983):14.

Autobiography

Cruikshank, Margaret. "Notes on Recent Lesbian Autobiographical Writing." *Journal of Homosexuality* 8:1 (Fall 1982):19-26.

de Monteflores, Carmen. "Invisible Audiences: Writing Fiction as a Form of Coming Out" (written by author of *Singing Softly/Cantando Bajito*). *Out/Look #10*, 3:2 (Fall 1990):65-8.

Smith, Sidonie. "Self, Subject, and Resistance: Marginalities and Twentieth-Century Autobiographical Practice." *Tulsa Studies in Women's Literature,* "Women Writing Autobiography" 9:1 (Spring 1990):11-24.

Zimmerman, Bonnie. "The Politics of Transliteration: Lesbian Personal Narratives." *Signs,* "The Lesbian Issue" 9:4 (Summer 1984):663-82.

Bars

Jay, Karla. "Life in the Underworld: the Lesbian Bar as Metaphor." *Resources for Feminist Research* (Canada), "The Lesbian Issue/Etre Lesbienne" 12:1 (March 1983):18-20.

Journal of Homosexuality, "Lesbians Over 60 Speak for Themselves," vol. 16, nos. 3/4, 1988.

Kaplan, Esther. "All Dressed Up, No Place to Go?" (compares late 1980s "girl bar" style with other and earlier lesbian styles). *Village Voice* 34:26 (June 27, 1989):29+.

Kennedy, Lisa. "Bar Belles: Sex Tips for Girls" (compares late 1980s "girl bar" style with other and earlier lesbian styles). *Village Voice* 34:26 (June 27, 1989):28-9+.

Kulp, Denise. "Lesbian Bar Culture" (session at National Women's Studies Association Conference, University of Washington, 1985). *off our backs* 15:9 (October 1985):10.

Mushroom, Merril. "Bar Dyke Sketches: 1959." *Common Lives/Lesbian Lives* 5 (Fall 1982):17-22.

Ottey, Shan. "Black Lesbian: Alienation and Aloneness" (interview with African-American lesbian writer Roxanne E.B. Roberts; includes discussion of being African-American in a lesbian bar). *off our backs* 5:5 (May-June 1975):15.

Stevens, Wendy J.E. "Tess's Last Night Out" (closure of lesbian bar in Washington, D.C.). *off our backs* 9:11 (December 1979):15.

Battering (see Violence Against Lesbians and Gay Men; Violence Against Women; Violence Among Lesbians)

Bisexuality (see also: Labels/Identity)

Allen, Susanna. "Bisexuality: the Best of Both Worlds." *Spare Rib* (Great Britain) 10 (April 1973):25-6.

Benn, Melissa. "The Passion of Decency: Thoughts on Feminism and Bisexuality." *Spare Rib* (Great Britain) 198 (February 1989):18-20.

Blumstein, Philip and Pepper Schwartz. "Bisexuality in Women." *Archives of Sexual Behavior* 5:2 (March 1976):171-81.

------. "Bisexuality: Some Social Psychological Issues" (differences between bisexual men and women). *Journal of Social Issues* 33:2 (1977):30-45.

Bressler, Lauren C. and Abraham D. Lavender. "Sexual Fulfillment of Heterosexual, Bisexual, and Homosexual Women." *Journal of Homosexuality,* "Historical, Literary, and Erotic Aspects of Lesbianism" 12:3/4 (May 1986):109-22.

"Britain: a New Intimacy" (bisexual women write about AIDS and sexual practices, from *Bisexual Lives* (Great Britain) (1988)). *Connexions,* "Women and AIDS" 33 (1990):26.

Clausen, Jan. "My Interesting Condition: What Does It Mean When a Lesbian Falls in Love with a Man?" *Out/Look #7,* 2:3 (Winter 1990):10-21.

"CLIT Statement #2" (Collective Lesbian International Terrors, group formed "to counterattack recent media insults against lesbians"). *off our backs* 4:8 (July 1974):10-11.

Coleman, Eli. "Bisexual Women in Marriages." *Journal of Homosexuality,* "Bisexualities: Theory and Research" 11:1/2 (Spring 1985):87-100.

------. "The Married Lesbian." *Marriage and Family Review* 14:3-4 (1989):119-35.

Dixon, Joan. "Sexuality and Relationship Changes in Married Females Following the Commencement of Bisexual Activity." *Journal of Homosexuality,* "Bisexualities: Theory and Research" 11:1/2 (Spring 1985):115-34.

Douglas, Carol Anne. "Lesbian Teacher OK" (federal jury grants damages to woman fired for "bisexuality"). *off our backs* 11:11 (December 1981):9.

Dworkin, Andrea. "Biological Superiority: the World's Most Dangerous and Deadly Idea" (separatism). *Heresies #6,* 2:2 (Summer 1978):46-51.

"Falling in Love Again" (interview with Charlotte Wolff about her study on and interviews with 150 bisexual women and men). *Spare Rib* (Great Britain) 63 (October 1977):38-9.

Green, G. Dorsey and Merilee Clunis. "Married Lesbians." *Women & Therapy,* "Lesbianism: Affirming Nontraditional Roles" 8:1/2 (1989):41-9.

Gross, Amy. "We're the Thorn in Everyone's Side: an Inquiry into Bisexuality." *Mademoiselle* 77 (September 1973):138-9+.

Harrison, Barbara Grizzuti. "Lesbians, Bisexuals, and the Struggle for Power in the Women's Movement" (focuses on the National Organization for Women). *New York* 7:13 (April 1, 1974):30.

------. "Sexual Chic, Sexual Fascism, and Sexual Confusion." *New York* 7:13 (April 1, 1974):25-30.

Hutchins, Lorraine. "Biatribe -- a Feminist Bisexual Politic for Change." *off our backs* 18:2 (February 1988):16-18.

------. "Bisexuality Conference" (East Coast Bisexual Network Fourth Annual Conference on Bisexuality, New York City). *off our backs* 17:7 (July 1987):10-11.

Journal of Homosexuality, "Bisexual and Homosexual Identities: Critical Theoretical Issues," vol. 9, nos. 2/3, Winter 1983/Spring 1984.

------, "Bisexualities: Theory and Research," vol. 11, nos. 1/2, Spring 1985.

------, "Controversy Over the Bisexual and Homosexual Identities: Commentaries and Reactions," vol. 10, nos. 3/4, Winter 1984.

Kaplan, Gisela T. and Lesley J. Rogers. "Breaking Out of the Dominant Paradigm: a New Look at Sexual Attraction." *Journal of Homosexuality*, "Controversy Over the Bisexual and Homosexual Identities: Commentaries and Reactions" 10:3/4 (Winter 1984):71-5.

Kelly, Janis. "Into the Eighties" (predicts that "sex . . . will become less important as a way of defining ourselves" and "lesbians will still feel free to mess around with men"). *off our backs*, "Ten Years Growing!" 10:2 (February 1980):6.

Klemesrud, Judy. "The Bisexuals." *New York* 7:13 (April 1, 1974):31-6.

LaTorre, Ronald A. and Kristina Wendenburg. "Psychological Characteristics of Bisexual, Heterosexual, and Homosexual Women." *Journal of Homosexuality* 9:1 (Autumn 1983):87-99.

Lavender, Abraham D. and Lauren C. Bressler. "Nondualists as Deviants: Female Bisexuals Compared to Female Heterosexuals-Homosexuals." *Deviant Behavior* 2 (1981):155-65.

MacDonald, A.P. "Bisexuality: Some Comments on Research and Theory." *Journal of Homosexuality* 6:3 (Spring 1981):21-35.

Murphy, Marilyn. "Thinking About Bisexuality." *Resources for Feminist Research* (Canada), "Confronting Heterosexuality/Confronter l'hétérosexualité" 19:3&4 (September/December 1990):87-8.

Nichols, Margaret. "Bisexuality in Women: Myths, Realities, and Implications for Therapy." *Women & Therapy* 7:2/3 (1989):235-52.

Paul, Jay P. "The Bisexual Identity: an Idea without Social Recognition." *Journal of Homosexuality,* "Bisexual and Homosexual Identities: Critical Theoretical Issues" 9:2/3 (Winter 1983/Spring 1984):45-63.

Roelofs, Sarah. "Thoughts on Bisexuality -- a Response" (to Melissa Benn, in *Spare Rib* (Great Britain) 198 (February 1989)). *Spare Rib* 199 (March 1989)48-9.

Smart, Corinna. "Counselling Practice: Counselling Homosexual/ Bisexual People with Particular Reference to Young Lesbian Women." *International Journal of Adolescence and Youth* 1:4 (1989):379-93.

Smith, Elaine M., Susan R. Johnson, and Susan M. Guenther. "Health Care Attitudes and Experiences During Gynecologic Care Among Lesbians and Bisexuals." *American Journal of Public Health* 75:9 (1985):1085-87.

Black Lesbians (see African-American Lesbians; Lesbians Around the World)

Body Image (see also: Fat Liberation)

Brown, Rita Mae. "The Good Fairy" (how lesbian-feminism changes women's body language). *Quest* 1:1 (Summer 1974):58-64.

Corinne, Tee A. "Bodies: a Collage" (essay and photographs). *Woman of Power,* "Women's Bodies" 18 (Fall 1990):70-2.

Dworkin, Sari H. "Not in Man's Image: Lesbians and the Cultural Oppression of Body Image." *Women & Therapy,* "Lesbianism: Affirming Nontraditional Roles" 8:1/2 (1989):27-39.

Lee, Beckie. "I Have a Beard." *Common Lives/Lesbian Lives* 19 (Spring 1986):51-5.

Rice, Carla. "Pandora's Box and Cultural Paradox: (Hetero)Sexuality, Lesbianism and Bulimia." *Resources for Feminist Research* (Canada), "Confronting Heterosexuality/Confronter l'hétérosexualité" 19:3&4 (September/December 1990):54-9.

sardyke, lahl. "joyous separatism" (letter to "A Readers' Forum -- Separatism: Beyond the Debate" about whom one upsets by having short or long hair). *Lesbian Ethics* 3:2 (Fall 1988):8-10.

Skinner, Judith. "A Shock to the System" (body hair, electrolysis, and feminist politics). *Gossip* (Great Britain) 3 (no date):52-7.

Striegelmoore, R.H., N. Tucker, and J. Hsu. "Body-Image Dissatisfaction and Disordered Eating in Lesbian College-Students." *International Journal of Eating Disorders* 9:5 (1990):493-500.

Wallsgrove, Ruth. (letter about fat oppression as part of nexus of oppressions under capitalist patriarchy). *Gossip* (Great Britain) 6 (1988):13-15.

Pumping Iron II -- The Women (film):
Millar, Ruth. "Pumping Iron: a Feminist Response" (to the film "Pumping Iron II -- the Women"). *Gossip* (Great Britain) 2 (1986):76-9.

------. (response to Lynnette Mitchell, "Skinny Lizzie Strikes Back: an Apologia for Thin Women's Liberation," *Gossip* (Great Britain) 3 (no date):40-4; see also, related letters in *Gossip* 4 (no date):7-14). *Gossip* 4 (no date):10-11.

Mitchell, Lynnette. "Skinny Lizzie Strikes Back: an Apologia for Thin Women's Liberation" (response to Ruth Millar, "Pumping Iron: a Feminist Response," *Gossip* (Great Britain) 2 (1986):76-9). *Gossip* 3 (no date):40-4.

Butch/Femme (see also: Bars; Fashion; Labels/Identity; History: 1940's and '50s; S/M)

Andrews, Isabel. (letter to "Reader's Forum"). *Lesbian Ethics* 2:2 (Fall 1986): 99-100.

Ardill, Susan and Sue O'Sullivan. "Butch/Femme Obsessions." *Feminist Review* (Great Britain), "Perverse Politics: Lesbian Issues" 34 (Spring 1990):79-85.

Bart, Pauline. "Reader's Forum -- My Brief Career as a Femme." *Lesbian Ethics* 2:2 (Fall 1986):92-5.

Belote, Deborah and Joan Jesting. "Demographic and Self-Report Characteristics of Lesbians." *Psychological Reports* 39 (October 1976):621-2.

Blackman, Inge and Kathryn Perry. "Skirting the Issue: Lesbian Fashion for the 1990s." *Feminist Review* (Great Britain), "Perverse Politics: Lesbian Issues" 34 (Spring 1990):67-78.

Brody, Rachel. "Butch/Femme: Knowing Myself and Trusting in Desire." *Common Lives/Lesbian Lives* 11 (Spring 1984):56-60.

Brown, Jan. "Sex, Lies, and Penetration: a Butch Finally 'Fesses Up." *Out/Look #7,* 2:3 (Winter 1990):30-4.

Case, Sue-Ellen. "Towards a Butch-Femme Aesthetic" (the problem of a female subject position). *Discourse: Journal for Theoretical Studies in Media and Culture* 11:1 (Fall-Winter 1988-89):55-73.

Clarke, Caro. "Weighing In." *Gossip* (Great Britain) 6 (1988):56-67.

Clarke, Dee. (letter to "Reader's Forum"). *Lesbian Ethics* 2:2 (Fall 1986):96-9.

DancingFire, Laura Rose. "Meditation of a Possible *Femme.*" *Common Lives/Lesbian Lives* 14 (Winter 1984):10-19.

Dejanikus, Tacie. "Charges of Exclusion & McCarthyism at Barnard Conference" (Towards a Politics of Sexuality (Barnard College Sexuality Conference), New York City, April 1982). *off our backs* 12:6 (June 1982):5+.

Douglas, Carol Anne. "Towards a Politics of Sexuality" (Towards a Politics of Sexuality (Barnard College Sexuality Conference), New York City, April 1982). *off our backs* 12:6 (June 1982):2-3.

Duggan, Lisa. "The Anguished Cry of an '80s Fem: 'I Want to Be a Drag Queen.'" *Out/Look* 1:1 (Spring 1988):62-5.

Forster, Jackie. "A Restricted Country" (interview with author Joan Nestle). *Spare Rib* (Great Britain) 195 (October 1988):10-12.

Grahn, Judy. "Butches and Femmes" (excerpt from *Another Mother Tongue*). *13th Moon,* "Narrative Forms" 8:1/2 (1984):127-32.

Hollibaugh, Amber and Cherríe Moraga. "What We're Rollin' Around in Bed With -- Sexual Silences in Feminism: a Conversation Toward Ending Them." *Heresies #12,* "The Sex Issue" 3:4 (1981):58-62.

Jeffreys, Sheila. "Butch and Femme: Now and Then." *Gossip* (Great Britain) 5 (no date):65-95.

Journal of Homosexuality, "Lesbians Over 60 Speak for Themselves," vol. 16, nos. 3/4, 1988.

Kennedy, Lisa. "Bar Belles: Sex Tips for Girls" (compares late 1980s "girl bar" style with other and earlier lesbian styles). *Village Voice* 34:26 (June 27, 1989):28-9+.

Koertge, Noretta. "Reader's Forum -- Butch Images: 1956-1986." *Lesbian Ethics* 2:2 (Fall 1986):102-3.

Livia, Anna. "'I Would Rather Have Been Dead Than Gone Forever': Butch and Femme as Responses to Patriarchy." *Gossip* (Great Britain) 5 (no date):53-64.

------. "Lesbian Ethics Workshop Reports: Butch and Femme." *Gossip* (Great Britain) 6 (1988):95-102.

Lynch, Jean M. and Mary Ellen Reilly. "Role Relationships: Lesbian Perspectives." *Journal of Homosexuality* 12:2 (Winter 1985-86):53-69.

Mariedaughter, Paula. "Too Butch for Straights, Too Femme for Dykes." *Lesbian Ethics* 2:1 (Spring 1986):96-100.

Marychild. "Calling All Dykes . . . Come In Please" (member of Collective Lesbian International Terrors (CLIT) comments on negative power dynamics of role-playing; asserts that women who role-play are not "dykes"). *off our backs* 4:8 (July 1974):21-2.

Mushroom, Merril. "Bar Dyke Sketches: 1959." *Common Lives/Lesbian Lives* 5 (Fall 1982):17-22.

------. "Confessions of a Butch Dyke." *Common Lives/Lesbian Lives* 9 (Fall 1983):38-45.

------. "How to Engage in Courting Rituals 1950s Butch Style in the Bar." *Common Lives/Lesbian Lives* 4 (Summer 1982):6-10.

Nestle, Joan. "Butch-fem Relationships: Sexual Courage in the 1950s." *Heresies #12*, "The Sex Issue" 3:4 (1981):21-4.

Penelope, Julia. "Heteropatriarchal Semantics: Just Two Kinds of People in the World." *Lesbian Ethics* 2:2 (Fall 1986):58-80.

------. "WHOSE Past Are We Reclaiming?" *Common Lives/Lesbian Lives* 13 (Autumn 1984):16-36.

"A Reunion" (reflections on a 1975 meeting of "middle-aged" and "elderly" lesbians who knew each other from the Toronto bar scene in the 1950s and '60s). *Research for Feminist Research* (Canada), "The Lesbian Issue/Etre Lesbienne" 12:1 (March 1983):40-1.

Ruston, Bev Jo, and Linda Strega. "Heterosexism Causes Lesbophobia Causes Butch-Phobia, Part II of The Big Sell-Out: Lesbian Femininity." *Lesbian Ethics* 2:2 (Fall 1986):22-41.

Smith, Elizabeth A. "Butches, Femmes, and Feminists: the Politics of Lesbian Sexuality" (includes discussion of the Daughters of Bilitis magazine *The Ladder*). *NWSA Journal* 1:3 (Spring 1989):398-421.

Strega, Linda. "The Big Sell-Out: Lesbian Femininity." *Lesbian Ethics* 1:3 (Fall 1985):73-84.

Taylor, Alan. "Conceptions of Masculinity and Femininity as a Basis for Stereotypes of Male and Female Homosexuals." *Journal of Homosexuality* 9 (Autumn 1983):37-54.

West, Cheryl. "Lesbian Daughter" (of a lesbian mother). *Sage,* "Mothers and Daughters II" 4:2 (Fall 1987):42-4.

Wilson, Elizabeth. "Deviant Dress" (in the late 1980s and the 1950s). *Feminist Review* (Great Britain) 35 (Summer 1990):67-74.

Zita, Jacquelyn. "'Real Girls' and Lesbian Resistance." *Lesbian Ethics* 3:1 (Spring 1988):85-96.

Cancer (see also: Health)

FM. "Intercourse & Cervical Cancer." *off our backs* 10:8 (August-September 1980):4-5; note: cover reads 10:7.

Greene, Laureen A. "Breaking the Barriers of Silence: an Interview with Audre Lorde" (discusses surviving as an African-American woman in the United States, and living with cancer). *Woman of Power,* "Life Cycles: Conscious Birthing, Living, and Dying" 14 (Summer 1989):39-41.

Lorde, Audre. "Breast Cancer: a Black Lesbian Feminist Experience." *Sinister Wisdom,* "On Being Old and Age" 10 (Summer 1979):44-61.

------. "A Burst of Light" (selection from book of same title, about living with cancer). *Spare Rib* (Great Britain) 198 (February 1989):6-10.

------. "Refusing to Hide the Scars" (excerpt from *The Cancer Journals*). *Spare Rib* (Great Britain) 122 (September 1982):6-8.

Robinson, Jean. "Lesbians and Cervix Cancer: the Need for Research." *Spare Rib* (Great Britain) 179 (June 1987):9.

Rosenblum, Barbara. "Living in an Unstable Body" (breast cancer). *Out/Look* 1:1 (Spring 1988):42-51.

Celibacy

Ardill, Susan and Sue O'Sullivan. "Sex in the Summer of '88" (sex and pornography controversies, including anti-gay Clause 28; *A Restricted Country,* book by Joan Nestle; *She Must Be Seeing Things,* video by Sheila McLaughlin). *Feminist Review* (Great Britain), "The Past Before Us: Twenty Years of Feminism" 31 (Spring 1989):126-34.

Beckett, Judith E. "Recollections of a Sexual Life, Revelations of a Celibate Time." *Lesbian Ethics* 3:1 (Spring 1988):23-36.

Dejanikus, Tacie. "Charges of Exclusion & McCarthyism at Barnard Conference" (Towards a Politics of Sexuality (Barnard College Sexuality Conference), New York City, April 1982). *off our backs* 12:6 (June 1982):5+.

Douglas, Carol Anne. "Towards a Politics of Sexuality" (Towards a Politics of Sexuality (Barnard College Sexuality Conference), New York City, April 1982). *off our backs* 12:6 (June 1982):2-3.

Hunt, Mary E. "Celibacy -- the Case Against: Liberating Lesbian Nuns." *Out/Look* 1:2 (Summer 1988):68-74.

"Letter from a Lover Who Didn't Make Love." *off our backs* 14:2 (February 1984):9-10.

Lootens, Tricia. "Lovers Who Don't Make Love" (special section, "Love/Sex"). *off our backs* 14:2 (February 1984):6-8.

Yarborough, Susan. "Lesbian Celibacy." *Sinister Wisdom* 11 (Fall 1979):24-9.

Censorship (see also: Mass Media; Pornography)

"Austria: Lesbian, Gay Publications Confiscated." *off our backs* 20:10 (November 1990):7.

CAD. "Book Burning" (75 students at Bishop's University in Lenoxville, Québec, Canada, burn student services handbook because it includes a chapter on lesbians and gay men). *off our backs* 10:10 (November 1980):9.

------. "Lesbian/Gay Trips, Cruises & Marches" (U.S. and international news briefs). *off our backs* 10:3 (March 1980):18-19+.

Farry, Marcel. "Censorship -- Who's Calling the Shots" (film). *Spare Rib* (Great Britain) 219 (December/January 1990/91):31-2.

"Gay TV" (show featuring a lesbian couple censored in Seattle, Washington). *off our backs* 9:2 (February 1979):8.

Goldsby, Jackie. "What It Means to Be Colored Me." *Out/Look #9*, 3:1 (Summer 1990):9-17.

Konek, Carol Wolfe. "Dangerous Discussions" (lesbians not permitted to display literature, and lesbianism banned as discussion topic at forums but discussed anyhow, at the United Nations Women's Decade Forum and Conference in Nairobi, Kenya, 1987). *Heresies* 25 (1990):83+.

MacDonald, Ingrid. "Customary Bias: Canada Customs Is Preventing Positive Images of Lesbian Sex." *Broadside* (Canada) 8 (July 1987):4.

"Out for Ourselves" (excerpt of book by and about Irish lesbians and gays). *Spare Rib* (Great Britain) 170 (September 1986):20-4.

Ross, Becki. "Launching Lesbian Cultural Offensives" (a response to interception of lesbian books by Canadian customs officials). *Resources for Feminist Research* (Canada) 17:2 (June 1988):12-15.

Smith, Barbara. "The NEA Is the Least of It" (silencing through overt censorship, as the National Endowment for the Arts, and through internalized oppression). *Ms.: The World of Women* 1:3 (November/December 1990):65-7.

Thomas, June. "Commonwealth Censorship of Gay Books" (England, New Zealand, Canada). *off our backs* 16:2 (February 1986):5.

------. "Harassment by Customs" (lesbian and gay magazines and books from U.S. seized at Canadian border). *off our backs* 17:4 (April 1987):4.

  Body Politic (Canadian gay newspaper):
  "*Body Politic* Acquitted" (of charges of "immorality"). *off our backs* 9:3 (March 1979):8.

CAD. "Gay Under the Crown" (legal attempts to censor Canadian gay liberation journal). *off our backs* 10:4 (April 1980):15.

Bookworld (Canada):
> Valverde, Mariana. "Freedom's Just Another Word; On One Side, the Devil of Censorship; On the Other, a Deep Blue Sea of Free Trade: Canada's Bookworld Is Threatened by Dangers of Which We in Britain Should Take Note." *New Statesman* (Great Britain) 113 (June 26, 1987):25-6.

A Challenge to Love: Gay and Lesbian Catholics in the Church (book):
"Another Book Ban" (by the Vatican). *Christian Century* 101:19 (May 30, 1984):568.

A Comedy in Six Unnatural Acts (film by Jan Oxenberg):
Garvey, Ellen. "Police Cancel Lesbian Film" (scheduled to show at a bar in Provincetown, Massachusetts; cancellation based on advertisements for film and its title). *off our backs* 6:4 (June 1976):7.

Dworkin, Andrea (activist and writer):
Braeman, Elizabeth and Carol Cox. "Andrea Dworkin: From a War Zone" (interview about Dworkin's book *Letters From a War Zone: Writings 1976-1989). off our backs* 20:1 (January 1990):8-9+.

Finley, Karen (performance artist):
Sawyer, Robin. "Censorship: NEA Denies Grants to Lesbians & Gays" (Holly Hughes, John Fleck, and Tim Miller, plus pro-gay straight feminist Karen Finley). *off our backs* 20:8 (August/September 1990):5.

Gay's the Word Bookstore (Great Britain):
Thomas, June. "Gagging 'Gay's the Word.'" *off our backs* 15:4 (April 1985):3.

------. "Literary Trials and Tribulations" (British customs officials raid
April 1984; hearing February 1985). *off our backs* 15:8 (August-
September 1985):15.

Hughes, Holly (performance artist):
Hornaday, Ann. "Holly Hughes, Playing the Ironies." *Ms.: The
World of Women* 1:3 (November/December 1990):64.

Sawyer, Robin. "Censorship: NEA Denies Grants to Lesbians &
Gays" (Holly Hughes, John Fleck, and Tim Miller, plus pro-gay
straight feminist Karen Finley). *off our backs* 20:8
(August/September 1990):5.

Maedchen in Uniform (film):
Kelly, Janis. "Maedchen in Uniform" (Huntington, New York theater
cancels lesbian discussion panel and film). *off our backs* 6:3
(May 1976):10.

National Endowment for the Arts:
Bennett, Linda. "NEA Funds for Gay Film Fest?" *off our backs* 20:1
(January 1990):6.

Sawyer, Robin. "Censorship: NEA Denies Grants to Lesbians &
Gays" (Holly Hughes, John Fleck, and Tim Miller, plus pro-gay
straight feminist Karen Finley). *off our backs* 20:8
(August/September 1990):5.

Smith, Barbara. "The NEA Is the Least of It" (silencing through
overt censorship, as the National Endowment for the Arts, and
through internalized oppression). *Ms.: The World of Women* 1:3
(November/December 1990):65-7.

Nestle, Joan (writer):
Metz, Holly. "Lesbian Writer Fights Feminist Censors." *Progressive*
53 (August 1989):16+.

<u>*The Well of Loneliness*</u> (novel):

Brown, Beverly. "Talking About *The Well of Loneliness* -- 'A Disgusting Book When Properly Read': the Obscenity Trial." *Hecate* (Australia) 10:2 (1984):7-19.

Chicana Lesbians (see also: Latina/Chicana Lesbians; Lesbians of Color; Racism)

Anzaldúa, Gloria. "La Conciencia de la Mestiza: the Mestiza Consciousness." *Woman of Power* 10 (Summer 1988):32-3+.

Castillo-Speed, Lillian. "Chicana Studies: a Selected List of Materials Since 1980" (including lesbian materials). *Frontiers,* "Las Chicanas" 11:1 (1990):66-84.

<u>Anzaldúa, Gloria</u> (writer):

"'Conversations at the Bookfair' Interview with Gloria Anzaldúa." *Trivia,* "Two-Part Issue -- The 3rd International Feminist Bookfair -- Part II: Language/Difference: Writing in Tongues" 14 (Spring 1989):37-45.

Culpepper, Emily Erwin. "New Tools for Theology: Writings by Women of Color" (draws on works of Audre Lorde, Pat Parker, Beverly Smith, and Gloria Anzaldúa, but never explicitly discusses lesbianism). *Journal of Feminist Studies in Religion* 4:2 (Fall 1988):39-50.

Freedman, Diane P. "Living on the Borderland: the Poetic Prose of Gloria Anzaldúa and Susan Griffin." *Women and Language* 12:1 (Spring 1989):1-14.

Valverde, Maya. "Borderlands: Transformation at the Crossroads" (interview). *Woman of Power* 10 (Summer 1988):30-3.

<u>Moraga, Cherríe</u> (writer):

Allison, Dorothy, Tomás Almaguer, and Jackie Goldsby. "'Writing Is the Measure of My Life . . . ': an Interview with Cherríe Moraga." *Out/Look* 1:4 (Winter 1989):53-7.

Yarbro-Bejarano, Yvonne. "Cherríe Moraga's *Giving Up the Ghost:* the Representation of Female Desire." *Third Woman* 3:1-2 (1986):113-20.

Child Abuse (see also: Incest)

Glendenning, Christina. "'When You Grow Up an Abused Child . . .'" *Sinister Wisdom* 15 (Fall 1980):37-9.

Kris. "Another Kind of Coming Out" (child sexual abuse in the British black community). *Gossip* (Great Britain) 2 (1986):80-9.

Kushner, Leah Pesa. "Dear Nancy" (letter from an abuse/incest survivor to her sister). *Common Lives/Lesbian Lives* 5 (Fall 1982):97-103.

Linden, Robin Ruth. "Notes on Age, Rage and Language." *Sinister Wisdom,* "On Being Old and Age" 10 (Summer 1979):29-30.

Schwartz, Patricia Roth. "Lesbian Love in Limbo." *off our backs* 20:6 (June 1990):18-20.

Wolverton, Terry, et al. "Two Scenes from 'An Oral Herstory of Lesbianism'" (script of experimental play). *Sinister Wisdom* 12 (Winter 1980):61-6.

Child Custody (see also: Adoption; Children of Lesbians; Foster Care; Parenting; Reproduction)

Agger, Ellen. "Lesbian Mothers and Custody Rights." *Fireweed* (Canada) 1 (Autumn 1978):64-7.

Armanno, Benna. "The Lesbian Mother: Her Right to Child Custody." *Golden Gate Law Review* 4:1 (Fall 1973):1-18.

Arnup, Katherine. "'Mothers Just Like Others': Lesbians, Divorce, and Child Custody in Canada." *Canadian Journal of Women and the Law* (Canada) 3:1 (1989):18-32.

Basile, R.A. "Lesbian Mothers.I" (homophobia of U.S. judicial system). *Women's Rights Law Reporter* 2:2 (December 1974):3-18.

Bradney, Anthony. "'Children Need Fathers?'" *Family Law* 16 (November 1986):351-2.

Brownmiller, Jan. "Lesbian Mother Suit" (lesbian loses custody, plans to appeal). *off our backs* 5:11 (January-February 1976):9.

Brownstone, Harvey. "The Homosexual Parent in Custody Disputes" (U.S. and Canadian case law). *Queen's Law Journal* 5 (1980):199+.

CAD. "'Maybe' for Lesbian Mom" (in Massachusetts). *off our backs* 10:10 (November 1980):9.

"Child Custody -- Spouse's Homosexuality Not Grounds for Change of Custody." *Seton Hall Law Review* 10:3 (Spring 1980):751-2.

Clemens, Margaret A. "In the 'Best Interests of the Child' and the Lesbian Mother: a Proposal for Legislative Change in New York." *Albany Law Review* 48:4 (Summer 1984):1021-44.

Cole, Geraldine, Pam Keeley, and Joan Pitell. "Lesbian Mothers Fight Back: Lesbian Mothers' National Defense Fund." *Quest* 5 (Summer 1979):62-9.

Cordova, Jeanne. "For Lesbian Mothers, the Battle Is In the Courtroom." *Majority Report* 5 (June 28, 1975):6-7.

"Custody and Homosexual Parents." *Women's Rights Law Reporter* 2:2 (December 1974):19-25.

"Custody: Lesbian Mothers in the Courts." *Gonzaga Law Review* 16 (1980):147+.

"Custody Run-Around" (Rachel Yassen in danger of losing custody of her daughter to her ex-husband, in Colorado). *off our backs* 6:7 (October 1976):5.

Davies, Rosalie C. "Representing the Lesbian Mother" (review of case law and suggested legal strategies). *Family Advocate* 1 (Winter 1979):21+.

Douglas, Carol Anne. "Lesbians and Motherhood" (report from the 14th National Conference on Women and the Law). *off our backs* 13:5 (May 1983):6.

Esposito, Shaun C. "Custody -- Mother's Homosexuality and Accompanying Embarrassment to Children Held Not Proper Grounds for Removal of Custody." *Journal of Family Law* 18:3 (Spring 1980):629-82.

Ettelbrick, Paula L. "Under the Law -- Does a Sperm Donor Have Parental Rights to a Lesbian Couple's Child?" *Visibilities* 2:2 (March/April 1988):17.

Feator, Penelope. "Women & the Law: Reaching Definitions & Making Demands" (National Conference on Women and the Law, Detroit, Michigan, March 1982; includes section on lesbian child custody). *off our backs* 12:6 (June 1982):6-7.

Fitz-Randolph, Julia. "Lesbian Mothers Fight Back: a Fundraising Strategy." *Quest* 5:1 (Spring 1979):69-74.

Foley, M.J. "Lesbian Mother's Custody Upheld" (Tennessee). *off our backs* 17:5 (May 1987):24.

Goldi. "Lesbian Mother Breakthrough" (American Psychology Association states that sexual orientation should not determine child custody or placement of a foster child). *off our backs* 6:9 (December 1976):10.

Goodman, Ellen. "Homosexuality of a Parent: a New Issue in Custody Disputes" (Australia). *Monash University Law Review* 5 (1979):305+.

Green, Richard. "The Best Interests of the Child with a Lesbian Mother."
Bulletin of American Academy of Psychiatry and the Law 10:1
(March 1982):7-15.

Gross, Wendy L. "Judging the Best Interests of the Child: Child Custody
and the Homosexual Parent." *Canadian Journal of Women and
the Law* (Canada) 1:2 (1986):505-31.

Harne, Lynne. "Lesbian Mothers' Custody Conference." *Spare Rib* (Great
Britain) 129 (April 1983):22-3.

Harris, Barbara S. "Lesbian Mother Child Custody: Legal and Psychiatric
Aspects." *Bulletin of American Academic Psychiatry and the
Law* 5 (1977):75+.

Harrison, Kate. "Child Custody and Parental Sexuality: Just Another
Factor?" *Refractory Girl* (Australia), "Feminists and Kids" 20-21
(October 1980):7-14.

Henry, Alice. "Child Custody" (summary of recent cases). *off our backs*
6:6 (September 1976):8.

------. "Courts and Closets." *off our backs* 7:8 (August-September
1977):8.

Hitchens, Donna J. "Social Attitudes, Legal Standards and Personal
Trauma in Child Custody Cases." *Journal of Homosexuality*
5:1-2 (Fall 1979-Winter 1980):89-96.

Hitchens, D.J. and B. Price. "Trial Strategy in Lesbian Mother Custody
Cases: the Use of Expert Testimony." *Golden Gate University
Law Review* 9 (1978-79):451+.

Hunter, Nan and Nancy Polikoff. "Lesbian Mothers Fight Back: Political
and Legal Strategies." *Quest* 5:1 (Spring 1979):54-7.

Hunter, N.D. and N.D. Polikoff. "Custody Rights of Lesbian Mothers:
Legal Theory and Litigation Strategy." *Buffalo Law Review* 25
(1976):691+.

"Judges Overturn Lesbian Custody Ruling" (lesbian mother in England loses custody granted in first hearing). *Spare Rib* (Great Britain) 216 (September 1990):44.

Kelly, Janis. "Lesbian Challenging Loss of Parental Rights" (Virginia). *off our backs* 10:4 (April 1980):14.

Klein, Mary. "Unfair in Love and Custody" (lesbian loses custody to her ex-lover, to whom she gave legal guardianship when she was critically ill). *off our backs* 10:3 (March 1980):17.

Knowles, Stevye. "(Lesbian) Mom and Apple Pie." *Women: a Journal of Liberation,* "Women Loving Women" 5:2 (1977):67-9.

Kraft, Philip. "Lesbian Child Custody." *Harvard Women's Law Journal* 6 (Spring 1983):183-92.

"Lesbian Custody" (recent cases). *off our backs* 7:2 (March 1977):11.

"Lesbian Custody Case" (Washington State Supreme Court to hear appeal after lesbians win custody). *off our backs* 8:2 (February 1978):3.

"Lesbian Mother Custody Victories" (recent cases). *off our backs* 6:5 (July-August 1976):11.

"Lesbian Mums on Holiday" (group goes together to Oaklands Women's Holiday Centre, continue to meet as lesbian mothers' network). *Spare Rib* (Great Britain) 134 (September 1983):6-7.

"Lesbian Sues for Custody" (of child born to her ex-lover during their relationship). *off our backs* 19:4 (April 1989):9.

Lewin, Ellen. "Lesbianism and Motherhood: Implications for Child Custody." *Human Organization* 40:1 (Spring 1981):6-14.

Linda. "The Politics of Parenting -- Lesbian Mothers Out on a Limb?" *Spare Rib* (Great Britain) 181 (August 1987):57.

LS. "Sperm Donor Can Sue for Custody" (Supreme Court ruling involving lesbian mother Linden Crouch and donor Kevin McIntyre). *off our backs* 20:6 (June 1990):20.

Lyons, Terrie A. "Lesbian Mothers' Custody Fears." *Women and Therapy,* "Women Changing Therapy: New Assessments, Values and Strategies in Feminist Therapy" 2:2/3 (Summer-Fall 1983):231-40.

MacNaughton, C. "Who Gets the Kids?" *Body Politic* (Canada) 34 (1977):12+.

Middleton, Kate. "Custody Battles -- Not Child's Play." *Broadside* (Canada) 1:6 (1979):8.

"Non-Biological Parents' Rights." *off our backs* 13:6 (June 1983):15.

"Parental Rights -- Adoption -- Natural Mother's Admitted Lesbian Relationship Was Insufficient to Justify Severance of Her Parental Rights." *Journal of Family Law* 20:4 (August 1982):771-4.

Payne, Anne T. "The Law and the Problem Parent: Custody and Parental Rights of Homosexual, Mentally Retarded, Mentally Ill and Incarcerated Parents." *Journal of Family Law* 16 (1977-78):797+.

Pies, Cheri and Francine Hornstein. "Baby M and the Gay Family." *Out/Look* 1:1 (Spring 1988):79-85.

Rand, Catherine, Dee L.R. Graham, and Edna I. Rawlings. "Psychological Health and Factors the Court Seeks to Control in Lesbian Mother Custody Trials." *Journal of Homosexuality* 8 (Fall 1982):27-39.

Ratterman, Debbie. "Lesbian Co-Mothers." *off our backs* 17:10 (November 1987):3.

Reese, Susan Elizabeth. "The Forgotten Sex: Lesbians, Liberation and the Law." *Willamette Law Journal* 11 (1975):354+.

Richman, Vicki. "Can A Mother Love Another Woman?" *Majority Report* 7 (October 29-November 11, 1977):1+.

Riley, Marilyn. "The Avowed Lesbian Mother and Her Right to Child Custody -- a Constitutional Challenge That Can No Longer Be Denied." *San Diego Law Review* 12 (1975):799-865.

Rivera, Rhonda R. "Our Straight-Laced Judges: the Legal Position of Homosexual Persons in the U.S." *Hastings Law Journal* 30 (1979):799+.

Rowen, Anne J. "Notes from the Battlefield: Lesbian Custody." *Common Lives/Lesbian Lives* 2 (Winter 1981):97-106.

Shepard, Alicia C. "A New Right for Lesbian 'Fathers'? Visit Sought to Lover's Child." *National Law Journal* 7 (October 1, 1984):9.

Sheppard, Annamay T. "Lesbian Mothers II: Long Night's Journey into Day." *Women's Rights Law Reporter* 8:4 (Fall 1985):219-46.

Smart, Barbara A. "*Bezio v. Patenaude:* the 'Coming Out' Custody Controversy of Lesbian Mothers in Court." *New England Law Review* 16 (1980-81):331-65.

Stephens, Eleanor. "Out of the Closets and Into the Courts" (discrimination against lesbian mothers in custody battles). *Spare Rib* (Great Britain) 50 (September 1976):6-8.

Sturgis, Susanna J. "Concert Supports Lesbian Mother Case" (Meg Christian and Judy Reagan play at concert; ACLU defending "Jane Doe" in Virginia). *off our backs* 10:5 (May 1980):14.

Susoeff, Steve. "Assessing Children's Best Interests When a Parent Is Gay or Lesbian: Toward a Rational Custody Standard." *UCLA Law Review* 32 (April 1985):852-903.

Sutton, Stuart A. "The Lesbian Family: Rights in Conflict Under the Uniform Parentage Act." *Golden Gate University Law Review* 10:1 (1980):1007-41.

TAL. "Lesbian Joint Custody Ruled Not Binding" (in California Superior Court). *off our backs* 20:3 (March 1990):17.

Thompson, Janus Fletcher. "Parent's Sexual Lifestyle Not Determinative in Custody Proceeding" (Stroman v. Williams, 1987). *South Carolina Law Review* 40:1 (Autumn 1988):116-21.

Van Gelder, Lindsy. "Lesbian Custody: a Tragic Day in Court." *Ms.* 5 (September 1976):72-3+.

Wyland, Francie. "Lesbian Mothers" (speech delivered for International Women's Week, March 1982, Calgary, Alberta, by member of Lesbian Mothers' Defence Fund of Toronto). *Resources for Feminist Research* (Canada), "The Lesbian Issue/Etre Lesbienne" 12:1 (March 1983):41-3.

Child Sexual Abuse (see Incest)

Children of Lesbians (see also: Adoption; Child Custody; Foster Care; Parenting; Reproduction)

Baptiste, David A., Jr. "Psychotherapy with Gay/Lesbian Couples and Their Children in 'Stepfamilies': a Challenge for Marriage and Family Therapists." *Journal of Homosexuality,* "Psychotherapy with Homosexual Men and Women: Integrated Identity Approaches for Clinical Practice" 14:1/2 (1987):213-22.

Bernice. "Triad" (lesbian mother and her two daughters). *Women: a Journal of Liberation* 6:3 (1979):30-1.

Bradney, Anthony. "'Children Need Fathers?'" *Family Law* 16 (November 1986):351-2.

Casey, Eileen. "Legally Kidnapped Children of Lesbians." *off our backs* 7 (October 29-November 11, 1977):5.

Clay, James W. "Working with Lesbian and Gay Parents and Their Children." *Young Children* 45:3 (March 1990):31-5.

Coleman, Eli. "The Married Lesbian." *Marriage and Family Review* 14:3-4 (1989):119-35.

Cramer, D. "Gay Parents and Their Children: a Review of Research and Practical Implications." *Journal of Counseling and Development* 64 (1986):504-7.

Doe, Jane. "I Left My Husband for the Woman I Loved." *Ms.* 16 (January 1988):80-3.

"Gay Motherhood: Rewards and Problems." *Science News* 116 (September 22, 1979):198.

Gibbs, Elizabeth D. "Psychosocial Development of Children Raised by Lesbian Mothers: a Review of Research." *Woman & Therapy,* "Lesbianism: Affirming Nontraditional Roles" 8:1/2 (1989):65-75.

Golombok, Susan and John Rust. "The Warnock Report and Single Women: What About the Children?" (criticism of decision not to sanction artificial insemination for single heterosexual women and lesbians based on decision that children are better off in two-parent heterosexual families). *Journal of Medical Ethics* 12 (December 1986):182-6.

Golombok, Susan, A. Spencer, and M. Rutter. "Children in Lesbian and Single-Parent Households: Psychosexual and Psychiatric Appraisal." *Journal of Child Psychology and Psychiatry* 24 (October 1983):551-72.

Gottman, Julie Schwartz. "Children of Gay and Lesbian Parents" (review of research literature). *Marriage and Family Review* 14:3-4 (1989):177-96.

Green, R. "Sexual Identity of 37 Children Raised by Homosexual or Transsexual Parents" (finds no difference from children of heterosexual parents). *American Journal of Psychiatry* 135 (1978):692-7.

Green, Richard, Jane Barclay Mandel, Mary E. Hotvedt, James Gray, and Laurel Smith. "Lesbian Mothers and Their Children: a Comparison with Solo Parent Heterosexual Mothers and Their Children." *Archives of Sexual Behavior* 15:2 (1986):167-84.

Hall, Marny. "Lesbian Families: Cultural and Clinical Issues." *Social Work* 23:5 (September 1978):380-5.

Hanscombe, Gillian. "The Right to Lesbian Parenthood." *Journal of Medical Ethics* 9 (September 1983):133-5.

Harris, Mary B. and Pauline H. Turner. "Gay and Lesbian Parents." *Journal of Homosexuality* 12:2 (Winter 1985/86):101-14.

Hoeffer, B. "Children's Acquisition of Sex Role Behavior in Lesbian-Mother Families." *American Journal of Orthopsychiatry* 51:3 (July 1981):536-44.

Huggins, Sharon L. "A Comparative Study of Self-Esteem of Adolescent Children of Divorced Lesbian Mothers and Divorced Heterosexual Mothers." *Journal of Homosexuality,* "Homosexuality and the Family" 18:1/2 (1989):123-36.

Javaid, G.A. "The Sexual Development of the Adolescent Daughter of a Homosexual Mother." *Journal of the American Academy of Child Psychiatry* 22 (March 1983):196-201.

Journal of Homosexuality, "Homosexuality and the Family," vol. 18, nos. 1/2, 1989.

Kirkpatrick, M., C. Smith, and R. Roy. "Lesbian Mothers and Their Children: a Comparative Survey." *American Journal of Orthopsychiatry* 51:3 (July 1981):545-51.

Kweskin, Sally L. and Alicia S. Cook. "Heterosexual and Homosexual Mothers' Self-Described Sex-Role Behavior and Ideal Sex-Role Behavior in Children." *Sex Roles* 8:9 (September 1982):967-75.

Lee, Anna. "The Tired Old Question of Male Children." *Lesbian Ethics* 1:2 (Spring 1985):106-8.

Lewis, K.G. "Children of Lesbians: Their Point of View." *Social Work* 25:3 (May 1980):198-203.

Liljesfraund, Petra. "Children without Fathers: Handling the Anonymous Donor Question." *Out/Look* 1:3 (Fall 1988):24-9.

Lorde, Audre. "Turning the Beat Around" (speech delivered at the Hunter College Lesbian and Gay Community Center's Forum on Lesbian and Gay Parents of Color, October 1986). *Black/Out* 1:3/4 (1987):13-16.

Malcolm, Sarah. "I Am a Second-Generation Lesbian." *Ms.* 6:4 (October 1977):13-16.

Miller, Judith Ann, R. Brooke Jacobsen, and Jerry Bigner. "The Child's Home Environment for Lesbian vs. Heterosexual Mothers: a Neglected Area of Research." *Journal of Homosexuality* 7:1 (Autumn 1981):49-56.

Nungesser, Lonnie G. "Theoretical Bases for Research on the Acquisition of Social Sex Roles by Children of Lesbian Mothers." *Journal of Homosexuality* 5:3 (Spring 1980):177-88.

Osman, Shelomo. "My Stepfather Is a She." *Family Process* 11 (June 1972):209-18.

Polikoff, N.D. "This Child Does Have Two Mothers: Redefining Parenthood to Meet the Needs of Children in Lesbian-Mother and Other Nontraditional Families." *Georgetown Law Journal* 78:3 (1990):459-575.

Riddle, D.L. "Relating to Children: Gays as Role Models." *Journal of Social Issues* 34:3 (1978):38-58.

Ross, Joellyn L. "Challenging Boundaries: an Adolescent in a Homosexual Family." *Journal of Family Psychology* 2:2 (December 1988):227-40.

Sorrel, Lorraine. "Lesbian Co-Parents and Their Daughters Share Experiences" (Baltimore Lesbian Mothers' Support Group conference, May 1984, Baltimore, Maryland). *off our backs* 14:7 (July 1984):2-3+.

Stevens, Lynne. "3rd Int'l Women's Film & Video Festival" (includes film about lesbian mothers and their children). *off our backs* 9:4 (April 1979):21+.

"The Three of Us Together: My Mother, Ann Britt and I" (trans. from *Pan,* Danish lesbian/gay bimonthly, February/March 1984). *Connexions* 27 (1988):2-3.

West, Cheryl. "Lesbian Daughter" (of a lesbian mother). *Sage,* "Mothers and Daughters II" 4:2 (Fall 1987):42-4.

Wigutoff, Sharon. "Children's Books: 'Libland' or Wasteland?" *off our backs* 12:6 (June 1982):14-15.

"'Your Mum's a Lessy-bin!'" (Lesbian Mothers', Lovers', and Children's Weekend, April 1982, New Zealand; from *bitches, witches, and dykes,* New Zealand lesbian feminist quarterly, June 1982). *Connexions,* "Global Lesbianism 2" 10 (Fall 1983):12-13.

<u>Dobkin, Alix</u> (musician):
Armstrong, Toni, Jr. "A Mother-Daughter Conversation: Alix Dobkin & Adrian Hood" (Jewish separatist musician and her daughter). *Hot Wire* 5:2 (May 1989):36-9.

Reagon, Toshi (African-American musician):

Yount, Rena. "Each in Her Own Generation: Bernice & Toshi
    Reagon" (African-American singer/songwriters who are mother
    and daughter). *Hot Wire* 5:2 (May 1989):34-5+.

Class and Classism (see also: Economics; Work)

Bravmann, Scott. "Telling (Hi)stories: Rethinking the Lesbian and Gay
    Historical Imagination" (problems of race, class, and gender in
    recovering lesbian and gay history). *Out/Look #8,* 2:4 (Spring
    1990):68-74.

Bunch, Charlotte. "Not for Lesbians Only." *Quest,* "Theories of
    Revolution" 2:2 (Fall 1975):50-6.

CAD. "Lesbian Mother Not Harmful" (custody returned to lesbian mother
    by Michigan Supreme Court). *off our backs* 9:3 (March 1979):8.

Cardea, C. "The Lesbian Revolution and the 50-minute Hour: a Working
    Class Look at Therapy and the Movement." *Lesbian Ethics* 1:3
    (1985):46-68.

Carter, Colevia. "Classism, Racism . . . the Enemy is Closer to Home"
    (response to Burning Cloud (Consuelo Sison), Nisqually Nation.
    "Open Letter from Filipina/Indian Dyke," *off our backs* 8:11
    (December 1978):8-9). *off our backs* 9:2 (February 1979):17.

CLIT (Collective Lesbian International Terrors). "CLIT Statement #3"
    (militant feminism and separatism, with discussion of classism
    and racism). *off our backs* 6:7 (October 1976):10-11.

D'Angelo, Maria. "Gaps Within the Womyn's Movement." *Common
    Lives/Lesbian Lives* 4 (Summer 1982):78-80.

Desmoines, Harriet. "Notes for a Magazine II" (founding concepts for
    Sinister Wisdom; discusses politically left revolutionary politics,
    racism, and classism). *Sinister Wisdom* 1:1 (Summer 1976):27-
    34.

Dykewomon, Elana. "Notes for a Magazine: On Passing." *Sinister Wisdom,* "Passing" 35 (Summer/Fall 1988):3-6.

Gambill, Sue Dove and Rachel deVries. "Rediscovering the Heart." *Sinister Wisdom* 24 (Winter 1983):41-55.

Gyn, Gloria. "Writing and Politicking as Privilege." *Sinister Wisdom* 5 (Winter 1978):71-2.

Hammond, Harmony. "Class Notes" (assumptions of class and heterosexuality in art). *Heresies #3,* "Lesbian Art and Artists" 1:3 (Fall 1977):34-6.

Hemmings, Susan and Manny. "Lesbians National . . . and International" (National Lesbian Conference on Sex and Sexual Practice, London, England, April 1983, and International Lesbian Service Conference, Paris, France, April 1983). *Spare Rib* (Great Britain) 131 (June 1983):12-13.

Henry, Alice. "Workshop Reports" (from the second national Women in Print Conference, Washington, D.C., October 1981; includes reports on "Creating a Lesbian Literature: How Conscious Are We?" of race, class, age, and disability; "Lesbian/Feminism and Radical Feminism in the 1980s"; and "Lesbian Feminists and Heterosexual Feminists"). *off our backs* 11:11 (December 1981):3+.

Hollibaugh, Amber. "Writers as Activists: Moving Working-Class Oral Protest Onto the Printed Page." *Out/Look #10,* 3:2 (Fall 1990):69-72.

Hollibaugh, Amber and Cherríe Moraga. "What We're Rollin' Around in Bed With -- Sexual Silences in Feminism: a Conversation Toward Ending Them." *Heresies #12,* "The Sex Issue" 3:4 (1981):58-62.

JMax. "And In This Corner . . . " (classism among lesbians/women). *Lesbian Ethics* 3:3 (Summer 1989):74-8.

JMax, et al. "And In This Corner . . . " (brief writings about class and classism). *Lesbian Ethics* 4:1 (Spring 1990):98-105.

Klepfisz, Irena. "The Distance Between Us: Feminism, Consciousness, and the Girls at the Office." *Sinister Wisdom* 28 (Winter 1985):48-72.

Lee, Anna. "Interstices of Race and Class: Creating Intimacy" (building community). *Lesbian Ethics* 4:1 (Spring 1990):77-83.

Lootens, Tricia. "Third Women in Print Conference" (May 1985, Berkeley, California; workshop issues reported include classism, erotica, lesbian nuns, women of color, pornography, censorship, raid on British gay bookstore). *off our backs* 15:8 (August-September 1985):8-9+.

Maria, C. "Separatism Is Not a Luxury: Some Thoughts on Separatism and Class." *Lesbian Ethics* 4:1 (Spring 1990):66-76.

Poppe, Terri. "Professionalism: To What Degree?" (commentary on the first national gay health conference, Washington, D.C., May 1978). *off our backs* 8:7 (July 1978):22.

"Questionnaire: What Misunderstandings or Cross-Purposes Have Arisen in Your Group Due to Racial, Sexual, Class, Religious, or Age Differences?" *Heresies #20*, "Activists" 5:4 (1985):82-5.

Quinn, Alice. "Insanity and Control: a Class Trap." *Quest* 1:2 (Fall 1974):35-49.

Rich, Adrienne. "Resisting Amnesia" (importance of reporting all aspects of history). *Ms.* 15:9 (March 1987):66-7.

Silveira, Jeannette. "Strategy and Class" (letter to "A Readers' Forum -- Separatism: Beyond the Debate," about how to use resources of separatists of all classes to revolutionary ends, rather than accusing some of not being true separatists because of where and with whom they work). *Lesbian Ethics* 3:2 (Fall 1988):22-5.

Springer, Christina. "The National Women's Music Festival: Bringing Non-Dominant Women to Full Boil." *off our backs* 20:5 (May 1990):9.

Stevens, May. "Class." *Conditions: six* 2:3 (Summer 1980):13-14.

Tobin, Ann. "Lesbianism and the Labour Party: The GLC Experience" (Gay and Lesbian Center). *Feminist Review* (Great Britain), "Perverse Politics: Lesbian Issues" 34 (Spring 1990):56-66.

Tuddé, Oedipussy. "The Agent Within" (how divisions within lesbian community help patriarchy co-opt the movement; written by a sociologist, member of the Collective Lesbian International Terrors (CLIT)). *off our backs* 4:8 (July 1974):15-16.

Weston, Kathleen M. and Lisa B. Rofel. "Sexuality, Class, and Conflict in a Lesbian Workplace." *Signs,* "The Lesbian Issue" 9:4 (Summer 1984):623-46.

White, Judy. "Women Divided?" (racism, classism, lesbian-heterosexual split in the Women's Liberation Movement; and the Congress to Unite Women, New York City, May 1970). *off our backs* 1:5 (May 1970):5.

Brady, Maureen (writer):
Brady, Maureen. "An Explanation of Class and Race Dynamics in the Writing of *Folly*" (lesbian novel; article written by the author). *13th Moon,* "Working Class Experience" 7:1/2 (1983):145-51.

Desert Hearts (film):
Grundberg, Sibyl. "Deserted Hearts: Lesbians Making It in the Movies" (includes discussion of class in the movie *Desert Hearts*). *Gossip* (Great Britain) 4 (no date):27-39.

Dworkin, Andrea (activist and writer):
Braeman, Elizabeth and Carol Cox. "Andrea Dworkin: From a War Zone" (interview about Dworkin's book *Letters From a War Zone: Writings 1976-1989*). *off our backs* 20:1 (January 1990):8-9+.

Folly (novel):

Brady, Maureen. "An Explanation of Class and Race Dynamics in the Writing of *Folly*" (lesbian novel; article written by the author). *13th Moon,* "Working Class Experience" 7:1/2 (1983):145-51.

Lorde, Audre (African-American writer):

Stato, Joanne. "I Am Your Sister Celeconference: Tribute to Audre Lorde" (Boston, Massachusetts, October 1990). *off our backs* 20:11 (December 1990):1-5+.

Miner, Valerie (writer):

Henry, Alice and Lorraine Sorrel. "Valerie Miner on Political Fiction, Feminist Criticism & Class" (interview). *off our backs* 13:1 (January 1983):15-17.

Nolan, Faith (African-American musician):

Brand, Dionne. "Faith Nolan: 'I'm a working class, Black lesbian. In everything I do I have to fight for that voice to be heard'" (written by musician). *Hot Wire* 5:1 (January 1989):39+.

Coming Out (see also: Labels/Identity)

Atatimur, Sara. "Untitled Piece" (autobiographical narrative by a blind woman about civil disobedience at the Pentagon and coming out). *Common Lives/ Lesbian Lives* 3 (Spring 1982):27+.

Bronwen. "Life Is Just a Phase I'm Going Through" (coming out as a lesbian at school). *Spare Rib* (Great Britain) 115 (February 1982):54-5.

Cantor, Carla. "'Coming Out' in the Jewish Family." *Lilith* 14:3 (Summer 1989/5749):23-5.

Carmen, Gail, Sheila, and Pratibha. "Becoming Visible: Black Lesbian Discussions." *Feminist Review* (Great Britain), "Many Voices, One Chant: Black Feminist Perspectives" 17 (Autumn 1984):53-72.

Chiaramonte, Lee. "Against a Separate Background: Visibility As a Learned Experience." *Visibilities* 2:3 (May/June 1988):4+.

Clarke, Cheryl. "Coming Out" (speech for Gay Pride Day, New York City, June 1986). *Black/Out* 1:2 (Fall 1986):11+.

Curties, Debra. "Coming Out and the Lesbian Community." *Women: a Journal of Liberation,* "Women Loving Women" 5:2 (1977):41-6.

de Monteflores, Carmen. "Invisible Audiences: Writing Fiction as a Form of Coming Out" (written by author of *Singing Softly/Cantando Bajito*). *Out/Look #10,* 3:2 (Fall 1990):65-8.

de Monteflores, Carmen and Stephen J. Schultz. "Coming Out: Similarities and Differences for Lesbians and Gay Men." *Journal of Social Issues,* "Psychology and the Gay Community" 34:3 (1978):59-72.

Doe, Jane. "I Left My Husband for the Woman I Loved." *Ms.* 16 (January 1988):80-3.

Dunlap, Mary C. "Under the Law -- The Pro's and Con's of Outing" (making someone else's lesbian/gay identity public). *Visibilities* 4:5 (September/October 1990):18-19.

Elliott, Phyllis. "Lesbian Identity and Self-Disclosure." *Resources for Feminist Research* (Canada), "The Lesbian Issue/Etre Lesbienne" 12:1 (March 1983):51-2.

Fischer, Clare B. "A Bonding of Choice: Values and Identity Among Lesbian and Gay Religious Leaders." *Journal of Homosexuality,* "Homosexuality and Religion" 18:3/4 (1989/90):145-74.

Fishman, Louise, ed. "The Tapes" (edited comments of 10 visual artists who met as a group in New York City, Winter 1977). *Heresies #3,* "Lesbian Art and Artists" 1:3 (Fall 1977):15-21.

Gambill, Sue. "Being Out or In: Interviews with Twelve Cincinnati Lesbians." *Common Lives/Lesbian Lives* 20 (Summer 1986):31-55.

Golding, Sue. "Knowledge Is Power" (conceptions, labels, and uses of women's sexuality -- especially lesbianism -- since beginning of the Women's Liberation Movement). *Fireweed,* (Canada) "Lesbiantics" 13 (1982):80-100.

Grier, Barbara. "Neither Profit Nor Salvation" (keynote speech, Lesbian Day, San Jose State University Women's Week Festival, March 1977, about all lesbians' "moral obligation" to come out of the closet). *Sinister Wisdom* 5 (Winter 1978):28-33.

Groves, Patricia A. "Coming Out: Issues for the Therapist Working with Women in the Process of Lesbian Identity Formation." *Women & Therapy* 4:1 (Summer 1985):17-22.

Groves, Patricia A. and L.A. Ventura. "The Lesbian Coming Out Process: Therapeutic Concerns." *Personnel and Guidance Journal* 62:3 (November 1983):146-9.

Johnson, Susan R. and Susan M. Guenther. "The Role of 'Coming Out' by the Lesbians in the Physician-Patient Relationship." *Women & Therapy,* "Women, Power, and Therapy: Issues for Women" 6:1/2 (Spring/Summer 1987):231-8.

Journal of Homosexuality, "Lesbians Over 60 Speak for Themselves," vol. 16, nos. 3/4, 1988.

Krestan, Jo-Ann. "Lesbian Daughters and Lesbian Mothers: the Crisis of Disclosure from a Family Systems Perspective." *Journal of Psychotherapy and the Family* 3:4 (1987):113-30.

"Lesbian Self-Disclosure in the Workplace" (report on paper given by Sharon Dewey at the National Women's Studies Association conference, June 1989, Towson State University, Maryland). *off our backs* 19:8 (August-September 1989):10.

Lewis, Lou-Ann. "The Coming Out Process for Lesbians: Integrating a Stable Identity." *Social Work* 29:5 (September-October 1984):464-9.

Lutz, J. "The Effect of Delay of Labeling on Memory." *Journal of General Psychology* 109 (October 1983):211-7.

McCray, Chirlane. "I Am a Lesbian" (personal narrative in the self-proclaimed "magazine for today's black woman"). *Essence* 10:5 (September 1979):90-1+.

Mara, Jane. "A Lesbian Perspective." *Women and Therapy*, "Women Changing Therapy: New Assessments, Values and Strategies in Feminist Therapy" 2:2/3 (Summer/Fall 1983):145-55.

Plummer, Ken. "Lesbian and Gay Youth in England." *Journal of Homosexuality*, "Gay and Lesbian Youth: Part II" 17:3/4 (1989):195-224.

Robinson, Bryan E., Lynda Henley Walters, and Patsy Skeen. "Response of Parents to Learning That Their Child Is Homosexual and Concern Over AIDS: a National Study" (of 402 parents of lesbians and gay men). *Journal of Homosexuality*, "Homosexuality and the Family" 18:1/2 (1989):59-80.

Savin-Williams, Ritch. "Coming Out to Parents and Self-Esteem Among Gay and Lesbian Youths." *Journal of Homosexuality*, "Homosexuality and the Family" 18:1/2 (1989):1-36.

Schneider, Margaret. "Sappho Was a Right-On Adolescent: Growing Up Lesbian" (study of 25 lesbians, age 15-20; many are members of Lesbian and Gay Youth Toronto). *Journal of Homosexuality*, "Gay and Lesbian Youth: Part I" 17:1/2 (1989):111-30.

Sea. "From Jesus to Sappho: Coming Out to Lesbianism and Into Feminism." *off our Backs* 12:8 (August-September 1982):24-5.

"Three Black Women Talk About Sexuality and Racism." *Spare Rib* (Great Britain) 135 (October 1983):6-8.

Valverde, Mariana. "Beyond Guilt: Lesbian-Feminism and 'Coming Out.'"
Resources for Feminist Research (Canada), "The Lesbian
Issue/Etre Lesbienne" 12:1 (March 1983):65-7.

Van Gelder, Lindsy. "America's Gay Women." *Rolling Stone* 382
(November 11, 1982):13-18.

Veronica. "Reflections in the Seventh Year." *Women: a Journal of
Liberation,* "Women Loving Women" 5:2 (1977):1-3.

Bauman, Batya (Jewish lesbian):
Bauman, Batya. "Ten Women Tell . . . The Ways We Are: Batya
Bauman" (Jewish lesbian). *Lilith* 1:2 (Winter 1976-77/5737):9-
10.

Chowdurry, Dupitara (Indian lesbian):
Islam, Sharmem. "Breaking Silence: Coming Out in India"
(interview with Nandini Datta and Dupitara Chowdurry).
Sojourner 14:10 (June 1989):20-1.

Datta, Nandini (Indian lesbian):
Islam, Sharmem. "Breaking Silence: Coming Out in India"
(interview with Nandini Datta and Dupitara Chowdurry).
Sojourner 14:10 (June 1989):20-1.

Dworkin, Andrea (activist and writer):
Braeman, Elizabeth and Carol Cox. "Andrea Dworkin: From a War
Zone" (interview about Dworkin's book *Letters From a War
Zone: Writings 1976-1989). off our backs* 20:1 (January
1990):8-9+.

Gidlow, Elsa (poet):
Gidlow, Elsa. "Memoirs" (coming out in the early 20th century;
introduction by Rayna Rapp). *Feminist Studies* 6:1 (Spring
1980):103-27.

Larkin, Joan (poet):
Larkin, Joan. "Coming Out: 'My Story Is Not About All Lesbians
. . .'" *Ms.* 4:9 (March 1976):72-4+.

<u>Community</u> (see also: Rural Lesbians)

Banks, Johnette E. "A House Divided" (factionalization of the African-American lesbian community). *Black/Out* 1:3/4 (1987):40.

Bowen, Angela. "From the Editor" (about African-American lesbians and gay men as "family"). *Black/Out,* "We Are Family" 2:2 (Summer 1989):2+.

Card, Claudia. "Defusing the Bomb: Lesbian Ethics and Horizontal Violence" (builds on ideas of "attending" and "community" in Sarah Lucia Hoagland's book *Lesbian Ethics,* to discuss lesbian battering). *Lesbian Ethics* 3:3 (Summer 1989):91-100.

Chapman, Frances and Bernice. "A Conference Is Bringing Together" (Midwest Gay Pride Conference, Iowa City, Iowa, and Lesbian Extravaganza, East Lansing, Michigan; topics covered include building community, athletics, parenting, publications, gay art and politics (talk by Rita Mae Brown), music, and theater). *off our backs* 5:5 (May-June 1975):4-5+.

Curties, Debra. "Coming Out and the Lesbian Community." *Women: a Journal of Liberation,* "Women Loving Women" 5:2 (1977):41-6.

D'Augelli, A.R. "The Development of a Helping Community for Lesbians and Gay Men -- a Case-Study in Community Psychology." *Journal of Community Psychology* 17:1 (1989):18-29.

D'Emilio, John. "Making and Unmaking Minorities: the Tensions Between Gay Politics and History." *New York University Review of Law & Social Change* 14:4 (Fall 1986):915-22.

Dorrell, B. "Being There: a Support Network of Lesbian Women." *Journal of Homosexuality* 20:3-4 (1990):89-98.

Dykewomon, Elana. "Lesbian Theory and Social Organization: the Knots of Process." *Sinister Wisdom,* "With an Emphasis on Lesbian Theory" 37 (Spring 1989):29-34.

Evans, Lee. "The Spread of Consumerism: Good Buy Community." *Sinister Wisdom,* "With an Emphasis on Lesbian Theory" 37 (Spring 1989):9-19.

Fischer, Clare B. "A Bonding of Choice: Values and Identity Among Lesbian and Gay Religious Leaders." *Journal of Homosexuality,* "Homosexuality and Religion" 18:3/4 (1989/90):145-74.

Frye, Marilyn. "The Possibility of Community." *Lesbian Ethics* 4:1 (Spring 1990):84-7.

Hartwell, Shirley. "The Lie of the Feminist Right Wing Ethic" (i.e., the denial of existing hierarchies, "the tyranny of structurelessness"). *Trivia,* "Breaking Forms" 16/17 (1990):68-80.

Hollander, Judith Porges. "Restructuring Lesbian Social Networks: Evaluation of an Intervention." *Journal of Gay and Lesbian Psychotherapy* 1:2 (1989):63-71.

Krieger, Susan. "Lesbian Identity and Community: Recent Social Science Literature." *Signs* 8:1 (Autumn 1982):91-108.

Langguth, Paula E. "With the Community's Support: Lesbian Filmmakers Support the Community." *Visibilities* 2:2 (March/April 1988):4-10.

Lee, Anna. "Interstices of Race and Class: Creating Intimacy" (building community). *Lesbian Ethics* 4:1 (Spring 1990):77-83.

Levy, Eileen F. "Lesbian Motherhood: Identity and Social Support." *Affilia* 4 (Winter 1989):40-53.

Lockard, Denyse. "The Lesbian Community: an Anthropological Approach." *Journal of Homosexuality,* "Anthropology and Homosexual Behavior" 11:3/4 (Summer 1985):83-96.

McCoy, Sherry and Maureen Hicks. "A Psychological Retrospective on Power in the Contemporary Lesbian-Feminist Community." *Frontiers,* "Lesbian History" 4:3 (Fall 1979):65-9.

"New Jewish Agenda and Lesbian Communities." *Feminisms* 1:1 (Winter 1988):5.

Pitts, Brenda G. "Beyond the Bars: the Development of Leisure-Activity Management in the Lesbian and Gay Population in America." *Leisure Information Quarterly* 15:3 (1989):4-7.

Ross, Becki. "Identity, Community and Lesbianism." *Resources for Feminist Research* (Canada), "Confronting Heterosexuality/Confronter l'hétérosexualité" 19:3&4 (September/December 1990):3-4.

Rupp, Leila J. "The Women's Community in the National Women's Party, 1945 to the 1960s." *Signs,* "Communities of Women" 10:4 (Summer 1985):715-40.

Sandoval, Chela. "Comment on Krieger's 'Lesbian Identity and Community: Recent Social Science Literature'" (objects to Krieger's generalizations, on the basis that lesbians of color build/perceive community differently; Krieger's article appears in *Signs* 8:1 (Autumn 1982):91-108). *Signs,* "The Lesbian Issue" 9:4 (Summer 1984):725-9.

Silber, Linda. "Negotiating Sexual Identity: Non-Lesbians in a Lesbian Feminist Community." *Journal of Sex Research* 27:1 (February 1990):131-9.

Spinster, Sidney. "Lesbian Culture: the Intimate Touch." *Hot Wire* 1:3 (July 1985):50-1.

White, Toni. "Casa Nuestra: Oasis for Desert Dykes" (Tucson, Arizona). *off our backs* 11:2 (February 1981):24.

Winter, Bronwyn. "La 'communauté lesbienne' et l'idéologie
hétéropatriarcale: les pièges du libéralisme." *Resources for
Feminist Research* (Canada), "Confronting
Heterosexuality/Confronter l'hétérosexualité" 19:3&4
(September/December 1990):49-53.

Yates, Dicey. "Dear Dyke Separatist Strangers" (posits that only dyke
separatist community can save the Earth from destruction by
men). *Lesbian Ethics* 3:2 (Fall 1988):26-47.

Australia:

"A Radicalesbian Lifestyle" (interview with lesbians living in
Canterbury Castle, a lesbian collective household). *Refractory
Girl* (Australia), "Lesbian Issue" 5 (Summer 1974):12-15.

Boston, Massachusetts:

Penn, Donna. "Identity and Consciousness in the Boston Lesbian
Community, 1929-1969." *NWSA Journal* 1:4 (Summer
1989):765-8.

Great Britain:

Egerton, Jayne. "Out But Not Down: Lesbians' Experience of
Housing" (squatting, alternative housing communities, and
national housing policy in Great Britain). *Feminist Review*
(Great Britain) 36 (Autumn 1990):75-88.

Ohio:

Roma, Catherine. "What's Round on the Outside and Hi in the
Middle?: Women's Culture in Ohio." *Hot Wire* 5:3 (September
1989):20-2+.

San Francisco, California:

Brandt, Kate. "The San Francisco Bay Area: Is It the 'Mecca' for
Lesbian Feminist Culture?" *Hot Wire* 3:1 (November 1986):
20-2+.

Washington, D.C.:

Seeger, Nancy and Rena Yount. "A Trip Through the Women's Communities of Washington, D.C." *Hot Wire* 6:1 (January 1990):40-4+.

Smith, Leslie and Toni White. "'Ourstory/Herstory': the Washington, D.C. Feminist Community from 1969 to 1979." *off our backs,* "Ten Years Growing!" 10:2 (February 1980):12-13+.

Conferences (see also: Music Festivals)

After the Second Sex, 1984:

Douglas, Carol Anne. "After the Second Sex: New Directions" (conference on Simone de Beauvoir, including workshop on lesbian criticism of her work, University of Pennsylvania, April 1984). *off our backs* 14:5 (May 1984):12.

Amazon Autumn III: Lesbian Fall Festival, 1979:

Marie Geraldine. "Lesbian Fall Festival" (Amazon Autumn III, New Jersey, November 1979). *off our backs* 9:11 (December 1979):18.

American Library Association Conference, 1978:

Olson, Ray. "Gay Film Work: Affecting But Too Evasive" (films shown at the American Library Association Conference, Chicago, Illinois, 1978, by the ALA Task Force on Gay Liberation). *Jump Cut* 20 (May 1979):9-12.

Anarcha-Feminist Conference, 1978:

Fridley, Mary. "Anarcha-Feminism: Growing Stronger" (first anarcha-feminist conference, Ithaca, New York, June 1978). *off our backs* 8:7 (July 1978):20.

Asian/Pacifica Lesbian Network Retreat, 1989:

Islam, Sharmem and Sarah Devi. "Asian Lesbian Conference" (University of California, Santa Cruz, September 1989). *Sojourner* 15:4 (December 1989):11.

Oikawa, Mona. "Safer Sex in Santa Cruz" (workshop at the First National Asian/Pacifica Lesbian Network Retreat, Santa Cruz, California, 1989). *Fireweed* (Canada), "Awakening Thunder: Asian Canadian Women" 30 (February 1990):31-4.

Asian Pacific Lesbian Conference, 1990:
"Lesbian Refused Admission to U.S." (Dutch woman of South Asian descent stopped on her way to the Asian Pacific Lesbian Conference in San Francisco, California). *off our backs* 20:3 (March 1990):17.

Asian/Pacifica Lesbian Network Meeting, 1990:
Bennett, Linda. "Asian/Pacifica Lesbian Network" (plans to meet in Hawaii, March 1990). *off our backs,* "20th Anniversary" 20:2 (February 1990):8.

Association for Women in Science, 1979:
Segerberg, Marsha. "Re/de/e/volving: Feminist Theories of Science" (symposia, Houston, Texas, January 1979). *off our backs* 9:3 (March 1979):12.

Association of Women's Music and Culture, 1990:
Harper, Jorjet. "The 1990 AWMAC Conference" (Association of Women's Music and Culture, San Francisco, California, March 1990). *Hot Wire* 6:2 (May 1990):34-5.

Baltimore Lesbian Mothers' Support Group Conference, 1984:
Sorrel, Lorraine. "Lesbian Co-parents and Their Daughters Share Experiences" (Baltimore Lesbian Mothers' Support Group Conference, Baltimore, Maryland, May 1984). *off our backs* 14:7 (July 1984):2-3+.

Becoming a Whole Woman: a Women's Health Festival, 1974:
Spalter-Roth, Bobbie. "Health Festival" (section on "Women Loving Women" in article about "Becoming a Whole Woman: a Women's Health Festival," Washington, D.C., June 1974). *off our backs* 4:8 (July 1974):6+.

Beyond Suffrage, the U.S. National Agenda Conference, 1976:
Kelly, Janis, Carol Anne Douglas, and Alice Henry. "Women's
    Agenda" ("Beyond Suffrage, the U.S. National Agenda"
    conference, Washington D.C., October 1976; including talk by
    Charlotte Bunch of the National Gay Task Force and performance
    by lesbian singer Maxine Feldman). *off our backs* 6:8
    (November 1976):8+.

Black Lesbian Gathering, 1988:
Louise, Vivienne. "Defining Ourselves: Black Lesbian Gathering"
    (Nia Collective, Sausalito, California, November 1988). *off our
    backs* 19:2 (February 1989):3.

Breaking the Links of Lies, 1985:
Doucette, Joan. "Breaking the Links of Lies" (lesbian sexuality
    conference). *Resources for Feminist Research* (Canada) 14
    (March 1985):9-10.

British Labour Party Conference, 1986:
Parker, Jan. "Victory for Lesbians at Labour Conference" (Labour
    Party debates lesbian/gay rights at annual conference). *Spare Rib*
    (Great Britain) 172 (November 1986):44.

British Lesbian Student Conference, 1982:
Hindley, Emma and Sarah Pritchard. "British Lesbian Student
    Conference." *off our backs* 12:8 (August-September 1982):14.

Combatting Racism in the Women's Movement, 1980:
Moira, Fran. "Combatting Racism in the Women's Movement"
    (forum sponsored by the D.C. Area Feminist Alliance,
    Washington, D.C., May 1980). *off our backs* 10:6 (June
    1980):4-5.

Common Differences: Third World Women and Feminist
    Perspectives Conference, 1983:
Disch, Estelle. "Common Differences: Third World Women and
    Feminist Perspectives" (Conference, University of Illinois at
    Urbana Champaign, April 1983; includes section on "Sexuality
    vs. Hunger"). *off our backs* 13:7 (July 1983):5-6.

Lootens, Tricia. "Common Differences: One Feminist's Perspective" (on the Common Differences: Third World Women and Feminist Perspectives Conference, University of Illinois at Urbana Champaign, April 1983; interview). *off our backs* 13:7 (July 1983):7.

Conference on Counselling Gay and Lesbian Youth, Canada, 1989:

Lenskyj, Helen. "Often Invisible: Conference on Counselling Gay and Lesbian Youth" (Toronto, Ontario, Canada, March 1989). *Resources for Feminist Research* (Canada) 18:2 (June 1989): 37-8.

Conference On Homosexuality, East Germany, 1986:

Bobinska, Monika. "East Europe on Gays" (first official conference on homosexuality in Leipzig, East Germany; discusses Poland and East Germany). *Spare Rib* (Great Britain) 167 (June 1986):47.

Congress to Unite Women, 1970:

White, Judy. "Women Divided?" (racism, classism, lesbian-heterosexual split in the women's liberation movement; and the Congress to Unite Women, New York City, May 1970). *off our backs* 1:5 (May 1970):5.

Dynamics of Color Conference, 1989:

"Racism: Lesbian Artists Have Their Say" (the Dynamics of Color Art Exhibition, part of the Dynamics of Color Conference, San Francisco, California, October 1989). *Out/Look #8,* 2:4 (Spring 1990):38-43.

Encuentra Feminista Latinoamericano y del Caribe, 1981:

Tinker, Catherine. "Encuentra Feminista" (La Primer Encuentra Feminista Latinoamericano y del Caribe, Bogotá, Colombia, July 1981). *off our backs* 12:3 (March 1982):2.

Encuentro Lésbico-Feminista de Latinoamerica y el Caribe, Costa Rica, 1990:

Sagot, Ana Elena Obando Montserrat. "Meeting with Repression: 2nd Encuentro Lésbico-Feminista de Latinoamerica y el Caribe" (San Jose, Costa Rica, April 1990). *off our backs* 20:8 (August/September 1990):2.

Encuentro of Feminist Lesbians, Mexico, 1987:

Popp, Elena. "First Encuentro of Feminist Lesbians" (Cuernavaca, Mexico, October 1987). *off our backs* 18:3 (March 1988):32-3.

Feminist Futures: The First National Conference By, For and About Women in Their 20s, 1989:

Davis, Rebecca. "Young Women Fight Movement Racism" (Feminist Futures: The First National Conference By, For and About Women in Their 20s, Washington, D.C., November 1989). *New Directions for Women* 19:1 (January/February 1990):5.

The First World Meeting of Prostitutes, 1976:

Carol and Laura. "Hookers" (letter by two lesbian prostitutes, regarding The First World Meeting of Prostitutes, Washington, D.C., June 1976; conference covered in *off our backs* 6:5, July-August 1976). *off our backs* 6:6 (September 1976):28.

Gathering of Lesbian and Gay Writers Living in Europe, 1987:

Robins, Peter. "Not All Cider with Bosie; the First Formal Gathering of Lesbian and Gay Writers Living in Europe Took Place Recently in London." *New Statesman* 113 (May 15, 1987):26-7.

Gay Academic Union Conference, 1982:

Bart, Pauline, Itala Rutter, and a friend. "Alienation and Estrangement in G.A.U. Land" (written by three lesbian feminists, about the Gay Academic Union Conference, Chicago, Illinois, October 1982). *off our backs* 13:2 (February 1983):23.

Gay Arts Festival, 1972:

Lang, Frances. "Gay Arts Festival" (Catholic University, August 1972; festival included reading and lecture by Rita Mae Brown and reading by Lee Lally; Brown responds to article in *off our backs* 3:2 (October 1972):21). *off our backs* 3:1 (September 1972):22.

Gay Nurses Alliance Convention, 1978:

MNM. "Our Dykes in White" (Gay Nurses Alliance first annual convention, Boston, Massachusetts, 1978). *off our backs* 8:5 (May 1978):10.

Gay Workers Conference, England, 1974:

Benton, Sarah. "Gay Workers Acknowledge Debt to Women's Movement" (first national Gay Workers' Conference, Leeds, England May 1974). *Spare Rib* (Great Britain) 37 (July 1975):22.

Great Southeastern Lesbians Conference, 1975:

Parks, Adrienne. "Great Southeastern Lesbians" (conference, Atlanta, Georgia, May 1975). *off our backs* 5:6 (July 1975):25.

The Homosexual Community Counseling Center Conference on Gay Couple Counseling, 1974:

"Gay Couple Counseling -- Proceedings of a Conference: Panel of Female Couples" (sponsored by The Homosexual Community Counseling Center, New York City, May 1974). *Homosexual Counseling Journal* 1:3 (July 1974):125-38.

Hunter College Lesbian and Gay Community Center Forum on Lesbian and Gay Parents of Color, 1986:

Lorde, Audre. "Turning the Beat Around" (speech delivered at the Hunter College Lesbian and Gay Community Center's Forum on Lesbian and Gay Parents of Color, October 1986). *Black/Out* 1:3/4 (1987):13-16.

I Am Your Sister, 1990:

Folayan, Ayofemi. "I Am Your Sister: a Tale of Two Conferences" (celebrating African-American writer/activist Audre Lorde, Boston, Massachusetts, October 1990; disabled women's access limited). *off our backs* 20:11 (December 1990):1-2.

Stato, Joanne. "I Am Your Sister Celeconference: Tribute to Audre Lorde" (Boston, Massachusetts, October 1990). *off our backs* 20:11 (December 1990):1-5+.

International Conference on Homosexuality and Medicine, England, 1986:

O'Sullivan, Sue. "Where Were the Lesbian Doctors?" (at the 1st International Conference on Homosexuality and Medicine, London, England, August 1986). *Spare Rib* (Great Britain) 172 (November 1986):8.

International Feminist Bookfair, England, 1984:

Lorde, Audre. "No, We Never Go Out of Fashion . . . for Each Other" (discussion among three black feminists and Audre Lorde at International Feminist Bookfair, England, June 1984). *Spare Rib* 149 (December 1984):26-9.

International Feminist Bookfair, Canada, 1988:

Harper, Jorjet. "Lesbian Visibility: High Priority at Summer Conferences" (3rd International Feminist Bookfair, Montréal, Québec, Canada, June 1988; and National Women's Studies Association conference, Minneapolis, Minnesota, June 1988). *Hot Wire* 5:1 (January 1989):40-2.

Thomas, June. "3rd International Feminist Book Fair: Promoting Lesbian Writing" (Montréal, Québec, Canada, June 1988). *off our backs* 18:10 (November 1988):3.

International Feminist Bookfair, Spain, 1990:

O'Sullivan, Sue. "The Sexual Schism: the British in Barcelona" (lesbian erotica and pornography attacked at panel meeting of the International Feminist Bookfair, Barcelona, Spain, Summer 1990). *off our backs* 20:9 (October 1990):9-11.

International Gay Association, 1981:

Douglas, Carol Anne. "International Lesbian & Gay Conferences: a Split" (formation of the International Lesbian Information Service and the International Gay Association). *off our backs* 11:6 (June 1981):7.

International Lesbian and Gay Association Conference, 1986:

Bosley, Anne Marie. "ILGA Conference (International Lesbian and Gay Association Conference, "Gays and Lesbians Facing Crisis," July 1986; organization changed name to include "Lesbian"). *Spare Rib* (Great Britain) 170 (September 1986):48.

International Lesbian and Gay People of Colour Conference, England, 1990:

Williams, Natalie. "Lesbian and Gay People of Colour Gather in London" (Sixth International Lesbian and Gay People of Colour Conference, London, England, November 1990). *Spare Rib* (Great Britain) 219 (December/January 1990/91):66-7.

International Lesbian Information Service Conference, Belgium, 1982:

"International Lesbian Conference" (International Lesbian Information Service Conference, Lichtaart, Belgium, December 30, 1981-January 3, 1982). *off our backs* 12:3 (March 1982):5.

International Lesbian Information Service Conference, France, 1983:

Hemmings, Susan and Manny. "Lesbians National . . . and International" (National Lesbian Conference on Sex and Sexual Practice, London, England, April 1983, and International Lesbian Information Service Conference, Paris, France, April 1983). *Spare Rib* (Great Britain) 131 (June 1983):12-13.

Manny. "International Lesbian Conference." *off our backs* 13:7 (July 1983):14.

International Lesbian Information Service Conference, Switzerland, 1986:

Mason-John, Valery, Nicky Serrano Prado, and Maritxu Soriano Muguruza. "Two Views on Lesbian Conference" (8th International Lesbian Information Service Conference, Geneva, Switzerland, March 1986). *Spare Rib* (Great Britain) 166 (May 1986):13.

"Notice to the Entire Lesbian Movement: Terrorism at the End of the 8th ILIS Conference . . . " (and letters about incident). *Gossip* (Great Britain) 3 (no date):9-16.

Shalom, Chaya. "The Only Dyke from Israel" (to attend the International Lesbian Information Service conference, Geneva, Switzerland, 1986). *off our backs* 16:8 (August-September 1986):26.

International Scientific Conference on Gay and Lesbian Studies,1987:

Adams, Mary Louise. "Homosexuality, Which Homosexuality?": International Scientific Conference on Gay and Lesbian Studies -- Amsterdam, December 15-18, 1987." *Resources for Feminist Research* (Canada) 17 (June 1988):57-9.

International Summit for Women, Canada, 1990:

Tavormina, Patrizia. "International Summit for Women: Many Dimensions of Lesbians and Power" (Montréal, Québec, Canada, June 1990; meeting to prepare for the 1995 United Nations Conference). *off our backs* 20:8 (August/September 1990):24.

International Tribunal of Crimes Against Women, Belgium, 1976:

Dejanikus, Tacie. "NY Tribunal: Crimes Versus Women" (The New York Tribunal on Crimes Against Women, February 1976; simultaneous tribunals held around the U.S., to coincide with the International Tribunal on Crimes Against Women in Europe). *off our backs* 6:2 (April 1976):8.

Grazia. "The Tribunal of Crimes Against Women" (International Tribunal of Crimes Against Women, Brussels, Belgium, March 1976; including official and unofficial lesbian workshops). *off our backs* 6:3 (May 1976):9.

Japanese Lesbian Conference, 1985:
Bishop, Marla. "Japanese Lesbians" (first lesbian conference, November 1985). *Spare Rib* (Great Britain) 164 (March 1986):47.

Latin American Feminist Meeting, 1985:
Ortega, Eliana and Nancy Saporta Sternbach. "Gracias a la Vida: Recounting the Third Latin American Feminist Meeting in Bertioga, Brazil, July 31-August 4, 1985." *off our backs* 16:1 (January 1986):1-5.

Lesbian and Gay Studies Conference, 1988:
Quinn, Liz. "Gay Studies Program" (first conference of the Yale University Lesbian and Gay Studies Center, October 1988). *off our backs* 18:1 (January 1988):8.

"Selections from the Symposia on Lesbian and Gay Studies in the Academy, Whitney Humanities Center, October 30-31, 1987 and October 28-30, 1988" (Yale University). *Yale Journal of Criticism* 3:1 (Fall 1989):187-260.

Lesbian Ethics Workshop, Great Britain, 1988:
Clarke, Caro. "Lesbian Ethics Workshop Reports: Working with Non-Lesbians." *Gossip* (Great Britain) 6 (1988):92-5.

Lesbian Extravaganza, 1975:
Chapman, Frances and Bernice. "A Conference Is Bringing Together" (Midwest Gay Pride Conference, Iowa City, Iowa, and Lesbian Extravaganza, East Lansing, Michigan; topics covered include building community, athletics, parenting, publications, gay art and politics (talk by Rita Mae Brown), music, and theater). *off our backs* 5:5 (May-June 1975):4-5+.

Lesbian/Feminist Dialogue, 1972:

Chapman, Frances. "Talking It Out in New York City: Is the Sexual Political?" ("Lesbian/Feminist Dialogue," conference at Columbia University, New York City, December 1972). *off our backs* 3:5 (January 1973):6.

Lesbian Lives' Conference, 1985:

Blessing, Shana Rowan. "Lesbian Lives' Conference" (Hunter College, New York City, November 1985). *off our backs* 16:4 (April 1986):5.

Lesbian Mothers' Conference, 1978:

Poppe, Terre. "Lesbian Mothers' Conference." *off our backs* 8:9 (October 1978):11+.

Lesbian Studies 1988: a Cross Canada Exchange:

Donald, Christine. "Pioneering Lesbian Studies" (Lesbian Studies 1988: a Cross Canada Exchange, Montréal, Quebec, Canada, November 1988). *Broadside* (Canada) 10:3 (December 1988-January 1989):3.

Lesbian Writers' Conference, 1974:

Chapman, Frances. "Women Loving Words and Other Women" (first annual Lesbian Writers' Conference). *off our backs* 4:10 (October 1974):7.

Lesbian Writers' Conference, 1975:

Lewin, Mimi. "Lesbian Writers Come Together" (second annual Lesbian Writers' Conference, Chicago, Illinois, September 1975). *off our backs* 5:9 (November 1975):18+.

Lesbians, Gays and Feminists at the Bar, 1986:

Schneider, Elizabeth, Mary Dunlap, Michael Lavery, and John DeWitt Gregory. "Lesbians, Gays and Feminists at the Bar: Translating Personal Experience into Effective Legal Argument -- a Symposium" (Brooklyn Law School, New York, 1986). *Women's Rights Law Reporter* 10:2-3 (1988):107-41.

Lesbians With Children Conference, 1979:

Speltz, Kara. "In a Dragon's Mouth: Lesbian Motherhood" (Third
Annual Lesbians with Children Conference, Cambridge,
Massachusetts, October 1979). *off our backs* 9:11 (December
1979):17.

Medical and Social Attitudes Toward Homosexuality, England, 1975:

Carne, Roz. "Homosexuality: Sexual 'Problem' or Political
Problem?" (conference of gays and representatives of the medical
profession/social counselling services to discuss medical and
social attitudes toward homosexuality, Bradford University, Great
Britain, April 1975). *Spare Rib* (Great Britain) 36 (June
1975):19.

Midwest Gay Pride Conference, 1975:

Chapman, Frances and Bernice. "A Conference Is Bringing Together"
(Midwest Gay Pride Conference, Iowa City, Iowa, and Lesbian
Extravaganza, East Lansing, Michigan; topics covered include
building community, athletics, parenting, publications, gay art
and politics (talk by Rita Mae Brown), music, and theater). *off
our backs* 5:5 (May-June 1975):4-5+.

Midwest Lesbian Conference, 1974:

Grosvenor, T.G. "Midwest Lesbian Conference" (Michigan State
University, May 1974). *off our backs* 4:7 (June 1974):6-7.

Modern Language Association Convention, 1975:

Arnold, June, Sandy Boucher, Susan Griffin, Melanie
Kaye(/Kantrowitz), and Judith McDaniel. "Lesbians and
Literature" (Modern Language Association panel, San Francisco,
California, December 1975). *Sinister Wisdom*, "Lesbian Writing
and Publishing" 1:2 (Fall 1976):20-33; Audre Lorde's speech
also in *Woman of Power* 14 (Summer 1989):40-1.

Modern Language Association Convention, 1977:

Daly, Mary, Audre Lorde, Judith McDaniel, Adrienne Rich, and Julia Penelope Stanley. "The Transformation of Silence into Language and Action" (Lesbians and Literature Panel of the Modern Language Association Convention, Chicago, Illinois, December 1977). *Sinister Wisdom* 6 (Summer 1978):4-25.

Modern Language Association Convention, 1978:

Desmoines, Harriet. "There Goes the Revolution . . . " (paper from the Modern Language Association Panel, "Lesbians and Literature: Transcending the Boundary Between the Personal the the Political," 1978). *Sinister Wisdom* 9 (Spring 1979):20-3.

Harris, Bertha. "Melancholia, and Why It Feels Good . . . " (part of 1978 Modern Language Association Panel, "Lesbians and Literature: Transcending the Boundary Between the Personal and the Political"). *Sinister Wisdom* 9 (Spring 1979):24-6.

Klepfisz, Irena. "Criticism: Form and Function in Lesbian Literature" (part of 1978 Modern Language Association Panel, "Lesbians and Literature: Transcending the Boundary Between the Personal and the Political"). *Sinister Wisdom* 9 (Spring 1979):27-30.

National Assembly on the Future of the Family (NOW Fund), 1979:

Polikoff, Nancy. "Assembly Removes Family Issue from the Right But . . . " *off our backs* 10:3 (March 1980):12.

National Coalition Against Domestic Violence Conference, 1980:

LAW. "Battered Women's Conference" (National Coalition Against Domestic Violence Conference, Washington, D.C., February 1980; including section on battered lesbians). *off our backs* 10:4 (April 1980):4.

National Coalition Against Domestic Violence Conference, 1983:
"Statement on Lesbian Battering and Sexual Violence: To the
    Lesbian Nation" (statement distributed by the lesbian caucus of
    the National Coalition Against Domestic Violence, developed by
    the caucus at the NCADV conference in Washington, D.C.,
    September 1983). *off our backs* 14:1 (January 1984):15.

National Coalition Against Domestic Violence Meeting, 1988:
"NCADV Meets" (National Coalition Against Domestic Violence,
    Seattle, Washington, July 1988; includes section on lesbian
    battering). *off our backs* 18:9 (October 1988):1-3+.

Nicarthy, Ginny. "NCADV Meets (part 2)" (National Coalition
    Against Domestic Violence, July 1988, Seattle; includes section
    on lesbian battering). *off our backs* 18:10 (November 1988):16-
    17.

National Coalition of Black Lesbians and Gays, 1988:
Black/Out, "Tenth Anniversary Edition: NCBLG Celebrates
    Homecoming" (National Coalition of Black Lesbians and Gays),
    vol. 2, no. 1, Fall 1988.

National Coalition of Lesbian and Gay Groups and Individuals
    Conference, 1980:
CAD. "Gay . . . Actions" (news briefs; new coalition inspired by the
    October 1979 march on Washington, Oberlin College, March
    1980). *off our backs* 10:5 (May 1980):9.

National Conference on Socialist Feminism, 1975:
"Lesbianism and Socialist Feminism" (statement delivered at the
    First National Conference on Socialist Feminism, Yellow
    Springs, Ohio, July 1975; addresses racism, classism, ageism,
    lesbian parenting, and homophobia in the socialist feminist
    movement). *off our backs* 5:8 (September-October 1975):19.

Moira, Fran. "Focus on Criticism and Women's Place" (at the First
    National Conference on Socialist Feminism, Yellow Springs,
    Ohio, July 1975; article includes "Lesbian Overview"). *off our
    backs* 5:7 (August 1975):3-4.

National Conference on Women and the Law, 1976:
Rankin, Teresa. "Gays' (Lack of) Rights" (part of report on the
    Seventh National Conference on Women and the Law, Temple
    University, March 1976). *off our backs* 6:2 (April 1976):3.

National Conference on Women and the Law, 1982:
Feator, Penelope. "Women & the Law: Reaching Definitions &
    Making Demands" (National Conference on Women and the
    Law, Detroit, Michigan, March 1982; includes section on
    lesbian child custody). *off our backs* 12:6 (June 1982):6-7.

National Gathering of the United Church of Christ's Coalition for
    Lesbian/Gay Concerns, 1986:
Comstock, Gary David. "Aliens in the Promised Land'?: Keynote
    Address for the 1986 National Gathering of the United Church of
    Christ's Coalition for Lesbian/Gay Concerns." *Journal of
    Homosexuality,* "Homosexuality and Religion" 18:3/4
    (1989/1990):133-44.

National Gay Health Conference, 1978:
Fridley, Mary. "The Health Closet: Opening the Door on Gay Health
    Issues" (first national gay health conference, Washington, D.C.,
    May 1978). *off our backs* 8:7 (July 1978):14+.

National Homosexual Conference, India, 1981:
"Indian Gay Conference" (Hyderabad, India, November 1981). *off our
    backs* 12:6 (June 1982):10.

National Lesbian Conference, 1991:
Calla. "Southeast Meets to Plan for the National Lesbian
    Conference." *off our backs* 19:4 (April 1989):8.

Curb, Rosemary. "Lesbian Conference Sets Bold Agenda." *New
    Directions for Women* 19:1 (January/February 1990):6.

------. "National Lesbian Conference: Spinning On to Atlanta"
    (Georgia, April 1991). *off our backs* 20:7 (July 1990):6.

Elliott, Farar. "Lesbians Plan National Gathering." *off our backs* 19:5 (May 1989):6-7.

Folayan, Ayofemi. "Lesbian Agenda Planning Continues" (for National Lesbian Conference, to be held in Atlanta, Georgia, April 1991). *off our backs* 19:9 (October 1989):15.

Platt, Mary Frances. "Serious Shit at the NLC" (planning for the National Lesbian Conference, April 1991, especially regarding disabled accessibility and education). *off our backs* 20:5 (May 1990):11.

National Lesbian Conference on Sex and Sexual Practice, England, 1983:
Hemmings, Susan and Manny. "Lesbians National . . . and International" (National Lesbian Conference on Sex and Sexual Practice, London, England, April 1983, and International Lesbian Information Service Conference, Paris, France, April 1983). *Spare Rib* (Great Britain) 131 (June 1983):12-13.

National Lesbian Feminist Conference, 1976:
"Lesbians Shut Out" (of the University of Indiana, Bloomington, which cancelled the scheduled National Lesbian Feminist Conference, planned for July 1976). *off our backs* 6:5 (July-August, 1976):11.

National Lesbian Feminist Organization Conference, 1978:
MNM. "NLFO" (National Lesbian Feminist Organization founding conference, Los Angeles, California, May 1978). *off our backs* 8:5 (May 1978):10.

National Lesbian Rights Conference, 1988:
Stowe, Ayofemi. "'Power Into Action': The National Lesbian Rights Conference" (of the National Organization for Women, San Diego, California, October 1988). *off our backs* 18:11 (December 1988):8+.

National Women's Conference, 1977:

AH and JK. "National Women's Conference" (Houston, Texas, November 1977; includes report on lesbian caucus). *off our backs* 8:1 (January 1978):2-3.

"National Women's Conference Resolutions" (Houston, Texas, November 1977; includes resolution on "sexual preference"). *off our backs* 8:1 (January 1978):4-5.

National Women's Film Circuit, 1978:

Poppe, Terri. "2nd National Women's Film Festival" (The National Women's Film Circuit, Washington D.C., May 1978). *off our backs* 8:5 (May 1978):14-15.

National Women's Studies Association Conference, 1979:

Bunch, Charlotte. "Visions and Revisions: Women and the Power to Change" (part of final panel of the first National Women's Studies Association conference, Lawrence, Kansas, May 30-June 3, 1979). *Women's Studies Newsletter* 7:3 (Summer 1979):20-1.

National Women's Studies Association Conference, 1981:

Manahan, Nancy. "Future Old Maids and Pacifist Agitators: the Story of Tracy Mygatt and Frances Witherspoon" (part of "Lesbian Survival Strategies, 1850-1950" panel at the National Women's Studies Association Conference in Storrs, Connecticut, 1981). *Women's Studies Quarterly* 10:1 (Spring 1982):10-13.

National Women's Studies Association Conference, 1984:

Douglas, Carol Anne. "Lesbian Nuns: Breaking Silence" (National Women's Studies Association Conference workshop, Rutgers University, New Brunswick, New Jersey, June 1984). *off our backs* 14:10 (November 1984):19.

National Women's Studies Association Conference, 1985:

Kulp, Denise and Karen Mudd. "Common Causes: Uncommon Coalitions" (Charlotte Bunch, Barbara MacDonald, Barbara Smith, and Merle Woo at National Women's Studies Association conference symposium, University of Washington, 1985). *off our backs* 15:8 (August-September 1985):4-5+.

<u>National Women's Studies Association Conference, 1988</u>:

Brant, Beth. "Lesbian Alliances: Heterosexism in the Eighties -- The Call of the Heron" (speech at the National Women's Studies Association conference, Minneapolis, Minnesota, June 1988). *Sojourner* 14:3 (November 1988):15.

CAD. "Lesbian Plenary: Combatting Heterosexism" (at 10th annual National Women's Studies Association Conference, June 1988, University of Minnesota in Minneapolis; panel members Beth Brant, Michelle Parkerson, Joan Nestle, Gloria Anzaldúa). *off our backs* 18:8 (August-September 1988):3+.

Harper, Jorjet. "Lesbian Visibility: High Priority at Summer Conferences" (3rd International Feminist Bookfair, Montréal, Québec, Canada, June 1988; and National Women's Studies Association conference, Minneapolis, Minnesota, June 1988). *Hot Wire* 5:1 (January 1989):40-2.

Ruby, Jennie. "The Black Diaspora" (Michelle Parkerson, Audre Lorde, and Cheryl Clarke speaking on diversity of self-expression among African-American women, in a session at the 10th annual National Women's Studies Association conference, University of Minnesota in Minneapolis, June 1988, "African American Women and the Black Diaspora"). *off our backs* 18:8 (August-September 1988):10.

Ruby, Jennie. "Lesbian Theory: Pursuing Lesbian Meaning" (Lesbian Theory session of the National Women's Studies' Association conference in Minneapolis, June 1988; includes reports on the following papers: Betty Tallen, "Lesbian Feminist Theory: a View from the Political Theory Trenches"; Lee Evans, "Lesbians, Community, and Patriarchal Consumer Values"; Elana Dykewomon, "The Knots of Process"; Anna Lee, "New Age Spirituality Is the Invention of Heteropatriarchy"; Sarah Hoagland, "Lesbian Agency" and "Lesbian Space"; and Jeffner Allen on writing). *off our backs* 18:9 (October 1988):18-19.

National Women's Studies Association Conference, 1989:
CAD. "Lesbian Relationships" (workshop at National Women's Studies Association Conference, Towson State University, Maryland, June 1989). *off our backs* 19:9 (October 1989):23.

Ruby, Jennie. "Lesbian Theory" (workshop at National Women's Studies Association conference, Towson State University, Maryland, June 1989; reports on Betty Tallen, "A Lesbian-Feminist Critique of 12-Step Programs"; Jeffner Allen, "Passions in the Gardens of Delight"; and Sarah Lucia Hoagland on Lesbian Ethics). *off our backs* 19:8 (August-September 1989):8.

National Women's Studies Association Conference, 1990:
CAD. "Theories of Sexuality Forum" (at the National Women's Studies Association Conference, Akron, Ohio, June 1990). *off our backs* 20:8 (August/September 1990):17.

Frye, Marilyn. "Do You Have to Be a Lesbian to Be a Feminist?" (speech delivered at the National Women's Studies Association Conference, Akron, Ohio, June 1990, about treating sexuality in women's studies courses). *off our backs* 20:8 (August/September 1990):21-3.

"Homophobia Workshops" (at the National Women's Studies Association Conference, Akron, Ohio, June 1990). *off our backs* 20:8 (August/September 1990):17-20.

National Women's Studies Conference, United Kingdom, 1984:
Duelli Klein, Renate. "Third National Women's Studies Conference, Bradford, U.K., March 31-April 1, 1984" (includes reports on lesbian studies workshop and lesbian invisibility presentation). *Women's Studies International Forum* 7:3 (1984):i-iv.

New Agenda: A Blueprint for the Future of Women's Sports, 1983:
Krebs, Paula. "At the Starting Blocks: Women Athletes' New Agenda" (New Agenda: A Blueprint for the Future of Women's Sports, conference, Washington, D.C., November 1983). *off our backs* 14:1 (January 1984):1-3.

New York Tribunal on Crimes Against Women, 1976:

Dejanikus, Tacie. "NY Tribunal: Crimes Versus Women" (The New
York Tribunal on Crimes Against Women, February 1976;
simultaneous tribunals held around the U.S., to coincide with the
International Tribunal on Crimes Against Women in Europe).
off our backs 6:2 (April 1976):8.

NOW national conference, 1973:

Pollner, Fran. "Lesbian Dynamics" (at sixth national conference of
the National Organization for Women). *off our backs* 3:6
(February-March 1973):7.

NOW national conference, 1982:

Krebs, Paula. "Is the Smeal Era Over for NOW?: NOW Votes for
New Officers" (lesbian and minority issues prioritized at 15th
annual conference as delegates confront NOW leadership). *off our
backs* 12:10 (November 1982):2-3.

NOW Conference on Sexuality, 1974:

Moira, Fran. "NOW: It'll Be a Long Time Coming" (report on
lesbian workshop at mostly heterosexual "NOW Conference on
Sexuality," October 1974). *off our backs* 4:11 (November
1974):3.

NOW Sexuality Task Force Conference, 1977:

Douglas, Carol Anne. "Women's Community Conference" (of the
NOW Sexuality Task Force). *off our backs* 7:5 (May 1977):8+.

NOW Sexuality Task Force Conference, 1978:

Douglas, Carol Anne. "Woman-Identified Conference" ("Woman-
Identified Women: Speaking for Ourselves," conference of the
Sexuality Task Force of the National Organization for Women,
George Washington University, Washington, D.C., April 1978).
off our backs 8:5 (May 1978):13.

NOW Sexuality Task Force Conference, 1979:

Douglas, Carol Anne and Diana Onley-Campbell. "Lesbians Are
Everywhere" (third annual conference of NOW Sexuality Task
Force). *off our backs* 9:7 (July 1979):18 and 9:8 (August-
September 1979):27.

Old Lesbian Conference and Celebration II, 1989:

Rosenblatt, Kate. "Old Lesbians Meet" (Old Lesbian Conference and Celebration II, San Francisco State University, August 1989). *off our backs* 19:10 (November 1989):5.

Organization for the Study of Communication, Language, and Gender, 1990:

Pierce, Dean. "Who Speaks for Lesbian/Gay Adolescents: Voices to be Silenced, Voices to be Heard" (speech delivered at the annual meeting of the Organization for the Study of Communication, Language, and Gender, 1990). *Women and Language* 13:2 (Winter 1990):37-41.

OUT Write Lesbian and Gay Writers Conference, 1990:

Chrichton, E.G. "'There's So Much to Say': OUT Write '90 Makes History" (first national conference of lesbian and gay writers, San Francisco, California, March 1990). *Out/Look #9,* 3:1 (Summer 1990):2-5.

Grahn, Judy. "'Gay or Lesbian Writer': Hardly an Alienated Occupation" (keynote address at OUT Write '90, national lesbian and gay writers conference, San Francisco, California, March 1990). *Out/Look #9,* 3:1 (Summer 1990):38-41.

Passages, 1988:

Douglas, Carol Anne. "Passages: Lesbian Aging" (fourth annual conference in Washington, D.C.). *off our backs* 18:4 (April 1988):16.

Passages V: A Multiracial Conference on Aging and Ageism for All Lesbians, 1989:

Ruby, Jennie. "Passages V: A Multiracial Conference on Aging and Ageism for All Lesbians" (Washington, D.C., March 1989). *off our backs* 19:5 (May 1989):8-9.

Passages, 1990:

CAD. "Passages: Aging Lesbians Meet" (keynote speech by Charlotte Bunch; Washington, D.C., March 1990). *off our backs* 20:5 (May 1990):8.

Pulling Together: Being with Children in Shelter Conference, 1981:

Lootens, Tricia. "Homophobia: Thin End of Antifeminist Wedge" (Lesbian Caucus meeting of the Pulling Together: Being with Children in Shelter Conference, Washington, D.C., December 1981). *off our backs* 12:3 (March 1982):30.

------. "Lesbian-Baiting in the Women's Movement" (statement by lesbians in the battered women's shelter movement, at the Pulling Together: Being with Children in Shelter Conference, Washington, D.C., December 1981). *off our backs* 12:3 (March 1982):17.

Radical Women National Conference, 1990:

Hindin, Roanne. "Radical Women National Conference: the Third Wave of Feminism" (Santa Monica, California, February 1990). *off our backs* 20:6 (June 1990):9.

Post, Dianne. "Radical Women National Conference: a Cold Shower" (Santa Monica, California, February 1990). *off our backs* 20:6 (June 1990):10-11.

Reproductive Rights National Network Conference, 1983:

Towey, Shawn. "Reproductive Rights National Network Meets: Racism and Heterosexism Discussed" (Reproductive Rights National Network Conference, Philadelphia, Pennsylvania, April 1983). *off our backs* 13:7 (July 1983):15.

Richmond Women's Festival, 1974:

Moira, Fran. "Richmond Women's Festival: an Overflow of Men, Wine and Blood" (Richmond, Virginia, July 1974; gathering held in public park, attended by many anti-feminist men and straight women; Flo Kennedy, Margaret Sloan, and Kay Gardner spoke and/or performed). *off our backs* 4:9 (August/September 1974):11.

<u>The Scholar and the Feminist Conference, 1980</u>:

Mutari, Ellen. "Class, Race, Sexual Preference Differences" (seventh annual The Scholar and the Feminist Conference, Barnard College, New York City, April 1980). *off our backs* 10:9 (June 1980):10.

<u>The Second Sex -- Thirty Years Later: a Commemorative Conference on Feminist Theory, 1979</u>:

Lorde, Audre. "The Role of Difference" (presentation on "The Personal is Political" panel of The Second Sex -- Thirty Years Later: a Commemorative Conference on Feminist Theory, September 1979; Lorde responds to lack of presence and discussion of lesbians/women of color). *off our backs* 9:12 (December 1979):5+.

<u>The Sexual Liberals and the Attack on Feminism Conference, 1987</u>:

Douglas, Carol Anne. "Commentary: Hope for Feminism" (response to The Sexual Liberals and the Attack on Feminism conference, New York University Law School, April 1987). *off our backs* 17:5 (May 1987):21.

Kulp, Denise. "Redefining Feminism and Excluding Women" (response to The Sexual Liberals and the Attack on Feminism conference, New York University Law School, April 1987). *off our backs* 17:5 (May 1987):22.

<u>Southeastern Lesbian and Gay Conference, 1988</u>:

Segrest, Mab. "Southern Reflections: Nothing Can Stop Us Now! But From What?" (keynote address to 12th annual Southeastern Lesbian and Gay Conference, Atlanta, Georgia, 1988). *Out/Look* 1:4 (Winter 1989):10-15.

<u>Third World Lesbian & Gay Conference, 1981</u>:

Abdullahad, Tania and Leigh H. Mosley. "Third World Lesbian & Gay Conference" (second annual national conference, Chicago, Illinois, November 1981; includes workshop reports on "mature lesbians," "urban black lesbians," "media," "grassroots," "racism & sexism"). *off our backs* 12:2 (February 1982):4.

Moraga, Cherríe. "A Unified Rainbow of Strength" (speech to the
Second National Third World Lesbian/Gay Conference, Chicago,
Illinois, November 1981). *off our backs* 12:2 (February 1982):
4-6.

Third World Lesbian Writers Conference, 1979:
Isis. "Herstory in the Making" (first Third World Lesbian Writers
Conference, New York City, February 1979). *off our backs* 9:4
(April 1979):20.

Through the Looking Glass: a Gynergetic Experience, 1976:
Landrine, Hope and Joan Regensburger. "Through the Looking Glass:
a Conference of Myopics" (report challenging the "feminist"
politics of Through the Looking Glass: a Gynergetic Experience,
Boston, Massachusetts, April 1976). *off our backs* 6:4 (June
1976):12.

Towards a Politics of Sexuality (Barnard College Sexuality
Conference), 1982:
Charbonneau, Claudette. "Sexual Confusion at Barnard" (Barnard
College Sexuality Conference), New York City, April 1982).
off our backs 12:6 (June 1982):25+.

Dejanikus, Tacie. "Charges of Exclusion & McCarthyism at Barnard
Conference" (Towards a Politics of Sexuality (Barnard College
Sexuality Conference), New York City, April 1982). *off our
backs* 12:6 (June 1982):5+.

Douglas, Carol Anne. "Towards a Politics of Sexuality" (Towards a
Politics of Sexuality (Barnard College Sexuality Conference),
New York City, April 1982). *off our backs* 12:6 (June 1982):
2-4+.

Moira, Fran. "Barnard Finale" (Towards a Politics of Sexuality
(Barnard College Sexuality Conference), New York City, April
1982). *off our backs* 12:6 (June 1982):24.

------. "Lesbian Sex Mafia ('I S/M') Speakout" (Towards a Politics of Sexuality (Barnard College Sexuality Conference), New York City, April 1982). *off our backs* 12:6 (June 1982):23-4.

------. "Politically Correct, Politically Incorrect Sexuality" (Towards a Politics of Sexuality (Barnard College Sexuality Conference), New York City, April 1982). *off our backs* 12:6 (June 1982): 22-3.

United Nations Forum and Conference for Women, Kenya, 1985:
"End of Decade Conference: Lesbian Voice" (United Nations Forum and Conference for Women). *New Directions for Women* 14:5 (September/October 1985):13.

Gevins, Adi. "To See Them in Person!" (interview with Kenyan woman distributing family planning information at the international women's conference in Nairobi, about lesbians at the conference). *Connexions,* "Forum '85: Nairobi, Kenya" 17-18 (Summer/Fall 1985):17.

United Nations Women's Decade Forum and Conference, Kenya, 1987:
Konek, Carol Wolfe. "Dangerous Discussions" (lesbians not permitted to display literature, and lesbianism banned as discussion topic at forums but discussed anyhow, at the United Nations Women's Decade Forum and Conference in Nairobi, Kenya, 1987). *Heresies* 25 (1990):83+.

West Coast Lesbian Conference, 1973:
Pollner, Fran. "Lesbian Conference -- 1200 Strong?" (West Coast Lesbian Conference, Los Angeles, California, April 1973). *off our backs* 3:8 (May 1973):10-11.

West Coast Old Lesbian Conference and Celebration, 1987:
MacDonald, Barbara. "A Movement of Old Lesbians" (keynote address, West Coast Old Lesbian Conference and Celebration, Dominguez Hills State University, California, April 1987). *off our backs* 17:7 (July 1987):3+.

Mountaingrove, Ruth. "West Coast Old Lesbian Conference and Celebration" (Dominguez Hills State University, California, April 1987). *off our backs* 17:7 (July 1987):1-2+.

Women Against Violence Against Women Conference, England, 1982:

Garthwaite, Al. "English WAVAW Conference: Pressure to Be Straight" (Women Against Violence Against Women). *off our backs* 12:2 (February 1982):2-3.

Women and AIDS, 1990:

Watstein, Sarah Barbara. "Because AIDS Is: a Report on a 'Women and AIDS' Conference." *Visibilities* 4:2 (March/April 1990): 10-11.

Women and Health Conference, West Germany, 1980:

"European Self-Help Conference" (Women and Health Conference organized by Feministisches Frauen Gesundheits Zentrum, Hanover, West Germany, April 1980). *off our backs* 10:8 (August-September 1980):5; note: cover reads 10:7.

Women & the Draft: a Forum, 1980:

Brooke. "Women & the Draft: a Forum" (following President Jimmy Carter's moves to require all young women and men to register for the draft; Washington, D.C., March 1980). *off our backs* 10:4 (April 1980):6+.

Women and the Law Conference, 1974:

Dell, Mae. "Women and the Law" (conference, New York University, February 1974; includes section on "Gay Rights"). *off our backs* 4:4 (March 1974):24-5.

Women and the Law Conference, 1990:

Ertman, Martha. "Women and the Law Conference" (Detroit, Michigan, March 1990; topics include legal needs of lesbians of color and violence against lesbians and gay men). *off our backs* 20:7 (July 1990):2-5.

Women in America: Legacies of Race and Ethnicity, 1988:

Lorde, Audre. "Women, Power, and Difference" (talk delivered at the Women in America: Legacies of Race and Ethnicity conference, Georgetown University, Washington, D.C., April 1988; Lorde discusses living in St. Croix, the U.S. Virgin Islands). *Sojourner* 15:3 (November 1989):18-19.

Women in Mid-Life Crises Conference, 1976:

Henry, Alice. "Mid-Life Crises" (Women in Mid-Life Crises Conference, Cornell University, Ithaca, New York, October 1976; noted for lack of discussion of lesbian issues). *off our backs* 6:9 (December 1976):6.

Women in Print Conference, 1985:

Lootens, Tricia. "Third Women in Print Conference" (May 1985, Berkeley, California; reports on workshops including classism, erotica, lesbian nuns, women of color, pornography, censorship, raid on British gay book store). *off our backs* 15:8 (August-September 1985):8-9+.

The Women's Movement: Forum, 1978:

Brooke. "A Feminist Future?" ("The Women's Movement: Forum," conference sponsored by The Matriarchists, New York City, September 1978; speakers included Robin Morgan, Gloria Steinem, Dianne Feeley, Willamette Brown, Elizabeth Shanklin, Jean O'Leary, Judith Levy, Kate Millett, Arlie Scott, Midge Costanza, Marisa de Los Angeles, Flo Kennedy, and Ti-Grace Atkinson; picketed by group accusing forum of token inclusion of women of color). *off our backs* 8:10 (November 1978):10-12.

Women's Weekend, 1974:

Devoe, Margaret. "A Weekend Away" ("Women's Weekend," Northeastern New Jersey, April 1974); includes section on sexual identity and lesbian points of view). *off our backs* 4:6 (May 1974):4-5.

Country Lesbians (see Rural Lesbians)

Cross-Dressing (see Transvestism)

Dance (see Art)

Daughters of Bilitis (DOB)

Esterberg, Kristin Gay. "From Illness to Action: Conceptions of
Homosexuality in *The Ladder,* 1956-1965." *Journal of Sex
Research* 27:1 (February 1990):65-80.

Smith, Elizabeth A. "Butches, Femmes, and Feminists: the Politics of
Lesbian Sexuality" (includes discussion of the Daughters of
Bilitis magazine *The Ladder*). *NWSA Journal* 1:3 (Spring
1989):398-421.

Gittings, Barbara:
Samoy, Stephanie Castillo. "*Visibilities* Highlights . . . Barbara
Gittings" (activist since the 1950s). *Visibilities* 4:5
(September/October 1990):28.

Lyon, Phyllis:
Dorrance, John. "Gay Panther" (co-founder of DOB). *San Francisco*
26 (December 1984):32-3.

Death and Dying (see also: Acquired Immune Deficiency Syndrome;
Health; Suicide; Violence Against Lesbians and Gay Men)

Biller, Ray and Susan Rice. "Experiencing Multiple Loss of Persons with
AIDS: Grief and Bereavement Issues." *Health and Social Work*
15:4 (November 1990):283-90.

Corinne, Tee A. "Remembering as a Way of Life" (lesbian 'National
Treasures,' including June Arnold, Jeannete Foster, Valerie
Taylor, Barbara Grier, Audre Lorde, Anita Cornwell, Sarah
Aldridge, Sonny Wainwright). *Common Lives/Lesbian Lives* 19
(Spring 1986):15-18.

Gamble, Richard H. "Estate Planning for the Unmarried Person: an Estate Planner's Dilemma; the Law Favors Marriage But Many Contemporary Americans Don't." *Trusts and Estates* 125 (April 1986):25-8.

Moore, Tracy. "Because She Died . . . " *Common Lives/Lesbian Lives* 2 (Winter 1981):42-9.

Ritter, K.Y. and C.W. O'Neill. "Moving Through Loss -- The Spiritual Journey of Gay Men and Lesbian Women." *Journal of Counseling and Development* 68:1 (1989):9-15.

Templer, Donald I., et al. "The Death Anxiety of Gays." *Omega: Journal of Death and Dying* 14:3 (1984):211-14.

Detective Novels

Rich, B. Ruby. "The Lady Dicks: Genre Benders Take the Case" (new trend of feminist and lesbian detective novels). *Village Voice Literary Supplement* 75 (June 1989):24-7.

Semple, Linda. "Lesbians in Detective Fiction." *Gossip* (Great Britain) 5 (no date):47-52.

------. "Sisters in Crime" (brief history of women mystery writers, with look at "new wave" of lesbian-feminist mysteries). *Spare Rib* (Great Britain) 197 (December 1988/January 1989):28-30.

Miner, Valerie:

Cranny-Francis, Anne. "Gender and Genre: Feminist Rewritings of Detective Fiction" (includes lesbian writers Valerie Miner and Barbara Wilson). *Women's Studies International Forum* 11:1 (1988):69-84.

Stein, Gertrude:

Holland, Jeanne. "Uncovering Woman's Body in Gertrude Stein's Subject-Cases: The Background of a Detective Story." *College English* 52:5 (September 1990):540-51.

Wilson, Barbara:

Cranny-Francis, Anne. "Gender and Genre: Feminist Rewritings of Detective Fiction" (includes lesbian writers Valerie Miner and Barbara Wilson). *Women's Studies International Forum* 11:1 (1988):69-84.

Disabled Lesbians and Disability

Anne, Sheila. "Womyn or Children First? Lesbian Space Elusive at East Coast Fest: Separatist Positive Perspective" (controversy over baby boys attending and lack of wheelchair accessibility at the 1st annual East Coast Lesbian Festival in West Stockbridge, Massachusetts, September 1989). *off our backs* 19:9 (October 1989):27-8.

Anonymous, with Kim Schive and Nancy Becker. "Alternatives to Print: On the Other Hand" (access to feminist education for deaf people). *Sinister Wisdom,* "Lesbian Writing and Publishing" 13 (Spring 1980):97-8.

Atatimur, Sara. "Untitled Piece" (autobiographical narrative by a blind woman about civil disobedience at the Pentagon and coming out). *Common Lives/Lesbian Lives* 3 (Spring 1982):27+.

Beckett, Elsa. "Lesbians with Disability." *Healthright: a Journal of Women's Health, Family Planning and Sexuality* 1:4 (August 1982):31.

Clare, Elizabeth. "Think Twice Before You Call Me Courageous." *Sinister Wisdom,* "Passing" 35 (Summer/Fall 1988):19-23.

Doucette, Joan. "Breaking the Links of Lies" (lesbian sexuality conference). *Resources for Feminist Research* (Canada) 14 (March 1985):9-10.

------. "Redefining Difference: Disabled Lesbians Resist." *Resources for Feminist Research* (Canada) 18:2 (June 1989):17-21.

Dykewomon, Elana. "Notes for a Magazine: On Passing." *Sinister Wisdom,* "Passing" 35 (Summer/Fall 1988):3-6.

Fithian, Nancy. "Michigan Womyn's Music Festival; Disabled Lesbian Conference." *off our backs* 11:9 (October 1981):15.

Folayan, Ayofemi. "I Am Your Sister: a Tale of Two Conferences" (celebrating African-American writer/activist Audre Lorde, Boston, Massachusetts, October 1990; disabled women's access limited). *off our backs* 20:11 (December 1990):1-2.

------. "National Black Gay and Lesbian Leadership Forum: a Conference Report" (Atlanta, Georgia, February 1990). *off our backs* 20:4 (April 1990):2-3.

Harper, Jorjet. "Accessibility, Male Children an Issue at Lesbian Fest" (First Annual East Coast Lesbian Festival, West Stockbridge, Massachusetts, Summer 1989). *Hot Wire* 6:1 (January 1990):29+.

Hemmings, Susan and Manny. "Lesbians National . . . and International" (National Lesbian Conference on Sex and Sexual Practice, London, England, April 1983, and International Lesbian Service Conference, Paris, France, April 1983). *Spare Rib* (Great Britain) 131 (June 1983):12-13.

Henry, Alice. "Workshop Reports" (from the second national Women in Print Conference, Washington, D.C., October 1981; includes reports on "Creating a Lesbian Literature: How Conscious Are We?" of race, class, age, and disability; "Lesbian/Feminism and Radical Feminism in the 1980s"; and "Lesbian Feminists and Heterosexual Feminists"). *off our backs* 11:11 (December 1981):3+.

Hugs, Diane. "Where Have All the Lesbians Gone?" (difference between caring and "co-ing," and between alcoholism and disability). *Sinister Wisdom,* "On Disability" 39 (Winter 1989-90):73-5.

Lambert, Sandra. "Disability and Intimacy." *Common Lives/Lesbian Lives* 26 (Spring 1988):5-15.

McVey, Judy. "The Southern [Women's Music and Comedy] Festival and Disability." *Hot Wire* 3:1 (November 1986):30-1+.

Nestle, Joan. "New York Illness Support Group: What Being a Lesbian Means in the Deepest Sense." *off our backs*, "Women and Disability" 11:5 (May 1981):8+.

"On Disability," *Sinister Wisdom*, Number 39, Winter 1989-90.

"Out of the Closets and Into the Streets." *Hysteria* 1 (Spring 1982):4-5.

Platt, Mary Frances. "Serious Shit at the NLC" (planning for the National Lesbian Conference, April 1991, especially regarding disabled accessibility and education). *off our backs* 20:5 (May 1990):11.

------. "A View from This Wheelchair" (of East Coast Lesbian Festival, West Stockbridge, Massachusetts, September 1989). *off our backs* 20:5 (May 1990):11.

Ruth, Barbara. "Resources of Interest to Lesbians with Disabilities" (lists of books, periodicals, lesbian land, arts organizations, general organizations). *Sinister Wisdom*, "On Disability" 39 (Winter 1989-90):128-31.

Schwarz, Judith. "On Being Physically Different." *Sinister Wisdom* 7 (Fall 1978):41-50.

Springer, Christina. "The National Women's Music Festival: Bringing Non-Dominant Women to Full Boil." *off our backs* 20:5 (May 1990):9.

Stato, Joanne. "I Am Your Sister Celeconference: Tribute to Audre Lorde" (Boston, Massachusetts, October 1990). *off our backs* 20:11 (December 1990):1-5+.

------. "14th Michigan Womyn's Music Festival" (the politics of the event -- who attended and what was discussed, including lesbians of color, racism, S/M, disability, and music). *off our backs* 19:9 (October 1989):20-1.

Steiner, Jody and Laurie Rothfeld. "ASL Interpreting for Concerts" (American Sign Language). *Hot Wire* 2:1 (November 1985):8-9+.

Sugars, Stephanie. "Illness in Our Community: My Body as Other." *Common Lives/Lesbian Lives* 5 (Fall 1982):93-6.

van Deurs, Kady and Eileen Pagan. "Catalogue for Women Who Are Blind" (list of "Womanbooks for Women Who Are Blind and/or Physically Challenged"). *Sinister Wisdom*, "Lesbian Writing and Publishing" 13 (Spring 1980):100.

Waite, Rosie. "They Didn't Know What to Say to Me." *Gossip* (Great Britain) 1 (1986):46-53.

Zakarewsky, G.T. "Patterns of Support Among Gay and Lesbian Deaf Persons." *Sexuality and Disability* 2:3 (1979):178-91.

Zana/Raven. "Two Pieces on Dis-Ability: And What of Those Who Remain Unhealed?; The Perfect Matriarchal Future." *Lesbian Ethics* 3:1 (Spring 1988):97-101.

Atattimur, Sara Deniz (activist and musician):
Foty, Caroline. "Community Mourns Loss: Sara Deniz Atattimur, January 7, 1962 - November 27, 1989" (obituary of blind musician and disabled rights activist). *off our backs* 20:3 (March 1990):9.

Edell, Therese (musician):
Sequoia. "Access -- Therese Edell: Composer and Desktop Music Publisher" (with multiple sclerosis). *Hot Wire* 6:1 (January 1990):48-9+.

<u>Kowalski, Sharon</u> (arranged chronologically; SK's parents were
    awarded legal guardianship after SK was severely disabled in an
    auto accident; they denied visitation rights to SK's lover, Karen
    Thompson; KT sued for guardianship and better care for SK and
    lost; KT was awarded guardianship of SK by a State Appellate
    Court in December 1991):

Linsley, Jeann. "A Right to Care." *Ms.* 14:3 (September 1985):19.

"No Visits to Lover." *off our backs* 16:1 (January 1986):15.

Foty, Caroline. "Courts Separate Lesbian Couple." *Progressive* 50
    (July 1986):15-6.

Shear, Marie. "Court Separates Couple." *New Directions for Women*
    16 (November-December 1987):9.

TAL. "Kowalski Update." *off our backs* 18:8 (August-September
    1988):7.

Gibbs, Nancy R. "Tragic Tug of War: a Lesbian's Fight to See Her
    Disabled Lover Becomes a Cause Celebre." *Time* 132 (August
    22, 1988):71.

Stowe, Ayofemi. "'Power Into Action': The National Lesbian Rights
    Conference" (of the National Organization for Women, San
    Diego, California, October 1988; Karen Thompson spoke). *off
    our backs* 18:11 (December 1988):8+.

CAD. "Sharon Kowalski to Get Rehabilitation." *off our backs* 19:1
    (January 1989):15; note: covers reads 18:11 (December 1988).

"Move Toward Freedom for Sharon Kowalski." *off our backs* 19:2
    (February 1989):5.

Payton, Sarah. "Sharon Kowalski Freed." *Spare Rib* (Great Britain)
    198 (February 1989):44.

"Lovers Reunited After Three Years." *off our backs* 19:3 (March 1989):16.

Foty, Caroline. "Private Choices, Public Consequences." *Woman of Power* 13 (Spring 1989):60-3.

"Kowalski Update." *off our backs* 19:8 (August-September 1989):19.

Panzerino, Connie (activist):
Graetz, Susan. "'It's What You Do with What You've Got': an Interview with Connie Panzerino." *Woman of Power* 1 (Spring 1984):72-4.

Domestic Partnership (see also: Legal Issues; Legislation; Relationships)

Bennett, Linda. "Lesbian Family Registry" (lesbian/gay couples register with National Family Registry of the Human Rights Campaign Fund to increase visibility). *off our backs,* "20th Anniversary" 20:2 (February 1990):8.

Ettelbrick, Paula L. "Gay Marriage: a Must or a Bust? -- Since When Was Marriage the Path to Liberation?" (published before the San Francisco Domestic Partners Initiative was defeated on the public ballot November 1989). *Out/Look #6,* 2:2 (Fall 1989):9+.

------. "Under the Law -- How Can We Create a Lesbian Family?" *Visibilities* 2:3 (May/June 1988):16-17.

------. "Under the Law -- Protecting Relationships." *Visibilities* 2:1 (January/February 1988):18-20.

Findlen, Barbara. "Gay Marriage: Lifting the Bans" (American Civil Liberties Union support for legal recognition). *Ms.* 15:8 (February 1987):29.

Holzberg, Bryan. "Court Rules 'Marriage' Not Valid: No Divorce for Lesbian Pair." *National Law Journal* 2 (July 28, 1980):4.

Poverny, Linda M. and Wilbur A. Finch, Jr. "Gay and Lesbian Domestic Partnerships: Expanding the Definition of Family." *Social Casework* 69:2 (February 1988):116-21.

Ryder, Bruce. "Equality Rights and Sexual Orientation: Confronting Heterosexual Family Privilege." *Canadian Journal of Family Law* (Canada) 9:1 (Fall 1990):39-97.

Sagmeister, Nancy. "In Sickness and in Health: Spousal Benefits for Gays and Lesbians." *Our Times* 6 (September 1987):33-4.

"UUA Endorses Gay Rites" (Unitarian Universalist Association approves unions in place of heterosexual-only marriages). *Christian Century* 101:25 (August 15-22, 1984):768-9.

Van Gelder, Lindsy. "Marriage as a Restricted Club." *Ms.* 12:8 (February 1984):59-60.

Canada:

"Canada: I Will Not Be Shelved" (interview with Karen Andrews, librarian fighting for employee spousal benefits for her lover; case based on Canada's Bill 7; reprint from Canadian monthly, *Rites* (March 1988)). *Connexions,* "Lesbian Activism" 29 (1989):18-20.

Eaton, Mary and Cynthia Peterson. "Andrew v. Ontario (Minister of Health" (Ontario, Canada High Court of Justice decides that lesbian partners are not spouses for purposes of the Ontario Health Insurance Plan). *Canadian Journal of Women and the Law* (Canada) 2:2 (1987-88):416-21.

Rule, Jane. "You Be Normal, Or Else . . . " (benefits denied to lesbian and gay couples). *Resources for Feminist Research* (Canada), "Confronting Heterosexuality/Confronter l'hétérosexualité" 19:3&4 (September/December 1990):86.

Denmark:

"Denmark: Gay Marriage OK, Adoption Not." *off our backs* 19:10 (November 1989):11.

Great Britain:

"Spousal Benefits for Lesbian Lovers." *Spare Rib* (Great Britain) 174
(January 1987):46.

Ithaca, New York:

"Ithaca Enacts Domestic Partnership Ordinance." *off our backs* 20:9
(October 1990):4.

The Netherlands:

"Netherlands: Court Overturns Gay Marriage Ban." *off our backs* 20:4
(April 1990):6.

Niles, Illinois:

Meyers, Cheryl. "Lesbians Jailed" (for sit-in at marriage license
bureau where they were denied a license; caused controversy in
the gay/lesbian community, because some thought the protest
jeopardized a pending "gay civil rights bill" in Congress). *off our
backs* 5:9 (November 1975):11.

Seattle, Washington:

TAL. "Partners Gain Benefits." *off our backs* 20:5 (May 1990):16.

Domestic Violence (see Violence Among Lesbians)

Drama (see Literature: Prose; Theater)

Drug Abuse (see Substance Abuse and Recovery)

Eating Disorders (see Body Image)

Economics (see also: Classism; Work)

Allen, Jeffner. "Lesbian Economics." *Trivia* 8 (Winter 1986):37-53.

Amana, Rue. "Becoming a 'Real' Dyke: Employment and Housing"
(moving out of cities as the lesbian dream; returning to cities to
work with People With AIDS). *Canadian Woman Studies*
(Canada), "Women & Housing" 11:2 (Fall 1990):43+.

Anderson, Shelley. "Falling Borders, Rising Hopes: Europe in 1992"
(effects of legal and economic integration of European Economic
Community). *Out/Look #10,* 3:2 (Fall 1990):30-5.

Bunch, Charlotte. "Lesbian Feminist Politics" (excerpt from speech
delivered at the Sojourner Truth School, course on "Tactics and
Strategies for the Women's Movement"). *off our backs* 3:7
(April 1973):17.

Claudia. "about class" (letter to "A Readers' Forum -- Separatism: Beyond
the Debate," calling for all lesbians to acknowledge class
background and bias). *Lesbian Ethics* 3:2 (Fall 1988):12.

de Margo, Louise. "Reflections d'Une Lesbienniste, en Marge de Colloque
des Périodiques Féministes Tenu a Orangeville, du 9 au 12 mai"
(dangers of cooptation for feminists in receiving government or
private foundation funding). *Canadian Woman Studies* (Canada),
"Women and Media/Les Femmes et les Media" 8:1 (Spring
1987):65.

Egerton, Jayne. "Out But Not Down: Lesbians' Experience of Housing"
(squatting, alternative housing communities, and national
housing policy in Great Britain). *Feminist Review* (Great
Britain) 36 (Autumn 1990):75-88.

Evans, Lee. "The Spread of Consumerism: Good Buy Community." *Sinister Wisdom,* "With an Emphasis on Lesbian Theory" 37 (Spring 1989):9-19.

Frank, Wendy. "Women and Insurance." *Visibilities* 4:1 (January/February 1990):12-13.

"Gay Group Issued Pride Credit Card." *off our backs* 20:9 (October 1990):4.

"Gay Money" (New York City gas station refuses to accept bills stamped "Gay Money"). *off our backs* 9:2 (February 1979):8.

"'Gay' Multinationals" (corporations polled about whether they discriminate against lesbians and gays). *off our backs* (February 1979):8.

Helmbold, Lois Rita. "Shopping Bag Lesbians." *Common Lives/Lesbian Lives* 5 (Fall 1982):69-71.

"IRS Homophobic" (tax-exempt status denied to lesbian feminist newspaper). *off our backs* 6:10 (January 1977):18.

Lesbian, Amber. "Made in Amazon Nation." *Lesbian Ethics* 2:2 (Fall 1986):84-5.

Nittera, Dee Dee. "Money Changes Everything" (therapy as part of "the misery industry"). *Sinister Wisdom* 36 (Winter 1988/89):76-86.

Ruby, Jennie. "Lesbian Theory: Pursuing Lesbian Meaning" (Lesbian Theory session of the National Women's Studies' Association conference in Minneapolis, Minnesota, June 1988; includes reports on the following papers: Betty Tallen, "Lesbian Feminist Theory: a View from the Political Theory Trenches"; Lee Evans, "Lesbians, Community, and Patriarchal Consumer Values"; Elana Dykewomon, "The Knots of Process"; Anna Lee, "New Age Spirituality Is the Invention of Heteropatriarchy"; Sarah Hoagland, "Lesbian Agency" and "Lesbian Space"; and Jeffner Allen on writing). *off our backs* 18:9 (October 1988):18-19.

Sagmeister, Nancy. "In Sickness and in Health: Spousal Benefits for Gays and Lesbians." *Our Times* (Canada) 6 (September 1987):33-4.

Smith, Margaret 'Chase'. "Crookery" (theft as a way to make a living and challenge the heteropatriarchy). *Lesbian Ethics* 3:2 (Fall 1988):48-53.

"Spousal Benefits for Lesbian Lovers." *Spare Rib* (Great Britain) 174 (January 1987):46.

Tilchen, Maida. "The State of Music: a Lesson from History" (cooptation of lesbian's efforts by straight male capitalists). *Hot Wire* 3:2 (March 1987):32-3.

Trebilcot, Joyce. "Dyke Economics: Hortense and Gladys on Money." *Lesbian Ethics* 3:1 (Spring 1988):37-47.

Fier, Debbie (musician):
Armstrong, Toni L. "Making Our Dreams Our Jobs: Making Ends Meet Through Music." *Hot Wire* 3:2 (March 1987):34-9.

Fineberg, Jean (musician):
Armstrong, Toni L. "Making Our Dreams Our Jobs: Making Ends Meet Through Music." *Hot Wire* 3:2 (March 1987):34-9.

Flower, Robin (musician):
Armstrong, Toni L. "Making Our Dreams Our Jobs: Making Ends Meet Through Music." *Hot Wire* 3:2 (March 1987):34-9.

MacDonald, Betty (musician):
Armstrong, Toni L. "Making Our Dreams Our Jobs: Making Ends Meet Through Music." *Hot Wire* 3:2 (March 1987):34-9.

Musica Femina (musical group):
Armstrong, Toni L. "Making Our Dreams Our Jobs: Making Ends Meet Through Music." *Hot Wire* 3:2 (March 1987):34-9.

Pelham, Ruth (musician):
Armstrong, Toni L. "Making Our Dreams Our Jobs: Making Ends
Meet Through Music." *Hot Wire* 3:2 (March 1987):34-9.

Rhiannon (musician):
Armstrong, Toni L. "Making Our Dreams Our Jobs: Making Ends
Meet Through Music." *Hot Wire* 3:2 (March 1987):34-9.

Trull, Teresa (musician):
Armstrong, Toni L. "Making Our Dreams Our Jobs: Making Ends
Meet Through Music." *Hot Wire* 3:2 (March 1987):34-9.

Walker, Leonie (co-founder of Women Managing Wealth/the Alva
Belmont Project, a program of the Ms. Foundation):
Kriegel, Phyllis. "Coming Out About Money." *New Directions for
Women* 19:5 (September/October 1990):4.

Education: Lesbians in Academe/Lesbians in the Classroom
(see also: Education: Pedagogy and Curriculum; Lesbian Studies)

Barale, Michele Aina. "The Lesbian Academic: Negotiating New
Boundaries." *Women & Therapy,* "Lesbianism: Affirming
Nontraditional Roles" 8:1/2 (1989):183-94.

Bart, Pauline, Itala Rutter, and a friend. "Alienation and Estrangement in
G.A.U. Land" (written by three lesbian feminists, about the Gay
Academic Union Conference, Chicago, Illinois, October 1982).
off our backs 13:2 (February 1983):23.

Beck, Evelyn Torton. "Self-Disclosure and the Commitment to Social
Change." *Women's Studies International Forum,* "Women in
Academe" 6:2 (1983):159-64.

Biemiller, Lawrence. "Georgetown University Homosexuals Cite
Constitution, Morality in Quest for Recognition." *Chronicle of
Higher Education* 29 (January 30, 1985):13.

------. "Homosexual Academics Say 'Coming Out' Could Jeopardize Careers." *Chronicle of Higher Education* 25 (October 20, 1982):9-10.

------. "Homosexual Groups at Georgetown University Get Court Backing." *Chronicle of Higher Education* 30 (August 7, 1985):1.

------. "Homosexual Students at Southern Methodist Wage Battle for Recognition" (Southern Methodist University, Dallas, Texas). *Chronicle of Higher Education* 27 (January 4, 1984):10+.

Bleich, David. "Homophobia and Sexism as Popular Values" (based on college freshman writing exercise). *Feminist Teacher* 4:2-3 (Fall 1989):21-8.

Branzburg, Judith V. "Private Lives in the Public Classroom." *Radical Teacher,* "Gay and Lesbian Studies" 24 (no date: c.1983):10-11.

Brittingham, Midge Wood. "Shared Interest" (guidelines for setting up lesbian/gay alumni groups, based on Oberlin College's alumni association). *Currents* 16:4 (April 1990):42-3.

Brown, Douglas F. "The Health Service and Gay Students." *Journal of the American College Health Association* 24:5 (June 1976):272-3.

Bulkin, Elly. "Heterosexism and Women's Studies." *Radical Teacher* 17 (November 1980):25-31.

Bunch, Charlotte. "Feminism and Education: Not by Degrees." *Quest* 5:1 (Summer 1979):7-18; also *New Directions for Women* 10 (September-October 1981):8-9 and 10 (November/December 1981):19.

Burns, William David. "Breaking Silence: Why Don't Gays Keep Quiet?" *Change* 22:3 (May-June 1990):42-3.

132

CAD. "Book Burning" (75 students at Bishop's University in Lenoxville, Québec, Canada, burn student services handbook because it includes a chapter on lesbians and gay men). *off our backs* 10:10 (November 1980):9.

------. "Dr. Strange Love" (news briefs about anti-lesbian/gay discrimination in U.S. and Great Britain). *off our backs* 8:3 (March 1978):10.

Chamberlain, Pam. "Homophobia in the Schools." *Radical Teacher,* "Teaching Sexuality" 29 (September 1985):3-6.

Clay, James W. "Working with Lesbian and Gay Parents and Their Children." *Young Children* 45:3 (March 1990):31-5.

Coughlin, Ellen. "Homosexual Professors Find Bias Plagues Their Life on Campuses." *Chronicle of Higher Education* 19 (September 24, 1979):1+.

Crew, Louie and Karen Keener. "Homophobia in the Academy: a Report of the Committee on Gay/Lesbian Concerns." *College English* 43:7 (November 1981):682-9.

Crumpacker, Laurie and Eleanor M. Vander Haegan. "Pedagogy and Prejudice: Strategies for Confronting Homophobia in the Classroom." *Women's Studies Quarterly* 15:3&4 (Fall/Winter 1987):65-73.

Daugelli, A.R. "Lesbians and Gay Men on Campus: Visibility, Empowerment, and Educational Leadership." *Peabody Journal of Education* 66:3 (1989):124-42.

DeFries, Zira. "Pseudohomosexuality in Female Students." *American Journal of Psychiatry* 133 (April 1976):400-4.

D'Emilio, John. "The Campus Environment for Gay and Lesbian Life." *Academe* 76:1 (January-February 1990):16-19.

Devlin, Diane. "The Plight of the Gay Student" (confrontations with high school and college officials). *off our backs* 1:6 (May 30, 1970):11.

Douglas, Carol Anne. "English Teachers Pro-Gay" (National Council of Teachers of English boycotts Holiday Inn, saying that the hotel's employment policies discriminate against lesbians and gays). *off our backs* 11:2 (February 1981):11.

------. "It Don't Gay in Minneapolis" (school board bans lesbian/gay panel from speaking in elementary schools). *off our backs* 11:2 (February 1981)11.

------. "Lesbian Teacher OK" (federal jury grants damages to woman fired for "bisexuality"). *off our backs* 11:11 (December 1981):9.

Dressler, Joshua. "Study of Law Students' Attitudes Regarding the Rights of Gay People to Be Teachers." *Journal of Homosexuality* 4:4 (Summer 1979):315-40.

Edwards, Elizabeth. "Educational Institutions of Extended Families? The Reconstruction of Gender in Women's Colleges in the Late Nineteenth and Early Twentieth Centuries." *Gender and Education* 2:1 (1990):17-35.

Fein, Sara Beck and Elane M. Nuehring. "Perspectives on the Gender-Integrated Gay Community: Its Formal Structure and Social Functions" (college level). *Homosexual Counseling Journal* 2:4 (October 1975):150-63.

"'Feminism 101': Holly Near on Tour for NWSA" (National Women's Studies Association fundraising concert tour, January 1981). *Women's Studies Newsletter* 8:4 (Fall/Winter 1980):14.

Fields, Cheryl. "Allegations of Lesbianism Being Used to Intimidate, Female Academics Say." *Chronicle of Higher Education* 27 (October 26, 1983):1+.

Frye, Marilyn. "Do You Have to Be a Lesbian to Be a Feminist?" (speech delivered at the National Women's Studies Association Conference, Akron, Ohio, June 1990, about treating sexuality in women's studies courses). *off our backs* 20:8 (August/September 1990):21-3.

"Gay, Lesbian and Bisexual Student Services to Open." *Feminisms* 3:2 (March/April 1990):6.

Gelwick, Beverly Prosser, et al. "Life-Styles of 6 Professional Women Engaged in College Student Development Careers: the Lesbian Professional." *Journal of College Student Personnel* 25:5 (September 1984):419-21.

Gevisser, Mark. "Legitimate or Liberate? Lesbian and Gay Students Choose" (college activism). *The Nation* 246:12 (March 26, 1988):413-14.

Gyn, Gloria. "Writing and Politicking as Privilege." *Sinister Wisdom* 5 (Winter 1978):71-2.

Henderson, Ann Fleck. "Homosexuality in the College Years: Developmental Differences Between Men and Women." *Journal of American College Health* 32:5 (April 1984):216-19.

Hindley, Emma and Sarah Pritchard. "British Lesbian Student Conference." *off our backs* 12:8 (August-September 1982):14.

"How to Be a Lesbian at School" (report on paper given by Renee Hansen at the National Women's Studies Association conference, Towson State University, Maryland, June 1989). *off our backs* 19:8 (August-September 1989):10.

Johnson, Angela. "Lesbians and Gays in the Schools: Teachers, Students and Courses of Study." *off our backs* 19:6 (June 1989):12-13+.

Khayatt, Didi. "Legalized Invisibility: the Effect of Bill 7 on Lesbian Teachers" (prohibits discrimination based on sexual orientation in Canada). *Women's Studies International Forum* 13:3 (1990):185-93.

Kirschenbaum, Carol. "Instant Activism: a Moment of Truth for Austin's Gays" (University of Texas, Austin). *Ms.* 14 (October 1985):80-1.

Klein, Melanie. "Anti-Semitism, Homophobia, and the Good White Knight." *off our backs,* education issue 12:5 (May 1982):30.

KM. "Queer Haters in Idaho" (legislation barring teachers from advocating or condoning homosexuality). *off our backs* 16:4 (April 1986):9.

Krebs, Paula. "Rumor Can Get You Fired in West Virginia" (teacher fired for her "reputation around town" for being a lesbian). *off our backs* 15:1 (January 1985):5.

"The Lesbian Educator: a Social-Legal History for Today's Activist" (report on paper given by Karen M. Harbeck at the National Women's Studies Association conference, Towson State University, Maryland, June 1989). *off our backs* 19:8 (August-September 1989):11.

"A Lesbian Perspective" (on the 1st National Women's Studies Conference). *off our backs* 9:8 (August-September 1979):33.

"Lesbians Fight College" (College of the Redwoods bans gay student groups). *off our backs* 7:2 (March 1977):11.

Lorde, Audre. "The Uses of Anger" (keynote speech at 3rd National Women's Studies Association conference, "Women Respond to Racism," Storrs, Connecticut, 1981). *Women's Studies Quarterly* 9:3 (Fall 1981):7-10.

Lubenow, Gerald C. "Gays and Lesbians on Campus." *Newsweek* 99 (April 5, 1982):75-7.

McCurdy, Jack. "University, Opposed to Lesbians, Bars Women's Studies Meeting" (National Women's Studies Association 1982 conference denied meeting space at University of San Francisco because of lesbian membership). *Chronicle of Higher Education* 22 (March 2, 1981):22.

McDaniel, Judith. "Is There Room for Me in the Closet?, or My Life as the Only Lesbian Professor." *Heresies #7,* 2:3 (Spring 1979):36-9.

McDaniel, Judith, et al. "We Were Fired: Lesbian Experiences in Academe." *Sinister Wisdom* 20 (1982):30-43.

McNaron, Toni A. H. "'Out' at the University: Myth and Reality." *Women's Studies Newsletter* 8:4 (Fall/Winter 1980):20-1.

Malinovich, Myriam Miedzian. "Opinion: on Lesbianism and Peer Group Pressure." *Mademoiselle* 82 (April 1976):84-6.

Newton, Esther. "Academe's Homophobia: It Damages Careers and Ruins Lives." *Chronicle of Higher Education* 33 (March 11, 1987):104.

Olson, Myrna R. "A Study of Gay and Lesbian Teachers" (about pressures to be in the closet, and dangers of coming out to colleagues). *Journal of Homosexuality* 13:4 (Summer 1987):73-82.

Palmieri, Patricia A. "Here Was Fellowship: a Social Portrait of Academic Women at Wellesley College, 1895-1920." *History of Education Quarterly* 23:2 (Summer 1983):195-214.

Phi Delta Kappan, "The Homosexual Teacher," vol. 59, no. 2, October 1977.

Powell, Robert Earl. "Homosexual Behavior and the School Counselor." *School Counselor* 34:3 (January 1987):202-8.

Radical Teacher, on African-American women, no. 17, November 1980.

------, "Gay and Lesbian Studies," no. 24, no date: c.1983.

Rich, Adrienne. "Disobedience Is What NWSA is Potentially About" (keynote speech at 3rd National Women's Studies Association conference, "Women Respond to Racism," Storrs, Connecticut, 1981). *Women's Studies Quarterly* 9:3 (Fall 1981):4-6.

Rickgarn, Ralph L. "Developing Support Systems for Gay and Lesbian Staff Members." *Journal of College and University Student Housing* 14:1 (Summer 1984):32-6.

RJ. "Harassment on Campus" (homophobic literature distributed at the University of Chicago). *off our backs* 17:4 (April 1987):4.

------. "Sex-Ed Guidelines Stalled" (controversy over discussing homosexuality in California classrooms). *off our backs* 17:4 (April 1987):4.

Rofes, Eric. "Opening Up the Classroom Closet: Responding to the Educational Needs of Gay and Lesbian Youth." *Harvard Educational Review* 59:4 (November 1989):444-53.

Secor, Cynthia. "Lesbians -- the Doors Open." *Change* 7:1 (February 1975):13-17.

"SF - Counseling Ok'd" (Board of Education in San Francisco, California approves program for lesbian and gay youth). *off our backs* 20:8 (August/September 1990):6.

Sievers, Sharon L. "What Have We Won, What Have We Lost? [One of] Three Personal Perspectives on Feminist Education at Cal State, Long Beach." *Frontiers,* "Tenth Anniversary Issue" 8:3 (1986):43-5.

Stanfill, Rebecca. "Confessions of a Lesbian Teacher" (high school). *off our backs* 18:9 (October 1988):14.

"Stanford Recognizes Domestic Partners" (Stanford University, Palo Alto, California). *off our backs* 20:10 (November 1990):18.

"UCLA's Gay Sisterhood" (Lambda Delta Lambda Sorority). *Time* 131 (March 14, 1988):31.

Van Dyne, Larry. "Homosexual Academics Organize, Seek End to Discrimination." *Chronicle of Higher Education* 8 (December 10, 1973):7.

Vance, N. Scott. "Former Basketball Coach Settles Lawsuit Against University of South Carolina" (coach had resigned amid published allegations of lesbianism and also sued *Sports Illustrated*). *Chronicle of Higher Education* 26 (August 3, 1983):15+.

"Victory for Gay Student Group" (court rules University of Arkansas must allow Gay and Lesbian Student Association to exist). *off our backs* 18:9 (October 1988):11.

Watkins, Beverly. "Widespread Bias Against Homosexuals Called Bar to Work in Sociology." *Chronicle of Higher Education* 23 (September 2, 1981):23.

Wine, Jeri Dawn. "The Lesbian Continuum in Academe." *Resources for Feminist Research* (Canada) 16:4 (December 1987):27-9.

------. "On Prejudice and Possibility: Lesbians in Canadian Academe." *Atlantis* (Canada) 14:1 (Fall 1988):45-55.

Wolverton, Terry. "Lesbian Art Project" (Natalie Barney Art Collective, Los Angeles, California). *Heresies #7,* "Women Working Together" 2:3 (Spring 1979):14-19.

Beck, Evelyn Torton (Jewish activist, educator, and writer):
Mayhew, Paula Hooper. "Visionary and Activist: an Interview with Evelyn Torton Beck, Director of Women's Studies, the University of Maryland." *Women's Studies International Forum* 9:2 (1986):137-40.

<u>The Briggs Initiative</u> (failed initiative that would have prohibited gay school teachers in California):
CAD. "Gays Struggle" (for support from politicians in opposition to the Briggs Initiative). *off our backs* 8:10 (November 1978):6.

David, Pam and Lois Helmbold. "San Francisco: Courts and Cops Against Gays" (written by two women in the movement against the Briggs Initiative, members of Lesbians Against Police Violence). *Radical America* 13:4 (July-August 1979):27-33.

Douglas, Carol Anne. "Gays Battle Briggotry." *off our backs* 8:8 (August-September 1978):7.

MNM. "Chalking One Up" (Bay Area Coalition Against the Briggs Initiative holds speakout, San Francisco, California, March 1978). *off our backs* 8:5 (May 1978):10.

Ward, Michael and Mark Freeman. "Defending Gay Rights: the Campaign Against the Briggs Amendment in California." *Radical America* 13:4 (July-August 1979):11-26.

<u>Cruikshank, Margaret</u> (editor of *Lesbian Studies* and educator):
Cruikshank, Margaret. "A Slice of My Life." *Frontiers* 3:3 (1978):49-51.

------. "How a College Administrator Who Couldn't Join the Boys' Club Joined the Fired Lesbians Caucus Instead." *off our backs*, education issue 12:5 (May 1982):29.

<u>Daly, Mary</u> (philosopher and theologian):
"Snools Deny Daly Tenure: Hags Revolt" (theologian Mary Daly denied full professorship at Boston College). *off our backs* 19:5 (May 1989):11.

Sturgis, Susanna. "Priests Monitor Hag" (Professor Mary Daly, author of *Gyn/Ecology*, harassed at Boston College, where she teaches). *off our backs* 9:4 (April 1979):11.

Dove, Frances:

Vicinus, Martha. "'One Life to Stand Beside Me': Emotional
    Conflicts in First-Generation College Women in England"
    (Constance Maynard and Louisa Lumsden, Anne Richardson,
    Marion Wakefield, Ralph Gray, Frances Dove). *Feminist Studies*
    8:3 (Fall 1982):603-28.

Gozemba, Pat (educator):

Radoslovich, Jean. "An Interview with Pat Gozemba" (steering
    committee member of the National Women's Studies
    Association, member of the Boston Area Lesbian and Gay
    History Project, and English professor). *Maenad,* "The
    Lesbian/Heterosexual Split" 2:2 (Winter 1982):98-107.

Lumsden, Louisa:

Vicinus, Martha. "'One Life to Stand Beside Me': Emotional
    Conflicts in First-Generation College Women in England"
    (Constance Maynard and Louisa Lumsden, Anne Richardson,
    Marion Wakefield, Ralph Gray, Frances Dove). *Feminist Studies*
    8:3 (Fall 1982):603-28.

Maynard, Constance:

Vicinus, Martha. "'One Life to Stand Beside Me': Emotional
    Conflicts in First-Generation College Women in England"
    (Constance Maynard and Louisa Lumsden, Anne Richardson,
    Marion Wakefield, Ralph Gray, Frances Dove). *Feminist Studies*
    8:3 (Fall 1982):603-28.

Richardson, Anne:

Vicinus, Martha. "'One Life to Stand Beside Me': Emotional
    Conflicts in First-Generation College Women in England"
    (Constance Maynard and Louisa Lumsden, Anne Richardson,
    Marion Wakefield, Ralph Gray, Frances Dove). *Feminist Studies*
    8:3 (Fall 1982):603-28.

<u>Wakefield, Marion</u>:

Vicinus, Martha. "'One Life to Stand Beside Me': Emotional Conflicts in First-Generation College Women in England" (Constance Maynard and Louisa Lumsden, Anne Richardson, Marion Wakefield, Ralph Gray, Frances Dove). *Feminist Studies* 8:3 (Fall 1982):603-28.

<u>Woo, Merle</u> (Asian/Pacifica activist, educator, and writer):

Sorrel, Lorraine. "Perb Orders Woo Rehired" (by U.C. Berkeley; Woo's contract had been improperly terminated in 1982). *off our backs* 13:2 (February 1983):14.

Education: Pedagogy and Curriculum (see also: Education: Lesbians in Academe/Lesbians in the Classroom; Lesbian Studies)

Andrews, Jane. "Don't Pass Us By: Keeping Lesbian and Gay Issues on the Agenda." *Gender and Education* 2:3 (1990):351-5.

Annas, Pam, Ephrain Barradas, Ann Froines, Ron Schreiber. "Heterosexism and the Classroom" *Radical Teacher*, "Gay and Lesbian Studies" 24 (no date, c.1983):15-16.

Beck, Evelyn Torton. "Self-Disclosure and the Commitment to Social Change." *Women's Studies International Forum*, "Women in Academe" 6:2 (1983):159-64.

------. "Teaching About Jewish Lesbians in Literature: from *Zeitel and Rickel* to *The Tree of Begats.*" *off our backs*, education issue 12:5 (May 1982):20.

Berg, Allison, et al. "Breaking the Silence -- Sexual Preference in the Composition Classroom" (confronting heterosexist assumptions in freshman composition courses, based on program at Indiana University). *Feminist Teacher* 4:23 (Fall 1989):29-32.

Bleich, David. "Homophobia and Sexism as Popular Values" (based on college freshman writing exercise). *Feminist Teacher* 4:2-3 (Fall 1989):21-8.

Buhrke, R.A. "Female Student Perspectives on Training in Lesbian and Gay Issues." *Counseling Psychologist* 17:4 (October 1989):629-36.

------. "Incorporating Lesbian and Gay Issues into Counselor Training -- a Resource Guide." *Journal of Counseling and Development,* "Lesbian, Gay and Bisexual Issues in Counseling" 68:1 (September-October 1989):77-80.

Bulkin, Elly. "Heterosexism and Women's Studies." *Radical Teacher* 17 (November 1980):25-31.

------. "Teaching Lesbian Poetry." *Women's Studies Newsletter* 8:2 (Spring 1980):5-8.

Bunch, Charlotte. "Understanding Feminist Theory: Training to Think More of Teaching Theory" (part 2). *New Directions for Women* 10:6 (November/December 1981):19; also *Quest* (Summer 1979).

Chamberlain, Pam. "Homophobia in the Schools." *Radical Teacher,* "Teaching Sexuality" 29 (September 1985):3-6.

Chism, Nancy Van Note, et al. "Teaching in a Diverse Environment: Knowledge and Skills Needed by TAs" (teaching assistants). *New Directions for Teaching and Learning,* "Teaching Assistant Training in the 1990s" 39 (Fall 1989):23-36.

Crumpacker, Laurie and Eleanor M. Vander Haegan. "Pedagogy and Prejudice: Strategies for Confronting Homophobia in the Classroom." *Women's Studies Quarterly* 15:3&4 (Fall/Winter 1987):65-73.

Ellis, Michael J. "Eliminating Our Heterosexist Approach to Sex Education: a Hope for the Future." *Journal of Sex Education and Therapy* 11:1 (Spring/Summer 1985):63+.

Freedman, Estelle. "Small Group Pedagogy: Consciousness Raising in Conservative Times." *NWSA Journal* 2:4 (Autumn 1990):603-23.

Greenberg, Yael. "Dumbo, Fag and God: Teaching Jewish Children in Mainstream Religious Schools." *off our backs* 12:6 (June 1982):17.

Halter, Marilyn. "Remembering the Women of the 1960's, Teaching the 1960s." *Radical History Review* 44 (1989):93-107.

Holzman, Lois. "What Do Teachers Have to Teach?" (making high school students aware of homophobia). *Feminist Teacher* 1:2 (1985):10-12.

Hull, Gloria T. and Barbara Smith. "'Keep Black Women at the Center': a Conversation Between Gloria T. Hull and Barbara Smith" (co-editors, with Patricia Bell Scott, of *But Some of Us Are Brave: Black Women's Studies*). *off our backs*, "education issue" 12:5 (May 1982):22-3.

Interracial Books for Children Bulletin, "Homophobia and Education: How to Deal with Name-Calling," vol. 14, nos. 3/4, 1983.

Lenskyj, Helen. "Beyond Plumbing and Prevention: Feminist Approaches to Sex Education." *Gender and Education* 2:2 (1990):217-30.

Newman, Bernie S. "Including Curriculum Content on Lesbian and Gay Issues." *Journal of Social Work Education* 25:3 (Fall 1989):202-11.

Rofes, Eric. "Opening Up the Classroom Closet: Responding to the Educational Needs of Gay and Lesbian Youth." *Harvard Educational Review* 59:4 (November 1989):444-53.

Rosser, Sue V. "Multiple Perspectives: Teaching About Sexuality and Reproduction." *Women's Studies Quarterly* 12:4 (Winter 1984):31-3.

Russell, Tanya G. "AIDS Education, Homosexuality, and the Counselor's Role." *School Counselor* 36:5 (May 1989):333-7.

Sang, Barbara E. "New Directions in Lesbian Research, Theory, and Education." *Journal of Counseling and Development,* "Gay, Lesbian, and Bisexual Issues in Counseling" 68:1 (September-October 1989):92-6.

Smith, Barbara and Gloria T. Hull. "'Keep Black Women at the Center': a Conversation Between Gloria T. Hull and Barbara Smith" (co-editors, with Patricia Bell Scott, of *But Some of Us Are Brave: Black Women's Studies*). *off our backs,* "education issue" 12:5 (May 1982):22-3.

Squirrell, Gillian. "Teachers and Issues of Sexual Orientation." *Gender and Education* 1:1 (March 1989):17-34.

Stevens, Carolyn. "The History of Sexuality in Britain and America 1800-1975: Course Method and Bill of Rights" (professor writes about class she taught at Antioch College; includes course outline and bibliography). *Women's Studies Quarterly,* "Teaching the New Women's History" 16:1&2 (Spring/Summer 1988):87-96.

Thomas, Becky. "Teaching About Lesbians in Women's Studies Introductory Classes." *Feminisms* 3:3 (May/June 1990):6.

Wells, Joel W. "Teaching About Gay and Lesbian Sexual and Affectional Orientation Using Explicit Films to Reduce Homophobia." *Journal of Humanistic Education and Development* 23:1 (September 1989):18-34.

Beck, Evelyn Torton (Jewish activist, educator, and writer):
Mayhew, Paula Hooper. "Visionary and Activist: an Interview with Evelyn Torton Beck, Director of Women's Studies, the University of Maryland." *Women's Studies International Forum* 9:2 (1986):137-40.

Freedman, Estelle (educator and co-author of *Intimate Matters: a History of Sexuality in America*):
Marty, Debian. "Estelle Freedman on Teaching Feminist Studies and *Intimate Matters*" (interview). *Feminisms* 3:2 (March/April 1990):3-5.

Khurana, Ritu (young lesbian):
Fraser, Jean. "Photography in Education: 'Someone to Talk to'" (interview with Ritu Khurana and Mel Burns, who participated in workshop involving young lesbian and gay photographers producing educational materials). *Ten.8* (Great Britain) 32 (Spring 1989):50-6.

Employment (see Work)

Environmentalism

Copper, Baba, with Peggy Cleveland. "Country Women Talking." *Common Lives/Lesbian Lives* 2 (Winter 1981):17-25.

Winston, Rachel. "New Age Rage: Crystal Mining Depletes Environment" (supportive response to Angela Johnson, "Prepackaged Spiritualism," *off our backs* 19:1 (January 1989):10; note: cover reads 18:11 (December 1988)). *off our backs* 19:2 (February 1989):20.

The Future Is Female Project:
Cheatham, Annie and Mary Clare Powell. "The Future Is Female Project." *Woman of Power* 2 (Summer 1985):43-7.

Equal Rights Amendment (ERA) (see also: National Organization for Women)

Gabriner, Vicki. "ERA: the Year of the Rabble" (lesbian leaders in the ERA campaign). *Quest* 1:2 (Fall 1974):62-73.

Hall, Ran. "Dear Martha" (lesbians and reformism in NOW and the ERA campaign). *Common Lives/Lesbian Lives* 6 (Winter 1982):40-3.

Henry, Alice. "ERA: Who Cares?" (10,000 supporters march for state ratification, Springfield, Illinois, May 1976). *off our backs* 6:6 (September 1976):10.

JK. "Roar on the Right" ("Family Day Rally" held by right-wing, anti-ERA groups, simultaneous with the National Women's Conference in Houston, Texas, November 1977). *off our backs* 8:1 (January 1978):3.

Kelly, Janis. "Relighting Feminist Fires: National Women's Independence Day." *off our backs* 11:8 (August-September 1981):18-19.

Rein, Marcy and Wendy Stevens. "Even Our Closets Won't Be Safe" (links between Anita Bryant's Save Our Children Campaign in Florida and Phyllis Schlafly's "Stop-ERA"). *off our backs* 7:6 (July/August 1977):5.

Rupp, Leila J. "The Women's Community in the National Woman's Party, 1945 to the 1960s." *Signs,* "Communities of Women" 10:4 (Summer 1985):715-40.

"State ERA Lacks Gay Rights Provisions" (Rhode Island). *off our backs* 13:6 (June 1983):15.

<u>Families of Lesbians</u> (see also: Adoption; Child Custody; Children
of Lesbians; Foster Care; Parenting)

Bernstein, Robert A. "The Real Pro-Family Policy" (father of a lesbian in
her 20's writes that "without Stonewall, I would probably be
estranged from my own daughter" -- part of "Messages to the
Movement . . . Where We Are Twenty Years After Stonewall").
Out/Look #5, 2:1 (Summer 1989):53-5.

Claverie, Laura. "The View from a Different Window" (coping with a
child's homosexuality). *New Orleans* 21 (February 1987):42-4.

Doe, Jane. "I Left My Husband for the Woman I Loved." *Ms.* 16 (January
1988):80-3.

Fishman, Louise, ed. "The Tapes" (edited comments of 10 visual artists
who met as a group in New York City, Winter 1977). *Heresies
#3,* "Lesbian Art and Artists" 1:3 (Fall 1977):15-21.

Fite, Karen and Nikola Trumbo. "Betrayals Among Women: Barriers to a
Common Language." *Lesbian Ethics* 1:1 (Fall 1984):70-89.

Gidlow, Elsa. "Whose Problem Is Lesbianism?" *Women: a Journal of
Liberation,* "Women Loving Women" 5:2 (1977):38-40.

Holtzen, D.W. and A.A. Agresti. "Parental Responses to Gay and Lesbian
Children: Differences in Homophobia, Self-Esteem, and Sex-
Role Stereotyping." *Journal of Social and Clinical Psychology*
9:3 (1990):390-9.

Johnson, M.M. et al. "Sexual Preferences, Feminism and Women's
Perceptions of Their Parents." *Sex Roles* 7:1 (January 1981):1-
18.

Jolly, Constance Shepard. "From Fear and Doubt to Pride and Love: a
Family's Odyssey." *New Directions for Women* 14 (November-
December 1985):12-13+.

Journal of Homosexuality, "Homosexuality and the Family," vol. 18, nos. 1/2, 1989.

Journal of Homosexuality, "Lesbians Over 60 Speak for Themselves," vol. 16, nos. 3/4, 1988.

Krestan, Jo-Ann. "Lesbian Daughters and Lesbian Mothers: the Crisis of Disclosure from a Family Systems Perspective." *Journal of Psychotherapy and the Family* 3:4 (1987):113-30.

MacLean, Judy. "The Untapped Lobby: Lesbian Daughters and Gay Sons of Politicians." *Out/Look #5*, 2:1 (Summer 1989):62-7.

Martin, A. Damien and Emery S. Hetrick. "The Stigmatization of the Gay and Lesbian Adolescent." *Journal of Homosexuality*, "Psychopathology and Psychotherapy in Homosexuality" 15:1/2 (1988):163-84.

Morales, Edward S. "Ethnic Minority Families and Minority Gays and Lesbians." *Marriage and Family Review* 14:3-4 (1989):217-39.

Murphy, B.C. "Lesbian Couples and Their Parents -- The Effects of Perceived Parental Attitudes on the Couple." *Journal of Counseling and Development* 68:1 (1989):46-51.

Neisen, Joseph H. "Resources for Families with a Gay/Lesbian Member" (survey asking where 90 families turned for support). *Journal of Homosexuality*, "Psychotherapy with Homosexual Men and Women: Integrated Identity Approaches for Clinical Practice" 14:1/2 (1987):239-52.

"Parents of Gays, Lesbians 'Too Controversial'" (to participate in Missouri's "Adopt-a-Highway" program). *off our backs* 20:9 (October 1990):4.

Robinson, Bryan E., et al. "Gay Men's and Women's Perceptions of Early Family Life and Their Relationships with Parents." *Family Relations* 31 (January 1982):79-84.

Robinson, Bryan E., Lynda Henley Walters, and Patsy Skeen. "Response of Parents to Learning That Their Child Is Homosexual and Concern Over AIDS: a National Study" (of 402 parents of lesbians and gay men). *Journal of Homosexuality,* "Homosexuality and the Family" 18:1/2 (1989):59-80.

Savin-Williams, Ritch. "Parental Influences on the Self-Esteem of Gay and Lesbian Youths: a Reflected Appraisals Model." *Journal of Homosexuality,* "Gay and Lesbian Youth: Part I" 17:1/2 (1989):93-110.

Thompson, Norman L., Jr., et al. "Parent-Child Relationship and Sexual Identity in Male and Female Homosexuals and Heterosexuals." *Journal of Consulting and Clinical Psychology* 41:1 (August 1973):120-7.

Wyers, Norman L. "Homosexuality in the Family: Lesbian and Gay Spouses." *Social Work* 32:2 (March-April 1987):143-8.

Allen, Indra Dean (musician):

"Mothers and Daughters" (includes annotated reading list, and articles about musicians and their families). *Hot Wire* 4:2 (March 1988):34-9.

Ishatova, Dovida (musician):

"Mothers and Daughters" (includes annotated reading list, and articles about musicians and their families). *Hot Wire* 4:2 (March 1988):34-9.

Sloan-Hunter, Margaret (musician):

"Mothers and Daughters" (includes annotated reading list, and articles about musicians and their families). *Hot Wire* 4:2 (March 1988):34-9.

<u>Fashion</u> (see also: Butch/Femme; S/M)

Blackman, Inge and Kathryn Perry. "Skirting the Issue: Lesbian Fashion for the 1990s." *Feminist Review* (Great Britain), "Perverse Politics: Lesbian Issues" 34 (Spring 1990):67-78.

Duggan, Lisa. "The Anguished Cry of an '80s Fem: 'I Want to Be a Drag Queen.'" *Out/Look* 1:1 (Spring 1988):62-5.

Klausner, Kim. "On Wearing Skirts." *Out/Look #8,* 2:4 (Spring 1990):18+.

Kulp, Denise. "'Dyke Aesthetics': Dressed to Cool." *off our backs* 14:7 (July 1984):24-5.

Rolley, Katrina. "Cutting a Dash: The Dress of Radclyffe Hall and Una Troubridge." *Feminist Review* (Great Britain) 35 (Summer 1990):54-66.

"S/M Aesthetic." *Out/Look* 1:4 (Winter 1989):42-3.

Stein, Arlene. "All Dressed Up, But No Place to Go? Style Wars and the New Lesbianism." *Out/Look* 1:4 (Winter 1989):34-42.

Tuddé, Oedipussy. "Fashion Politics and the Fashion in Politics" (how mass media coopts subculture and its politics, in part through integrating anti-establishment fashion, written by a member of Collective Lesbian International Terrors (CLIT)). *off our backs* 4:8 (July 1974):17-19.

Wallsgrove, Ruth. "Lipstick Etc." *off our backs* 20:10 (November 1990):13.

Wilson, Elizabeth. "Deviant Dress" (in the late 1980s and the 1950s). *Feminist Review* (Great Britain) 35 (Summer 1990):67-74.

Fat Liberation (see also: Body Image)

Clarke, Caro. "Weighing In." *Gossip* (Great Britain) 6 (1988):56-67.

Denne, Diane. "Being a Fat Separatist." *Common Lives/Lesbian Lives* 9 (Fall 1983):61-4.

Dworkin, Sari H. "Not in Man's Image: Lesbians and the Cultural Oppression of Body Image." *Women & Therapy,* "Lesbianism: Affirming Nontraditional Roles" 8:1/2 (1989):27-39.

Hayman, Angela. "Fat Oppression." *Gossip* (Great Britain) 3 (no date):58-64.

Jo, Bev. "If Looks Could Kill: Fat Oppression." *Lesbian Ethics* 3:1(Spring 1988):48-54.

Kelly. "They Are Trying to Kill Us (But It's For Our Own Good)." *Common Lives/Lesbian Lives* 1 (Fall 1981):32-6.

Lawrence, Sheena Ann. "From a Fat Dyke . . . " *Common Lives/Lesbian Lives* 6 (Winter 1982):71-3.

Stein, Judith. "Thoughts on Fitting In . . . " (as a fat, Jewish lesbian). *Common Lives/Lesbian Lives* 17 (Fall 1985):69-70.

Valley Fat Dykes. "Concerning Fat Dykes: a Fat 'Womonifesto.'" *Common Lives/Lesbian Lives* 20 (Summer 1986):81-2.

------. "Miss Fat Manners' Rules of Etiquette." *Common Lives/Lesbian Lives* 20 (Summer 1986):83-4.

FAT LIP Readers' Theatre:
Bock, Laura. "FAT LIP Readers' Theatre." *Women of Power,* "Humor" 17 (Summer 1990):32-3.

Pumping Iron -- The Women (film):

Millar, Ruth. "Pumping Iron: a Feminist Response" (to the film *Pumping Iron II -- the Women*). *Gossip* (Great Britain) 2 (1986):76-9.

------. (response to Lynnette Mitchell, "Skinny Lizzie Strikes Back: an Apologia for Thin Women's Liberation" *Gossip* (Great Britain) 3 (no date):40-4; see also, related letters in *Gossip* 4 (no date):7-14). *Gossip* 4 (no date):10-11.

Mitchell, Lynnette. "Skinny Lizzie Strikes Back: an Apologia for Thin Women's Liberation" (response to Ruth Millar, "Pumping Iron: a Feminist Response," *Gossip* (Great Britain) 2 (1986):76-9). *Gossip* 3 (no date):40-4.

Film and Video (see also: Television; Vampires)

Ardill, Susan and Penny Ashbrook. "Lesbian Wastelands and Desert Hearts: Lesbians in Film." *Spare Rib* (Great Britain) 169 (August 1986):20-2.

Becker, Edith, Michelle Citron, Julia Lesage, and B. Ruby Rich. "Introduction" (to special section, "Lesbians and Film"). *Jump Cut* 24/5 (March 1981):17-21.

Bennett, Linda. "NEA Funds for Gay Film Fest?" (National Endowment for the Arts). *off our backs* 20:1 (January 1990):6.

Charboneau, Claudette and Lucy Winer. "Lesbians in 'Nice Films.'" *Jump Cut*, "Lesbians and Film" 24/5 (March 1981):25-6.

Christianson, Joseph. "Closet Drama: the Sound and the Flurry Surrounding Winnipeg's International Festival of Gay and Lesbian Films" (Canada). *Border Crossing* 6 (Summer 1987):27-8.

Clarke, Caro. "Lesbian Ethics Workshop Reports: Lesbians in Film." *Gossip* (Great Britain) 6 (1988):13-16.

Collis, Rose and Linda Semple. "A Queer Feeling When I Look at You" (third Lesbian and Gay Film Festival, London, England, October 1988). *Spare Rib* (Great Britain) 195 (October 1988):22-3.

Cook, Alberta I. "More Suits After Plath Pact?" (Dr. Jane Anderson's libel suit about her portrayal as a suicidal lesbian in a film about Sylvia Plath: Anderson v. Avco Embassy Pictures Corp.). *National Law Journal* 9 (February 16, 1987):6.

Dyer, Richard. "Gays in Film." *Jump Cut*, "Lesbians and Film" 24/5 (March 1981):15-16.

------. "Less and More Than Women and Men: Lesbian and Gay Cinema in Weimar Germany." *New German Critique* 51 (Fall 1990):5-60.

Farber, Stephen. "Hollywood Comes Out of the Closet." *Saturday Review* 8 (October 1981):48-51.

Farry, Marcel. "Censorship -- Who's Calling the Shots." *Spare Rib* (Great Britain) 219 (December/January 1990/91):31-2.

Jump Cut, "Lesbians and Film," nos. 24/5, March 1981.

Fishbein, Leslie. "Women on the Fringe: a Film Series." *Film and History* 8:3 (1978):49-58.

"France: Lesbians of the Main Screen" (trans. from French lesbian monthly, *Lesbia*, no. 67 (December 1988); interview with co-founder of Ciné-club of Paris, France). *Connexions*, "Lesbian Activism" 29 (1989):12-13.

Hammer, Barbara. "Lesbian Filmmaking -- Self-Birthing." *Film Reader* 5 (1982):60-6.

------. "Use of Time in Women's Cinema." *Heresies #3*, "Lesbian Art and Artists" 1:3 (Fall 1977):86-9.

Horne, Larry and John Ramirez. "The UCLA Gay and Lesbian Media Conference." *Camera Obscura* 11 (Fall 1983):121-31.

Kilday, Gregg. "Hollywood's Homosexuals." *Film Comment,* "When the Gaze Is Gay" 22:2 (March/April 1986):40-3.

Langguth, Paula E. "With the Community's Support: Lesbian Filmmakers Support the Community." *Visibilities* 2:2 (March/April 1988):4-10.

Leveritt, Annie. "The Seventh Annual Women in the Director's Chair: Women's Film and Video Festival" (not exclusively lesbian). *Hot Wire* 3:3 (July 1987):30-1+.

Martineau, Barbara Halpern. "Out of Sight, Out of Mind, Out of Pocket: Lesbian Representation in Documentary Film." *Resources for Feminist Research* (Canada), "The Lesbian Issue/Etre Lesbienne" 12:1 (March 1983):34-7.

Olson, Ray. "Gay Film Work: Affecting But Too Evasive" (films shown at the American Library Association Conference, Chicago, Illinois, 1978, by the ALA Task Force on Gay Liberation). *Jump Cut* 20 (May 1979):9-12.

Pally, Marcia. "Women in Love." *Film Comment,* "When the Gaze is Gay" 22:2 (March/April 1986):35-9.

Parkerson, Michelle. "No More Mammy Stories: an Overview of Black Women Filmmakers" (not exclusively lesbian). *Gallerie: Women's Art* (1989 annual):12-15.

Patton, Cindy. "The Cum Shot: 3 Takes on Lesbian and Gay Sexuality" (in film). *Out/Look* 1:3 (Fall 1988):72-7.

Poppe, Terri. "2nd National Women's Film Festival" (The National Women's Film Circuit, Washington D.C., May 1978). *off our backs* 8:5 (May 1978):14-15.

Rich, B. Ruby. "The Crisis of Naming in Feminist Film Criticism." *Jump Cut* 19 (December 1978):9-12.

------. "In the Name of Feminist Film Criticism" (discusses lesbian and straight film and film criticism). *Heresies #9,* 3:1 (1980):74-81.

Russo, Vito. "A State of Being." *Film Comment,* "When the Gaze is Gay" 22:2 (March/April 1986):32-4.

Shear, Marie. "Media Watch: Leaving Out Lavender." *New Directions for Women,* "Women in the Arts" 15 (September-October 1986):7.

Smyth, Cherry. "The Pleasure Threshold: Looking at Lesbian Pornography on Film." *Feminist Review* (Great Britain), "Perverse Politics: Lesbian Issues" 34 (Spring 1990):152-9.

Spires, Randy. "The 1986 International Gay Film Festival." *Canadian Woman Studies* (Canada), "Women and Media/Les Femmes et les Media" 8:1 (Spring 1987):90-1.

Stevens, Lynne. "3rd Int'l Women's film & Video Festival" (includes film about lesbian mothers and their children). *off our backs* 9:4 (April 1979):21+.

Stuart, Jan. "A Queer Kind of Film" (First Lesbian and Gay Experimental Film Festival). *Film Comment* 23 (November-December 1987):4.

Sulter, Maud. "Black Codes: the Misrepresentation of Blacklesbians in Film" (considers "Born in Flames," "The Color Purple," "Mark of Lilith," "Mona Lisa," "Passion of Remembrance," and "She's Gotta Have It"). *Gossip* (Great Britain) 5 (no date):29-36.

Swedborg, Deborah. "What Do We See When We See Woman/Woman Sex in Pornographic Movies?" *NWSA Journal* 1:4 (Summer 1989):602-16.

Watstein, Sarah Barbara. "Documenting the Undocumented -- Films and Videos on Women and AIDS." *Visibilities* 4:5 (September/October 1990):20-1.

Weiss, Andrea. "Filmography of Lesbian Works." *Jump Cut,* "Lesbians and Film" 24/5 (March 1981):22+.

------. "Lesbian as Outlaw: New Forms and Fantasies in Women's Independent Cinema." *Conditions: eleven/twelve* 4:2/3 (Spring/Summer 1985):117-32.

------. "Lesbian Cinema and Romantic Love." *Jump Cut,* "Lesbians and Film" 24/5 (March 1981):30.

Wells, Joel W. "Teaching About Gay and Lesbian Sexual and Affectional Orientation Using Explicit Films to Reduce Homophobia." *Journal of Humanistic Education and Development* 23:1 (September 1989):18-34.

Whitelaw, Liz. "Lesbians in the Mainscreen." *Gossip* (Great Britain) 5 (no date):37-46.

Whitaker, Judy. "Hollywood Transformed" (interviews with lesbians who grew up in the environment of film and television). *Jump Cut,* "Lesbians and Film" 24/5 (March 1981):33-5.

Williamson, Judith. "In the Pink" (gay and lesbian films at London's Tyneside Festival, including "The Lesbian Vampire on Film," "Underground Canada," and "Novembermoon"). *New Statesman* (Great Britain) 114 (October 9, 1987):22-3.

Another Way:
"Another Way" (Hungarian film directed by Karoly Makk, based on popular novel, *Outside the Law and Inside,* by Erzsebet Galgoczi, 1981). *Connexions,* "Global Lesbianism 2" 10 (Fall 1983):26-7.

Armatage, Kay (filmmaker):
Armatage, Kay. "Feminist Film-Making: Theory and Practice" (director discusses her two films: "Jill Johnston October 1975" and "Gertrude and Alice in Passing"). *Canadian Woman Studies* (Canada) 1:3 (Spring 1979):49-50.

Blood and Roses: Under the Spell of the Lesbian Vampire:

Collis, Rose. "Blood Sisters" (interview with Andrea Weiss about her film *Blood and Roses: Under the Spell of the Lesbian Vampire*). *Spare Rib* (Great Britain) 183 (October 1987):40-1.

Born in Flames:

Sulter, Maud. "Black Codes: the Misrepresentation of Blacklesbians in Film" (considers "Born in Flames," "The Color Purple," "Mark of Lilith," "Mona Lisa," "Passion of Remembrance," and "She's Gotta Have It"). *Gossip* (Great Britain) 5 (no date):29-36.

Charbonneau, Patricia (co-star of *Desert Hearts*):

Armstrong, Toni L. "*Desert Hearts* Heartthrob: Patricia Charbonneau." *Hot Wire* 3:2 (March 1987):2-5+.

Clod, Bente (filmmaker and writer):

Anderson, Marguerite. "An Interview with Bente Clod: Danish Writer, Poet, Filmmaker and Feminist." *Resources for Feminist Research* (Canada) 17 (December 1988):23-6.

The Color Purple:

Sulter, Maud. "Black Codes: the Misrepresentation of Blacklesbians in Film" (considers "Born in Flames," "The Color Purple," "Mark of Lilith," "Mona Lisa," "Passion of Remembrance," and "She's Gotta Have It"). *Gossip* (Great Britain) 5 (no date):29-36.

A Comedy in Six Unnatural Acts:

CAD. "Gays and Media" (*Windows, Cruising, A Comedy in Six Unnatural Acts*). *off our backs* 10:6 (June 1980):9.

Cruising:

CAD. "Lesbian/Gay Trips, Cruises & Marches" (U.S. and international news briefs; "Cruising"). *off our backs* 10:3 (March 1980):18-19+.

------. "Gays and Media" (*Windows, Cruising, A Comedy in Six Unnatural Acts*). *off our backs* 10:6 (June 1980):9.

Daughters of Darkness:
Zimmerman, Bonnie. "_Daughters of Darkness:_ Lesbian Vampires."
Jump Cut, "Lesbians and Film" 24/5 (March 1981):23-4.

Deitch, Donna (filmmaker; director of _Desert Hearts_):
Aufderheide, Patricia. "_Desert Hearts:_ an Interview with Donna
Deitch" (director). _Cinéaste_ 15:1 (1986):18-19.

Harper, Jorjet. "_Desert Hearts:_ Donna Deitch" (director/producer). _Hot
Wire_ 3:1 (November 1986):23-5.

Kort, Michele. "Independent Filmmaker Donna Deitch." _Ms._ 14:5
(November 1985):66-7.

Desaulniers, Michelle (video artist):
Dascher, Helge. "Mémoire, reconnaissance: Entrevue avec Michelle
Desaulniers et Diane Trépanière." _Canadian Woman Studies_
(Canada), "Feminism and Visual Art/Le féminisme et l'art
visuel" 11:1 (Spring 1990):75-7.

Desert Hearts:
Armstrong, Toni L. "_Desert Hearts_ Heartthrob: Patricia
Charbonneau." _Hot Wire_ 3:2 (March 1987):2-5+.

Aufderheide, Patricia. "_Desert Hearts:_ an Interview with Donna
Deitch" (director). _Cinéaste_ 15:1 (1986):18-19.

Baim, Tracy (with Toni L. Armstrong). "Finally, Good News at the
Movies: _One Fine Day_ and _Desert Hearts._" _Hot Wire_ 2:2 (March
1986):42-4+.

Claessens, Dorothy. (letter about _Desert Hearts_ and _Coup de Foudre_
(a.k.a. _Entre Nous_ in the U.S.); response to Sibyl Grundberg,
"Deserted Hearts: Lesbians Making It in the Movies," _Gossip_
(Great Britain) 4 (no date):27-39). _Gossip_ 6 (1988):9-11.

Grundberg, Sibyl. "Deserted Hearts: Lesbians Making It in the
Movies" (includes discussion of class in the movie _Desert
Hearts_). _Gossip_ (Great Britain) 4 (no date):27-39.

Harper, Jorjet. *"Desert Hearts:* Donna Deitch" (director/producer). *Hot Wire* 3:1 (November 1986):23-5.

Internicola, Dorene. "Desert Hearts: Sexy Film of Women in Love." *New Directions for Women* 15:5 (September/October 1986):6.

Kulp, Denise. "Whatever's For Us: Lesbians in Popular Culture" (television show, *My Two Loves;* film, *Desert Hearts;* theatre, Lily Tomlin's *The Search for Signs of Intelligent Life in the Universe*). *off our backs* 16:6 (June 1986):24-5.

Desire: Sexuality in Germany 1910-45:
Shaw, Nancy. "On a Trumped-Up Charge: Two Video Films" (including video film *Desire: Sexuality in Germany 1910-45* by Stuart Marshall, about gays and lesbians under Nazism). *Vanguard* (Canada) 18:3 (Summer 1989):20-5.

Diabolo Menthe:
Mitchell, Lynette. (letter about *Coup de Foudre* (a.k.a. *Entre Nous* in the United States) and *Diabolo Menthe* by Diane Kurys). *Gossip* (Great Britain) 6 (1988):11-13.

Entre Nous (Coup de Foudre):
Claessens, Dorothy. (letter about *Desert Hearts* and *Coup de Foudre* (a.k.a. *Entre Nous* in the U.S.); response to Sibyl Grundberg, "Deserted Hearts: Lesbians Making It in the Movies," *Gossip* (Great Britain) 4 (no date):27-39). *Gossip* 6 (1988):9-11.

Mitchell, Lynette. (letter about *Coup de Foudre* (a.k.a. *Entre Nous* in the United States) and *Diabolo Menthe* by Diane Kurys). *Gossip* (Great Britain) 6 (1988):11-13.

Firewords:
Williamson, Janice. *"Firewords:* Dorothy Hénaut -- National Film Board, Studio D" (film about three radical feminist Québécois writers: Louky Bersianik, Nicole Brossard, Jovette Marchessault). *Resources for Feminist Research* (Canada) 15 (December 1986/January 1987):25-7.

Förster, Annette (Dutch film critic):
Donem, Suzanna. "Lesbian Lives on Screen" (interview). *Sojourner*
    15:3 (November 1989):20-1.

Garbo, Greta (actor):
Adam, Margie. "Greta Garbo's 'Mysterious' Private Life." *Out/Look*
    #10, 3:2 (Fall 1990):25.

Hair:
Chasin, Susan. "A Special Event: '*Hair* . . . For the Next
    Generation.'" *Visibilities* 2:5 (September/October 1988):12-13.

Hammer, Barbara (filmmaker):
Zita, Jacquelyn. "Films of Barbara Hammer: Counter-Currencies of a
    Lesbian Iconography." *Jump Cut,* "Lesbians and Film" 24/5
    (March 1981):26-30.

Iris (film distribution collective):
Moira, Fran. "Iris -- Movie Marathon" (U.S. tour; includes lesbian
    films). *off our backs* 5:8 (September-October 1975):11.

Reid, Frances. "IRIS Films: Documenting the Lives of Lesbians."
    Heresies #3, "Lesbian Art and Artists" 1:3 (Fall 1977):100-1.

Schmitz, Marlene and Margie Crow. "Iris -- Reel Women" (collective
    working on a film about lesbian mothers and organizing a
    "National Women's Film Circuit"). *off our backs* 5:7 (August
    1975):12.

JEB (photographer):
Johnson, Angela. "JEB's Fabulous Multi-Image Slide Presentation:
    For Love and For Life" (slide show and video of the March on
    Washington for Lesbian and Gay Rights, October 1987). *off our
    backs* 18:11 (December 1988):12-13.

Lianna:
Rubin, Barbara. "'Coming Out' for Lianna Means Separation,
    Growth" (*Lianna,* directed by John Sayles). *New Directions for
    Women* 12:3 (May/June 1983):7.

Maedchen in Uniform:

Goldschen, Lisa Ohm. "The Filmic Adaptation of the Novel *Das Kind Manuela:* Christa Winsloe's Child Heroine Becomes a Madchen in Uniform." *Neue Germanistik* (Minneapolis, Minnesota) 4:2 (Spring 1986):3-12.

Kelly, Janis. "Maedchen in Uniform" (Huntington, New York theater cancels lesbian discussion panel and film). *off our backs* 6:3 (May 1976):10.

Rich, B. Ruby. "*Maedchen in Uniform:* From Repressive Tolerance to Erotic Liberation" (German lesbian history through discussion of Leontine Sagan's film). *Radical America* 15:6 (November-December 1981):17-36.

Mark of Lilith:

Sulter, Maud. "Black Codes: the Misrepresentation of Blacklesbians in Film" (considers "Born in Flames," "The Color Purple," "Mark of Lilith," "Mona Lisa," "Passion of Remembrance," and "She's Gotta Have It"). *Gossip* (Great Britain) 5 (no date):29-36.

Mona Lisa:

Sulter, Maud. "Black Codes: the Misrepresentation of Blacklesbians in Film" (considers "Born in Flames," "The Color Purple," "Mark of Lilith," "Mona Lisa," "Passion of Remembrance," and "She's Gotta Have It"). *Gossip* (Great Britain) 5 (no date):29-36.

Nightwood:

Levine, Nancy J. "'I've Always Suffered from Sirens': the Cinema and Djuna Barnes' *Nightwood*" (novel). *Women's Studies: an Interdisciplinary Journal* 16:3-4 (1989):271-81.

Novembermoon:

Leveritt, Annie and Celia Guse. "*Novembermoon*" (film about Nazi occupation of France, with lesbian main characters). *Hot Wire* 2:3 (July 1986):40-1.

On Golden Pond:

Sperry, Jackie. "Is Love Political?" (anti-lesbian jokes in "On Golden Pond"). *Common Lives/Lesbian Lives* 7 (Spring 1983):102-6.

One Fine Day:

Baim, Tracy (with Toni L. Armstrong). "Finally, Good News at the Movies: *One Fine Day* and *Desert Hearts.*" *Hot Wire* 2:2 (March 1986):42-4+.

Ottinger, Ulrike (filmmaker):

Hansen, Miriam. "Visual Pleasure, Fetishism and the Problem of Feminine/Feminist Discourse: Ulrike Ottinger's *Ticket of No Return.*" *New German Critique* 31 (Winter 1984):95-108.

Oxenberg, Jan (filmmaker):

CAD. "Gays and Media" (*Windows, Cruising, A Comedy in Six Unnatural Acts*). *off our backs* 10:6 (June 1980):9.

Citron, Michelle. "Films of Jan Oxenberg: Comic Critique." *Jump Cut,* "Lesbians and Film" 24/5 (March 1981):31-2.

Garvey, Ellen. "Police Cancel Lesbian Film" (*A Comedy in Six Unnatural Acts,* scheduled to show at a bar in Provincetown, Massachusetts; cancellation based on advertisements for film and its title). *off our backs* 6:4 (June 1976):7.

Kelly, Janis and Terri Poppe. "Jan Oxenberg -- Filmmaker" (interview). *off our backs* 6:10 (January 1977):12-13.

Parkerson, Michelle (African-American filmmaker):

Leveritt, Annie and Toni L. Armstrong. "Filmmaker, Activist, Writer: Michelle Parkerson" (co-chair, National Coalition of Black Lesbians and Gays). *Hot Wire* 3:3 (July 1987):26-8.

Parkerson, Michelle. "Beyond Chiffon" (1950s drag show at The Jewel Box, including male impersonator Miss Stormé DeLarvie, about whom Parkerson made the film "Stormé". *Black/Out* 1:3/4 (1987):21-2.

Ruby, Jennie. "The Black Diaspora" (Michelle Parkerson, Audre Lorde, and Cheryl Clarke speaking on diversity of self-expression among African-American women, in a session at the 10th annual National Women's Studies Association conference, University of Minnesota in Minneapolis, June 1988, "African American Women and the Black Diaspora"). *off our backs* 18:8 (August-September 1988):10.

Passion of Remembrance:

Sulter, Maud. "Black Codes: the Misrepresentation of Blacklesbians in Film" (considers "Born in Flames," "The Color Purple," "Mark of Lilith," "Mona Lisa," "Passion of Remembrance," and "She's Gotta Have It"). *Gossip* (Great Britain) 5 (no date):29-36.

Personal Best:

Kidd, Dorothy. "Getting Physical: Compulsory Heterosexuality and Sport" (discusses the film *Personal Best*). *Canadian Woman Studies* (Canada), "Sport" 4:3 (Spring/May 1983):62-5.

Picard, Jane (separatist filmmaker, founding member of the $10 Movie Company):

Weller, Marilyn. "An Interview with Jane Picard." *Maenad*, "The Lesbian/Heterosexual Split" 2:2 (Winter 1982):87-97.

Pumping Iron II -- the Women:

Millar, Ruth. "Pumping Iron: a Feminist Response" (to the film *Pumping Iron II -- the Women*). *Gossip* (Great Britain) 2 (1986):76-9.

Schiller, Greta (filmmaker):

"Jazz Jivin' and Hell Divin' Women" (film *Tiny and Ruby: Hell-Divin' Women*" by Greta Schiller and Andrea Weiss). *Spare Rib* (Great Britain) 195 (October 1988):24.

Shame:

Harper, Jorjet. "The Women's Action/Adventure Film: 'Shame' (about a gang rape in a small town in western Australia). *Hot Wire* 5:2 (May 1989):24-5.

She Must Be Seeing Things:

Ardill, Susan and Sue O'Sullivan. "Sex in the Summer of '88" (sex and pornography controversies, including anti-gay Clause 28; *A Restricted Country,* book by Joan Nestle; *She Must Be Seeing Things,* video by Sheila McLaughlin). *Feminist Review* (Great Britain), "The Past Before Us: Twenty Years of Feminism" 31 (Spring 1989):126-34.

de Lauretis, Teresa. "Sexual Indifference and Lesbian Representation" (discusses novels *The Well of Loneliness, Nightwood,* and *The Lesbian Body,* and the film *She Must Be Seeing Things). Theatre Journal* 40:2 (May 1988):155-77.

"Whatever Happened at the Lesbian Archive?" (dispute in collective over showing of film with S/M content, "She Must Be Seeing Things," and over alleged racism in hiring). *Spare Rib* (Great Britain) 199 (March 1989):17.

She's Gotta Have It:

Sulter, Maud. "Black Codes: the Misrepresentation of Blacklesbians in Film" (considers "Born in Flames," "The Color Purple," "Mark of Lilith," "Mona Lisa," "Passion of Remembrance," and "She's Gotta Have It"). *Gossip* (Great Britain) 5 (no date):29-36.

Ticket of No Return:

Hansen, Miriam. "Visual Pleasure, Fetishism and the Problem of Feminine/Feminist Discourse: Ulrike Ottinger's *Ticket of No Return." New German Critique* 31 (Winter 1984):95-108.

Tiny and Ruby: Hell-Divin' Women:

"Jazz Jivin' and Hell Divin' Women" (film *Tiny and Ruby: Hell-Divin' Women"* by Greta Schiller and Andrea Weiss). *Spare Rib* (Great Britain) 195 (October 1988):24.

Tomlin, Lily (comic actor):

Langguth, Paula E. "Tomlin Film Engaged in Lawsuit." *Visibilities* 1:1 (Summer 1987):19.

<u>Trépanière, Diane</u> (video artist):

Dascher, Helge. "Mémoire, reconnaissance: Entrevue avec Michelle Desaulniers et Diane Trépanière." *Canadian Woman Studies* (Canada), "Feminism and Visual Art/Le féminisme et l'art visuel" 11:1 (Spring 1990):75-7.

Waiting For the Moon:

Blake, Angie. "Jill Godmilow's *Waiting for the Moon*" (film about Gertrude Stein and Alice B. Toklas). *off our backs* 17:6 (June 1987):20-1.

"Waiting for the Moon, Film by Jill Godmilow" (about Gertrude Stein and Alice B. Toklas). *New Directions for Women* 16 (September-October 1987):8.

<u>Weiss, Andrea</u> (filmmaker):

Collis, Rose. "Blood Sisters" (interview with Andrea Weiss about her film *Blood and Roses: Under the Spell of the Lesbian Vampire*). *Spare Rib* (Great Britain) 183 (October 1987):40-1.

"Jazz Jivin' and Hell Divin' Women" (film *Tiny and Ruby: Hell-Divin' Women"* by Greta Schiller and Andrea Weiss). *Spare Rib* (Great Britain) 195 (October 1988):24.

Windows:

Beverly, Brooke, and Wendy Stevens. "Why Protest Windows?" (movie about a psychotic lesbian who hires a man to rape a straight woman). *off our backs* 10:4 (April 1980):9+.

CAD. "Gays and Media" (*Windows, Cruising, A Comedy in Six Unnatural Acts*). *off our backs* 10:6 (June 1980):9.

Stevens, Lynne. "The Window: a Look Inside" (protest against "Windows," movie about a psychotic lesbian who hires a man to rape a straight woman). *off our backs* 10:3 (March 1980):16-17.

Working Girls:
Bishop, Marla and Lucy O'Brien. "Working Girls" (interview with director Lizzie Borden about her film about a lesbian working in a heterosexual brothel). *Spare Rib* (Great Britain) 175 (February 1987):37-9.

Foster Care (see also: Adoption; Child Custody; Children of Lesbians; Parenting)

DAR. "Foster Equality Day" (protesting discrimination against lesbians and gay men who want to be foster parents). *off our backs* 16:7 (July 1986):9.

Ricketts, Wendell and Roberta Achtenberg. "Adoption and Foster Parenting for Lesbians and Gay Men: Creating New Traditions in Family." *Marriage and Family Review* 14:3-4 (1989):83-118.

Massachusetts:
"Gay Foster Care Update" (prohibition of gay/lesbian foster care). *off our backs* 18:10 (November 1988):7.

"Gays and Lesbians Foster?" *off our backs* 20:8 (August/September 1990):6.

"Unmarried Foster Parents OK in Massachusetts." *off our backs* 20:5 (May 1990):6.

New Hampshire:
"Gay Foster Parents" (anti-gay foster-parent bill). *off our backs* 17:3 (Mary 1987):11.

KM. "Close Call in New Hampshire" (State House of Representatives narrowly upholds lesbian and gay foster care). *off our backs* 16:4 (April 1986):9.

Ratterman, Debbie. "Gay Foster Parents" (banned). *off our backs* 17:10 (November 1987):3.

Friendship

Clare, Elizabeth. "Friends, Lovers and Passion." *Sinister Wisdom,* "On Friendship" 40 (Spring 1990):96-8.

Copper, Baba. "Different Kinds of Love Quarrels." *Common Lives/Lesbian Lives* 17 (Fall 1985):32-5.

Daly, Mary. "Sparking: The Fire of Female Friendship" (excerpt from *Gyn/ecology*). *Chrysalis* 6 (1978):27-35.

Dykewomon, Elana. "Notes for a Magazine -- Friendship: This Issue." *Sinister Wisdom,* "On Friendship" 40 (Spring 1990):3-9.

Dykewomon, Elana, Susan Levinkind, Valerie Stoehr, Jasmine Marah, Caryatis Cardea, Cath Thompson, Susanjill Kahn, and Naja Sorella. "*Sinister Wisdom* Friendship Discussion." *Sinister Wisdom,* "On Friendship" 40 (Spring 1990):17-35.

Hunt, Linda C. "Sustenance and Balm: The Question of Female Friendship in *Shirley* and *Vilette.*" *Tulsa Studies in Women's Literature* 1:1 (Spring 1982):55-66.

Johnson, Loretta. "In a Penal Colony." *Sinister Wisdom,* "On Friendship" 40 (Spring 1990):15-16.

Libertin, Mary. "Female Friendship in Women's Verse: Toward a New Theory of Female Poetics" (argues that the point in defining lesbian writing is not evidence of genital contact). *Women's Studies* 9:3 (1982):291-308.

Palladino, Diane and Yanela Stephenson. "Perceptions of the Sexual Self: Their Impact on Relationships Between Lesbian and Heterosexual Women." *Women & Therapy,* "Diversity and Complexity in Feminist Therapy: Part II" 9:3 (1990):231-53.

Raymond, Janice. "A Genealogy of Female Friendship." *Trivia* 1 (Fall 1982):5-26.

Rose, Suzanna and Laurie Roades. "Feminism and Women's Friendships" (friendships among lesbian, straight, feminist, and non-feminist women). *Psychology of Women Quarterly* 11 (June 1987):243-54.

Sinister Wisdom, "On Friendship," no. 40, Spring 1990.

Raymond, Janice (author of *A Passion for Friends*):
Griffin, Connie. "A Passion for Female Friends: an Interview with Janice Raymond." *Woman of Power* 7 (Summer 1987):68-71.

Gay Bashing (see Violence Against Lesbians and Gay Men)

Gay Liberation Movement (see also: Political Organizing; Political Theory)

Apuzzo, Virginia M. "Brand X: Why We Need to Be More Generic" ("Is this a movement for social change, or is it a movement to make it okay to be gay or lesbian?" -- part of "Messages to the Movement . . . Where We Are Twenty Years After Stonewall"). *Out/Look #5,* 2:1 (Summer 1980):60-1.

Bearchell, Chris. "Why I Am a Gay Liberationist: Thoughts on Sex, Freedom, the Family and the State" (gay liberation and lesbian-feminism, and Canada's gay/lesbian liberation journal, *The Body Politic*). *Resources for Feminist Research* (Canada), "The Lesbian Issue/Etre Lesbienne" 12:1(March 1983):57-60.

Bernstein, Robert A. "The Real Pro-Family Policy" (father of a lesbian in her 20's writes that "without Stonewall, I would probably be estranged from my own daughter" -- part of "Messages to the Movement . . . Where We Are Twenty Years After Stonewall"). *Out/Look #5,* 2:1 (Summer 1989):53-5.

Blow, Richard. "Those Were the Gays: What Now for the Gay Movement?" *New Republic* 197 (November 2, 1987):14-16.

Bosley, Anne Marie. "ILGA Conference (International Lesbian and Gay Association Conference, "Gays and Lesbians Facing Crisis," July 1986; organization changed name to include "Lesbian"). *Spare Rib* (Great Britain) 170 (September 1986):48.

Brackx, Amy. "Out Into the Open: Ten Years of the Gay Movement." *Spare Rib* (Great Britain) 84 (July 1979):42-6.

Chapman, Frances and Bernice. "A Conference Is Bringing Together" (Midwest Gay Pride Conference, Iowa City; Lesbian Extravaganza, East Lansing, Michigan). *off our backs* (May-June 1975):4-5+.

Douglas, Carol Anne. "Election '88" (section on "Lesbian and Gay Rights" in various states and nationally). *off our backs* 18:11 (December 1988):1-2.

------. "International Lesbian & Gay Conferences: a Split" (formation of International Lesbian Information Service and the International Gay Association). *off our backs* 11:6 (June 1981):7.

Elshtain, Jean Bethke. "Homosexual Politics: the Paradox of Gay Liberation." *Salmagundi,* "Homosexuality: Sacrilege, Vision, Politics" 58-59 (Fall 1982-Winter 1983):252-80.

"For a New Coalition" (National March for Lesbian and Gay Rights, October 11, 1987). *The Nation* 245:13(October 24, 1987):433.

"Gay Gala" (Christopher Street Gay Liberation Days commemorating the 1969 Stonewall Riots, New York City, June 1970). *off our backs* 1:7 (June 26, 1970):14.

"Gay Rights Bills in State Senates" (anti-discrimination legislation passes in state houses in Iowa and Massachusetts). *off our backs* 19:6 (June 1989):7.

"Gays on the March" (unsympathetic cover story on the surge of lesbian and gay pride/visibility). *Time* 106 (September 8, 1975):32-43.

Gomez, Jewelle. "We Haven't Come Such a Long Way, Baby" (part of "Messages to the Movement . . . Where We Are Twenty Years After Stonewall"). *Out/Look #5,* 2:1 (Summer 1989):55-6.

Graff, Holly. "Anita's Closet Isn't Big Enough! -- Gay and Lesbian Rights: a Socialist Feminist Perspective." *Women: a Journal of Liberation,* "Women Loving Women" 5:2 (1977):58-9.

Horowitz, Paul. "Beyond the Gay Nation: Where Are We Marching?" (National March for Lesbian and Gay Rights, Washington, D.C., October 11, 1987). *Out/Look* 1:1 (Spring 1988):7+.

"How Gay Is Gay?: Homosexual Men and Women Are Making Progress Toward Equality" (cover story). *Time* 113 (April 23, 1979):72-6.

Humm, A. "The Personal Politics of Lesbian and Gay Liberation." *Social Policy* 11:2 (September-October 1980):40-5.

Johnston, Jill. "Lesbian/Feminism Reconsidered." *Salmagundi,* "Homosexuality: Sacrilege, Vision, Politics" 58-59 (Fall 1982-Winter 1983):76-88.

Negrin, Su. "(Hetero)Sexual Politics" (except from *Begin at Start: Some Thoughts on Personal Liberation and World Change). Edcentric* 31-2 (November 1974):47-9.

A Radicalesbian. "Sister Love" (lesbians in first annual Christopher Street Gay Liberation Day, commemorating 1969 Stonewall Riots, New York City, June 1970). *off our backs* 1:9&10 (July 31, 1970):3.

Samoy, Stephanie Castillo. "*Visibilities* Highlights . . . Barbara Gittings" (activist since the 1950s). *Visibilities* 4:5 (September/October 1990):28.

Vaid, Urvashi. "We Have a Blueprint; Now We Need Tools" (part of "Messages to the Movement . . . Where We Are Twenty Years After Stonewall"). *Out/Look #5*, 2:1 (Summer 1989):59-60.

Wallsgrove, Ruth. "Signs of the Times: a Short Natural History of Some Favorite Feminist and Gay Liberation Symbols." *Spare Rib* (Great Britain) 120 (July 1982):10.

Weir, Lorna and Eve Zaremba. "Boys and Girls Together: Feminism and Gay Liberation." *Broadside* (Canada) 4:1 (1982):6-7.

<u>Gay Men and Lesbians</u> (see also: Gay Liberation Movement)

CAD. "Working with Gay Men" (problems with). *off our backs* 10:6 (June 1980):9.

Cruikshank, Margaret and Dan Allen. "Team Teaching Gay/Lesbian Studies." *Radical Teacher,* "Gay and Lesbian Studies" 24 (no date, c.1983):22-3.

de Monteflores, Carmen and Stephen J. Schultz. "Coming Out: Similarities and Differences for Lesbians and Gay Men." *Journal of Social Issues,* "Psychology and the Gay Community" 34:3 (1978):59+.

Fein, Sara Beck and Elane M. Nuehring. "Perspectives on the Gender-Integrated [College] Gay Community: Its Formal Structure and Social Functions." *Homosexual Counseling Journal* 2:4 (October 1975):150-63.

Kulp, Denise. "On Working with My Brothers: Why a Lesbian Does AIDS Work." *off our backs* 18:8 (August-September 1988):22.

"Lesbian Space in London [Gay] Center." *Spare Rib* (Great Britain) 143 (June 1984):24-5.

Miller, Barbara. "AIDS -- Should We Care?" *Spare Rib* (Great Britain) 141 (April 1984):28.

Parker, Jan and Suzanne Arnold. "*Gay News:* Good News for Lesbians?" (two *Spare Rib* writers talk to Gillian Hanscombe and Allison Hennigan, writers for *Gay News*). *Spare Rib* (Great Britain) 130 (May 1983):49-51.

Schaefer, Siegrid. "Sociosexual Behavior in Male and Female Homosexuals: a Study in Sex Differences" (West Germany). *Archives of Sexual Behavior* 6 (1977):355+.

Warren, C.A.B. "Women Among Men: Females in the Male Homosexual Community." *Archives of Sexual Behavior* 5:2 (1976):157-69.

Gender Roles (see Androgyny; Butch/Femme; Transsexualism; Transvestism)

Health (see also: Acquired Immune Deficiency Syndrome; Cancer; Disabled Lesbians and Disability)

"55% Not Out" (lesbians and bisexual women to their gynecologist). *off our backs* 16:1 (January 1986):14.

Bennett, Linda. "Lesbian Health Care" (non-profit organization formed in Washington, D.C.). *off our backs,* "20th Anniversary" 20:2 (February 1990):8.

Brown, Douglas F. "The Health Service and Gay Students." *Journal of the American College Health Association* 24:5 (June 1976):272-3.

CAD. "D.C. -- Barry Listens" (Washington, D.C. mayor Marion Barry supports community efforts on behalf of African-American lesbians and gays, gay clinic, and enforcement of anti-discrimination laws). *off our backs* 9:3 (March 1979):8.

Cochran, S.D. and V.M. Mays. "Disclosure of Sexual Preference to Physicians by Black Lesbian and Bisexual Women." *Western Journal of Medicine* 149:5 (1988):616-19.

Eaton, Mary and Cynthia Peterson. "Andrew v. Ontario Minister of Health" (Ontario, Canada High Court of Justice decides that lesbian partners are not spouses for purposes of the Ontario Health Insurance Plan). *Canadian Journal of Women and the Law* (Canada) 2:2 (1987-88):416-21.

"European Self-Help Conference" (Women and Health Conference organized by Feministisches Frauen Gesundheits Zentrum, Hanover, West Germany, April 1980). *off our backs* 10:8 (August-September 1980):5; note: cover reads 10:7.

Foloyan, Ayofemi. "National Black Gay and Lesbian Leadership Forum: a Conference Report" (Atlanta, Georgia, February 1990). *off our backs* 20:4 (April 1990):2-3.

Freedman, Mark. "Far From Illness: Homosexuals May be Healthier Than Straights." *Psychology Today* 8:10 (March 1975):28-32.

Fridley, Mary. "The Health Closet: Opening the Door on Gay Health Issues" (first national gay health conference, Washington, D.C., May 1978). *off our backs* 8:7 (July 1978):14+.

Harvey, S.M., C. Carr, and S. Bernheime. "Lesbian Mothers -- Health-Care Experiences." *Journal of Nurse-Midwifery* 34:3 (1989):115-9.

Hemmings, Susan. "Overdose of Doctors: Susan Hemmings on Dykes at the Doctors." *Spare Rib* (Great Britain) 162 (January 1986):20-1.

Hitchcock, Janice. "Bibliography: Lesbian Health." *Women's Studies: an Interdisciplinary Journal* 17:1-2 (1989):139-44.

Johnson, Susan R., Susan M. Guenther, Douglas W. Laube, and William C. Keettel. "Factors Influencing Lesbian Gynecologic Care: a Preliminary Study." *American Journal of Obstetrics and Gynecology* 140:1 (May 1981):21+.

Leaman, Thomas L. "The Lesbian Patient, Part II: When She Is Your Patient." *The Female Patient* 12:5 (May 1987):12+.

"Lesbian Health" (3rd International Meeting: Women and Health, Geneva, Switzerland, June 1981). *ISIS International Bulletin* 20 (1981):17.

"Lesbianism 101" (cites article by male physician giving advice to help other doctors meet lesbians' needs). *off our backs* 17:10 (November 1987):5.

Mary and June. "Lesbian Nurses" (letter). *Spare Rib* (Great Britain) 164 (March 1986):6.

Nestle, Joan. "New York Illness Support Group: What Being a Lesbian Means in the Deepest Sense." *off our backs,* "Women and Disability" 11:5 (May 1981):8+.

O'Donnell, Mary. "Lesbian Health Care: Issues and Literature." *Science for the People* 10 (May-June 1978):8-19.

O'Sullivan, Sue. "Where Were the Lesbian Doctors?" (at the 1st International Conference on Homosexuality and Medicine, London, England, August 1986). *Spare Rib* (Great Britain) 172 (November 1986):8.

Poppe, Terri. "Professionalism: To What Degree?" (commentary on the first nationall gay health conference, Washington, D.C., May 1978). *off our backs* 8:7 (July 1978):22.

Potter, Sandee. "Social Work, Traditional Health Care Systems and Lesbian Invisibility." *Journal of Social Work & Human Sexuality* 3:2-3 (1985):59-68.

Raymond, Chris Anne. "Lesbians Call for Greater Physician Awareness, Sensitivity to Improve Patient Care." *JAMA, The Journal of the American Medical Association* 259 (January 1, 1988):18.

Schwanberg, Sandra L. "Attitudes Towards Homosexuality in American Health Care Literature 1983-1987." *Journal of Homosexuality* 19:3 (1990):117-36.

------. "Changes in Labeling Homosexuality in Health Sciences Literature: a Preliminary Investigation." *Journal of Homosexuality* 12:1 (Fall 1985):51-73.

Shaw, Nancy Stoller. "New Research Issues in Lesbian Health." *Women's Studies: an Interdisciplinary Journal* 17:1-2 (1989):125-38.

Smith, Elaine M., Susan R. Johnson, and Susan M. Guenther. "Health Care Attitudes and Experiences During Gynecologic Care Among Lesbians and Bisexuals." *American Journal of Public Health* 75:9 (1985):1085-7.

Sorella, Naja. "A/part of the Community" (environmental illness, and the fact that "Lesbians put their . . . energy into AIDS" and not into other chronic illness as well). *Sinister Wisdom,* "On Disability" 39 (Winter 1989-90):104-7.

Sorrel, Lorraine and Vickie Leonard. "Gay Health Activists Meet in L.A." (National Lesbian and Gay Health Conference, Los Angeles, California, March 1987). *off our backs* 17:8 (August-September 1987):4.

Stevens, Patricia and Joanne Hall. "Stigma in Lesbian Women: Identifiability, Health Beliefs, and Health Care Interactions." *Image: Journal of Nursing Scholarship* 20:2 (Summer 1988):69-73.

Thomas, June. "Lesbian/Gay Health Conference: Moving Lesbian and Gay Health Care into the Mainstream" (seventh annual conference, George Washington University, March 1986). *off our backs* 16:5 (May 1986):1-3+.

Winnow, Jackie. "Lesbians Evolving Healthcare: Our Lives Depend On It." *Sinister Wisdom,* "On Disability" 39 (Winter 1989-90):53-63.

------. "Lesbians Working on AIDS: Assessing the Impact on Health Care for Women." *Out/Look #5,* 2:1 (Summer 1989):10-18.

"Workshop Reports: Lesbian Health" (from the Third International
	Meeting, Women and Health, Geneva, Switzerland, June 1981).
	ISIS International Bulletin 20 (1981):17-19.

Zeidenstein, L. "Gynecological and Childbearing Needs of Lesbians."
	Journal of Nurse-Midwifery 35:1 (1990):10-18.

Heterosexism (see Homophobia/Heterosexism)

History (see also: Archives)

General/Theory:
Aptheker, Bettina. "Imagining Our Lives: the Novelist as Historian"
	(including *Patience and Sarah* by Isabel Miller/Alma Routsong).
	Woman of Power, "ReVisioning History" 16 (Spring 1990):32-
	5.

Bearchell, Chris. "Bar-Hopping" (history of lesbian bars in Toronto,
	Ontario, Canada). *Body Politic* (Canada) 77 (October 1981):25-7.

Bravmann, Scott. "Telling (Hi)stories: Rethinking the Lesbian and
	Gay Historical Imagination" (problems of race, class, and gender
	in recovering lesbian and gay history). *Out/Look #8*, 2:4 (Spring
	1990):68-74.

CAD. "History Open House" (Washington, D.C.-based Women's
	Center History Project, including the group Lesbian Heritage,
	D.C.). *off our backs* 9:11 (December 1979):15.

Cleary, Cindy. "Affecting Our Lives: the Importance of Oral History
	to Lesbians." *Common Lives/Lesbian Lives* 1 (Fall 1981):71-3.

Cook, Blanche Wiesen. "The Historical Denial of Lesbianism."
	Radical History Review 20 (Spring/Summer 1979):60-5.

----------."'Women Alone Stir My Imagination': Lesbianism and the
	Cultural Tradition." *Signs* 4:4 (Summer 1979):718-39.

Corinne, Tee A. "Remembering as a Way of Life" (lesbian "national treasures," including writers June Arnold, Jeannette Foster, Valerie Taylor, Barbara Grier, Audre Lorde, Anita Cornwell, Sarah Aldridge, Sonny Wainwright). *Common Lives/Lesbian Lives* 19 (Spring 1986):15-18.

Crowden, John J. "The Love That Dares Now Speak Its Name" (bibliography on sexuality, history, gender identity, gay liberation, research, psychotherapy, social attitudes). *Choice* 11 (April 1974):209-27.

Day, Susie. "Joan Nestle: 'Taking Pride in Lesbian Herstory.'" *Sojourner* 14:10 (June 1989):17-19.

DeCecco, J.P. "Definition and Meaning of Sexual Orientation." *Journal of Homosexuality* 6:4 (Summer 1981):51-67.

D'Emilio, John. "Gay Politics, Gay Community: San Francisco's Experience." *Socialist Review* 55, 11:1 (January/February 1981):77-104.

------. "Making and Unmaking Minorities: the Tensions Between Gay Politics and History." *New York University Review of Law & Social Change* 14:4 (Fall 1986):915-22.

------. "Not a Simple Matter: Gay History and Gay Historians" (round table: "What has/n't changed in American historical practice?"). *Journal of American History* 76 (September 1989):435-43.

di Leonardo, Micaela. "Warrior Virgins and Boston Marriages: Spinsterhood in History and Culture" (implications of spinsterhood in various cultures around the world: Boston marriages, Kwantung marriage resistance, Nuer Woman-Marriage, Hausa housewives and prostitutes). *Feminist Issues* 5:2 (Fall 1985):47-68.

Doughty, Frances. "Lesbian Biography, Biography of Lesbians." *Frontiers,* "Lesbian History" 4:3 (Fall 1979):76-9.

Duggan, Lisa. "Lesbianism and American History: A Brief Source Review." *Frontiers,* "Lesbian History" 4:3 (Fall 1979):80-5.

Everard, M. "Lesbian History: A History of Change and Disparity." *Journal of Homosexuality,* "Historical, Literary, and Erotic Aspects of Lesbianism" 12:3/4 (May 1986):123-37.

Faderman, Lillian. "Lesbian Magazine Fiction in the Early Twentieth Century." *Journal of Popular Culture* 11:4 (Spring 1978):800-17.

------. "Who Hid Lesbian History?" *Frontiers,* "Lesbian History" 4:3 (Fall 1979):74-6.

Ferguson, Ann, Jacquelyn N. Zita, and Kathryn Pine Adelson. "On 'Compulsory Heterosexuality and Lesbian Existence': Defining the Issues" (three responses to Adrienne Rich's essay in *Signs* 5:4 (Summer 1980):631-60). *Signs,* "French Feminism and Theory" 7:1 (Autumn 1981):158-99.

Freedman, Estelle. "Separatism as Strategy: Female Institution Building and American Feminism, 1870-1930." *Feminist Studies* 5:3 (Fall 1979):512-29.

Freedman, Estelle and John D'Emilio. "Problems Encountered in Writing the History of Sexuality: Sources, Theory and Interpretation." *Journal of Sex Research* 27:4 (November 1990):481-95.

Frontiers: a Journal of Women's Studies, "Lesbian History," vol. 4, no. 3, Fall 1979.

Gorman, Phyllis. "Central Ohio Lesbian History Project." *Feminisms* 1:2 (Spring 1988):10.

Hoagland, Sarah Lucia. "Remembering Lesbian Lives." *Sinister Wisdom* 14 (Summer 1980):52-6.

Hunnisett, Rowena J. "Developing Phenomenological Method for Researching Lesbian Existence." *Canadian Journal of Counselling* (Canada) 20:4 (October 1986):255-68.

Interrante, Joe. "From Homosexual to Gay to ?: Recent Work in Gay History." *Radical America* 15:6 (November-December 1981):79-86.

Jeffreys, Sheila. "Butch and Femme: Now and Then." *Gossip* (Great Britain) 5 (no date):65-95.

The Lesbians Making History Collective. "People Think This Can't Happen in Canada." *Fireweed* (Canada) "Lesbiantics" 28 (Spring 1989):81-6.

Livia, Anna. "With Gossip Aforethought." *Gossip* (Great Britain) 1 (1986):60-7.

Miller, Patricia McClelland. "The Individual Life" (issues and strategies for lesbian biography). *Frontiers,* "Lesbian History" 4:3 (Fall 1979):70-4.

Padgug, Robert A. "Sexual Matters: Conceptualizing Sexuality in History." *Radical History Review* 20 (Spring/Summer 1979):3-23.

Rich, Adrienne. "Resisting Amnesia" (importance of reporting all aspects of history). *Ms.* 15:9 (March 1987):66-7; also *Woman of Power,* "ReVisioning History" 16 (Spring 1990):15-21.

Richards, Dell. "The Making of 'Lesbian Lists': Uncovering a Rich Lesbian Past" (by the author of the almanac *Lesbian Lists*). *Hot Wire* 6:2 (May 1990):16-17.

Rook, June. "The Need for a Lesbian History." *WIN: Peace and Freedom Through Nonviolent Action,* "Lesbian Culture" 11:22 (June 26, 1975):18-19.

Rupp, Leila J. "'Imagine My Surprise': Women's Relationships in Historical Perspective." *Frontiers* 5:3 (Fall 1980):61-70.

Schwarz, Judith. "Researching Lesbian History." *Sinister Wisdom* 5 (Winter 1978):55-9.

Schwarz, Judith, et al. "Questionnaire on Issues in Lesbian History." *Frontiers,* "Lesbian History" 4:3 (Fall 1979):1-12.

Terry, Jenny. "Locating Ourselves in the History of Sexuality." *Outlook* 1:2 (Summer 1988):86-8.

Thomas, June. "Public-Private Diary: Finding Black Women's History" (interview with Gloria T. Hull, editor of *Give Us Each Day: the Diary of Alice Dunbar Nelson* (1873-1935)). *off our backs* 15:5 (May 1985):20-2.

Vicinus, Martha. "Sexuality and Power: a Review of Current Work in the History of Sexuality." *Feminist Studies* 8:1 (Winter 1982):34-56.

Vitale, Sylvia Witts. "A Herstorical Look at Some Aspects of Black Sexuality." *Heresies #12,* "The Sex Issue" 3:4 (1981):63-5.

Pre-16th Century:
Brown, Judith C. "Lesbian Sexuality in Renaissance Italy: the Case of Sister Benedetta Carlinni." *Signs,* "The Lesbian Issue" 9:4 (Summer 1984):751-8.

Crompton, Louis. "The Myth of Lesbian Impunity: Capital Laws from 1270-1791." *Journal of Homosexuality* 6:1/2 (Fall/Winter 1980/81):11-25.

D'Angelo, Mary Rose. "Women Partners in the New Testament" (as belonging to "lesbian continuum"; e.g., Tryphaena and Tryphosa, Evodia and Syntyche, Martha and Mary). *Journal of Feminist Studies in Religion* 6:1 (Spring 1990):65-86.

Grahn, Judy. "The Queen of Bulldikery" (a history of the "bulldike"). *Chrysalis* 10 (no date; c. Winter 1980):35-41.

Matter, E. Ann. "My Sister, My Spouse: Woman-Identified Women in Medieval Christianity." *Journal of Feminist Studies in Religion* 2:2 (Fall 1986):81-93.

Sitka, Chris. "Lesbian Rebirth" (ancient matriarchy, contemporary technology, and parthenogenesis). *Lesbian Ethics* 4:1 (Spring 1990):4-27.

16th Century:

"Demons, Duelers and Poets" (trans. from *Fem*, Mexican feminist bimonthly, vol.7, no.26). *Connexions*, "Global Lesbianism 2" 10 (Fall 1983):21.

Differences, "Sexuality in Greek and Roman Society," vol. 2, no. 1, Spring 1990.

"Lesbians and the Inquisition: Love and Languishing" (in Brazil). *Connexions*, "Global Lesbianism" 3 (January 1982):15+.

Shapiro, Susan C. "Amazons, Hermaphrodites, and Plain Monsters: the 'Masculine' Woman in English Satire and Social Criticism from 1580-1640." *Atlantis* (Canada) 13 (Fall 1987):65-76.

17th Century:

Bell, Rudolph and Judith Butler. "Renaissance Sexuality and the Florentine Archives: an Exchange." *Renaissance Quarterly* 40:3 (Autumn 1987):485-511.

Clarke, M.L. "The Making of a Queen: the Education of Christina of Sweden" (not specifically lesbian account of this "masculine" Scandinavian monarch). *History Today* 28:4 (April 1978):228-35.

Crompton, Louis. "Homosexuals and the Death Penalty in Colonial America." *Journal of Homosexuality* 1:3 (Spring 1976):277-93.

------. "The Myth of Lesbian Impunity: Capital Laws from 1270-1791." *Journal of Homosexuality* 6:1/2 (Fall/Winter 1980/81):11-25.

"Demons, Duelers and Poets" (trans. from *Fem,* Mexican feminist bimonthly, vol.7, no.26). *Connexions,* "Global Lesbianism 2" 10 (Fall 1983):21.

Kendall, Kathryn. "From Lesbian Heroine to Devoted Wife: Or, What the Stage Would Allow." *Journal of Homosexuality,* "Historical, Literary, and Erotic Aspects of Lesbianism" 12:3/4 (May 1986):9-22.

Roberts, J.R. "'leude behauior each with other vpon a bed': the Case of Sarah Norman and Mary Hammond." *Sinister Wisdom* 14 (Summer 1980):57-62.

Shapiro, Susan C. "Amazons, Hermaphrodites, and Plain Monsters: the 'Masculine' Woman in English Satire and Social Criticism from 1580-1640." *Atlantis* 13 (Fall 1987):65-76.

18th Century:
Coward, D.D. "Attitudes to Homosexuality in Eighteenth Century France" (homosexuality as not uncommon among aristocracy, with little punishment). *Journal of European Studies* 10:4 (1980):231-55.

Crompton, Louis. "The Myth of Lesbian Impunity: Capital Laws from 1270-1791." *Journal of Homosexuality* 6:1/2 (Fall/Winter 1980/81):11-25.

Eriksson, Brigitte (trans.). "A Lesbian Execution in Germany, 1721: the Trial Records." *Journal of Homosexuality* 6:1/2 (Fall/Winter 1980/81):27-40.

Hunt, Margaret. "The De-Eroticization of Women's Liberation: Social Purity Movements and the Revolutionary Feminism of Sheila Jeffreys." *Feminist Review* (Great Britain), "Perverse Politics: Lesbian Issues" 34 (Spring 1990):23-46.

19th Century:

Archer, Koré. "This Great Drama" (Ellen Craft, escaped slave from Georgia, and Sarah Edmonds, Canadian passing woman who spied for the Union Army). *Sinister Wisdom,* "Passing" 35 (Summer/Fall 1988):86-94.

Bullough, Vern L. and Martha Voght. "Homosexuality and its Confusion with the Secret Sin in Pre-Freudian America." *Journal of the History of Medicine and Allied Sciences* 28 (April 1973):143-55.

"Bus Tour Through Berlin: Once Upon a Time . . . " *Connexions,* "Special Introductory Issue" 0 (May 1, 1981):14-15.

Canarina, John. "The Legendary Dame Ethel Smyth" (British composer, suffragette). *Helicon Nine* 4 (Spring 1981):6-13.

Chauncey, George. "From Sexual Inversion to Homosexuality: Medicine and the Changing Conceptualization of Female Deviance." *Salmagundi,* "Homosexuality: Sacrilege, Vision, Politics" 58-59 (Fall 1982-Winter 1983):114-46.

"China: A Well of Strength" (19th- and early 20th-century sisterhoods of marriage resistors in Guangdong province; trans. and excerpted from Chen Dongyuan, *A History of Chinese Women's Lives* (Shangai, 1937) and Xiaoming Xiong, *The History of Homosexuality in China* (Hong Kong, 1984)). *Connexions,* "Lesbian Activism" 29 (1989):29.

Cook, Blanche Wiesen. "Female Support Networks and Political Activism: Lillian Wald, Crystal Eastman, Emma Goldman." *Chrysalis* 3 (1977):43-61.

D'Emilio, John. "Gay Politics, Gay Community: San Francisco's Experience." *Socialist Review #55,* 11:1 (January/February 1981):77-104.

Engelstein, Laura. "Lesbian Vignettes: a Russian Triptych from the 1890s." *Signs* 15:4 (1990):813-31.

Faderman, Lillian. "Female Same-Sex Relationships in Novels by Longfellow, Holmes, and James." *New England Quarterly* 51:3 (1978):309-32.

------. "The Morbidification of Love Between Women by 19th Century Sexologists." *Journal of Homosexuality* 4:1 (Autumn 1978):73-90.

Finn, Barbara R. "Anna Howard Shaw and Women's Work" (American suffragist and equal work opportunity activist; her relationship -- not necessarily sexual -- with Lucy Anthony). *Frontiers,* "Lesbian History" 4:3 (Fall 1979):21-5.

Freedman, Estelle. "Separatism as Strategy: Female Institution Building and American Feminism: 1870-1930." *Feminist Studies* 5:3 (Fall 1979):512-29.

----------."Sexuality in Nineteenth-Century America: Behavior, Ideology and Politics." *Reviews in American History* (December 1982):196-215.

Hunt, Margaret. "The De-Eroticization of Women's Liberation: Social Purity Movements and the Revolutionary Feminism of Sheila Jeffreys." *Feminist Review* (Great Britain), "Perverse Politics: Lesbian Issues" 34 (Spring 1990):23-46.

Kawan, Hildegard and Barbara Weber. "Reflections on a Theme: the German Women's Movement, Then and Now" (1848-1933, and the 1980s). *Women's Studies International Quarterly* 4:4 (1981):421-33.

Kendall, Kathryn. "From Lesbian Heroine to Devoted Wife: Or, What the Stage Would Allow." *Journal of Homosexuality,* "Historical, Literary, and Erotic Aspects of Lesbianism" 12:3/4 (May 1986):9-22.

Langley, Juliet A. "'Audacious Fancies': a Collection of Letters from Charlotte Perkins Gilman to Martha Luther." *Trivia* 6 (Winter 1985):52-69.

Maglin, Nan Bauer. "Vida to Florence: 'Comrade and Companion'"
(American writers Vida Dutten Scudder and Florence Converse).
Frontiers "Lesbian History" 4:3 (Fall 1979):13-20.

Mannocchi, Phyllis F. "Vernon Lee and Kit Anstruther-Thomson: a
Study of Love and Collaboration Between Romantic Friends"
(Vernon Lee, writer, critic, and historian (1856-1935);
Clementina (Kit) Anstruther-Thomson, artist (1857-1921)).
Women's Studies 12:2 (1986):129-48.

Mullaney, Marie Marmo. "Sexual Politics in the Career and Legend
of Louise Michel" (French revolutionary, member of Paris
Commune). *Signs* 15:2 (Winter 1990):300-22.

"Out in the Outback" (Edward de Lacy Evans, passing woman in
Australia for 20 years and through three marriages with women;
discovered in 1879). *Connexions,* "Global Lesbianism 2" 10
(Fall 1983):20.

Palmieri, Patricia A. "Here Was Fellowship: a Social Portrait of
Academic Women at Wellesley College, 1895-1920." *History of
Education Quarterly* 23:2 (Summer 1983):195-214.

Sahli, Nancy. "Smashing: Women's Relationships Before the Fall."
Chrysalis 8 (Summer 1979):17-27.

Schwarz, Judith. "*Yellow Clover:* Katharine Lee Bates and Katharine
Coman" (Bates was a poet; both were professors at Wellesley
College). *Frontiers* 4:1 (Spring 1979):59-67.

Shade, William. "'A Mental Passion': Female Sexuality in Victorian
America." *International Journal of Women's Studies* 1:1
(January/February 1978):13-29.

Simmons, Christina. "Companionate Marriage and the Lesbian
Threat." *Frontiers,* "Lesbian History" 4:3 (Fall 1979):54-9.

Smith-Rosenberg, Carroll. "The Female World of Love and Ritual."
Signs 1:1 (Autumn 1975):1-29.

Stevens, Carolyn. "The History of Sexuality in Britain and America 1800-1975: Course Method and Bill of Rights" (professor writes about class she taught at Antioch College; includes course outline and bibliography). *Women's Studies Quarterly,* "Teaching the New Women's History" 16:1&2 (Spring/Summer 1988):87-96.

Summers, Anne. "Marion/Bill Edwards" (passing woman who married a woman, born 1881). *Refractory Girl* (Australia), "Lesbian Issue" 5 (Summer 1974):21-2.

Thomas, June. "Public-Private Diary: Finding Black Women's History" (interview with Gloria T. Hull, editor of *Give Us Each Day: the Diary of Alice Dunbar Nelson* (1873-1935)). *off our backs* 15:5 (May 1985):20-2.

Vicinus, Martha. "Distance and Desire: English Boarding-School Friendships." *Signs,* "The Lesbian Issue" 9:4 (Summer 1984):600-22.

------. "'One Life to Stand Beside Me': Emotional Conflicts in First-Generation College Women in England" (Constance Maynard and Louisa Lumsden, Anne Richardson, Marion Wakefield, Ralph Gray, Frances Dove). *Feminist Studies* 8:3 (Fall 1982):603-28.

1900-1920:

"Bus Tour Through Berlin: Once Upon a Time . . . " *Connexions,* "Special Introductory Issue" 0 (May 1, 1981):14-15.

Canarina, John. "The Legendary Dame Ethel Smyth" (British composer, suffragette). *Helicon Nine* 4 (Spring 1981):6-13.

Chauncey, George. "From Sexual Inversion to Homosexuality: Medicine and the Changing Conceptualization of Female Deviance." *Salmagundi,* "Homosexuality: Sacrilege, Vision, Politics" 58-59 (Fall 1982-Winter 1983):114-46.

"China: A Well of Strength" (19th- and early 20th-century sisterhoods of marriage resisters in Guangdong province; trans. and excerpted from Chen Dongyuan, *A History of Chinese Women's Lives* (Shangai, 1937) and Xiaoming Xiong, *The History of Homosexuality in China* (Hong Kong, 1984)). *Connexions,* "Lesbian Activism" 29 (1989):29.

Claus, Ruth F. "Confronting Homosexuality: A Letter from Frances Wilder" (to Edward Carpenter, October 25, 1915). *Signs* 2:4 (Summer 1977):928-33.

Cook, Blanche Wiesen. "Female Support Networks and Political Activism: Lillian Wald, Crystal Eastman, Emma Goldman." *Chrysalis* 3 (1977):43-61.

D'Emilio, John. "Gay Politics, Gay Community: San Francisco's Experience." *Socialist Review #55,* 11:1 (January/February 1981):77-104.

Duberman, Martin Bauml. "'I Am Not Contented': Female Masochism and Lesbianism in Early Twentieth-Century New England: Archives." *Signs* 5:4 (Summer 1980):825-41.

Dyer, Richard. "Less and More Than Women and Men: Lesbian and Gay Cinema in Weimar Germany." *New German Critique* 51 (Fall 1990):5-60.

Edwards, Elizabeth. "Educational Institutions or Extended Families? The Reconstruction of Gender in Women's Colleges in the Late Nineteenth and Early Twentieth Centuries." *Gender and Education* 2:1 (1990):17-35.

Finn, Barbara R. "Anna Howard Shaw and Women's Work" (American suffragist and equal work opportunity activist; her relationship -- not necessarily sexual -- with Lucy Anthony). *Frontiers,* "Lesbian History" 4:3 (Fall 1979):21-5.

Freedman, Estelle. "Separatism as Strategy: Female Institution Building and American Feminism: 1870-1930." *Feminist Studies* 5:3 (Fall 1979):512-29.

Kawan, Hildegard and Barbara Weber. "Reflections on a Theme: the German Women's Movement, Then and Now" (1848-1933, and the 1980s). *Women's Studies International Quarterly* 4:4 (1981):421-33.

Maglin, Nan Bauer. "Vida to Florence: 'Comrade and Companion'" (American writers Vida Dutten Scudder and Florence Converse). *Frontiers* "Lesbian History" 4:3 (Fall 1979):13-20.

Manahan, Nancy. "Future Old Maids and Pacifist Agitators: the Story of Tracy Mygatt and Frances Witherspoon" (part of "Lesbian Survival Strategies, 1850-1950" panel at the National Women's Studies Association Convention in Storrs, Connecticut, 1981). *Women's Studies Quarterly* 10:1 (Spring 1982):10-13.

Mannocchi, Phyllis F. "Vernon Lee and Kit Anstruther-Thomson: a Study of Love and Collaboration Between Romantic Friends" (Vernon Lee, writer, critic, and historian (1856-1935); Clementina (Kit) Anstruther-Thomson, artist (1857-1921)). *Women's Studies* 12:2 (1986):129-48.

Orenstein, Gloria F. "Natalie Barney's Parisian Salon: the *Savoir Faire* and *Joie de Vivre* of a Life of Love and Letters." *13th Moon* 5:1/2 (1980):76-94.

Palmieri, Patricia A. "Here Was Fellowship: a Social Portrait of Academic Women at Wellesley College, 1895-1920." *History of Education Quarterly* 23:2 (Summer 1983):195-214.

Rolley, Katrina. "Cutting a Dash: The Dress of Radclyffe Hall and Una Troubridge." *Feminist Review* (Great Britain) 35 (Summer 1990):54-66.

Rooke, Patricia T. "Public Figure, Private Woman: Same Sex Support Structures in the Life of Charlotte Whitton" (Canadian social worker and politician). *International Journal of Women's Studies* 6:5 (November-December 1983):412-28.

Sawabe, Hitomi (trans. Eleanor Batchelder and Fumiko Ohno). "Yuriko, Da Svidanya (Goodbye, Yuriko): the Youth of Yoshiko Yuasa" (excerpt, in Japanese and English, of book about writer and translator Yoshiko Yuasa). *Conditions: seventeen* (1990):20-9.

Schwarz, Judith. "*Yellow Clover:* Katharine Lee Bates and Katharine Coman" (Bates was a poet; both were professors at Wellesley College). *Frontiers* 4:1 (Spring 1979):59-67.

"Sixty Places to Talk, Dance and Play" (flourishing lesbian and gay culture in turn of the twentieth century Germany, until the rise of the Third Reich). *Connexions,* "Global Lesbianism" 3 (January 1982):16-18.

Stevens, Carolyn. "The History of Sexuality in Britain and America 1800-1975: Course Method and Bill of Rights" (professor writes about class she taught at Antioch College; includes course outline and bibliography). *Women's Studies Quarterly,* "Teaching the New Women's History" 16:1&2 (Spring/Summer 1988):87-96.

Summers, Anne. "Marion/Bill Edwards" (passing woman who married a woman, born 1881). *Refractory Girl* (Australia), "Lesbian Issue" 5 (Summer 1974):21-2.

Thomas, June. "Public-Private Diary: Finding Black Women's History" (interview with Gloria T. Hull, editor of *Give Us Each Day: the Diary of Alice Dunbar Nelson* (1873-1935)). *off our backs* 15:5 (May 1985):20-2.

Vicinus, Martha. "Distance and Desire: English Boarding-School Friendships." *Signs,* "The Lesbian Issue" 9:4 (Summer 1984):600-22.

<u>1920s and '30s</u>:

Bérubé, Allan. "Coming Out Under Fire: the Untold Story of the World War II Soldiers Who Fought on the Front Lines of Lesbian and Gay Liberation." *Mother Jones* 8:2 (February/March 1983):23-9.

Bullough, Vern and Bonnie Bullough. "Lesbianism in the 1920s and 1930s: a Newfound Study." *Signs* 2:4 (Summer 1977):895-904.

"Bus Tour Through Berlin: Once Upon a Time . . . " *Connexions,* "Special Introductory Issue" 0 (May 1, 1981):14-15.

Chauncey, George. "From Sexual Inversion to Homosexuality: Medicine and the Changing Conceptualization of Female Deviance." *Salmagundi,* "Homosexuality: Sacrilege, Vision, Politics" 58-59 (Fall 1982-Winter 1983):114-46.

"China: A Well of Strength" (19th- and early 20th-century sisterhoods of marriage resisters in Guangdong province; trans. and excerpted from Chen Dongyuan, *A History of Chinese Women's Lives* (Shangai, 1937) and Xiaoming Xiong, *The History of Homosexuality in China* (Hong Kong, 1984)). *Connexions,* "Lesbian Activism" 29 (1989):29.

Cook, Blanche Wiesen. "Female Support Networks and Political Activism: Lillian Wald, Crystal Eastman, Emma Goldman." *Chrysalis* 3 (1977):43-61.

Curtin, Kaier. "Roaring Twenties Scandal: Yiddish Lesbian Play Rocks Broadway" (*The God of Vengeance* by Sholom Asch; written 1907; performed on Broadway 1922; cast arrested). *Lilith* 19 (Spring 1988/5748):13-14.

D'Emilio, John. "Gay Politics, Gay Community: San Francisco's Experience." *Socialist Review #55,* 11:1 (January/February 1981):77-104.

Dyer, Richard. "Less and More Than Women and Men: Lesbian and Gay Cinema in Weimar Germany." *New German Critique* 51 (Fall 1990):5-60.

Faderman, Lillian. "Love Between Women in 1928: Why Progressivism Is Not Always Progress." *Journal of Homosexuality*, "Historical, Literary, and Erotic Aspects of Lesbianism" 12:3/4 (May 1986):23-42.

Freedman, Estelle. "Separatism as Strategy: Female Institution Building and American Feminism: 1870-1930." *Feminist Studies* 5:3 (Fall 1979):512-29.

Garber, Eric. "Gladys Bentley: the Bulldagger Who Sang the Blues." *Out/Look* 1:1 (Spring 1988):52-61.

Kawan, Hildegard and Barbara Weber. "Reflections on a Theme: the German Women's Movement, Then and Now" (1848-1933, and the 1980s). *Women's Studies International Quarterly* 4:4 (1981):421-33.

King, Lillie. "Great Aunt Ruby Helen MacCloon and Her Life-Mate, Myrtle Heim." *Common Lives/Lesbian Lives* 18 (Winter 1985):4-7.

"Lesbians in the Butzow Concentration Camp." *Connexions* 3 (January 1982):17.

Lesselier, Claudie. "Social Categorizations and Construction of a Lesbian Subject." *Feminist Issues* 7:1 (Spring 1987):89-94.

Maglin, Nan Bauer. "Vida to Florence: 'Comrade and Companion'" (American writers Vida Dutten Scudder and Florence Converse). *Frontiers* "Lesbian History" 4:3 (Fall 1979):13-20.

Manahan, Nancy. "Future Old Maids and Pacifist Agitators: the Story of Tracy Mygatt and Frances Witherspoon" (part of "Lesbian Survival Strategies, 1850-1950" panel at the National Women's Studies Association Convention in Storrs, Connecticut, 1981). *Women's Studies Quarterly* 10:1 (Spring 1982):10-13.

Minton, Henry L. "Femininity in Men and Masculinity in Women: American Psychiatry and Psychology Portray Homosexuality in the 1930s." *Journal of Homosexuality* 13:1 (Fall 1986):1-22.

Orenstein, Gloria F. "Natalie Barney's Parisian Salon: the *Savoir Faire* and *Joie de Vivre* of a Life of Love and Letters." *13th Moon* 5:1/2 (1980):76-94.

Penn, Donna. "Identity and Consciousness in the Boston Lesbian Community, 1929-1969." *NWSA Journal* 1:4 (Summer 1989):765-8.

Rich, B. Ruby. "*Maedchen in Uniform:* From Repressive Tolerance to Erotic Liberation" (German lesbian history through discussion of Leontine Sagan's film). *Radical America* 15:6 (November-December 1981):17-36.

Rolley, Katrina. "Cutting a Dash: The Dress of Radclyffe Hall and Una Troubridge." *Feminist Review* (Great Britain) 35 (Summer 1990):54-66.

Rooke, Patricia T. "Public Figure, Private Woman: Same Sex Support Structures in the Life of Charlotte Whitton" (Canadian social worker and politician). *International Journal of Women's Studies* 6:5 (November-December 1983):412-28.

Rupp, Leila J. "'Imagine My Surprise': Women's Relationships in Historical Perspective." *Frontiers* 5:3 (Fall 1980):61-70.

Sawabe, Hitomi (trans. Eleanor Batchelder and Fumiko Ohno). "Yuriko, Da Svidanya (Goodbye, Yuriko): the Youth of Yoshiko Yuasa" (excerpt, in Japanese and English, of book about writer and translator Yoshiko Yuasa). *Conditions: seventeen* (1990):20-9.

"Sixty Places to Talk, Dance and Play" (flourishing lesbian and gay culture in turn of the twentieth century Germany, until the rise of the Third Reich). *Connexions,* "Global Lesbianism" 3 (January 1982):16-8.

Stevens, Carolyn. "The History of Sexuality in Britain and America 1800-1975: Course Method and Bill of Rights" (professor writes about class she taught at Antioch College; includes course outline and bibliography). *Women's Studies Quarterly,* "Teaching the New Women's History" 16:1&2 (Spring/Summer 1988):87-96.

Terry, Jennifer. "Lesbians Under the Medical Gaze: Scientists Search for Remarkable Differences" (1930s). *Journal of Sex Research* 27:3 (1990):317-39.

Thomas, June. "Public-Private Diary: Finding Black Women's History" (interview with Gloria T. Hull, editor of *Give Us Each Day: the Diary of Alice Dunbar Nelson* (1873-1935)). *off our backs* 15:5 (May 1985):20-2.

1940s and '50s (see also: Butch/Femme; Daughters of Bilitis; Pulp Novels):
Bannon, Ann. "Speaking to Women Through Fiction: Then and Now" (by the author of the 1950s "Beebo Brinker" pulp novel series). *Hot Wire* 1:1 (November 1984):50.

Benno, Susanna. "Sappho in Soft Cover: Notes in Lesbian Pulp." *Fireweed* (Canada) 11 (1981):35-43.

Bérubé, Allan. "Coming Out Under Fire: the Untold Story of the World War II Soldiers Who Fought on the Front Lines of Lesbian and Gay Liberation." *Mother Jones* 8:2 (February/March 1983):23-9.

Bérubé, Allan and John D'Emilio. "The Military and Lesbians During the McCarthy Years." *Signs,* "The Lesbian Issue" 9:4 (Summer 1984):759-75.

Brandt, Kate. "Lisa Ben: A Lesbian Pioneer." *Visibilities* 4:1 (January/February 1990):8-11.

Bulkin, Elly. "An Old Dyke's Tale: an Interview with Doris Lunden" (African-American lesbian, born in 1936, came out in 1953). *Conditions: six* 2:3 (Summer 1980):26-44; also *Conditions: sixteen,* "Retrospective" (1989):63-82.

Davis, Madeline and Elizabeth Lapovsky Kennedy. "Oral History and the Study of Sexuality in the Lesbian Community: Buffalo, New York, 1940-1960." *Feminist Studies* 12:1 (Spring 1986):7-26.

D'Emilio, John. "Gay Politics, Gay Community: San Francisco's Experience." *Socialist Review #55,* 11:1 (January/February 1981):77-104.

Dorrance, John. "Gay Panther" (Phyllis Lyon, co-founder of the Daughters of Bilitis). *San Francisco* 26 (December 1984):32-3.

Esterberg, Kristin Gay. "From Illness to Action: Conceptions of Homosexuality in *The Ladder,* 1956-1965" (magazine of the Daughters of Bilitis). *Journal of Sex Research* 27:1 (February 1990):65-80.

Jeffreys, Sheila. "Butch and Femme: Now and Then." *Gossip* (Great Britain) 5 (no date):65-95.

King, Lillie. "Great Aunt Ruby Helen MacCloon and Her Life-Mate, Myrtle Heim." *Common Lives/Lesbian Lives* 18 (Winter 1985):4-7.

"Lesbians in the Butzow Concentration Camp." *Connexions* 3 (January 1982):17.

Lesselier, Claudie. "Social Categorizations and Construction of a Lesbian Subject." *Feminist Issues* 7:1 (Spring 1987):89-94.

Maglin, Nan Bauer. "Vida to Florence: 'Comrade and Companion'" (American writers Vida Dutten Scudder and Florence Converse). *Frontiers,* "Lesbian History" 4:3 (Fall 1979):13-20.

Manahan, Nancy. "Future Old Maids and Pacifist Agitators: the Story of Tracy Mygatt and Frances Witherspoon" (part of "Lesbian Survival Strategies, 1850-1950" panel at the National Women's Studies Association Convention in Storrs, Connecticut, 1981). *Women's Studies Quarterly* 10:1 (Spring 1982):10-13.

Mushroom, Merril. "Bar Dyke Sketches: 1959." *Common Lives/Lesbian Lives* 5 (Fall 1982):17-22.

------. "How to Engage in Courting Rituals 1950s Butch Style in the Bar." *Common Lives/Lesbian Lives* 4 (Summer 1982):6-10.

Parkerson, Michelle. "Beyond Chiffon" (1950s drag show at The Jewel Box, including male impersonator Miss Stormé DeLarvie, about whom Parkerson made the film *Stormé*). *Black/Out* 1:3/4 (1987):21-2.

Penn, Donna. "Identity and Consciousness in the Boston Lesbian Community, 1929-1969." *NWSA Journal* 1:4 (Summer 1989):765-8.

Rooke, Patricia T. "Public Figure, Private Woman: Same Sex Support Structures in the Life of Charlotte Whitton" (Canadian social worker and politician). *International Journal of Women's Studies* 6:5 (November-December 1983):412-28.

Rupp, Leila J. "The Women's Community in the National Woman's Party: 1945 to the 1960s." *Signs,* "Communities of Women" 10:4 (Summer 1985):715-40.

Samoy, Stephanie Castillo. "*Visibilities* Highlights . . . Barbara Gittings" (activist since the 1950s). *Visibilities* 4:5 (September/October 1990):28.

Sawabe, Hitomi (trans. Eleanor Batchelder and Fumiko Ohno). "Yuriko, Da Svidanya (Goodbye, Yuriko): the Youth of Yoshiko Yuasa" (excerpt, in Japanese and English, of book about writer and translator Yoshiko Yuasa). *Conditions: seventeen* (1990):20-9.

Smith, Elizabeth A. "Butches, Femmes, and Feminists: the Politics of Lesbian Sexuality" (includes discussion of the Daughters of Bilitis magazine *The Ladder*). *NWSA Journal* 1:3 (Spring 1989):398-421.

Stevens, Carolyn. "The History of Sexuality in Britain and America 1800-1975: Course Method and Bill of Rights" (professor writes about class she taught at Antioch College; includes course outline and bibliography). *Women's Studies Quarterly,* "Teaching the New Women's History" 16:1&2 (Spring/Summer 1988):87-96.

Wilson, Elizabeth. "Deviant Dress" (in the late 1980s and the 1950s). *Feminist Review* (Great Britain) 35 (Summer 1990):67-74.

1960s and '70s (see also: Equal Rights Amendment; Gay Liberation Movement; Lesbians and the Right; Periodicals; Publishing)
Biggs, Mary. "From Harriet Monroe to *AQ* [*Amazon Quarterly*]: Selected Women's Literary Journals, 1912-1972." *13th Moon,* "Narrative Forms" 8:1/2 (1984):183-216.

Collective Lesbian International Terrors. "CLIT Statement #4 - Necropolis, USA: a Dying Empire Fucks Itself" (CLIT Reviews the Nineteen Seventies). *off our backs* 10:8 (August-September 1980):16-18; note: cover reads 10:7.

Esterberg, Kristin Gay. "From Illness to Action: Conceptions of Homosexuality in *The Ladder,* 1956-1965" (magazine of the Daughters of Bilitis). *Journal of Sex Research* 27:1 (February 1990):65-80.

Halter, Marilyn. "Remembering the Women of the 1960s, Teaching the 1960s." *Radical History Review* 44 (1989):93-107.

Wallsgrove, Ruth. "Signs of the Times: a Short Natural History of Some Favorite Feminist and Gay Liberation Symbols." *Spare Rib* (Great Britain) 120 (July 1982):10.

The Holocaust

"Bus Tour Through Berlin: Once Upon a Time . . . " *Connexions,* "Special Introductory Issue" 0 (May 1, 1981):14-15.

"Germany: Not Just Memories" (trans. and excerpted from *Bulletin des Archives Lesbiennes* no. 7 (June 1988) and West German feminist monthly, *Emma* (December 1988)). *Connexions,* "Lesbian Activism" 29 (1989):28-9.

Haeberle, E.J. "Swastika, Pink Triangle and Yellow Star -- the Destruction of Sexology and the Persecution of Homosexuals in Nazi Germany" (mostly about men). *Journal of Sex Research,* "History and Sexuality" 17:3 (August 1981):270-87.

"Lesbians in the Butzow Concentration Camp." *Connexions* 3 (January 1982):17.

"Sixty Places to Talk, Dance and Play" (flourishing lesbian and gay culture in turn of the twentieth century Germany, until the rise of the Third Reich). *Connexions,* "Global Lesbianism" 3 (January 1982):16-18.

Desire: Sexuality in Germany 1910-45 (film about gays and lesbians under Nazism):
Shaw, Nancy. "On a Trumped-Up Charge: Two Video Films." *Vanguard* (Canada) 18:3 (Summer 1989):20-5.

Novembermoon (film film about Nazi occupation of France, with lesbian main characters):
Leveritt, Annie and Celia Guse. "*Novembermoon.*" *Hot Wire* 2:3 (July 1986):40-1.

Williamson, Judith. "In the Pink" (gay and lesbian films at London's Tyneside Festival, including *The Lesbian Vampire on Film, Underground Canada,* and *Novembermoon*). *New Statesman* (Great Britain) 114 (October 9, 1987):22-3.

Homophobia/Heterosexism (see also: Child Custody; Domestic Partnership; Education: Lesbians in Academe/Lesbians in the Classroom; Foster Care; The Holocaust; Immigration; Legal Issues; Legislation; Lesbians and the Right; Military; Political Protest; Prison; Psychology; Psychotherapy; Religion; Suicide; Violence Against Lesbians and Gay Men; Work)

"Aimez-vous les Hommes?" (trans. of editorial on heterosexism from *La Vie en Rose,* feminist journal from Montréal, Québec, Canada). *Broadside* (Canada) 4:2 (1982):14.

Albro, Joyce C. and Carol Tully. "A Study of Lesbian Lifestyles in the Homosexual Micro-Culture and the Heterosexual Macro-Culture." *Journal of Homosexuality* 4:4 (Summer 1979):331-54.

Anderson, Shelley. "Thailand: Tomboys, Ladies, and Amphibians." *Connexions,* "Lesbian Activism" 29 (1989):6.

Annas, Pam, Ephrain Barradas, Ann Froines, Ron Schreiber. "Heterosexism and the Classroom" *Radical Teacher,* "Gay and Lesbian Studies" 24 (no date, c.1983):15-16.

Anne, Lynne, Pam and Sharon. "If Not N.O.W., Who?" (homophobia in the National Organization for Women). *off our backs* 1:11 (September 30, 1970):2.

"Argentina: Shrouded in Silence." *Connexions,* "Global Lesbianism" 3 (January 1982):12-14.

Arguelles, Lourdes and B. Ruby Rich. "Homosexuality, Homophobia, and Revolution: Notes Toward an Understanding of the Cuban Lesbian and Gay Male Experience, Part I" (for Part II, see Rich, B. Ruby, this section). *Signs,* "The Lesbian Issue" 9:4 (Summer 1984):683-99.

Armstrong, Toni L. "Red, White and (Visa) Blues: Immigration Headaches for Performers." *Hot Wire* 3:2 (March 1987):20-1.

Ayres, Caroline. "Gallup Findings on Gays." *off our backs* 13:2 (February 1983):16.

Bader, Eleanor. "Church Wages War on Dissenters" (including Archbishop Raymond Hunthausen, for allowing gay rights group to hold Mass, Father Charles Curran, for not strongly condemning homosexuality). *New Directions for Women* 15 (November-December 1986):1+.

Bebbington, Laura. "The Mexico International Women's Year Conference" (International Women's Year Tribune's attempt to censor lesbian feminist participation). *Meanjin Quarterly* (Australia) 34 (December 1975):373-9.

Berger, Raymond M. "Passing: Impact on the Quality of Same-Sex Couple Relationships." *Social Work* 35:4 (July 1990):328-32.

Bernache-Baker, Barbara. "The Sexual Attitudes and Behavior of Private and Public School Students: a Comparative Study" (wide-ranging lifestyle study, considers homophobia). *Adolescence* 22 (Summer 1987):259-69.

Biemiller, Lawrence. "Homosexual Academics Say 'Coming Out' Could Jeopardize Careers." *Chronicle of Higher Education* 25 (October 20, 1982):9-10.

Black, Pam. "When a Friend Tells She's Gay." *Mademoiselle* 89 (March 1983):248-9.

Bleich, David. "Homophobia and Sexism as Popular Values" (based on college freshman writing exercise). *Feminist Teacher* 4:2-3 (Fall 1989):21-8.

Bowry, Gill. "Lesbians in Cuba." *off our backs* 19:3 (March 1989):6-7.

Brandt, Kate. "Back to the Closet?" (U.S. Immigration and Naturalization Service discrimination against lesbian and gay performers). *Hot Wire* 3:2 (March 1987):22+.

Brant, Beth. "Lesbian Alliances: Heterosexism in the Eighties -- The Call of the Heron" (speech at the National Women's Studies Association conference, Minneapolis, Minnesota, June 1988). *Sojourner* 14:3 (November 1988):15.

Brooke. "The State of Feminism" (lesbian and straight separatism as bad for the movement). *off our backs,* "Ten Years Growing!" 10:2 (February 1980):8+.

Brown, Laura S. "Confronting Internalized Oppression in Sex Therapy with Lesbians." *Journal of Homosexuality,* "Historical, Literary, and Erotic Aspects of Lesbianism" 12:3/4 (May 1986):99-108.

Brown, Marvin and Donald M. Amoroso. "Attitudes Toward Homosexuality Among West Indian Male and Female College Students." *Journal of Social Psychology* 97 (December 1975):163-8.

Brown, Rita Mae. "The Good Fairy" (how lesbian-feminism changes women's body language, which is typically "deformed by the patriarchy"). *Quest* 1:1 (Summer 1974):58-64.

Bulkin, Elly. "Heterosexism and Women's Studies." *Radical Teacher* 17 (November 1980):25-31.

------. "An Interchange on Feminist Criticism on 'Dancing Through the Minefield'" (Judith Kegan Gardiner, Elly Bulkin, and Rena Grasso Patterson comment on Annette Kolodny's article, "Dancing Through the Minefield: Some Observations on the Theory, Practice, and Politics of a Feminist Literary Criticism"; Bulkin's contribution discusses heterosexism and racism in Kolodny's essay; Kolodny's response is on pp.665-75). *Feminist Studies* 8:3 (Fall 1982):635-54.

Bunch, Charlotte. "Not for Lesbians Only." *Quest*, "Theories of Revolution" 2:2 (Fall 1975):50-6.

CAD. "Death Penalty for Lesbians and Gays?" (reports of homophobic incidents around the U.S.). *off our backs* 11:4 (April 1981):9.

------. "Dr. Strange Love" (news briefs about anti-lesbian/gay discrimination in the U.S. and Great Britain). *off our backs* 8:3 (March 1978):10.

------. "Herstorians Harassed" (threats to founders of the Lesbian Herstory Archives). *off our backs* 11:11 (December 1981):9.

------. "Lesbian Plenary: Combatting Heterosexism" (at 10th annual National Women's Studies Association convention, University of Minnesota in Minneapolis, June 1988; panel members Beth Brant, Michelle Parkerson, Joan Nestle, Gloria Anzaldúa). *off our backs* 18:8 (August-September 1988):3+.

Cameron, Deborah. "Ten Years On: 'Compulsory Heterosexuality and Lesbian Existence'" (essay by Adrienne Rich, in *Signs* 5:4 (Summer 1980):631-60). *Women: a Cultural Review* (Great Britain) 1:1 (April 1990):35-7.

Carne, Roz. "Homosexuality: Sexual 'Problem' or Political Problem?" (conference of gays and representatives of the medical profession/social counseling services to discuss medical and social attitudes toward homosexuality, Bradford University, Great Britain, April 1975). *Spare Rib* (Great Britain) 36 (June 1975):19.

Cartledge, Sue and Susan Hemmings. "How Did We Get This Way? Sue Cartledge and Susan Hemmings Look at Explanations of Lesbianism." *Spare Rib* (Great Britain) 86 (September 1979):43-7.

Cavin, Susan. "Lesbian Origins Sex Ratio Theory" (challenges heterosexism in the social sciences). *Sinister Wisdom* 9 (Spring 1979):14-19.

Chamberlain, Pam. "Homophobia in the Schools." *Radical Teacher*, "Teaching Sexuality" 29 (September 1985):3-6.

Child, Sabrina. "NLGTF Notes Hate Crime Rise" (National Lesbian and Gay Task Force). *off our backs* 19:7 (July 1989):7.

"Chile" (excerpt from article in *Women's News*, Irish feminist bimonthly, (December/January 1989)). *Connexions*, "Lesbian Activism" 29 (1989):15.

Clark, Joan L. and Madge Rinehardt. "Silencing of Gay Issues in the Christian Churches." *Insight: a Quarterly of Lesbian/Gay Christian Opinion* 3:3 (Summer 1979):5-13.

Cliff, Michelle. "Notes on Speechlessness." *Sinister Wisdom* 5 (Winter 1978):5-9.

"Colombia: Attacks on Gays" (murder of lesbians and gays by paramilitary troops). *off our backs* 17:5 (May 1987):18.

Cook, Blanche Wiesen. "The Historical Denial of Lesbianism." *Radical History Review* 20 (Spring/Summer 1979):60-5.

Crew, Louie and Karen Keener. "Homophobia in the Academy: a Report of the Committee on Gay/Lesbian Concerns." *College English* 43:7 (November 1981):682-9.

Crew, Louie and R. Norton. "The Homophobic Imagination: an Editorial." *College English* 36:3 (1974):272-90.

Crowden, John J. "The Love That Dares Now Speak Its Name" (bibliography on sexuality, history, gender identity, gay liberation, research, psychotherapy, social attitudes). *Choice* 11 (April 1974):209-27.

DancingFire, Laura Rose. "The Love That Dared Not Speak Its Name" (speech delivered at the 1988 March for Justice, Louisville, Kentucky). *Common Lives/Lesbian Lives* 34 (Spring 1990):87-90.

D'Augelli, Anthony R. "Lesbian Women in a Rural Helping Network: Exploring Informal Helping Resources." *Women & Therapy,* "Lesbianism: Affirming Nontraditional Roles" 8:1/2 (1989):119-30.

Douglas, Carol Anne. "It Don't Gay in Minneapolis" (school board bans lesbian/gay panel from speaking in elementary schools). *off our backs* 11:2 (February 1981)11.

------. "Spain: a Kiss is Just a Kiss" (lesbian kiss-in protesting arrest of two women for kissing in public). *off our backs* 17:5 (May 1987):18.

Dressler, Joshua. "Study of Law Students' Attitudes Regarding the Rights of Gay People to Be Teachers." *Journal of Homosexuality* 4:4 (Summer 1979):315-40.

Durocher, Constance. "Heterosexuality: Sexuality or Social System?" (in English and French, "L'hétérosexualité: sexualité ou système social?"). *Resources for Feminist Research* (Canada), "Confronting Heterosexuality/Confronter l'hétérosexualité" 19:3&4 (September/December 1990):13-22.

Dykewomon, Elana. "Notes for a Magazine: On Passing." *Sinister Wisdom,* "Passing" 35 (Summer/Fall 1988):3-6.

Egerton, Jayne. "Out But Not Down: Lesbians' Experience of Housing" (squatting, alternative housing communities, and national housing policy in Great Britain). *Feminist Review* (Great Britain) 36 (Autumn 1990):75-88.

Ettelbrick, Paula L. "Yellow Pages Shuts the Closet Door." *Visibilities* 2:6 (November/December 1988):14-16.

FE. "Williams-Sonoma Sued for Firing Lesbians of Color." *off our backs* 20:3 (March 1990):17.

Fields, Cheryl. "Allegations of Lesbianism Being Used to Intimidate, Female Academics Say." *Chronicle of Higher Education* 27 (October 26, 1983):1+.

Fite, Karen and Nikola Trumbo. "Betrayals Among Women: Barriers to a Common Language." *Lesbian Ethics* 1:1 (Fall 1984):70-89.

Friend, Richard A. "Older Lesbian and Gay People: Responding to Homophobia." *Marriage and Family Review* 14:3-4 (1989):241-63.

Frye, Marilyn. "Assignment: NWSA -- Bloomington -- 1980: Speak on 'Lesbian Perspectives on Women's Studies'" (National Women's Studies Association). *Sinister Wisdom* 14 (Summer 1980):3-7.

Gambill, Sue. "Being Out or In: Interviews with Twelve Cincinnati Lesbians." *Common Lives/Lesbian Lives* 20 (Summer 1986):31-55.

Gartrell, N. "Combatting Homophobia in the Psychotherapy of Lesbians." *Women & Therapy* 3 (1984):13-29.

"Gay Foster Care Update" (prohibition of gay/lesbian foster parents in Massachusetts). *off our backs* 18:10 (November 1988):7.

"Gays Under Attack" (in Turkey). *Spare Rib* (Great Britain) 182 (September 1987):42.

Gennino, Angela. "Keeping the Path Straight" (Sierra Club refusal to officially recognize "Gay/Lesbian Sierrans"). *Mother Jones* 10:8 (October 1985):14.

"Germany: Not Just Memories" (trans. and excerpted from *Bulletin des Archives Lesbiennes* No. 7 (June 1988) and West German feminist monthly, *Emma* (December 1988)). *Connexions*, "Lesbian Activism" 29 (1989):28-9.

Gidlow, Elsa. "Whose Problem Is Lesbianism?" *Women: a Journal of Liberation*, "Women Loving Women" 5:2 (1977):38-40.

Glenn, Audrey A. and Richard K. Russell. "Heterosexual Bias Among Counselor Trainees." *Counselor Education and Supervision* 25:3 (March 1986):222-9.

Goldstein, Melville. "Some Tolerant Attitudes Toward Female Homosexuality Throughout History" (male homosexuals as "threat to the dominant order" and therefore more persecuted than lesbians; see Saunders, Robert J., "Comment on Melville Goldstein's 'Some Tolerant Attitudes Toward Female Homosexuality,'" *Journal of Psychohistory* 10:4 (1983):520-1, for critical response). *Journal of Psychohistory* 9:4 (Spring 1982):437-60.

Gomez, Jewelle and Barbara Smith. "Talking About It: Homophobia in the Black Community." *Feminist Review* (Great Britain), "Perverse Politics: Lesbian Issues" 34 (Spring 1990):47-55.

Gottlieb, Rhonda and Debra Kessler. "Where Are All the Militant Dykes?" (resurgence of lesbian invisibility in the Women's Liberation Movement). *off our backs*, "Ten Years Growing!" 10:2 (February 1980):9.

Gross, Amy. "Women in Love: If Lesbians Make You Nervous . . . " *Mademoiselle* (February 1978):126-7+.

Hall, Marny. "The Lesbian Corporate Experience." *Journal of Homosexuality,* "Historical, Literary, and Erotic Aspects of Lesbianism" 12:3/4 (May 1986):59-76.

Hammond, Harmony. "Class Notes" (assumptions of class and heterosexuality in art). *Heresies #3,* "Lesbian Art and Artists" 1:3 (Fall 1977):34-6.

Harrison, James. "The Dynamics of Sexual Anxiety." *Christianity and Crisis,* "Homosexuality" 37:9&10 (May 30 & June 13, 1977):136-40.

Hart, Vada. "Lesbians and AIDS." *Gossip* (Great Britain) 2 (1986):90-6.

Hemmings, Susan. "Overdose of Doctors: Susan Hemmings on Dykes at the Doctors." *Spare Rib* (Great Britain) 162 (January 1986):20-1.

Hemmings, Susan and Manny. "Lesbians National . . . and International" (National Lesbian Conference on Sex and Sexual Practice, London, England, April 1983, and International Lesbian Service Conference, Paris, France, April 1983). *Spare Rib* (Great Britain) 131 (June 1983):12-13.

Henry, Alice. "Mexican Lesbian Speaks Out" (about her writing, homophobia, and political organizing in Mexico, remaining anonymous for fear of repression). *off our backs* 16:1 (January 1986):8.

Herek, Gregory M. "Attitudes Toward Lesbians and Gay Men: a Factor-Analytic Study." *Journal of Homosexuality* 10:1/2 (Fall 1984):39-52.

------. "Beyond Homophobia: A Social Psychological Perspective on Attitudes Toward Lesbians and Gay Men." *Journal of Homosexuality,* "Homophobia: an Overview" 10:1/2 (Fall 1984):1-21.

------. "The Social Psychology of Homophobia: toward a Practical Theory." *New York University Review of Law & Social Change* 14:4 (Fall 1986):923-34.

Herman, Ellen. "The Romance of Lesbian Motherhood." *Sojourner* 13:7 (March 1988):12-13.

"Heterosexism and the Lesbian Experience." *Broadside* (Canada) 4:9 (July 1983):5.

Hetrick, Emery S. and A. Damien Martin. "Developmental Issues and Their Resolution for Gay and Lesbian Adolescents." *Journal of Homosexuality*, "Psychotherapy with Homosexual Men and Women: Integrated Identity Approaches for Clinical Practice" 14:1/2 (1987):25-44.

Heyward, Carter. "Heterosexist Theology: Being Above It All." *Journal of Feminist Studies in Religion* 3:1 (Spring 1987):29-38.

Hiltner, Seward. "Neglected Phenomenon of Female Homosexuality" (review of recent literature, and argument for tolerance and to remember that there are female as well as male homosexuals). *Christian Century* 91:21 (May 29, 1974):591-3.

Hobart Women's Action Group. "Sexism and the Women's Liberation Movement" (heterosexism in the movement). *Refractory Girl* (Australia), "Lesbian Issue" 5 (Summer 1974):30-3.

Holtzen, D.W. and A.A. Agresti. "Parental Responses to Gay and Lesbian Children: Differences in Homophobia, Self-Esteem, and Sex-Role Stereotyping." *Journal of Social and Clinical Psychology* 9:3 (1990):390-9.

Holzman, Lois. "What Do Teachers Have to Teach?" (making high school students aware of homophobia). *Feminist Teacher* 1:2 (1985):10-12.

"A Homophobia Workshop" (step-by-step guide, developed by Suzanne
      Pharr and the Lesbian Task Force of the National Coalition
      Against Domestic Violence). *off our backs* 14:1 (January
      1984):12-14.

"Homophobia Workshops" (at the National Women's Studies Association
      Conference, Akron, Ohio, June 1990). *off our backs* 20:8
      (August/September 1990):17-20.

Hooks, Bell. "Reflections on Homophobia and Black Communities."
      Out/Look 1:2 (Summer 1988):22-5.

"'I Am Everything'" (interview with 25-year-old Brazilian lesbian; trans.
      from *Mulherio,* Brazilian feminist bimonthly,
      September/October 1982). *Connexions,* "Global Lesbianism 2"
      10 (Fall 1983):14-15.

Interracial Books for Children Bulletin, "Homophobia and Education:
      How to Deal with Name-Calling," vol. 14, nos. 3/4, 1983.

Islam, Sharmem. "Breaking Silence: Coming Out in India" (interview
      with Nandini Datta and Dupitara Chowdurry). *Sojourner* 14:10
      (June 1989):20-1.

Jennings, Paula. "Lesbian Liberation Later" (homophobia in the women's
      movement). *Gossip* (Great Britain) 3 (no date):77-81.

Journal of Homosexuality, "Homophobia: an Overview," vol. 10, nos.
      1/2, Fall 1984.

Kite, Mary E. and Kay Deaux. "Gender Belief Systems -- Homosexuality
      and the Implicit Inversion Theory." *Psychology of Women
      Quarterly* 11 (March 1987):83-96.

Kitzinger, Celia. "Heteropatriarchal Language: the Case Against
      'Homophobia.'" *Gossip* (Great Britain) 5 (no date):15-20.

Klein, Melanie. "Anti-Semitism, Homophobia, and the Good White
      Knight." *off our backs,* education issue 12:5 (May 1982):30.

KM. "Fighting to Hold Gains in Washington State" (fighting to defeat initiative that would rescind state executive order banning discrimination based on sexual orientation). *off our backs* 16:4 (April 1986):9.

Laner, Mary Riege and J. Byrne. "Sexual Preference or Personal Style? Why Lesbians Are Disliked." *Journal of Homosexuality* 5 (Summer 1980):339-56.

Law, Sylvia A. "Homosexuality and the Social Meaning of Gender" (homophobia as related to disapprobation of violation of gender norms). *Wisconsin Law Review* 2 (1988):187-235.

LEL. "Lesbians Who Work with Children" (letter seeking advice for combatting homophobia from other lesbians who work with children). *Spare Rib* (Great Britain) 171 (October 1986):5.

Lenskyj, Helen. "Combatting Homophobia in Sports." *off our backs* 20:6 (June 1990):2-3.

Leonard, Leigh Megan. "A Missing Voice in Feminist Legal Theory: the Heterosexual Presumption." *Women's Rights Law Reporter* 12 (Spring 1990):39-49.

Leonard, Vickie and Carol Anne Douglas. "Working Together: a Heterosexual Radical Feminist and a Lesbian Radical Feminist" (members of *off our backs* collective). *Maenad*, "The Lesbian/Heterosexual Split" 2:2 (Winter 1982):55-60.

"Lesbians in the News . . . in Nairobi" (lesbian press conference held after delegate to international conference defied a "pack and go" order). *Connexions*, "Forum '85: Nairobi, Kenya" 17-18 (Summer/Fall 1985):16.

"Lesbians Sue Boss" (for being forced to quit because of a hostile work environment). *off our backs* 6:7 (October 1976):5.

Loiacano, Darryl K. "Gay Identity Issues among Black Americans: Racism, Homophobia, and the Need for Validation." *Journal of Counseling and Development,* "Lesbian, Gay and Bisexual Issues in Counseling" 68:1 (September-October 1989):21-5.

Lootens, Tricia. "Homophobia: Thin End of Antifeminist Wedge" (Lesbian Caucus meeting of the Pulling Together: Being with Children in Shelter Conference, Washington, D.C., December 1981). *off our backs* 12:3 (March 1982):30.

------. "Lesbian-Baiting in the Women's Movement" (statement by lesbians in the battered women's shelter movement, at the Pulling Together: Being with Children in Shelter Conference, Washington, D.C., December 1981). *off our backs* 12:3 (March 1982):17.

------. "Northampton [Massachusetts] Lesbians Unify Against Threats." *off our backs* 13:3 (March 1983):27.

------. "Third Women in Print Conference" (Berkeley, California, May 1985; workshop issues reported include classism, erotica, lesbian nuns, women of color, pornography, censorship, raid on British gay bookstore). *off our backs* 15:8 (August-September 1985):8-9+.

Lorde, Audre. "The Role of Difference" (presentation on "The Personal is Political" panel of The Second Sex -- Thirty Years Later: a Commemorative Conference on Feminist Theory, September 1979; Lorde responds to lack of presence and discussion of lesbians/women of color). *off our backs* 9:12 (December 1979):5+.

McCray, Chirlane. "I Am a Lesbian" (personal narrative in the self-proclaimed "magazine for today's black woman"). *Essence* 10:5 (September 1979):90-1+.

McCurdy, Jack. "University, Opposed to Lesbians, Bar Women's Studies Meeting" (National Women's Studies Association 1982 conference denied meeting space by University of San Francisco, because of lesbian membership). *Chronicle of Higher Education* 22 (March 2, 1981):22.

MacDonald, A.P., Jr. and Richard G. Games. "Some Characteristics of Those Who Hold Positive and Negative Attitudes Toward Homosexuals." *Journal of Homosexuality* 1 (Fall 1974):9-27.

MacDonald, Ingrid. "Customary Bias: Canada Customs Is Preventing Positive Images of Lesbian Sex." *Broadside* (Canada) 8 (July 1987):4.

Maenad, "The Lesbian/Heterosexual Split," vol. 2, no. 2, Winter 1982.

Mara, Jane. "A Lesbian Perspective." *Women and Therapy,* "Women Changing Therapy: New Assessments, Values and Strategies in Feminist Therapy" 2:2/3 (Summer/Fall 1983):145-55.

Martin, A. Damien and Emery S. Hetrick. "The Stigmatization of the Gay and Lesbian Adolescent." *Journal of Homosexuality,* "Psychopathology and Psychotherapy in Homosexuality" 15:1/2 (1988):163-84.

"Mexican Lesbian Group" (Grupo Lesbico Patlamali de Guadalajara). *off our backs* 18:9 (October 1988):11.

Milham, Jim, Christopher L. San Miguel, and Richard Kellogg. "A Factor-Analytic Conceptualization of Attitudes Toward Male and Female Homosexuality." *Journal of Homosexuality* 2 (Fall 1976):3-10.

Minkowitz, Donna. "Listen Up!" (article addressed to heterosexuals, about recent examples of homophobia and how to combat prejudice). *Village Voice* 34:26 (June 27, 1989):32.

Minnigerode, Fred A. "Attitudes Toward Homosexuality: Feminist Attitudes and Sexual Conservatism." *Sex Roles* 2:4 (December 1976):347-52.

Mohin, Lilian (letter responding to Celia Kitzinger, "Heteropatriarchal Language: the Case Against 'Homophobia,'" *Gossip* (Great Britain) 5 (no date):15-20). *Gossip* 6 (1988):19-20.

Morin, S.F. "Heterosexual Bias in Psychological Research on Lesbianism and Male Homosexuality." *American Psychologist* 32 (August 1977):629-37.

Mudd, Karen. "Houston Homophobe Defeated" (by incumbent mayor, Houston, Texas). *off our backs* 15:11 (December 1985):5.

"Mythmaking in the Women's Movement" (the lesbian/heterosexual split). *Refractory Girl* (Australia), "Lesbian Issue" 5 (Summer 1974):34-8.

National Gay Task Force. "We All Have a Stake in Curing Homophobia." *New Directions for Women* 9:2 (March/April 1980):9.

Nava, Mica. "'Everybody's Views Were Just Broadened': a Girls' Project and Some Responses to Lesbianism." *Feminist Review* (Great Britain) 10 (Spring 1982):37-59.

Oliver, Maureen. "Lesbians Attacked in Stockholm" (European Bus Tour Against British Section (Clause) 28). *Spare Rib* (Great Britain) 198 (February 1989):45-6.

Olson, Myrna R. "A Study of Gay and Lesbian Teachers" (about pressures to be in the closet, and dangers of coming out to colleagues). *Journal of Homosexuality* 13:4 (Summer 1987):73-82.

O'Sullivan, Sue. "How Cuba Doesn't Cope with Sexuality." *Spare Rib* (Great Britain) 125 (December 1982):52-5.

Padesky, Christine A. "Attaining and Maintaining Positive Lesbian Self-Identity: a Cognitive Therapy Approach." *Women & Therapy,* "Lesbianism: Affirming Nontraditional Roles" 8:1/2 (1989):145-56.

Page, Stewart and Mary Yee. "Conception of Male and Female Homosexual Stereotypes Among University Undergraduates" (concludes that female "gender nonconformity" is more acceptable than male). *Journal of Homosexuality* 12:1 (Fall 1985):109-18.

Palladino, Diane and Yanela Stephenson. "Perceptions of the Sexual Self: Their Impact on Relationships Between Lesbian and Heterosexual Women." *Women & Therapy,* "Diversity and Complexity in Feminist Therapy: Part II" 9:3 (1990):231-53.

Parker, Jan. "Lesbians -- Laying Down the Law" (how present laws affect lesbians; why lesbian/gay rights legislation is important for everyone). *Spare Rib* (Great Britain) 175 (February 1987):15-19.

Parkerson, Michelle. "Lesbian Alliances: Heterosexism in the Eighties -- Challenging Otherness" (speech at the National Women's Studies Association conference, Minneapolis, Minnesota, June 1988). *Sojourner* 14:3 (November 1988):14.

Peeples, Edward, Jr., Tunstall, Walter W. and Everett Eberhardt. "The Veil of Hurt" (survey of 508 gay, lesbian, and bisexual African-American and European-American people in Richmond and Alexandria, Virginia, regarding discrimination in business and the public sector). *Southern Exposure* 13:5 (1985):24-7.

Penelope, Julia. "The Mystery of Lesbians: I" (separatist lesbian-feminism as opposed to reformism of 1980s feminism). *Lesbian Ethics* 1:1(Fall 1984):7-33; also *Gossip* (Great Britain) 1 (1986):9-45.

------. "The Mystery of Lesbians: II" (separatist political theory). *Lesbian Ethics* 1:2 (Spring 1985):29-67; also *Gossip* (Great Britain) 2 (1986):16-68.

Pheterson, Gail. "Alliances Between Lesbians: Overcoming Internalized Oppression and Internalized Domination" ("Feminist Alliance Project" in the Netherlands addressing racism, anti-Semitism, and heterosexism). *Signs* 12:1 (Autumn 1986):146-60.

Ponse, Barbara. "Secrecy in the Lesbian World." *Urban Life* 5:3 (October 1976):313-38.

"Questionnaire: What Misunderstandings or Cross-Purposes Have Arisen in Your Group Due to Racial, Sexual, Class, Religious, or Age Differences?" *Heresies #20,* "Activists" 5:4 (1985):82-5.

"Racism and Homophobia: Letters to *Plexus* and *off our backs.*" *off our backs* 9:10 (November 1979):12-13.

Ratterman, Debra. "Lesbians Beaten" (by ex-boyfriend of one of the two). *off our backs* 18:11 (December 1988):3.

------. "Massachusetts Fosters Discrimination" (lesbians and gays denied right to be foster parents). *off our backs* 16:3 (March 1986):16.

Resources for Feminist Research (Canada), vol. 19, nos. 3&4, September/December 1990.

"Revolutionary People's Constitutional Convention: Lesbian Testimony" (homophobia in the New Left). *off our backs* 1:11 (September 30, 1970):4-5.

Rich, Adrienne. "Compulsory Heterosexuality and Lesbian Existence." *Signs* 5:4 (Summer 1980):631-60.

------. "Resisting Amnesia" (importance of reporting all aspects of history). *Ms.* 15:9 (March 1987):66-7.

Rich, B. Ruby and Lourdes Arguelles. "Homosexuality, Homophobia, and Revolution: Notes Toward an Understanding of the Cuban Lesbian and Gay Male Experience, Part II." *Signs* 11:1 (Autumn 1985):120-36.

RJ. "Harassment on Campus" (homophobic literature distributed at the University of Chicago). *off our backs* 17:4 (April 1987):4.

Robertson, Vicki. "British Lesbians Attacked by Police." *off our backs* 11:7 (July 1981):10.

Robinson, Rose. "A Fine Romance" (legal case regarding seating of lesbian couple at Papa Choux restaurant). *Ms.* 13 (September 1984):25.

Roche, Judy. "Boise Police Turn Against Their Own." *Ms.* 6:5 (November 1977):20.

Rosen, Steven A. "Police Harassment of Homosexual Women and Men in New York City, 1960-80." *Columbia Human Rights Law Review* 12 (Fall-Winter 1981):159-90.

Rosenthal, A. "Heterosexism and Clinical Assessment." *Smith College Studies in Social Work* 52 (March 1982):145-59.

Ross, Becki. "Heterosexuals Only Need Apply: the Secretary of State's Regulation of Lesbian Existence." *Resources for Feminist Research* (Canada), "Feminist Perspectives on the Canadian State/Perspectives Féministes sur l'État Canadien" 17:3 (September 1988):35-8.

Rotenberg, Lorie. "Impact of Homophobia, Heterosexism and Closetedness on Intimacy Dynamics in Lesbian Relationships." *Resources for Feminist Research* (Canada) 18:2 (June 1989):1-2.

Rule, Jane. "Homophobia and Romantic Love." *Conditions: three* 1:3 (Spring 1978):34-8.

------. "You Be Normal, Or Else . . . " *Resources for Feminist Research* (Canada), "Confronting Heterosexuality/Confronter l'hétérosexualité" 19:3&4 (September/December 1990):86.

Ruston, Bev Jo, and Linda Strega. "Heterosexism Causes Lesbophobia Causes Butch-Phobia, Part II of The Big Sell-Out: Lesbian Femininity." *Lesbian Ethics* 2:2 (Fall 1986):22-41.

Saunders, Robert J. "Comment on Melvin Goldstein's 'Some Tolerant Attitudes Toward Female Homosexuality'" (see Goldstein, *Journal of Psychohistory* 9:4 (1982):437-60). *Journal of Psychohistory* 10:4 (1983):520-1.

Schenck, Judith. "The Gala Fight: 1977" (violent attack on lesbians in a bar). *Common Lives/Lesbian Lives* 2 (Winter 1981):86-9.

Sedgwick, Eve Kosofsky. "Privilege of Unknowing" ("ignorance" of those in power about the disempowered, and the power of that ignorance; analyzes Diderot's *La Religieuse* for examples of this dynamic; "the epistemology of the closet"; potential for backlash in response to anti-homophobia of the 1980s). *Genders* 1 (Spring 1988):102-24.

Shabazz, Naeemah. "Homophobia: Myths and Realities." *Heresies #8*, "Third World Women: the Politics of Being Other" 2:4 (1979):34-6.

Shear, Marie. "Media Watch: Leaving Out Lavender." *New Directions for Women* 15:5 (September/October 1986):7.

Silas, Faye A. "Bias in the Booth? Lesbians Sue Restaurant." *ABA Journal* 69 (November 1983):1621.

Smith, Barbara. "The NEA Is the Least of It" (silencing through overt censorship, as the National Endowment for the Arts, and through internalized oppression). *Ms.: The World of Women* 1:3 (November/December 1990):65-7.

------. "Visions and Revisions: Women and the Power to Change" (part of final panel at the First National Women's Studies Conference, Lawrence, Kansas, May 30-June 3, 1979). *Women's Studies Newsletter* 7:3 (Summer 1979):19-20.

Smith, Elaine M., Susan R. Johnson, and Susan M. Guenther. "Health Care Attitudes and Experiences During Gynecologic Care Among Lesbians and Bisexuals." *American Journal of Public Health* 75:9 (1985):1085-7.

Sophie, Joan. "Internalized Homophobia and Lesbian Identity." *Journal of Homosexuality,* "Psychotherapy with Homosexual Men and Women: Integrated Identity Approaches for Clinical Practice" 14:1/2 (1987):53-66.

Staats, Gregory R. "Stereotype Content and Social Distance: Changing Views of Homosexuality." *Journal of Homosexuality* 4:1 (Autumn 1978):15-28.

Stein, Terry S. "Theoretical Considerations in Psychotherapy with Gay Men and Lesbians." *Journal of Homosexuality,* "Psychopathology and Psychotherapy in Homosexuality" 15:1/2 (1988):75-96.

Sternbach, Nancy Saporta. "Argentina 'In Democracy': Feminism 1985" (including section on "Women's Groups and Homophobia"). *off our backs* 16:1 (January 1986):6-8.

Strega, Linda. "The Big Sell-Out: Lesbian Femininity" (internalized homophobia). *Lesbian Ethics* 1:3 (Fall 1985):73-84.

Taylor, Alan. "Conceptions of Masculinity and Femininity as a Bases for Stereotypes of Male and Female Homosexuals." *Journal of Homosexuality* 9 (Autumn 1983):37-54.

Thomas, June. "Homophobe of the Year" (lesbians thrown out of restaurant in Newark, Delaware present award to owner of establishment). *off our backs* 16:1 (January 1986):18.

------. "Literary Trials and Tribulations" (British customs officials raid
Gay's the Word Bookstore, April 1984; hearing February 1985).
off our backs 15:8 (August-September 1985):15.

Thompson, George H. and William R. Fishburn. "Attitudes Toward
Homosexuality Among Graduate Counseling Students."
Counselor Education and Supervision 17:2 (December
1977):121-9.

Thompson, Martha. "On Confusing Heterosexism with Having a Male
Sex Partner." *off our backs* 9:10 (November 1979):30.

Towey, Shawn. "Reproductive Rights National Network Meets: Racism
and Heterosexism Discussed" (Reproductive Rights National
Network Conference, Philadelphia, Pennsylvania, April 1983).
off our backs 13:7 (July 1983):15.

Tyler, Robin. "Keeping the Land" (discrimination in renting land for
women's music festivals). *Hot Wire* 3:1 (November 1986):28-9.

Valverde, Mariana. "Heterosexism: a Challenge to the Left." *Canadian
Dimension* (Canada) 17:1 (March 1983):36-8.

Van Gelder, Lindsy. "Marriage as a Restricted Club." *Ms.* 12:8 (February
1984):59-60.

------. "Personal Politics: a Lesson in Straight Talk." *Ms.* 16 (November
1987):95.

Vance, N. Scott. "Former Basketball Coach Settles Lawsuit Against
University of South Carolina" (coach had resigned amid
allegations of lesbianism and also sued *Sports Illustrated*).
Chronicle of Higher Education 26 (August 3, 1983):15+.

Ward, Russell A. "Typifications of Homosexuals." *Sociological Quarterly*
20 (Summer 1979):411-24.

Watkins, Beverly. "Widespread Bias Against Homosexuals Called Bar to Work in Sociology." *Chronicle of Higher Education* 23 (September 2, 1981):23.

Watters, Alan T. "Heterosexual Bias in Psychological Research on Lesbianism and Male Homosexuality (1979-1983), Utilizing the Bibliographic and Taxonomic System of Morin." *Journal of Homosexuality* 13:1 (Fall 1986):35-58.

Weems, Renita J. "Just Friends" (written by a woman who is friends with a lesbian, about homophobia and the African-American community). *Essence* 20 (May 1989):60+.

Weinberger, Linda E. and Jim Millham. "Attitudinal Homophobia and Support of Traditional Sex Roles." *Journal of Homosexuality* 4:3 (Spring 1979):237-46.

Weiss, C. and R. Dain. "Ego Development and Sexual Attitudes in Heterosexual and Homosexual Men and Women" (no significant differences found; heterosexual men more homophobic than heterosexual women). *Archives of Sexual Behavior* 8:4 (July 1979):341-56.

Wells, Joel W. "Teaching About Gay and Lesbian Sexual and Affectional Orientation Using Explicit Films to Reduce Homophobia." *Journal of Humanistic Education and Development* 23:1 (September 1989):18-34.

White, Judy. "Women Divided?" (racism, classism, lesbian-heterosexual split in the Women's Liberation Movement; and the Congress to Unite Women, New York City, May 1970). *off our backs* 1:5 (May 1970):5.

White, T.A. "Attitudes of Psychiatric Nurses Toward Same Sex Orientations." *Nursing Research* 28 (September-October 1979):276-81.

Whitehead, Minnie M. and Kathleen M. Nokes. "An Examination of Demographic Variable, Nurturance, and Empathy Among Homosexual and Heterosexual Big Brother/Big Sister Volunteers" (shows no basis for discriminating against homosexual volunteers, as many Big Brother/Big Sister programs do). *Journal of Homosexuality* 29:4 (1990):89-101.

Wigutoff, Sharon. "Children's Books: 'Libland' or Wasteland?" *off our backs* 12:6 (June 1982):14-15.

Williams, Lewis. "The Churches: Lutherans, Presbyterians, Episcopalians, Unitarians, Where They Stand Today." *Vector* 7:8 (August 1971):1-2.

Wittig, Monique. "On the Social Contract" (of Jean-Jacques Rousseau, as heterosexual). *Feminist Issues* 9:1 (Spring 1989):3-12.

------. *"La Pensée Straight"* ("The Straight Mind"). *Questions Féministes* (février 1980):45-53.

------. "The Straight Mind" (*"La Pensée Straight"*). *Feminist Studies* 1:1 (Summer 1980):103-11.

Yarber, William L. and Bernadette Yee. "Heterosexuals' Attitudes Toward Lesbianism and Male Homosexuality: Their Affective Orientation Toward Sexuality and Sex Guilt." *Journal of American College Health* 31:5 (April 1983):203-8.

Young, Allen. "The Press as an Institution of Gay Oppression." *Edcentric* 31-2(November 1974):27+.

"Zap Repression!" (interview with 21-year-old Venezuelan lesbian; trans. from *Entendido,* Venezuelan gay monthly, February 1983). *Connexions,* "Global Lesbianism 2" 10 (Fall 1983):8.

Armstrong Amendment (exempts religious groups from anti-discrimination laws):
"Congress Undermines Gay Rights" (Armstrong amendment). *off our backs* 18:10 (November 1988):7.

DAR. "Senate Threatens DC" (Armstrong bill would cut federal
funding to the District of Columbia if D.C. wouldn't allow
religious groups exemption from anti-discrimination laws). *off
our backs* 18:8 (August-September 1988):5.

Bishop, Heather (musician):
Smith, Connie. "Canadian Viewpoint: Heather Bishop Interviewed"
(about U.S. Immigration and Naturalization Service
discrimination against women's music performers). *Hot Wire* 3:2
(March 1987):21-2.

Clause 28 (Great Britain):
Alderson, Lynn and Harriet Wistrich. "Clause 29: Radical Feminist
Perspectives" (anti-gay/lesbian ordinance commonly referred to as
Clause 28). *Trouble & Strife* (Great Britain) 13 (Spring 1988):3-
8.

Farraday, Annabel. "Lesbian Outlaws: Past Attempts to Legislate
Against Lesbians." *Trouble & Strife* (Great Britain) 13 (Spring
1988):9-16.

Cruikshank, Margaret (educator):
Cruikshank, Margaret. "How a College Administrator Who Couldn't
Join the Boys' Club Joined the Fired Lesbians Caucus Instead."
off our backs, education issue 12:5 (May 1982):29.

Diana Press:
Conner, K. Patrick. "Diana Press: a Story of Survival" (office
vandalized October 26, 1977). *Small Press Review #65,* 10:6
(June 1978):8-9.

Dworkin, Andrea (activist and writer):
Braeman, Elizabeth and Carol Cox. "Andrea Dworkin: From a War
Zone" (interview about Dworkin's book *Letters From a War
Zone: Writings 1976-1989). off our backs* 20:1 (January
1990):8-9+.

Hate Crimes Statistics Act:

AM. "Anti-Gay Violence Bill" (introduction in the U.S. House of
    Representatives). *off our backs* 17:10 (November 1987):3; note:
    cover reads 17:9.

King, Billie Jean (professional tennis player):

Roberts, Shelly. "Bad Form, Billie Jean" (reproaches tennis star
    Billie Jean King for publicly denouncing her admitted lesbian
    relationship). *Newsweek* 97:21 (May 25, 1981):19.

The Ladder (magazine of the Daughters of Bilitis):

Esterberg, Kristin Gay. "From Illness to Action: Conceptions of
    Homosexuality in *The Ladder*, 1956-1965." *Journal of Sex
    Research* 27:1 (February 1990):65-80.

On Golden Pond (film):

Sperry, Jackie. "Is Love Political?" (anti-lesbian jokes in the film On
    Golden Pond). *Common Lives/Lesbian Lives* 7 (Spring
    1983):102-6.

Personal Best (film):

Kidd, Dorothy. "Getting Physical: Compulsory Heterosexuality and
    Sport" (discusses the film *Personal Best*). *Canadian Woman
    Studies* (Canada), "Sport" 4:3 (Spring/May 1983):62-5.

Rich, Adrienne (writer):

Thompson, Martha E. "Comment on Rich's 'Compulsory
    Heterosexuality and Lesbian Existence'" (Adrienne Rich's essay
    appears in *Signs*, 5:4 (Summer 1980):631-60). *Signs* 6:4
    (Summer 1981):790-4.

Windows (film):

Stevens, Lynne. "The Window: a Look Inside" (protest against
    Windows, film about a psychotic lesbian who hires a man to
    rape a straight woman). *off our backs* 10:3 (March 1980):16-17.

Humor

Anderson, Jamie. "Humor in Women's Music." *Hot Wire* 6:1 (January 1990):46-7+.

Brannon, Rebecca. "Madison's Fourth Annual Lesbian Variety Show: I Got This Way from Kissing Girlz" (Madison, Wisconsin, November 1989). *Hot Wire* 6:2 (May 1990):36-8.

Daly, Mary. "Spiraling Into the Nineties." *Woman of Power,* "Humor" 17 (Summer 1990):6-12.

Gomez, Jewelle. "Black Women's Humour." *Black/Out,* "We Are Family" 2:2 (Summer 1989):14+.

Grey, Morgan and Julia Penelope. "Found Goddesses" (excerpt from forthcoming book, *The Book of Found Goddesses, from Asphalta to Vulva*). *Lesbian Ethics* 2:2 (Fall 1986):42-9.

Harper, Jorjet. "Southern: the 'Live and Let Live' Festival" (Southern Women's Music and Comedy Festival, Georgia, Summer 1990). *Hot Wire* 6:3 (September 1990):40-2.

Jochild, Meg. "Lesbian Jokes" (some examples). *Common Lives/Lesbian Lives* 4 (Summer 1982):76.

Livia, Anna. "Hippo Cream and Car Spray" (attempts to define women's/lesbian humor vs. oppressive humor; includes short humorous script, "Car Spray"). *Lesbian Ethics* 3:3 (Summer 1989):30-46.

Stanley, Julia Penelope and Susan W. Robbins. "Lesbian Humor." *Women: a Journal of Liberation* 5:1 (1976):26-9.

Bechdel, Alison (cartoonist):
Chiaramonte, Lee. "Prophet to Watch Out For: Alison Bechdel." *Visibilities* 2:2 (March/April 1988):11-13.

"Confabulation: Alison Bechdel and Kris Kovick" (conversation between cartoonists). *Hot Wire* 6:3 (September 1990):2-4+.

Harper, Jorjet and Toni L. Armstrong. "'Dykes to Watch Out For' Cartoonist Alison Bechdel." *Hot Wire* 3:3 (July 1987):2-5.

Thomas, June. "Drawing on the Lesbian Community: an Interview with Alison Bechdel" (creator of "Dykes to Watch Out For" comic strip). *off our backs* 18:8 (August-September 1988):1+.

Clinton, Kate (comic):
Armstrong, Toni L. "I Love Women Who Laugh: Comedy in Women's Music & Culture" (Trudy Wood, Kate Clinton, Robin Tyler, and Linda Moakes). *Hot Wire* 3:3 (July 1987):32-5.

Barrett, Carolann. "Be Bold and Be Bad" (interview). *Woman of Power,* "Humor" 17 (Summer 1990):60-3.

Blakley, Mary Kay. "Kate Clinton on the Feminist Comedy Circuit." *Ms.* 13 (October 1984):128.

Clinton, Kate. "Making Light: Another Dimension -- Some Notes on Feminist Humor." *Trivia* 1 (Fall 1982):37-42.

Zipter, Yvonne. "Making Conversation with Kate Clinton." *Hot Wire* 1:1 (November 1984):10.

FAT LIP Readers Theatre:
Bock, Laura. "FAT LIP Readers Theatre." *Women of Power,* "Humor" 17 (Summer 1990):32-3.

Grant, Monica (comic):
Grant, Monica. "White Courtesy Phones, Monogamy, and Other . . . Reflections from a Rookie." *Hot Wire* 6:2 (May 1990):46-7.

Harris, Hilary (comic):
Harris, Hilary. "The Second Wave" (about coming of age in a world of festivals where she can perform). *Hot Wire* 3:2 (March 1987):52-3.

Kennedy, Flo (activist):

Kennedy, Flo. "Color Me Flo" (excerpt from 1976 autobiography). *Woman of Power*, "Humor" 17 (Summer 1990):16-19.

Kovick, Kris (cartoonist):

"Confabulation: Alison Bechdel and Kris Kovick" (conversation between cartoonists). *Hot Wire* 6:3 (September 1990):2-4+.

Lavner, Lynn (comic and musician):

Lavner, Lynn. "From Amsterdam to Miami Beach: a Gay Cabaret Musician Plays Two Religious Conferences." *Hot Wire* 4:1 (November 1987):24-5+.

Wenzel, Lynn. "Spirited Women Music Makers Hit High Note" (comic Lynn Lavner, and musicians The Washington Sisters, Jasmine, Dianne Davidson, Faith Nolan, Heather Bishop, Kitty Barber, Two Nice Girls, Jamie Anderson, Martie van der Voort, and Deuce). *New Directions for Women* 18:4 (July/August 1989):14-16.

Moakes, Linda (comic):

Armstrong, Toni L. "I Love Women Who Laugh: Comedy in Women's Music & Culture" (Trudy Wood, Kate Clinton, Robin Tyler, and Linda Moakes). *Hot Wire* 3:3 (July 1987):32-5.

Moakes, Linda. "Warning: Humor May Be Hazardous to Your Illness." *Hot Wire* 2:2 (March 1986):24-6.

Tomlin, Lily (comic actor):

Langguth, Paula E. "Tomlin Film Engaged in Lawsuit." *Visibilities* 1:1 (Summer 1987):19.

Tyler, Robin (comic):

Armstrong, Toni L. "I Love Women Who Laugh: Comedy in Women's Music & Culture" (Trudy Wood, Kate Clinton, Robin Tyler, and Linda Moakes). *Hot Wire* 3:3 (July 1987):32-5.

------. "The P.T. Barnum of Women's Music and Culture: Robin Tyler." *Hot Wire* 4:2 (March 1988):2-6.

Ryan, Lori. "The Razor Edge of Truth -- a Conversation With Robin Tyler." *Visibilities* 2:6 (November/December 1988):8-11.

Wood, Trudy (comic):
Armstrong, Toni L. "I Love Women Who Laugh: Comedy in Women's Music & Culture" (Trudy Wood, Kate Clinton, Robin Tyler, and Linda Moakes). *Hot Wire* 3:3 (July 1987):32-5.

Identity (see Labels/Identity)

Immigration

Angela, Angie and Demetria Iazetto. "Commari: Excerpts of a Dialogue." *Sinister Wisdom,* "il viaggio delle donne" 41 (Summer/Fall 1990):82-8.

Armstrong, Toni L. "Red, White, and (Visa) Blues: Immigration Headaches for Performers." *Hot Wire* 3:2 (March 1987):20-1.

"Australia: Gay Immigration Curb." *off our backs* 20:4 (April 1990):6.

"Australia: 'Serious' Gays OK" (non-Australian couples together more than four years allowed to stay in Australia). *off our backs* 17:3 (March 1987):9.

Brandt, Kate. "Back to the Closet?" (U.S. Immigration and Naturalization Service discrimination against lesbian and gay performers). *Hot Wire* 3:2 (March 1987):22+.

CAD. "Lesbian/Gay Trips, Cruises & Marches" (U.S. and international news briefs). *off our backs* 10:3 (March 1980):18-19+.

------. "Victory into Defeat" (civil rights issues around the U.S., including immigration issues). *off our backs* 9:11 (December 1979):7.

Capone, Janet and Denise Leto. "Notes for a Magazine -- Il Viaggio Delle Donne: Italian-American Women Reach Shore." *Sinister Wisdom,* "il viaggio delle donne" 41 (Summer/Fall 1990):3-6.

Capra, Joan. "The Italian Jewish Connection, or, The History of America." *Sinister Wisdom,* "il viaggio delle donne" 41 (Summer/Fall 1990):101-4.

Foley, M.J. "Gay Refugee Denied Visa" (by U.S.; refugee fleeing Cuba). *off our backs* 17:5 (May 1987):24.

Gannon, Aixa. "Homosexuality in Cuba: a Threat to Public Morality?" (interview with Cuban lesbian who emigrated to the U.S. in May 1980). *Connexions,* "In Search of Work and Refuge" 2 (Fall 1981):18-19.

"Gays Can Immigrate" (to U.S.; change in policy). *off our backs* 6:7 (October 1976):5.

"Immigration Bill Reintroduced" (to repeal laws barring gay and lesbian entry into the U.S.). *off our backs* 13:7 (July 1983):16.

Islam, Sharmem. "Asian Lesbian Refused Entry to U.S." (on her way to Asian Pacific Lesbian Conference, University of California, Santa Cruz, September 1989). *Sojourner* 15:4 (December 1989):11.

"Lesbian Refused Admission to U.S." (Dutch woman of South Asian descent stopped on her way to the Asian Pacific Lesbian Conference in San Francisco, California). *off our backs* 20:3 (March 1990):17.

Manny. "International Lesbian Conference" (International Lesbian Information Service Conference, Paris, France, April 1983). *off our backs* 13:7 (July 1983):14.

Reynolds, William T. "The Immigration Act and the Rights of Homosexual Aliens." *Journal of Homosexuals,* "Homosexuality and the Law" 5:1-2 (Fall 1979-Winter 1980):79-87.

Ruth. "Cuban Lesbians in USA" (interview with two women who recently moved to Seattle, Washington). *off our backs* 11:4 (April 1981):12.

Singerman, Deborah. "Australia: Gay & Lesbian Immigration Task Force." *off our backs* 19:7 (July 1989):12.

Sinister Wisdom, "il viaggio delle donne" (Italian-American Issue), no. 41, Summer/Fall 1990.

Stanford, Liz. "Lesbians Seek Exile" (from Pakistan, Mozambique, Spain, Nicaragua, and Cuba). *off our backs* 10:5 (May 1980):6.

Thomas, June. "Harassment by INS" (U.S. Immigration and Naturalization Service; of women's music performers from Canada). *off our backs* 17:4 (April 1987):4.

Wheatley, Mickey. "Lesbian and Gay Aliens Denied Naturalization." *Loyola of Los Angeles International and Comparative Law Journal* 8:1 (Winter 1985):161-82.

Zehra. "Lesbians and Immigration." *Spare Rib* (Great Britain) 176 (March 1987):37.

Bishop, Heather (musician):
Smith, Connie. "Canadian Viewpoint: Heather Bishop Interviewed" (about U.S. Immigration and Naturalization Service discrimination against women's music performers). *Hot Wire* 3:2 (March 1987):21-2.

Gessen, Masha (Soviet Jew, editor of lesbian/gay weekly *Next,*):
"Lesbian Challenges Immigration Laws" (1952 McCarran-Walter Immigration and Nationality Act). *off our backs* 19:6 (June 1989):7.

<u>Incest</u> (see also: Child Abuse)

Coveney, Lal and Leslie Kay. "A Symposium on Feminism, Sexuality, and Power" (Five College Women's Studies Committee and Faculty Seminar, Mt. Holyoke College). *off our backs* 17:1 (January 1987):12-13.

"Experiences of Lesbian Survivors of Incest." *Common Lives/Lesbian Lives* 2 (Winter 1981):62-8.

Fukaya, Michiyo. "Will the Real Me Please Stand Up?" *Common Lives/Lesbian Lives* 10 (Winter 1983):89-98.

"Incest and Other Sexual Taboos: a Dialogue Between Men and Women." *Out/Look #6,* 2:2 (Fall 1989):50-7.

Kris. "Another Kind of Coming Out" (child sexual abuse in the British black community). *Gossip* (Great Britain) 2 (1986):80-9.

Kushner, Leah Pesa. "Dear Nancy" (letter from an incest/child abuse survivor to her sister). *Common Lives/Lesbian Lives* 5 (Fall 1982):97-103.

Lee, Anne. "Untitled Incest Piece." *Common Lives/Lesbian Lives* 2 (Winter 1981):73-9.

Pelc, Mary, Naomi Dykestein, and Susan Marie. "Lesbian Survivors of Incest." *off our backs* 12:9 (October 1982):16-17.

Rothblum, Esther D. "Depression Among Lesbians: an Invisible and Unresearched Phenomenon." *Journal of Gay & Lesbian Psychotherapy* 1:3 (1990):67-87.

Schwartz, Patricia Roth. "Lesbian Love in Limbo." *off our backs* 20:6 (June 1990):18-20.

Thundercloud RDOC, Flying. "Voices" (incest and psychotherapy). *Common Lives/Lesbian Lives* 15/16 (Summer 1985):35-9.

Vincent, R. Judith. "On Mother/Daughter Incest." *Sojourner* 14:1 (September 1988):9.

Internalized Homophobia (see Homophobia/Heterosexism)

International Lesbian-Feminism (see also: Lesbians Around the World)

Aspen, Kristan. "The International Congress on Women in Music." *Hot Wire* 4:2 (March 1988):12-13.

Bebbington, Laura. "The Mexico International Women's Year Conference" (International Women's Year Tribune's attempts to censor lesbian feminist participation). *Meanjin Quarterly* (Australia) 34 (December 1975):373-9.

Bosley, Anne Marie. "ILGA Conference" (International Lesbian and Gay Association Conference, "Gays and Lesbians Facing Crisis," July 1986; organization changed name to include "Lesbian"). *Spare Rib* (Great Britain) 170 (September 1986):48.

CAD. "Gayintern" (formation of the International Gay Association, a civil rights organization). *off our backs* 8:10 (November 1978):6.

Connexions: an International Women's Quarterly, "Global Lesbianism," no. 3, January 1982.

------, "Global Lesbianism 2," no. 10, Fall 1983.

Dorothea, Zami and Valerie. "ILIS -- Striving for International Lesbian Movements" (International Lesbian Information Service conference, Geneva, Switzerland, 1986). *off our backs* 16:8 (August-September 1986):1-2+.

Douglas, Carol Anne. "ILGA Suspends South African Gay Group" (International Lesbian and Gay Association, on charges by predominantly black South African gay group that the Gay Association of South Africa (GASA) collaborates with the South African Government). *off our backs* 18:1 (January 1988):3.

------. "International Lesbian & Gay Conferences: a Split" (formation of the International Lesbian Information Service and the International Gay Association). *off our backs* 11:6 (June 1981):7.

"End of Decade Conference: Lesbian Voice" (United Nations Forum and Conference for Women). *New Directions for Women* 14:5 (September/October 1985):13.

Fink, Sue. "Report from Israel: the First International Women's Music Festival." *Hot Wire* 3:2 (March 1987):24-6.

Gevins, Adi. "To See Them in Person!" (interview with Kenyan woman distributing family planning information at the Nairobi international women's conference, about lesbians at the conference). *Connexions,* "Forum '85: Nairobi, Kenya" 17-18 (Summer/Fall 1985):17.

Grazia. "The Tribunal of Crimes Against Women" (International Tribunal of Crimes Against Women, Brussels, Belgium, March 1976; including official and unofficial lesbian workshops). *off our backs* 6:3 (May 1976):9.

Haggard, Judith. (letter about vandalism of nuclear bunkers at International Lesbian Information Service conference in Geneva, Switzerland, March 1986; see "Notice to the Entire Lesbian Movement: Terrorism at the End of the 8th ILIS Conference . . . " *Gossip* (Great Britain) 3 (no date):9-16). *Gossip* 6 (1988):15-7.

Hemmings, Susan and Manny. "Lesbians National . . . and International" (National Lesbian Conference on Sex and Sexual Practice, London, England, April 1983, and International Lesbian Service Conference, Paris, France, April 1983). *Spare Rib* (Great Britain) 131 (June 1983):12-13.

"ILIS Action" (fifth International Lesbian Information Service conference, Paris, France, April 1983). *Connexions,* "Global Lesbianism 2" 10 (Fall 1983):10-11.

"International Lesbian Conference" (International Lesbian Information Service Conference, Lichtaart, Belgium, December 30, 1981-January 3, 1982). *off our backs* 12:3 (March 1982):5.

"International Lesbian Conference: Focus on Autonomy" (trans. from *CLIT (Concentré Lesbien Irrestiblement Toxique) 007,* Switzerland). *Connexions,* "Global Lesbianism" 3 (January 1982):27.

Kelly, Janis. "The Global Impact of AIDS on Women" (includes section on lesbians and AIDS). *off our backs* 18:8 (August-September 1988):20-1.

Konek, Carol Wolfe. "Dangerous Discussions" (lesbians not permitted to display literature, lesbianism banned as discussion topic at forums but discussed anyhow, at the United Nations Women's Decade Forum and Conference in Nairobi, Kenya, 1987). *Heresies* 25 (1990):83+.

"Lesbian Voice" (at Nairobi international women's conference). *New Directions for Women* 14 (September-October 1985):13.

"Lesbians in the News . . . at Nairobi" (lesbian press conference held after delegates to the international conference in Nairobi defied a "pack-and-go" order). *Connexions,* "Forum '85: Nairobi, Kenya" 17-18 (Summer/Fall 1985):16.

"Lesbians of the World Unite" (International Lesbian Information Service; excerpt from *Gay News,* British biweekly, January 22-February 4, 1981). *Connexions,* "Special Introductory Issue" 0 (May 1, 1981):12-13.

Mason-John, Valery, Nicky Serrano Prado, and Maritxu Soriano Muguruza. "Two Views on Lesbian Conference" (8th International Lesbian Information Service Conference, Geneva, Switzerland, March 1986). *Spare Rib* (Great Britain) 166 (May 1986):13.

Mesec, Rose and Olga Nada. "First International Lesbian Conference." *off our backs* 11:3 (March 1981):13+.

Nissim, Rina. "Organizing the Conference" (International Lesbian Information Service Conference, Geneva, Switzerland, 1986). *off our backs* 6:8 (August-September 1986):27.

"Notice to the Entire Lesbian Movement: Terrorism at the End of the 8th ILIS Conference . . . " (International Lesbian Information Service). *Gossip* (Great Britain) 3 (no date):9-16.

Parmar, Pratibha and Sue O'Sullivan. "The Second International Feminist Bookfair" (Oslo, Norway, June 1986; includes section on "Global Day/Lesbian Day"). *Spare Rib* (Great Britain) 169 (August 1986):18-19.

Shalom, Chaya. "The Only Dyke from Israel" (to attend the National Lesbian Information Service Conference, Geneva, Switzerland, 1986). *off our backs* 16:8 (August-September 1986):26.

Tavormina, Patrizia. "International Summit for Women: Many Dimensions of Lesbians and Power" (Montréal, Québec, Canada, June 1990; meeting to prepare for the 1995 United Nations Conference). *off our backs* 20:8 (August/September 1990):24.

Winbury, Gale. "International Feminist Conference" (sponsored by the National Organization for Women, Cambridge, Massachusetts, June 1973; article includes section on "international lesbians"). *off our backs* 3:9 (July-August 1973):9.

Borren, Sylvia (founding member of the International Lesbian Information Service):
"The Decade Has Been Good for Us" (interview). *Connexions,* "Forum '85: Nairobi, Kenya" 17-18 (Summer/Fall 1985):14-15.

<u>Bunch, Charlotte</u> (activist and writer):

Douglas, Carol Anne. "Charlotte Bunch on Global Feminism" (interview). *off our backs* 17:9 (October 1987):10-12.

Griffin, Connie and Linda Roach. "International Feminism: 'a Passionate Politics' -- an Interview with Charlotte Bunch." *Woman of Power*, "International Feminism" 7 (Summer 1987):6-9+.

Schultz, Debra. "Bunch, One-Woman Coalition." *New Directions for Women* 16 (November-December 1987):4+.

Interviews

<u>Adam, Margie</u> (musician):

Glickman, Donna. "Margie Adam: One Voice in a Constellation." *off our backs* 6:3 (May 1976):18.

<u>Allen, Paula Gunn</u> (Native American writer):

Caputi, Jane. "Interview with Paula Gunn Allen." *Trivia*, "Breaking Forms" 16/17 (1990):50-67.

Wynne, Patrice. "Recovering Spiritual Reality in Native American Traditions: an Interview with Paula Gunn Allen." *Woman of Power*, "ReVisioning the Dark" 8 (Winter 1988):68-70.

Alive! (all-women jazz ensemble):

Maeda, Sheri and Sarie Feld. "Alive!" *off our backs* 13:8 (August-September 1983):30.

<u>Andrews, Karen</u> (librarian in Canada fighting for employee spousal benefits for her lover):

"Canada: I Will Not Be Shelved" (reprint from Canadian monthly, *Rites* (March 1988)). *Connexions*, "Lesbian Activism" 29 (1989):18-20.

Anzaldúa, Gloria (Chicana essayist and poet):
"Conversations at the Bookfair: Interview with Gloria Anzaldúa."
Trivia, "Two-Part Issue -- The 3rd International Feminist
Bookfair -- Part II: Language/Difference: Writing in Tongues" 14
(Spring 1989):37-45.

Valverde, Maya. "Borderlands: Transformation at the Crossroads."
Woman of Power 10 (Summer 1988):30-3.

Arauz, Rita (Nicaraguan activist and Sandinista):
"Nicaragua: Moving Forward Together" (AIDS activism and
education in Nicaragua). *Connexions,* "Women and AIDS" 33
(1990):13.

Attom, Patches, Alix Dobkin, and Kay Gardner (band members of
Lavender Jane Loves Women, the first lesbian record album):
Moira, Fran and Anne Williams. "Lavender Jane Loves . . . " *off our
backs* 4:5 (April 1974):6-7.

Bannon, Ann (pulp novelist):
Lootens, Tricia. "Ann Bannon: a Writer of Lost Lesbian Fiction
Finds Herself and Her Public." *off our backs* 13:11 (December
1983):14-15+.

Bechdel, Alison (cartoonist):
Harper, Jorjet and Toni L. Armstrong. "'Dykes to Watch Out For
Cartoonist Alison Bechdel." *Hot Wire* 3:3 (July 1987):2-5.

Thomas, June. "Drawing on the Lesbian Community: an Interview
with Alison Bechdel." *off our backs* 18:8 (August-September
1988):1+.

Beck, Evelyn Torton (Jewish writer, educator, and activist):
Cantor, Aviva. "*Lilith* interviews Evelyn Torton Beck." *Lilith* 10
(Winter 1982-3/5743):10-14.

Mayhew, Paula Hooper. "Visionary and Activist: an Interview with Evelyn Torton Beck, Director of Women's Studies, the University of Maryland." *Women's Studies International Forum* 9:2 (1986):137-40.

Moira, Fran. "A Nice Jewish Girl: Evi Beck." *off our backs* 12:8 (August-September 1982):8-11.

<u>Berson, Ginny, Meg Christian, Judy Dlugacz, Cyndi Gair, and Helaine Harris</u> (Olivia Records collective members):
Crow, Margie, Margaret Devoe, Madeline Janover, and Fran Moira. "The Muses of Olivia: Our Own Economy, Our Own Song." *off our backs* 4:9 (August/September 1974):2-3.

<u>Bishop, Heather</u> (Canadian musician):
Armstrong, Toni Jr. "A Taste of the Canadian Prairies: Heather Bishop." *Hot Wire* 6:2 (May 1990):2-4+.

Smith, Connie. "Canadian Viewpoint: Heather Bishop Interviewed" (about U.S. Immigration and Naturalization Service discrimination against women's music performers). *Hot Wire* 3:2 (March 1987):21-2.

<u>Bladebridge, Persimmon</u> (Canadian sculptor):
Mintz, Chavah. "Persimmon Bladebridge." *Fireweed* (Canada), "Lesbiantics" 13 (1982):135-40.

Rooney, F. "Interview: Persimmon." *Resources for Feminist Research* (Canada) 13:4 (1984):30-2.

<u>Bloch, Alice</u> (Jewish writer):
Sturgis, Susanna J. "An Interview with Alice Bloch." *off our backs* 11:11 (December 1981):22-3.

<u>Borden, Lizzie</u> (filmmaker):
Bishop, Marla and Lucy O'Brien. "Working Girls" (interview with director of film about a lesbian working in a heterosexual brothel). *Spare Rib* (Great Britain) 175 (February 1987):37-9.

Borrn, Sylvia (founding member of the International Lesbian
    Information Service, Switzerland):
"The Decade Has Been Good for Us." *Connexions,* "Forum '85:
    Nairobi, Kenya" 17-18 (Summer/Fall 1985):14-15.

Brady, Maureen (author of *Folly*):
Klepfisz, Irena. "Spinsters, Ink: an Interview with Maureen Brady and
    Judith McDaniel." *Sinister Wisdom,* "Lesbian Writing and
    Publishing." 13 (Spring 1980):77-81.

Sorrel, Lorraine and Susan Sojourner. "Maureen Brady: Envisioning
    Possibilities." *off our backs* 13:4 (April 1983):14-16.

Brantenberg, Gerd (Norwegian author of *Egalia's Daughters*):
Wilson, Barbara. "An Interview with Gerd Brantenberg." *off our
    backs* 16:4 (April 1986):18-19.

Bright, Susie (editor of lesbian erotic magazine *On Our Backs*):
Gonsalves, Sharon. "Exploring Our Sexual Fantasies: Women's
    Erotica -- Susie Bright: On the Line." *Sojourner* 14:2 (October
    1988):30-1.

Brossard, Nicole (Canadian writer):
Lockey, Ottie. "Interview with Nicole Brossard." *Broadside* (Canada)
    2:8 (June 1981):10-11.

Brown, Rita Mae (writer):
Armstrong, Toni L. "Rita Mae Brown." *Hot Wire* 2:3 (July 1986):2-
    5.

Urbanska, Wanda. "Conversation with Rita Mae Brown." *Los
    Angeles Herald Examiner,* California Living section (May 3,
    1981):5.

Bulkin, Elly (writer, and co-editor of *Lesbian Poetry*):
Sorrel, Lorraine and Sue Sojourner. "Lesbian Poetry." *off our backs*
    10:8 (August-September 1981):20-1.

Bunch, Charlotte (activist and writer):
Doughty, Frances. "Frances Doughty Talks to Charlotte Bunch About Women's Publishing." *Sinister Wisdom,* "Lesbian Writing and Publishing" 13 (Spring 1980):71-7.

Douglas, Carol Anne. "Charlotte Bunch on Global Feminism." *off our backs* 17:9 (October 1987):10-12.

Griffin, Connie and Linda Roach. "International Feminism: 'a Passionate Politics' -- an Interview with Charlotte Bunch." *Woman of Power,* "International Feminism" 7 (Summer 1987):6-9+.

Schultz, Debra. "Interview." *Belles Lettres* 3 (November-December 1987):7.

Butcher, Linda (welder):
Tabor, Martha. "Linda Butcher: Striking While the Iron's Hot." *off our backs* (February 1979):14-15+.

Byrd, Stephanie (poet):
"A Conversation With Stephanie Byrd." *Visibilities* 3:2 (March/April 1989):7-10.

Carter, Colevia (activist, member of AIDS outreach program of the National Coalition of Black Lesbians and Gays):
Hutchins, Loraine. "Colevia Carter -- Women and AIDS." *off our backs* 17:1 (January 1987):20-1.

Castelón, Alida and Lourdes Pérez (organizers of the first lesbian *Encuentro* in Cuernavaca, Mexico, October 1987):
"Mexico: the First Lesbian *Encuentro*" (reprint from Canadian monthly, *Rites* 4:4 (September 1987)). *Connexions,* "Lesbian Activism" 29 (1989):26-7.

Charbonneau, Patricia (actress, starred in film "Desert Hearts"):
Armstrong, Toni L. "'Desert Hearts' Heartthrob: Patricia Charbonneau." *Hot Wire* 3:2 (March 1987):2-5+.

<u>Chowdurry, Dupitara and Nandini Datta</u> (Indian lesbians):
Islam, Sharmem. "Breaking Silence: Coming Out in India."
Sojourner 14:10 (June 1989):20-1.

<u>Christian, Meg</u> (musician):
Davenport, Katherine. "Interview: Meg Talks." *off our backs* 11:3
(March 1981):19+.

Edelson, Carol and Fran Pollner. "Meg Christian." *off our backs* 3:7
(April 1973):2-3.

Pollock, Mary. "Recovery and Integrity: the Music of Meg
Christian" (and substance abuse). *Frontiers* 9:2 (1987):29-34.

<u>Christian, Meg, Ginny Berson, Judy Dlugacz, Cyndi Gair, and
Helaine Harris</u> (Olivia Records collective members):
Crow, Margie, Margaret Devoe, Madeline Janover, and Fran Moira.
"The Muses of Olivia: Our Own Economy, Our Own Song."
off our backs 4:9 (August/September 1974):2-3.

<u>Chrystos</u> (Native American poet and activist):
Claudia, Karen and Lorraine Sorrel. "Chrystos: Not Vanishing --
& In Person" (interview and review of her book *Not Vanishing*).
off our backs 19:3 (March 1989):18-19.

<u>Clark, Judy</u> (political prisoner):
Moira, Fran. "Judy Clark: 75 to Life, but Life Goes On." *off our
backs* 14:11 (December 1984):2-8.

<u>Clark, Judy, Linda Evans, and Laura Whitehorn</u> (political prisoners):
Kalman, Marilyn and Rachel Lederman. "Talking with Three Lesbian
Political Prisoners" (interview by two activist lawyers). *Sinister
Wisdom,* "With an Emphasis on Lesbian Theory" 37 (Spring
1989):100-10.

<u>Cleyrerque, Berthe</u> (author Natalie Barney's cook):
Orenstein, Gloria Feman. "The Salon of Natalie Clifford Barney: an
interview with Berthe Cleyrerque." *Signs* 4:3 (Spring 1979):484-
96.

Clinton, Kate (comic):

Barrett, Carolann. "Be Bold and Be Bad." *Woman of Power,* "Humor" 17 (Summer 1990):60-3.

Clod, Bente (Danish writer and filmmaker):

Anderson, Marguerite. "An Interview with Bente Clod: Danish Writer, Poet, Filmmaker and Feminist." *Resources for Feminist Research* (Canada) 17 (December 1988):23-6.

Cohen, Jocelyn Helaine, Nancy Taylor, and Victoria Poore (of Helaine Victoria Press postcard company):

Tilchen, Maida. "Helaine Victoria Press." *Sinister Wisdom,* "Lesbian Writing and Publishing" 13 (Spring 1980):87-90.

Corinne, Tee (artist, photographer, and writer):

Henry, Alice. "Images of Lesbian Sexuality." *off our backs* 13:4 (April 1983):10-12.

Coventry Lesbian Theatre Group (Great Britain):

Mohin, Lilian. "Herstory Interview with Members of the Coventry Lesbian Theatre Group: Lou Hart, Jane Skeates, Vicki Ryder and Suzanne Ciechomski." *Gossip* (Great Britain) 4 (no date):59-85.

Crawford, Muriel and Anyda Marchant (founders of The Naiad Press):

Damon, Gene (Barbara Grier, current owner of Naiad). "The Naiad Press." *Sinister Wisdom,* "Lesbian Writing and Publishing" 1:2 (Fall 1976):116-19.

Culver, Casse (musician):

Moira, Fran. "Casse Culver: 'Integrated Separatism'" (interview with musician Casse Culver and her concert producer Spotts, including conversation about violence against women). *off our backs* 4:11 (November 1974):12-13.

Daly, Mary (philosopher and theologian):

Cosstick, Vicky. "Mary Daly, Feminist Philosopher." *New Directions for Women* 8:1 (Anniversary 1979):1+.

Douglas, Carol Anne. "Mary Daly Speaks & Sparks." *off our backs* 9:5 (May 1979):22-3.

Datta, Nandini and Dupitara Chowdurry (Indian lesbians):
Islam, Sharmem. "Breaking Silence: Coming Out in India." *Sojourner* 14:10 (June 1989):20-1.

de Madrugada, Llena and Deidre McCalla (musicians):
Segrest, Mab. "'It's Hard to Play the Flute When Your Lip is Quivering': Interviews with Deirdre McCalla and Llena de Madrugada." *Sinister Wisdom* 6 (Summer 1978):93-8.

Deitch, Donna (filmmaker; director of *Desert Hearts*):
Aufderheide, Patricia. "*Desert Hearts:* an Interview with Donna Deitch." *Cinéaste* 15:1 (1986):18-19.

Harper, Jorjet. "*Desert Hearts':* Donna Deitch." *Hot Wire* 3:1 (November 1986):23-5.

Delphy, Christine (French activist and writer):
Cottingham, Laura. "Christine Delphy: French Feminist" (includes section on "Lesbianism in France"). *off our backs* 14:3 (March 1984):10-11+.

Deming, Barbara (civil rights/peace activist and writer):
Robson, Ruthann. "An Interview with Barbara Deming." *Kalliope* 6:1 (1984):37-45.

Desaulniers, Michelle and Diane Trépanière (Canadian video artists):
Dascher, Helge. "Mémoire, reconnaissance: Entrevue avec Michelle Desaulniers et Diane Trépanière." *Canadian Woman Studies* (Canada), "Feminism and Visual Art/Le féminisme et l'art visuel" 11:1 (Spring 1990):75-7.

Dickson, Roz (Haitian activist):
Lootens, Tricia. "Common Differences: One Feminist's Perspective" (on the Common Differences: Third World Women and Feminist Perspectives Conference, University of Illinois, April 1983; interview). *off our backs* 13:7 (July 1983):7.

Dlugacz, Judy, Meg Christian, Ginny Berson, Cyndi Gair, and
   Helaine Harris (Olivia Records collective members):
Crow, Margie, Margaret Devoe, Madeline Janover, and Fran Moira.
   "The Muses of Olivia: Our Own Economy, Our Own Song." *off
   our backs* 4:9 (August/September 1974):2-3.

Dobkin, Alix (separatist musician):
Claudia, Karen. "Alix Dobkin as Separatist/Symbol/Songwriter." *off
   our backs* 18:2 (February 1988):14-15.

Dobkin, Alix. "Hi Phranc, This Is Alix Calling." *Hot Wire* 6:1
   (January 1990):16-18+.

Douglas, Carol Anne. "'A' is for Alix Dobkin." *off our backs* 11:10
   (November 1981):22-3.

Miller, Rosalie J. "A Conversation With Alix Dobkin." *Visibilities*
   3:3 (May/June 1989):4-9.

Dobkin, Alix, Patches Attom, and Kay Gardner (band members of
   Lavender Jane Loves Women, the first lesbian record album):
Moira, Fran and Anne Williams. "Lavender Jane Loves . . . " *off our
   backs* 4:5 (April 1974):6-7.

Dworkin, Andrea (activist and writer):
Braeman, Elizabeth and Carol Cox. "Andrea Dworkin: From a War
   Zone" (about Dworkin's book *Letters From a War Zone:
   Writings 1976-1989*). *off our backs* 20:1 (January 1990):8-9+.

"Interview on 'Womanpower': Andrea Dworkin." *Woman of Power* 1
   (Spring 1984):24-6+.

Loach, Loretta. "Where Angels Fear to Tread" (interview about
   Dworkin's anti-pornography work). *Spare Rib* (Great Britain)
   167 (June 1986):40-2.

Stoil, Julie-Maya. "Profile: 'Woman as Warrior' -- Radical Visionary
   for Justice: Andrea Dworkin." *Woman of Power* 3
   (Winter/Spring 1986):26-9+.

Wilson, Elizabeth. "Interview with Andrea Dworkin." *Feminist Review* (Great Britain) "Sexuality" 11 (Summer 1982):23+.

Edel, Deb and Joan Nestle (co-founders of The Lesbian Herstory Archive):
Hodges, Beth. "An Interview with Joan and Deb of the Lesbian Herstory Archives (Part 1)." *Sinister Wisdom* 11 (Fall 1979):3-13.

------. "Preserving Our Words and Pictures (Part 2)" (of interview in *Sinister Wisdom* 11). *Sinister Wisdom*, "Lesbian Writing and Publishing" 13 (Summer 1980):101-5.

Evans, Linda, Judy Clark, and Laura Whitehorn (political prisoners):
Kalman, Marilyn and Rachel Lederman. "Talking with Three Lesbian Political Prisoners" (interview by two activist lawyers). *Sinister Wisdom*, "With an Emphasis on Lesbian Theory" 37 (Spring 1989):100-10.

Eyega, Zeinab (Sudanese feminist living in exile):
Salomyn, Shay. "Black Women in Sudan." *off our backs* 20:3 (March 1990):8.

Ferron (musician):
Einhorn, Jennifer H. "Ferron's Sweet Deal" (interview). *Sojourner* 15:2 (October 1989):31.

Fishman, Louise (painter):
Gilliland, Elizabeth. "An Interview with Louise Fishman." *Kalliope* 11:1 (1989):29-42.

Flores, Brenda (Sandinista):
Irving, Kim. "Nicaragua: Lesbian Sandinista." *off our backs* 17:6 (June 1987):9.

Förster, Annette (Dutch film critic):
Donem, Suzanna. "Lesbian Lives on Screen." *Sojourner* 15:3 (November 1989):20-1.

Forster, Jackie (editor of now-defunct British lesbian magazine,
    Sappho, and writer):
Sojourner, Susan and Lorraine Sorrel. "Creating Sappho's Family."
    off our backs 12:10 (November 1982):20-1.

Wilmer, Val. "A Salute to *Sappho*" (magazine that ceased publishing
    just short of its tenth anniversary). *Spare Rib* (Great Britain) 116
    (March 1982):31-2.

François, Jocelyne (French novelist):
Shaw, Nanette. "Interview with Jocelyne François." *13th Moon,*
    "Narrative Forms" 8:1/2 (1984):52-60.

Freedman, Estelle (educator and co-author of *Intimate Matters: The
    History of Sexuality in America*):
Marty, Debian. "Estelle Freedman on Teaching Feminist Studies and
    Intimate Matters." *Feminisms* 3:2 (March/April 1990):3-5.

Fried, Nancy and Christina Schlesinger (artists):
Levin, Jenifer. "An Interview with Artists Nancy Fried and Christina
    Schlesinger." *Visibilities* 1:1 (Summer 1987):8+.

Gair, Cyndi, Judy Dlugacz, Meg Christian, Ginny Berson, and
    Helaine Harris (Olivia Records collective members):
Crow, Margie, Margaret Devoe, Madeline Janover, and Fran Moira.
    "The Muses of Olivia: Our Own Economy, Our Own Song." *off
    our backs* 4:9 (August/September 1974):2-3.

Gardner, Kay (musician):
Armstrong, Toni L. "Kay Gardner." *Hot Wire* 2:2 (March 1986):2-6.

Gardener, Kay, Alix Dobkin, and Patches Attom (band members of
    Lavender Jane Loves Women, the first lesbian record album):
Moira, Fran and Anne Williams. "Lavender Jane Loves . . . " *off our
    backs* 4:5 (April 1974):6-7.

Gearhart, Sally (author of *The Wanderground*):
"Discovering the Underground: an Interview with Sally Gearhart." *off
    our backs* 10:1 (January 1980):24-5+.

Gordon, Rebecca (activist and writer):

Thomas, June. "Women in Nicaragua: an Interview with Rebecca Gordon" (including section on "lesbian identity"). *off our backs* 17:3 (March 1987):4-5.

Gozemba, Pat (educator):

Radoslovich, Jean. "An Interview with Pat Gozemba." *Maenad,* "The Lesbian/Heterosexual Split" 2:2 (Winter 1982):98-107.

Grahn, Judy (writer):

Aal, Katharyn Machan. "Judy Grahn on Women's Poetry Readings: History and Performance (Part I)." *Sinister Wisdom* 25 (Winter 1984):67-76.

------. "Judy Grahn on Women's Poetry Readings: History and Performance (Part II)." *Sinister Wisdom* 27 (Fall 1984):54-61.

Beckett, Judith. "Profile: 'Woman as Warrior -- Warrior/Dyke': Judy Grahn." *Woman of Power* 3 (Winter/Spring 1986):56-9.

Constantine, Lynne and Suzanne Scott. "*Belles Lettres* Interview." *Belles Lettres* 2 (March-April 1987):7.

Green, G. Dorsey (therapist and writer):

Douglas, Carol Anne. "Lesbian Couples." *off our backs* 18:7 (July 1988):12-13.

Greenfield, Gloria, Pat McGloin, and Deborah Snow (editors of now-defunct Persephone Press):

Rich, Cynthia. "Persephone Press." *Sinister Wisdom,* "Lesbian Writing and Publishing" 13 (Spring 1980):81-5.

Griffin, Susan (writer):

Pavel, Margaret. "Interview on 'Womanpower': Susan Griffin." *Woman of Power* 1 (Spring 1984):34-8.

Grosberg, Carol:
Jay, Karla. "Carol Grosberg on Lesbian Theater." *Margins,* "Lesbian
Feminist Writing and Publishing" 23 (August 1975):55-7; also
WIN: Peace and Freedom Through Nonviolent Action, "Lesbian
Culture" 11:22 (June 26, 1975):15-17.

Hacker, Marilyn (poet):
Hammond, Karla. "An Interview with Marilyn Hacker." *Frontiers* 5:3
(Fall 1980):22-7.

Hampton, Mabel (born 1903; co-founder of the Lesbian Herstory
Archives):
Nestle, Joan. "Surviving and More: Interview with Mabel Hampton."
Sinister Wisdom, "On Being Old and Age" 10 (Summer
1979):19.

Rushin, Kate. "Mabel Hampton: 'Cracking Open the Door.'"
Sojourner 13:12 (August 1988):21.

Harris, Helaine, Cyndi Gair, Judy Dlugacz, Meg Christian, and
Ginny Berson (Olivia Records collective members):
Crow, Margie, Margaret Devoe, Madeline Janover, and Fran Moira.
"The Muses of Olivia: Our Own Economy, Our Own Song." *off
our backs* 4:9 (August/September 1974):2-3.

Heyward, Carter (Episcopalian priest and theologian):
Saz, Marnette. "Pioneer Priest Assesses Last 20 Years." *New
Directions for Women* 13:4 (July/August 1984):5.

Higbie, Barbara and Teresa Trull (musicians):
Armstrong, Toni L. "Interview with Teresa Trull and Barbara
Higbie." *Hot Wire* 1:3 (July 1985):2-6+.

Hinojosa, Claudia (founding member of Mexican feminist magazine,
Fem):
"Things Have Changed: Copenhagen and Nairobi Compared."
Connexions, "Forum '85: Nairobi, Kenya" 17-18 (Summer/Fall
1985):7-9.

Hoagland, Sarah Lucia (separatist philosopher):
Collis, Rose. "For Lesbians Only -- an Interview with Sarah
    Hoagland." *Spare Rib* (Great Britain) 197 (December
    1988/January 1989):31.

Hughes, Holly (performance artist):
Schneider, Rebecca. "Holly Hughes: Polymorphous Perversity and
    the Lesbian Scientist." *Drama Review* 33 (Spring 1989):171+.

Hull, Gloria T. (African-American critic and writer):
Thomas, June. "Public-Private Diary: Finding Black Women's
    History." *off our backs* 15:5 (May 1985):20-2.

Ifateyo, Ajowa (founder of *Upfront*, national black women's quarterly,
    and former editor of *The Running Spear*, African People's
    Socialist Party newspaper):
Douglas, Carol Anne. "Ajowa Ifateyo: Speaking Up Front." *off our
    backs* 14:10 (November 1984):10-12.

Israel, Pat (women's music festival organizer):
McPherson, Cathy. "Front Row Centre: the New England Women's
    Musical Retreat on Wheels: an Interview with Pat Israel."
    Resources for Feminist Research (Canada) 14 (March 1985):45-
    7.

Jay, Karla (critic and writer):
Douglas, Carol Anne. "*Gay Report:* Jay Report." *off our backs* 9:7
    (July 1979):16-17+.

Johnson, Chris, Janet Soule, and Chris Straayer (editors of the Metis
    Press):
"Metis Press." *Sinister Wisdom,* "Lesbian Writing and Publishing"
    13 (Spring 1980):91-4.

Johnson, Eva (aboriginal, black playwright):

Poggi, Stephanie, Jennifer Abod, Jacqui Alexander, and Evelynn Hammonds. "Claiming My Mothers, Exposing Aboriginal Consciousness to the World: an Interview with Aboriginal, Black Lesbian Playwright Eva Johnson." *Black/Out,* "We Are Family" 2:2 (Summer 1989):48-53.

Johnson, Sonia (U.S. Presidential candidate in 1984 and writer):

Armstrong, Toni Jr., Laura Post, and Sara Wolfersberger. "Sonia Johnson Speaks of Creating a 'Women's World.'" *Hot Wire* 6:3 (September 1990):37-9.

Constantine, Lynne M. and Suzanne Scott. "*Belles Lettres* Interview." *Belles Lettres* 3 (November-December 1987):6.

Kulp, Denise. "Sonia Johnson: 'The Answer Is Feminism.'" *off our backs* 14:9 (October 1984):20-3.

Salkind, Betsy and Vanessa Cruz. "Sonia Johnson: Breaking Free" (see response in *Sojourner* 13:6 (February 1988)). *Sojourner* 13:5 (January 1988):16-17.

Johnston, Jill (author of *Lesbian Nation,* columnist for *The Village Voice*):

Dulaney, Maedell. "Jill Johnston." *off our backs* 3:9 (July-August 1973):14-15.

Kimber, Kim (coordinator of the New England Women's Musical Retreat day stage):

Grace, Cindee. "Talking with the NEWMR Day Stage Coordinator: Kim Kimber." *Hot Wire* 2:2 (March 1986):39.

Kishwar, Madhu (editor of Indian feminist magazine *Manushi*):

Douglas, Carol Anne. "Feminism in India." *off our backs* 10:5 (May 1980):2-4.

Klepfisz, Irena (Jewish writer and Holocaust survivor):

Johnson, Barbara. "*Belles Lettres* Interview" (about *The Tribe of Dina*). *Belles Lettres* 2 (September-October 1987):5.

Kelly, Janis and Amy Stone. "Irena Klepfisz." *off our backs* 13:11 (December 1983):10-11.

Lesbians Against the Right (activists from Vancouver, British Columbia, Canada):
Steele, Lisa. "Fighting the Right." *Fuse* (Canada) 5:6/7 (August/September 1981):211-15.

Lesboten (German rock band):
"Never a Love Song." *Connexions,* "Global Lesbianism 2" 10 (Fall 1983):29.

Livia, Anna (British writer and publisher):
Smith, Jean. "Writing *Relatively Norma.*" *Spare Rib* (Great Britain) 130 (May 1983):25.

Thomas, June. "Anna Livia: Lesbian Author, Publisher." *off our backs* 18:11 (December 1988):10+.

Lorde, Audre (African-American writer):
Chiaramonte, Lee. "Letter From Berlin: Audre Lorde Answers Questions on Writing, Voice and Being a Woman Warrior." *Visibilities* 2:5 (September/October 1988):4-7.

Cornwell, Anita. "'So Who's Giving Guarantees?' An Interview with Audre Lorde." *Sinister Wisdom* 4 (Fall 1977):15-21.

Greene, Laureen A. "Breaking the Barriers of Silence: an Interview with Audre Lorde" (discusses surviving as an African-American woman in the United States, and living with cancer). *Woman of Power,* "Life Cycles: Conscious Birthing, Living, and Dying" 14 (Summer 1989):39-41.

Harper, Jorjet and Toni L. Armstrong. "Audre Lorde." *Hot Wire* 5:1 (January 1989):2-6.

"An Interview: Audre Lorde and Adrienne Rich." *Signs* 6:4 (Summer 1981):713-36.

Moira, Fran and Lorraine Sorrel. "Audre Lorde: Lit from Within."
off our backs 12:4 (April 1982):2-3.

Parmer, Pratibha and Jackie Kay. "Frontiers: Interview [with] Black
Author and Activist, Audre Lorde." *Spare Rib* (Great Britain) 188
(March 1988):37-41.

Loulan, JoAnn (therapist and author of books on lesbian sex and
relationships):
Armstrong, Toni Jr. "Education as Entertainment: Lesbian Sexpert
JoAnn Loulan." *Hot Wire* 6:1 (January 1990):2-5.

Wallsgrove, Ruth and Alice Henry. "JoAnn Loulan Interview."
off our backs 15:10 (November 1985):18-19.

Lunden, Doris (African-American lesbian, born in 1936, came out in
1953):
Bulkin, Elly. "An Old Dyke's Tale: an Interview with Doris Lunden."
Conditions: six 2:3 (Summer 1980):26-44; also *Conditions:
sixteen,* "Retrospective" (1989):63-82.

McCalla, Deidre (African-American musician):
Armstrong, Toni L. "Deidre McCalla." *Hot Wire* 4:3 (July 1988):
2-5+.

McCalla, Deidre and Llena de Madrugada (musicians):
Segrest, Mab. "'It's Hard to Play the Flute When Your Lip is
Quivering': Interviews with Deidre McCalla and Llena de
Madrugada." *Sinister Wisdom* 6 (Summer 1978):93-8.

McDaniel, Judith (writer):
Klepfisz, Irena. "Spinsters, Ink: an Interview with Maureen Brady and
Judith McDaniel." *Sinister Wisdom,* "Lesbian Writing and
Publishing." 13 (Spring 1980):77-81.

Sturgis, Susanna J. "Judith McDaniel: Writer, Organizer, Witness"
(plus, "A Preface to the Interview: a Statement by Judith
McDaniel"). *off our backs* 16:3 (March 1986):25-7.

McEwen, Christian (editor of lesbian poetry anthology, *Naming the Waves*):
Whitlock, Monica. "Naming the Waves." *Spare Rib* (Great Britain) 189 (April 1988):26-7.

McGloin, Pat, Gloria Greenfield, and Deborah Snow (editors of now-defunct Persephone Press):
Rich, Cynthia. "Persephone Press." *Sinister Wisdom*, "Lesbian Writing and Publishing" 13 (Spring 1980):81-5.

McKenzie, Michelle and Araba Mercer (members of Sheba Publishers, England):
Ross, Becki. "Black Women of Letters" (from Canadian monthly *Rites* (November 1988)). *Connexions*, "Women on Work" 30 (1989):24-5.

McNeill, Pearlie (Australian novelist living in London, England):
Ferrier, Carole. "Interview with Pearlie McNeill." *Hecate* (Australia) 16:1/2 (1990):102-10.

MacManus, Yvonne and Jo Anne Prather (founders of Timely Books Press):
Kinard, Lee. "Timely Books." *Sinister Wisdom*, "Lesbian Writing and Publishing" 13 (Spring 1980):86-7.

Marchant, Anyda and Muriel Crawford (founders of The Naiad Press):
Damon, Gene (Barbara Grier, current owner of Naiad). "The Naiad Press." *Sinister Wisdom*, "Lesbian Writing and Publishing" 1:2 (Fall 1976):116-19.

Marchessault, Jovette and Michelle Rossignol (playwright and director of "The Saga of the Wet Hens"):
Bell, Gay. "Where Nest the Wet Hens: Interviews of Michelle Rossignol and Jovette Marchessault." *Broadside* (Canada) 3:4 (1982):12-13.

<u>Mercer, Araba and Michelle McKenzie</u> (members of Sheba
Publishers, Great Britain):
Ross, Becki. "Black Women of Letters" (from Canadian monthly
Rites (November 1988)). *Connexions,* "Women on Work" 30
(1989):24-5.

<u>Merck, Mandy</u> (editor of British lesbian and gay television series
"Out On Tuesday"):
"Lesbians Hit Prime Time." *Spare Rib* (Great Britain) 213 (June
1990):39-42.

<u>Miner, Valerie</u> (writer):
Henry, Alice and Lorraine Sorrel. "Valerie Miner on Political
Fiction, Feminist Criticism & Class." *off our backs* 13:1
(January 1983):15-17.

Kinnaird, Linda. "All Good Women?" *Spare Rib* (Great Britain) 184
(November 1987):52-3.

<u>Moraga, Cherríe</u> (Chicana activist and writer):
Allison, Dorothy, Tomás Almaguer, and Jackie Goldsby. "'Writing Is
the Measure of My Life . . . ': an Interview with Cherríe
Moraga." *Out/Look* 1:4 (Winter 1989):53-7.

<u>Moraga, Cherríe and Barbara Smith</u> (co-editor and publisher of *This
Bridge Called My Back: Writings by Radical Women of Color*):
Sorrel, Lorraine. "*This Bridge* Moves Feminists." *off our backs* 12:4
(April 1982):4-5+.

<u>Mountaingrove, Jean and Ruth Mountaingrove</u> (founders of
Womanspirit magazine):
Danab, Mint and Athame Mountainclimber. "An Interview with Ruth
and Jean Mountaingrove." *Sinister Wisdom* 8 (Winter 1979):73-
6.

<u>Mountaingrove, Ruth and Jean Mountaingrove</u> (founders of
  Womanspirit magazine):
Danab, Mint and Athame Mountainclimber. "An Interview with Ruth
  and Jean Mountaingrove." *Sinister Wisdom* 8 (Winter 1979):73-
  6.

<u>Namjoshi, Suniti</u> (Indian-Canadian writer):
Dibblin, Jane. "Suniti Interviewed . . . " *Spare Rib* (Great Britain)
  147 (October 1984):20-2.

<u>Near, Holly</u> (musician and activist):
Armstrong, Toni Jr. "A Personal Chat with Holly Near About her
  New Autobiography" (*Fire in the Rain . . . Singer in the
  Storm*). *Hot Wire* 6:3 (September 1990):2-5+.

Feld, Sarie and Sheri Maeda. "Holly Near: Reaching More People
  with the Speed of Light." *off our backs* 12:11 (December
  1982):20-1.

<u>Nestle, Joan</u> (writer, co-founder of the Lesbian Herstory Archives):
Forster, Jackie. "A Restricted Country." *Spare Rib* (Great Britain)
  195 (October 1988):10-12.

<u>Nestle, Joan and Deb Edel</u> (co-founders of The Lesbian Herstory
  Archive):
Hodges, Beth. "Preserving Our Words and Pictures." *Sinister
  Wisdom,* "Lesbian Writing and Publishing" 13 (Summer
  1980):101-5.

<u>Norman, Pat</u> (activist):
Bowen, Angela. "Pat Norman, the Y.E.S. Woman: an Interview"
  (San Francisco Youth Environment Studies Training Center).
  Black/Out, "We Are Family" 2:2 (Summer 1989):41+.

<u>Ova</u> (British music group):
Thomas, June. "Ova: Stroppy Women." *off our backs* 16:9 (October
  1986):19.

Oxenberg, Jan (filmmaker):
Kelly, Janis and Terri Poppe. "Jan Oxenberg -- Filmmaker." *off our backs* 6:10 (January 1977):12-13.

Panzerino, Connie (disabled lesbian activist):
Graetz, Susan. "'It's What You Do With What You've Got': an Interview with Connie Panzerino." *Woman of Power* 1 (Spring 1984):72-4.

Parker, Pat (poet and activist):
Woodwoman, Libby. "Pat Parker Talks About Her Life and Her Work." *Margins*, "Lesbian Feminist Writing and Publishing" 23 (August 1975):60-1.

Patton, Cindy (author of *Sex and Germs: The Politics of AIDS*):
O'Sullivan, Sue. "Mapping: Lesbians, AIDS and Sexuality -- an Interview with Cindy Patton." *Feminist Review* (Great Britain), "Perverse Politics: Lesbian Issues" 34 (Spring 1990):120-33.

Pérez, Lourdes and Alida Castelón (organizers of the first lesbian *Encuentro* in Cuernavaca, Mexico, October 1987):
"Mexico: the First Lesbian *Encuentro*" (reprint from Canadian monthly, *Rites* 4:4 (September 1987)). *Connexions*, "Lesbian Activism" 29 (1989):26-7.

Phranc (Jewish folksinger):
Dobkin, Alix. "Hi Phranc, This Is Alix Calling." *Hot Wire* 6:1 (January 1990):16-18+.

Picard, Jane (separatist filmmaker):
Willer, Marilyn. "An Interview with Jane Picard." *Maenad*, "The Lesbian/Heterosexual Split" 2:2 (Winter 1982):87-97.

Poore, Victoria, Jocelyn Helaine Cohen, and Nancy Taylor (of Helaine Victoria Press postcard company):
Tilchen, Maida. "Helaine Victoria Press." *Sinister Wisdom*, "Lesbian Writing and Publishing" 13 (Spring 1980):87-90.

Prather, Jo Anne and Yvonne MacManus (co-founders of Timely
    Books Press):
Kinard, Lee. "Timely Books." *Sinister Wisdom,* "Lesbian Writing
    and Publishing" 13 (Spring 1980):86-7.

Raymond, Janice (author of *A Passion for Friends*):
Griffin, Connie. "A Passion for Female Friends: an Interview with
    Janice Raymond." *Woman of Power* 7 (Summer 1987):68-71.

Red Elk, Lois (American Indian Movement Activist, discussing
    lesbian presence at an AIM protest):
Stern, Carol. "Lois Red Elk." *Heresies #13,* "Feminism and
    Ecology" 4:1 (1981):19-20.

Rich, Adrienne (writer):
Bulkin, Elly. "An Interview with Adrienne Rich, Part 1."
    Conditions: one 1:1 (April 1977):50-65.

------. "An Interview with Adrienne Rich, Part 2." *Conditions: two*
    1:2 (October 1977):53-66.

"An Interview: Audre Lorde and Adrienne Rich." *Signs* 6:4 (Summer
    1981):713-36.

Lockey, Ottie. (interview with Adrienne Rich). *Broadside* (Canada)
    2:8 (June 1981):10-11.

Packwood, Marilyn. "Adrienne Rich." *Spare Rib* (Great Britain) 103
    (February 1981):14-16.

Wilson, Jean. "Adrienne Rich: Journey Towards a Common
    Language." *Broadside* (Canada) 2:9 (July 1981):8-9.

Ro Ro, Angela (Brazilian singer):
"'Don't Label Me; I Label Myself'" (trans. from *Chana Com Chana,*
    Brazilian lesbian journal (Spring 1981)). *Connexions,* "Global
    Lesbianism" 3 (January 1982):10-11.

Roberts, Roxanne E.B. (writer):
Ottey, Shan. "Black Lesbian: Alienation and Aloneness." *off our
    backs* 5:5 (May-June 1975):15.

Rossignol, Michelle and Jovette Marchessault (director and
    playwright of "The Saga of the Wet Hens"):
Bell, Gay. "Where Nest the Wet Hens: Interviews of Michelle
    Rossignol and Jovette Marchessault." *Broadside* (Canada) 3:4
    (1982):12-13.

Rule, Jane (Canadian writer):
Collis, Rose. "Breaking the Rules." *Spare Rib* (Great Britain) 185
    (December 1987):16-18.

Hancock, Geoff. "An Interview with Jane Rule." *Canadian Fiction
    Magazine* (Canada) 23 (1976): 57-112.

Sagot, Montserrat (Costa Rican feminist):
Douglas, Carol Anne. "Feminism in the Barrios of Costa Rica." *off
    our backs* 20:3 (March 1990):1-3+.

Sarton, May (writer):
Bakerman, Jane S. "'Work is My Rest': a Conversation with May
    Sarton." *Moving Out* 7:2 & 8:1 (1978):8-12+.

Carter, Nancy Corson. "An Interview with May Sarton." *Kalliope*
    5:2 (1983):37-48.

Shelley, D. "Conversation with May Sarton." *Women and Literature*
    7:2 (Spring 1979):33-41.

Schlesinger, Christina and Nancy Fried (artists):
Levin, Jenifer. "An Interview with Artists Nancy Fried and Christina
    Schlesinger." *Visibilities* 1:1 (Summer 1987):8+.

Schulman, Sarah (writer):
Cassidy, Cristi. "A Conversation with Sarah Schulman." *Visibilities*
    3:1 (January/February 1989):8+.

Kulp, Denise. "Sarah Schulman: On the Road to . . . " (interviewed during promotional tour for her novel, *Girls, Visions and Everything*). *off our backs* 16:11 (December 1986):20-1+.

Shanbaum, Susann and Nancy Vogl (musicians):
Feld, Sarie. "Nancy Vogl and Susann Shanbaum." *off our backs* 12:11 (December 1982):22-3.

Shelley, Martha (poet and member of the Women's Press Collective):
"Women's Press Collective." *Sinister Wisdom,* "Lesbian Writing and Publishing" 1:2 (Fall 1976):120-1.

Shocked, Michelle (musician):
Nordheim, Christie and Julie A. Kreiner. "On Coming Out: Michelle Shocked." *Hot Wire* 6:3 (September 1990):20-1.

Smith, Barbara (African-American activist and writer, founder of Kitchen Table Press):
Parkerson, Michelle. "Some Place That's Our Own -- an Interview with Barbara Smith." *off our backs* 14:4 (April 1984):10-12+.

Smith, Barbara and Cherríe Moraga (publisher and co-editor of *This Bridge Called My Back: Writings by Radical Women of Color*):
Sorrel, Lorraine. "*This Bridge* Moves Feminists." *off our backs* 12:4 (April 1982):4-5+.

Smith, Beverly (African-American writer and activist):
Bellos, Linda. "Beverly Smith in Conversation" (about African-American women's literature, and needlework). *Spare Rib* (Great Britain) 121 (August 1982):8.

Walker-Crawford, Vivienne. "Interview with Beverly Smith." *Common Lives/Lesbian Lives* 11 (Spring 1984):10-16.

Snow, Deborah, Gloria Greenfield, and Pat McGloin (editors of now-defunct Persephone Press):
Rich, Cynthia. "Persephone Press." *Sinister Wisdom,* "Lesbian Writing and Publishing" 13 (Spring 1980):81-5.

Soule, Janet, Chris Johnson, and Chris Straayer (editors of Metis Press):
"Metis Press." *Sinister Wisdom,* "Lesbian Writing and Publishing" 13 (Spring 1980):91-4.

Straayer, Chris, Chris Johnson, and Janet Soule (editors of the Metis Press):
"Metis Press." *Sinister Wisdom,* "Lesbian Writing and Publishing" 13 (Spring 1980):91-4.

Suwannanond, Unchana (Thai lesbian-feminist activist):
Berhane-Selassie, Tsehai, Alice Henry, Sona Osman, and Ruth Wallsgrove. "Feminism in Thailand: 'It Will Take My Whole Life, I Think.'" *off our backs* 15:3 (March 1985):2-4.

T., Marilyn (rap artist):
Stato, Joanne. "Lesbian Rap Artist: an Interview with Marilyn T." *off our backs* 19:9 (October 1989):22.

Taylor, Nancy, Jocelyn Helaine Cohen, and Victoria Poore (of Helaine Victoria Press postcard company):
Tilchen, Maida. "Helaine Victoria Press." *Sinister Wisdom,* "Lesbian Writing and Publishing" 13 (Spring 1980):87-90.

Taylor, Valerie (pulp novelist):
Corinne, Tee and Caroline Overman. "Valerie Taylor Interview." *Common Lives/Lesbian Lives* 25 (Winter 1988):61-72.

Tillery, Linda (African-American musician):
Gautreaux, Michele. "Sweet Linda Divine: an Interview with Linda Tillery." *Hot Wire* 1:2 (March 1985):2-5.

Tillery, Linda and Adrienne Torf (musicians):
Feld, Sarie and Sheri Maeda. "Linda Tillery and Adrienne Torf: Looking at Issues." *off our backs* 13:10 (November 1983):22-3.

<u>Tillery, Linda and Mary Watkins</u> (African-American musicians):
Pollock, Mary S. "The Politics of Women's Music: a Conversation with Linda Tillery and Mary Watkins." *Frontiers* 10:1 (1988):14-19.

<u>Torf, Adrienne and Linda Tillery</u> (musicians):
Feld, Sarie and Sheri Maeda. "Linda Tillery and Adrienne Torf: Looking at Issues." *off our backs* 13:10 (November 1983):22-3.

<u>Toder, Nancy</u> (writer):
Kelly, Janis. "Interview with Nancy Toder, Author of *Choices: a Novel About Lesbian Love.*" *off our backs* 10:11 (December 1980):16.

<u>Tremblay, Lucie Blue</u> (Canadian musician):
Armstrong Toni L. "Lucie Blue Tremblay." *Hot Wire* 3:1 (November 1986):2-5.

<u>Trépanière, Diane and Michelle Desaulniers</u> (Canadian video artists):
Dascher, Helge. "Mémoire, reconnaissance: Entrevue avec Michelle Desaulniers et Diane Trépanière." *Canadian Woman Studies* (Canada), "Feminism and Visual Art/Le féminisme et l'art visuel" 11:1 (Spring 1990):75-7.

<u>Trull, Teresa</u> (musician):
Armstrong, Toni, Jr. "The Best of Both Worlds: Teresa Trull." *Hot Wire* 5:2 (May 1989):2-5.

Stato, Joanne. "Teresa Trull: Excellence in Music." *off our backs* 19:11 (December 1989):20-2+.

<u>Trull, Teresa and Barbara Higbie</u> (musicians):
Armstrong, Toni L. "Interview with Teresa Trull and Barbara Higbie." *Hot Wire* 1:3 (July 1985):2-6+.

<u>Tyler, Robin</u> (comedian and music festival producer):
Armstrong, Toni L. "The P.T. Barnum of Women's Music and Culture: Robin Tyler." *Hot Wire* 4:2 (March 1988):2-6.

Ryan, Lori. "The Razor Edge of Truth -- a Conversation With Robin Tyler." *Visibilities* 2:6 (November/December 1988):8-11.

Vogl, Nancy and Susann Shanbaum (musicians):
"Nancy Vogl and Susann Shanbaum." *off our backs* 12:11 (December 1982):22-3.

Wan, Choi (feminist journalist from Hong Kong):
Norrgard, Lenore. "Opening the Hong Kong Closet" (interview with Choi Wan and Josephine, journalists and members of the Association for the Advancement of Feminism). *Out/Look #7*, 2:3 (Winter 1990):56-61.

Washington Sisters (African-American musicians Sondra and Sharon Washington):
Armstrong, Toni L. "The Washington Sisters." *Hot Wire* 4:1 (November 1987):2-4+.

JAG. "A Dialogue: The Washington Twins." *Hot Wire* 1:1 (November 1984):20.

Watkins, Mary and Linda Tillery (African-American musicians):
Pollock, Mary S. "The Politics of Women's Music: a Conversation with Linda Tillery and Mary Watkins." *Frontiers* 10:1 (1988):14-19.

Weiss, Andrea (filmmaker):
Collis, Rose. "Blood Sisters" (interview about Weiss' film *Blood and Roses: Under the Spell of the Lesbian Vampire*). *Spare Rib* (Great Britain) 183 (October 1987):40-1.

Whitehorn, Laura, Judy Clark, and Linda Evans (political prisoners):
Kalman, Marilyn and Rachel Lederman. "Talking with Three Lesbian Political Prisoners" (interview by two activist lawyers). *Sinister Wisdom,* "With an Emphasis on Lesbian Theory" 37 (Spring 1989):100-10.

Wicks, Marlene (co-founder of *off our backs*):
Dejanikus, Tacie, Carol Anne Douglas, and Susan R. Crites. "Marlene Wicks: Co-Founder of *oob*." *off our backs*, "Ten Years Growing!" 10:2 (February 1980):4+.

Williamson, Cris (musician):
Armstrong, Toni, Jr. "Cris" (interview in which Williamson says "No one knows if I am [a lesbian] or not . . . It has nothing to do with my music, whether people think it or not"). *Hot Wire* 5:3 (September 1989):2-6+.

Clark, Terri. "Interview with Cris." *off our backs* 10:5 (May 1980):15.

Wilson, Barbara (writer, and founder of Seal Press):
Leonard, Vickie and Denise Kulp. "An Interview with Barbara Wilson." *off our backs* 14:11(December 1984):26-7+.

Thomas, June. "Barbara Wilson Talks About: Feminist Publishing, Crime and Punishment." *off our backs* 20:1 (January 1990):10-11.

Winterson, Jeanette (British author):
Kay, Jackie. "Unnatural Passions" (interview conducted shortly after the movie version of her novel *Oranges Are Not the Only Fruit* was televised in England). *Spare Rib* (Great Britain) 209 (February 1990):26-9.

Scott, Suzanne and Lynne M. Constantine. "*Belles Lettres* Interview: Jeanette Winterson." *Belles Lettres* 5:4 (Summer 1990):24-6.

Wittig, Monique (French writer):
"Entretien Avec Monique Wittig." *L'Art Vivant* 45 (December 1973-January 1974):24-5.

Wolff, Charlotte (psychiatrist and writer):
"Falling in Love Again" (interview about Wolff's study on and interviews with 150 bisexual women and men). *Spare Rib* (Great Britain) 63 (October 1977):38-9.

Steakley, James D. "Love Between Women and Love Between Men: an Interview with Charlotte Wolff." *New German Critique* 23 (Spring-Summer 1981):73-81.

Ziff, Trisha (British hairdresser):
Zalsberg, Kitty. "Hairdressing" (in London's East End). *Spare Rib* (Great Britain) 93 (April 1980):6-8.

Italian-American Lesbians (see also: Immigration)

Angela, Angie and Demetria Iazetto. "Commari: Excerpts of a Dialogue." *Sinister Wisdom,* "il viaggio delle donne" 41 (Summer/Fall 1990):82-8.

Capone, Janet and Denise Leto. "Notes for a Magazine -- Il Viaggio Delle Donne: Italian-American Women Reach Shore." *Sinister Wisdom,* "il viaggio delle donne" 41 (Summer/Fall 1990):3-6.

Capra, Joan. "The Italian Jewish Connection, or, The History of America." *Sinister Wisdom,* "il viaggio delle donne" 41 (Summer/Fall 1990):101-4.

Sinister Wisdom, "il viaggio delle donne" (Italian-American Issue), no. 41, Summer/Fall 1990.

Jewish Lesbians (see also: Anti-Semitism; The Holocaust; Religion; Spirituality)

Beck, Evelyn Torton. "Self-Disclosure and the Commitment to Social Change." *Women's Studies International Forum,* "Women in Academe" 6:2 (1983):159-64.

------. "Teaching About Jewish Lesbians in Literature: from *Zeitel and Rickel* to *The Tree of Begats.*" *off our backs,* education issue 12:5 (May 1982):20.

Bolton, Elizabeth. "Double Takes and Mazel Tovs" (Jewish lesbian wedding). *Broadside* (Canada) 8 (January 1987):6.

Brown, Laura S. "How Is This Feminist Different From All Other Feminists? Or, My Journey from Pirke Avot to Feminist Therapy Ethics." *Women & Therapy* 10:4 (1990):41-55.

Cantor, Carla. "'Coming Out' in the Jewish Family." *Lilith* 14:3 (Summer 1989/5749):23-5.

Capra, Joan. "The Italian Jewish Connection, or, The History of America." *Sinister Wisdom,* "il viaggio delle donne" 41 (Summer/Fall 1990):101-4.

Cooper, Aaron. "No Longer Invisible: Gay and Lesbian Jews Build a Movement." *Journal of Homosexuality,* "Homosexuality and Religion" 18:3/4 (1989/1990):83-94.

Goldin, Sally. "An Invitation to Passover" (includes an "Alternative Women's Pesach Hagaddah"). *Common Lives/Lesbian Lives* 10 (Winter 1983):4-12.

Greenberg, Yael. "Dumbo, Fag and God: Teaching Jewish Children in Mainstream Religious Schools." *off our backs* 12:6 (June 1982):17.

Kaye/Kantrowitz, Melanie. "The Issue is Power: Some Notes on Jewish Women in Therapy." *Women & Therapy,* "Jewish Women in Therapy: Seen But Not Heard" 10:4 (1990):7-18.

------. "Observations: The Next Step." *NWSA Journal* 2:2 (Spring 1990):236-44.

Klepfisz, Irena. "Jewish Progressives and the Jewish Community" (*Tikkun* conference address, about lesbian, gay, and progressive Jews). *Tikkun* 4 (May-June 1989):83+.

Morris, Bonnie. "Anti-Semitism in the Women's Movement: a Jewish Lesbian Speaks." *off our backs* 20:11 (December 1990):12-13.

Mushroom, Merril. "Merril Mushroom Is a Jew." *Common Lives/Lesbian Lives* 7 (Spring 1983):78-85.

"New Jewish Agenda and Lesbian Communities." *Feminisms* 1:1 (Winter 1988):5.

"*Nice Jewish Girls: a Lesbian Anthology*" (excerpts of contributions by Melanie Kaye/Kantrowitz, Maxine Feldman, Evelyn Torton Beck, Susan J. Wolfe, Irena Klepfisz, Bernice Mennis, Rachel Wahlon, Elana Dykewomon, and Harriet Malinowitz). *Spare Rib* (Great Britain) 127 (February 1983):20-3.

Nugent, Robert and Jeannine Grammick. "Homosexuality: Protestant, Catholic, and Jewish Issues; a Fishbone Tale." *Journal of Homosexuality,* "Homosexuality and Religion" 18:3/4 (1989/1990):7-46.

Orbach, William. "Homosexuality and Jewish Law." *Journal of Family Law* 14:3 (1976):353-82.

Sarah, Elizabeth. "Re-thinking Feminism: Some Thoughts on the Limitations of 'Basics'-Training." *Women's Studies International Forum* 8:1 (1985):9-13.

Saslow, J.M. "Hear Oh Israel: We Are Jews, We Are Gay." *The Advocate* 465 (1987):38.

Shmate: a Journal of Progressive Jewish Thought, "Lesbian and Gay Jews," vol. 1, no. 2, June/July 1982.

Shulman, Sheila. "Lesbian Feminists and the Great Baby Con." *Gossip* (Great Britain) 1 (1986):68-90; also *Spinster* (Great Britain) 4 (1980).

------. "Some Thoughts on Biblical Prophecy and Feminist Vision." *Gossip* (Great Britain) 6 (1988):68-79.

Sinister Wisdom, "The Tribe of Dina: a Jewish Women's Anthology," nos. 29/30, 1986/5746.

Skurnik, Jennifer A. "Jewish Lesbians: a Cultural Celebration" (Washington, D.C., October 1982). *off our backs* 12:10 (November 1982):23.

Sloan, Judy. "Reclaiming a Past: a Search Into Jewish Identity" (actor discusses reintegrating "Sophie," a Jewish character, into performance for lesbian-feminist audiences). *Hot Wire* 3:3 (July 1987):46-8+.

Smith, Adrienne J. "Reflections of a Jewish Lesbian-Feminist Activist-Therapist; Or, First of All I Am Jewish, the Rest Is Commentary." *Women & Therapy,* "Jewish Women in Therapy: Seen But Not Heard" 10:4 (1990):57-64.

Smith, Beverly, with Judith Stein and Priscilla Golding. "'The Possibility of Life Between Us': A Dialogue Between Black and Jewish Women." *Conditions: seven* 3:1 (Spring 1981):25-46.

Stein, Judith A. "Telling *Bobbeh Meisehs* ['Old Wives' Tales']: Notes on Identity and the Creation of Jewish Lesbian Culture." *Common Lives/Lesbian Lives* 8 (Summer 1983):7-13.

------. "Thoughts on Fitting In . . . " (as a fat, Jewish lesbian). *Common Lives/Lesbian Lives* 17 (Fall 1985):69-70.

Bauman, Batya:
Bauman, Batya. "Ten Women Tell . . . The Ways We Are: Batya Bauman." *Lilith* 1:2 (Winter 1976-77/5737):9-10.

Beck, Evelyn Torton (educator and writer):
Cantor, Aviva. "*Lilith* Interviews Evelyn Torton Beck" (editor of *Nice Jewish Girls: a Lesbian Anthology*). *Lilith* 10 (Winter 1982-3/5743):10-14.

Mayhew, Paula Hooper. "Visionary and Activist: an Interview with Evelyn Torton Beck, Director of Women's Studies, the University of Maryland." *Women's Studies International Forum* 9:2 (1986):137-40.

Moira, Fran. "A Nice Jewish Girl: Evi Beck" (interview with the editor of *Nice Jewish Girls: a Lesbian Anthology*). *off our backs* 12:8 (August-September 1982):8-11.

Bloch, Alice (writer):
Sturgis, Susanna J. "An Interview with Alice Bloch" (writer). *off our backs* 11:11 (December 1981):22-3.

Brin, Rabbi Deborah (rabbi):
"Lesbian Rabbi Resigns" (Rabbi Deborah Brin of Downsview, Ontario, Canada, after coming out and feeling "oppressive" working environment develop). *off our backs* 20:10 (November 1990):9.

Dobkin, Alix (musician):
Armstrong, Toni L. "March on Washington for Lesbian & Gay Rights: New Jewish Agenda Havdallah Service & Concert" (including Alix Dobkin, Ronnie Gilbert, and Ruth Pelham). *Hot Wire* 4:2 (March 1988):20-1+.

Dobkin, Alix. "Hi Phranc, This Is Alix Calling" (conversation between musicians Alix Dobkin and Phranc). *Hot Wire* 6:1 (January 1990):16-18+.

Gilbert, Ronnie (musician):
Armstrong, Toni L. "March on Washington for Lesbian & Gay Rights: New Jewish Agenda Havdallah Service & Concert" (including Alix Dobkin, Ronnie Gilbert, and Ruth Pelham). *Hot Wire* 4:2 (March 1988):20-1+.

The God Of Vengeance (play):
Curtin, Kaier. "Roaring Twenties Scandal: Yiddish Lesbian Play Rocks Broadway" ("The God of Vengeance" by Sholom Asch; written 1907; performed on Broadway 1922; cast arrested). *Lilith* 19 (Spring 1988/5748):13-14.

Klepfisz, Irena (writer and Holocaust survivor):

Beck, Evelyn Torton. "From Nightmare to Vision: an Introduction to the Essays of Irena Klepfisz" (abridged version of introduction to Klepfisz's 1990 book *Dreams of an Insomniac: Jewish Feminist Essays, Speeches and Diatribes*). *Belles Lettres* 6:1 (Fall 1990):2-5.

Johnson, Barbara. "*Belles Lettres* Interview" (with Irena Klepfisz about *The Tribe of Dina: a Jewish Women's Anthology*, which Klepfisz co-edited with Melanie Kaye/Kantrowitz). *Belles Lettres* 2 (September-October 1987):5.

Kelly, Janis and Amy Stone. "Irena Klepfisz" (interview about *Keeper of Accounts*, dealing with Klepfisz' experience as a Holocaust survivor). *off our backs* 13:11 (December 1983):10-11.

Lavner, Lynn (comic):

Lavner, Lynn. "From Amsterdam to Miami Beach: a Gay Cabaret Musician Plays Two Religious Conferences." *Hot Wire* 4:1 (November 1987):24-5+.

Pelham, Ruth (musician):

Armstrong, Toni L. "March on Washington for Lesbian & Gay Rights: New Jewish Agenda Havdallah Service & Concert" (including Alix Dobkin, Ronnie Gilbert, and Ruth Pelham). *Hot Wire* 4:2 (March 1988):20-1+.

Phranc (musician):

Dobkin, Alix. "Hi Phranc, This Is Alix Calling" (conversation between musicians Alix Dobkin and Phranc). *Hot Wire* 6:1 (January 1990):16-18+.

Rich, Adrienne (poet):

Carruthers, Mary. "Adrienne Rich's 'Sources.'" *River Styx*, "Women's Issues" 15 (1984):69-74.

Judicial System (see Legal Issues)

<u>Labels/Identity</u> (see also: Androgyny; Bisexuality; Butch/Femme;
Coming Out; Transsexualism)

Albright, Mia. "What Is a Lesbian?" *Sinister Wisdom* 2 (Winter
1977):10-14.

Anzaldúa, Gloria. "Border Crossings" ("hybrid" multicultural writing
style; by Chicana poet/essayist). *Trivia*, "Two-Part Issue -- The
3rd International Feminist Bookfair -- Part II: Language/
Difference: Writing in Tongues" 14 (Spring 1989):46-51.

Brandt, Kathleen. "It Could Happen to You: a Straight Woman Talks
With Lesbian Friends." *Maenad*, "The Lesbian/Heterosexual
Split" 2:2 (Winter 1982):44-54.

Bristow, Ann R. and Pearn, Pam Langford. "Comment on Krieger's
'Lesbian Identity and Community: Recent Social Science
Literature'" (in *Signs* 8:1 (Autumn 1982):91-108). *Signs*, "The
Lesbian Issue" 9:4 (Summer 1984):729-32.

Brossard, Nicole (trans. Marlene Wildeman). "Kind Skin My Skin."
Trivia 12 (Spring 1988):43-4.

Bunch, Charlotte. "Self Definition and Political Survival." *Quest* 1:3
(Winter 1975):2-15.

Cartledge, Sue and Susan Hemmings. "How Did We Get This Way? Sue
Cartledge and Susan Hemmings Look at Explanations of
Lesbianism." *Spare Rib* (Great Britain) 86 (September 1979):43-
7.

Cass, Vivienne C. "Homosexual Identity: a Concept in Need of
Definition." *Journal of Homosexuality*, "Bisexual and
Homosexual Identities: Critical Theoretical Issues" 9:2/3 (Winter
1983/Spring 1984):105-26.

Chan, C.S. "Issues of Identity Development Among Asian-American Lesbians and Gay Men." *Journal of Counseling and Development,* "Gay, Lesbian, and Bisexual Issues in Counseling" 68:1 (September-October 1989):16-20.

Chauncey, George. "From Sexual Inversion to Homosexuality: Medicine and the Changing Conceptualization of Female Deviance." *Salmagundi,* "Homosexuality: Sacrilege, Vision, Politics" 58-59 (Fall 1982-Winter 1983):114-46.

Clark, Wendy. "The Dyke, The Feminist, and The Devil." *Feminist Review* (Great Britain), "Sexuality" 11 (Summer 1982):30-9.

Clausen, Jan. "My Interesting Condition: What Does It Mean When a Lesbian Falls in Love with a Man?" *Out/Look #7,* 2:3 (Winter 1990):10-21.

Cooper, Margaret. "Rejecting 'Femininity': Some Research Notes on Gender Identity Development in Lesbians." *Deviant Behavior* 11:4 (October-December 1990):371-80.

Cotter, Julia, Claudia Leight, Colleen Livingston, Sharon Mulgrew, and Karen Whitman. "Once More With Feeling . . . and Rationality: Feminists in Heterosexual Relationships." *Women: A Journal of Liberation* 3:1 (1972):30-2.

DeCecco, J.P. "Definition and Meaning of Sexual Orientation." *Journal of Homosexuality* 6:4 (Summer 1981):51-67.

DeFries, Zira. "Political Lesbianism and Sexual Politics." *Journal of the American Academy of Psychoanalysis* 6 (1978):71-8.

------. "Pseudohomosexuality in Female Students." *American Journal of Psychiatry* 133 (April 1976):400-4.

Desmoines, Harriet. "Notes for a Magazine II" (founding concepts for *Sinister Wisdom* ; discusses politically left revolutionary politics, racism, and classism). *Sinister Wisdom* 1:1 (Summer 1976):27-34.

Devoe, Margaret. "A Weekend Away" ("Women's Weekend," New Jersey, April 1974; includes section on sexual identity and lesbian points of view). *off our backs* 4:6 (May 1974):4-5.

Douglas, Carol Anne. "Confessions of an Ex-Heterosexual." *off our backs* 9:9 (October 1979):13+.

------. "What the Hell Is a Radical Feminist." *off our backs*, "Ten Years Growing!" 10:2 (February 1980):15.

Dworkin, Andrea. "Biological Superiority: the World's Most Dangerous and Deadly Idea" (separatism). *Heresies #6*, 2:2 (Summer 1978):46-51.

Elliott, Phyllis. "Lesbian Identity and Self-Disclosure." *Resources for Feminist Research* (Canada), "The Lesbian Issue/Etre Lesbienne" 12:1 (March 1983):51-2.

English, Deirdre, Amber Hollibaugh and Gayle Rubin. "Talking Sex: a Conversation on Sexuality and Feminism." *Feminist Review* (Great Britain), "Sexuality" 11 (Summer 1982):40-52; also *Socialist Review #58*, 11:4 (July-August 1981):43-62.

Faderman, Lillian. "The 'New Gay' Lesbians" (identity development through radical feminism). *Journal of Homosexuality,* "Controversy Over the Bisexual and Homosexual Identities: Commentaries and Reactions" 10:3/4 (Winter 1984):85-96.

Fenwomyn, Carol. "Lesbian Ethics Workshop Reports: 'Love Your Enemy?': Political Lesbianism." *Gossip* (Great Britain) 6 (1988):110-16.

Golding, Sue. "Knowledge Is Power" (conceptions, uses, and labels of women's sexuality -- especially lesbianism -- since beginning of the Women's Liberation Movement). *Fireweed,* (Canada) "Lesbiantics" 13 (1982):80-100.

Grier, Barbara. "What Is a Lesbian?" *Sinister Wisdom* 2 (Winter 1977):10-14.

Harris, Bertha. "Lesbian/Feminist Parley: Closing the Label Gap."
    Village Voice (December 28, 1972):15+.

------. "What Is a Lesbian?" *Sinister Wisdom* 2 (Winter 1977):10-14.

Harrison, Barbara G. "Sexual Chic, Sexual Fascism, and Sexual
    Confusion." *New York* 7:13 (April 1, 1974):31-6.

Imray, L. "From Heterosexual Feminist to Political Lesbian: the Painful
    Transition." *Women's Studies International Forum* 7:1
    (1984):39-41.

James, Selma. "From the Mother Country: One English Woman's Words
    on the U.S. and British Women's Movements" (section on
    "U.S.: 'Political Lesbians'"). *off our backs* 2:7 (March 1972):4.

Johnston, Jill. "Are Lesbians 'Gay'?" *Ms.* 3:12 (June 1975):85-6.

Journal of Homosexuality, "Bisexual and Homosexual Identities: Critical
    Theoretical Issues," vol. 9, nos. 2/3, Winter 1983/Spring 1984.

Journal of Homosexuality, "Controversy Over the Bisexual and
    Homosexual Identities: Commentaries and Reactions," vol. 10,
    nos. 3/4, Winter 1984.

Kelly, Janis. "Into the Eighties" (predicts that "sex . . . will become less
    important as a way of defining ourselves" and "lesbians will still
    feel free to mess around with men"). *off our backs*, "Ten Years
    Growing!" 10:2 (February 1980):6.

Khayatt, Didi. "Personal Politics and Sexuality" (by Egyptian-Canadian
    lesbian). *Resources for Feminist Research* (Canada),
    "Confronting Heterosexuality/Confronter l'hétérosexualité"
    19:3&4 (September/December 1990):8-12.

Kitzinger, Celia and Rex Stainton Rogers. "A Q-Methodological Study of
    Lesbian Identities." *European Journal of Social Psychology*
    15:2 (1985):167-87.

Koedt, Anne. "Lesbianism and Feminism." *Women: A Journal of Liberation* 3:1 (1972):33-6.

Krieger, Susan. "Lesbian Identity and Community: Recent Social Science Literature." *Signs* 8:1 (Autumn 1982):91-108.

------. "Reply to Sandoval and Bristow and Pearn" (*Signs,* "The Lesbian Issue" 9:4 (Summer 1984):725-31, response to Krieger's "Lesbian Identity and Community: Recent Social Science Literature," *Signs* 8:1 (Autumn 1982):91-108). *Signs,* "The Lesbian Issue" 9:4 (Summer 1984):732-3.

Leonard, Vickie and Carol Anne Douglas. "Working Together: a Heterosexual Radical Feminist and a Lesbian Radical Feminist" (members of the *off our backs* collective). *Maenad,* "The Lesbian/Heterosexual Split" 2:2 (Winter 1982):55-60.

"Lesbians and Their Girlfriends" (critique, focused on lesbian identity politics, of *Refractory Girl* (Australia) No.5, special issue on lesbianism). *Refractory Girl* 6 (June 1974):40-2.

Lesselier, Claudie. "Social Categorizations and Construction of a Lesbian Subject." *Feminist Issues* 7:1 (Spring 1987):89-94.

Levy, Eileen F. "Lesbian Motherhood: Identity and Social Support." *Affilia* 4 (Winter 1989):40-53.

Loiacano, Darryl K. "Gay Identity Issues among Black Americans: Racism, Homophobia, and the Need for Validation." *Journal of Counseling and Development,* "Lesbian, Gay and Bisexual Issues in Counseling" 68:1 (September-October 1989):21-5.

MacDonald, Ingrid. "'We'll Deconstruct When They Deconstruct.'" *Resources for Feminist Research* (Canada), "Confronting Heterosexuality/Confronter l'hétérosexualité" 19:3&4 (September/December 1990):89-90.

Martin, Annette. "My Own Story" (growing up African-American and lesbian). *Common Lives/Lesbian Lives* 1 (Fall 1981):15-19.

Marychild. "Calling All Dykes . . . Come In Please" (member of Collective Lesbian International Terrors (CLIT) comments on negative power dynamics of role-playing; asserts that women who role-play are not "dykes"). *off our backs* 4:8 (July 1974):21-2.

Moberly, Elizabeth. "Homosexuality: Restating the Conservative Case" (shaping of the debate over "the homosexual question"). *Salmagundi*, "Homosexuality: Sacrilege, Vision, Politics," 58-59 (Fall 1982-Winter 1983):281-99.

Nichols, Margaret and Sandra R. Leiblum. "Lesbianism as a Personal Identity and Social Role: a Model." *Affilia* 1 (Spring 1985):48-59.

Overall, Christine. "Ascribing Sexual Orientations." *Atlantis* (Canada) 13:2 (Spring/printemps 1988):48-57.

Palzkill, Birit. "Between Gymshoes and High-Heels: the Development of a Lesbian Identity and Existence in Top Class Sport." *International Review for the Sociology of Sport* 25:3 (1990):221-34.

Pas, Faux. "Lesbian Separatism: What Do We Mean?" (letter to "A Readers' Forum -- Separatism: Beyond the Debate," questioning how "radical" (root) different varieties of separatism are). *Lesbian Ethics* 3:2 (Fall 1988):10-11.

Penelope, Julia. "The Mystery of Lesbians: I" (separatist lesbian-feminism as opposed to reformism of 1980s feminism). *Lesbian Ethics* 1:1 (Fall 1984):7-33 and *Gossip* (Great Britain) 1 (1986):9-45.

Penn, Donna. "Identity and Consciousness in the Boston Lesbian Community, 1929-1969." *NWSA Journal* 1:4 (Summer 1989):765-8.

Radicalesbians. "Woman-Identified Woman" (definition of "lesbian"). *Radical Therapist* 2 (April/May 1972):11.

Rich, Adrienne. "Compulsory Heterosexuality and Lesbian Existence."
    Signs 5:4 (Summer 1980):631-60.

Richardson, Diane. "The Dilemma of Essentiality in Homosexual
    Theory." *Journal of Homosexuality,* "Bisexual and Homosexual
    Identities: Critical Theoretical Issues" 9:2/3 (Winter 1983/Spring
    1984):79-90.

Roberts, J.R. "Notes on the Etymology and Usage of 'Dyke'"
    (supplement to Roberts' "In America They Call Us Dykes,"
    Sinister Wisdom 9 (Spring 1979):3-11). *Sinister Wisdom* 11
    (Fall 1979):61-3.

Ross, Becki. "Identity, Community and Lesbianism." *Resources for
    Feminist Research* (Canada), "Confronting Heterosexuality/
    Confronter l'hétérosexualité" 19:3&4 (September/December
    1990):3-4.

Rushin, Kate. "What's In a Name?" (discusses the following labels:
    African-American, Afro-American, Colored, Black, People of
    Color, Negro). *Black/Out,* "We Are Family" 2:2 (Summer
    1989):15.

Sandoval, Chela. "Comment on Krieger's 'Lesbian Identity and
    Community: Recent Social Science Literature'" (in *Signs* 8:1
    (Autumn 1982):91-108). *Signs,* "The Lesbian Issue" 9:4
    (Summer 1984):725-9.

Schwanberg, Sandra L. "Changes in Labeling Homosexuality in Health
    Sciences Literature: a Preliminary Investigation." *Journal of
    Homosexuality* 12:1 (Fall 1985):51-73.

Shapiro, Michael. "Gays and Lesbians" ("gay" as generic vs. male term).
    American Speech 65:2 (Summer 1990):191-2.

Shelley, Martha. "What Is a Lesbian?" *Sinister Wisdom* 2 (Winter
    1977):10-14.

Silber, Linda. "Negotiating Sexual Identity: Non-Lesbians in a Lesbian Feminist Community." *Journal of Sex Research* 27:1 (February 1990):131-9.

Silverstein, C. "The Ethical and Moral Implications of Sexual Classification -- a Commentary" (removal of homosexuality as a mental illness from psychology DSM). *Journal of Homosexuality* 9:4 (Summer 1984):29-38.

Spinster, Sidney. "Lesbian Culture: the Intimate Touch." *Hot Wire* 1:3 (July 1985):50-1.

Thompson, Martha. "On Confusing Heterosexism with Having a Male Sex Partner." *off our backs* 9:10 (November 1979):30.

Trebilcot, Joyce. "Dyke Methods, or Principles for the Discovery/Creation of Withstanding" (of patriarchy by wimmin). *Hypatia* 3:2 (Summer 1988):1-13.

Van Gelder, Lindsy. "America's Gay Women." *Rolling Stone* 382 (November 11, 1982):13-18.

Wilson, Elizabeth. "Forbidden Love" (proposes individual sexual identity as opposed to conformity to role playing or "non-sexual" lesbian-feminism). *Feminist Studies* 10:2 (Summer 1984):213-26.

Wine, Jeri Dawn. "The Lesbian Continuum in Academe." *Resources for Feminist Research* (Canada) 16:4 (December 1987):27-9.

Wolverton, Terry, et al. "Two Scenes from 'An Oral Herstory of Lesbianism'" (script of experimental play). *Sinister Wisdom* 12 (Winter 1980):61-6.

Zimmerman, Bonnie. "The Politics of Transliteration: Lesbian Personal Narratives." *Signs,* "The Lesbian Issue" 9:4 (Summer 1984):663-82.

<u>Beck, Evelyn Torton</u> (Jewish activist, educator, and writer):
Beck, Evelyn Torton. "Daughters and Mothers: an Autobiographical
Sketch." *Sinister Wisdom* 14 (Summer 1980):76-80.

<u>de Beauvoir, Simone</u> (French philosopher):
Ferguson, A. "Lesbian Identity: Beauvoir and History." *Women's
Studies International Forum* 8:3 (1985):203-8.

<u>Garbo, Greta</u> (actor):
Adam, Margie. "Greta Garbo's 'Mysterious' Private Life." *Out/Look
#10*, 3:2 (Fall 1990):25.

<u>Gozemba, Pat</u> (educator):
Radoslovich, Jean. "An Interview with Pat Gozemba" (steering
committee member of the National Women's Studies
Association, member of the Boston Area Lesbian and Gay
History Project, and English professor). *Maenad*, "The
Lesbian/Heterosexual Split" 2:2 (Winter 1982):98-107.

<u>Rich, Adrienne</u> (writer):
Cameron, Deborah. "Ten Years On: 'Compulsory Heterosexuality and
Lesbian Existence'" (essay by Adrienne Rich, in *Signs* 5:4
(Summer 1980):631-60). *Women: a Cultural Review* (Great
Britain) 1:1 (April 1990):35-7.

Gentile, Mary. "Adrienne Rich and Separatism: the Language of
Multiple Realities." *Maenad*, "The Lesbian/Heterosexual Split"
2:2 (Winter 1982):136-46.

<u>Wittig, Monique</u> (French critic and writer):
Wittig, Monique. "On the Social Contract" (of Jean-Jacques
Rousseau, as heterosexual). *Feminist Issues* 9:1 (Spring
1989):3-12.

<u>Language</u> (see also: Labels/Identity; Literary Critical Theory)

Alicen, Debbie. "Intertextuality: the Language of Lesbian Relationships."
Trivia 3 (Fall 1983):6-26.

Ashley, Leonard. "Dyke Diction: the Language of Lesbians." *Maledicta* 6:1-2 (Summer-Winter 1982):123-62.

Boone, B. "Gay Language as Political Praxis." *Social Text* 1 (Winter 1979):59.

Brown, Rita Mae. "The Good Fairy" (how lesbian-feminism changes women's body language, typically "deformed by the patriarchy"). *Quest* 1:1 (Summer 1974):58-64.

Canadian Woman Studies/Les Cahiers de la Femme, Canada, "Sexuality and Symbol/*Symbolisme et Sexualité,*" vol. 3, no. 2, 1981.

"CLIT Statement #2" (Collective Lesbian International Terrors, group formed "to counterattack recent media insults against lesbians"). *off our backs* 4:8 (July 1974):10-11.

Cunningham, Joyce. "Bad Language: Negating, CR, Space, Guilt-Tripping." *Gossip* (Great Britain) 2 (1986):97-8.

Daly, Mary. "On Lust and the Lusty" (excerpt from *Pure Lust: Elemental Feminist Philosophy*). *Trivia* 3 (Fall 1983):47-69.

Daly, Mary, Julia Penelope Stanley, Audre Lorde, Judith McDaniel and Adrienne Rich. "The Transformation of Silence into Language and Action" (Lesbians and Literature Panel of the Modern Language Association Convention, Chicago, Illinois, December 1977). *Sinister Wisdom* 6 (Summer 1978):4-25.

Desmoines, Harriet. "Notes for a Magazine II" (founding concepts for *Sinister Wisdom*; discusses politically left revolutionary politics, racism, and classism). *Sinister Wisdom* 1:1 (Summer 1976): 27-34.

Frye, Marilyn. "Lesbian 'Sex.'" *Sinister Wisdom,* "Passing" 35 (Summer/Fall 1988):46-54.

------. "To Be and Be Seen: Metaphysical Misogyny." *Sinister Wisdom* 17 (1981):57-70.

Grahn, Judy. "The Queen of Bulldikery" (a history of the "bulldike"). *Chrysalis* 10 (no date; c. Winter 1980):35-41.

Grimard-Leduc, Micheline. "The Mind-Drifting Islands" (excerpt from *L'île des Amantes;* discusses lesbians as an exiled island people based on Amazon heritage). *Trivia* 8 (Winter 1986):28-36.

Hayes, Joseph J. "Language and Language Behavior of Lesbian Women and Gay Men: a Selected Bibliography, Part 1." *Journal of Homosexuality* 4:2 (Winter 1978):201-12.

Hayes, Joseph J. "Language and Language Behavior of Lesbian Women and Gay Men: a Selected Bibliography, Part 2." *Journal of Homosexuality* 4:3 (Spring 1978):299-309.

Interrante, Joe. "From Homosexual to Gay to ?: Recent Work in Gay History." *Radical America* 15:6 (November-December 1981):79-86.

Kitzinger, Celia. "Heteropatriarchal Language: the Case Against 'Homophobia.'" *Gossip* (Great Britain) 5 (no date):15-20.

Lesselier, Claudie. "Social Categorizations and Construction of a Lesbian Subject." *Feminist Issues* 7:1 (Spring 1987):89-94.

Livia, Anna. "With Gossip Aforethought." *Gossip* (Great Britain) 1 (1986):60-7.

Lorde, Audre, Mary Daly, Julia Penelope Stanley, Judith McDaniel, and Adrienne Rich. "The Transformation of Silence into Language and Action" (Lesbians and Literature Panel of the Modern Language Association Convention, Chicago, Illinois, December 1977). *Sinister Wisdom* 6 (Summer 1978):4-25; Audre Lorde's speech also in *Woman of Power* 14 (Summer 1989):40-1.

McDaniel, Judith, Mary Daly, Julia Penelope Stanley, Audre Lorde, and Adrienne Rich. "The Transformation of Silence into Language and Action" (Lesbians and Literature Panel of the Modern Language Association Convention, Chicago, Illinois, December 1977). *Sinister Wisdom* 6 (Summer 1978):4-25.

MacDonald, Ingrid. "'We'll Deconstruct When They Deconstruct." *Resources for Feminist Research* (Canada), "Confronting Heterosexuality/Confronter l'hétérosexualité" 19:3&4 (September/December 1990):89-90.

Mohin, Lilian (letter responding to Celia Kitzinger, "Heteropatriarchal Language: the Case Against 'Homophobia,'" *Gossip* (Great Britain) 5 (no date):15-20). *Gossip* 6 (1988):19-20.

Moirai, Catherine Risingflame, with Merril Mushroom. "White Lies and Common Language: Notes for Lesbian Writers and Readers." *Common Lives/Lesbian Lives* 5 (Fall 1982):46-58.

Penelope, Julia (see also: Stanley, Julia Penelope). "Heteropatriarchal Semantics: Just Two Kinds of People in the World." *Lesbian Ethics* 2:2 (Fall 1986):58-80.

------. "Láadan -- Age, Bodily Secretions, Lesbians . . . Developing the Language." *Hot Wire* 6:2 (May 1990):18-19+.

------. (letter responding to Celia Kitzinger, "Heteropatriarchal Language: the Case Against 'Homophobia,'" *Gossip* (Great Britain) 5 (no date):15-20). *Gossip* 6 (1988):20-2.

------. "The Mystery of Lesbians: II" (separatist political theory). *Lesbian Ethics* 1:2 (Spring 1985):29-67 and *Gossip* (Great Britain) 2 (1986):16-68.

Ponse, Barbara. "Secrecy in the Lesbian World." *Urban Life* 5:3 (October 1976):313-38.

Rich, Adrienne, Mary Daly, Julia Penelope Stanley, Audre Lorde, and Judith McDaniel. "The Transformation of Silence into Language and Action" (Lesbians and Literature Panel of the Modern Language Association Convention, Chicago, Illinois, December 1977). *Sinister Wisdom* 6 (Summer 1978):4-25.

Roberts, J.R. "In America They Call Us Dykes: Notes on the Etymology and Usage of 'Dyke.'" *Sinister Wisdom* 9 (1979):3-11.

------. "Notes on the Etymology and Usage of 'Dyke'" (supplement to Roberts' "In America They Call Us Dykes," *Sinister Wisdom* 9 (Spring 1979):3-11). *Sinister Wisdom* 11 (Fall 1979):61-3.

Rosenfeld, Marthe. "Language and the Vision of a Lesbian-Feminist Utopia in Wittig's *Les Guérillères.*" *Frontiers,* "NWSA -- Selected Conference Proceedings, 1980" 6:1-2 (Spring-Summer 1981):6-9.

Shapiro, Michael. "Gays and Lesbians" ("gay" as generic vs. male term). *American Speech* 65:2 (Summer 1990):191-2.

Spears, Richard A. "On the Etymology of Dike." *American Speech* 60:4 (1985):318-27.

Stanley, Julia Penelope (see also: Penelope, Julia). "A Cursory and Precursory History of Language, and the Telling of It." *Sinister Wisdom* 1:1 (July 1976):5-12.

------. "Homosexual Slang." *American Speech* 45:1/2 (1970):45-59.

------. "When We Say 'Out of the Closets!'" (gay (male) slang as oppressive to women, and attempts to salvage and redefine terms). *College English* 36:3 (November 1974):385-91.

Stanley, Julia Penelope, Mary Daly, Audre Lorde, Judith McDaniel, and Adrienne Rich. "The Transformation of Silence into Language and Action" (Lesbians and Literature Panel of the Modern Language Association Convention, Chicago, Illinois, December 1977). *Sinister Wisdom* 6 (Summer 1978):4-25.

Stato, Joanne. "Spelling [woman symbol] Reminding Myself" ("woman" vs. "womyn"). *off our backs* 19:11 (December 1989):6.

Trebilcot, Joyce. "Conceiving Women: Notes on the Logic of Feminism." *Sinister Wisdom* 11 (Fall 1979):43-50.

------. "Dyke Methods." *Hypatia* 3:2 (Summer 1988):1-13.

Warland, Betsy. "cutting re/marks." *Sinister Wisdom,* "Lesbian Voices" 42 (Winter 1990/1991):94-112.

Wells, Joel W. "Sexual Language Usage in Different Interpersonal Contexts: a Comparison of Gender and Sexual Orientation." *Archives of Sexual Behavior* 18:2 (April 1989):127-43.

------. "The Sexual Vocabularies of Heterosexual and Homosexual Males and Females for Communicating Erotically with a Sexual Partner." *Archives of Sexual Behavior* 19:2 (April 1990):139-47.

Wittig, Monique. "La Pensée Straight" ("The Straight Mind"). *Questions Féministes* (France) (février 1980):45-53.

------. "The Mark of Gender" (pronouns and gendered language in Wittig's novels). *Feminist Issues* 5:2 (Fall 1985):3-12.

------. "The Point of View: Universal or Particular." *Feminist Issues* 3 (Fall 1983):63-9.

------. "The Straight Mind" (originally published as "La Pensée Straight," *Questions Féministes* (février 1980):45-53). *Feminist Issues* 1:1 (Summer 1980):103-11.

Zita, Jacquelyn. "'Real Girls' and Lesbian Resistance." *Lesbian Ethics* 3:1 (Spring 1988):85-96.

Barnes, Djuna (writer):

Hokensen, Jan. "The Pronouns of Gomorrha: a Lesbian Prose
Tradition" (lesbian modernist writers -- including Virginia
Woolf, Gertrude Stein, Djuna Barnes, and Colette -- and post-
modernist writers -- including Monique Wittig, June Arnold, and
Bertha Harris). *Frontiers* 10:1 (1988):62-9.

Brossard, Nicole (Canadian writer):

Wildeman, Marlene. "The Lesbian Feminist Literary Ethics of Nicole
Brossard in *La Lettre Aérienne.*" *Gossip* (Great Britain) 6
(1988):44-55.

Colette (French writer):

Hokensen, Jan. "The Pronouns of Gomorrha: a Lesbian Prose
Tradition" (lesbian modernist writers -- including Virginia
Woolf, Gertrude Stein, Djuna Barnes, and Colette -- and post-
modernist writers -- including Monique Wittig, June Arnold, and
Bertha Harris). *Frontiers* 10:1 (1988):62-9.

Rich, Adrienne (writer):

Ferguson, Ann, Jacquelyn N. Zita, and Kathryn Pine Adelson. "On
'Compulsory Heterosexuality and Lesbian Existence': Defining
the Issues" (three responses to Rich's essay in *Signs* 5:4
(Summer 1980):631-60). *Signs,* "French Feminism and Theory"
7:1 (Autumn 1981):158-99.

Gentile, Mary. "Adrienne Rich and Separatism: the Language of
Multiple Realities." *Maenad,* "The Lesbian/Heterosexual Split"
2:2 (Winter 1982):136-46.

Templeton, Alice. "The Dream and the Dialogue: Rich's Feminist
Poetics and Gadamer's Hermeneutics." *Tulsa Studies in Women's
Literature* 7:2 (Fall 1988):283-96.

Stein, Gertrude (writer):

Hokensen, Jan. "The Pronouns of Gomorrha: a Lesbian Prose
   Tradition" (lesbian modernist writers -- including Virginia
   Woolf, Gertrude Stein, Djuna Barnes, and Colette -- and post-
   modernist writers -- including Monique Wittig, June Arnold, and
   Bertha Harris). *Frontiers* 10:1 (1988):62-9.

Wittig, Monique (French critic and writer):

Creet, Julia M. "Speaking in Lesbian Tongues -- Monique Wittig and
   the Universal Point of View." *Resources for Feminist Research*
   (Canada) 16 (December 1987):16-20.

Rosenfeld, Marthe. "The Linguistic Aspect of Sexual Conflict:
   Monique Wittig's *Le Corps Lesbien.*" *Mosaic* (Canada) 17:2
   (Spring 1984):235-41.

Wolff, Charlotte (psychiatrist and writer):

Steakley, James D. "Love Between Women and Love Between Men:
   an Interview with Charlotte Wolff." *New German Critique* 23
   (Spring-Summer 1981):73-81.

Woolf, Virginia (British writer):

Hokensen, Jan. "The Pronouns of Gomorrha: a Lesbian Prose
   Tradition" (lesbian modernist writers -- including Virginia
   Woolf, Gertrude Stein, Djuna Barnes, and Collette -- and post-
   modernist writers -- including Monique Wittig, June Arnold, and
   Bertha Harris). *Frontiers* 10:1 (1988):62-9.

Latina/Chicana Lesbians (see also: Chicana Lesbians; Lesbians of
   Color; Lesbians Around the World; Racism)

Anzaldúa, Gloria. "Border Crossings" ("hybrid" multicultural writing
   style; by Chicana poet/essayist). *Trivia,* "Two-Part Issue -- The
   3rd International Feminist Bookfair -- Part II: Language/
   Difference: Writing in Tongues" 14 (Spring 1989):46-51.

de Monteflores, Carmen. "Invisible Audiences: Writing Fiction as a Form
   of Coming Out." *Out/Look #10,* 3:2 (Fall 1990):65-8.

Elizarde, Margarita. "Lesbianas de Color." *off our backs* 9:6 (June 1979):10+.

Hidalgo, Hilda A. and Elia Hidalgo Christensen. "The Puerto Rican Lesbian and the Puerto Rican Community." *Journal of Homosexuality* 2 (Winter 1977):109-22.

Johnson, Lynell. "Women of Color and AIDS." *Black/Out,* "Tenth Anniversary Edition: NCBLG Celebrates Homecoming" 2:1 (Fall 1988):27-8.

Jones, Brooke. "Cuban Lesbians" (in refugee center at Fort Indiantown Gap, Pennsylvania). *off our backs* 10:9 (October 1980):6+.

Malone, Bridget. "Latin Lesbians in Iowa City: an Interview." *Common Lives/Lesbian Lives* 15/16 (Summer 1985):121-35.

Ortega, Eliana and Nancy Saporta Sternbach. "Gracias a la Vida: Recounting the Third Latin American Feminist Meeting in Bertioga, Brazil, July 31-August 4, 1985." *off our backs* 16:1 (January 1986):1-5.

Ortiz, Terri. "The Evolution of a *Boricua* Lesbian Feminist." *Sojourner* 13:2 (October 1987):19.

Paz, Juana Maria. "Womyn and Colour: a Puerto Rican Dyke Examines Her Roots." *off our backs* 9:6 (June 1979):9+.

Ruth. "Cuban Lesbians in U.S.A." *off our backs* 10:4 (April 1981):12.

Legal Issues (see also: Child Custody; Domestic Partnership; Equal Rights Amendment; Foster Care; Homophobia/Heterosexism; Immigration; Legislation; Work)

Alibrando, Julie. "Up Lambda" (lesbian files sex discrimination complaint against gay bookstore in Washington, D.C. after she was fired and her job was given to a man). *off our backs* 6:9 (December 1976):12.

Anderson, Shelley. "Falling Borders, Rising Hopes: Europe in 1992" (effects of legal and economic integration of European Economic Community). *Out/Look #10,* 3:2 (Fall 1990):30-35.

Arriola, Elvia Rosales. "Sexual Identity and the [U.S.] Constitution: Homosexual Persons as a Discrete and Insular Minority." *Women's Rights Law Reporter* 10 (Winter 1988):143-76.

Ayres, Caroline. "'Immediate Family' Clause Under Attack" (attempted eviction of a lesbian couple from their apartment). *off our backs* 13:2 (February 1983):16.

Bloom, Lisa. "We Are All Part of One Another: Sodomy Laws and Morality on Both Sides of the Atlantic." *New York University Review of Law & Social Change,* "Symposium: Sex, Politics and the Law; Lesbians and Gay Men Take the Offensive" 14:4 (Fall 1986):995-1016.

Bullough, Vern L. "Lesbianism, Homosexuality and the American Civil Liberties Union" (impact of ACLU taking up lesbian/gay rights cause). *Journal of Homosexuality* 13:1 (Fall 1986):23-34.

CAD. "Blows Struck -- Gay Struggle Continues" (murder of openly gay San Francisco Supervisor Harvey Milk; gay rights struggles around the U.S.). *off our backs* 9:1 (January 1979):10.

------. "California Dreaming" (gay rights struggles in California and Washington, D.C.). *off our backs* 9:4 (April 1979):11.

------. "Democrats Smile at Gays" (Carter administration and Democratic Party make "some moves toward opposing discrimination against lesbians and gays"). *off our backs* 10:8 (August-September 1980):15; note: cover reads 10:7.

------. "Gayintern" (lesbian and gay rights struggles around the world). *off our backs* 9:11 (December 1979):7.

------. "Gays Struggle" (news briefs about gay rights struggles around the world). *off our backs* 8:10 (November 1978):6.

------. "Gays Win Some" (gay issues in elections in California, Washington, Florida, New York, and Washington D.C.; tentative plans for a lesbian and gay march on Washington D.C. in 1979). *off our backs* 8:11 (December 1978):11.

------. "Victory into Defeat" (civil rights issues around the U.S., including immigration issues). *off our backs* 9:11 (December 1979):7.

Coffey, Mary Anne. "Of Father Born: a Lesbian Feminist Critique of the Ontario Law Reform Commission Recommendations on Artificial Insemination." *Canadian Journal of Women and the Law* (Canada) 1:2 (1986):424-33.

"The Constitutionality of Laws Forbidding Private Homosexual Conduct." *Michigan Law Review* 72 (August 1974):1613-36.

Cox, Gail Diane. "Gay Lawyers Seek a National Voice." *National Law Journal* 11:14 (December 12, 1988):23.

Crozier, Alana. "The Canadian Criminal Justice System and Lesbianism: a Research Note on the Relationship Between Systematic Exclusion and Criminal Victimization." *Resources for Feminist Research* (Canada) 4 (December 1985-January 1986):18-19.

Dell, Mae. "Women and the Law" (conference, New York University, February 1974; includes section on "Gay Rights"). *off our backs* 4:4 (March 1974):24-5.

"Developments in the Law: Sexual Orientation and the Law." *Harvard Law Review* 102:7 (May 1989):1508-1671.

Dixon, Edie. "Supreme Court Avoids Gay Rights." *off our backs* 15:4 (April 1985):2.

Douglas, Carol Anne. "Election '88" (section on "Lesbian and Gay Rights" in various states). *off our backs* 18:11 (December 1988):1-2.

------. "Lesbian Teacher OK" (federal jury grants damages to woman fired for "bisexuality"). *off our backs* 11:11 (December 1981):9.

Dunlap, Mary C.. "Under the Law -- The Pro's and Con's of Outing." *Visibilities* 4:5 (September/October 1990):18-19.

Egerton, Jayne. "Nothing Natural" (legal obstacles to lesbian parenting in Great Britain). *New Statesman & Society* 3:127 (1990):12-14.

Ertman, Martha. "Women and the Law Conference" (Detroit, Michigan, March 1990; topics include legal needs of lesbians of color and violence against lesbians and gay men). *off our backs* 20:7 (July 1990):2-5.

Ettelbrick, Paula L. "Passing Lesbian/Gay Rights Laws Is Just the First Step." *Visibilities* 2:5 (September/October 1988):16-17.

------. "Under the Law." *Visibilities* 4:1 (January/February 1990):18-19.

------. "Under the Law -- Bias Crimes Laws." *Visibilities* 2:4 (July/August 1988):14-15.

------. "Under the Law -- Does a Sperm Donor Have Parental Rights to a Lesbian Couple's Child?" *Visibilities* 2:2 (March/April 1988):17.

------. "Under the Law -- How Can We Create a Lesbian Family?" *Visibilities* 2:3 (May/June 1988):16-17.

------. "Under the Law -- The Lesbian Rights Project Goes National." *Visibilities* 3:4 (July/August 1989):14-15.

------. "Under the Law -- Protecting Relationships." *Visibilities* 2:1 (January/February 1988):18-20.

------. "Under the Law -- Reproductive Choice." *Visibilities* 3:3 (May/June 1989):16-17.

------. "Under the Law -- Who Comes First When There Is No Marriage?" *Visibilities* 3:5 (September/October 1989):18-19.

Falk, P.J. "Lesbian Mothers -- Psychosocial Assumptions in Family-Law." *American Psychologist* 44:6 (1989):941-7.

Farley, William P, Patrick Sweeney and June Besek. "Civil Rights: Discrimination on the Basis of Sexual Preference." *Annual Survey of American Law* (1980):60-4.

FE. "Williams-Sonoma Sued for Firing Lesbians of Color." *off our backs* 20:3 (March 1990):17.

Feyler, Nan. "The Use of the State Constitutional Right to Privacy to Defeat State Sodomy Laws." *New York University Review of Law & Social Change,* "Symposium: Sex, Politics and the Law; Lesbians and Gay Men Take the Offensive" 14:4 (Fall 1986):973-94.

Gamble, Richard H. "Estate Planning for the Unmarried Person: an Estate Planner's Dilemma; the Law Favors Marriage But Many Contemporary Americans Don't." *Trusts and Estates* 125 (April 1985):25-8.

"Gay Canada" (New Democratic Party passes resolution calling for anti-discrimination law to protect lesbians and gays). *off our backs* (February 1979):8.

"Gay D.C." (discrimination in Washington, D.C. by the Office of Human Rights). *off our backs* 9:2 (February 1979):8.

"Gays on the March" (unsympathetic cover story on the surge of gay pride/visibility). *Time* 106 (September 8. 1975):32-43.

Gomez, Jose. "The Public Expression of Lesbian-Gay Personhood as Protected Speech." *Law & Inequality* 1:1 (June 1983):121-53.

Grosvenor, T.G. "Midwest Lesbian Conference" (Michigan State University, May 1974). *off our backs* 4:7 (June 1974):6-7.

Halley, Janet E. "The Politics of the Closet: Towards Equal Protection for Gay, Lesbian, and Bisexual Identity." *UCLA Law Review* 36:5 (June 1989):915-76.

Heatherly, Gail E. "Gay and Lesbian Rights: Employment Discrimination." *Annual Survey of American Law* (1985):901-2.

Hedgpeth, Judith M. "Employment Discrimination Law and the Rights of Gay Persons." *Journal of Homosexuality,* "Homosexuality and the Law" 5:1-2 (Fall 1979-Winter 1980):67-78.

Henry, Alice. "Current Lesbian Rights Issues" (16th National Conference on Women and the Law, New York City, March 1985). *off our backs* 15:6 (June 1985):25.

Herek, G.M. "Hate Crimes Against Lesbians and Gays -- Issues for Research and Policy." *American Psychologist* 44:6 (1989):948-55.

Hughes, Janice. "Civil Disobedience: National March on Washington for Lesbian and Gay Rights" (and rally protesting Bowers v. Hardwick Supreme Court ruling, Washington, D.C., October 1987). *off our backs* 17:11 (December 1987):15+.

Journal of Homosexuality, "Homosexuality and the Law," vol. 5, nos. 1-2, Fall 1979-Winter 1980.

------, "Research on the Violations of Civil Liberties of Homosexual Men and Women," vol. 2, no. 4, Summer 1977.

Kelly, Janis. "Nearly Everybody Loses" (sex discrimination complaint against Lambda Rising gay bookstore in Washington, D.C.). *off our backs* 6:10 (January 1977):18.

------. "Supreme Court, Sodomy, and Me" (U.S. Supreme Court affirms states' rights to outlaw certain sexual acts). *off our backs* 6:3 (May 1976):10.

Leonard, A.S. "Gay Lesbian Rights: Report From the Legal Front."
Nation 251:1 (1990):12-15.

Leonard, Leigh Megan. "A Missing Voice in Feminist Legal Theory: the
Heterosexual Presumption." *Women's Rights Law Reporter* 12
(Spring 1990):39-49.

Leopold, Margaret and Wendy King. "Compulsory Heterosexuality,
Lesbians and the Law: the Case for Constitutional Protection."
Canadian Journal of Women and the Law (Canada) 1:1
(1985):163-86.

"Lesbian Charged with Manslaughter in New York" (woman appealing
conviction for shooting her roommate's boyfriend). *off our backs*
10:3 (March 1980):9.

"The Lesbian Educator: a Social-Legal History for Today's Activist"
(report on paper given by Karen M. Harbeck at the National
Women's Studies Association conference, June 1989, Towson
State University, Maryland). *off our backs* 19:8 (August-
September 1989):11.

"Lesbian Mother Accused of Molesting Daughter" (doctor making charge
based on "violence of [mother's] lifestyle"). *off our backs* 6:4
(June 1976):7.

"Lesbians Fight Oppressive Laws" (in Czechoslovakia). *New Directions
for Women* 19:5 (September/October 1990):9.

"Lesbians Sue Boss" (for being forced to quit because of a hostile work
environment). *off our backs* 6:7 (October 1976):5.

McDonald, Tracy. "Gay Bashing an Attack on Civil Rights"
(Massachusetts State Attorney General's office brief). *off our
backs* 17:5 (May 1987):16.

Morrow, Becky. "Military Ban on Homosexuals Is Widely Litigated."
New Jersey Law Journal 106 (November 20, 1980):21.

New York University Review of Law & Social Change, "Symposium: Sex, Politics and the Law; Lesbians and Gay Men Take the Offensive," vol. 14, no. 4, Fall 1986.

"NGTF Attacks Gov't Order" (National Gay Task Force calls for end to executive order restricting government employment of lesbians and gays). *off our backs* 13:6 (June 1983):15.

Perkins, Penny. "Under the Law -- Lesbians and Sodomy Laws." *Visibilities* 4:2 (March/April 1990):18-19.

Post, Dianne and Amanda Bailey. "Legal System: Friend or Foe?" *Common Lives/Lesbian Lives* 7 (Spring 1983):55-7.

Rankin, Teresa. "Gays' (Lack of) Rights" (part of report on the Seventh National Conference on Women and the Law, Temple University, March 1976). *off our backs* 6:2 (April 1976):3.

Reese, Susan Elizabeth. "The Forgotten Sex: Lesbians, Liberation and the Law." *Willamette Law Journal* 11 (1975):354+.

Richards, David A.J. "Constitutional Privacy and Homosexual Love." *New York University Review of Law & Social Change,* "Symposium: Sex, Politics and the Law: Lesbians and Gay Men Take the Offensive" 14:4 (Fall 1986):895-905.

Riegler, Waultrad. "Austria: Lesbian Graffiti Wins" (court upholds contract allowing pro-lesbian slogan on bus ad). *off our backs* 20:6 (June 1990):4.

Rivera, Rhonda R. "Our Straight-Laced Judges: the Legal Position of Homosexual Persons in the U.S." *Hastings Law Journal* 30 (1979):799+.

Robson, Ruthann. "Looking for Lesbian Legal Theory -- a Surprising Journey." *Sinister Wisdom,* "Lesbian Voices" 42 (Winter 1990/1991):32-9.

Rothblum, Esther D. "Introduction: Lesbianism as a Model of a Positive
Lifestyle for Women." *Women & Therapy,* "Lesbianism:
Affirming Nontraditional Roles" 8:1/2 (1989):1-12.

Schneider, Elizabeth. "Lesbians, Gays and Feminists at the Bar:
Translating Personal Experience into Effective Legal Argument
-- a Symposium" (held at the Brooklyn Law School, New York).
Women's Rights Law Reporter 10 (Winter 1988):107-41.

Solomon, Donald M. "The Emergence of Associational Rights for
Homosexual Persons." *Journal of Homosexuality,*
"Homosexuality and the Law" 5:1-2 (Fall 1979-Winter
1980):147-55.

"State ERA Lacks Gay Rights Provisions" (Rhode Island). *off our backs*
13:6 (June 1983):15.

Stoil, Julie-Maya. "Profile: 'Woman as Warrior' -- Radical Visionary for
Justice: Andrea Dworkin" (activist and writer). *Woman of Power*
3 (Winter/Spring 1986):26-9+.

Sutton, Stuart A. "The Lesbian Family: Rights in Conflict Under the
Uniform Parentage Act." *Golden Gate University Law Review*
10:1 (1980):1007-41.

Thomas, Paul K. "Marriage Annulments for Gay Men and Lesbian
Women: New Canonical and Psychological Insight." *The Jurist*
43:2 (Spring 1983):318-42.

"Victory for Gay Student Group" (court rules University of Arkansas
must allow a Gay and Lesbian Student Association to exist). *off
our backs* 18:9 (October 1988):11.

Weise, Beth Reba. "Scandinavia: Feminist Utopia or Patriarchal
Stronghold?" *off our backs* 20:3 (March 1990):4-7.

Wertheimer, David M. "Treatment and Service Interventions for Lesbian
and Gay Male Crime Victims." *Journal of Interpersonal Violence*
5:3 (1990):384-400.

Wills, Sue. "The Psychologist and the Lesbian." *Refractory Girl*
(Australia) 9 (Winter 1975):41-5.

Wise, Donna L. "Challenging Sexual Preference Discrimination in
Private Employment." *Ohio State Law Journal* 41:2 (Fall
1980):501-31.

"Women and the Law" (conference, Georgetown University, Washington,
D.C.; includes section on "Lesbian Rights -- a Lawst Cause?").
off our backs 5:4 (April-May 1975):18.

WS. "Playing Your Cards Right" (meeting with mayor and police
officials in Washington, D.C. lead to agreement to enforce anti-
discrimination laws). *off our backs* 9:11 (December 1979):15.

Anderson v. Avco Embassy Pictures Corp.:
Cook, Alberta I. "More Suits After Plath Pact?" (Dr. Jane Anderson's
libel suit regarding her portrayal as a suicidal lesbian in a film
about poet Sylvia Plath: Anderson v. Avco Embassy Pictures
Corp.). *National Law Journal* 9 (February 16, 1987):6.

Bowers v. Hardwick:
Dunlap, Mary C. "In the Supreme Court of the United States,
October Term, 1985, Michael J. Bowers, petitioner, v. Michael
Hardwick, et al., Respondents. Brief Amicus Curiae for the
Lesbian Rights Project, Women's Legal Defense Fund, Equal
Rights Advocates, Inc., and the National Women's Law Center."
New York University Review of Law & Social Change,
"Symposium: Sex, Politics and the Law; Lesbians and Gay Men
Take the Offensive" 14:4 (Fall 1986):949-72.

Ettelbrick, Paula L. "The Hardwick Decision" (Bowers v. Hardwick,
Supreme Court decision upholding states' rights to maintain and
prosecute sodomy laws). *Visibilities* 1:1 (Summer 1987):5+.

"Sodomy Laws Targeted" (by civil liberties and gay rights groups,
after the Bowers v. Hardwick U.S. Supreme Court ruling). *off
our backs* 17:3 (March 1987):11.

"Supreme Court: the Good (Sexual Harassment Ruling); the Bad
(Sodomy Ruling); the Ugly (Rehnquist Nomination)." *off our
backs* 16:8 (August-September 1986):3+.

Watkins v. United-States Army:
Leonard, A.S. "Watkins v. United-States Army and the Employment
Rights of Lesbians and Gay Men." *Labor Law Journal* 40:7
(1989):438-45.

Legislation (see also: Domestic Partnership; Equal Rights Amendment;
Foster Care; Immigration; Legal Issues)

CAD. "Gay Picture Gaier Than Usual" (civil rights legislation around the
U.S.). *off our backs* 9:3 (March 1979):8.

FE. "Gay Rights Bills Around the Country" (U.S.). *off our backs* 20:3
(March 1990):17.

"Gay Rights Bills" (news from various states). *off our backs* 17:5 (May
1987):13.

"News From the States." *off our backs* 13:7 (July 1983):16.

Parker, Jan. "Lesbians -- Laying Down the Law" (how present laws
affect lesbians; why lesbian/gay rights legislation is important
for everyone). *Spare Rib* (Great Britain) 175 (February 1987):15-
19.

"State Gay Rights Bills Fail." *off our backs* 13:6 (June 1983):15.

"State Legislatures Consider Gay Rights." *off our backs* 17:6 (June
1987):1.

California:
CAD. "Civil Rights Win, Lose" (win in Wisconsin; lose in Palo
Alto, California and Austin, Texas). *off our backs* 11:11
(December 1981):9.

------. "Lesbian Slides" (slide show on the campaign against the Briggs Initiative, which would prohibit gay teachers in California). *off our backs* 9:3 (March 1979):8.

Quinn, Liz. "Gay Rights Victories" (Washington, D.C., Boulder, Colorado, and San Anselmo, California). *off our backs* 18:1 (January 1988):8.

Sorrel, Lorraine. "Voters Overturn Gay Rights" (failure of domestic partners legislation on 1989 ballot in San Francisco, overturning law approved by the City Council). *off our backs* 19:11 (December 1989):7.

Canada:
CAD. "Canadian Law Changes." *off our backs* 9:4 (April 1979):11.

Khayatt, Didi. "Legalized Invisibility: the Effect of Bill 7 on Lesbian Teachers" (prohibits discrimination based on sexual orientation). *Women's Studies International Forum* 13:3 (1990):185-93.

"Recognizing Gay Rights." *off our backs,* 20:2 (February 1990):7.

Colorado:
Quinn, Liz. "Gay Rights Victories" (Washington, D.C., Boulder, Colorado, and San Anselmo, California). *off our backs* 18:1 (January 1988):8.

Florida:
CAD. "Dade Replay" (ballot initiative for lesbian and gay rights in Dade County, where voters had already opted to discriminate against lesbians and gays). *off our backs* 8:10 (November 1978):6.

Great Britain:
Farraday, Annabel. "Lesbian Outlaws: Past Attempts to Legislate Against Lesbians" (historical context of Clause 28). *Trouble & Strife* (Great Britain) 13 (Spring 1988):9-16.

Henry, Alice. "New British Law Against Lesbians and Gays" (Clause 28). *off our backs* 18:3 (March 1988):5.

Roelofs, Sarah. "The Rights We Lost" (Clause 28). *Spare Rib* (Great Britain) 197 (December 1988/January 1989):7.

Illinois:

CAD. "Gay . . . Antichrists" (news briefs; city council removes sexual orientation from human rights ordinance in Duluth, Minnesota; lesbian/gay rights bills pending in Illinois and Baltimore, Maryland). *off our backs* 10:5 (May 1980):9.

Ireland:

"Ireland: Gay Sex Legal." *off our backs* 20:9 (October 1990):7.

Iowa:

"Gay Rights Bills in State Senates" (anti-discrimination legislation passes in state houses in Iowa and Massachusetts). *off our backs* 19:6 (June 1989):7.

Kansas:

MNM. "Get It in Righting" (news briefs about activism on behalf of lesbian and gay rights bills in New York City, Wichita, Kansas, Boston, Massachusetts, and Woodstock, New York). *off our backs* 8:5 (May 1978):17.

Maryland:

"Baltimore Victory." *off our backs* 18:8 (August-September 1988):5.

CAD. "Gay . . . Antichrists" (news briefs; city council removes sexual orientation from human rights ordinance in Duluth, Minnesota; lesbian/gay rights bills pending in Illinois and Baltimore, Maryland). *off our backs* 10:5 (May 1980):9.

Massachusetts:

Bennett, Linda. "Gay Rights Law Survives Challenge." *off our backs* 20:1 (January 1990):5.

MNM. "Get It in Righting" (news briefs about activism on behalf of lesbian and gay rights bills in New York City, Wichita, Kansas, Boston, Massachusetts, and Woodstock, New York). *off our backs* 8:5 (May 1978):17.

"Gay Civil Rights Bill Victory." *Sojourner* 15:3 (November 1989):29.

"Gay Rights Bills in State Senates" (anti-discrimination legislation passes in state houses in Iowa and Massachusetts). *off our backs* 19:6 (June 1989):7.

"Mass -- Rights Law Stands" (Supreme Judicial Court rules referendum to overturn lesbian and gay rights law is unconstitutional). *off our backs* 20:8 (August/September 1990):6.

Sorrel, Lorraine. "Massachusetts Gay Victory." *off our backs* 19:11 (December 1989):7.

Thomas, June. "MA Bill Stalled." *off our backs* 18:1 (January 1988):8.

Michigan:
"Michigan Sodomy Law Challenged" (in Circuit Court, and is struck down). *off our backs* 20:9 (October 1990):4.

Minnesota:
CAD. "Gay . . . Antichrists" (news briefs; city council removes sexual orientation from human rights ordinance in Duluth, Minnesota; lesbian/gay rights bills pending in Illinois and Baltimore, Maryland). *off our backs* 10:5 (May 1980):9.

New York:
"Gay Rights Bill Fails." *off our backs* 13:7 (July 1983):16.

KM. "Controversy in New York" (City Council committee passes gay rights bill). *off our backs* 16:4 (April 1986):9.

MNM. "Get It in Righting" (news briefs about activism on behalf of lesbian and gay rights bills in New York City, Wichita, Kansas, Boston, Massachusetts, and Woodstock, New York). *off our backs* 8:5 (May 1978):17.

North Carolina:
Bennett, Linda. "Greensboro Quits Discriminating" (against lesbians and gay men in the work place). *off our backs* 20:1 (January 1990):6.

Oregon:
Ratterman, Debbie. "Gay Rights Order" (state employment anti-discrimination law). *off our backs* 17:10 (November 1987):3.

Rhode Island:
"RI -- Near Win for Gays." *off our backs* 20:8 (August/September 1990):6.

Texas:
CAD. "Civil Rights Win, Lose" (win in Wisconsin; lose in Palo Alto, California and Austin, Texas). *off our backs* 11:11 (December 1981):9.

United States (Federal):
AM. "Anti-Gay Violence Bill" (introduction of the Hate Crimes Statistics Act in the U.S. House of Representatives). *off our backs* 17:10 (November 1987):3; note: cover reads 17:9.

"Congress Undermines Gay Rights" (Armstrong amendment exempting religious groups from anti-discrimination laws). *off our backs* 18:10 (November 1988):7.

DAR. "Hate Crimes Bill" (U.S. House of Representatives passes bill requiring Department of Justice to keep statistics, including cases involving anti-gay violence.) *off our backs* 18:8 (August-September 1988):5.

------. "Senate Threatens DC" (Armstrong bill would cut federal funding to the District of Columbia if D.C. wouldn't allow religious groups exemption from anti-discrimination laws). *off our backs* 18:8 (August-September 1988):5.

Maguire, Amanda. "Anti-Gay Violence Bill" (introduction of the Hate Crimes Statistics Act in the U.S. House of Representatives). *off our backs* 17:10 (May 1987):3.

Washington:
KM. "Fighting to Hold Gains in Washington State" (fighting to defeat initiative that would rescind state executive order banning discrimination based on sexual orientation). *off our backs* 16:4 (April 1986):9.

Washington, D.C.:
CAD. "D.C. -- Barry Listens" (mayor Marion Barry supports community efforts on behalf of African-American lesbians and gays, gay clinic, and enforcement of anti-discrimination laws). *off our backs* 9:3 (March 1979):8.

DAR. "Senate Threatens DC" (Armstrong bill would cut federal funding to the District of Columbia if D.C. wouldn't allow religious groups exemption from anti-discrimination laws). *off our backs* 18:8 (August-September 1988):5.

Quinn, Liz. "Gay Rights Victories" (Washington, D.C., Boulder, Colorado, and San Anselmo, California). *off our backs* 18:1 (January 1988):8.

Wisconsin:
CAD. "Civil Rights Win, Lose" (win in Wisconsin; lose in Palo Alto, California and Austin, Texas). *off our backs* 11:11 (December 1981):9.

Lesbian Studies (see also: Education: Lesbians in Academe/Lesbians
   in the Classroom; Education: Pedagogy and Curriculum)

Adams, Mary Louise. "Homosexuality, Which Homosexuality?":
   International Scientific Conference on Gay and Lesbian Studies --
   Amsterdam, December 15-18, 1987." *Resources for Feminist
   Research* (Canada) 17 (June 1988):57-9.

Adamson, Nancy. "Lesbian Issues in Women's Studies Courses."
   Resources for Feminist Research (Canada), "The Lesbian
   Issue/Etre Lesbienne" 12:1(March 1983):5-7.

Boxer, Marilyn J. "For and About Women: the Theory and Practice of
   Women's Studies in the United States." *Signs* 7:3 (Spring
   1982):661-95.

Branzburg, Judith V. "Private Lives in the Public Classroom." *Radical
   Teacher,* "Gay and Lesbian Studies" 24 (no date: c.1983):10-11.

Buhrke, R.A. "Female Student Perspectives on Training in Lesbian and
   Gay Issues." *Counseling Psychologist* 17:4 (1989):629-36.

Bulkin, Elly. "A Whole New Poetry Beginning Here: Teaching Lesbian
   Poetry." *College English* 40 (1979):874-88.

CAD. "Lesbian Plenary: Combatting Heterosexism" (at 10th annual
   National Women's Studies Association convention, University
   of Minnesota in Minneapolis, June 1988; panel members Beth
   Brant, Michelle Parkerson, Joan Nestle, Gloria Anzaldúa). *off
   our backs* 18:8 (August-September 1988):3+.

Castillo-Speed, Lillian. "Chicana Studies: a Selected List of Materials
   Since 1980" (including lesbian materials). *Frontiers,* "Las
   Chicanas" 11:1 (1990):66-84.

Criste, Charlotte. "Lesbian Research Projects" (lesbian sessions at first
   National Women's Studies Association conference, Kansas,
   1979). *Women's Studies Newsletter* 7:3 (1979):15.

Crowden, John J. "The Love That Dares Now Speak Its Name" (bibliography on sexuality, history, gender identity, gay liberation, research, psychotherapy, social attitudes). *Choice* 11 (April 1974):209-27.

Cruikshank, Margaret. "Lesbian Studies: Some Preliminary Notes." *Radical Teacher* 17 (November 1980):18-19.

------. "Looking Back on Lesbian Studies." *Frontiers,* (Special Tenth Anniversary Issue) "The Women's Studies Movement: a Decade Inside the Academy" 8:3 (1986):107-9.

Cruikshank, Margaret and Dan Allen. "Team Teaching Gay/Lesbian Studies." *Radical Teacher,* "Gay and Lesbian Studies" 24 (no date: c.1983):22-3.

Donald, Christine. "Pioneering Lesbian Studies" (Lesbian Studies 1988: a Cross Canada Exchange, Montréal, Quebec, November 1988). *Broadside* (Canada) 10:3 (December 1988-January 1989):3.

Donovan, Josephine. "Humanities: Women's Studies Scholarship: the Voice of the Mother." *Women's Annual* 5 (1984-85):43-58.

Duelli Klein, Renate. "Third National Women's Studies Conference, Bradford University, U.K., March 31-April 1, 1984" (includes reports on lesbian studies workshop and lesbian invisibility presentation). *Women's Studies International Forum* 7:3 (1984):i-iv.

Freedman, Estelle and John D'Emilio. "Problems Encountered in Writing the History of Sexuality: Sources, Theory and Interpretation." *Journal of Sex Research* 27:4 (November 1990):481-95.

Frye, Marilyn. "Assignment: NWSA -- Bloomington -- 1980: Speak on 'Lesbian Perspectives on Women's Studies.'" *Sinister Wisdom* 14 (Summer 1980):3-7.

------. "Do You Have to Be a Lesbian to Be a Feminist?" (speech delivered at the National Women's Studies Association Conference, Akron, Ohio, June 1990, about treating sexuality in women's studies courses). *off our backs* 20:8 (August/September 1990):21-3.

Garber, Linda. "Lesbian Studies: Still Coming Out." *The Women's Review of Books* 6:5 (February 1989):17-18.

Gross, Michael. "The Science of 'Strange Females': a Course on Hormones and Homosexuality." *Women's Studies Quarterly* 12 (Winter 1984):6-10.

Heller, Scott. "Gay- and Lesbian-Studies Movement Gains Acceptance in Many Areas of Scholarship and Teaching." *Chronicle of Higher Education* 37:8 (October 24, 1990):A4.

Hunnisett, Rowena J. "Developing Phenomenological Methods for Researching Lesbian Existence." *Canadian Journal of Counseling* (Canada) 20:4 (October 1986):255-68.

Keener, K.M. "Out of the Archives and Into the Academy: Opportunities for Research and Publication in Lesbian Literature." *College English* 44:3 (March 1982):301-13.

Lenskyj, Helen. "On the Treatment of the Sexualities in Research." *Resources for Feminist Research* (Canada), "Confronting Heterosexuality/Confronter l'hétérosexualité" 19:3&4 (September/December 1990):90-3.

"Lesbian Scholar Honored" (with tenured professorship at the University of Utrecht, by Dutch Queen Beatrix). *off our backs* 19:1 (January 1989):7; note: cover reads vol.18, no.11 (December 1988).

McClave, Heather. "Scholarship and the Humanities." *Women's Annual* 3 (1982-3):205-29.

McNaron, Toni. "Finding and Studying Lesbian Culture." *Women's Studies Newsletter* 5:4 (Fall 1977):18-20.

Miller, Patricia McClelland. "The Individual Life" (issues and strategies for lesbian biography). *Frontiers,* "Lesbian History" 4:3 (Fall 1979):70-4.

Moraga, Cherríe and Barbara Smith. "Lesbian Literature: a Third World Perspective." *Radical Teacher,* "Gay and Lesbian Studies" 24 (no date; c.1983):12-14.

Polikoff, Nancy. "Lesbian Studies Flourish at National Women's Studies Conference." *off our backs* 10:7 (July 1980):16-19.

Quinn, Liz. "Gay Studies Program" (first conference of the Yale University Lesbian and Gay Studies Center, October 1988). *off our backs* 18:1 (January 1988):8.

Radical Teacher, "Gay and Lesbian Studies," no. 24, no date: c.1983.

Roscoe, Will. "Making History: The Challenge of Gay and Lesbian Studies." *Journal of Homosexuality* 15:3/4 (1988):1-40.

Rosier, Pat. "Lesbian Issues in Women's Studies." *Women's Studies Journal* 1 (April 1985):45-60.

Sang, Barbara E. "New Directions in Lesbian Research, Theory, and Education." *Journal of Counseling and Development,* "Gay, Lesbian, and Bisexual Issues in Counseling" 68:1 (September-October 1989):92-6.

"Selections from the Symposia on Lesbian and Gay Studies in the Academy, Whitney Humanities Center, October 30-31, 1987 and October 28-30, 1988" (Yale University). *Yale Journal of Criticism* 3:1 (Fall 1989):187-260.

Stern, Simon. "Lesbian and Gay Studies: a Selective Bibliography." *Yale Journal of Criticism* 3:1 (Fall 1989):253-60.

Thomas, Becky. "Teaching About Lesbians in Women's Studies Introductory Classes." *Feminisms* 3:3 (May/June 1990):6.

Wine, Jeri. "Lesbian Academics in Canada." *Resources for Feminist Research* (Canada), "The Lesbian Issue/Etre Lesbienne" 12:1 (March 1983):9-11.

Zimmerman, Bonnie. "Lesbianism 101." *Radical Teacher* 17 (November 1980):20-4.

Lesbians and the Right (see also: Censorship; Homophobia/Heterosexism; Political Organizing; Political Protest; Political Theory; Religion)

CAD. "Dr. Strange Love" (news briefs about anti-lesbian/gay discrimination in U.S. and Great Britain). *off our backs* 8:3 (March 1978):10.

------. "Gay . . . Antichrists" (fundamentalist anti-gay activism). *off our backs* 10:5 (May 1980):9.

Dworkin, Andrea. "Antifeminism." *Trivia* 2 (Spring 1983):6-35.

Glazer, Shelley. "Fight the Right" (speech at Fight the Right Festival, Toronto, Ontario, Canada, May 1982). *Broadside* (Canada) 3:8 (1982):7.

JK. "Roar on the Right" ("Family Day Rally" held by right-wing, anti-ERA groups, simultaneous with the National Women's Conference in Houston, Texas, November 1977). *off our backs* 8:1 (January 1978):3.

Lesbians Against the Right. "Dykes in the Streets -- a March for Power, Pride and Visibility." *Broadside* (Canada) 3:1 (1981):6.

Marston, Brenda. "1 Nation Under God, Inc." (two-day fundamentalist demonstration in Washington D.C. sponsored by Washington for Jesus). *off our backs* 10:6 (June 1980):9.

Meredith, Diana and Ellen Wexler. "Lesbians and the Right." *Resources for Feminist Research* (Canada), "The Lesbian Issue/Etre Lesbienne" 12:1 (March 1983):63-5.

Steele, Lisa. "Fighting the Right" (interview with two lesbian activists from Vancouver, British Columbia, Canada). *Fuse* (Canada) 5:6/7 (August/September 1981):211-15.

Weir, Lorna. "Lesbians Against the Right" (Lesbians Against the Right Day, Toronto, Ontario, Canada, May 1981). *Broadside* (Canada) 2:8 (June 1981):9.

Weir, Lorna and Brenda Steiger. "Coming Together in a Hot Gym" (Lesbians Against the Right, Toronto, Ontario, Canada). *Broadside* (Canada) 2:10 (August/September 1981):7.

Briggs Initiative (failed initiative that would have prohibited lesbian and gay school teachers in California):
David, Pam and Lois Helmbold. "San Francisco: Courts and Cops Against Gays" (written by two women in the movement against the Briggs Initiative, members of Lesbians Against Police Violence). *Radical America* 13:4 (July-August 1979):27-33.

Douglas, Carol Anne. "Gays Battle Briggotry" (Briggs anti-gay teacher initiative in California). *off our backs* 8:8 (August-September 1978):7.

Ward, Michael and Mark Freeman. "Defending Gay Rights: the Campaign Against the Briggs Amendment in California." *Radical America* 13:4 (July-August 1979):11-26.

Bryant, Anita (entertainer and anti-gay activist):
Graff, Holly. "Anita's Closet Isn't Big Enough! -- Gay and Lesbian Rights: a Socialist Feminist Perspective." *Women: a Journal of Liberation,* "Women Loving Women" 5:2 (1977):58-9.

Douglas, Carol Anne. "In the Wake of Dade . . . " (Anita Bryant and lesbian/gay liberation). *off our backs* 7:8 (August-September 1977):3.

Fischli, Ronald. "Anita Bryant's Stand Against 'Militant Homosexuality': Religious Fundamentalism and the Democratic Process." *Central States Speech Journal* 30 (August 1979): 262-71.

McGraw, James R. "Anita and the Gays." *Christianity and Crisis* 37:11 (June 27, 1977):147-9.

Narot, Ruth and Rosemary Bramble. "Anita's Closet Isn't Big Enough!: Lesbian Community Center Speech" (Baltimore, Maryland). *Women: a Journal of Liberation,* "Women Loving Women" 5:2 (1977):58.

Rein, Marcy and Wendy Stevens. "Even Our Closets Won't Be Safe" (links between Anita Bryant's Save Our Children Campaign in Florida and Phyllis Schlafly's "Stop-ERA"). *off our backs* 7:6 (July/August 1977):5.

"Sunkist Marriage Goes Sour." *Broadside* (Canada) 1:9 (1979):9.

Van Gelder, Lindsy. "Anita Bryant on the March: the Lessons of Dade County." *Ms.* 6:3 (September 1977):75-8+.

Lesbians Around the World (see also: Immigration; International Lesbian-Feminism)

Connexions: an International Women's Quarterly, "Global Lesbianism," no. 3, January 1982.

------, "Global Lesbianism 2," no. 10, Fall 1983.

------, "Lesbian Activism," no. 29, 1989.

Africa (see also: African-American Lesbians; Middle East):
Douglas, Elaine. "On Being a Lesbian in East Africa." *Visibilities* 3:6 (November/December 1989):10-13.

Johnson, A. "Inside Gay Africa." *Black/Out* 1:2 (Fall 1986):1.

Krige, Eileen Jensen. "Woman-Marriage, with Special Reference to the Lovendu -- Its Significance for the Definition of Marriage." *Africa* 44:1 (1974):11-37.

Lahzem. "Rainbow Solidarity" (group of North African lesbians and gays living in France, formed in Paris in Fall 1982). *Connexions,* "Global Lesbianism 2" 10 (Fall 1983):4.

Obbo, Christine. "Dominant Male Ideology and Female Options: Three East African Case Studies" (woman-marriage). *Africa* 46:4 (1976):371-89.

Algeria:
Badra. "An Authentic Identity." *Connexions,* "Global Lesbianism 2" 10 (Fall 1983):3-4.

Egypt (see Middle East)

Kenya:
Gevins, Adi. "To See Them in Person!" (interview with Kenyan woman distributing family planning information at the international women's conference in Nairobi, about lesbians at the conference). *Connexions,* "Forum '85: Nairobi, Kenya" 17-18 (Summer/Fall 1985):17.

Konek, Carol Wolfe. "Dangerous Discussions" (lesbians not permitted to display literature, and lesbianism banned as discussion topic at forums but discussed anyhow, at the United Nations Women's Decade Forum and Conference in Nairobi, Kenya, 1987). *Heresies* 25 (1990):83+.

<u>Lesotho:</u>

Gay, Judith. "'Mummies and Babies' and Friends and Lovers in Lesotho." *Journal of Homosexuality,* "Anthropology and Homosexual Behavior" 11:3/4 (Summer 1985):97-116.

Mueller, Martha and Linda Hopkins. "Momma-Baby Relationships: Female Bonding in Lesotho." *Women's Studies International Quarterly* (Great Britain), "Cross-Cultural Perspectives on Women" 2:4 (1978):439-48.

<u>Mozambique:</u>

Stanford, Liz. "Lesbians Seek Exile" (from Pakistan, Mozambique, Spain, Nicaragua, and Cuba). *off our backs* 10:5 (May 1980):6.

<u>South Africa:</u>

Douglas, Carol Anne. "ILGA Suspends South African Gay Group" (International Lesbian and Gay Association, on charges by predominantly black South African gay group that the Gay Association of South Africa (GASA) collaborates with the South African Government). *off our backs* 18:1 (January 1988):3.

Duckitt, John H. and Laetitia du Toit. "Personality Profiles of Homosexual Men and Women" (in South Africa). *The Journal of Psychology* 123:5 (September 1989):497-505.

"South Africa" (from "Black Gays and Lesbians in South Africa" in Canadian monthly *Rites* (October 1987)). *Connexions,* "Lesbian Activism" 29 (1989):15.

"South Africa and Lesotho: Three Lesbian Conversations" (interviews with two black and three white lesbians). *Connexions,* "Global Lesbianism" 3 (January 1982):22-4.

Stato, Joanne. "I Am Your Sister Celeconference: Tribute to Audre Lorde" (Boston, Massachusetts, October 1990). *off our backs* 20:11 (December 1990):1-5+.

Sudan:

Salomyn, Shay. "Black Women in Sudan" (interview with Zeinab Eyega, Sudanese feminist living in exile). *off our backs* 20:3 (March 1990):8.

Australia and New Zealand:

Allen, Susanna. "Bisexuality: the Best of Both Worlds." *Spare Rib* (Great Britain) 10 (April 1973):25-6.

"Australia: Gay Immigration Curb." *off our backs* 20:4 (April 1990):6.

"Australia: 'Serious' Gays OK" (non-Australian couples together more than four years allowed to stay in Australia). *off our backs* 17:3 (March 1987):9.

Buhrich, Neil and Carlson Loke. "Homosexuality, Suicide, and Parasuicide in Australia." *Journal of Homosexuality,* "Psychopathology and Psychotherapy in Homosexuality" 15:1/2 (1988):113-30.

CAD. "Australian State Bans Discriminations vs. Gays" (New South Wales). *off our backs* 13:2 (February 1983):12.

Dominy, Michèle D. "Lesbian-Feminist Gender Conceptions: Separatism in Christchurch, New Zealand." *Signs* 11:2 (Winter 1986):274-89.

Ferrier, Carole. "Interview with Pearlie McNeill" (Australian author living in London, England). *Hecate* (Australia) 16:1/2 (1990):102-10.

Goodman, Ellen. "Homosexuality of a Parent: a New Issue in Custody Disputes" (Australia). *Monash University Law Review* (Australia) 5 (1979):305+.

Hammer, Barbara. "Into a Woman's World" (interview with Chinese Malay who moved to Australia at age 17). *Connexions,* "Global Lesbianism 2" 10 (Fall 1983):19.

Harper, Jorjet. "The Women's Action/Adventure Film: 'Shame' (about a gang rape in a small town in Western Australia). *Hot Wire* 5:2 (May 1989):24-5.

Harrison, Kate. "Child Custody and Parental Sexuality: Just Another Factor?" *Refractory Girl* (Australia), "Feminists and Kids" 20-21 (October 1980):7-14.

Kallenberg, Tracy. "Where Is the Justice?" (letter from lesbian imprisoned for murder, regarding judicial and prison systems, and lesbians in prison). *Connexions*, "Women Inside and Out" 14 (Fall 1984):29.

"Mythmaking in the Women's Movement" (the lesbian/heterosexual split). *Refractory Girl* (Australia), "Lesbian Issue" 5 (Summer 1974):34-8.

"New Zealand: an Island of Many Cultures." *Connexions*, "Global Lesbianism" 3 (January 1982):25.

"Out in the Outback" (Edward de Lacy Evans, passing woman in Australia for 20 years and through three marriages with women; discovered in 1879). *Connexions*, "Global Lesbianism 2" 10 (Fall 1983):20.

Poggi, Stephanie, Jennifer Abod, Jacqui Alexander, and Evelynn Hammonds. "Claiming My Mothers, Exposing Aboriginal Consciousness to the World: an Interview with Aboriginal, Black Lesbian Playwright Eva Johnson." *Black/Out*, "We Are Family" 2:2 (Summer 1989):48-53.

Refractory Girl (Australia), "Lesbian Issue" (includes extensive bibliography of pre-1970s fiction/nonfiction books and artwork), no. 5, Summer 1974.

Singerman, Deborah. "Australia: Gay & Lesbian Immigration Task Force." *off our backs* 19:7 (July 1989):12.

------. "Australia: Lesbian Discrimination Fought" (by New South Wales Anti-Discrimination Board and its report "What Is Lesbian Discrimination?"). *off our backs* 20:7 (July 1990):9.

Smith, Jean. "Writing *Relatively Norma*" (interview with author Anna Livia). *Spare Rib* (Great Britain) 130 (May 1983):25.

Steffensen, Jyanni. "Things Change . . . And About Time Too: a Critical Review of Women's Erotic Writing." *Hecate* (Australia) 15:2 (1989):26-33.

Summers, Anne. "Marion/Bill Edwards" (passing woman who married a woman, born 1881). *Refractory Girl* (Australia), "Lesbian Issue" 5 (Summer 1974):21-2.

Thomas, June. "Anna Livia: Lesbian Author, Publisher." *off our backs* 18:11 (December 1988):10+.

------. "Commonwealth Censorship of Gay Books" (England, New Zealand, Canada). *off our backs* 16:2 (February 1986):5.

"Uma" (excerpt of interview with New Zealander of Indian descent). *Connexions*, "Global Lesbianism 2" 10 (Fall 1983):5-7.

Viano, Emilio. "Maintaining Respectability: Life Styles of Gay Women in an Urban Environment." *Australian and New Zealand Journal of Criminology* 8 (September-December 1975):275+.

Wakeling, Louise Katherine, Margaret Bradstock, and Mary Fallon. "Poetry Doesn't Sell." *Connexions*, "Women's Words" 13 (Summer 1984):26-7.

"'Your Mum's a Lessy-bin!'" (Lesbian Mothers', Lovers', and Children's Weekend, New Zealand, April 1983; from *bitches, witches, and dykes,* New Zealand lesbian feminist quarterly, June 1982). *Connexions*, "Global Lesbianism 2" 10 (Fall 1983):12-13.

Canada:

"Aimez-vous les Hommes?" (translation of editorial on heterosexism from *La Vie en Rose,* Montreal feminist journal). *Broadside* (Canada) 4:2 (1982):14.

Amana, Rue. "Becoming a 'Real' Dyke: Employment and Housing" (moving out of cities as the lesbian dream; returning to cities to work with People With AIDS). *Canadian Woman Studies* (Canada), "Women & Housing" 11:2 (Fall 1990):43+.

Amazones d'hier, Lesbiennes d'aujourd'hui. "Radical Lesbianism" (excerpt included in "A Readers' Forum -- Separatism: Beyond the Debate"). *Lesbian Ethics* 3:2 (Fall 1988):17-20.

Andersen, Marguerite. "Nicole Brossard: un Imaginaire Tonique" (Québécois writer). *Resources for Feminist Research* (Canada) 15 (December 1986/January 1987):22-4.

Archer, Koré. "This Great Drama" (Ellen Craft, escaped slave from Georgia, and Sarah Edmonds, Canadian passing woman who spied for the Union Army). *Sinister Wisdom,* "Passing" 35 (Summer/Fall 1988):86-94.

Armatage, Kay. "Feminist Film-Making: Theory and Practice" (director discusses her two films, "Jill Johnston October 1975" and "Gertrude and Alice in Passing"). *Canadian Woman Studies* (Canada) 1:3 (Spring 1979):49-50.

Armstrong, Toni Jr. "A Taste of the Canadian Prairies: Heather Bishop" (musician). *Hot Wire* 6:2 (May 1990):2-4+.

Armstrong, Toni L. "Lucie Blue Tremblay" (musician). *Hot Wire* 3:1 (November 1986):2-5.

Arnup, Katherine. "'Mothers Just Like Others': Lesbians, Divorce and Child Custody in Canada." *Canadian Journal of Women and the Law* (Canada) 3:1 (1989):18-32.

"At Least They Have a Mutual Enemy" (basic article debunking some myths about lesbians and about LOOT, Lesbian Organization of Toronto; part of group of short articles on "A Decade of Gay Liberation"). *Saturday Night* (Canada) 94:2 (March 1979):4.

Bearchell, Chris. "Bar-Hopping" (history of lesbian bars in Toronto, Ontario). *Body Politic* (Canada) 77 (October 1981):25-7.

Bell, Gay. "Where Nest the Wet Hens: Interviews of Michelle Rossignol and Jovette Marchessault" (director and playwright of "The Saga of the Wet Hens"). *Broadside* (Canada) 3:4 (1982):12-13.

Bertrand, Luce. "L'Homosexualité N'est Pas Une Maladie . . . Elle ne Peut Donc pas se Guérir" ("Homosexuality Is Not an Illness . . . It Therefore Cannot be Cured"). *Canadian Woman Studies* (Canada), "Sexuality and Symbol/Symbolisme et Sexualité" 3:2 (1981):57-8.

Biggs, Mary. "Career with Compromise" (writer Jane Rule). *Women's Review of Books* 2 (May 1985):13-15.

"*Body Politic* Acquitted" (Canadian gay newspaper acquitted of charges of "immorality"). *off our backs* 9:3 (March 1979):8.

Bolton, Elizabeth. "Double Takes and Mazel Tovs" (Jewish lesbian wedding). *Broadside* (Canada) 8 (January 1987):6.

Bourbonnais, Nicole. "Femme Métonymique, Femme Métaphorique: la Poésie d'Anne Hébert et de Renée Vivien." *Atlantis* (Canada) 11 (Spring 1986):108-14.

Brady, Maureen. "'A Vision of Central Value': the Novels of Jane Rule." *Resources for Feminist Research* (Canada), "The Lesbian Issue/Etre Lesbienne" 12:1(March 1983):13-16.

Brossard, Nicole. "Traversing Fiction." *Fireweed* (Canada) 1 (Autumn 1978):20-1.

------. "The Writer." *Fireweed* (Canada), "Women and Language" 5&6 (Winter 1979-80 and Spring 1980):106-17.

Brownstone, Harvey. "The Homosexual Parent in Custody Disputes" (U.S. and Canadian case law). *Queen's Law Journal* (Canada) 5 (1980):199+.

Brunet, Ariane and Louise Turcotte. "Separatism and Radicalism: an Analysis of the Differences and Similarities" (U.S.-American separatism and French Canadian radical lesbianism). *Lesbian Ethics* 2:1 (Spring 1986):41-9.

CAD. "Book Burning" (75 students at Bishop's University in Lenoxville, Québec, Canada, burn student services handbook because it includes a chapter on lesbians and gay men). *off our backs* 10:10 (November 1980):9.

------. "Canada: Lesbian Rights" (Conservative Party voices support for lesbian and gay rights). *off our backs* 16:4 (April 1986):13.

------. "Canadian Law Changes." *off our backs* 9:4 (April 1979):11.

------. "Gay . . . Intern" (news briefs; *The Body Politic* appeals ruling that it must face trial for transmitting indecent material through the mail; Alberta Human Rights Commission does not recommend adding sexual orientation to the Human Rights code). *off our backs* 10:5 (May 1980):9.

------. "Gay Under the Crown" (legal attempts to censor gay liberation journal *The Body Politic*). *off our backs* 10:4 (April 1980):15.

------. "Lesbian/Gay Trips, Cruises & Marches" (U.S. and international news briefs; gay liberation journal *The Body Politic*). *off our backs* 10:3 (March 1980):18-19+.

"Canada: I Will Not Be Shelved" (interview with librarian fighting for employee spousal benefits for her lover; case based on Canada's Bill 7; from Canadian monthly, *Rites* (March 1988)). *Connexions*, "Lesbian Activism" 29 (1989):18-20.

Canadian Fiction Magazine, Canada, on Jane Rule, no. 23, 1976.

Canadian Theatre Review, Canada, "Homosexuality and the Theatre" (not specifically about lesbians; written by gay men), no. 12, Fall 1976.

Canadian Woman Studies/Les Cahiers de la Femme, Canada, "Sexuality and Symbol/*Symbolisme et Sexualité,*" vol. 3, no. 2, 1981.

Chitty, Elizabeth. "You Can't Rock the Boat with Cold Fact" (feminist response to lesbian-feminist sexual imagery). *Fuse* (Canada) 4:2 (January 1980):117+.

Christianson, Joseph. "Closet Drama: the Sound and the Flurry Surrounding Winnipeg's International Festival of Gay and Lesbian Films." *Border Crossings* (Canada) 6 (Summer 1987):27-8.

Clarke, Caro. "Weighing In." *Gossip* (Great Britain) 6 (1988):56-67.

Coffey, Mary Anne. "Of Father Born: a Lesbian Feminist Critique of the Ontario Law Reform Commission Recommendations on Artificial Insemination." *Canadian Journal of Women and the Law* (Canada) 1:2 (1986):424-33.

Le Colectif: Amazones d'Hier, Lesbiennes d'Aujourd'hui. "Lesbianisme Radical." *Resources for Feminist Research* (Canada) 15 (December 1986/January 1987):5-7.

------, trans. Denise Blais. "Radical Lesbianism." *Gossip* (Great Britain) 4 (no date):21-6.

Collis, Rose. "Breaking the Rules" (interview with author Jane Rule). *Spare Rib* (Great Britain) 185 (December 1987):16-18.

Crozier, Alana. "The Canadian Criminal Justice System and Lesbianism: a Research Note on the Relationship Between Systematic Exclusion and Criminal Victimization." *Resources for Feminist Research* (Canada) 14 (December 1985-January 1986):18-19.

Dascher, Helge. "Mémoire, reconnaissance: Entrevue avec Michelle Desaulniers et Diane Trépanière" (video artists). *Canadian Woman Studies* (Canada), "Feminism and Visual Art/Le féminisme et l'art visuel" 11:1 (Spring 1990):75-7.

de Margo, Louise. "Reflections d'Une Lesbienniste, en Marge de Colloque des Périodiques Féministes Tenu a Orangeville, du 9 au 12 mai" (dangers of cooptation for feminists in receiving government or private foundation funding). *Canadian Woman Studies* (Canada), "Women and Media/Les Femmes et les Media" 8:1 (Spring 1987):65.

"Deacons Suspended" (lesbians in Anglican Church of Canada). *Christian Century* 103 (April 2, 1986):322.

Dibblin, Jane. "Suniti Interviewed . . . " (Suniti Namjoshi, Indian-Canadian author). *Spare Rib* (Great Britain) 147 (October 1984):20-2.

Dineen, Claire and Jackie Crawford. "Lesbian Mothering." *Fireweed* (Canada), "Lesbiantics" 28 (Spring 1989):24-35.

Donald, Christine. "Pioneering Lesbian Studies" (Lesbian Studies 1988: a Cross Canada Exchange, Montréal, Quebec, Canada, November 1988). *Broadside* (Canada) 10:3 (December 1988-January 1989):3.

Dufault, Roseanne L. "Louise Maheux-Forcier's *Amadou*: Reflections on Some Critical Blindspots." *Québec Studies* (Canada) 11 (1990-1991):103-10.

Durocher, Constance. "Heterosexuality: Sexuality or Social System?" (in English and French, "L'hétérosexualité: sexualité ou système social?"). *Resources for Feminist Research* (Canada), "Confronting Heterosexuality/Confronter l'hétérosexualité" 19:3&4 (September/December 1990):13-22.

Eaton, Mary and Cynthia Peterson. "Andrew v. Ontario (Minister of Health)" (Ontario, Canada High Court of Justice decides that lesbian partners are not spouses for purposes of the Ontario Health Insurance Plan). *Canadian Journal of Women and the Law* (Canada) 2:2 (1987-88):416-21.

Edwards, Val. "The Invisible Community -- Lesbians in Toronto." *Broadside* (Canada) 1:10 (1979):4-5.

Fireweed: a Feminist Quarterly, Canada, "Lesbiantics," no. 13, 1982.

"Gay Canada" (New Democratic Party passes resolution calling for anti-discrimination law to protect lesbians and gays). *off our backs* (February 1979):8.

Genge, Susan. "Sexual Orientation and Union Protection." *Resources for Feminist Research* (Canada), "Women and Trade Unions" 10:2 (July 1981):28-9.

Glazer, Shelley. "Fight the Right" (speech at Fight the Right Festival, Toronto, May 1982). *Broadside* (Canada) 3:8 (1982):7.

Godard, Barbara. "Nicole Brossard: *Amantes* and *La Mer.*" *Broadside* (Canada) 2:6 (April 1981):14.

Gould, Karen. "Setting Words Free: Feminist Writing in Quebec" (lesbian and straight; includes discussion of Nicole Brossard and Louky Bersianik). *Signs* 6:4 (Summer 1981):617-42.

Gross, Wendy L. "Judging the Best Interests of the Child: Child Custody and the Homosexual Parent." *Canadian Journal of Women and the Law* (Canada) 1:2 (1986):505-31.

Hancock, Geoff. "An Interview with Jane Rule" (writer). *Canadian Fiction Magazine* (Canada) 23 (1976):57-112.

"Heterosexism and the Lesbian Experience." *Broadside* (Canada) 4:9 (July 1983):5.

Hollerith, J.P. "Reading, Raging and Writing: Some Thoughts on Speculative Fiction and Radical Feminism." *Gossip* (Great Britain) 4 (no date):51-8.

Israelstam, S. "Knowledge and Opinions of Alcohol Intervention Workers in Ontario, Canada, Regarding Issues Affecting Male Gays and Lesbians." *International Journal of the Addictions* 23:3 (1988):227-52.

Khayatt, Didi. "Legalized Invisibility: the Effect of Bill 7 on Lesbian Teachers" (prohibits discrimination based on sexual orientation in Canada). *Women's Studies International Forum* 13:3 (1990):185-93.

------. "Personal Politics and Sexuality" (by Egyptian-Canadian lesbian). *Resources for Feminist Research* (Canada), "Confronting Heterosexuality/Confronter l'hétérosexualité" 19:3&4 (September/December 1990):8-12.

Kuhns, Connie. "Live! From Canada: Canada's Own Heather Bishop" (musician). *Hot Wire* 4:1 (November 1987):48-9.

------. "Live! From Canada: Canadian Women's Music Festivals" (a brief history and overview). *Hot Wire* 5:2 (May 1989):48-51.

Lenskyj, Helen. "Beyond Plumbing and Prevention: Feminist Approaches to Sex Education." *Gender and Education* 2:2 (1990):217-30.

Leopold, Margaret and Wendy King. "Compulsory Heterosexuality, Lesbians and the Law: the Case for Constitutional Protection." *Canadian Journal of Women and the Law* (Canada) 1:1 (1985):163-86.

"Lesbian Rabbi Resigns" (Rabbi Deborah Brin of Downsview, Ontario, after coming out and feeling "oppressive" working environment develop). *off our backs* 20:10 (November 1990):9.

"Lesbian Thespians: Gay Sweatshop." *Broadside* (Canada) 7 (December 1985/January 1986):13.

Lesbians Against the Right. "Dykes in the Streets -- a March for Power, Pride and Visibility." *Broadside* (Canada) 3:1 (1981):6.

The Lesbians Making History Collective. "People Think This Can't Happen in Canada." *Fireweed* (Canada), "Lesbiantics" 28 (Spring 1989):81-6.

"Lesbians of Colour: Loving and Struggling -- a Conversation Between Three Lesbians of Colour." *Fireweed* (Canada), "Women of Colour" 16 (Spring 1983):66-72.

MacDonald, Ingrid. "Customary Bias: Canada Customs Is Preventing Positive Images of Lesbian Sex." *Broadside* (Canada) 8 (July 1987):4.

MacNaughton, C. "Who Gets the Kids?" *Body Politic* (Canada) 34 (1977):12+.

Meigs, Mary. "Lesbians in the Visual Arts." *Resources for Feminist Research* (Canada), "The Lesbian Issue/Etre Lesbienne" 12:1 (March 1983):28-30.

------. "Lily Briscoe: a Self-Portrait" (excerpt from artist's memoirs, of the same title). *Broadside* (Canada) 10 (Spring 1981):31-45.

------. "Lily Briscoe: a Self Portrait -- an excerpt from the memoirs of Mary Meigs." *Fireweed* (Canada), "Writing" 10 (Spring 1981):31-45.

------. "Mary Meigs: a Self-Portrait" (excerpt from *Lily Briscoe: a Self-Portrait*). *Broadside* (Canada) 3:1 (1981):10-11.

Meredith, Diana. "Lesbians and Abortion." *Broadside* (Canada) 4:2 (1982):7.

Middleton, Kate. "Custody Battles -- Not Child's Play." *Broadside* (Canada) 1:6 (1979):8.

Mintz, Chavah. "Persimmon Bladebridge" (interview with sculptor). *Fireweed* (Canada), "Lesbiantics" 13 (1982):135-40.

Oikawa, Mona. "Safer Sex in Santa Cruz" (workshop at the First National Asian/Pacifica Lesbian Network Retreat, Santa Cruz, California, 1989). *Fireweed* (Canada), "Awakening Thunder: Asian Canadian Women" 30 (February 1990):31-4.

------. "Some Thoughts on Being a Sansei Lesbian Feminist." *Fireweed* (Canada) "Lesbiantics" 28 (Spring 1989):95-104.

"Queer Bashing" (charges of obscenity made against Canadian gay/lesbian newspaper *The Body Politic*). *Broadside* (Canada) 3:8 (1982):2.

"Recognizing Gay Rights" (in Canada). *off our backs*, 20:2 (February 1990):7.

RFR/DRF -- Resources for Feminist Research/Documentation sur le Recherche Féministe (cited throughout as *Resources for Feminist Research*), Canada, "The Lesbian Issue/Etre Lesbienne," vol. 12, no. 1, March/mars 1983.

Rooke, Patricia T. "Public Figure, Private Woman: Same Sex Support Structures in the Life of Charlotte Whitton" (social worker and civic politician). *International Journal of Women's Studies* 6:5 (November-December 1983):412-28.

Rooney, F. "Interview: Persimmon" (Bladebridge, sculptor)." *Resources for Feminist Research* (Canada) 13:4 (1984):30-2.

Ross, Becki. "Heterosexuals Only Need Apply: the Secretary of State's Regulation of Lesbian Existence." *Resources for Feminist Research* (Canada), "Feminist Perspectives on the Canadian State/Perspectives Féministes sur l'État Canadien" 17:3 (September 1988):35-8.

------. "The House that Jill Built: Lesbian Feminist Organizing in Toronto, 1976-1980" (Ontario). *Feminist Review* (Great Britain) 35 (Summer 1990):75-91.

------. "Identity, Community and Lesbianism." *Resources for Feminist Research* (Canada), "Confronting Heterosexuality/Confronter l'hétérosexualité" 19:3&4 (September/December 1990):3-4.

------. "Launching Lesbian Cultural Offensives" (a response to interception of lesbian books by Canadian customs officials). *Resources for Feminist Research* (Canada) 17:2 (June 1988):12-15.

Rule, Jane. "Making the Real Visible: Lesbian and Writer." *Fireweed* (Canada), "Lesbiantics" 13 (1982):101-4.

Rumscheidt, Barbara. "Institutionalizing Christian Heterosexism in Maritime Conference of the United Church of Canada." *Resources for Feminist Research* (Canada), "Confronting Heterosexuality/Confronter l'hétérosexualité" 19:3&4 (September/December 1990):75-80.

Ryder, Bruce. "Equality Rights and Sexual Orientation: Confronting Heterosexual Family Privilege." *Canadian Journal of Family Law* (Canada) 9:1 (Fall 1990):39-97.

Sagmeister, Nancy. "In Sickness and in Health: Spousal Benefits for Gays and Lesbians." *Our Times* (Canada) 6 (September 1987):33-4.

Sand, Cy-Thea. "Readers as Rebels: the Story of the Vancouver Lesbian Literary Collective." *Radical Reviewer* 4 (Fall 1981):6-7.

Schneider, Margaret. "Sappho Was a Right-On Adolescent: Growing Up Lesbian" (study of 25 lesbians, age 15-20; many are members of Lesbian and Gay Youth Toronto). *Journal of Homosexuality*, "Gay and Lesbian Youth: Part I" 17:1/2 (1989):111-30.

Schuster, Marilyn R. "Strategies for Survival: The Subtle Subversion of Jane Rule" (writer). *Feminist Studies* 7 (Fall 1981):431-50.

Sequin, Lucie. "Nicole Brossard: Les Mots-étreintes" (writer). *Canadian Woman Studies* (Canada) 1:3 (Spring 1979):56-9.

Smith, Connie. "Canadian Viewpoint: Heather Bishop Interviewed" (about U.S. Immigration and Naturalization Service visa discrimination against women's music performers). *Hot Wire* 3:2 (March 1987):21-2.

Sonthoff, Helen. "Celebration: Jane Rule's Fiction." *Canadian Fiction Magazine* (Canada) 23 (1976):121-33.

Spires, Randy. "The 1986 International Gay Film Festival." *Canadian Woman Studies* (Canada), "Women and Media/Les Femmes et les Media" 8:1 (Spring 1987):90-1.

Springer, Judy. "Goddesses Unite: the Making of a Mural." *Canadian Woman Studies* (Canada), "Feminism & Visual Art/Le féminisme et l'art visuel" 11:1 (Spring 1990):97-8.

Steele, Lisa. "Fighting the Right" (interview with two activists from Vancouver, British Columbia). *Fuse* (Canada) 5:6/7 (August/September 1981):211-15.

Tavormina, Patrizia. "International Summit for Women: Many Dimensions of Lesbians and Power" (Montréal, Québec, Canada, June 1990; meeting to prepare for the 1995 United Nations Conference). *off our backs* 20:8 (August/September 1990):24.

Thomas, June. "Commonwealth Censorship of Gay Books" (England, New Zealand, Canada). *off our backs* 16:2 (February 1986):5.

------. "Harassment by Customs" (lesbian and gay magazines and books from U.S. seized at Canadian border). *off our backs* 17:4 (April 1987):4.

------. "Harassment by INS" (U.S. Immigration and Naturalization Service; of women's music performers from Canada). *off our backs* 17:4 (April 1987):4.

Tremble, Bob, Margaret Schneider, and Carol Appathurai. "Growing Up Gay or Lesbian in a Multicultural Context" (study based on Toronto). *Journal of Homosexuality,* "Gay and Lesbian Youth: Part II" 17:3/4 (1989):253-68.

Valverde, Mariana. "Freedom's Just Another Word; On One Side, the Devil of Censorship; On the Other, a Deep Blue Sea of Free Trade: Canada's Bookworld Is Threatened by Dangers of Which We in Britain Should Take Note." *New Statesman* (Great Britain) 113 (June 26, 1987):25-6.

------. "Heterosexism: a Challenge to the Left." *Canadian Dimension* (Canada) 17:1 (March 1983):36-8.

"Voices from the Periphery: First-Generation Lesbian Fiction in Canada." *Resources for Feminist Research* (Canada), "The Lesbian Issue/Etre Lesbienne" 12:1 (March 1983):22-6.

Weir, Lorna. "Lesbians Against the Right" (Lesbians Against the Right Day, Toronto, May 1981). *Broadside* (Canada) 2:8 (June 1981):9.

------. "Tit for Tat: Coalition Politics." *Broadside* (Canada) 3:4 (1982):10-11.

Weir, Lorna and Brenda Steiger. "Coming Together in a Hot Gym" (Lesbians Against the Right, Toronto, Ontario). *Broadside* (Canada) 2:10 (August/September 1981):7.

Weir, Lorna and Eve Zaremba. "Boys and Girls Together: Feminism and Gay Liberation." *Broadside* (Canada) 4:1 (1982):6-7.

Wildeman, Marlene. "The Lesbian Feminist Literary Ethics of Nicole Brossard in *La Lettre Aérienne.*" *Gossip* (Great Britain) 6 (1988):44-55.

Williamson, Janice. "'Firewords' -- Dorothy Hénaut -- National Film Board, Studio D" (film about three radical feminist Québécois writers: Louky Bersianik, Nicole Brossard, Jovette Marchessault). *Resources for Feminist Research* (Canada) 15 (December 1986/January 1987):25-7.

Williamson, Judith. "In the Pink" (gay and lesbian films at London's Tyneside Festival, including *The Lesbian Vampire on Film, Underground Canada,* and *Novembermoon* about two lesbians in Nazi concentration camps). *New Statesman* (Great Britain) 114 (October 9, 1987):22-3.

Wilson, Jean. "Nicole Brossard: Fictions and Realities." *Broadside* (Canada) 3:7 (1982):20.

Wine, Jeri Dawn. "Lesbian Academics in Canada." *Resources for Feminist Research* (Canada), "The Lesbian Issue/Etre Lesbienne" 12:8-9 (March 1983):9-11.

------. "The Lesbian Continuum in Academe." *Resources for Feminist Research* (Canada) 16:4 (December 1987):27-9.

------. "National Lesbian Forum." *Broadside* (Canada) 9 (February 1988):5.

------. "On Prejudice and Possibility: Lesbians in Canadian Academe."
Atlantis (Canada) 14:1 (Fall 1988):45-55.

Winter, Bronwyn. "La 'communauté lesbienne' et l'idéologie
hétéropatriarcale: les pièges du libéralisme." *Resources for
Feminist Research* (Canada), "Confronting
Heterosexuality/Confronter l'hétérosexualité" 19:3&4
(September/December 1990):49-53.

East Asia (see also: Asian/Pacifica Lesbians):
China:

"China: A Well of Strength" (19th- and early 20th-century
sisterhoods of marriage resisters in Guangdong province; trans.
and excerpted from Chen Dongyuan, *A History of Chinese
Women's Lives* (Shanghai, 1937) and Xiaoming Xiong, *The
History of Homosexuality in China* (Hong Kong, 1984)).
Connexions, "Lesbian Activism" 29 (1989):29.

"China: Shocks for Gays" (homosexuality treated as a disease). *off
our backs* 20:4 (April 1990):6.

Hammer, Barbara. "Into a Woman's World" (interview with Chinese
Malay woman who moved to Australia at age 17). *Connexions*,
"Global Lesbianism 2" 10 (Fall 1983):19.

Hong Kong:

"China: A Well of Strength" (19th- and early 20th-century
sisterhoods of marriage resisters in Guangdong province; trans.
and excerpted from Chen Dongyuan, *A History of Chinese
Women's Lives* (Shangai, 1937) and Xiaoming Xiong, *The
History of Homosexuality in China* (Hong Kong, 1984)).
Connexions, "Lesbian Activism" 29 (1989):29.

Lieh-Mak, F., K.M. O'Hoy, and S.L. Luk. "Lesbianism in the
Chinese of Hong Kong." *Archives of Sexual Behavior* 12
(February 1983):21-30.

Norrgard, Lenore. "Opening the Hong Kong Closet" (interview with Choi Wan and Josephine, journalists and members of the Association for the Advancement of Feminism). *Out/Look #7,* 2:3 (Winter 1990):56-61.

Sankar, Andrea. "Sisters and Brothers, Lovers and Enemies: Marriage Resistance in Southern Kwangtung" (Hong Kong). *Journal of Homosexuality,* "Anthropology and Homosexual Behavior" 11:3/4 (Summer 1985):69-81.

Japan:

Bishop, Marla. "Japanese Lesbians" (first lesbian conference, November 1985). *Spare Rib* (Great Britain) 164 (March 1986):47.

James, Mary. "So Full of Longing" (interview with Japanese lesbian-feminist, living in the United States for two years). *Connexions,* "Global Lesbianism 2" 10 (Fall 1983):16-17.

"Japan -- Regumi: a New Spelling of Our Name" (interview with a lesbian activist). *Connexions,* "Lesbian Activism" 29 (1989):24-5.

"The Lavender Kimono." *Connexions,* "Global Lesbianism" 3 (January 1982):21; also excerpted in *off our backs* 12:3 (March 1982):6.

"Lesbian Poets" (Miamoto Yuriko, Hirazuka Raicho, and Yoshia Nobuko; trans. from *CLIT 007,* Swiss lesbian-feminist quarterly, June 1983). *Connexions,* "Global Lesbianism 2" 10 (Fall 1983):18.

Robertson, Jennifer. "Gender-Bending in Paradise: Doing 'Female' and 'Male' in Japan" (Takarazuka Revue, all-female theater founded in 1914). *Genders* 5 (July 1989):50-69.

Sawabe, Hitomi (trans. Eleanor Batchelder and Fumiko Ohno). "Yuriko, Da Svidanya (Goodbye, Yuriko): the Youth of Yoshiko Yuasa" (excerpt, in Japanese and English, of book about writer and translator Yoshiko Yuasa). *Conditions: seventeen* (1990):20-9.

Europe:
Austria:
"Austria: Lesbian, Gay Publications Confiscated." *off our backs* 20:10 (November 1990):7.

H., Mia. "Austria: Lesbians Organize" (Women's Section of Homosexuelle Initiative, Vienna). *off our backs* 20:3 (March 1990):11.

Riegler, Waultrad. "Austria: Lesbian Graffiti Wins" (court upholds contract allowing pro-lesbian slogan on bus ad). *off our backs* 20:6 (June 1990):4.

Belgium:
Douglas, Carol Anne. "Dutch, Belgian Lesbian Movement Discussed" (interview with activists). *off our backs* 12:8 (August-September 1982):13.

Goddemaer, Nicky. "The 'She-Wolf'" (personal account of incarceration in juvenile hall). *Connexions,* "Women Inside and Out" 14 (Fall 1984):18-19.

Czechoslovakia:
Hyánková, Karla. (letter from lesbian activist about female to male transsexuals and their relationship to the status of violence against women in Czechoslovakia). *Connexions,* "Defy Violence" 34 (1990):2-3.

"Lesbians Fight Oppressive Laws" (in Czechoslovakia). *New Directions for Women* 19:5 (September/October 1990):9.

Denmark:

Bolz, Barbara. "Scandinavian 'People Like Us.'" *Visibilities* 3:1 (January/February 1989):3-7.

"Denmark: Gay Marriage OK, Adoption Not." *off our backs* 19:10 (November 1989):11.

Gilfillan, Caroline. "Lesbian Summer Camp" (Danish women's liberation movement group, "The Redstockings," hold annual camp on the island of Femø; article about first year of lesbian separatist camp simultaneous with camp open to heterosexuals). *Spare Rib* (Great Britain) 64 (November 1977):14-15.

"The Three of Us Together: My Mother, Ann Britt and I" (trans. from *Pan,* Danish lesbian/gay bimonthly, February/March 1984). *Connexions,* "Girls Speak Out!" 27 (1988):2-3.

Weise, Beth Reba. "Scandinavia: Feminist Utopia or Patriarchal Stronghold?" *off our backs* 20:3 (March 1990):4-7.

East Germany:

Bobinska, Monika. "East Europe on Gays" (first official conference on homosexuality in Leipzig, East Germany; discusses Poland and East Germany). *Spare Rib* (Great Britain) 167 (June 1986):47.

"East Germany: Lesbians Take Refuge in the Church" (lesbians legally allowed to meet under the auspices of the Protestant Church; trans. and excerpted from Swiss feminist quarterly, *Frauenzitig* 23, Fall 1987). *Connexions,* "Feminism and Religion" 28 (1988-89):28.

"East Germany: the Sunday Club" (only lesbian/gay group allowed to meet outside the Protestant Church or bars; trans. and excerpted from West German lesbian quarterly, *Lebenstich,* Spring 1988). *Connexions,* "Lesbian Activism" 29 (1989):22.

"Lesbians in Eastern Europe" (information about groups in East
Germany and Yugoslavia, from an article in *The Washington
Gay Blade,* December 23, 1988). *off our backs* 19:3 (March
1989):9.

"Love Through Letters" (interview with East German lesbian; trans.
from *Courage,* West German monthly, May 1978). *Connexions,*
"Women in Eastern Europe" 5 (Summer 1982):24-5.

Parsons, John. "East Germany Faces Its Past: a New Start for
Socialist Sexual Politics." *Out/Look #5,* 2:1 (Summer
1989):43-52.

Finland:

Bolz, Barbara. "Scandinavian 'People Like Us.'" *Visibilities* 3:1
(January/February 1989):3-7.

"Gayintern" (lesbian and gay rights struggles around the world). *off
our backs* 9:11 (December 1979):7.

Weise, Beth Reba. "Scandinavia: Feminist Utopia or Patriarchal
Stronghold?" *off our backs* 20:3 (March 1990):4-7.

France:

Barney, Natalie (trans. Margaret Porter). "Natalie Barney on Renée
Vivien." *Heresies #3,* "Lesbian Art and Artists" 1:3 (Fall
1977):65-71.

Bourbonnais, Nicole. "Femme Métonymique, Femme Métaphorique:
la Poésie d'Anne Hébert et de Renée Vivien." *Atlantis* (Canada)
11 (Spring 1986):108-14.

Cochran, Judy. "The Textual, Sexual Self: Self-Consciousness in
Violette Leduc's *La Bâtarde.*" *Atlantis* (Canada) 13:1 (Fall
1987):47-52.

Cottingham, Laura. "Christine Delphy: French Feminist" (interview with activist, writer, and co-editor of *Nouvelle Question Féministe;* includes section on "Lesbianism in France"). *off our backs* 14:3 (March 1984):10-11+.

Coward, D.D. "Attitudes to Homosexuality in Eighteenth-Century France" (homosexuality as not uncommon among aristocracy, with little punishment). *Journal of European Studies* 10:4 (1980):231-55.

Crowder, Diane Griffin. "Amazons and Mothers? Monique Wittig, Hélène Cixous and Theories of Writing." *Contemporary Literature* 24:2 (Summer 1983):117-44.

Dranch, Sherry A. "Reading Through the Veiled Text: Colette's *The Pure and the Impure.*" *Contemporary Literature* 24:2 (Summer 1983):176-89.

"France: Lesbians Invisible?" *off our backs* 20:7 (July 1990):9.

"France: Lesbians of the Main Screen" (trans. from French lesbian monthly, *Lesbia,* no. 67, December 1988; interview with co-founder of Ciné-club of Paris). *Connexions,* "Lesbian Activism" 29 (1989):12-13.

"France: To Recognize Rape as a Political Crime" (Marie André, lesbian/feminist raped by a group of men, who turned her own case into a political cause; from *Elles Voient Rouge,* French feminist periodical, no. 3, May 1980). *Connexions,* "Women Organizing Against Violence" 1 (Summer 1981):26-7.

Irigaray, Luce (trans. Carolyn Burke). "When our Lips Speak Together" (sexuality). *Signs* 6:1 (Autumn 1980):69-79.

Kuthy, S. "Courbet und die Zwei Feudinnen" ("Courbet and the Two Friends"; controversial depiction of lesbians by 19th century French painter Gustave Courbet). *Berner Kunstmitteilungen* (Switzerland) 222-223 (June-July 1983):1-9.

Lahzem. "Rainbow Solidarity" (group of North African lesbians and gays living in France, formed in Paris in Fall 1982). *Connexions,* "Global Lesbianism 2" 10 (Fall 1983):4.

LeBitoux, Jean. "To Be Twenty and Homosexual in France Today." *Journal of Homosexuality,* "Gay and Lesbian Youth: Part II" 17:3/4 (1989):291-8.

Lesselier, Claudie. "Social Categorizations and Construction of a Lesbian Subject." *Feminist Issues* 7:1 (Spring 1987):89-94.

Leveritt, Annie and Celia Guse. "*Novembermoon*" (film about Nazi occupation of France, with lesbian main characters). *Hot Wire* 2:3 (July 1986):40-1.

Maas, N. "Du Mlle. Giraud Ma Femme: A 1870 Lesbian Novel by Adolphe Belot." *Maatstaf* 32:2 (1984):48-68.

Mullaney, Marie Marmo. "Sexual Politics in the Career and Legend of Louise Michel" (French revolutionary, member of Paris Commune). *Signs* 15:2 (Winter 1990):300-22.

Radical Lesbian Front. "Political Lesbianism -- the Battle Rages" (trans. from *Masques,* French quarterly gay theoretical journal, Fall 1981). *Connexions,* "Global Lesbianism" 3 (January 1982):28-9.

Rex, Walter E. "Secrets from Suzanne: the Tangled Motives of *La Religieuse*" (by Denis Diderot). *The Eighteenth Century* 24:3 (Fall 1983):185-98.

Rosenfeld, Marthe. "Language and the Vision of Utopia in Wittig's *Les Guérillères.*" *Frontiers* 6:1-2 (Spring-Summer 1981):6-9.

------. "The Linguistic Aspect of Sexual Conflict: Monique Wittig's *Le Corps Lesbien.*" *Mosaic* (Canada) 17:2 (Spring 1984):235-41.

Shaktini, Namascar. "Displacing the Phallic Subject: Wittig's Lesbian Writing." *Signs* 8:1 (Autumn 1982):29-44.

Shaw, Nanette. "Interview with Jocelyne François" (French novelist). *13th Moon,* "Narrative Forms" 8:1/2 (1984):52-60.

------. "Jocelyne François: an Introduction" (to the French novelist). *13th Moon,* "Narrative Forms" 8:1/2 (1984):52-60.

Steakley, James D. "Love Between Women and Love Between Men: an Interview with Charlotte Wolff" (psychiatrist and writer). *New German Critique* 23 (Spring-Summer 1981):73-81.

VLASTA: Révue des Fictions Utopies Amazonienes, France, "Spécial: Monique Wittig," no. 4.

Wenzel, Hélène Vivienne. "The Text as Body/Politics: an Appreciation of Monique Wittig's Writings in Context." *Feminist Studies* 7:2 (Summer 1981):264-87.

Wickes, George (editor). "A Natalie Barney Garland" (recollections of Barney's life and work as gathered from interviews, memoirs, and books of Sylvia Beach, Romaine Brooks, Madame Gaston Bergery, Elizabeth Eyre, Virgil Thomsen, Truman Capote, and Janet Flanner). *Paris Review* (U.S.) 61 (Spring 1975):84-134.

Germany (see East Germany; West Germany)

Great Britain:

Alderson, Lynn and Harriet Wistrich. "Clause 29: Radical Feminist Perspectives" (anti-gay/lesbian ordinance commonly referred to as Clause 28). *Trouble & Strife* (Great Britain) 13 (Spring 1988):3-8.

Ardill, Susan and Sue O'Sullivan. "Butch/Femme Obsessions." *Feminist Review* (Great Britain), "Perverse Politics: Lesbian Issues" 34 (Spring 1990):79-85.

------. "Sex in the Summer of '88" (sex and pornography controversies, including anti-gay Clause 28; *A Restricted Country,* book by Joan Nestle; *She Must Be Seeing Things,* video by Sheila McLaughlin). *Feminist Review* (Great Britain), "The Past Before Us; Twenty Years of Feminism" 31 (Spring 1989):126-34.

------. "Upsetting an Applecart: Difference, Desire and Lesbian Sadomasochism." *Feminist Review* (Great Britain), "Socialist Feminism: Out of the Blue" 23 (Summer 1986):31-57.

Bardsley, Barney. "The Impersonators . . . Women Who Were Musical Halls' 'Men.'" *Spare Rib* (Great Britain) 126 (January 1983):49.

Bell, Ellen. "Britain: Women Abusing Women" (excerpt from *Trouble & Strife,* British feminist quarterly, 1989). *Connexions,* "Defy Violence" 34 (1990):28-30.

Benn, Melissa. "The Passion of Decency: Thoughts on Feminism and Bisexuality." *Spare Rib* (Great Britain) 198 (February 1989):18-20.

Blackman, Inge and Kathryn Perry. "Skirting the Issue: Lesbian Fashion for the 1990s." *Feminist Review* (Great Britain), "Perverse Politics: Lesbian Issues" 34 (Spring 1990):67-78.

Brackx, Amy. "Out Into the Open: Ten Years of the Gay Movement." *Spare Rib* (Great Britain) 84 (July 1979):42-6.

"Britain: a New Intimacy" (bisexual women write about AIDS and sexual practices, from *Bisexual Lives* (England) (1988)). *Connexions,* Women and AIDS" 33 (1990):26.

"Britain: 'Pass the Clingfilm, dear!'" (plastic wrap as safe sex paraphernalia; from *Square Peg,* England, 1987). *Connexions,* "Women and AIDS" 33(1990):28.

"Britain: Stop the Clause" (anti-lesbian/gay Clause 28; excerpted from British Feminist monthly *Outwrite* 65 (May 1988)). *Connexions,* "Lesbian Activism" 29 (1989):9.

CAD. "Dr. Strange Love" (news briefs about anti-lesbian/gay discrimination in U.S. and Great Britain). *off our backs* 8:3 (March 1978):10.

------. "Gays Struggle" (news briefs about gay rights struggles around the world). *off our backs* 8:10 (November 1978):6.

Carmen, Gail, Sheila, and Pratibha. "Becoming Visible: Black Lesbian Discussions." *Feminist Review* (Great Britain), "Many Voices, One Chant: Black Feminist Perspectives" 17 (Autumn 1984):53-72.

Clarke, Caro. "Lesbian Ethics Workshop Reports: Lesbians in Film." *Gossip* (Great Britain) 6 (1988):13-6.

------. "Lesbian Ethics Workshop Reports: Working with Non-Lesbians." *Gossip* (Great Britain) 6 (1988):92-5.

Collis, Rose. "Out on Tuesdays: Not for Beginners" (lesbian/gay magazine-format series on British television channel 4). *Spare Rib* (Great Britain) 198 (February 1989):33.

de Lauretis, Teresa. "The Essence of the Triangle, Or, Taking the Risk of Essentialism Seriously: Feminist Theory in Italy, the U.S., and Britain." *Differences,* "The Essential Difference: Another Look at Essentialism" 1:2 (Summer 1989):3-37.

Dixon, Janet. "Separatism" (excerpt from *Radical Records: Thirty Years of Lesbian and Gay History*). *Spare Rib* (Great Britain) 192 (June 1988):6-11.

Duelli Klein, Renate. "Third National Women's Studies Conference, Bradford, U.K., March 31-April 1, 1984" (includes reports on lesbian studies workshop and lesbian invisibility presentation). *Women's Studies International Forum* 7:3 (1984):i-iv.

"Editor's Introduction" (to *Gossip: a Journal of Lesbian Feminist Ethics,* about publishing and political and ethical issues in British lesbian-feminist community). *Gossip* (Great Britain) 1 (1986):5-7.

Edwards, Elizabeth. "Educational Institutions or Extended Families? The Reconstruction of Gender in Women's Colleges in the Late Nineteenth and Early Twentieth Centuries." *Gender and Education* 2:1 (1990):17-35.

Egerton, Jayne. "Nothing Natural" (legal obstacles to lesbian parenting in Great Britain). *New Statesman & Society* (Great Britain) 3:127 (1990):12-14.

------. "Out But Not Down: Lesbians' Experience of Housing" (squatting, alternative housing communities, and national housing policy in Great Britain). *Feminist Review* (Great Britain) 36 (Autumn 1990):75-88.

Etorre, Betsy. "Sappho Revisited: a New Look at Lesbianism" (links between feminism and lesbianism for some women). *Women's Studies International Quarterly* 3:4 (1980):415-28.

Farraday, Annabel. "Lesbian Outlaws: Past Attempts to Legislate Against Lesbians" (historical context of Clause 28). *Trouble & Strife* (Great Britain) 13 (Spring 1988):9-16.

Farry, Marcel. "Censorship -- Who's Calling the Shots" (film). *Spare Rib* (Great Britain) 219 (December/January 1990/91):31-2.

Feminist Review, Great Britain, "Sexuality," no. 11, Summer 1982.

Fenwomyn, Carol. "Lesbian Ethics Workshop Reports: 'Love Your Enemy?': Political Lesbianism." *Gossip* (Great Britain) 6 (1988):110-6.

Field, Rachael. "Lesbian Tradition" (about painting, by a lesbian painter). *Feminist Review* (Great Britain), "Perverse Politics: Lesbian Issues" 34 (Spring 1990):115-19.

Fraser, Jean. "Photography in Education: 'Someone to Talk to'" (interview with Ritu Khurana and Mel Burns, who participated in workshop involving young lesbian and gay photographers producing educational materials). *Ten.8* (Great Britain) 32 (Spring 1989):50-6.

Fritz, Leah. "Publishing and Flourishing" (Sheba Press Limited, Onlywomen Press, and other British non-lesbian feminist presses). *Women's Review of Books* 3 (February 1986):16-17.

Harne, Lynne. "Lesbian Mothers' Custody Conference." *Spare Rib* (Great Britain) 129 (April 1983):22-3.

Hart, Vada. "Lesbians and AIDS." *Gossip* (Great Britain) 2 (1986):90-6.

Henry, Alice. "New British Law Against Lesbians and Gays" (Clause 28). *off our backs* 18:3 (March 1988):5.

Hindley, Emma and Sarah Pritchard. "British Lesbian Student Conference." *off our backs* 12:8 (August-September 1982):14.

"Holland: Never Going Underground" (bus tour of Western Europe by Dutch lesbian/gay rights organization Labda, to benefit the movement against British anti-lesbian/gay Clause 28). *Connexions,* "Lesbian Activism" 29 (1989):7-8.

Hopkins, June. "Lesbian Signs on the Rorschach" (concludes homosexuality is not a "clinical entity"). *British Journal of Projective Psychology and Personality Study* (Great Britain) 15 (1970):7-14.

Hunt, Margaret. "The De-Eroticization of Women's Liberation: Social Purity Movements and the Revolutionary Feminism of Sheila Jeffreys." *Feminist Review* (Great Britain), "Perverse Politics: Lesbian Issues" 34 (Spring 1990):23-46.

Jeffreys, Sheila. "Butch and Femme: Now and Then." *Gossip* (Great Britain) 5 (no date; c.1987):65-95.

337

Jennings, Paula. "The Hunt Saboteurs in Fox Furs" (S/M). *Gossip* (Great Britain) 6 (1988):80-91.

Kris. "Another Kind of Coming Out" (child sexual abuse in the British black community). *Gossip* (Great Britain) 2 (1986):80-9.

"Lesbian Mums on Holiday" (group goes together to Oaklands Women's Holiday Centre, continue to meet as lesbian mothers' network). *Spare Rib* (Great Britain) 134 (September 1983):6-7.

"Lesbians Hit Prime Time" (interview with Mandy Merck, editor of lesbian and gay television series "Out On Tuesday"). *Spare Rib* (Great Britain) 213 (June 1990):39-42.

Lettice. "Lesbian Ethics Workshop: Separatism." *Gossip* (Great Britain) 6 (1988):107-10.

Livia, Anna. "'I Would Rather Have Been Dead Than Gone Forever': Butch and Femme as Responses to Patriarchy." *Gossip* (Great Britain) 5 (no date):53-64.

------. "Lesbian Ethics Workshop Reports: Butch and Femme." *Gossip* (Great Britain) 6 (1988):95-102.

------. "With Gossip Aforethought." *Gossip* (Great Britain) 1 (1986):60-7.

Lumsden, Andrew. "I.B.A. Gets an Overdue Earful from Lesbians and Gays" (Independent Broadcasting Authority). *New Statesman* (Great Britain) 111 (February 21, 1986):6.

Melville, Joy. "I'm Not a Feminist, But . . . " (feminist publishing in Great Britain). *New Society* (Great Britain) 68 (June 7, 1984):391-2.

------. "Women in Love with Women." *New Society* (Great Britain) 59 (January 28, 1982):137-40.

Nava, Mica. "'Everybody's Views Were Just Broadened': a Girls' Project and Some Responses to Lesbianism." *Feminist Review* (Great Britain) 10 (Spring 1982):37-59.

O'Sullivan, Susan. "Passionate Beginnings: Ideological Politics 1969-72." *Feminist Review* (Great Britain), "Sexuality" 11 (Summer 1982):70-86.

Oliver, Maureen. "Lesbians Attacked in Stockholm" (European bus Tour Against British Clause 28). *Spare Rib* (Great Britain) 198 (February 1989):45-6.

"OUTRAGE: New Lesbian and Gay Direct Action Group" (British group modeled after U.S. AIDS Coalition to Unleash Power (ACT-UP)). *Spare Rib* (Great Britain) 214 (July 1990):43.

"Ova Easy" (response by Women's Reproductive Rights Information Campaign to the Warnock Report, issued by a government commission, on reproductive technologies). *Connexions,* "Changing Technology" 15 (Winter 1985):8.

Parker, Jan. "Lesbians -- Laying Down the Law" (how present laws affect lesbians; why lesbian/gay rights legislation is important for everyone). *Spare Rib* (Great Britain) 175 (February 1987):15-19.

------. "Victory for Lesbians at Labour Conference" (Labour Party debates lesbian/gay rights at annual conference). *Spare Rib* (Great Britain) 172 (November 1986):44.

------. "When You're Out You're Out!" (lesbians kicked out of the military). *Spare Rib* (Great Britain) 119 (June 1982):6-8+.

Parker, Jan and Suzanne Arnold. "*Gay News:* Good News for Lesbians?" (two *Spare Rib* writers talk to Gillian Hanscombe and Allison Hennigan, writers for *Gay News*). *Spare Rib* (Great Britain) 130 (May 1983):49-51.

Parmar, Pratibha and Sunil Gupta. "Homosexualities Part Two: UK" (depiction of homosexuality in photography). *Ten.8* (Great Britain) 32 (Spring 1989):22-35.

Patel, Madhu. "The Struggle to Be Accepted as a Person" (coming out as an Asian lesbian). *Spare Rib* (Great Britain) 136 (November 1983):26.

Robertson, Vicki, "British Lesbians Attacked by Police." *off our backs* 11:7 (July 1981):10.

Roelofs, Sarah. "The Rights We Lost" (British Clause 28). *Spare Rib* (Great Britain) 197 (December 1988/January 1989):7.

Schonfeld, Rosemary. "Report from the Front Lines: Women's Music in Europe" (written by one half of the British duo OVA). *Hot Wire* 5:2 (May 1989):26-7.

Scott, Suzanne and Lynne M. Constantine. "*Belles Lettres* Interview: Jeanette Winterson" (author). *Belles Lettres* 5:4 (Summer 1990):24-6.

Semple, Linda. "Lesbians in Detective Fiction." *Gossip* (Great Britain) 5 (no date):47-52.

"Sharing Children." *Spare Rib* (Great Britain) 90 (January 1980):31-4.

Siegelman, Marion. "Adjustment of Homosexual and Heterosexual Women" (lesbians higher on goal-directedness and self acceptance, lower on depression than heterosexual women). *British Journal of Psychiatry* (Great Britain) 120 (1972):477-81.

Smartt, Dorothea and Val Mason-John. "Black Feminists Organising on Both Sides of the Atlantic." *Spare Rib* (Great Britain) 171 (October 1986):20-4.

"A Smell of Fascism in the Air" (report on anti-gay Clause 28, one
    year after it was passed into law). *Spare Rib* (Great Britain) 201
    (May 1989):14.

"Spousal Benefits for Lesbian Lovers." *Spare Rib* (Great Britain) 174
    (January 1987):46.

Stephens, Eleanor. "Out of the Closets and Into the Courts"
    (discrimination against lesbian mothers in custody battles). *Spare
    Rib* (Great Britain) 50 (September 1976):6-8.

Sulter, Maud. "Black Codes: the Misrepresentation of Black Lesbians
    in Film" (considers "Born in Flames," "The Color Purple,"
    "Mark of Lilith," "Mona Lisa," "Passion of Remembrance," and
    "She's Gotta Have It"). *Gossip* (Great Britain) 5 (no date):29-36.

Thomas, June. "Anna Livia: Lesbian Author, Publisher." *off our
    backs* 18:11 (December 1988):10+.

------. "Commonwealth Censorship of Gay Books" (England, New
    Zealand, Canada). *off our backs* 16:2 (February 1986):5.

------. "Literary Trials and Tribulations" (British customs officials raid
    Gay's the Word Bookstore, April 1984; hearing February 1985).
    off our backs 15:8 (August-September 1985):15.

Tobin, Ann. "Lesbianism and the Labour Party: The GLC
    Experience" (Gay and Lesbian Center). *Feminist Review* (Great
    Britain), "Perverse Politics: Lesbian Issues" 34 (Spring
    1990):56-66.

Valverde, Mariana. "Freedom's Just Another Word; On One Side, the
    Devil of Censorship; On the Other, a Deep Blue Sea of Free
    Trade: Canada's Bookworld Is Threatened by Dangers of Which
    We in Britain Should Take Note." *New Statesman* (Great Britain)
    113 (June 26, 1987):25-6.

"Veronica4Rose" (television show about lesbians). *Connexions,*
    "Global Lesbianism 2" 10 (Fall 1983):10.

Waite, Rosie. "They Didn't Know What to Say to Me." *Gossip* (Great Britain) 1 (1986):46-53.

Wallsgrove, Ruth. "A Guide to Lesbian Groups" (Sappho, Kenric, NOOL (National Organization of Lesbians), Lesbian Link, Lesbian Line, Gemma, Action for Lesbian Parents, Wages Due Lesbians, and Lesbian Left). *Spare Rib* (Great Britain) 74 (September 1978):26-9.

Wilmer, Val. "A Salute to *Sappho*" (interview with Jackie Forster, editor of magazine that ceased publishing just short of its tenth anniversary). *Spare Rib* (Great Britain) 116 (March 1982):31-2.

Wilson, Elizabeth. "Deviant Dress" (in the late 1980s and the 1950s). *Feminist Review* (Great Britain) 35 (Summer 1990):67-74.

------. "Forbidden Love." *Feminist Studies* 10:2 (Summer 1984):213-26.

Zehra. "Lesbians and Immigration." *Spare Rib* (Great Britain) 176 (March 1987):37.

England:

"ACT-UP" (plans for London chapter of the AIDS Coalition to Unleash Power). *Spare Rib* (Great Britain) 197 (December 1988/January 1989):18-19.

Anderson, Shelley. "Lesbian London." *Visibilities* 4:3 (May/June 1990):4-7.

Benton, Sarah. "Gay Workers Acknowledge Debt to Women's Movement" (first national Gay Workers' Conference, Leeds, May 1974). *Spare Rib* (Great Britain) 37 (July 1975):22.

Carne, Roz. "Homosexuality: Sexual 'Problem' or Political Problem?" (gays and representatives of the medical and counselling professions meet to discuss attitudes toward homosexuality, Bradford University, England, April 1975). *Spare Rib* (Great Britain) 36 (June 1975):19.

Carola, Elizabeth. "Agreeing to Differ? Lesbian Sadomasochism" (by member of Lesbians Against Sadomasochism, London). *Spare Rib* (Great Britain) 170 (September 1986):39-40.

Collis, Rose and Linda Semple. "A Queer Feeling When I Look at You" (third Lesbian and Gay Film Festival, London, October 11-November 6, 1988). *Spare Rib* (Great Britain) 195 (October 1988):22-3.

Durrell, Anna. "Uproar Over Violent Images" (S/M debates in London's lesbian/gay movement). *New Statesman* (Great Britain) 109 (June 14, 1985):16-17.

Emberley, Julia and Donna Landry. "Coverage of Greenham and Greenham as 'Coverage'" (Greenham Common Womyn's Peace Encampment). *Feminist Studies* 15:3 (Fall 1989):485-98.

"England: a Working Collective" (interview with a collective member of *Outwrite,* British feminist monthly newspaper). *Connexions,* "Media: Getting to Women" 16 (Spring 1985):3-4.

Ferrier, Carole. "Interview with Pearlie McNeill" (Australian author living in London, England). *Hecate* (Australia) 16:1/2 (1990):102-10.

Garthwaite, Al. "English WAVAW Conference: Pressure to Be Straight" (Women Against Violence Against Women). *off our backs* 12:2 (February 1982):2-3.

"Gay Adoption: in Britain" (promoted by Newcastle City Council, opposed by British Home Secretary). *off our backs* 20:11 (December 1990):6.

Hemmings, Susan and Manny. "Lesbians National . . . and International" (National Lesbian Conference on Sex and Sexual Practice, London, April 1983, and International Lesbian Service Conference, Paris, France, April 1983). *Spare Rib* (Great Britain) 131 (June 1983):12-13.

James, Selma. "From the Mother Country: One English Woman's Words on the U.S. and British Women's Movements" (section on "U.S.: 'Political Lesbians'"). *off our backs* 2:7 (March 1972):4.

"Judges Overturn Lesbian Custody Ruling" (lesbian mother in England loses custody granted in first hearing). *Spare Rib* (Great Britain) 216 (September 1990):44.

Kalioaka. "Greenham Common Wimmin's Peace Camp." *Woman of Power,* "International Feminism" 7 (Summer 1987):57-9+.

Kay, Jackie. "Unnatural Passions" (interview with Jeanette Winterson, conducted shortly after the movie version of her novel *Oranges Are Not the Only Fruit* was televised in England). *Spare Rib* (Great Britain) 209 (February 1990):26-9.

"Lesbian Blood Victory" (Nottingham Lesbian Line and others succeed in overturning refusal of lesbian blood donors at the National Blood Transfusion Service in England). *Spare Rib* (Great Britain) 170 (September 1986):47.

"Lesbian Space in London [Gay] Center." *Spare Rib* (Great Britain) 143 (June 1984):24-5.

Lorde, Audre. "No, We Never Go Out of Fashion . . . for Each Other" (discussion among four black feminists at International Feminist Bookfair, June 1984, England). *Spare Rib* (Great Britain) 149 (December 1984):26-9.

McNeil, Sarah. "English WAVAW Conference: Female Sexuality" (Women Against Violence Against Women). *off our backs* 12:2 (February 1982):2-3.

Mohin, Lilian. "Herstory Interview with Members of the Coventry Lesbian Theatre Group: Lou Hart, Jane Skeates, Vicki Ryder and Suzanne Ciechomski." *Gossip* (Great Britain) 4 (no date):59-85.

O'Sullivan, Sue. "Where Were the Lesbian Doctors?" (at the 1st International Conference on Homosexuality and Medicine, London, August 1986). *Spare Rib* (Great Britain) 172 (November 1986):8.

"OUTRAGE Protests Anti-Gay Murders" (in England; direct action group modeled after U.S. AIDS Coalition to Unleash Power (ACT-UP)). *Spare Rib* (Great Britain) 216 (September 1990):44.

Pam and Ruth. "London Lesbian Line -- Ten Years Old." *Spare Rib* (Great Britain) 178 (May 1987):6-7.

Parker, Jan. "Happy Birthday 837-8062" (fifth anniversary of London Lesbian Line; interview with collective members). *Spare Rib* (Great Britain) 123 (October 1982):49-51.

Plummer, Ken. "Lesbian and Gay Youth in England." *Journal of Homosexuality,* "Gay and Lesbian Youth: Part II" 17:3/4 (1989):195-224.

Robins, Peter. "Not All Cider with Bosie; the First Formal Gathering of Lesbian and Gay Writers Living in Europe Took Place Recently in London." *New Statesman* (Great Britain) 113 (May 15, 1987):26-7.

Romalis, Shelly. "Carrying Greenham Home: the London Women's Peace Support Network." *Atlantis* (Canada) 12 (Spring 1987):90-8.

Ross, Becki. "Black Women of Letters" (excerpt of interview
with Michelle McKenzie and Araba Mercer of Sheba
Publishers, England, from Canadian monthly *Rites*,
November 1988). *Connexions*, "Women on Work" 30
(1989):24-5.

"Sappho Invaded" (*Evening News* reporters trick lesbian
newspaper *Sappho* into revealing names of lesbian mothers
for a sensationalistic feature story). *off our backs* (February
1979):8.

"Sit-in" (at *London Evening News*, protesting articles opposing
lesbian artificial insemination). *off our backs* 8:2 (February
1978):3.

Vicinus, Martha. "Distance and Desire: English Boarding-School
Friendships." *Signs*, "The Lesbian Issue" 9:4 (Summer
1984):600-22.

"Whatever Happened at the Lesbian Archive?" (dispute in
collective over showing of film with S/M content, *She
Must Be Seeing Things*, and over alleged racism in hiring).
Spare Rib (Great Britain) 199 (March 1989):17.

Williams, Natalie. "Lesbian and Gay People of Colour Gather in
London" (Sixth International Lesbian and Gay People of
Colour Conference, London, England, November 1990).
Spare Rib (Great Britain) 219 (December/January
1990/91):66-7.

Williamson, Judith. "In the Pink" (gay and lesbian films at
London's Tyneside Festival, including *The Lesbian Vampire
on Film, Underground Canada*, and *Novembermoon* about
two lesbians in Nazi concentration camps). *New Statesman*
(Great Britain) 114 (October 9, 1987):22-3.

Northern Ireland:

CAD. "Lesbian/Gay Trips, Cruises & Marches" (U.S. and
international news briefs; first lesbian play performed in
Ulster, Northern Ireland). *off our backs* 10:3 (March
1980):18-19+.

"Ireland" ("Lesbian Line" in Belfast). *Connexions*, "Lesbian
Activism" 29 (1989):23.

Scotland:

Jennings, Paula. "Lesbian Liberation Later" (homophobia in the
women's movement). *Gossip* (Great Britain) 3 (no date):77-
81.

Greece:

Differences, "Sexuality in Greek and Roman Society," vol. 2, no. 1,
Spring 1990.

Hungary:

"Another Way" (Hungarian film, directed by Karoly Makk, based on
popular novel *Outside the Law and Inside* by Erzsebet Galgoczi,
1981). *Connexions*, "Global Lesbianism 2" 10 (Fall 1983):26-7.

"Hungary: Gay Group Approved" (first officially approved lesbian and
gay group in a communist country). *off our backs* 18:9 (October
1988):10.

Iceland:

Bolz, Barbara. "Scandinavian 'People Like Us.'" *Visibilities* 3:1
(January/February 1989):3-7.

Weise, Beth Reba. "Scandinavia: Feminist Utopia or Patriarchal
Stronghold?" *off our backs* 20:3 (March 1990):4-7.

Ireland:

Carlson, Helena M. and Leslie A. Baxter. "Androgyny, Depression
and Self-Esteem in Irish Homosexual and Heterosexual Males
and Females." *Sex Roles* 10 (March 1984):457-67.

Crone, Joni. "Lesbian Feminism in Ireland." *Women's Studies International Forum* 11:4 (1988):343-7.

"Ireland: Gay Sex Legal." *off our backs* 20:9 (October 1990):7.

"Lesbian's Stand" (Liz Noonan, lesbian feminist candidate in the General Election). *Spare Rib* (Great Britain) 108 (July 1981):15.

"Out for Ourselves" (excerpt of book by and about Irish lesbians and gays). *Spare Rib* (Great Britain) 170 (September 1986):20-4.

Wilson, Marie. "Irish Women's Eyes Aren't Smiling (Family, Contraception, and Homosexuality)." *off our backs* 11:1 (January 1981):8-9.

Italy (see also: Italian-American Lesbians):

Bell, Rudolph and Judith Butler. "Renaissance Sexuality and the Florentine Archives: an Exchange." *Renaissance Quarterly* 40:3 (Autumn 1987):485-511.

Carne, Rosalind. "Lesbians in Rome: All Our Childhood We Are Told to Keep Away from Men." *Spare Rib* (Great Britain) 40 (October 1975):26.

de Lauretis, Teresa. "The Essence of the Triangle, Or, Taking the Risk of Essentialism Seriously: Feminist Theory in Italy, the U.S., and Britain." *Differences,* "The Essential Difference: Another Look at Essentialism" 1:2 (Summer 1989):3-37.

Differences, "Sexuality in Greek and Roman Society," vol. 2, no. 1, Spring 1990.

Fiocchetto, Rosanna. "International Lesbianism: Italy." *Feminist Review* (Great Britain), "Perverse Politics: Lesbian Issues" 34 (Spring 1990):18-22.

The Netherlands:

Adams, Mary Louise. "Homosexuality, Which Homosexuality?": International Scientific Conference on Gay and Lesbian Studies -- Amsterdam, December 15-18, 1987." *Resources for Feminist Research* (Canada) 17 (June 1988):57-9.

Anderson, Sheeley. "Lesbian Amsterdam." *Visibilities* 3:3 (May/June 1989):10+.

CAD. "Lesbian/Gay Trips, Cruises & Marches" (U.S. and international news briefs). *off our backs* 10:3 (March 1980):18-19+.

Douglas, Carol Anne. "Dutch, Belgian Lesbian Movement Discussed" (interview with activists). *off our backs* 12:8 (August-September 1982):13.

Everard, Myriam. "Tribade of *Zielsvriendin*" (Aagje Deken, 18th century Dutch poet). *Groniek* 77 (1982):16-20.

"Gay Adoption: in Netherlands" (legalization considered by federal government, which legalized same-sex marriage in 1989). *off our backs* 20:11 (December 1990):6.

"Holland: Never Going Underground" (bus tour of Western Europe by Dutch lesbian/gay rights organization Labda, to benefit the movement against British anti-lesbian/gay Clause 28). *Connexions,* "Lesbian Activism" 29 (1989):7-8.

"Holland: Old Dykes' Home" (trans. from *Serpentine,* Dutch feminist monthly, November 1980). *Connexions,* "Global Lesbianism" 3 (January 1982):30.

"In Practice, Not Theory" (account by two Dutch members of the Dutch Venceremos Brigade, who went to Cuba to seek out lesbians). *Connexions,* "Global Lesbianism 2" 10 (Fall 1983):9.

Journal of Homosexuality, "Interdisciplinary Research on Homosexuality in the Netherlands." vol. 13, nos. 2/3, Winter 1986/Spring 1987.

"Keeping Everything" (formation of Dutch lesbian archives). *Connexions*, "Global Lesbianism" 10 (Fall 1983):11.

"Lesbian Scholar Honored" (by Dutch Queen Beatrix, with tenured professorship at the University of Utrecht). *off our backs* 19:1 (January 1989):7; note: cover reads vol. 18, no. 11 (December 1988).

"Mati" (name used by women in the Organization of Surinamese Homosexuals in Holland, SoHo). *Connexions*, "Global Lesbianism 2" 10 (Fall 1983):10.

"Netherlands: Court Overturns Gay Marriage Ban." *off our backs* 20:4 (April 1990):6.

"Netherlands: Gay News on TV." *off our backs* 17:3 (March 1987):9.

"Nobody Listens to Me" (interview with two teenage lesbians; trans. from *Sek*, Dutch lesbian and gay periodical, No.9, October 3, 1980). *Connexions*, "Young and Old Women" 7 (Winter 1983):10-11.

Pheterson, Gail. "Alliances Between Women: Overcoming Internalized Oppression and Internalized Domination" ("Feminist Alliance Project" in the Netherlands, addressing racism, anti-Semitism, and heterosexism). *Signs* 12:1 (Autumn 1986):146-60.

Pheterson, Gail and Leny Jansen. "Lesbian Struggle Against a Pillar or a Wall: A Dutch-American Dialogue." *Journal of Homosexuality* 13:2/3 (Winter 1986/Spring 1987):29-42.

Rosalind. "Parliamentary Pink" (Evelien Eshuis, lesbian
parliamentary member of the Dutch Communist Party, who
wears a pink triangle badge). *Connexions,* "Global Lesbianism
2" 10 (Fall 1983):28.

Schuyf, Judith. "Lesbian Emancipation in the Netherlands." *Journal
of Homosexuality* 13:2/3 (Winter 1986/Spring 1987):19-28.

Norway:

Bolz, Barbara. "Scandinavian 'People Like Us.'" *Visibilities* 3:1
(January/February 1989):3-7.

"Lesbian/Gay Trips, Cruises & Marches" (U.S. and international
news briefs). *off our backs* 10:3 (March 1980):18-19+.

Kvaleng, Inger Marie, Elizabeth Bjørk, and Berit Rossvold. "When
Penis Equals Sexuality" (trans. from Norwegian lesbian
quarterly, *Kvinnejournalen,* 1987). *Connexions,* "Women and
AIDS" 33 (1990):11-12.

Oliver, Maureen. "Lesbians Attacked in Stockholm" (European bus
Tour Against British Clause 28). *Spare Rib* (Great Britain) 198
(February 1989):45-6.

Weise, Beth Reba. "Scandinavia: Feminist Utopia or Patriarchal
Stronghold?" *off our backs* 20:3 (March 1990):4-7.

Wilson, Barbara. "An Interview with Gerd Brantenberg" (author of
Egalia's Daughters). *off our backs* 16:4 (April 1986):18-19.

Poland:

Bobinska, Monika. "East Europe on Gays" (first official conference
on homosexuality in Leipzig, East Germany; discusses Poland
and East Germany). *Spare Rib* (Great Britain) 167 (June
1986):47.

"In Poland" (trans. from *De Homokrant,* Belgian gay monthly,
October 1980). *Connexions,* "Women in Eastern Europe" 5
(Summer 1982):25.

Kokula, Ilse. "Poland: Going Public, Step-by-Step" (trans. and excerpted from West German lesbian quarterly, *Lebenstich* (Spring 1988)). *Connexions,* "Lesbian Activism" 29 (1989):11.

Russia (see USSR)

Spain:

Douglas, Carol Anne. "Spain: a Kiss is Just a Kiss" (lesbian kiss-in protesting arrest of two women for kissing in public). *off our backs* 17:5 (May 1987):18.

Morrissey, Carolyn. "Illegal Lesbians." *off our backs* 10:4 (April 1980):22.

O'Sullivan, Sue. "The Sexual Schism: the British in Barcelona" (lesbian erotica and pornography attacked at panel meeting of the International Feminist Bookfair, Barcelona, Spain, Summer 1990). *off our backs* 20:9 (October 1990):9-11.

Stanford, Liz. "Lesbians Seek Exile" (from Pakistan, Mozambique, Spain, Nicaragua, and Cuba). *off our backs* 10:5 (May 1980):6.

Sweden:

Bolz, Barbara. "Scandinavian 'People Like Us.'" *Visibilities* 3:1 (January/February 1989):3-7.

CAD. "Gayintern" (lesbian and gay rights struggles around the world). *off our backs* 9:11 (December 1979):7.

Clarke, M.L. "The Making of a Queen: the Education of Christina of Sweden" (non-lesbian account of this "masculine" monarch). *History Today* 28:4 (April 1978):228-35.

Garde, Pia. "How to Remember Her?" (Swedish poet, novelist and critic Karin Boye, b.1900). *Connexions,* "Global Lesbianism 2" 10 (Fall 1983):22-3.

"Sweden: Speaking the Truth in Schools" (Eva Hansson tours
Sweden with one-woman play about teenage lesbian love; trans.
and excerpted from Swedish feminist bimonthly
Kvinnobulletinen, January/February 1988). *Connexions,* "Girls
Speak Out!" 27 (1988):23.

Weise, Beth Reba. "Scandinavia: Feminist Utopia or Patriarchal
Stronghold?" *off our backs* 20:3 (March 1990):4-7.

Switzerland:
"'I Don't Make Love, I Work'" (anonymous article by a Swiss lesbian
who works as a heterosexual prostitute; trans. from *CLIT 007,*
Swiss lesbian quarterly, September 1982). *Connexions,* "Women
and Prostitution" 12 (Spring 1984):28.

"Sperm Smorgasbord: Switzerland" (trans. from *Frauenzitig,* Swiss
bimonthly, November 1988). *Connexions,* "Reproductive
Technologies" 32 (1990):21.

"Switzerland: What You Should Know About Lesbians" (pamphlet
imitating the format and tone of official government educational
materials, widely distributed in Switzerland; trans. from Swiss
lesbian quarterly *CLIT 007,* 1986). *Connexions,* "Lesbian
Activism" 29 (1989):14.

Turkey:
"Gays Under Attack." *Spare Rib* (Great Britain) 182 (September
1987):42.

West Germany:
Anonymous. "Lesbians in the GDR: Two Women." *New German
Critique* 23 (Spring/Summer 1981):83-96.

"Bus Tour Through Berlin: Once Upon a Time . . . " *Connexions,*
"Special Introductory Issue" 0 (May 1, 1981):14-15.

Dodds, Dinah. "The Lesbian Relationship in Bachmann's '*Ein Schritt
nach Gomorrha.*'" *Monatshefte* 72:4 (Winter 1980):431-8.

Dyer, Richard. "Less and More Than Women and Men: Lesbian and Gay Cinema in Weimar Germany." *New German Critique* 51 (Fall 1990):5-60.

Eriksson, Brigitte (trans.). "A Lesbian Execution in Germany, 1721: the Trial Records." *Journal of Homosexuality* 6:1/2 (Fall/Winter 1980/81):27-40.

"Germany: Not Just Memories" (trans. and excerpted from *Bulletin des Archives Lesbiennes* 7 (June 1988) and West German feminist monthly, *Emma* (December 1988)). *Connexions*, "Lesbian Activism" 29 (1989):28-9.

Goldschen, Lisa Ohm. "The Filmic Adaptation of the Novel *Das Kind Manuela:* Christa Winsloe's Child Heroine Becomes a Madchen in Uniform." *Neue Germanistik* 4:2 (Spring 1986):3-12.

Hansen, Miriam. "Visual Pleasure, Fetishism and the Problem of Feminine/Feminist Discourse: Ulrike Ottinger's *Ticket of No Return.*" *New German Critique* 31 (Winter 1984):95-108.

Jaeckel, Monika. "Feminist Catch-as-Catch-Can" (German lesbian-feminist discusses need to overcome conflicts between feminists). *Women's Studies International Forum* 8:1 (1985):5-8.

Kawan, Hildegard and Barbara Weber. "Reflections on a Theme: the German Women's Movement, Then and Now" (1848-1933, and the 1980s). *Women's Studies International Quarterly* 4:4 (1981):421-33.

Kimpel, Richard. "*The Mists of Avalon/Die Nebel von Avalon:* Marion Zimmer Bradley's German Bestseller." *Journal of American Culture* 9 (Fall 1986):25-8.

"Lesbians in the Butzow Concentration Camp." *Connexions*, "Global Lesbianism" 3 (January 1982):17.

Marx, Sabine. "Desire Cannot Be Fragmented" (trans. and excerpted from West German feminist quarterly, *Tarantel*, 1988). *Connexions*, "Women and AIDS" 33 (1990):6-9.

"Never a Love Song" (interview with members of German rock band Lesboten). *Connexions*, "Global Lesbianism 2" 10 (Fall 1983):29.

Rich, B. Ruby. "*Maedchen in Uniform:* From Repressive Tolerance to Erotic Liberation" (German lesbian history through discussion of Leontine Sagan's film). *Radical America* 15:6 (November-December 1981):17-36.

Schaefer, Siegrid. "Sociosexual Behavior in Male and Female Homosexuals: a Study in Sex Differences." *Archives of Sexual Behavior* 6 (1977):355+.

"Sixty Places to Talk, Dance and Play" (flourishing lesbian and gay culture in turn of the 20th century Germany, until the rise of the Third Reich). *Connexions*, "Global Lesbianism" 3 (January 1982):16-18.

Steakley, James D. "Love Between Women and Love Between Men: an Interview with Charlotte Wolff" (psychiatrist and writer). *New German Critique* 23 (Spring-Summer 1981):73-81.

"West Germany: Chaos in the Assembly" (outspoken lesbian activist Jutta Oesterle-Schwerin, Green Party member of House of Parliament in Bonn; trans. from West German feminist monthly *Emma*, No.1 (January 1989)). *Connexions*, "Lesbian Activism" 29 (1989):4-5.

"Young Lesbians in West Berlin: Be a Sweetie . . . Don't Tell Anyone." *Connexions*, "Global Lesbianism" 3 (January 1982):4-5.

<u>Western Europe:</u>

Anderson, Shelley. "Falling Borders, Rising Hopes: Europe in 1992" (effects of legal and economic integration of European Economic Community). *Out/Look #10,* 3:2 (Fall 1990):30-35.

"Holland: Never Going Underground" (bus tour of Western Europe by Dutch lesbian/gay rights organization Labda, to benefit the movement against British anti-lesbian/gay Clause 28). *Connexions,* "Lesbian Activism" 29 (1989):7-8.

Lesselier, Claudie. "Dykument" (trans. from *Archives Recherches Lesbiennes,* French lesbian quarterly, no.1, June 1984, with list of lesbian archives in Belgium, France, the Netherlands, Switzerland, West Germany). *Connexions,* "Media: Getting to Women" 16 (Spring 1985):19.

Robins, Peter. "Not All Cider with Bosie; the First Formal Gathering of Lesbian and Gay Writers Living in Europe Took Place Recently in London." *New Statesman* 113 (May 15, 1987):26-7.

Wilson, Barbara. "European Feminist Publishing." *off our backs* 14:5 (May 1984):14-15.

<u>Yugoslavia:</u>

"Lesbians in Eastern Europe" (information about groups in East Germany and Yugoslavia, from an article in *The Washington Gay Blade,* December 23, 1988). *off our backs* 19:3 (March 1989):9.

Olga. "In Search of Yugoslav Lesbians." *off our backs* 12:4 (April 1982):13+.

"Yugoslavia: We Love Women" (trans. and excerpted from West German lesbian quarterly, *Lebenstich,* Spring 1988). *Connexions,* "Lesbian Activism" 29 (1989):21.

Latin America and the Caribbean (see also: Chicana Lesbians; Latina/Chicana Lesbians)

Sagot, Ana Elena Obando Montserrat. "Meeting with Repression: 2nd Encuentro Lesbico-Feminista de Latinoamerica y el Caribe" (San Jose, Costa Rica, April 1990). *off our backs* 20:8 (August/September 1990):2.

Tinker, C. "Latin America's *Encuentro Feminista*" (open discussion of lesbianism at *El Primer Encuentro Feminista LatinoAmericano y del Caribe, Bogotá, Colombia,* Summer 1981). *Connexions,* "Global Lesbianism" 3 (January 1982):9.

Tinker, Catherine. "Encuentra Feminista" (La Primer Encuentra Feminista Latinoamericano y del Caribe, Bogotá, Colombia, July 1981). *off our backs* 12:3 (March 1982):2.

Wyland, Francie. "Talking with Lesbians in South America." *Fireweed* (Canada), "Lesbiantics" 13 (1982):12-18.

Argentina:

"Argentina: Gay Groups Banned." *off our backs* 20:10 (November 1990):7.

"Argentina: Shrouded in Silence." *Connexions,* "Global Lesbianism" 3 (January 1982):12-4; also *Spare Rib* (Great Britain) 133 (August 1983):20-2.

Gascon-Vera, Elena. "El Naufragio del Deseo: Esther Tusquets y Sylvia Molloy" ("The Failure of Desire: Esther Tusquets and Sylvia Molloy"; author Molloy wrote the short novel *En Breve Carcel*). *Plaza: Revista de Literatura* 11 (Autumn 1986):20-4.

Hozven, Roberto. "*En Breve Carcel:* Fé de Erratas" (short novel by Sylvia Molloy). *Discurso Literario: Revista de Temas Hispánicos* 5:1 (Autumn 1987):121-38.

Sternbach, Nancy Saporta. "Argentina 'In Democracy': Feminism 1985" (including section on "Women's Groups and Homophobia"). *off our backs* 16:1 (January 1986):6-8.

<u>Brazil</u>:

"'Don't Label Me; I Label Myself'" (interview with Angela Ro Ro, popular Brazilian singer; trans. from *Chana Com Chana*, Brazilian lesbian journal, Spring 1981). *Connexions*, "Global Lesbianism" 3 (January 1982):10-11.

Grupo de Acao Lesbico-Feminista. "Brazilian Lesbian Statement" (trans. from *Chana Com Chana*, Brazilian lesbian journal). *off our backs* 12:3 (March 1982):2.

"'I Am Everything'" (interview with 25-year-old Brazilian lesbian; trans. from *Mulherio*, Brazilian feminist bimonthly, September/October 1982). *Connexions*, "Global Lesbianism 2" 10 (Fall 1983):14-15.

"Lesbians and the Inquisition: Love and Languishing." *Connexions*, "Global Lesbianism" 3 (January 1982):15+.

Mendonça, Nana. "International Lesbianism: Brazil." *Feminist Review* (Great Britain), "Perverse Politics: Lesbian Issues" 34 (Spring 1990):8-11.

Ortega, Eliana and Nancy Saporta Sternbach. "Gracias a la Vida: Recounting the Third Latin American Feminist Meeting in Bertioga, Brazil, July 31-August 4, 1985." *off our backs* 16:1 (January 1986):1-5.

Parker, Richard. "Youth, Identity, and Homosexuality: the Changing Shape of Sexual Life in Contemporary Brazil." *Journal of Homosexuality*, "Gay and Lesbian Youth: Part II" 17:3/4 (1989):269-90.

Rodrigues, Marlene. "International Lesbianism: Letter from São Paolo." *Feminist Review* (Great Britain), "Perverse Politics: Lesbian Issues" 34 (Spring 1990):11-13.

Chile:

"Chile" (excerpt from *Women's News,* Irish feminist bimonthly,
(December/January 1989)). *Connexions,* "Lesbian Activism" 29
(1989):15.

Colombia:

"Colombia: Attacks on Gays" (murder of lesbians and gays by
paramilitary troops). *off our backs* 17:5 (May 1987):18.

Costa Rica:

Douglas, Carol Anne. "Feminism in the Barrios of Costa Rica"
(interview with Cost Rican feminist Montserrat Sagot). *off our
backs* 20:3 (March 1990):1-3+.

Cuba:

Arguelles, Lourdes and B. Ruby Rich. "Homosexuality,
Homophobia, and Revolution: Notes Toward an Understanding
of the Cuban Lesbian and Gay Male Experience, Part I" (for Part
II, see Rich, B. Ruby, this section). *Signs,* "The Lesbian Issue"
9:4 (Summer 1984):683-99.

Bowry, Gill. "Lesbians in Cuba." *off our backs* 19:3 (March 1989):6-
7.

Foley, M.J. "Gay Refugee Denied Visa" (by U.S.; refugee fleeing
Cuba). *off our backs* 17:5 (May 1987):24.

Gannon, Aixa. "Homosexuality in Cuba: a Threat to Public
Morality?" (interview with Cuban lesbian who emigrated to the
U.S. in May 1980). *Connexions,* "In Search of Work and
Refuge" 2 (Fall 1981):18-9.

"In Practice, Not Theory" (account by two Dutch members of the
Dutch Venceremos Brigade, who went to Cuba to seek out
lesbians). *Connexions,* "Global Lesbianism 2" 10 (Fall 1983):9.

Lancaster, Roger N. "Comment on Arguelles and Rich's 'Homosexuality, Homophobia and Revolution: Notes Toward an Understanding of the Cuban Lesbian and Gay Male Experience, Part II'" (from perspective of field work in Nicaragua, with reply by B. Ruby Rich and Lourdes Arguelles). *Signs* 12:1 (Autumn 1986):188-92.

O'Sullivan, Sue. "How Cuba Doesn't Cope with Sexuality." *Spare Rib* (Great Britain) 125 (December 1982):52-5.

Rich, B. Ruby and Lourdes Arguelles. "Homosexuality, Homophobia, and Revolution: Notes Toward an Understanding of the Cuban Lesbian and Gay Male Experience, Part II" (for Part I, see Arguelles, Lourdes, this section). *Signs* 11:1 (Autumn 1985):120-36.

Ruth. "Cuban Lesbians in USA" (interview with two women who recently moved to Seattle, Washington). *off our backs* 11:4 (April 1981):12.

Stanford, Liz. "Lesbians Seek Exile" (from Pakistan, Mozambique, Spain, Nicaragua, and Cuba). *off our backs* 10:5 (May 1980):6.

Steffens, Heidi. "Revolutions Are Never Easy: a Hard Look at Our Movement, Sexuality in Cuba, and What Happened on the Venceremos Brigade." *off our backs* 2:2 (October 1971):36-7.

Mexico:
CAD. "Gays Struggle" (news briefs about gay rights struggles around the world). *off our backs* 8:10 (November 1978):6.

de la Tierra, Tatiana. "Latina American Lesbian-Feminist: Together in Mexico." *Visibilities* 2:5 (September/October 1988):8-11.

"Demons, Duelers, and Poets" (lesbians in the 16th, 17th, and 20th centuries; trans. from *Fem*, Mexican feminist bimonthly, vol.7, no.26). *Connexions,* "Global Lesbianism 2" 10 (Fall 1983):2.

Granero, M. "Differences Between Homosexuals and Heterosexuals (Males and Females) in Fears, Assertivity and Self-Sufficiency." *Revista LatinoAmericana de Psychologia* (Mexico) 16:1 (1984):39-52.

Harper, Jorjet. "Sor Juana [Inez de la Cruz]: the Other Tenth Muse" (17th century poet and nun). *Hot Wire* 5:2 (May 1989):14-15+.

Henry, Alice. "Mexican Lesbian Speaks Out" (about her writing, homophobia, and political organizing in Mexico, remaining anonymous for fear of repression). *off our backs* 16:1 (January 1986):8.

"Mexican Gays Attacked" (at rally held by the Comité de Lesbianas y Homosexuales en Apoyo a Rosario Ibarra in Mexico City, March 1982). *off our backs* 12:6 (June 1982):10.

"Mexican Lesbian Group" (Grupo Lesbico Patlamali de Guadalajara). *off our backs* 18:9 (October 1988):11.

"Mexico: Lesbians Meet" (Second National Lesbian Conference, Mexico City, September 1988; from *Mujer a Mujer,* Mexico). *off our backs* 19:4 (April 1989):6.

"Mexico: the First Lesbian *Encuentro*" (interview with organizers Alida Castelón and Lourdes Pérez; Cuernavaca, Mexico, October 1987; from Canadian monthly, *Rites* 4:4 (September 1987)). *Connexions,* "Lesbian Activism" 29 (1989):26-7.

Popp, Elena. "First Encuentro of Feminist Lesbians" (Cuernavaca, October 1987). *off our backs* 18:3 (March 1988):32-3.

"Sor Juana [Inez de la Cruz]: Trials and Triumphs in the Convent" (17th century poet and nun; trans. from Venezuelan bimonthly *La Mala Vida,* May/June 1988). *Connexions,* "Feminism and Religion" 28 (1988-89):4-6.

"Things Have Changed: Copenhagen and Nairobi Compared"
(interview with Claudia Hinojosa, founding member of Mexican
feminist magazine *Fem*). *Connexions,* "Forum '85: Nairobi,
Kenya" 17-18 (Summer/Fall 1985):7-9.

Nicaragua:

Irving, Kim. "Nicaragua: Lesbian Sandinista" (interview with young
lesbian activist and Sandinista; from Canadian monthly *Rites,*
March 1987). *Connexions,* "Lesbian Activism" 29 (1989):10-11.

------. "Nicaragua: Lesbian Sandinista" (interview with Brenda Flores).
off our backs 17:6 (June 1987):9.

"Nicaragua: Moving Forward Together" (interview with Sandinista
activist Rita Arauz about AIDS activism and education in
Nicaragua). *Connexions,* "Women and AIDS" 33 (1990):13.

Stanford, Liz. "Lesbians Seek Exile" (from Pakistan, Mozambique,
Spain, Nicaragua, and Cuba). *off our backs* 10:5 (May 1980):6.

Thomas, June. "Women in Nicaragua: an Interview with Rebecca
Gordon" (author of *Letters from Nicaragua;* including section on
"lesbian identity"). *off our backs* 17:3 (March 1987):4-5.

Peru:

"Jock Shorts" (soccer team formed by lesbians in women's prison
near Lima, Peru). *Connexions,* "Global Lesbianism 2" 10 (Fall
1983):11.

"Peru: the Other Face of the Moon" (compiled and trans. from articles
in West German bimonthly *Tarantel,* January/February 1987 and
Canadian monthly *Rites,* October 1985). *Connexions,* "Lesbian
Activism" 29 (1989):16-17.

Puerto Rico:

Hidalgo, Hilda A. and Elia Hidalgo Christensen. "The Puerto Rican
Lesbian and the Puerto Rican Community." *Journal of
Homosexuality* 2 (Winter 1977):109-22.

Suriname:

"Mati" (name used by women in the Organization of Surinamese
Homosexuals in Holland, SoHo). *Connexions,* "Global
Lesbianism 2" 10 (Fall 1983):10.

Venezuela:

"Zap Repression!" (interview with 21-year-old Venezuelan lesbian;
trans. from *Entendido,* Venezuelan gay monthly, February 1983).
Connexions, "Global Lesbianism 2" 10 (Fall 1983):8.

Middle East:
Egypt:

Khayatt, Didi. "Personal Politics and Sexuality" (by Egyptian-
Canadian lesbian). *Resources for Feminist Research* (Canada),
"Confronting Heterosexuality/Confronter l'hétérosexualité"
19:3&4 (September/December 1990):8-12.

Israel:

Jan. "Israeli Lesbians." *off our backs* 8:7 (July 1978):4.

Katz, Sue. "The Vanilla Tourist" (the S/M debate in Israel's
"underground" lesbian community). *Common Lives/Lesbian
Lives* 30 (Spring 1989):31-8.

Pittsberg, Spike. "International Lesbianism: Israel." *Feminist
Review* (Great Britain), "Perverse Politics: Lesbian Issues" 34
(Spring 1990):14-18.

Shalom, Chaya. "The Only Dyke from Israel" (to attend the
International Lesbian Information Service conference, Geneva,
Switzerland, 1986). *off our backs* 16:8 (August-September
1986):26.

Turkey (see Europe)

South Asia (see also: Asian/Pacifica Lesbians):
India:

Dibblin, Jane. "Suniti Interviewed . . . " (Suniti Namjoshi, Indian-Canadian author). *Spare Rib* (Great Britain) 147 (October 1984):20-2.

CAD. "Indian Women Fight Possession, Violence" (includes section on "Lesbian Suicides"). *off our backs* 10:10 (November 1980):2.

Douglas, Carol Anne. "Feminism in India" (interview with Madhu Kishwar, editor of the Indian feminist magazine *Manushi*). *off our backs* 10:5 (May 1980):2-4.

Heske, Susan with Utsa and Kayal. "There Are, Always Have Been, Always Will Be Lesbians in India" (interview). *Conditions: thirteen* 5:1 (1986):135-46.

"India: Lesbian Police" (fired and reinstated due to public protest). *off our backs* 18:9 (October 1988):10.

"Indian Gay Conference" (Hyderabad, India, November 1981). *off our backs* 12:6 (June 1982):10.

Islam, Sharmem. "Breaking Silence: Coming Out in India" (interview with Nandini Datta and Dupitara Chowdurry). *Sojourner* 14:10 (June 1989):20-1.

"Young Lesbians in India: Bury Us Together" (lesbians today and in ancient history). *Connexions*, "Global Lesbianism" 3 (January 1982):7.

Pakistan:

Naheed, Kishwar (trans. *Diva* editorial board). "Of Lesbianism" (in relation to Pakistan and Muslim religious texts). *Diva: a Quarterly of South Asian Women* 1:2 (1988):24-9.

Stanford, Liz. "Lesbians Seek Exile" (from Pakistan, Mozambique, Spain, Nicaragua, and Cuba). *off our backs* 10:5 (May 1980):6.

Southeast Asia (see also: Asian/Pacifica Lesbians):
Indonesia:
"Young Lesbians in Indonesia: Trial and a Marriage" (trans. from
Tempo, a mainstream Indonesian newsmagazine, May 23 and 30,
1981). *Connexions*, "Global Lesbianism" 3 (January 1982):6;
also *off our backs* 12:3 (March 1982):5.

Malaysia:
Hammer, Barbara. "Into a Woman's World" (interview with Chinese
Malay woman who moved to Australia at age 17). *Connexions*,
"Global Lesbianism 2" 10 (Fall 1983):19.

Thailand:
Anderson, Shelley. "Thailand: Tomboys, Ladies, and Amphibians."
Connexions, "Lesbian Activism" 29 (1989):6.

Berhane-Selassie, Tsehai, Alice Henry, Sona Osman and Ruth
Wallsgrove. "Feminism in Thailand: 'It Will Take My Whole
Life, I Think . . . '" (interview with lesbian-feminist activist
Unchana Suwannanond). *off our backs* 15:3 (March 1985):2-4.

"Ladies Lodge" (low-cost hostel for lesbians traveling to Bangkok,
founded by the Asian Lesbian Network). *Sojourner* 15:1
(September 1989):15.

USSR:
Dorf, Julie. "On the Theme: Talking with the Editor of the Soviet
Union's First Gay and Lesbian Newspaper" (*Tema;* editor uses
pseudonym). *Out/Look#9*, 3:1 (Summer 1990):55-9.

Engelstein, Laura. "Lesbian Vignettes: a Russian Triptych from the
1890s." *Signs* 15:4 (1990):813-31.

Gessen, Masha. "We Have No Sex: Soviet Gays and AIDS in the Era
of Glasnost." *Out/Look #9*, 3:1 (Summer 1990):42-54.

"In the USSR" (trans. from *L'Alternative*, French-language
bimonthly about Eastern Europe, no. 3, March-April 1980).
Connexions, "Women in Eastern Europe" 5 (Summer 1982):25.

"Lesbians in Soviet Jails." *off our backs* 19:1 (January 1989):6; note: cover reads 18:11 (December 1988).

Shore, Rima. "Remembering Sophia Parnok (1885-1933)" (Russian writer). *Conditions: six* 2:3 (Summer 1980): 177-93.

Lesbians of Color (see also: African-American Lesbians; Asian/Pacifica Lesbians; Chicana Lesbians; Latina/Chicana Lesbians; Lesbians Around the World; Native American Lesbians; Racism)

Abdullahad, Tania and Leigh H. Mosley. "Third World Lesbian & Gay Conference" (second annual national conference, Chicago, Illinois, November 1981; includes workshop reports on "mature lesbians," "urban black lesbians," "media," "grassroots," "racism & sexism"). *off our backs* 12:2 (February 1982):4.

Anzaldúa, Gloria. "*En Rapport,* In Opposition: *Cobrando Cuentas a Las Nuestras.*" *Sinister Wisdom* 33 (Fall 1987):11-17.

------. "La Conciencia de la Mestiza: the Mestiza Consciousness." *Woman of Power* 10 (Summer 1988):32-3+.

Brant, Beth. (Letter about third world women and writing). *Sinister Wisdom* 19 (1982):32-6.

Burning Cloud (Consuelo Sison), Nisqually Nation. "Open Letter from Filipina/Indian Dyke." *off our backs* 8:11 (December 1978):8-9.

Carmen, Gail, Sheila, and Pratibha. "Becoming Visible: Black Lesbian Discussions." *Feminist Review* (Great Britain), "Many Voices, One Chant: Black Feminist Perspectives" 17 (Autumn 1984):53-72.

Disch, Estelle. "Common Differences: Third World Women and Feminist Perspectives" (Conference, University of Illinois at Urbana Champaign, April 1983; includes section on "Sexuality vs. Hunger"). *off our backs* 13:7 (July 1983):5-6.

DOC. "The First National Third World Lesbian and Gay Conference." *off our backs* 9:10 (November 1979):14.

Douglas, Carol Anne. "Feminist Theory: Notes From the Third Decade." *off our backs,* "20th Anniversary" 20:2 (February 1990):24.

Elizarde, Margarita. "Lesbianas de Color." *off our backs* 9:6 (June 1979):10+.

Ertman, Martha. "Women and the Law Conference" (Detroit, Michigan, March 1990; topics include legal needs of lesbians of color and violence against lesbians and gay men). *off our backs* 20:7 (July 1990):2-5.

Goldsby, Jackie. "What It Means to Be Colored Me." *Out/Look #9,* 3:1 (Summer 1990):9-17.

Hindin, Roanne. "Radical Women National Conference: the Third Wave of Feminism" (Santa Monica, California, February 1990). *off our backs* 20:6 (June 1990):9.

Hunter, Joyce. "Violence Against Lesbian and Gay Male Youths" (especially people of color, and related suicide attempts). *Journal of Interpersonal Violence* 5:3 (1990):295-300.

Isis. "Herstory in the Making" (first Third World Lesbian Writers Conference, New York City, February 1979). *off our backs* 9:4 (April 1979):20.

Kanuha, Valli. "Compounding the Triple Jeopardy: Battering in Lesbian of Color Relationships." *Women & Therapy,* "Diversity and Complexity in Feminist Therapy: Part I" 9:1/2 (1990):169-84.

"Lesbians of Colour: Loving and Struggling -- a Conversation Between Three Lesbians of Colour." *Fireweed* (Canada), "Women of Colour" 16 (Spring 1983):66-72.

Lootens, Tricia. "Third Women in Print Conference" (Berkeley, California, May 1985; workshop issues reported include classism, erotica, lesbian nuns, women of color, pornography, censorship, raid on British gay bookstore). *off our backs* 15:8 (August-September 1985):8-9+.

Lorde, Audre. "Women, Power, and Difference" (talk delivered at the Women in America: Legacies of Race and Ethnicity conference, Georgetown University, Washington, D.C., April 1988; Lorde discusses living in St. Croix, the U.S. Virgin Islands). *Sojourner* 15:3 (November 1989):18-19.

Miller, Cheryl. "Lesbians of Color: Celebrating Our Common Bonds and Differences." *Hot Wire* 4:2 (March 1988):28-9+.

Moraga, Cherríe. "A Unified Rainbow of Strength" (speech to the Second National Third World Lesbian/Gay Conference, Chicago, Illinois, November 1981). *off our backs* 12:2 (February 1982):4-6.

Moraga, Cherríe and Barbara Smith. "Lesbian Literature: a Third World Perspective." *Radical Teacher,* "Gay and Lesbian Studies" 24 (no date; c.1983):12-14.

Morales, Edward S. "Ethnic Minority Families and Minority Gays and Lesbians." *Marriage and Family Review* 14:3-4 (1989):217-39.

Morris, Bonnie. "Anti-Semitism in the Women's Movement: a Jewish Lesbian Speaks." *off our backs* 20:11 (December 1990):12-13.

Paz, Juana Maria. "Womyn and Colour: a Puerto Rican Dyke Examines Her Roots." *off our backs* 9:6 (June 1979):9+.

Pheterson, Gail. "Alliances Between Women: Overcoming Internalized Oppression and Internalized Domination" ("Feminist Alliance Project" in the Netherlands, addressing racism, anti-Semitism, and heterosexism). *Signs* 12:1 (Autumn 1986):146-60.

Post, Dianne. "Radical Women National Conference: a Cold Shower" (Santa Monica, California, February 1990). *off our backs* 20:6 (June 1990):10-11.

"Racism: Lesbian Artists Have Their Say" (the Dynamics of Color Art Exhibition, part of the Dynamics of Color Conference, San Francisco, California, October 1989). *Out/Look #8,* 2:4 (Spring 1990):38-43.

Sandoval, Chela. "Comment on Krieger's 'Lesbian Identity and Community: Recent Social Science Literature'" (objects to Krieger's generalizations, on the basis that lesbians of color build/perceive community differently; Krieger's article appears in *Signs,* 8:1 (Autumn 1982):91-108). *Signs,* "The Lesbian Issue" 9:4 (Summer 1984):725-29.

Springer, Christina. "The National Women's Music Festival: Bringing Non-Dominant Women to Full Boil." *off our backs* 20:5 (May 1990):9.

Stato, Joanne. "14th Michigan Womyn's Music Festival" (the politics of the event -- who attended, what was discussed, including lesbians of color, racism, S/M, disability, and music). *off our backs* 19:9 (October 1989):20-1.

"Uma" (excerpt of interview with New Zealander of Indian descent). *Connexions,* "Global Lesbianism 2" 10 (Fall 1983):5-7.

Weir, Lorna. "Tit for Tat: Coalition Politics." *Broadside* (Canada) 3:4 (1982):10-11.

Williams, Natalie. "Lesbian and Gay People of Colour Gather in London" (Sixth International Lesbian and Gay People of Colour Conference, London, England, November 1990). *Spare Rib* (Great Britain) 219 (December/January 1990/91):66-7.

Anzaldúa, Gloria (Chicana writer):

DeShazer, Mary K. "'Sisters in Arms' -- the Warrior Construct in Writings by Contemporary U.S. Women of Color" (including Gloria Anzaldúa and Audre Lorde). *NWSA Journal* 2:3 (Summer 1990):349-73.

Bunch, Charlotte (white activist and writer):

Schultz, Debra. "Bunch, One-Woman Coalition." *New Directions for Women* 16 (November-December 1987):4+.

Dickson, Roz (Haitian activist):

Lootens, Tricia. "Common Differences: One Feminist's Perspective" (on the Common Differences: Third World Women and Feminist Perspectives Conference, University of Illinois at Urbana Champaign, April 1983; interview). *off our backs* 13:7 (July 1983):7.

Johnson, Sonia (white writer):

Bowen, Angela, Jacqui Alexander, Jennifer Abod, and Terri Ortiz. "Taking Issue with Sonia" (response to interview with Sonia Johnson in *Sojourner* 13:5 (January 1988)). *Sojourner* 13:6 (February 1988):14-15.

Kitchen Table: Women of Color Press:

Jewell, Terri L. "Barbara Smith and Kitchen Table Women of Color Press." *Hot Wire* 6:2 (May 1990):20-2+.

Parkerson, Michelle. "Some Place That's Our Own -- an Interview with Barbara Smith." *off our backs* 14:4 (April 1984):10-12+.

Smith, Barbara. "A Press of Our Own: Kitchen Table: Women of Color Press." *Frontiers* 10:3 (1989):11-13.

Sorrel, Lorraine. "This Bridge Moves Feminists" (interview with Cherríe Moraga and Barbara Smith). *off our backs* 12:4 (April 1982):4-5+.

Lorde, Audre (African-American writer):

DeShazer, Mary K. "Sisters in Arms' -- the Warrior Construct in Writings by Contemporary U.S. Women of Color" (including Gloria Anzaldúa and Audre Lorde). *NWSA Journal* 2:3 (Summer 1990):349-73.

Stato, Joanne. "I Am Your Sister Celeconference: Tribute to Audre Lorde" (Boston, Massachusetts, October 1990). *off our backs* 20:11 (December 1990):1-5+.

Moraga, Cherríe (Chicana writer):

Sorrel, Lorraine. "This Bridge Moves Feminists" (interview with Cherríe Moraga and Barbara Smith). *off our backs* 12:4 (April 1982):4-5+.

Outwrite (British newspaper):

"England: a Working Collective" (interview with Hansa, a collective member of *Outwrite*). *Connexions,* "Media: Getting to Women" 16 (Spring 1985):3-4.

Smith, Barbara (African-American activist, publisher, writer):

Jewell, Terri L. "Barbara Smith and Kitchen Table Women of Color Press." *Hot Wire* 6:2 (May 1990):20-2+.

Kulp, Denise and Karen Mudd. "Common Causes: Uncommon Coalitions" (Charlotte Bunch, Barbara MacDonald, Barbara Smith, and Merle Woo at National Women's Studies Association conference symposium, University of Washington, 1985). *off our backs* 15:8 (August-September 1985):4-5+.

Parkerson, Michelle. "Some Place That's Our Own -- an Interview with Barbara Smith." *off our backs* 14:4 (April 1984):10-12+.

Smith, Barbara. "A Press of Our Own: Kitchen Table: Women of Color Press." *Frontiers* 10:3 (1989):11-13.

Sorrel, Lorraine. "This Bridge Moves Feminists" (interview with Cherríe Moraga and Barbara Smith). *off our backs* 12:4 (April 1982):4-5+.

<u>Woo, Merle</u> (Asian/Pacifica activist and writer):
Kulp, Denise and Karen Mudd. "Common Causes: Uncommon
    Coalitions" (Charlotte Bunch, Barbara MacDonald, Barbara
    Smith, and Merle Woo at National Women's Studies Association
    conference symposium, University of Washington, 1985). *off
    our backs* 15:8 (August-September 1985):4-5+.

<u>Linguistics</u> (see Language)

<u>Literary Critical Theory</u> (see also: Autobiography; Language;
    Literature: Prose; Poetry)

Alexander, Kate. "Lesbian Reading." *Gossip* (Great Britain) 6 (1988):37-
    43.

Allen, Jeffner. "Poetic Politics: How the Amazons Took the Acropolis"
    (the writing of Hélène Cixous and Monique Wittig as jumping
    off point for study of "amazon intertext" of lesbian and feminist
    writing). *Hypatia* 3:2 (Summer 1988):107-22.

Anzaldúa, Gloria. "Border Crossings" ("hybrid" multicultural writing style
    by Chicana poet/essayist). *Trivia,* "Two-Part Issue -- The 3rd
    International Feminist Bookfair -- Part II: Language/Difference:
    Writing in Tongues" 14 (Spring 1989):46-51.

Apthorp, Elaine Sargent. "Speaking of Silence: Willa Cather and the
    'Problem' of Feminist Biography." *Women's Studies* 18:1
    (1990):1-11.

Arnold, June, Sandy Boucher, Susan Griffin, Melanie Kaye(/Kantrowitz),
    and Judith McDaniel. "Lesbians and Literature" (Modern
    Language Association panel, San Francisco, California,
    December 1975). *Sinister Wisdom,* "Lesbian Writing and
    Publishing" 1:2 (Fall 1976):20-33.

Arnold, June and Bertha Harris. "Lesbian Fiction: a Dialogue" (concerned mainly with defining the term "lesbian fiction"). *Sinister Wisdom*, "Lesbian Writing and Publishing" 1:2 (Fall 1976):42-51.

Boucher, Sandy, June Arnold, Susan Griffin, Melanie Kaye(/Kantrowitz), and Judith McDaniel. "Lesbians and Literature" (Modern Language Association panel, San Francisco, California, December 1975). *Sinister Wisdom,* "Lesbian Writing and Publishing" 1:2 (Fall 1976):20-33.

Brossard, Nicole. "Traversing Fiction." *Fireweed* (Canada) 1 (Autumn 1978):20-1.

Bulkin, Elly. "Racism and Writing: Some Implications for White Lesbian Critics." *Sinister Wisdom,* "Lesbian Writing and Publishing" 13 (Spring 1980):3-22.

------. "An Interchange on Feminist Criticism on 'Dancing Through the Minefield'" (Judith Kegan Gardiner, Elly Bulkin, and Rena Grasso Patterson comment on Annette Kolodny's article, "Dancing Through the Minefield: Some Observations on the Theory, Practice, and Politics of a Feminist Literary Criticism"; Bulkin's contribution discusses heterosexism and racism in Kolodny's essay; Kolodny's response is on pp.665-75). *Feminist Studies* 8:3 (Fall 1982):635-54.

Case, Sue-Ellen. "Towards a Butch-Femme Aesthetic" (the problem of a female subject position). *Discourse: Journal for Theoretical Studies in Media and Culture* 11:1 (Fall-Winter 1988-89):55-73.

Cramer, Patricia. "Building a Tradition for Lesbian Feminist Literary Criticism: an Annotated Bibliography." *Feminist Teacher* 2:3 (1987):20-2.

Crowder, Diane Griffin. "Amazons and Mothers? Monique Wittig, Hélène Cixous, and Theories of Women's Writing." *Contemporary Literature* 24:2 (Summer 1983):117-44.

Dallery, Arleen B. "Sexual Embodiment: Beauvoir and French Feminism" (women's sexuality in Simone de Beauvoir, Hélène Cixous, Luce Irigaray and Julia Kristeva). *Women's Studies International Forum* 8:3 (1985):197-202.

Daly, Mary, Julia Penelope Stanley, Audre Lorde, Judith McDaniel and Adrienne Rich. "The Transformation of Silence into Language and Action" (Lesbians and Literature Panel of the Modern Language Association Convention, Chicago, Illinois, December 1977). *Sinister Wisdom* 6 (Summer 1978):4-25.

de Lauretis, Teresa. "The Essence of the Triangle, Or, Taking the Risk of Essentialism Seriously: Feminist Theory in Italy, the U.S., and Britain." *Differences,* "The Essential Difference: Another Look at Essentialism" 1:2 (Summer 1989):3-37.

------. "Sexual Indifference and Lesbian Representation" (discusses novels *The Well of Loneliness, Nightwood,* and *The Lesbian Body,* and the film *She Must Be Seeing Things*). *Theatre Journal* 40:2 (May 1988):155-77.

Desmoines, Harriet. "There Goes the Revolution . . . " (paper from the 1978 Modern Language Association Panel, "Lesbians and Literature: Transcending the Boundary Between the Personal the the Political"). *Sinister Wisdom* 9 (Spring 1979):20-3.

Dollemore, Jonathan. "The Dominant and the Deviants: A Violent Dialectic." *Critical Quarterly* 28:1/2 (Spring/Summer 1986):179-92.

Engelbrecht, Penelope J. "'Lifting Belly Is a Language': The Postmodern Lesbian Subject." *Feminist Studies* 16:1 (Spring 1990):85-114.

Farwell, Marilyn R. "Toward a Definition of the Lesbian Literary Imagination" (focuses on Adrienne Rich, Monique Wittig, and lesbian literary criticism). *Signs* 14:1 (Autumn 1988):100-18.

Fetterley, Judith F. "Writes of Passing" (lesbian as reader). *Gossip* (Great Britain) 5 (n.d.; c.1987):21-8; also *Gay Studies Newsletter* 14:1 (March 1987).

Foster, Thomas. "'The Very House of Difference': Gender as 'Embattled' Standpoint" (bases postmodern discussion of coalition politics on Audre Lorde's poetry). *Genders* 8 (July 1990):17-37.

Gomez, Jewelle. "Imagine a Lesbian . . . a Black Lesbian . . . " *Trivia* 12 (Spring 1988):45-60.

Griffin, Susan, June Arnold, Sandy Boucher, Melanie Kaye(/Kantrowitz), and Judith McDaniel. "Lesbians and Literature" (Modern Language Association panel, San Francisco, California, December 1975). *Sinister Wisdom,* "Lesbian Writing and Publishing" 1:2 (Fall 1976):20-33.

Harris, Bertha. "Melancholia, and Why It Feels Good . . . " (part of 1978 MLA Panel, "Lesbians and Literature: Transcending the Boundary Between the Personal and the Political"). *Sinister Wisdom* 9 (Spring 1979):24-6.

---------."What We Mean to Say: Notes Toward Defining the Nature of Lesbian Literature." *Heresies #3,* 1:3 (September 1977):5-8.

Henry, Alice and Lorraine Sorrel. "Valerie Miner on Political Fiction, Feminist Criticism & Class" (interview). *off our backs* 13:1 (January 1983):15-17.

Kaye(/Kantrowitz), Melanie. "Culture Making: Lesbian Classics in the Year 2000?" *Sinister Wisdom,* "Lesbian Writing and Publishing" 13 (Spring 1980):23-34.

-----, Susan Griffin, June Arnold, Sandy Boucher, and Judith McDaniel. "Lesbians and Literature" (Modern Language Association panel, San Francisco, California, December 1975). *Sinister Wisdom,* "Lesbian Writing and Publishing" 1:2 (Fall 1976):20-33.

Kennard, Jean E. "Ourself Behind Ourself: A Theory for Lesbian Readers." *Signs,* "The Lesbian Issue" 9:4 (Summer 1984):647-62.

Klepfisz, Irena. "Criticism: Form and Function in Lesbian Literature" (part of 1978 Modern Language Association Panel, "Lesbians and Literature: Transcending the Boundary Between the Personal and the Political"). *Sinister Wisdom* 9 (Spring 1979):27-30.

Kramarae, Cherie and Jane Kramer. "Feminist Novel Approaches to Conflict" (includes discussion of Sally Gearhart's *The Wanderground* and Marge Piercy's *Woman on the Edge of Time*). *Women & Language* 11 (Winter 1987):36-9.

Lesselier, Claudie (trans. Mary Jo Lakeland). "Social Categorizations and Construction of a Lesbian Subject." *Feminist Issues* 7 (Spring 1987):89-94.

Lorde, Audre, Mary Daly, Julia Penelope Stanley, Judith McDaniel, and Adrienne Rich. "The Transformation of Silence into Language and Action" (Lesbians and Literature Panel of the Modern Language Association Convention, Chicago, Illinois, December 1977). *Sinister Wisdom* 6 (Summer 1978):4-25; Audre Lorde's speech also in *Woman of Power* 14 (Summer 1989):40-1.

McDaniel, Judith, Susan Griffin, June Arnold, Sandy Boucher, and Melanie Kaye(/Kantrowitz). "Lesbians and Literature" (Modern Language Association panel, San Francisco, California, December 1975; McDaniel discusses *Mrs. Dalloway* by Virginia Woolf). *Sinister Wisdom,* "Lesbian Writing and Publishing" 1:2 (Fall 1976):20-33.

McDaniel, Judith, Mary Daly, Julia Penelope Stanley, Audre Lorde, and Adrienne Rich. "The Transformation of Silence into Language and Action" (Lesbians and Literature Panel of the Modern Language Association Convention, Chicago, Illinois, December 1977). *Sinister Wisdom* 6 (Summer 1978):4-25.

Marshall, Pam. "Desire Makes the Difference: Representation of Sexuality in the Structures of Narrative" (discusses the work of theorist Teresa de Lauretis, and Jane Rule's *Desert of the Heart*). *Phoebe* 1:2 (October 1989):82-5.

Newman, Kathy. "Re-membering an Interrupted Conversation: the Mother/Virgin Split" (Virginia Woolf, Tillie Olsen, Edith Wharton). *Trivia* 2 (Spring 1983):45-63.

Parks, Adrienne. "The Lesbian Feminist as Writer as Lesbian Feminist" (refusal of lesbian feminist writers to be coopted by aesthetic and/or academic convention). *Margins*, "Lesbian Feminist Writing and Publishing" 23 (August 1975):67-9.

Penelope, Julia. "Lesbians Reviewing/Reviewing Lesbians" (part of "Symposium" on feminist book reviewing). *Feminist Studies* 14:3 (Fall 1988):606-9.

Rich, Adrienne. "It Is the Lesbian In Us . . ." (". . . who is creative, for the dutiful daughter of the fathers in us is only a hack"). *Sinister Wisdom* 3 (Spring 1977):6-9.

------, Mary Daly, Julia Penelope Stanley, Audre Lorde, and Judith McDaniel. "The Transformation of Silence into Language and Action" (Lesbians and Literature Panel of the Modern Language Association Convention, Chicago, Illinois, December 1977). *Sinister Wisdom* 6 (Summer 1978):4-25.

Sand, Cy-Thea. "Lesbian Writing: Adventure into Autonomy." *Fireweed* (Canada), "Lesbiantics" 13 (1982):24-38.

Smith, Barbara. "Toward a Black Feminist Criticism." *Conditions: two* 1:2 (October 1977):25-44; also *Radical Teacher* 7 (March 1978):20-7; also *Women's Studies International Quarterly* 2:2 (1979):183-94; also *Conditions: sixteen*, "Retrospective" (1989):6-25.

Smith, Sidonie. "Self, Subject, and Resistance: Marginalities and Twentieth-Century Autobiographical Practice." *Tulsa Studies in Women's Literature,* "Women Writing Autobiography" 9:1 (Spring 1990):11-24.

Stanley, Julia Penelope, Mary Daly, Audre Lorde, Judith McDaniel, and Adrienne Rich. "The Transformation of Silence into Language and Action" (Lesbians and Literature Panel of the Modern Language Association Convention, Chicago, Illinois, December 1977). *Sinister Wisdom* 6 (Summer 1978):4-25.

Stimpson, Catharine. "Zero Degree Deviancy: the Lesbian Novel in English." *Critical Inquiry* 8 (Winter 1981):363-80.

Textual Practice, "Lesbian and Gay Cultures: Theories and Texts," vol. 4, no. 2, Summer 1990.

"What Is the Function of Criticism in the Movement?" (various writers and critics). *Sinister Wisdom,* "Lesbian Writing and Publishing" 1:2 (Fall 1976):64-5.

Wildeman, Marlene. "The Lesbian Feminist Literary Ethics of Nicole Brossard in *La Lettre Aérienne.*" *Gossip* (Great Britain) 6 (1988):44-55.

Wittig, Monique. "La Pensée 'Straight.'" *Questions Féministes* (France) (février 1980):45-53.

------. "The Point of View: Universal or Particular" (critique of concept of "feminine writing," with special attention to Djuna Barnes). *Feminist Issues* 3:2 (Fall 1983):63-9.

------. "The Straight Mind." *Feminist Issues* 1:1 (Summer 1980):103-11.

Zimmerman, Bonnie. "Is 'Chloe Liked Olivia' a Lesbian Plot?" *Women's Studies International Forum* 6:2 (1983):169-75.

------. "What Has Never Been: An Overview of Lesbian Feminist Criticism." *Feminist Studies* 7:3 (Fall 1981): 451-75.

Literature: Prose (see also: Autobiography; Censorship; Detective Novels; Language; Literary Critical Theory; Periodicals: Lesbian/Feminist/Gay; Poetry; Publishing; Pulp Novels; Science Fiction/Fantasy; Theater; Vampires)

Arnold, June and Bertha Harris. "Lesbian Fiction: A Dialogue." *Sinister Wisdom,* "Lesbian Writing and Publishing" 2:1 (Fall 1976):42-51.

Bannon, Ann. "Speaking to Women Through Fiction: Then and Now" (by the author of the 1950s "Beebo Brinker" pulp novel series). *Hot Wire* 1:1 (November 1984):50.

Beck, Evelyn Torton. "Teaching About Jewish Lesbians in Literature: From *Zeitel and Rickel* to *The Tree of Begats.*" *off our backs,* education issue 12:5 (May 1982):20.

Belles Lettres: a Review of Books, "Lesbian Writers," vol. 2, no. 4, March/April 1987.

Bellos, Linda. "Beverly Smith in Conversation" (about African-American women's literature, and needlework). *Spare Rib* (Great Britain) 121 (August 1982):8.

Benstock, Shari. "Beyond the Reaches of Feminist Criticism: a Letter from Paris" (genre, and Gertrude Stein and women writers contemporary with her). *Tulsa Studies in Women's Literature* 3 (Spring-Fall 1984):5-27.

Biggs, Mary. "From Harriet Monroe to *AQ* [*Amazon Quarterly*]: Selected Women's Literary Journals, 1912-1972." *13th Moon,* "Narrative Forms" 8:1/2 (1984):183-216.

Birtha, Becky. "Celebrating Themselves: Four Self-Published Black Lesbian Authors" (part 1: I. Introduction; II. Stephanie Byrd). *off our backs* 15:7 (July 1985):22.

------. "Celebrating Themselves: Four Self-Published Black Lesbian Authors" (part 3: V. Linda Brown, and "Books by Self-Identified Black Lesbians"). *off our backs* 15:9 (October 1985):16-17.

Boucher, Sandy, Susan Griffin, June Arnold, Melanie Kaye(/Kantrowitz), and Judith McDaniel. "Lesbians and Literature" (Modern Language Association panel, San Francisco, California, December 1975). *Sinister Wisdom,* "Lesbian Writing and Publishing" 1:2 (Fall 1976):20-33.

Brady, Maureen and Judith McDaniel. "Lesbians in the Mainstream: Images of Lesbians in Recent Commercial Fiction." *Conditions: six* 2:3 (Summer 1980):82-105.

Brant, Beth. (Letter about Third World women and writing). *Sinister Wisdom* 19 (1982):32-6.

Califia, Pat. "We Know What We Want: Lesbian Literature Meets the Sexual Revolution." *Sinister Wisdom,* "Lesbian Writing and Publishing" 1:2 (Fall 1976):67-72.

Chapman, Frances. "Women Loving Words and Other Women" (first annual Lesbian Writers' Conference). *off our backs* 4:10 (October 1974):7.

Chrichton, E.G. "'There's So Much to Say': OUT Write '90 Makes History" (first national conference of lesbian and gay writers, San Francisco, California, March 1990). *Out/Look #9,* 3:1 (Summer 1990):2-5.

Clarke, Cheryl, Jewelle Gomez, Evelyn Hammonds, Bonnie Johnson, and Linda Powell. "Black Women on Black Women Writers: Conversations and Questions." *Conditions: nine* 3:3 (Spring 1983):88-137.

Cook, Blanche Wiesen. "'Women Alone Stir My Imagination':
Lesbianism and the Cultural Tradition." *Signs* 4:4 (Summer
1979):718-39.

Coward, Rosalind. "Sexual Outlaws" (erotica in women's writing). *New
Statesman and Society* 2 (June 9, 1989):42-3.

Cruikshank, Cathy. "Lesbian Literature: Random Thoughts." *Margins,*
"Lesbian Feminist Writing and Publishing" 23 (August
1975):40-1.

Damon, Gene (Barbara Grier). "When It Changed Or, Growing Up Gay in
America with the Help of Literature." *Margins,* "Lesbian
Feminist Writing and Publishing" 23 (August 1975):16-18.

de Lauretis, Teresa. "Sexual Indifference and Lesbian Representation"
(discusses novels *The Well of Loneliness, Nightwood,* and *The
Lesbian Body,* and the film *She Must Be Seeing Things*).
Theatre Journal 40:2 (May 1988):155-77.

DeShazer, Mary K. "'Sisters in Arms' -- the Warrior Construct in
Writings by Contemporary U.S. Women of Color" (including
Gloria Anzaldúa and Audre Lorde). *NWSA Journal* 2:3 (Summer
1990):349-73.

Desmoines, Harriet, Bertha Harris, and Irena Klepfisz. "Lesbian Literature
and Criticism" (papers from Modern Language Association
panel, 1978). *Sinister Wisdom* 9 (Spring 1979):20-30.

Duncombe, Sue and Anne Picot. "The Two Faces of Antigone."
Refractory Girl (Australia) 6 (June 1974):31-4.

Dunn, Sara. "Voyages of the Valkyries: Recent Lesbian Pornographic
Writing." *Feminist Review* (Great Britain), "Perverse Politics:
Lesbian Issues" 34 (Spring 1990):161-70.

Faderman, Lillian. "Female Same-Sex Relationships in Novels by
Longfellow, Holmes, and James." *New England Quarterly* 51:3
(September 1978):309-32.

------. "Lesbian Magazine Fiction in the Early Twentieth Century." *Journal of Popular Culture* 11:4 (Spring 1978):800-17.

------. "Love Between Women in 1928: Why Progressivism Is Not Always Progress." *Journal of Homosexuality* 12:3/4 (May 1986):23-42.

Fassler, Barbara. "Theories of Homosexuality as Sources of Bloomsbury's Androgyny" (Virginia Woolf's circle of literary/artist friends). *Signs* 5:2 (Winter 1979):237-51.

Gomez, Jewelle. "Re-Casting the Mythology: Writing Vampire Fiction." *Hot Wire* 4:1 (November 1987):42-3+.

Grover, Jan Zita. "Words to Lust By" (lesbian erotica and pornography). *Women's Review of Books* 8 (November 1990):21-3.

Gubar, Susan. "Blessings in Disguise: Cross-dressing as Re-dressing for Female Modernists." *Massachusetts Review* 22:3 (Autumn 1981):477-508.

------. "Sapphistries" (influence of Sappho on various writers). *Signs* 10:1 (Autumn 1984):43-62.

Hart, Betty. "A Cry in the Wilderness: The Diary of Alice Dunbar Nelson." *Women's Studies Quarterly* 17:3&4 (Fall/Winter 1989):74-8.

Henry, Alice and Lorraine Sorrel. "Valerie Miner on Political Fiction, Feminist Criticism & Class" (interview). *off our backs* 13:1 (January 1983):15-17.

Hernton, Calvin. "Sexual Mountain and Black Women Writers" (lesbian and heterosexual writers). *Black Scholar* 16:4 (July 1985):2.

Hollibaugh, Amber. "Writers as Activists: Moving Working-Class Oral Protest Onto the Printed Page." *Out/Look #10,* 3:2 (Fall 1990):69-72.

Isis. "Herstory in the Making" (first Third World Lesbian Writers Conference, New York City, February 1979). *off our backs* 9:4 (April 1979):20.

Kaye(/Kantrowitz), Melanie. "Culture Making: Lesbian Classics in the Year 2000?" *Sinister Wisdom* 13 (Spring 1980):23-34.

Keener, K.M. "Out of the Archives and into the Academy: Opportunities for Research and Publication in Lesbian Literature." *College English* 44:3 (March 1982):301-13.

Kessler, C.F. and G. Rudenstein. "Mothers and Daughters in Literature: a Preliminary Bibliography." *Women's Studies* 6 (1979):223-34.

Levine, Nancy J. "'I've Always Suffered from Sirens': the Cinema and Djuna Barnes' *Nightwood.*" *Women's Studies: an Interdisciplinary Journal* 16:3-4 (1989):271-81.

Lewin, Mimi. "Lesbian Writers Come Together" (second annual Lesbian Writers' Conference, Chicago, Illinois, September 1975). *off our backs* 5:9 (November 1975):18+.

Livia, Anna. (letter about S/M, and lesbian sexuality in literature). *Lesbian Ethics* 2:2 (Fall 1986):105-6.

Margins, "Lesbian Feminist Writing and Publishing," no. 23, August 1975.

Millin, Sarah. "Pink Ink Since 1963: Best Gay-Lesbian Writings in Review." *Canadian Dimension* (Canada) 22 (November-December 1988):22+.

Moira, Fran. "Writing-On: Women Personified" (Washington, D.C. Lesbian-Feminist Writing Collective). *off our backs* 5:5 (May-June 1975):16.

Moraga, Cherríe and Barbara Smith. "Lesbian Literature: a Third World Perspective." *Radical Teacher,* "Gay and Lesbian Studies" 24 (no date; c.1983):12-14.

Penelope, Julia. "Lesbians Reviewing/Reviewing Lesbians" (part of "Symposium" on feminist book reviewing). *Feminist Studies* 14:3 (Fall 1988):606.

Powell, Leslie. "The Gay Writer: This Will Hurt You With the Publishers." *Progressive* 45 (November 1981):46-7.

Robins, Peter. "Not All Cider with Bosie; the First Formal Gathering of Lesbian and Gay Writers Living in Europe Took Place Recently in London." *New Statesman* 113 (May 15, 1987):26-7.

Rule, Jane. "Making the Real Visible: Lesbian and Writer." *Fireweed* (Canada), "Lesbiantics" 13 (1982):101-4.

------. "Sexuality in Literature." *Fireweed* (Canada), "Women and Language" 5&6 (Winter 1979-80 & Spring 1980):22-7.

Ruthchild, Nancy M. "Lesbian Books: a Long and Painful Search." *Mother Jones* 1:2 (April 1976):63-5.

Sand, Cy-Thea. "Lesbian Writing: Adventure into Autonomy." *Fireweed* (Canada) 13 (1982):24-38.

------. "Readers as Rebels: the Story of the Vancouver Lesbian Literary Collective." *Radical Reviewer* 4 (Fall 1981):6-7.

Segrest, Mab. "Lines I Dare to Write: Lesbian Writing in the South." *Southern Exposure,* "Festival: Celebrating Southern Literature" 9:2 (Summer 1981):53-62.

Shapiro, Susan C. "Amazons, Hermaphrodites, and Plain Monsters: the 'Masculine' Woman in English Satire and Social Criticism from 1580-1640." *Atlantis* (Canada) 13:1 (Fall 1987):65-76.

Shockley, A. "On Lesbian/Feminist Book Reviewing." *Sojourner* 9 (April 1984):18.

Shockley, Ann Allen. "The Black Lesbian in American literature: an Overview." *Conditions: five* 2:2 (Autumn 1979):133-42.

Sinister Wisdom, "Lesbian Writing and Publishing," vol. 1, no. 2, Fall 1976.

------, "Lesbian Writing and Publishing," no. 13, Spring 1980.

Smith, Barbara. "'Fractious, Kicking, Messy, Free': Feminist Writers Confront the Nuclear Abyss." *New England Review/Bread Loaf Quarterly* (Summer 1983):581-92.

Stanley, Julia P. "Uninhabited Angels: Metaphors for Love" (lesbian world and "real" world in lesbian novels). *Margins,* "Lesbian Feminist Writing and Publishing" 23 (August 1975):7-10.

Steffensen, Jyanni. "Things Change . . . And About Time Too: a Critical Review of Women's Erotic Writing." *Hecate* (Australia) 15:2 (1989):26-33.

Textual Practice, "Lesbian and Gay Cultures: Theories and Texts," vol. 4, no. 2, Summer 1990.

Thomas, June. "3rd International Feminist Book Fair: Promoting Lesbian Writing" (Montréal, Québec, Canada, June 1988). *off our backs* 18:10 (November 1988):3.

"Views: Publishers, Readers, Writers, Editors" (short essays and quotations about lesbian writing and publishing). *Sinister Wisdom,* "Lesbian Writing and Publishing" 13 (Spring 1980):35-50.

"Visions from the Periphery: First-Generation Lesbian Fiction in Canada." *Resources for Feminist Research* (Canada), "The Lesbian Issue/Etre Lesbienne" 12:1 (March 1983):22-6.

Wigutoff, Sharon. "Children's Books: 'Libland' or Wasteland?" *off our backs* 12:6 (June 1982):14-15.

Alcott, Louisa May:

Murphy, Ann B. "The Borders of Ethical, Erotic, and Artistic Possibilities in *Little Women.*" *Signs,* "The Ideology of Mothering: Disruption and Reproduction of Patriarchy" 15:3 (Spring 1990):562-85.

Aldridge, Sarah:

Corinne, Tee A. "Remembering as a Way of Life" (lesbian 'National Treasures', including June Arnold, Jeannete Foster, Valerie Taylor, Barbara Grier, Audre Lorde, Anita Cornwell, Sarah Aldridge, Sonny Wainwright). *Common Lives/Lesbian Lives* 19 (Spring 1986):15-18.

Anonymous:

Henry, Alice. "Mexican Lesbian Speaks Out" (about her writing, homophobia, and political organizing in Mexico, remaining anonymous for fear of repression). *off our backs* 16:1 (January 1986):8.

Anzaldúa, Gloria:

"Conversations at the Bookfair: Interview with Gloria Anzaldúa" (writer and activist). *Trivia,* "Two-Part Issue -- The 3rd International Feminist Bookfair -- Part II: Language/Difference: Writing in Tongues" 14 (Spring 1989):37-45.

Freedman, Diana P. "Living on the Borderland: the Poetic Prose of Gloria Anzaldúa and Susan Griffin." *Women and Language* 12:1 (Spring 1989):1-14.

Arnold, June:

Arnold, June, Sandy Boucher, Susan Griffin, Melanie Kaye(/Kantrowitz), and Judith McDaniel. "Lesbians and Literature" (Modern Language Association session, San Francisco, California, December 1975). *Sinister Wisdom,* "Lesbian Writing and Publishing" 2:1 (Fall 1976):20-33.

Arnold, June and Bertha Harris. "Lesbian Fiction: A Dialogue." *Sinister Wisdom,* "Lesbian Writing and Publishing" 2:1 (Fall 1976):42-51.

Corinne, Tee A. "Remembering as a Way of Life" (lesbian 'National Treasures', including June Arnold, Jeannete Foster, Valerie Taylor, Barbara Grier, Audre Lorde, Anita Cornwell, Sarah Aldridge, Sonny Wainwright). *Common Lives/Lesbian Lives* 19 (Spring 1986):15-18.

Hokensen, Jan. "The Pronouns of Gomorrha: a Lesbian Prose Tradition" (lesbian modernist writers -- including Virginia Woolf, Gertrude Stein, Djuna Barnes, and Colette -- and postmodernist writers -- including Monique Wittig, June Arnold, and Bertha Harris). *Frontiers* 10:1 (1988):62-9.

Arobateau, Red Jordan:
Shockley, Ann Allen. "Red Jordan Arobateau: A Different Kind of Black Lesbian Writer." *Sinister Wisdom* 21 (1982):35-9.

Barnes, Djuna:
Bessière, Jean. "Djuna Barnes Nouvelliste et Romancière: du Lieu Commun à l'Imprévisible sens *Spillway* et *Nightwood.*" *RLC - Revue de Littérature Comparée* 50:4 (October-December 1976):455-77.

Hokensen, Jan. "The Pronouns of Gomorrha: a Lesbian Prose Tradition" (lesbian modernist writers -- including Virginia Woolf, Gertrude Stein, Djuna Barnes, and Colette -- and post-modernist writers -- including Monique Wittig, June Arnold, and Bertha Harris). *Frontiers* 10:1 (1988):62-9.

Lanser, Susan Snider. "Speaking in Tongues: *The Ladies Almanack* and the Language of Celebration." *Frontiers,* "Lesbian History" 4:3 (Fall 1979):39-46.

Pochoda, Elizabeth. "Style's Hoax: A Reading of Djuna Barnes' *Nightwood.*" *Twentieth Century Literature* 22:2 (May 1976):179-91.

Barney, Natalie Clifford:

Orenstein, Gloria Feman. "Natalie Barney's Parisian Salon: the *Joie de Vivre* and *Savoir Faire* of a Life of Love and Letters." *13th Moon* 5:1/2 (1980):76-94.

------. "The Salon of Natalie Clifford Barney: an interview with Berthe Cleyrerque." *Signs* 4:3 (Spring 1979):484-96.

Sherman, Deborah. "The Paris Project and the Art of Lesbian Relationship" (theater group performing about Natalie Barney and her circle). *Heresies #22,* 6:2 (1987):9-13.

Wickes, George (editor). "A Natalie Barney Garland" (recollections of Barney's life and work as gathered from interviews, memoirs, and books of Sylvia Beach, Romaine Brooks, Madame Gaston Bergery, Elizabeth Eyre, Virgil Thomsen, Truman Capote, and Janet Flanner). *Paris Review* (U.S.) 61 (Spring 1975):84-134.

Belot, Adolphe:

Maas, N. "Du Mlle. Giraud Ma Femme: A 1870 Lesbian Novel by Adolphe Belot." *Maatstaf* 32:2 (1984):48-68.

Bersianik, Louky:

Gould, Karen. "Setting Words Free: Feminist Writing in Quebec" (lesbian and straight; includes discussion of Nicole Brossard and Louky Bersianik). *Signs* 6:4 (Summer 1981):617-42.

Williamson, Janice. "'Firewords' -- Dorothy Hénaut -- National Film Board, Studio D" (film about three radical feminist Québécois writers: Louky Bersianik, Nicole Brossard, Jovette Marchessault). *Resources for Feminist Research* (Canada) 15 (December 1986/January 1987):25-7.

Bloch, Alice:

Sturgis, Susanna J. "An Interview with Alice Bloch." *off our backs* 11:11 (December 1981):22-3.

<u>Bogus, SDiane</u>:
Birtha, Becky. "Celebrating Themselves: Four Self-Published Black
    Lesbian Authors" (part 2: III. Doris Davenport; IV. SDiane
    Bogus). *off our backs* 15:8 (August-September 1985):19-21.

<u>Boucher, Sandy</u>:
Boucher, Sandy, Susan Griffin, June Arnold, Melanie
    Kaye(/Kantrowitz), and Judith McDaniel. "Lesbians and
    Literature" (Modern Language Association panel, San Francisco,
    California, December 1975). *Sinister Wisdom,* "Lesbian Writing
    and Publishing" 1:2 (Fall 1976):20-33.

<u>Boye, Karin</u>:
Garde, Pia. "How to Remember Her?" (Swedish poet, novelist, and
    critic Karin Boye, b.1900). *Connexions,* "Global Lesbianism 2"
    10 (Fall 1983):22-3.

<u>Brady, Maureen</u>:
Brady, Maureen. "An Explanation of Class and Race Dynamics in the
    Writing of *Folly*" (lesbian novel discussed by the author). *13th
    Moon,* "Working Class Experience" 7:1/2 (1983):145-51.

Brady, Maureen and Judith McDaniel. "Lesbians in the Mainstream:
    Images of Lesbians in Recent Commercial Fiction." *Conditions:
    six* 2:3 (Summer 1980):82-105.

Sorrel, Lorraine and Susan Sojourner. "Maureen Brady: Envisioning
    Possibilities" (interview). *off our backs* 13:4 (April 1983):14-16.

<u>Brant, Beth</u>:
Brant, Beth. (Letter about Third World women and writing). *Sinister
    Wisdom* 19 (1982):32-6.

<u>Brantenberg, Gerd</u>:
Wilson, Barbara. "An Interview with Gerd Brantenberg" (Norwegian
    author of *Egalia's Daughters*). *off our backs* 16:4 (April
    1986):18-19.

Brome, Richard:

Rigaud, Nadia J. "L'Homosexualité Féminine dans *A Mad Couple Well Matched* (1639) de Richard Brome" ("Female Homosexuality in A Mad Couple Well Matched (1639) by Richard Brome"). *Bulletin de la Société d'Etudes Anglo-Américaines des XVIIe et XVIIIe Siècles* (France) 20 (June 1985):23-36.

Brontë, Charlotte:

Hunt, Linda C. "Sustenance and Balm: The Question of Female Friendship in *Shirley* and *Vilette.*" *Tulsa Studies in Women's Literature* 1:1 (Spring 1982):55-66.

Brossard, Nicole:

Anderson, Marguerite. "Nicole Brossard: un Imaginaire Tonique." *Resources for Feminist Research* (Canada) 15 (December 1986/January 1987):22-4.

Godard, Barbara. "*L'Amèr* or the Exploding Chapter: Nicole Brossard at the Site of Feminist Deconstruction." *Atlantis* (Canada) 9 (Spring 1984):23-34.

------. "Nicole Brossard: *Amantes* and *La Mer.*" *Broadside* (Canada) 2:6 (April 1981):14.

------. "Women Loving Women Writing: Nicole Brossard." *Resources for Feminist Research* (Canada), "The Lesbian Issue/Etre Lesbienne" 12:1 (March 1983):20-2.

Gould, Karen. "Setting Words Free: Feminist Writing in Quebec" (lesbian and straight; includes discussion of Nicole Brossard and Louky Bersianik). *Signs* 6:4 (Summer 1981):617-42.

Lockey, Ottie. (Interview with Canadian writer Nicole Brossard). *Broadside* (Canada) 2:8 (June 1981):10-11.

Sequin, Lucie. "Nicole Brossard: Les Mots-étreintes." *Canadian Woman Studies* (Canada) 1:3 (Spring 1979):56-9.

Wildeman, Marlene. "The Lesbian Feminist Literary Ethics of Nicole Brossard in *La Lettre Aérienne.*" *Gossip* (Great Britain) 6 (1988):44-55.

Williamson, Janice. "'Firewords' -- Dorothy Hénaut -- National Film Board, Studio D" (film about three radical feminist Québécois writers: Louky Bersianik, Nicole Brossard, Jovette Marchessault). *Resources for Feminist Research* (Canada) 15 (December 1986/January 1987):25-7.

Wilson, Jean. "Nicole Brossard: Fictions and Realities." *Broadside* (Canada) 3:7 (1982):20.

Brown, Linda:

Birtha, Becky. "Celebrating Themselves: Four Self-Published Black Lesbian Authors" (part 3: V. Linda Brown, and "Books by Self-Identified Black Lesbians"). *off our backs* 15:9 (October 1985):16-17.

Brown, Rita Mae:

Armstrong, Toni L. "Rita Mae Brown" (interview). *Hot Wire* 2:3 (July 1986):2-5.

Chew, Martha. "Rita Mae Brown: Feminist Theorist and Southern Novelist." *The Southern Quarterly* 22:1 (Fall 1983):61-80.

Fishbein, Leslie. "*Rubyfruit Jungle:* Lesbianism, Feminism, and Narcissism." *International Journal of Women's Studies* (Canada) 7:2 (March-April 1984):155-9.

Martindale, Kathleen. "Rita Mae Brown's *Six of One* and Anne Cameron's *The Journey:* Fictional Contributions to the Ethics of Feminist Nonviolence." *Atlantis* (Canada) 12:1 (Fall 1986):103-10.

Urbanska, Wanda. "Conversation with Rita Mae Brown." *Los Angeles Herald Examiner,* "California Living" section (May 3, 1981):5.

Byrd, Stephanie:

Birtha, Becky. "Celebrating Themselves: Four Self-Published Black Lesbian Authors" (part 1: I. Introduction; II. Stephanie Byrd). *off our backs* 15:7 (July 1985):22.

Cameron, Anne:

Martindale, Kathleen. "Rita Mae Brown's *Six of One* and Anne Cameron's *The Journey:* Fictional Contributions to the Ethics of Feminist Nonviolence." *Atlantis* (Canada) 12:1 (Fall 1986):103-10.

Cather, Willa:

Adams, T.D. "My Gay Antonía: The Politics of Willa Cather's Lesbianism." *Journal of Homosexuality* 12:3/4 (May 1986):89-98.

Apthorp, Elaine Sargent. "Speaking of Silence: Willa Cather and the 'Problem' of Feminist Biography." *Women's Studies* 18:1 (1990):1-11.

Epstein, Joseph. "Willa Cather: Listing Toward Lesbos." *New Criterion* 2:4 (December 1983):35-43.

Lambert, Deborah G. "The Defeat of a Hero: Autonomy and Sexuality in *My Antonia.*" *American Literature* 53:4 (January 1982):676-90.

Norton, Camille. "'Tomb Breakers': the Case Against Willa Cather." *Trivia* 3 (Fall 1983):27-46.

O'Brien, Sharon. "The Thing Not Named': Willa Cather as a Lesbian Writer." *Signs,* "The Lesbian Issue" 9:4 (Summer 1984):576-99.

Rubin, Larry. "The Homosexual Motif in Willa Cather's 'Paul's Case.'" *Studies in Short Fiction* 12 (Spring 1975):127-31.

Russ, Joanna. "To Write 'Like a Woman': Transformations of Identity in the Work of Willa Cather." *Journal of Homosexuality,* "Historical, Literary, and Erotic Aspects of Lesbianism" 12:3/4 (May 1986):77-88.

Sedgwick, Eve Kosofsky. "Across Gender, Across Sexuality: Willa Cather and Others" (focus on Cather's "cross gender" explorations of male homosocial bonding). *South Atlantic Quarterly* 88 (Winter 1989):53-72.

Women's Studies, on Willa Cather, vol. 11, no. 3, 1984.

Cliff, Michelle:

Dejanikus, Tacie and Loie Hayes. "Claiming an Identity: an Interview with Michelle Cliff." *off our backs* 11:6 (June 1981):18-20.

Clod, Bente:

Anderson, Marguerite. "An Interview with Bente Clod: Danish Writer, Poet, Filmmaker and Feminist." *Resources for Feminist Research* (Canada) 17 (December 1988):23-6.

Colette:

Dranch, Sherry A. "Reading Through the Veiled Text: Colette's *The Pure and the Impure.*" *Contemporary Literature* 24:2 (Summer 1983):176-89.

Hokensen, Jan. "The Pronouns of Gomorrha: a Lesbian Prose Tradition" (lesbian modernist writers -- including Virginia Woolf, Gertrude Stein, Djuna Barnes, and Colette -- and post-modernist writers -- including Monique Wittig, June Arnold, and Bertha Harris). *Frontiers* 10:1 (1988):62-9.

Converse, Florence:

Maglin, Nan Bauer. "Vida to Florence: 'Comrade and Companion'" (American writers Vida Dutten Scudder and Florence Converse). *Frontiers,* "Lesbian History" 4:3 (Fall 1979):13-20.

Davenport, Doris:

Birtha, Becky. "Celebrating Themselves: Four Self-Published Black
Lesbian Authors" (part 2: III. Doris Davenport; IV. SDiane
Bogus). *off our backs* 15:8 (August-September 1985):19-21.

de Monteflores, Carmen:

de Monteflores, Carmen. "Invisible Audiences: Writing Fiction as a
Form of Coming Out" (written by author of *Singing
Softly/Cantando Bajito*). *Out/Look #10*, 3:2 (Fall 1990):65-8.

Diderot, Denis:

Mylne, Vivienne. "What Suzanne Knew: Lesbianism and La
Religieuse." *Studies on Voltaire and the Eighteenth Century* 208
(1982):167-73.

Rex, Walter E. "Secrets from Suzanne: the Tangled Motives of *La
Religieuse.*" *The Eighteenth Century* 24:3 (Fall 1983):185-98.

Doolittle, Hilda (see H.D.)

Dutten, Vida:

Maglin, Nan Bauer. "Vida to Florence: 'Comrade and Companion'"
(American writers Vida Dutten Scudder and Florence Converse).
Frontiers, "Lesbian History" 4:3 (Fall 1979):13-20.

Fielding, Henry:

Castle, Terry. "Matters Not Fit to be Mentioned: Fielding's *The
Female Husband.*" *ELH* 49 (1982):602-22.

Forrest, Katherine V.:

Forrest, Katherine V. "Inspiration: Seven Stories of Creating Art --
'Curious Wine'" (novel by Forrest). *Hot Wire* 4:1 (November
1987):31.

Levin, Jenifer. "Aboard the *Scorpio IV* -- and Other Places -- with
Katherine V. Forrest." *Visibilities* 2:4 (July/August 1988):4-7.

François, Jocelyne:

Shaw, Nanette. "Interview with Jocelyne François." *13th Moon,* "Narrative Forms" 8:1/2 (1984):52-60.

------. "Jocelyne François: an Introduction." *13th Moon,* "Narrative Forms" 8:1/2 (1984):38-51.

Freeman, Mary Eleanor Wilkins:

Koppelman, Susan. "About 'Two Friends' and Mary Eleanor Wilkins Freeman" (includes reprint of the short story). *American Literary Realism, 1870-1910* 21:1 (Fall 1988):43-57.

Garden, Nancy:

Garden, Nancy. "Annie on My Mind" (by author of this book about two teenage lesbians). *Hot Wire* 4:3 (July 1988):46-7.

Gilman, Charlotte Perkins:

Langley, Juliet A. "'Audacious Fancies': a Collection of Letters from Charlotte Perkins Gilman to Martha Luther." *Trivia* 6 (Winter 1985):52-69.

Gomez, Jewelle:

Clarke, Cheryl, Jewelle Gomez, Evelyn Hammonds, Bonnie Johnson, and Linda Powell. "Black Women on Black Women Writers: Conversations and Questions." *Conditions: nine* 3:3 (Spring 1983):88-137.

Gomez, Jewelle. "Re-Casting the Mythology: Writing Vampire Fiction." *Hot Wire* 4:1 (November 1987):42-3+.

Griffin, Susan:

Freedman, Diana P. "Living on the Borderland: The Poetic Prose of Gloria Anzaldúa and Susan Griffin." *Women and Language* 12:1 (Spring 1989):1-14.

Griffin, Susan, Sandy Boucher, June Arnold, Melanie Kaye(/Kantrowitz), and Judith McDaniel. "Lesbians and Literature" (Modern Language Association panel, San Francisco, California, December 1975). *Sinister Wisdom,* "Lesbian Writing and Publishing" 1:2 (Fall 1976):20-33.

H.D.:

Dunn, Margaret M. "Altered Patterns and New Endings: Reflections of Change in Stein's *Three Lives* and H.D.'s *Palimpsest.*" *Frontiers* 9:2 (1987):54-9.

Hall, Radclyffe:

Brown, Beverly. "Talking About *The Well of Loneliness* -- 'A Disgusting Book When Properly Read': the Obscenity Trial." *Hecate* (Australia) 10:2 (1984):7-19.

Davis, R.G. "On Daring to Speak Its Name . . . " (letter about gay and lesbian themes in literature as taught and received in the 1930s; mentions *The Well of Loneliness*) *Encounter* 52 (February 1979):95-6.

Faderman, Lillian and Ann Williams. "Radclyffe Hall and the Lesbian Image." *Conditions: one* 1:1 (April 1977):31-41.

Franks, Claudia Stillman. "Stephen Gordon, Novelist: A Re-evaluation of Radclyffe Hall's *The Well of Loneliness.*" *Tulsa Studies in Women's Literature* 1:2 (Fall 1982):125-39.

Ingram, Angela. "'Unutterable Putrefaction' and 'Foul Stuff': Two 'Obscene' Novels of the 1920s" (*The Well of Loneliness* and *Sleeveless Errand*). *Women's Studies International Forum* 9:4 (1986):341-54.

Martinez, Inez. "The Lesbian Hero Bound: Radclyffe Hall's Portrait of Sapphic Daughters and Their Mothers." *Journal of Homosexuality* 8:3/4 (Spring-Summer 1983):127-38.

Newton, Esther. "The Mythic Mannish Lesbian: Radclyffe Hall and the New Woman." *Signs,* "The Lesbian Issue" 9:4 (Summer 1984):557-75.

Roe, Jill. "'Not At All Like Other Ladies': Radclyffe Hall." *Refractory Girl* (Australia), "Lesbian Issue" 5 (Summer 1974):24-8.

Rolley, Katrina. "Cutting a Dash: The Dress of Radclyffe Hall and Una Troubridge." *Feminist Review* (Great Britain) 35 (Summer 1990):54-66.

Sand, Cy-Thea. "Radclyffe Hall: A Feminist Analysis." *Maenad* 1 (Winter 1981):78-90.

Whitlock, Gillian. "Everything Is Out of Place: Radclyffe Hall and the Lesbian Literary Tradition." *Feminist Studies* 13:3 (Fall 1987):555-82.

------. "Talking About *The Well of Loneliness* -- 'A Martyr Reluctantly Canonised': the Lesbian Literary Tradition." *Hecate* (Australia) 10:2 (1984):20-39.

Harris, Bertha:
Arnold, June and Bertha Harris. "Lesbian Fiction: A Dialogue." *Sinister Wisdom,* "Lesbian Writing and Publishing" 2:1 (Fall 1976):42-51.

Desmoines, Harriet, Bertha Harris, and Irena Klepfisz. "Lesbian Literature and Criticism" (papers from Modern Language Association panel, 1978). *Sinister Wisdom* 9 (Spring 1979):20-30.

Hokensen, Jan. "The Pronouns of Gomorrha: a Lesbian Prose Tradition" (lesbian modernist writers -- including Virginia Woolf, Gertrude Stein, Djuna Barnes, and Colette -- and post-modernist writers -- including Monique Wittig, June Arnold, and Bertha Harris). *Frontiers* 10:1 (1988):62-9.

Jewett, Sarah Orne:

Donovan, Josephine. "The Unpublished Love Poems of Sarah Orne Jewett." *Frontiers,* "Lesbian History" 4:3 (Fall 1979):26-31.

Johnston, Jill:

Dulaney, Maedell. "Jill Johnston" (interview). *off our backs* 3:9 (July-August 1973):14-15.

Wolfe (Robbins), Susan J. "Stylistic Experimentation in Millett, Johnston and Wittig." *Fireweed* (Canada), "Women and Language" 5&6 (Winter 1979-80 and Spring 1980):134-42.

Kaye/Kantrowitz, Melanie:

Kaye(/Kantrowitz), Melanie. "Culture Making: Lesbian Classics in the Year 2000?" *Sinister Wisdom* 13 (Spring 1980):23-34.

------, Susan Griffin, Sandy Boucher, June Arnold, and Judith McDaniel. "Lesbians and Literature" (Modern Language Association panel, San Francisco, California, December 1975). *Sinister Wisdom,* "Lesbian Writing and Publishing" 1:2 (Fall 1976):20-33.

Leduc, Violette:

Cochran, Judy. "The Textual, Sexual Self: Self-Consciousness in Violette Leduc's *La Bâtarde.*" *Atlantis* (Canada) 13:1 (Fall 1987):47-52.

Lee, Vernon:

Mannocchi, Phyllis F. "Vernon Lee and Kit Anstruther-Thomson: a Study of Love and Collaboration Between Romantic Friends" (Vernon Lee, writer, critic, and historian (1856-1935); Clementina (Kit) Anstruther-Thomson, artist (1857-1921)). *Women's Studies* 12:2 (1986):129-48.

Livia, Anna:

Livia, Anna. (letter about S/M, and lesbian sexuality in literature). *Lesbian Ethics* 2:2 (Fall 1986):105-6.

Smith, Jean. "Writing *Relatively Norma*" (interview with author Anna Livia). *Spare Rib* (Great Britain) 130 (May 1983):25.

Thomas, June. "Anna Livia: Lesbian Author, Publisher." *off our backs* 18:11 (December 1988):10+.

Lorde, Audre:

Christian, Barbara. "No More Buried Lives -- the Theme of Lesbianism in Lorde, Naylor, Shange, Walker." *Feminist Issues* 5 (Spring 1985):3-20.

Corinne, Tee A. "Remembering as a Way of Life" (lesbian 'National Treasures', including June Arnold, Jeannete Foster, Valerie Taylor, Barbara Grier, Audre Lorde, Anita Cornwell, Sarah Aldridge, Sonny Wainwright). *Common Lives/Lesbian Lives* 19 (Spring 1986):15-18.

Lorde, Audre, Adrienne Rich, and Alice Walker. "In the Name of All Women: the National Book Award Speech" (read by Rich, who won the award; all three authors were nominated and agreed that whoever won would accept "in the name of all the women whose voices have gone and still go unheard in a patriarchal world"). *Margins,* "Lesbian Feminist Writing and Publishing" 23 (August 1975):23.

Ruby, Jennie. "The Black Diaspora" (Michelle Parkerson, Audre Lorde, and Cheryl Clarke speaking on diversity of self-expression among African-American women, in a session at the 10th annual National Women's Studies Association conference, University of Minnesota in Minneapolis, June 1988, "African American Women and the Black Diaspora"). *off our backs* 18:8 (August-September 1988):10.

Lynch, Lee:

Lynch, Lee. "Inspiration: Seven Stories of Creating Art -- 'The Swashbuckler' and other Fiction." *Hot Wire* 4:1 (November 1987):27+.

McDaniel, Judith:

McDaniel, Judith, Susan Griffin, Sandy Boucher, June Arnold, and
Melanie Kaye(/Kantrowitz). "Lesbians and Literature" (Modern
Language Association panel, San Francisco, California,
December 1975; McDaniel discusses *Mrs. Dalloway* by Virginia
Woolf). *Sinister Wisdom,* "Lesbian Writing and Publishing" 1:2
(Fall 1976):20-33.

Sturgis, Susanna J. "Judith McDaniel: Writer, Organizer, Witness"
(interview, plus, "A Preface to the Interview: a Statement by
Judith McDaniel"). *off our backs* 16:3 (March 1986):25-7.

McNeill, Pearlie:

Ferrier, Carole. "Interview with Pearlie McNeill" (Australian author
living in London, England). *Hecate* (Australia) 16:1/2
(1990):102-10.

Maheux-Forcier, Louise:

Dufault, Roseanne L. "Louise Maheux-Forcier's *Amadou*: Reflections
on Some Critical Blindspots." *Quebec Studies* 11 (1990-
1991):103-10.

Marchessault, Jovette:

Williamson, Janice. "'Firewords' -- Dorothy Hénaut -- National Film
Board, Studio D" (film about three radical feminist Québécois
writers: Louky Bersianik, Nicole Brossard, Jovette
Marchessault). *Resources for Feminist Research* (Canada) 15
(December 1986/January 1987):25-7.

Miller, Isabel:

Aptheker, Bettina. "Imagining Our Lives: the Novelist as Historian"
(including *Patience and Sarah* by Isabel Miller/Alma Routsong).
Woman of Power, "ReVisioning History" 16 (Spring 1990):32-
5.

Millett, Kate:

Wolfe (Robbins), Susan J. "Stylistic Experimentation in Millett,
Johnston and Wittig." *Fireweed* (Canada), "Women and
Language" 5&6 (Winter 1979-80 and Spring 1980):134-42.

Miner, Valerie:

Henry, Alice and Lorraine Sorrel. "Valerie Miner on Political
    Fiction, Feminist Criticism & Class" (interview). *off our backs*
    13:1 (January 1983):15-17.

Kinnaird, Linda. "All Good Women?" (interview with Valerie Miner).
    Spare Rib (Great Britain) 184 (November 1987):52-3.

Molloy, Sylvia:

Gascon-Vera, Elena. "El Naufragio del Deseo: Esther Tusquets y
    Sylvia Molloy" ("The Failure of Desire: Esther Tusquets and
    Sylvia Molloy"; author Molloy wrote the short novel *En Breve
    Carcel*). *Plaza: Revista de Literatura* 11 (Autumn 1986):20-4.

Hozven, Roberto. "*En Breve Carcel:* Fé de Erratas" (short novel by
    Argentine writer Sylvia Molloy). *Discurso Literario: Revista de
    Temas Hispánicos* 5:1 (Autumn 1987):121-38.

Moraga, Cherríe:

Allison, Dorothy, Tomás Almaguer, and Jackie Goldsby. "'Writing Is
    the Measure of My Life . . . ': an Interview with Cherríe
    Moraga." *Out/Look* 1:4 (Winter 1989):53-7.

Moraga, Cherríe and Barbara Smith. "Lesbian Literature: a Third
    World Perspective." *Radical Teacher,* "Gay and Lesbian Studies"
    24 (no date; c.1983):12-14.

Morrison, Toni:

Smith, Barbara. "Toward a Black Feminist Criticism." *Conditions:
    two* 1:2 (October 1977):25-44; also *Radical Teacher* 7 (March
    1978):20-7; also *Women's Studies International Quarterly* 2:2
    (1979):183-94; also *Conditions: sixteen*, "Retrospective"
    (1989):6-25.

Namjoshi, Suniti:

Dibblin, Jane. "Suniti Interviewed . . . " *Spare Rib* (Great Britain)
    147 (October 1984):20-2.

<u>Naylor, Gloria</u>:

Christian, Barbara. "No More Buried Lives -- the Theme of Lesbianism in Lorde, Naylor, Shange, Walker." *Feminist Issues* 5 (Spring 1985):3-20.

Mills, Bronwyn. "Gloria Naylor: Dreaming the Dream." *Sojourner* 13:9 (May 1988):17.

<u>Parnok, Sophia</u>:

Shore, Rima. "Remembering Sophia Parnok (1885-1933)" (Russian writer). *Conditions: six* 2:3 (Summer 1980):177-93.

<u>Rule, Jane</u>:

Biggs, Mary. "Career with Compromise" (Canadian author Jane Rule). *Women's Review of Books* 2 (May 1985):13-15.

Brady, Maureen. "'A Vision of Central Value': the Novels of Jane Rule." *Resources for Feminist Research* (Canada), "The Lesbian Issue/Etre Lesbienne" 12:1(March 1983):13-6.

Canadian Fiction Magazine, Canada, on Jane Rule, no. 23, 1976.

Collis, Rose. "Breaking the Rules" (interview). *Spare Rib* (Great Britain) 185 (December 1987):16-18.

Hancock, Geoff. "An Interview with Jane Rule." *Canadian Fiction Magazine* (Canada) 23 (1976):57-112.

Marshall, Pam. "Desire Makes the Difference: Representation of Sexuality in the Structures of Narrative" (discusses the work of theorist Teresa de Lauretis, and Jane Rule's *Desert of the Heart*). *Phoebe* 1:2 (October 1989):82-5.

Niemi, Judith. "Jane Rule and the Reviewers." *Margins,* "Lesbian Feminist Writing and Publishing" 23 (August 1975):34-7.

Rule, Jane. "Making the Real Visible: Lesbian and Writer." *Fireweed,* (Canada) "Lesbiantics" 13 (1982):101-4.

------. "Sexuality in Literature." *Fireweed* (Canada), "Women and Language" 5&6 (Winter 1979-80 & Spring 1980):22-7.

Schuster, Marilyn R. "Strategies for Survival: The Subtle Subversion of Jane Rule." *Feminist Studies* 7 (Fall 1981):431-50.

Sonthoff, Helen. "Celebration: Jane Rule's Fiction." *Canadian Fiction Magazine* (Canada) 23 (1976): 121-33.

Sackville-West, Vita:
DeSalvo, Louise A. "Lighting the Cave: the Relationship Between Vita Sackville-West and Virginia Woolf." *Signs* 8:2 (Winter 1982):195-214.

Knopp, Sherron E. "'If I Saw You Would You Kiss Me?': Sapphism and the Subversiveness of Virginia Woolf's *Orlando*" (discusses the relationship between Virginia Woolf and Vita Sackville-West). *PMLA* 103:1 (January 1988):24-34.

Sarton, May:
Bakerman, Jane S. "'Kinds of Love': Love and Friendship in Novels of May Sarton." *Critique - Studies in Modern Fiction* 20:2 (1978):83-91.

------. "'Work is My Rest': A Conversation with May Sarton." *Moving Out* 7:2 & 8:1 (1978):8-12+.

Carter, Nancy Corson. "An Interview with May Sarton." *Kalliope* 5:2 (1983):37-48.

Hershman, Marcie. "May Sarton at 70: 'A Viable Life Against the Odds.'" *Ms.* 11:4 (October 1982):23-6.

Shelley, D. "Conversation with May Sarton." *Women and Literature* 7:2 (Spring 1979):33-41.

Springer, Marlene. "As We Shall Be: May Sarton and Aging." *Frontiers* 5:3 (Fall 1980):46-9.

Woodward, K. "May Sarton and Fictions of Old Age." *Women and Literature* 1 (1980):108-27.

Schulman, Sarah:

Cassidy, Cristi. "A Conversation with Sarah Schulman." *Visibilities* 3:1 (January/February 1989):8+.

Kulp, Denise. "Sarah Schulman: 'On the Road to . . .'" (interview). *off our backs* 16:11 (December 1986):20-1+.

Scott, Claudia:

Devries, R. "Work and Death of Lesbian Writer." *New Women's Times* 8:10 (November 1982):S.15.

Shange, Ntozake:

Christian, Barbara. "No More Buried Lives -- the Theme of Lesbianism in Lorde, Naylor, Shange, Walker." *Feminist Issues* 5 (Spring 1985):3-20.

Smith, Lillian:

Murray, Hugh. "Lillian Smith: a Neglected Southern Heroine." *Journal of Ethnic Studies* 17:1 (Spring 1989):136-40.

Stein, Gertrude:

Benstock, Shari. "Beyond the Reaches of Feminist Criticism: a Letter from Paris" (genre, and Gertrude Stein and women writers contemporary with her). *Tulsa Studies in Women's Literature* 3 (Spring-Fall 1984):5-27.

Blake, Angie. "Jill Godmilow's 'Waiting for the Moon'" (film about Gertrude Stein and Alice B. Toklas). *off our backs* 17:6 (June 1987):20-1.

Dunn, Margaret M. "Altered Patterns and New Endings: Reflections of Change in Stein's *Three Lives* and H.D.'s *Palimpsest.*" *Frontiers* 9:2 (1987):54-9.

Engelbrecht, Penelope J. "'Lifting Belly Is a Language': the Postmodern Lesbian Subject." *Feminist Studies* 16:1 (Spring 1990):85-114.

Fifer, Elizabeth. "Is Flesh Advisable?: the Interior Theater of Gertrude Stein." *Signs* 4:3 (Spring 1979):472-83.

Hokensen, Jan. "The Pronouns of Gomorrha: a Lesbian Prose Tradition" (lesbian modernist writers -- including Virginia Woolf, Gertrude Stein, Djuna Barnes, and Colette -- and post-modernist writers -- including Monique Wittig, June Arnold, and Bertha Harris). *Frontiers* 10:1 (1988):62-9.

Holland, Jeanne. "Uncovering Woman's Body in Gertrude Stein's Subject-Cases: The Background of a Detective Story." *College English* 52:5 (September 1990):540-51.

Thurman, Judith. "A Rose Is a Rose Is a Rose" (biographical essay). *Ms.* 2:8 (February 1974):50-7+.

"*Waiting for the Moon,* Film by Jill Godmilow" (about Gertrude Stein and Alice B. Toklas). *New Directions for Women* 16 (September-October 1987):8.

Wight, Doris T. "Woman as Eros-Rose in Gertrude Stein's *Tender Buttons* and Contemporaneous Portraits." *Transactions of the Wisconsin Academy of Sciences, Arts, and Letters* 4 (1986):34-40.

Taber, Gladys:
Grier, Barbara. "Proud, Disputed Names" (author Gladys Taber). *Sinister Wisdom* 14 (Summer 1980):64-7.

Toder, Nancy:
Kelly, Janis. "Interview with Nancy Toder, Author of *Choices: a Novel About Lesbian Love.*" *off our backs* 10:11 (December 1980):16.

Walker, Alice:

Christian, Barbara. "No More Buried Lives -- the Theme of
   Lesbianism in Lorde, Naylor, Shange, Walker." *Feminist Issues*
   5 (Spring 1985):3-20.

Henderson, Mae G. "*The Color Purple:* Revisions and Redefinitions"
   (deals in part with Shug and Celie's lesbian relationship). *Sage,*
   "Women as Writers" 2:1 (Spring 1985):14-18.

Walker, Alice, Adrienne Rich, and Audre Lorde. "In the Name of All
   Women: the National Book Award Speech" (read by Rich, who
   won the award; all three authors were nominated and agreed that
   whoever won would accept "in the name of all the women whose
   voices have gone and still go unheard in a patriarchal world").
   Margins, "Lesbian Feminist Writing and Publishing" 23
   (August 1975):23.

Warner, Sylvia Townsend:

Castle, Terry. "Sylvia Townsend Warner and the Counterplot of
   Lesbian Fiction." *Textual Practice,* "Lesbian and Gay Cultures:
   Theories and Texts" 4:2 (1990):213-35.

Wilson, Barbara:

Leonard, Vickie and Denise Kulp. "An Interview with Barbara
   Wilson" (writer, and founder of Seal Press). *off our backs* 14:11
   (December 1984):26-7+.

Winsloe, Christa:

Goldschen, Lisa Ohm. "The Filmic Adaptation of the Novel *Das
   Kind Manuela:* Christa Winsloe's Child Heroine Becomes a
   Madchen in Uniform." *Neue Germanistik* (U.S.) 4:2 (Spring
   1986):3-12.

Winterson, Jeanette:

Kay, Jackie. "Unnatural Passions" (interview conducted shortly after
   the movie version of her novel *Oranges Are Not the Only Fruit*
   was televised in England). *Spare Rib* (Great Britain) 209
   (February 1990):26-9.

Scott, Suzanne and Lynne M. Constantine. "*Belles Lettres* Interview: Jeanette Winterson." *Belles Lettres* 5:4 (Summer 1990):24-6.

Wittig, Monique:

Allen, Jeffner. "Poetic Politics: How the Amazons Took the Acropolis." *Hypatia* 3:2 (Summer 1988):107-22.

Creet, Julia M. "Speaking in Lesbian Tongues -- Monique Wittig and the Universal Point of View." *Resources for Feminist Research* (Canada) 16 (December 1987):16-20.

Hokensen, Jan. "The Pronouns of Gomorrha: a Lesbian Prose Tradition" (lesbian modernist writers -- including Virginia Woolf, Gertrude Stein, Djuna Barnes, and Colette -- and post-modernist writers -- including Monique Wittig, June Arnold, and Bertha Harris). *Frontiers* 10:1 (1988):62-9.

Lew, Margaret. "Relocating the Hedge Transforms the House: Monique Wittig and Pueblo Architecture." *Trivia* 12 (Spring 1988):6-35.

Louppe, Larence. "Entretien avec Monique Wittig" (interview). *L'Art Vivant* 45 (December 1973-January 1974):24-5.

Rosenfeld, Marthe. "Language and the Vision of a Lesbian-Feminist Utopia in Wittig's *Les Guérillères.*" *Frontiers,* "NWSA -- Selected Conference Proceedings, 1980" 6:1-2 (Spring-Summer 1981):6-9.

------. "The Linguistic Aspect of Sexual Conflict: Monique Wittig's *Le Corps Lesbien.*" *Mosaic* (Canada) 17:2 (Spring 1984):235-41.

Shaktini, Namascar. "Displacing the Phallic Subject: Wittig's Lesbian Writing." *Signs* 8:1 (Winter 1982):29-44.

Thiébaux, Marcelle. "A Mythology for Women: Monique Wittig's *Les Guérillères.*" *13th Moon* 4:1 (1978):37-45.

VLASTA: Révue des Fictions Utopies Amazonienes, France, "Spécial: Monique Wittig," no. 4.

Wenzel, Hélène Vivienne. "The Text as Body/Politics: an Appreciation of Monique Wittig's Writings in Context." *Feminist Studies* 7:2 (Summer 1981):264-87.

Wittig, Monique. "The Mark of Gender" (pronouns and gendered language in Wittig's novels). *Feminist Issues* 5:2 (Fall 1985):3-12.

Wolfe (Robbins), Susan J. "Stylistic Experimentation in Millett, Johnston and Wittig." *Fireweed* (Canada), "Women and Language" 5&6 (Winter 1979-80 and Spring 1980):134-42.

Woolf, Virginia:

Adams, Kate. "Root and Branch: Mrs. Ramsay and Lily Briscoe in *To the Lighthouse.*" *San Jose Studies* 9:2 (Spring 1983):93-109.

DeSalvo, Louise A. "Lighting the Cave: the Relationship Between Vita Sackville-West and Virginia Woolf." *Signs* 8:2 (Winter 1982):195-214.

Fassler, Barbara. "Theories of Homosexuality as Sources of Bloomsbury's Androgyny" (Virginia Woolf's circle of literary/artist friends). *Signs* 5:2 (Winter 1979):237-51.

Hokensen, Jan. "The Pronouns of Gomorrha: a Lesbian Prose Tradition" (lesbian modernist writers -- including Virginia Woolf, Gertrude Stein, Djuna Barnes, and Colette -- and post-modernist writers -- including Monique Wittig, June Arnold, and Bertha Harris). *Frontiers* 10:1 (1988):62-9.

Knopp, Sherron E. "'If I Saw You Would You Kiss Me?': Sapphism and the Subversiveness of Virginia Woolf's *Orlando*" (discusses the relationship between Virginia Woolf and Vita Sackville-West). *PMLA* 103:1 (January 1988):24-34.

McDaniel, Judith, Susan Griffin, Sandy Boucher, June Arnold, and
Melanie Kaye(/Kantrowitz). "Lesbians and Literature" (Modern
Language Association panel, San Francisco, California,
December 1975; McDaniel discusses *Mrs. Dalloway* by Virginia
Woolf). *Sinister Wisdom,* "Lesbian Writing and Publishing" 1:2
(Fall 1976):20-33.

McNaron, Toni H. "Echoes of Virginia Woolf" (conflict between
respect for intelligence of the men near her and the centrality of
women in Woolf's life). *Women's Studies International Forum*
6:5 (1983):501-7.

Rosenman, Ellen Bayuk. "Sexual Identity and *A Room of One's
Own:* 'Secret Economies' in Virginia Woolf's Feminist
Discourse." *Signs* 14:3 (Spring 1989):634-50.

Squier, Susan M. "Tradition and Revision in Woolf's *Orlando:* Defoe
and 'The Jessamy Brides.'" *Women's Studies* 12:2 (1986):167-77.

Zwerding, Alex. "Virginia Woolf: In and Out of Bloomsbury."
Sewanee Review 83:3 (Summer 1975):510-23.

Yuasa, Yoshiko:
Sawabe, Hitomi (trans. Eleanor Batchelder and Fumiko Ohno).
"Yuriko, Da Svidanya (Goodbye, Yuriko): the Youth of Yoshiko
Yuasa" (excerpt, in Japanese and English, of book about writer
and translator Yoshiko Yuasa). *Conditions: seventeen* (1990):20-
9.

Mass Media (see also: Art; Censorship; Film and Video; Periodicals:
Lesbian/Feminist/Gay; Photography; Publishing; Radio;
Television)

Abdullahad, Tania and Leigh H. Mosley. "Third World Lesbian & Gay
Conference" (second annual national conference, Chicago,
Illinois, November 1981; includes workshop reports on "mature
lesbians," "urban black lesbians," "media," "grassroots," "racism
& sexism"). *off our backs* 12:2 (February 1982):4.

Bosch, Ise. "Breaking the Last Taboo" (lesbian scene in magazine ads for liqueur). *Mother Jones* 14 (May 1989):49.

CAD. "Gay . . . Communicating" (Federal Communications Commission ruling on gay programming; publication delay for performance arts quarterly *High Performance* because a printer refused to print Tee Corinne's erotic lesbian photograph). *off our backs* 10:5 (May 1980):9.

------. "Lesbian/Gay Trips, Cruises & Marches" (U.S. and international news briefs). *off our backs* 10:3 (March 1980):18-19+.

Chasin, Susan T. "Media and the Incredible Invisible Lesbian." *Visibilities* 3:5 (September/October 1989):10+.

"CLIT Statement #2" (Collective Lesbian International Terrors, group formed "to counterattack recent media insults against Lesbians"). *off our backs* 4:8 (July 1974):10-11.

"Collective Lesbian International Terrors" (CLIT, formed "to counterattack recent media insults against Lesbians"). *off our backs* 4:6 (May 1974):16.

de Margo, Louise. "Reflections d'Une Lesbienniste, en Marge de Colloque des Périodiques Féministes Tenu a Orangeville, du 9 au 12 mai" (dangers of cooptation for feminists in receiving government or private foundation funding). *Canadian Woman Studies* (Canada), "Women and Media/Les Femmes et les Media" 8:1 (Spring 1987):65.

"God, Gays, & the Media." *off our backs* 13:2 (February 1983):16.

Horne, Larry and John Ramirez. "The UCLA Gay and Lesbian Media Conference." *Camera Obscura* 11 (Fall 1983):121-31.

Juhasz, Alexandra. "The Contained Threat: Women in Mainstream AIDS Documentary." *Journal of Sex Research* 27:1 (February 1990):25-46.

Mertzel, Nancy. "Lesbians Enter the Information Age." *Visibilities* 4:6
(November/December 1990):10-13.

"No Ads for Lesbians or Gays" (Wisconsin Supreme Court rules that
newspaper can turn down lesbian and gay ads). *off our backs* 20:8
(August/September 1990):5.

Shear, Marie. "Media Watch: Leaving Out Lavender." *New Directions for
Women,* "Women in the Arts" 15:5 (September/October
1986):7.

Tuddé, Oedipussy. "Fashion Politics and the Fashion in Politics" (how
mass media coopts subculture and its politics, in part through
integrating anti-establishing fashion, written by a member of
Collective Lesbian International Terrors (CLIT)). *off our backs*
4:8 (July 1974):17-19.

Young, Allen. "The Press as an Institution of Gay Oppression." *Edcentric*
31-2 (November 1974):27+.

CBS:
CAD. "Journalists Hit CBS" (response to documentary, "Gay
Power, Gay Politics," about gay politics that emphasized public
sex and sadomasochism). *off our backs* 10:10 (November
1980):9.

------. "Not CBS" (boycott of network in response to documentary,
"Gay Power, Gay Politics," about gay politics that emphasized
public sex and sadomasochism). *off our backs* 10:8 (August-
September 1980):15; note: cover reads 10:7.

Christian Science Monitor:
"Christine Madsen Suit Against *Christian Science Monitor* Asks
Court Rule on Reporter Privacy Right as Lesbian." *Media
Report to Women* 12 (July/August 1984):7-8.

Evening News (Great Britain):

"Sappho Invaded" (British *Evening News* reporters trick lesbian
newspaper *Sappho* into revealing names of lesbian mothers for a
sensationalistic feature story). *off our backs* (February 1979):8.

"Sit-in" (protesting articles opposing lesbian artificial insemination).
off our backs 8:2 (February 1978):3.

Greenham Common Womyn's Peace Encampment (Great Britain):
Emberley, Julia and Donna Landry. "Coverage of Greenham and
Greenham as 'Coverage'" (Greenham Common Womyn's Peace
Encampment). *Feminist Studies* 15:3 (Fall 1989):485-98.

Hickok, Lorena (journalist and companion of Eleanor Roosevelt):
Beasley, M. "Lorena M. Hickok: Her Journalistic Influence on
Eleanor Roosevelt" (discusses the possible sexual nature of their
close relationship). *Journalism Quarterly* 57 (Summer
1980):281-6.

Johnson, Sonia (U.S. Presidential candidate in 1984 and writer):
"Sonia Johnson Seeks Legal Determination that Media Access to
Voters Is Integral Part of Election Process." *Media Report to
Women* 12 (November-December 1984):1+.

Madsen, Christine (journalist):
"Christine Madsen Suit Against *Christian Science Monitor* Asks
Court Rule on Reporter Privacy Right as Lesbian." *Media
Report to Women* 12 (July/August 1984):7-8.

Paz, Juana Maria (Latina activist and writer):
"Juana Maria Paz's Experience Shows Her: People Need and Want to
Communicate But Only Know Mass Media's Way." *Media
Report to Women* 12:1 (January-February 1984):14.

Media (see Art; Censorship; Film and Video; Mass Media; Periodicals:
Lesbian/Feminist/Gay; Photography; Publishing; Radio;
Television)

Military

"ACLU Sues Army." *off our backs* 13:6 (June 1983):15.

"Army Homophobia" (brief report on recent dishonorable discharges and court-martials). *off our backs* 18:9 (October 1988):11.

Atkins, Gary L. "Lesbians and Gays: Forced March in the Military." *The Nation* 248 (January 2, 1989):16+.

Bérubé, Allan. "Coming Out Under Fire: the Untold Story of the World War II Soldiers Who Fought on the Front Lines of Gay and Lesbian Liberation." *Mother Jones* 8:2 (February/March 1983):23-9.

Bérubé, Allan and John D'Emilio. "The Military and Lesbians During the McCarthy Years" (includes reprint of "Indoctrination of WAVE Recruits on Subject of Homosexuality" (1952), 284-95). *Signs: the Lesbian Issue* 9:4 (Summer 1984):759-75.

Brooke. "Women & the Draft: a Forum" (following President Jimmy Carter's moves to require all young women and men to register for the draft; Washington, D.C., March 1980). *off our backs* 10:4 (April 1980):6+.

CAD. "Army Dykes: 6 x More Than Gays?" *off our backs* 10:10 (November 1980):9.

------. "Lesbian Sailors Charged." *off our backs* 10:8 (August-September 1980):15; note: cover reads 10:7.

"Civil Rights Victory within Military" (Navy reinstates good service record of woman who had testified on behalf of a lesbian). *off our backs* 20:9 (October 1990):4.

Cursi, Jackie. "Leaping Lesbians" (personal experience of lesbian who was a member of the Women's Army Corps in 1964). *Lesbian Ethics* 2:2 (Fall 1986):81-3.

Dejanikus, Tacie and Janis Kelly. "Military Witchhunt" (general feature article, not about a specific incident). *off our backs* 5:5 (May-June 1975):2-3.

Dunlap, Mary C. "Under the Law -- Lesbians and Gay Men In and Out of the Military." *Visibilities* 4:4 (July/August 1990):14-15.

Harry, Joseph. "Homosexual Men and Women Who Served Their Country." *Journal of Homosexuality* 10:1/2 (Fall 1984):117-25.

Journal of Homosexuality, "Lesbians Over 60 Speak for Themselves," vol. 16, nos. 3/4, 1988.

Leonard, A.S. "Watkins v. United-States Army and the Employment Rights of Lesbians and Gay Men." *Labor Law Journal* 40:7 (1989):438-45.

"Lesbians in the Armed Forces." *off our backs* 13:2 (February 1983):16.

McCrary, Jerel and Lewis Gutierrez. "The Homosexual Person in the Military and in National Security Employment." *Journal of Homosexuality,* "Homosexuality and the Law" 5:1-2 (Fall 1979-Winter 1980):115-46.

McDonald, Tracy. "Lesbian Demoted" (for not divulging names of former lovers). *off our backs* 17:5 (May 1987):16.

Maguire, Amanda. "Lesbian Socks It to the Army Reserves" (reinstated after being kicked out for coming out publicly). *off our backs* 17:10 (November 1987):3.

Morrow, Becky. "Military Ban on Homosexuals Is Widely Litigated." *New Jersey Law Journal* 106 (November 20, 1980):21.

Parker, Jan. "When You're Out You're Out!" (lesbians kicked out of the military). *Spare Rib* (Great Britain) 119 (June 1982):6-8+.

Steinhauser, Thomas C. "Give Me a Responsible Job and Leave Me Alone." *Armed Forces Journal* 99 (May 1972):40-1.

TAL. "Gays Still Banned from Military." *off our backs* 20:4 (April 1990):11.

Wilson, Donna L. "Women and Homophobia in the Armed Services: an Annotated Bibliography (Part One)." *Minerva* 7:1 (Spring 1989):63-84.

------. "Women and Homophobia in the Armed Services: an Annotated Bibliography (Part Two)." *Minerva* 7:2 (1989):60-8.

Pratt, Margo (discharged from the military):
Robertson, Heather. "A Lesbian Ordeal." *Saturday Night* (Canada) 101 (August 1986):22-7.

Monogamy (see also: Domestic Partnership; Relationships)

Bart, Pauline B. "Non? Monogamy?" *Lesbian Ethics* 1:2 (Spring 1985):79-105.

Geller, Gloria. "The Issue of Nonmonogamy Among Lesbians." *Resources for Feminist Research* (Canada), "The Lesbian Issue/Etre Lesbienne" 12:1 (March 1983):44-5.

Kassoff, Elizabeth. "Nonmonogamy in the Lesbian Community." *Women & Therapy,* "Lesbianism: Affirming Nontraditional Roles" 8:1/2 (1989):167-82.

Maggie. "Lesbians and Monogamy." *Spare Rib* (Great Britain) 98 (September 1980):4.

Mountaingrove, Ruth. "Some Notes on Non-Monogamy." *Common Lives/Lesbian Lives* 30 (Spring 1989):101-6.

Spalter-Roth, Bobbie. "Health Festival" (section on "Women Loving Women" in article about "Becoming a Whole Woman: a Women's Health Festival," Washington, D.C., June 1974). *off our backs* 4:8 (July 1974):6+.

Wallgrove, Ruth. "To Be Or Not To Be -- the 'Shoulds' of Lesbianism and Non-monogamy." *off our backs* 14:2 (February 1984):14-5.

Music (see also: Music Festivals; Radio)

Anderson, Eileen. "Compulsory Performance: Rescuing My Lesbian Self from the Shell of the Prodigy" (art and artists under patriarchy; written by a trained classical musician). *Lesbian Ethics* 3:3 (Summer 1989):7-29.

Anderson, Jamie. "Humor in Women's Music." *Hot Wire* 6:1 (January 1990):46-7+.

Armstrong, Toni L. "The Great White Folk Music Myth." *Hot Wire* 4:3 (July 1988):22.

------. "Red, White, and (Visa) Blues: Immigration Headaches for Performers." *Hot Wire* 3:2 (March 1987):20-1.

Armstrong, Toni, Jr.. "What Is Women's Music -- an Endangered Species: Women's Music By, For, and About Women." *Hot Wire* 5:3 (September 1989):17-19+.

Armstrong, Toni, Jr., Lucy Diamond, and Kathy McKue. "Behind the Scenes: Vada Vernée, Karen Hester, and Carrie Barton" (*Hot Wire* photographer, women's music producer, and bassist, respectively). *Hot Wire* 5:1 (January 1989):50-2.

Brandt, Kate. "Back to the Closet?" (U.S. Immigration and Naturalization Service discrimination against lesbian and gay performers). *Hot Wire* 3:2 (March 1987):22+.

Brodsky, Marla B. "Music and Sexuality." *Hot Wire* 4:3 (July 1988):42-3.

Chapman, Frances and Bernice. "A Conference Is Bringing Together" (Midwest Gay Pride Conference, Iowa City, Iowa, and Lesbian Extravaganza, East Lansing, Michigan; topics covered include building community, athletics, parenting, publications, gay art and politics (talk by Rita Mae Brown), music, and theater). *off our backs* 5:5 (May-June 1975):4-5+.

Cline, Cheryl. "'Bitch': the Women's Rock Mag with Bite." *Hot Wire* 3:3 (July 1987):44-5.

Diamond, Lucy. "Behind the Scenes: Betsy York" (producer and distributor). *Hot Wire* 1:2 (March 1985):52-3.

------. "Behind the Scenes: Brynna Fish and Leslie Ann Jones" (producer/booker and recording engineer). *Hot Wire* 4:1 (November 1987):56-7.

------. "Behind the Scenes: Pokey Anderson, Merle Bicknell, and Tam Martin" (producer/disc jockey, distributor, and booking agent). *Hot Wire* 3:3 (July 1987):54-5+.

------. "Behind the Scenes: Polly Laurelchild" (concert producer). *Hot Wire* 2:1 (November 1985):56-7.

Friends of the Hammer (Fabiola Rodriguez, Cappy Kotz, and Phrin Prickett). "*The Return of the Hammer* and Its Sequel: Lesbian Musical Theater." *Hot Wire* 5:2 (May 1989):30-1.

Gardner, Kay. "Early Women's Music and the Squirrel." *Hot Wire* 2:2 (March 1986):56-8.

------. "How Did We Get Into This Mess? an Unblinking Look at the Status of Women's Music Today." *Hot Wire* 2:3 (July 1986):56-8.

Grace, Cindee. "Women's Music, Magic, and Matrism." *Hot Wire* 1:1 (November 1984):22.

Harper, Jorjet. "Towards a Lesbian Aesthetic: Is There Such a Thing as True 'Women's Music.'" *Hot Wire* 6:1 (January 1990):14-15+.

"Jazz Jivin' and Hell Divin' Women" (film *Tiny and Ruby: Hell-Divin' Women*" by Greta Schiller and Andrea Weiss). *Spare Rib* (Great Britain) 195 (October 1988):24.

Karlin, Liz. "The 'Shrinking' Audience: Learning from the Mainstream." *Hot Wire* 3:2 (March 1987):48-50.

Kimber, Kim. "The Women's Music Archives: Preserving Our Musical Heritage." *Hot Wire* 2:1 (November 1985):44-5.

MacAuslan, Janna and Kristan Aspen. "In Search of Dykes and Divas" (opera). *Hot Wire* 1:2 (March 1985):12-13+.

Penelope, Julia. "Women - and Lesbian - Only Spaces: Thought Into Action." *off our backs* 20:5 (May 1990):14-16.

Pipik, Jane E. "Woman-Identified Music: Moving On." *Heresies #10,* "Women and Music" 3:2 (1980):88-90.

Seeger, Nancy and Rena Yount. "A Trip Through the Women's Communities of Washington, D.C." *Hot Wire* 6:1 (January 1990):40-4+.

Shapiro, Lynne D. "Lesbian Music Takes Off." *WIN: Peace and Freedom Through Nonviolent Action,* "Lesbian Culture" 11:22 (June 26, 1975):12-14.

Steiner, Jody and Laurie Rothfeld. "ASL Interpreting for Concerts" (American Sign Language). *Hot Wire* 2:1 (November 1985):8-9+.

Swaney, Alexandra. "Pioneering Women's Music in Montana." *Hot Wire* 1:2 (March 1985):44-6.

Thomas, June. "Harassment by INS" (U.S. Immigration and
Naturalization Service; of women's music performers from
Canada). *off our backs* 17:4 (April 1987):4.

Tilchen, Maida. "The State of Music: a Lesson from History" (cooptation
of lesbian's efforts by straight male capitalists). *Hot Wire* 3:2
(March 1987):32-3.

Yount, Rena. "Happy Tenth Birthday to Woman Sound" (sound
engineering company). *Hot Wire* 1:3 (July 1985):32-5.

------. "Roadwork: Putting Women's Culture on the Road." *Hot Wire* 2:2
(March 1986):32-5.

Abera, Nurudafina Pili:
Trowbridge, Jennifer. "Feel the Beat: Four Percussionists"
(Nurudafina Pili Abera, Carolyn Brandy, Nydia "Liberty" Mata,
and Edwina Lee Tyler). *Hot Wire* 5:2 (May 1989):18-23.

Abyss:
Baim, Tracy and Paula Walowitz. "Rock and Women's Music" (Carol
McDonald and Witch, Holy War, The Fabulous Dyketones, and
Abyss). *Hot Wire* 1:3 (July 1985):40-3.

Adam, Margie:
Glickman, Donna. "Margie Adam: One Voice in a Constellation." *off
our backs* 6:3 (May 1976):18.

Manning, Janet Earley. "Adam Dazzles on Discs, in Concert." *New
Directions for Women* 11:2 (March/April 1982):7.

Alive! (see also Rhiannon):
Maeda, Sheri and Sarie Feld. "Alive!" (interview with three members
of five-woman jazz ensemble). *off our backs* 13:8 (August-
September 1983):30.

Allen, Indra Dean:

"Mothers and Daughters" (includes annotated reading list, and articles on the following musicians (underlined) and their families: Dovida Ishatova and Henia Goodman; Margaret and Kathleen Sloan-Hunter; Indra Dean Allen, her mother Donna Allen, and Indra's two sisters). *Hot Wire* 4:2 (March 1988):34-9.

Anderson, Jamie:

Wenzel, Lynn. "Spirited Women Music Makers Hit High Note" (comedian Lynn Lavner, and musicians The Washington Sisters, Jasmine, Dianne Davidson, Faith Nolan, Heather Bishop, Kitty Barber, Two Nice Girls, Jamie Anderson, Martie van der Voort, and Deuce). *New Directions for Women* 18:4 (July/August 1989):14-16.

Armatrading, Joan:

Fudger, Marion. "Joan Armatrading" (deals in part with African-Americans, feminists, and gays/lesbians wanting Armatrading to support their politics explicitly). *Spare Rib* (Great Britain) 53 (December 1976):6-8.

Atattimur, Sara Deniz:

Foty, Caroline. "Community Mourns Loss: Sara Deniz Atattimur, January 7, 1962 - November 27, 1989" (obituary of blind musician and disabled rights activist). *off our backs* 20:3 (March 1990):9.

Attom, Patches:

Moira, Fran and Anne Williams. "Lavender Jane Loves . . . " (interview with musicians Patches Attom, Alix Dobkin, and Kay Gardner, who made the first lesbian record album). *off our backs* 4:5 (April 1974):6-7.

Barber, Kitty:

Wenzel, Lynn. "Spirited Women Music Makers Hit High Note"
(comic Lynn Lavner, and musicians The Washington Sisters,
Jasmine, Dianne Davidson, Faith Nolan, Heather Bishop, Kitty
Barber, Two Nice Girls, Jamie Anderson, Martie van der Voort,
and Deuce). *New Directions for Women* 18:4 (July/August
1989):14-16.

Barton, Carrie:

Armstrong, Toni, Jr., Lucy Diamond, and Kathy McKue. "Behind the
Scenes: Vada Vernée, Karen Hester, and Carrie Barton" (*Hot Wire*
photographer, women's music producer, and bassist,
respectively). *Hot Wire* 5:1 (January 1989):50-2.

Ben, Lisa:

Brandt, Kate. "Lisa Ben: A Lesbian Pioneer." *Visibilities* 4:1
(January/February 1990):8-11.

Bishop, Heather:

Armstrong, Toni Jr. "A Taste of the Canadian Prairies: Heather
Bishop." *Hot Wire* 6:2 (May 1990):2-4+.

Kuhns, Connie. "Live! From Canada: Canada's Own Heather
Bishop." *Hot Wire* 4:1 (November 1987):48-9.

Smith, Connie. "Canadian Viewpoint: Heather Bishop Interviewed"
(about U.S. Immigration and Naturalization Service visa
discrimination against women's music performers). *Hot Wire* 3:2
(March 1987):21-2.

Wenzel, Lynn. "Spirited Women Music Makers Hit High Note"
(comic Lynn Lavner, and musicians The Washington Sisters,
Jasmine, Dianne Davidson, Faith Nolan, Heather Bishop, Kitty
Barber, Two Nice Girls, Jamie Anderson, Martie van der Voort,
and Deuce). *New Directions for Women* 18:4 (July/August
1989):14-16.

<u>Blazing Star</u>:

Willenborg, Erleen. "Organizing with Music: Blazing Star." *Heresies #9,* 3:1 (1980):32-3.

<u>Brandy, Carolyn</u>:

Trowbridge, Jennifer. "Feel the Beat: Four Percussionists" (Nurudafina Pili Abera, Carolyn Brandy, Nydia "Liberty" Mata, and Edwina Lee Tyler). *Hot Wire* 5:2 (May 1989):18-23.

<u>Christian, Meg</u>:

Crow, Margie, Margaret Devoe, Madeline Janover, and Fran Moira. "The Muses of Olivia: Our Own Economy, Our Own Song" (interview with Olivia Records collective members: Cyndi Gair, Helaine Harris, Meg Christian, Judy Dlugacz, and Ginny Berson). *off our backs* 4:9 (August/September 1974):2-3.

Davenport, Katherine. "Interview: Meg [Christian] Talks." *off our backs* 11:3 (March 1981):19+.

Edelson, Carol and Fran Pollner. "Meg Christian" (interview). *off our backs* 3:7 (April 1973):2-3.

Frances. "Product of Persistence" (Meg Christian's "I Know You Know," the first album produced by Olivia Records). *off our backs* 5:5 (May-June 1975):17.

Manning, Janet Earley. "Meg and Cris at Carnegie: Night to Remember" (Meg Christian and Cris Williamson performing at Carnegie Hall to celebrate Olivia Records 10th anniversary). *New Directions for Women* 12:1 (January/February 1983):1+.

Pollock, Mary S. "Recovery and Integrity: the Music of Meg Christian" (and substance abuse). *Frontiers* 9:2 (1987):29-34.

Sturgis, Susanna J. "Concert Supports Lesbian Mother Case" (Meg Christian and Judy Reagan play at concert; ACLU defending "Jane Doe" in Virginia). *off our backs* 10:5 (May 1980):14.

Culver, Casse:

Moira, Fran. "Casse Culver: 'Integrated Separatism'" (interview with musician Casse Culver and her concert producer Spotts, including conversation about violence against women). *off our backs* 4:11 (November 1974):12-13.

D.C. Area Feminist Chorus:

Sturgis, Susanna J. "[Washington] D.C. Area Feminist Chorus." *Hot Wire* 2:1 (November 1985):48-9+.

Davidson, Dianne:

Hanrahan, Noelle. "Dianne Davidson: Southern, Feminist, and Proud." *Sojourner* 14:8 (April 1989):34-5.

Wenzel, Lynn. "Spirited Women Music Makers Hit High Note" (comic Lynn Lavner, and musicians The Washington Sisters, Jasmine, Dianne Davidson, Faith Nolan, Heather Bishop, Kitty Barber, Two Nice Girls, Jamie Anderson, Martie van der Voort, and Deuce). *New Directions for Women* 18:4 (July/August 1989):14-16.

Davis, Hunter:

"Redwood Records: Mary Watkins, Nancy Vogl, Hunter Davis, Linda Tillery, Ferron, Holly Near, Connie Kaldor, Judy Small, Ronnie Gilbert" (profiles of artists on Redwood Records label). *Hot Wire* 2:3 (July 1986):30-5+.

de Madrugada, Llena:

Segrest, Mab. "'It's Hard to Play the Flute When Your Lip Is Quivering': Interviews with Deirdre McCalla and Llena de Madrugada." *Sinister Wisdom* 6 (Summer 1978):93-8.

The Deadly Nightshade:

Hooke, Helen. "Twenty Years of Making Music" (by member of the 1970s group The Deadly Nightshade). *Hot Wire* 6:2 (May 1990):42-3.

Deuce:

Wenzel, Lynn. "Spirited Women Music Makers Hit High Note"
(comic Lynn Lavner, and musicians The Washington Sisters,
Jasmine, Dianne Davidson, Faith Nolan, Heather Bishop, Kitty
Barber, Two Nice Girls, Jamie Anderson, Martie van der Voort,
and Deuce). *New Directions for Women* 18:4 (July/August
1989):14-16.

Dobkin, Alix:

Armstrong, Toni L. "March on Washington for Lesbian & Gay
Rights: New Jewish Agenda Havdallah Service & Concert"
(including Alix Dobkin, Ronnie Gilbert, and Ruth Pelham). *Hot
Wire* 4:2 (March 1988):20-1+.

Armstrong, Toni, Jr. "A Mother-Daughter Conversation: Alix
Dobkin & Adrian Hood." *Hot Wire* 5:2 (May 1989):36-9.

Claudia, Karen. "Alix Dobkin as Separatist/Symbol/Songwriter." *off
our backs* 18:2 (February 1988):14-15.

Dobkin, Alix. "Hi Phranc, This Is Alix Calling." *Hot Wire* 6:1
(January 1990):16-18+.

------. "The Old Girls' Network." *Hot Wire* 1:2 (March 1985):47-9.

Douglas, Carol Anne. "'A' is for Alix Dobkin" (interview with Alix
Dobkin and Denslow Brown). *off our backs* 11:10 (November
1981):22-3.

Miller, Rosalie J. "A Conversation With Alix Dobkin." *Visibilities*
3:3 (May/June 1989):4-9.

Moira, Fran and Anne Williams. "Lavender Jane Loves . . . "
(interview with musicians Patches Attom, Alix Dobkin, and Kay
Gardner, who made the first lesbian record album). *off our backs*
4:5 (April 1974):6-7.

Edell, Therese:

Ball, Charlene. "This Longest Concert: Therese Edell's 40th Birthday Bash." *Hot Wire* 6:3 (September 1990):28-9+.

Sequoia. "Access -- Therese Edell: Composer and Desktop Music Publisher" (with multiple sclerosis). *Hot Wire* 6:1 (January 1990):48-9+.

Etheridge, Melissa:

Einhorn, Jennifer H. "Melissa Etheridge: New Queen of Devastation" (discusses her in context of women's music, but does not explicitly label her a lesbian artist). *Sojourner* 14:9 (May 1989):34-5.

The Fabulous Dyketones:

Baim, Tracy and Paula Walowitz. "Rock and Women's Music" (Carol McDonald and Witch, Holy War, The Fabulous Dyketones, and Abyss). *Hot Wire* 1:3 (July 1985):40-3.

Priolo, Char. "10 Years of '50s 'Rock & Role' Music: The Fabulous Dyketones." *Hot Wire* 3:3 (July 1987):36-7+.

Fanny:

Koerber, Carmel. "Honkey Tonk Women" (Fanny -- all women rock band featuring June and Jean Millington). *Spare Rib* (Great Britain) 6 (December 1972):9-10.

Feldman, Maxine:

Kelly, Janis, Carol Anne Douglas, and Alice Henry. "Women's Agenda" ("Beyond Suffrage, the U.S. National Agenda" conference, Washington D.C., October 1976; including talk by Charlotte Bunch of the National Gay Task Force and performance by singer Maxine Feldman). *off our backs* 6:8 (November 1976):8+.

Ferron:

Einhorn, Jennifer H. "Ferron's Sweet Deal" (interview). *Sojourner* 15:2 (October 1989):31.

Kulp, Denise. "Ferron: Expanding Visions." *off our backs* 14:6 (June 1984):16-17.

"Redwood Records: Mary Watkins, Nancy Vogl, Hunter Davis, Linda Tillery, Ferron, Holly Near, Connie Kaldor, Judy Small, Ronnie Gilbert" (profiles of artists on Redwood Records label). *Hot Wire* 2:3 (July 1986):30-5+.

Stan, Adelle-Marie. "Folk Evolution: a 1980s Sound with Timeless Roots" (lesbian folksinger Ferron; also the Roches, Christine Lavin, Suzanne Vega). *Ms.* 14 (April 1986):24-7.

Fier, Debbie:

Armstrong, Toni L. "Making Our Dreams Our Jobs: Making Ends Meet Through Music" (Teresa Trull, Robin Flower, Ruth Pelham, Debbie Fier, Betty MacDonald, Musica Femina, Rhiannon, Jean Fineberg). *Hot Wire* 3:2 (March 1987):34-9.

Fineberg, Jean:

Armstrong, Toni L. "Making Our Dreams Our Jobs: Making Ends Meet Through Music" (Teresa Trull, Robin Flower, Ruth Pelham, Debbie Fier, Betty MacDonald, Musica Femina, Rhiannon, Jean Fineberg). *Hot Wire* 3:2 (March 1987):34-9.

Fink, Sue:

Fink, Sue. "Report from Israel: the First International Women's Music Festival." *Hot Wire* 3:2 (March 1987):24-6.

Flower, Robin:

Armstrong, Toni L. "Making Our Dreams Our Jobs: Making Ends Meet Through Music" (Teresa Trull, Robin Flower, Ruth Pelham, Debbie Fier, Betty MacDonald, Musica Femina, Rhiannon, Jean Fineberg). *Hot Wire* 3:2 (March 1987):34-9.

Brandt, Kate. "Torn Between Two Audiences: Robin Flower." *Hot Wire* 3:3 (July 1987):38-9.

Gardner, Kay:

Armstrong, Toni L. "Kay Gardner" (musician and proponent of
music's healing properties). *Hot Wire* 2:2 (March 1986):2-6.

Gardner, Kay. "Early East Coast Women's Music and the Squirrel."
Hot Wire 2:2 (March 1986):56-8.

------. "How Did We Get Into This Mess? an Unblinking Look at the
Status of Women's Music Today." *Hot Wire* 2:3 (July 1986):56-
8.

------. "How to Get Airplay on Non-Commercial Radio." *Hot Wire*
6:3 (September 1990):50-1.

Moira, Fran and Anne Williams. "Lavender Jane Loves . . . "
(interview with musicians Patches Attom, Alix Dobkin, and Kay
Gardner, who made the first lesbian record album). *off our backs*
4:5 (April 1974):6-7.

Gilbert, Ronnie:

Armstrong, Toni L. "March on Washington for Lesbian & Gay
Rights: New Jewish Agenda Havdallah Service & Concert"
(including Alix Dobkin, Ronnie Gilbert, and Ruth Pelham). *Hot
Wire* 4:2 (March 1988):20-1+.

"AWMAC Banquet Speaker: Ronnie Gilbert" (Association of
Women's Music and Culture, San Francisco, California, March
1990). *Hot Wire* 6:2 (May 1990):35.

"Redwood Records: Mary Watkins, Nancy Vogl, Hunter Davis, Linda
Tillery, Ferron, Holly Near, Connie Kaldor, Judy Small, Ronnie
Gilbert" (profiles of artists on Redwood Records label). *Hot Wire*
2:3 (July 1986):30-5+.

Wenzel, Lynn. "Ronnie Gilbert's Career: Singing for Our Lives,
from Anti-Fascism to Feminism." *New Directions for Women*
18:1 (January/February 1989):12-13.

Graetz, Susan:

Reynolds, Cindy. "Profile: 'Woman as Warrior' -- 'To Know
    Somebody Worth the Strain': Susan Graetz" (peace activist
    involved in Women's Encampment for a Future of Peace and
    Justice in New York, and musician and founder of On Our Way
    Productions, who committed suicide in 1985). *Woman of Power*
    3 (Winter/Spring 1986):63-5.

Grant, Monica:

Grant, Monica. "White Courtesy Phones, Monogamy, and Other . . .
    Reflections from a Rookie." *Hot Wire* 6:2 (May 1990):46-7.

Higbie, Barbara:

Armstrong, Toni L. "Interview with Teresa Trull and Barbara
    Higbie." *Hot Wire* 1:3 (July 1985):2-6+.

Holy War:

Baim, Tracy and Paula Walowitz. "Rock and Women's Music" (Carol
    McDonald and Witch, Holy War, The Fabulous Dyketones, and
    Abyss). *Hot Wire* 1:3 (July 1985):40-3.

Homi, Julie:

Post, Laura. "Two Roads to Solo Keyboard Work: Julie Homi and
    Adrienne Torf." *Hot Wire* 6:2 (May 1990):28-30+.

Hooke, Helen:

Hooke, Helen. "Twenty Years of Making Music" (by member of the
    1970s group The Deadly Nightshade). *Hot Wire* 6:2 (May
    1990):42-3.

Ishatova, Dovida:

"Mothers and Daughters" (includes annotated reading list, and articles
    on the following musicians (underlined) and their families:
    Dovida Ishatova and Henia Goodman; Margaret and Kathleen
    Sloan-Hunter; Indra Dean Allen, her mother Donna Allen, and
    Indra's two sisters). *Hot Wire* 4:2 (March 1988):34-9.

Jasmine:

Wenzel, Lynn. "Spirited Women Music Makers Hit High Note"
(comic Lynn Lavner, and musicians The Washington Sisters,
Jasmine, Dianne Davidson, Faith Nolan, Heather Bishop, Kitty
Barber, Two Nice Girls, Jamie Anderson, Martie van der Voort,
and Deuce). *New Directions for Women* 18:4 (July/August
1989):14-16.

Kaldor, Connie:

"Redwood Records: Mary Watkins, Nancy Vogl, Hunter Davis, Linda
Tillery, Ferron, Holly Near, Connie Kaldor, Judy Small, Ronnie
Gilbert" (profiles of artists on Redwood Records label). *Hot Wire*
2:3 (July 1986):30-5+.

Labrys:

Jordan, Elena. "Labrys: the Duo and the Label." *Hot Wire* 4:1
(November 1987):22-3.

Ladyslipper Music:

Sturgis, Susanna J. "Ladyslipper: Meeting the Challenges of
Feminist Business" (women's music distributor and producer).
Hot Wire 1:2 (March 1985):36-8.

Lavner, Lynn:

Lavner, Lynn. "From Amsterdam to Miami Beach: a Gay Cabaret
Musician Plays Two Religious Conferences." *Hot Wire* 4:1
(November 1987):24-5+.

Wenzel, Lynn. "Spirited Women Music Makers Hit High Note"
(comic Lynn Lavner, and musicians The Washington Sisters,
Jasmine, Dianne Davidson, Faith Nolan, Heather Bishop, Kitty
Barber, Two Nice Girls, Jamie Anderson, Martie van der Voort,
and Deuce). *New Directions for Women* 18:4 (July/August
1989):14-16.

Lesboten:

"Never a Love Song" (interview with members of German rock
band). *Connexions,* "Global Lesbianism 2" 10 (Fall 1983):29.

McCalla, Deidre:

Armstrong, Toni L. "Deidre McCalla" (interview). *Hot Wire* 4:3 (July 1988):2-5+.

Segrest, Mab. "'It's Hard to Play the Flute When Your Lip Is Quivering': Interviews with Deidre McCalla and Llena de Madrugada." *Sinister Wisdom* 6 (Summer 1978):93-8.

McDonald, Carol:

Baim, Tracy and Paula Walowitz. "Rock and Women's Music" (Carol McDonald and Witch, Holy War, The Fabulous Dyketones, and Abyss). *Hot Wire* 1:3 (July 1985):40-3.

MacDonald, Betty:

Armstrong, Toni L. "Making Our Dreams Our Jobs: Making Ends Meet Through Music" (Teresa Trull, Robin Flower, Ruth Pelham, Debbie Fier, Betty MacDonald, Musica Femina, Rhiannon, Jean Fineberg). *Hot Wire* 3:2 (March 1987):34-9.

MacKay, Karen:

MacKay, Karen. "A Matter of Tradition" (written by a banjo player, singer/songwriter; learning from "Aunt Jennie" Wilson). *Hot Wire* 1:3 (July 1985):14-16.

Marilyn T. (see T., Marilyn)

Mata, Nydia "Liberty":

Trowbridge, Jennifer. "Feel the Beat: Four Percussionists" (Nurudafina Pili Abera, Carolyn Brandy, Nydia "Liberty" Mata, and Edwina Lee Tyler). *Hot Wire* 5:2 (May 1989):18-23.

Millington, Jean:

Bull, Barbara. "Sisters" (Filipina-American rock musicians June and Jean Millington). *Hot Wire* 1:3 (July 1985):22-3+.

Koerber, Carmel. "Honkey Tonk Women" (Fanny -- all women rock band featuring June and Jean Millington). *Spare Rib* (Great Britain) 6 (December 1972):9-10.

Millington, June:

Bull, Barbara. "Sisters" (Filipina-American rock musicians June and Jean Millington). *Hot Wire* 1:3 (July 1985):22-3+.

Feld, Sarie. "June Millington in Concert and Conversation." *off our backs* 12:7 (July 1982):18.

Koerber, Carmel. "Honkey Tonk Women" (Fanny -- all women rock band featuring June and Jean Millington). *Spare Rib* (Great Britain) 6 (December 1972):9-10.

Millington, June. "Music, Life, and Politics." *Hot Wire* 3:1 (November 1986):48-50.

Post, Laura. "The Institute for the Musical Arts" (founded by June Millington). *Hot Wire* 5:3 (September 1989):46-8.

Musica Femina:

Armstrong, Toni L. "Making Our Dreams Our Jobs: Making Ends Meet Through Music" (Teresa Trull, Robin Flower, Ruth Pelham, Debbie Fier, Betty MacDonald, Musica Femina, Rhiannon, Jean Fineberg). *Hot Wire* 3:2 (March 1987):34-9.

Perry, Chris. "*Musica Femina:* More Than a Flute and Guitar Duo" (classical music duo). *Hot Wire* 1:3 (July 1985):18-19.

Near, Holly:

Armstrong, Toni Jr. "A Personal Chat with Holly Near About her New Autobiography" (*Fire in the Rain . . . Singer in the Storm*). *Hot Wire* 6:3 (September 1990):2-5+.

Chasin, Susan T. "Holly Near: a Year of Change." *Visibilities* 2:3 (May/June 1988):10.

Faber, Nancy. "Never in the Closet or on the Charts (Yet), Holly Near Sings Uncompromisingly of Gay Love." *People Weekly* 16 (July 13, 1981):103-4.

Feld, Sarie and Sheri Maeda. "Holly Near: Reaching More People with the Speed of Light." *off our backs* 12:11 (December 1982):20-1.

"'Feminism 101': Holly Near on Tour for NWSA" (fundraising concert tour for the National Women's Studies Association, January 1981). *Women's Studies Newsletter* 8:4 (Fall/Winter 1980):14.

Fishel, Elizabeth. "Holly Near: Putting Politics to Music." *Ms.* 5 (October 1976):31-3+.

Hollis, Flo. "Workshop with Holly" (singer/songwriter and activist Holly Near). *off our backs* 8:7 (July 1978):24.

Landau, Deborah. "[Holly] Near Journeys Far For World-Wide Peace." *New Directions for Women* 11 (November-December 1982):4+.

"Redwood Records: Mary Watkins, Nancy Vogl, Hunter Davis, Linda Tillery, Ferron, Holly Near, Connie Kaldor, Judy Small, Ronnie Gilbert" (profiles of artists on Redwood Records label). *Hot Wire* 2:3 (July 1986):30-5+.

Schmitz, Marlene. "Holly Near: You Can Know All She Is." *off our backs* 6:4 (June 1976):21.

Van Gelder. "Woman of the Year: Holly Near." *Ms.* 13:7 (January 1985):72-3.

Nolan, Faith:

Brand, Dionne. "Faith Nolan: 'I'm a working class, Black lesbian. In everything I do I have to fight for that voice to be heard.'" *Hot Wire* 5:1 (January 1989):39+.

Wenzel, Lynn. "Spirited Women Music Makers Hit High Note" (comic Lynn Lavner, and musicians The Washington Sisters, Jasmine, Dianne Davidson, Faith Nolan, Heather Bishop, Kitty Barber, Two Nice Girls, Jamie Anderson, Martie van der Voort, and Deuce). *New Directions for Women* 18:4 (July/August 1989):14-16.

Olivia Records:

Crow, Margie, Margaret Devoe, Madeline Janover, and Fran Moira. "The Muses of Olivia: Our Own Economy, Our Own Song" (interview with Olivia Records collective members: Cyndi Gair, Helaine Harris, Meg Christian, Judy Dlugacz, and Ginny Berson). *off our backs* 4:9 (August/September 1974):2-3.

Dlugacz, Judy. "If It Weren't for the Music: 15 Years of Olivia Records" (part 1; written by co-founder of the women's music label). *Hot Wire* 4:3 (July 1988):28-31+.

------. "If It Weren't for the Music: 15 Years of Olivia Records" (part 2; written by co-founder of the women's music label). *Hot Wire* 5:1 (January 1989):20-3.

Edelman, Sue. "Olivia Records Celebrates 15 Years." *Sojourner* 13:8 (April 1988):33-4.

Feld, Sarie. "Olivia's Birthday at Carnegie Hall: Olivia's 10th." *off our backs* 13:1 (January 1983):25.

Frances. "Product of Persistence" (Meg Christian's "I Know You Know," the first album produced by Olivia Records). *off our backs* 5:5 (May-June 1975):17.

Harper, Jorjet. "15th Anniversary Bash: Olivia Records at Carnegie Hall." *Hot Wire* 5:2 (May 1989):32-3.

Levin, Monica. "Happy Birthday Olivia Records" (15th anniversary). *New Directions for Women* 17:5 (September/October 1988):12.

Manning, Janet Earley. "Meg and Cris at Carnegie: Night to Remember" (Meg Christian and Cris Williamson performing at Carnegie Hall, to celebrate Olivia Records 10th anniversary). *New Directions for Women* 12:1 (January/February 1983):1+.

Martin, Tam. "Olivia Records." *Hot Wire* 1:3 (July 1985):58-9.

Post, Laura. "The First Olivia Cruise: Maiden Voyage" (February 1990). *Hot Wire* 6:3 (September 1990):26-7+.

OVA:

Schonfeld, Rosemary. "Report from the Front Lines: Women's Music in Europe" (written by one half of the British duo OVA). *Hot Wire* 5:2 (May 1989):26-7.

Thomas, June. "Ova: Stroppy Women" (Jane Runnalls and Rosemary Schonfeld of the British group OVA, interviewed at the 1986 Michigan Womyn's Music Festival). *off our backs* 16:9 (October 1986):19.

Pelham, Ruth:

Armstrong, Toni L. "Making Our Dreams Our Jobs: Making Ends Meet Through Music" (Teresa Trull, Robin Flower, Ruth Pelham, Debbie Fier, Betty MacDonald, Musica Femina, Rhiannon, Jean Fineberg). *Hot Wire* 3:2 (March 1987):34-9.

------. "March on Washington for Lesbian & Gay Rights: New Jewish Agenda Havdallah Service & Concert" (including Alix Dobkin, Ronnie Gilbert, and Ruth Pelham). *Hot Wire* 4:2 (March 1988):20-1+.

Phranc:

Dobkin, Alix. "Hi Phranc, This Is Alix Calling." *Hot Wire* 6:1 (January 1990):16-18+.

"A Phemale Pholkie Named Phranc, Who Hopes to Laugh All the Way to the Bank." *People Weekly* 32 (August 14, 1989):62.

Reagan, Judy:

Sturgis, Susanna J. "Concert Supports Lesbian Mother Case" (Meg Christian and Judy Reagan play at concert; ACLU defending "Jane Doe" in Virginia). *off our backs* 10:5 (May 1980):14.

Reagon, Bernice Johnson:

Yount, Rena. "Each in Her Own Generation: Bernice & Toshi Reagon" (African-American singer/songwriters who are mother and daughter). *Hot Wire* 5:2 (May 1989):34-5+.

Reagon, Toshi:

Yount, Rena. "Each in Her Own Generation: Bernice & Toshi Reagon" (African-American singer/songwriters who are mother and daughter). *Hot Wire* 5:2 (May 1989):34-5+.

Redwood Records (see also Holly Near):

Armstrong, Toni L. "Redwood Records: More Than Just 'Holly's Label.'" *Hot Wire* 2:3 (July 1986):26-9+.

Lont, Cynthia M. "Subcultural Persistence: the Case of Redwood Records." *Women's Studies in Communication* 11 (Spring 1988):50-60.

"Redwood Records: Mary Watkins, Nancy Vogl, Hunter Davis, Linda Tillery, Ferron, Holly Near, Connie Kaldor, Judy Small, Ronnie Gilbert" (profiles of artists on Redwood Records label). *Hot Wire* 2:3 (July 1986):30-5+.

Reed, Ann:

"Ann Reed: TKO Over His Purple Badness Prince at Awards Night" (Folk Musician beat out pop musician Prince at Minnesota Music Awards, May 1990). *Hot Wire* 6:3 (September 1990):30-1.

Rhiannon (see also Alive!):

Armstrong, Toni L. "Making Our Dreams Our Jobs: Making Ends Meet Through Music" (Teresa Trull, Robin Flower, Ruth Pelham, Debbie Fier, Betty MacDonald, Musica Femina, Rhiannon, Jean Fineberg). *Hot Wire* 3:2 (March 1987):34-9.

Ro Ro, Angela:

"'Don't Label Me: I Label Myself'" (interview with popular Brazilian
singer; trans. from *Chana Com Chana,* Brazilian lesbian journal,
Spring 1981). *Connexions,* "Global Lesbianism" 3 (January
1982):10-11.

Rose, Betsy:

Rose, Betsy. "Bridge Building and Border Crossing." *Hot Wire* 1:3
(July 1985):54-5.

Sappho:

Harper, Jorjet. "Sappho's Musical Genius." *Hot Wire* 4:1 (November
1987):14-15+.

Shanbaum, Susann:

Feld, Sarie. "Nancy Vogl and Susann Shanbaum." *off our backs*
12:11 (December 1982):22-3.

Shocked, Michelle:

Nordheim, Christie and Julie A. Kreiner. "On Coming Out: Michelle
Shocked." *Hot Wire* 6:3 (September 1990):20-1.

Sloan-Hunter, Margaret:

"Mothers and Daughters" (includes annotated reading list, and articles
on the following musicians (underlined) and their families:
Dovida Ishatova and Henia Goodman; Margaret and Kathleen
Sloan-Hunter; Indra Dean Allen, her mother Donna Allen, and
Indra's two sisters). *Hot Wire* 4:2 (March 1988):34-9.

Small, Judy:

"Redwood Records: Mary Watkins, Nancy Vogl, Hunter Davis, Linda
Tillery, Ferron, Holly Near, Connie Kaldor, Judy Small, Ronnie
Gilbert" (profiles of artists on Redwood Records label). *Hot Wire*
2:3 (July 1986):30-5+.

Smyth, Dame Ethel:

Canarina, John. "The Legendary Dame Ethel Smyth" (British
composer, suffragist, friend of Virginia Woolf). *Helicon Nine* 4
(Spring 1981):6-13.

Swingshift:
"Swingshift" (lesbian jazz band). *Hot Wire* 1:2 (March 1985):23+.

T., Marilyn:
Stato, Joanne. "Lesbian Rap Artist: an Interview with Marilyn T."
off our backs 19:9 (October 1989):22.

Tillery, Linda:
Feld, Sarie. "Linda Tillery and Adrienne Torf: Looking at Issues"
(interview). *off our backs* 13:10 (November 1983):22-3.

Gautreaux, Michele. "Sweet Linda Divine: an Interview with Linda
Tillery." *Hot Wire* 1:2 (March 1985):2-5.

Pollock, Mary S. "The Politics of Women's Music: a Conversation
with Linda Tillery and Mary Watkins." *Frontiers* 10:1 (1988):14-
19.

"Redwood Records: Mary Watkins, Nancy Vogl, Hunter Davis, Linda
Tillery, Ferron, Holly Near, Connie Kaldor, Judy Small, Ronnie
Gilbert" (profiles of artists on Redwood Records label). *Hot Wire*
2:3 (July 1986):30-5+.

Torf, Adrienne:
Feld, Sarie. "Linda Tillery and Adrienne Torf: Looking at Issues"
(interview). *off our backs* 13:10 (November 1983):22-3.

Post, Laura. "Two Roads to Solo Keyboard Work: Julie Homi and
Adrienne Torf." *Hot Wire* 6:2 (May 1990):28-30+.

Tremblay, Lucie Blue:
Armstrong, Toni L. "Lucie Blue Tremblay" (interview). *Hot Wire*
3:1 (November 1986):2-5.

Trull, Teresa:
Armstrong, Toni L. "Interview with Teresa Trull and Barbara
Higbie." *Hot Wire* 1:3 (July 1985):2-6+.

------. Armstrong, Toni L. "Making Our Dreams Our Jobs: Making Ends Meet Through Music" (Teresa Trull, Robin Flower, Ruth Pelham, Debbie Fier, Betty MacDonald, Musica Femina, Rhiannon, Jean Fineberg). *Hot Wire* 3:2 (March 1987):34-9.

Armstrong, Toni, Jr. "The Best of Both Worlds: Teresa Trull." *Hot Wire* 5:2 (May 1989):2-5.

Brandt, Kate. "A Step Away: Teresa Trull." *Hot Wire* 4:2 (March 1988):22-4.

Stato, Joanne. "Teresa Trull: Excellence in Music." *off our backs* 19:11 (December 1989):20-2+.

Two Nice Girls:
Wenzel, Lynn. "Spirited Women Music Makers Hit High Note" (comic Lynn Lavner, and musicians The Washington Sisters, Jasmine, Dianne Davidson, Faith Nolan, Heather Bishop, Kitty Barber, Two Nice Girls, Jamie Anderson, Martie van der Voort, and Deuce). *New Directions for Women* 18:4 (July/August 1989):14-16.

Tyler, Edwina Lee:
Trowbridge, Jennifer. "Feel the Beat: Four Percussionists" (Nurudafina Pili Abera, Carolyn Brandy, Nydia "Liberty" Mata, and Edwina Lee Tyler). *Hot Wire* 5:2 (May 1989):18-23.

Vogl, Nancy:
Feld, Sarie. "Nancy Vogl and Susann Shanbaum." *off our backs* 12:11 (December 1982):22-3.

"Redwood Records: Mary Watkins, Nancy Vogl, Hunter Davis, Linda Tillery, Ferron, Holly Near, Connie Kaldor, Judy Small, Ronnie Gilbert" (profiles of artists on Redwood Records label). *Hot Wire* 2:3 (July 1986):30-5+.

van der Voort, Martie:

Wenzel, Lynn. "Spirited Women Music Makers Hit High Note"
(comic Lynn Lavner, and musicians The Washington Sisters,
Jasmine, Dianne Davidson, Faith Nolan, Heather Bishop, Kitty
Barber, Two Nice Girls, Jamie Anderson, Martie van der Voort,
and Deuce). *New Directions for Women* 18:4 (July/August
1989):14-16.

The Washington Sisters:

Armstrong, Toni L. "The Washington Sisters" (musicians Sondra and
Sharon Washington). *Hot Wire* 4:1 (November 1987):2-4+.

JAG. "A Dialogue: The Washington Twins" (Sondra and Sharon
Washington). *Hot Wire* 1:1 (November 1984):20.

Wenzel, Lynn. "Spirited Women Music Makers Hit High Note"
(comedian Lynn Lavner, and musicians The Washington Sisters,
Jasmine, Dianne Davidson, Faith Nolan, Heather Bishop, Kitty
Barber, Two Nice Girls, Jamie Anderson, Martie van der Voort,
and Deuce). *New Directions for Women* 18:4 (July/August
1989):14-16.

Watkins, Mary:

"Redwood Records: Mary Watkins, Nancy Vogl, Hunter Davis, Linda
Tillery, Ferron, Holly Near, Connie Kaldor, Judy Small, Ronnie
Gilbert" (profiles of artists on Redwood Records label). *Hot Wire*
2:3 (July 1986):30-5+.

Williamson, Cris:

Armstrong, Toni, Jr. "Cris" (interview in which Cris Williamson
says "No one knows if I am [a lesbian] or not . . . It has nothing
to do with my music, whether people think it or not"). *Hot Wire*
5:3 (September 1989):2-6+.

Clark, Terri. "Interview with Cris." *off our backs* 10:5 (May
1980):15.

Fong-Torres, Ben. "Changes in a Strange Paradise: Musician Cris Williamson Is Taking the Road Less Traveled to Stardom." *Mother Jones* 6 (April 1981):12-14+.

Manning, Janet Earley. "Meg and Cris at Carnegie: Night to Remember" (Meg Christian and Cris Williamson performing at Carnegie Hall to celebrate Olivia Records 10th anniversary). *New Directions for Women* 12:1 (January/February 1983):1+.

Williamson, Cris. (letter stating "I am a lesbian and I remain proud"; apologizing for "kneejerk response" to question about her sexuality in interview by Toni Armstrong Jr., *Hot Wire* September 1989). *Hot Wire* 6:1 (January 1990):6.

Williamson, Cris (with Cindy Anderson). "'Music and Life.'" *Hot Wire* 3:3 (July 1987):50-1.

Wilson, "Aunt Jennie":

MacKay, Karen. "A Matter of Tradition" (written by a banjo player, singer/songwriter; learning from "Aunt Jennie" Wilson). *Hot Wire* 1:3 (July 1985):14-16.

Witch:

Baim, Tracy and Paula Walowitz. "Rock and Women's Music" (Carol McDonald and Witch, Holy War, The Fabulous Dyketones, and Abyss). *Hot Wire* 1:3 (July 1985):40-3.

Music Festivals (see also: Music)

Andrews, Cathy. "Doing the Festivals, Or How I Spent My Summer." *Hot Wire* 6:3 (September 1990):43+.

Kuhns, Connie. "Live! From Canada: Canadian Women's Music Festivals" (brief history and overview). *Hot Wire* 5:2 (May 1989):48-51.

Parker, Pat. "Poetry at Women's Music Festivals: Oil and Water." *Hot Wire* 3:1 (November 1986):52-3+.

Tyler, Robin. "Keeping the Land" (discrimination in renting land for women's music festivals). *Hot Wire* 3:1 (November 1986):28-9.

Amazon Music Project:

Reuss, Natalie. "Redwoods, Lovely Women, New Culture: Amazon Music Project" (Santa Cruz, California). *off our backs* 4:10 (October 1974):24-5.

Association of Women's Music and Culture Conference:

Harper, Jorjet. "The 1990 AWMAC Conference" (San Francisco, California, March 1990). *Hot Wire* 6:2 (May 1990):34-5.

Campfest:

Hochberg, Marcy J. "One Producer, One Comfortable Festival: Campfest 1988" (Oxford, Pennsylvania). *Hot Wire* 5:1 (January 1989):28-9.

East Coast Lesbian Festival:

Anne, Sheila. "Womyn or Children First? Lesbian Space Elusive at East Coast Fest: Separatist Positive Perspective" (First Annual East Coast Lesbian Festival, West Stockbridge, Massachusetts, September 1989). *off our backs* 19:9 (October 1989):27-8.

Braeman, Elizabeth. "Womyn or Children First? The Debate Continues: In Defense of Separatists" (First Annual East Coast Lesbian Festival, West Stockbridge, Massachusetts, September 1989). *off our backs* 19:10 (November 1989):20.

Harper, Jorjet. "Accessibility, Male Children an Issue at Lesbian Fest" (First Annual East Coast Lesbian Festival, West Stockbridge, Massachusetts, Summer 1989). *Hot Wire* 6:1 (January 1990):29+.

------. "The First Annual East Coast Lesbians' Festival" (West Stockbridge, Massachusetts, Summer 1989). *Hot Wire* 6:1 (January 1990):28+.

Johnson, Angela. "Womyn or Children First? The Debate Continues: There Must Be a Better Way" (First Annual East Coast Lesbian Festival, West Stockbridge, Massachusetts, September 1989). *off our backs* 19:10 (November 1989):20.

Platt, Mary Frances. "A View from This Wheelchair" (First Annual East Coast Lesbian Festival, West Stockbridge, Massachusetts, September 1989). *off our backs* 20:5 (May 1990):11.

Gulf Coast Women's Festival:

Henson, Brenda. "Women's Music in the Deep South at the First Annual Gulf Coast Women's Festival" (Mississippi, Summer 1989). *Hot Wire* 6:1 (January 1990):38-9.

International Congress on Women in Music:

Aspen, Kristan. "The International Congress on Women in Music." *Hot Wire* 4:2 (March 1988):12-13.

International Women's Music Festival:

Fink, Sue. "Report from Israel: the First International Women's Music Festival." *Hot Wire* 3:2 (March 1987):24-6.

Lesbian Variety Show:

Brannon, Rebecca. "Madison's Fourth Annual Lesbian Variety Show: I Got This Way from Kissing Girlz" (Madison, Wisconsin, November 1989). *Hot Wire* 6:2 (May 1990):36-8.

Michigan Womyn's Music Festival:

Armstrong, Toni L. "Ninth Michigan Womyn's Music Festival." *Hot Wire* 1:1 (November 1984):36.

Creech, Kay. "Birth of a New Tradition: the Michigan Festival Concert Band." *Hot Wire* 6:1 (January 1990):32-3+.

Diamond, Lucy. "Behind the Scenes: Denise Notzon and Therese Edell" (promoter and announcer at Michigan Womyn's Music Festival). *Hot Wire* 2:2 (March 1986):54-5.

------. "Behind the Scenes: Sandy Ramsey and Barbara 'Boo' Price" (distributor and co-producer of Michigan Womyn's Music Festival). *Hot Wire* 2:3 (July 1986):54-5+.

Fithian, Nancy. "Michigan Womyn's Music Festival; Disabled Lesbian Conference." *off our backs* 11:9 (October 1981):15.

Fridley, Mary. "Women's Culture or Mass Culture" (political consciousness and the second Michigan Womyn's Music Festival, August 1977). *off our backs* 7:9 (November 1977):14.

Fugh-Berman, Adrienne J. "Neophyte at Michigan." *off our backs* 20:10 (November 1990):11+.

Garlington, Lee. "Making Music in Michigan Mud" (second Michigan Womyn's Music Festival, August 1977). *off our backs* 7:8 (October 1977):22-3.

Kane, Karen. "The Audio Angle: the Michigan Acoustic Stage." *Hot Wire* 5:1 (January 1989):10-11.

Stato, Joanne. "On Women's Space" (at Michigan Womyn's Music Festival and elsewhere). *off our backs* 20:9 (October 1990):14.

------. "14th Michigan Womyn's Music Festival" (the politics of the event -- who attended, what was discussed, including lesbians of color, racism, S/M, disability, and music). *off our backs* 19:9 (October 1989):20-1.

National Women's Music Festival:
Armstrong, Toni, Jr. "National Women's Music Festival: Showcase 1988" (Bloomington, Indiana). *Hot Wire* 5:1 (January 1989):26-7+.

Berson, Ginny. "First National Women's Music Festival -- Giving Music Back to Its Muses -- Women's Music Is Exploding" (Champaign, Illinois, June 1974). *off our backs* 4:8 (July 1974):2.

Diamond, Lucy. "Behind the Scenes: Dino Sierp and Karen Merry" (organizer of National Women's Music Festival in Bloomington, Indiana and distributor). *Hot Wire* 3:1 (November 1986):54-5.

Guse, C.W. "The Music Industry Conference: Third Annual Gathering at NWMF" (National Women's Music Festival, Bloomington, Indiana). *Hot Wire* 2:1 (November 1985):38-9.

Schmitz, Marlene. "National Music Festival's Third Refrain" (discussion of lesbian/heterosexual split there; Champaign-Urbana, Illinois, June 1976). *off our backs* 6:5 (July-August 1976):14.

Schmitz, Marlene and Carol Edelson. "National Women's Music Festival" (second annual, Champaign, Illinois). *off our backs* 5:6 (July 1975):1+.

Springer, Christina. "The National Women's Music Festival: Bringing Non-Dominant Women to Full Boil." *off our backs* 20:5 (May 1990):9.

Tilchen, Maida. "A Festival Album 1984 -- CelebraTen: NWMF's Tenth" (National Women's Music Festival). *Hot Wire* 1:1 (November 1984):32-4.

New England Women's Musical Retreat:

Grace, Cindee. "Talking with the NEWMR [New England Women's Musical Retreat] Day Stage Coordinator: Kim Kimber." *Hot Wire* 2:2 (March 1986):39.

McPherson, Cathy. "Front Row Centre: the New England Women's Musical Retreat on Wheels: an Interview with Pat Israel." *Resources for Feminist Research* (Canada) 14 (March 1985):45-7.

Organizers of the New England Women's Musical Retreat. "But I Don't Know What to Say to Her." *Resources for Feminist Research* (Canada) 14 (March 1985):45-7.

Sisterfire:

Diamond, Lucy. "Behind the Scenes: Ivy Young" (coordinator of Sisterfire Women's Music Festival). *Hot Wire* 1:3 (July 1985):56-7.

Seeger, Nancy. "Sisterfire: Why Did Roadwork Skip 1986?" (Sisterfire music festival did not take place in 1986). *Hot Wire* 3:1 (November 1986):26-7.

------. "Sisterfire '88" (Upper Marlboro, Maryland). *Hot Wire* 5:1 (January 1989):30-1.

------. "Welcome Back: Sisterfire 1987" (Sisterfire music festival did not take place in 1986). *Hot Wire* 4:1 (November 1987):38-40.

Yount, Rena. "Sisterfire" (music festival). *Hot Wire* 1:1 (November 1984):28.

Southern Women's Music and Comedy Festival:

Harper, Jorjet. "Southern: the 'Live and Let Live' Festival" (Southern Women's Music and Comedy Festival, Georgia, Summer 1990). *Hot Wire* 6:3 (September 1990):40-2.

Landau, Penny M. "First Southern Festival." *Hot Wire* 1:1 (November 1984):30.

McVey, Judy. "The Southern Festival and Disability." *Hot Wire* 3:1 (November 1986):30-1+.

West Coast Women's Music and Comedy Festival:

Elias, Ellen. "West Coast Women's Music and Comedy Festival." *Hot Wire* 2:2 (March 1986):36-7.

Wiminfest:

Boss, Carol. "Wiminfest '86" (Albuquerque, New Mexico). *Hot Wire* 3:2 (March 1987):23+.

Walowitz, Paula. "Report from Albuquerque: Wiminfest '89"
(Women in Movement in New Mexico). *Hot Wire* 6:1 (January
1990):36-7.

Women Take Liberty:
Curb, Rosemary. "Women Take Liberty in 1986" (women's music
festival and political rally at Statue of Liberty to commemorate
statue's 100th anniversary). *Hot Wire* 3:2 (March 1987):44-6.

Women's Choral Festival:
Guse, C.W. "The Third Annual Women's Choral Festival." *Hot Wire*
3:2 (March 1987):28-9+.

Roma, Cathy. "The Fifth National Women's Choral Festival"
(Kansas City, Missouri, October 1989). *Hot Wire* 6:2 (May
1990):44-5.

National Organization for Women (NOW) (see also: Equal
Rights Amendment)

Anne, Lynne, Pam and Sharon. "If Not NOW, Who?" (homophobia in
the National Organization for Women). *off our backs* 1:11
(September 30, 1970):2.

CAD. "Gay . . . Actions" (news briefs; New York NOW supports anti-
discrimination legislation protecting lesbians and gays but
refuses to endorse a gay rights march on Albany because one of
the keynote speakers is a representative of the North American
Man-Boy Love Association). *off our backs* 10:5 (May 1980):9.

Douglas, Carol Anne. "Woman-Identified Conference" ("Woman-Identified
Women: Speaking for Ourselves," conference of the Sexuality
Task Force of the National Organization for Women, George
Washington University, Washington, D.C., April 1978). *off our
backs* 8:5 (May 1978):13.

------. "Women's Community Conference" (of the NOW Sexuality Task
Force). *off our backs* 7:5 (May 1977):8+.

Douglas, Carol Anne and Diana Onley-Campbell. "Lesbians Are Everywhere" (third annual conference of NOW Sexuality Task Force). *off our backs* 9:7 (July 1979):18 and 9:8 (August-September 1979):27.

Hall, Ran. "Dear Martha" (lesbians and reformism in NOW and the Equal Rights Amendment campaign). *Common Lives/Lesbian Lives* 6 (Winter 1982):40-3.

Harrison, Barbara Grizzuti. "Lesbians, Bisexuals, and the Struggle for Power in the Women's Movement" (focuses on NOW). *New York* 7:13 (April 1, 1974):30.

Krebs, Paula. "Is the Smeal Era Over for NOW?: NOW Votes for New Officers" (lesbian and minority issues prioritized at 15th annual conference as delegates confront NOW leadership). *off our backs* 12:10 (November 1982):2-3.

Moira, Fran. "NOW: It'll Be a Long Time Coming" (report on lesbian workshop at mostly heterosexual NOW Conference on Sexuality, October 1974). *off our backs* 4:11 (November 1974):3.

"People Organize to Protest Recent NOW Resolution on Lesbian and Gay Rights." *Heresies #12*, "The Sex Issue" 3:4 (1981):92-3.

Pollner, Fran. "Lesbian Dynamics" (at sixth national conference of the National Organization for Women). *off our backs* 3:6 (February-March 1973):7.

Stowe, Ayofemi. "'Power Into Action': The National Lesbian Rights Conference" (of the National Organization for Women, San Diego, CA, October 1988). *off our backs* 18:11 (December 1988):8+.

Whitlock, Kay. "Power Brokerage and Single Issue Politics in NOW." *Quest* 5:2 (1980):36-55.

<u>Native American Lesbians</u> (see also: Lesbians of Color; Racism)

Allen, Paula Gunn. "Beloved Women: Lesbians in American Indian Culture." *Conditions: seven* 3:1 (Spring 1981):67-87; also *Conditions: sixteen,* "Retrospective" (1989):84-106.

Blackwood, Evelyn. "Sexuality and Gender in Certain North American Tribes: the Case of Cross-Gender Females." *Signs* 10:1 (Autumn 1984):27-42.

Brant, Beth. "Lesbian Alliances: Heterosexism in the Eighties -- The Call of the Heron" (speech at the National Women's Studies Association conference, Minneapolis, Minnesota, June 1988). *Sojourner* 14:3 (November 1988):15.

------. "Seeking My Own Vision: Two Remembrances -- Making Fry Bread, Moccasins from Home." *Common Lives/Lesbian Lives* 2 (Winter 1981):5-8.

Burning Cloud (Consuelo Sison), Nisqually Nation. "Open Letter from Filipina/Indian Dyke." *off our backs* 8:11 (December 1978):8-9.

CAD. "Lesbian Plenary: Combatting Heterosexism" (at 10th annual National Women's Studies Association convention, University of Minnesota in Minneapolis, June 1988; panel members Beth Brant, Michelle Parkerson, Joan Nestle, Gloria Anzaldúa). *off our backs* 18:8 (August-September 1988):3+.

Chrystos. "Nidishenok (Sisters)." *Maenad,* "The Lesbian/Heterosexual Split" 2:2 (Winter 1982):23-32.

Dirzhud-Rashid, Shani. "New Age Rage: Spiritual Path a Choice" (response to Angela Johnson, "Pre-packaged Spiritualism," *off our backs* 19:1 (January 1989):10; note: cover reads 18:11 (December 1988)). *off our backs* 19:2 (February 1989):19.

Grahn, Judy. "Strange Country This: Lesbianism and North American Indian Tribes." *Journal of Homosexuality,* "Historical, Literary, and Erotic Aspects of Lesbianism" 12:3/4 (May 1986):43-57.

Iami. "Reader's Forum: Playing Indian." *Lesbian Ethics* 3:1 (Spring 1988):80-2.

Sinister Wisdom, "A Gathering of Spirit" (Native American women), nos. 22/3, 1983.

Allen, Paula Gunn (writer):
Caputi, Jane. "Interview with Paula Gunn Allen." *Trivia,* "Breaking Forms" 16/17 (1990):50-67.

Wynne, Patrice. "Recovering Spiritual Reality in Native American Traditions: an Interview with Paula Gunn Allen." *Woman of Power,* "ReVisioning the Dark" 8 (Winter 1988):68-70.

Chrystos (poet):
Claudia, Karen and Lorraine Sorrel. "Chrystos: Not Vanishing -- & In Person" (interview and review of her book *Not Vanishing*). *off our backs* 19:3 (March 1989):18-19.

Red Elk, Lois (American Indian Movement activist):
Stern, Carol. "Lois Red Elk" (interview). *Heresies #13,* "Feminism and Ecology" 4:1 (1981):19-20.

Nonmonogamy (see Monogamy; Relationships)

Nonviolence (see also: Peace Activism)

Meyerdin, Jane. "In Response: On Nonviolence and Feminism" (response to Jeffner Allen's "Looking at Our Blood: a Lesbian Response to Men's Terrorization of Women," *Trivia* 4 (Spring 1984):11-30). *Trivia* 5 (Fall 1984):60-9.

Brown, Rita Mae (writer):
Martindale, Kathleen. "Rita Mae Brown's *Six of One* and Anne Cameron's *The Journey:* Fictional Contributions to the Ethics of Feminist Nonviolence." *Atlantis* (Canada) 12:1 (Fall 1986):103-10.

Cameron, Anne (writer):

Martindale, Kathleen. "Rita Mae Brown's *Six of One* and Anne Cameron's *The Journey:* Fictional Contributions to the Ethics of Feminist Nonviolence." *Atlantis* (Canada) 12:1 (Fall 1986):103-10.

Deming, Barbara (peace and civil rights activist):

Fritz, Leah. "Barbara Deming: the Rage of a Pacifist." *Ms.* 7:5 (November 1978):97-101.

Robson, Ruthann. "An Interview with Barbara Deming" (peace activist and writer). *Kalliope* 6:1 (1984):37-45.

Nuns

"Authors of Lesbian Nuns Banned in Boston." *National Catholic Reporter* 21 (April 26, 1985):2.

Brown, Hester. "Get Thee to the Motherhouse or the Meaning and Significance of Real Bread in the Mass" (community of nuns as role model for lesbian-feminist community). *Heresies #7,* 2:3 (Spring 1979):76-9.

Douglas, Carol Anne. "Lesbian Nuns: Breaking Silence" (NWSA conference workshop, Rutgers University, June 1984). *off our backs* 14:10 (November 1984):19.

Gramick, Jeannine, SSND. "Lesbian Nuns" (interview with two lesbian nuns, age 45 and 50). *Probe: National Assembly of Women Religious Newsletter* 7:6 (March 1978):5-6.

------. "Lesbian Nuns' Book: Ignored, Rapped, Sexploited." *National Catholic Reporter* 21 (September 6, 1985):14.

Hunt, Mary E. "Celibacy -- the Case Against: Liberating Lesbian Nuns." *Out/Look* 1:2 (Summer 1988):68-74.

Krebs, Paula. "Breaking Silence About *Lesbian Nuns*" (editing the book, and printing excerpts in *Penthouse*'s *Forum Magazine*). *off our backs* 15:5 (May 1985):1-4.

Lootens, Tricia. "Third Women in Print Conference" (Berkeley, California, May 1985; reports on workshops including classism, erotica, lesbian nuns, women of color, pornography, censorship, raid on British gay book store). *off our backs* 15:8 (August-September 1985):8-9+

Manahan, Nancy. "A Lesbian Ex-Nun Meets Her Sisters" (first national gathering of lesbian ex-nuns, at the 1983 Michigan Womyn's Music Festival). *Common Lives/ Lesbian Lives* 8 (Summer 1983):88-91.

------. "*Lesbian Nuns:* an End Note" (letter from co-editor). *off our backs* 15:9 (October 1985):28.

Matter, E. Ann. "Discourses of Desire: Sexuality and Christian Women's Visionary Narratives." *Journal of Homosexuality,* "Homosexuality and Religion" 18:3/4 (1989/1990):119-32.

Murphy, Sheila. "Counseling Lesbian Women Religious." *Women & Therapy* 5:4 (Winter 1986):7-17.

Nuscera, Maria. "Lesbian and Celibate: Journeys in the Dark." *Images* 2:1 (March 1984):2-3.

O'Shea, Kathleen. "Lesbian Nun: Breaking Silence Again" (letter; related letters from Jan Raymond, Pat Hynes and Sister Mary Joan). *off our backs* 15:6 (June 1985):27+.

Sowers, Prudence. "The Habits of Love." *The Advocate* 56 (May 27, 1982):29-30.

Stocker, Midge. "More Than a Controversy -- *Lesbian Nuns:* a Brief History" (selling of portions of book to *Penthouse Forum Magazine*). *Hot Wire* 2:2 (March 1986):52-3+.

Sturgis, Susanna J. "Breaking Silence, Breaking Faith: the Promotion of *Lesbian Nuns.*" *Lesbian Ethics* 1:3 (Fall 1985):89-107.

"Vows of Defiance." *Newsweek* (March 19, 1984):97-100.

Curb, Rosemary (co-editor of *Lesbian Nuns*):
Curb, Rosemary. "*Lesbian Nuns* Controversy: Rosemary Curb Responds." *off our backs* 15:9 (October 1985):27-8.

Doclar, Charlotte (contributor to *Lesbian Nuns*):
Doclar, Charlotte. "Lesbian Nuns: Charlotte Doclar's Story" (excerpt from *Lesbian Nuns*). *Ms.* 14 (August 1985):48-9.

Grier, Barbara (publisher of *Lesbian Nuns*):
Grier, Barbara. "Barbara Grier on *Lesbian Nuns.*" *off our backs* 15:8 (August-September 1985):29.

Old Lesbians and Ageing (see also: Ageism)

Abdullahad, Tania and Leigh H. Mosley. "Third World Lesbian & Gay Conference" (second annual national conference, Chicago, Illinois, November 1981; includes workshop reports on "mature lesbians," "urban black lesbians," "media," "grassroots," "racism & sexism"). *off our backs* 12:2 (February 1982):4.

Adelman, Marcy. "Quieting Our Fears: Lesbians and Aging." *Out/Look* 1:3 (Fall 1988):78-81.

------. "Stigma, Gay Life-Styles, and Adjustment to Aging: a Study of Later-Life Gay Men and Lesbians." *Journal of Homosexuality* 20:3-4 (1990):7-32.

Berger, Raymond M. "Realities of Gay and Lesbian Aging." *Social Work* 29:1 (January-February 1984):57-62.

------. "The Unseen Minority: Older Gays and Lesbians." *Social Work* 27:3 (May 1982):236-43.

CAD. "Passages: Aging Lesbians Meet" (keynote speech by Charlotte Bunch; Washington, D.C., March 1990). *off our backs* 20:5 (May 1990):8.

Cole, Ellen and Esther Rothblum. "Commentary on 'Sexuality and the Midlife Woman'" (by Sandra Leiblum, same issue, pp.495-508). *Psychology of Women Quarterly* 14:4 (December 1990):509-12.

Cook, Loree. "Lesbians and Gays Discuss Aging: Report on the Second National Conference on Lesbian and Gay Aging." *off our backs* 13:9 (October 1983):20-1.

Copper, Baba. "Some Notes from the Fifty-Ninth Year of This Life." *Sinister Wisdom*, "On Being Old and Age" 10 (Summer 1979):31-3.

Corinne, Tee A. "Remembering as a Way of Life" (lesbian 'National Treasures', including: June Arnold, Jeannete Foster, Valerie Taylor, Barbara Grier, Audre Lorde, Anita Cornwell, Sarah Aldridge, Sonny Wainwright). *Common Lives/Lesbian Lives* 19 (Spring 1986):15-18.

Cruikshank, M. "Lavender and Gray: a Brief Survey of Lesbian and Gay Aging Studies." *Journal of Homosexuality* 20:3-4 (1990):77-87.

Douglas, Carol Anne. "Passages: Lesbian Aging" (fourth annual conference in Washington, D.C.). *off our backs* 18:4 (April 1988):16.

Friend, Richard A. "The Individual and Social Psychology of Aging: Clinical Implications for Lesbians and Gay Men." *Journal of Homosexuality*, "Psychotherapy with Homosexual Men and Women: Integrating Identity Approaches for Clinical Practice" 14:1/2 (1987):307-32.

------. "Older Lesbian and Gay People: a Theory of Successful Aging." *Journal of Homosexuality* 20:3-4 (1990):99-118.

------. "Older Lesbian and Gay People: Responding to Homophobia." *Marriage and Family Review* 14:3-4 (1989):241-63.

Henry, Alice. "Mid-Life Crises" (Women in Mid-life Crises Conference, Cornell University, Ithaca, New York, October 1976; noted for lack of discussion of lesbian issues). *off our backs* 6:9 (December 1976):6.

"Holland: Old Dykes' Home" (trans. from *Serpentine,* Dutch feminist monthly, November 1980). *Connexions,* "Global Lesbianism" 3 (January 1982):30.

Howard, Elizabeth M. "Gay Elders." *Ms.* 13 (May 1985):24.

Journal of Homosexuality, "Lesbians Over 60 Speak for Themselves," vol. 16, nos. 3/4, 1988.

Kehoe, Monika. "The Hidden Sorority: Lesbians Over 60." *On the Issues* 12 (1989):22-4+.

------. "A Portrait of the Older Lesbian." *Journal of Homosexuality,* "Historical, Literary, and Erotic Aspects of Lesbianism" 12:3/4 (May 1986):157-62.

------. "Lesbians Over 65: a Triply Invisible Minority." *Journal of Homosexuality,* "Historical, Literary, and Erotic Aspects of Lesbianism" 12:3/4 (May 1986):139-52.

Kimmel, Douglas C. "Adult Development and Aging: a Gay Perspective." *Journal of Social Issues,* "Psychology and the Gay Community" 34:3 (1978):113-30.

Kirkpatrick, Martha. "Middle Age and the Lesbian Experience." *Women's Studies Quarterly* 17:1&2 (Spring/Summer 1989):87-96.

Laner, Mary Riege. "Growing Older Female: Heterosexual and Homosexual." *Journal of Homosexuality* 4:3 (Spring 1979):267-75.

MacDonald, Barbara. "A Movement of Old Lesbians" (keynote address, West Coast Old Lesbian Conference and Celebration, Dominguez Hills State University, California, April 1987). *off our backs* 17:7 (July 1987):3+.

------. "A Movement of Old Lesbians." *Sojourner* 14:5 (January 1989):20-1.

Mountaingrove, Ruth. "West Coast Old Lesbian Conference and Celebration" (Dominguez Hills State University, California, April 1987). *off our backs* 17:7 (July 1987):1-2+.

Mudd, Karen. "Lesbians Talk About Aging." *off our backs* 15:3 (March 1985):17.

Pasternak, Judith. "SAGE Meets Needs of Gay Seniors" (Senior Action in a Gay Environment, 10-year-old service organization). *New Directions for Women* 17:6 (November/December 1988):5.

Penelope, Julia. "Láadan -- Age, Bodily Secretions, Lesbians . . . Developing the Language." *Hot Wire* 6:2 (May 1990):18-19+.

Rich, Cynthia. "Roots in the Sand: Growing Older in the Desert" (excerpt from *Desert Years: Undreaming the American Dream*). *Out/Look #6*, 2:2 (Fall 1989):74-8.

Rosenblatt, Kate. "Old Lesbians Meet" (Old Lesbian Conference and Celebration II, San Francisco State University, August 1989). *off our backs* 19:10 (November 1989):5.

Ruby, Jennie. "Passages V: A Multiracial Conference on Aging and Ageism for All Lesbians" (Washington, D.C., March 1989). *off our backs* 19:5 (May 1989):8-9.

Sang, Barbara. "Reflections of Midlife Lesbians on Their Adolescence." *Journal of Women & Aging,* "Women, Aging and Ageism" 2:2 (1990):111-17.

Sinister Wisdom, "On Being Old & Age," no. 10, Summer 1979.

Star, Susan Leigh. "Introduction: Notes for a Magazine." *Sinister Wisdom*, "On Being Old and Age" 10 (Summer 1979):4-8.

Tully, C. Thorpe. "Caregiving: What Do Midlife Lesbians View as Important?" *Journal of Gay & Lesbian Psychotherapy* 1:1 (1989):87-103.

Hampton, Mabel (co-founder of the Lesbian Herstory Archives):

Nestle, Joan. "Surviving and More: Interview with Mabel Hampton" (77-year-old African-American lesbian). *Sinister Wisdom,* "On Being Old and Age" 10 (Summer 1979):19+.

Rushin, Kate. "Mabel Hampton: 'Cracking Open the Door'" (85-year-old African-American lesbian). *Sojourner* 13:12 (August 1988):21.

Lunden, Doris:

Bulkin, Elly. "An Old Dyke's Tale: an Interview with Doris Lunden" (African-American lesbian, born in 1936, came out in 1953). *Conditions: six* 2:3 (Summer 1980):26-44; also *Conditions: Sixteen,* "Retrospective" (1989):63-82.

Sarton, May (writer):

Springer, Marlene. "As We Shall Be: May Sarton and Aging." *Frontiers* 5:3 (Fall 1980):46-9.

Woodward, K. "May Sarton and Fictions of Old Age." *Women and Literature* 1 (1980):108-27.

Parenting (see also: Adoption; Child Custody; Children of Lesbians; Foster Care; Reproduction)

Agger, Ellen and Francie Wyland. "Lesbian Mothers Fight Back: Wages Due Lesbians." *Quest* 5:1 (Spring 1979):57-62.

Beck, Evelyn Torton. "Daughters and Mothers: an Autobiographical Sketch." *Sinister Wisdom* 14 (Summer 1980):76-80.

------. "The Motherhood That Dare Not Speak Its Name." *Women's Studies Quarterly* 11 (Winter 1983):8-11.

Bernice. "Triad" (lesbian mother and her two daughters). *Women: a Journal of Liberation* 6:3 (1979):30-1.

"Changing with My Daughter: a Lesbian Discovers with Her Daughter That Politics Start at Home." *Spare Rib* (Great Britain) 60 (July 1977):44-6.

"Choosing to Have Children: a Lesbian Perspective." *Women: a Journal of Liberation,* "Women and Conflict" 6:2 (1979):36-42.

Clausen, Jan. "A Flommy Looks at Lesbian Parenting." *off our backs* 16:8 (August-September 1986):16-17+.

Coffey, Mary Anne. "Seizing the Means of Reproduction: Proposal for an Exploratory Study of Alternative Fertilization and Parenting Strategies Among Lesbian Women." *Resources for Feminist Research* (Canada) 18:3 (September 1989):76-9.

Connor, Janet, Debbie Lubarr, Barbara Newman, and Shirley Royster. "Lesbian Mothers Come Out" (lesbians who have older children, not presently "choosing children"). *Sojourner* 13:5 (January 1988):20.

Copper, Baba. "Different Kinds of Love Quarrels." *Common Lives/Lesbian Lives* 17 (Fall 1985):32-5.

------. "Mothers and Daughters of Invention." *Trivia* 11 (Fall 1987):8-20.

------. "We Have to Ask the Question: What Is Happening?" (separatism and parenting). *Common Lives/Lesbian Lives* 9 (Fall 1983):22-32.

Cramer, D. "Gay Parents and Their Children: a Review of Research and Practical Implications." *Journal of Counseling and Development* 64 (1986):504-507.

457

Dejanikus, Tacie. "The Politics of Lesbians Having Children." *off our backs* 14:11 (December 1984):20-1.

DiLapi, Elena Marie. "Lesbian Mothers and the Motherhood Hierarchy" (society's views of who is a fit mother). *Journal of Homosexuality,* "Homosexuality and the Family" 18:1/2 (1989):101-22.

Dineen, Claire and Jackie Crawford. "Lesbian Mothering." *Fireweed* (Canada), "Lesbiantics" 28 (Spring 1989):24-35.

Doe, Jane. "I Left My Husband for the Woman I Loved." *Ms.* 16 (January 1988):80-3.

Egerton, Jayne. "Nothing Natural" (legal obstacles to lesbian parenting in Great Britain). *New Statesman & Society* 3:127 (1990):12-14.

Erlichman, Karen Lee. "Lesbian Mothers: Ethical Issues in Social Work Practice." *Women & Therapy,* "Lesbianism: Affirming Nontraditional Roles" 8:1/2 (1989):207-24.

Ettelbrick, Paula L. "Under the Law -- How Can We Create a Lesbian Family?" *Visibilities* 2:3 (May/June 1988):16-17.

Evans, Beverly K. "Mothering as a Lesbian Issue." *Journal of Feminist Family Therapy* 2:1 (1990):43-52.

Falk, P.J. "Lesbian Mothers -- Psychosocial Assumptions in Family-Law." *American Psychologist* 44:6 (1989):941-7.

Ferguson, Ann. "Motherhood and Sexuality: Some Feminist Questions." *Hypatia* 1:2 (Fall 1986):3-22.

Fishman, Louise, ed. "The Tapes" (edited comments of 10 visual artists who met as a group in New York City, Winter 1977). *Heresies #3,* "Lesbian Art and Artists" 1:3 (Fall 1977):15-21.

"Gay Motherhood: Rewards and Problems." *Science News* 116 (September 22, 1979):198.

Goodman, Bernice. "The Lesbian Mother" (similarities between lesbian and heterosexual mothers). *American Journal of Orthopsychiatry* 43 (1973):283-4.

Green, Richard, Jane Barclay Mandel, Mary E. Hotvedt, James Gray, and Laurel Smith. "Lesbian Mothers and Their Children: a Comparison with Solo Parent Heterosexual Mothers and Their Children." *Archives of Sexual Behavior* 15:2 (1986):167-84.

Hall, Marny. "Lesbian Families: Cultural and Clinical Issues." *Social Work* 23:5 (September 1978):380-5.

Hanscombe, Gillian. "The Rights to Lesbian Parenthood." *Journal of Medical Ethics* 9 (September 1983):133-5.

Harper, Jorjet. "Accessibility, Male Children an Issue at Lesbian Fest" (First Annual East Coast Lesbian Festival, West Stockbridge, Massachusetts, Summer 1989). *Hot Wire* 6:1 (January 1990):29+.

Harris, Mary B. and Pauline H. Turner. "Gay and Lesbian Parents." *Journal of Homosexuality* 12:2 (Winter 1985/86):101-14.

Harvey, S.M., C. Carr, and S. Bernheime. "Lesbian Mothers -- Health-Care Experiences." *Journal of Nurse-Midwifery* 34:3 (1989):115-19.

Herman, Ellen. "The Romance of Lesbian Motherhood." *Sojourner* 13:7 (March 1988):12-13.

Joseph, Gloria I. "Black Mothers and Daughters: Traditional and New Perspectives" (includes discussion of lesbian mothers). *Sage,* "Mothers and Daughters" 1:2 (Fall 1984):17-21.

Journal of Homosexuality, "Homosexuality and the Family," vol. 18, nos. 1/2, 1989.

Journal of Homosexuality, "Lesbians Over 60 Speak for Themselves," vol.16, nos.3/4, 1988.

Kirkpatrick, Martha. "Clinical Implications of Lesbian Mother Studies." *Journal of Homosexuality,* "Psychotherapy with Homosexual Men and Women: Integrated Identity Approaches and Clinical Practice" 14:1/2 (1987):201-12.

Kirkpatrick, Martha, Catherine Smith and Ron Roy. "Lesbian Mothers and Their Children: a Comparative Survey." *American Journal of Orthopsychiatry* 51:3 (July 1981):545-51.

------. "A New Look at Lesbian Mothers." *Human Behavior* 7 (1978):60-1.

Knowles, Stevye. "(Lesbian) Mom and Apple Pie." *Women: a Journal of Liberation,* "Women Loving Women" 5:2 (1977):67-9.

Kweskin, Sally L. and Alicia S. Cook. "Heterosexual and Homosexual Mothers' Self-Described Sex-Role Behavior and Ideal Sex-Role Behavior in Children." *Sex Roles* 8:9 (September 1982):967-75.

"The Lesbian As Mother" (generally positive article, but printed as part of the magazine's "Medicine" section). *Newsweek* 82 (September 24, 1973):75-6.

"Lesbian Mother Accused of Molesting Daughter" (doctor making charge based on "violence of [mother's] lifestyle"). *off our backs* 6:4 (June 1976):7.

"Lesbian Mothers." *off our backs* 2:9 (May-June 1972):20.

Lesbian Mothers' and Friends' Support Group. "Why Are Lesbian Mothers in the Closet?" *off our backs* 7:6 (July-August 1977):6.

"Lesbian Mothers: Robin and Joyce and Family." *Ms.* 2:4 (October 1973):81-2.

"Lesbian Mums on Holiday" (group goes together to Oaklands Women's Holiday Centre, continue to meet as lesbian mothers' network). *Spare Rib* (Great Britain) 134 (September 1983):6-7.

Levy, Eileen F. "Lesbian Motherhood: Identity and Social Support."
Affilia 4:4 (Winter 1989):40-53.

Linda. "The Politics of Parenting -- Lesbian Mothers Out on a Limb?"
Spare Rib (Great Britain) 181 (August 1987):57.

LJ. "Homosexuality and Abortion" (lesbian mothers and gay families
barred from participating in the White House Conference on the
Family). *off our backs* 9:11 (December 1979):17.

Lois. "Life as Mother: Lesbian Motherhood." *ISIS International Bulletin*
23 (June 1982):22-5.

Lorde, Audre. "Manchild: a Black Lesbian Feminist's Response."
Conditions: four 1:4 (Winter 1979):30-6; also *Conditions:
sixteen,* "Retrospective" (1989):28-35.

------. "Turning the Beat Around" (speech delivered at the Hunter College
Lesbian and Gay Community Center's Forum on Lesbian and
Gay Parents of Color, October 1986). *Black/Out* 1:3/4
(1987):13-16.

McNeill, Pearlie. "Oh, Susannah!" (personal account of lesbian-feminist
co-parenting). *Gossip* (Great Britain) 2 (1986):69-75.

McShea, Marie. "Great Expectations" (personal account of lesbian-
feminist co-parenting). *Gossip* (Great Britain) 3 (no date):45-51.

Martin, Del and Phyllis Lyon. "Lesbian Mothers." *Ms.* 2:4 (October
1973):78-80.

Miller, Judith Ann, R. Brooke Jacobsen, and Jerry Bigner. "The Child's
Home Environment for Lesbian vs. Heterosexual Mothers: a
Neglected Area of Research." *Journal of Homosexuality* 7:1
(Autumn 1981):49-56.

Mosely, Leigh. "Lesbian Co-Parents and Their Daughters Share
Experiences" (conference, Baltimore, Maryland, May 1983). *off
our backs* 14:7 (July 1984):2-3+.

Mucklow, Bonnie M. and Gladys K. Phelan. "Lesbian and Traditional Mothers' Responses to Adult Response to Child Behavior and Self-Concept." *Psychological Reports* 44:3 (June 1979):880-2.

Pagelow, M. "Heterosexual and Lesbian Single Mothers: a Comparison of Problems, Coping, and Solutions." *Journal of Homosexuality* 5:3 (Spring 1980):189-204.

Pies, Cheri. "Lesbians and the Choice to Parent." *Marriage and Family Review* 14:3-4 (1989):137-54.

------. "Lesbians Choosing Children: the Use of Social Group Work in Maintaining and Strengthening the Primary Relationship" (between the two lesbian lovers). *Journal of Social Work and Human Sexuality* 5:2 (1987):79-88.

Polikoff, Nancy. "Assembly Removes Family Issue from the Right But . . . " (National Assembly on the Future of the Family, sponsored by the NOW Fund, New York City, November 1979). *off our backs* 10:3 (March 1980):12.

------. "Lesbian Mothers, Lesbian Families: Legal Obstacles, Legal Challenges." *New York University Review of Law & Social Change,* "Symposium: Sex, Politics and the Law; Lesbians and Gay Men Take the Offensive" 14:4 (Fall 1986):907-14.

Pollack, Sandra. "Lesbian Parents: Claiming Our Visibility." *Women & Therapy,* "Motherhood: a Feminist Perspective" 10:1/2 (1990):181-94.

Poppe, Terre. "Lesbian Mothers Conference." *off our backs* 8:9 (October 1978):11+.

Quest, "Organizers' Dialogue: Lesbian Mothers Fight Back," vol. 5, Summer 1979.

Ratterman, Debbie. "Lesbian Co-Mothers." *off our backs* 17:10 (November 1987):3.

Richardson, D. "Do Lesbians Make Good Parents?" *Community Care* 224 (1978):16-17.

Riddle, D.L. "Relating to Children: Gays as Role Models." *Journal of Social Issues* 34:3 (1978):38-58.

Robson, Ruthann. "A Son: Nightmares and Dreams of a Radical Feminist." *Trivia* 6 (Winter 1985):70-9.

Rohrbaugh, Joanna Bunker. "Choosing Children: Psychological Issues in Lesbian Parenting." *Women & Therapy,* "Lesbianism: Affirming Nontraditional Roles" 8:1/2 (1989):51-64.

"Sappho Invaded" (British *Evening News* reporters trick lesbian newspaper *Sappho* into revealing names of lesbian mothers for a sensationalistic feature story). *off our backs* (February 1979):8.

Schafer, Teya. "Mothering in the Lesbian Community." *off our backs* 14:7 (July 1984):4-5.

Schmitz, Marlene and Margie Crow. "Iris -- Reel Women" (nationwide film distribution collective, working on a film about lesbian mothers and organizing a "National Women's Film Circuit"). *off our backs* 5:7 (August 1975):12.

Segrest, Mab. "Southern Reflections: Nothing Can Stop Us Now! But From What?" (keynote address to 12th annual Southeastern Lesbian and Gay Conference, Atlanta, Georgia, 1988). *Out/Look* 1:4 (Winter 1989):10-15.

Shah, Diane K., Linda Walters, and Tony Clifton. "Lesbian Mothers." *Newsweek* 93 (February 12, 1979):61.

"Sharing Children." *Spare Rib* (Great Britain) 90 (January 1980):31-4.

Shavelson, Eileen, M.K. Biaggio, H.H. Cross, and R. Lehman. "Lesbian Women's Perceptions of Their Parent-Child Relationships." *Journal of Homosexuality* 5:3 (Spring 1980):205-15.

Sheppard, Annamay T. "Lesbian Mothers II: Long Night's Journey into Day." *Women's Rights Law Reporter* 8:4 (Fall 1985):219-46.

Shulman, Sheila. "Lesbian Feminists and the Great Baby Con." *Gossip* (Great Britain) 1 (1986):68-90; also *Spinster* (Great Britain) 4 (1980).

Sojourner, Susan and Lorraine Sorrel. "Creating Sappho's Family" (interview with Jackie Forster, co-author of *Rocking the Cradle-- Lesbian Mothers: a Challenge in Family Living*). *off our backs* 12:10 (November 1982):20-1.

Sorrel, Lorraine. "Lesbian Co-parents and Their Daughters Share Experiences" (Baltimore Lesbian Mothers' Support Group conference, Baltimore, Maryland, May 1984). *off our backs* 14:7 (July 1984):2-3+.

Speltz, Kara. "In a Dragon's Mouth: Lesbian Motherhood" (Third Annual Lesbians with Children Conference, Cambridge, Massachusetts, October 1979). *off our backs* 9:11 (December 1979):17.

St. Joan, Jackie. "Who Was Rembrandt's Mother?" (mother as leader image). *Quest* 2:4 (Spring 1976):67-79.

Steinhorn, A. "Lesbian Mothers -- the Invisible Minority: Role of the Mental Health Worker." *Women & Therapy,* "Therapeutic Issues with Lesbian Clients" 1:4 (Winter 1982):35-48.

Stevens, Lynne. "3rd Int'l Women's Film & Video Festival" (includes film about lesbian mothers and their children). *off our backs* 9:4 (April 1979):21+.

Stiglitz, Eloise. "Caught Between Two Worlds: the Impact of a Child on a Lesbian Couple's Relationship." *Women & Therapy,* "Motherhood: a Feminist Perspective" 10:1/2 (1990):99-116.

"Surge of Lesbian Moms to Present Legal Problems." *Jet* 75 (March 20, 1989):37.

Sutton, Stuart A. "The Lesbian Family: Rights in Conflict Under the Uniform Parentage Act." *Golden Gate University Law Review* 10:1 (1980):1007-41.

Taylor, Tobe. "'What If It's a Boy?'" *Sojourner* 14:4 (December 1988):8-10.

Thompson, Norman L., Jr., et al. "Parent-Child Relationship and Sexual Identity in Male and Female Homosexuals and Heterosexuals." *Journal of Consulting and Clinical Psychology* 41:1 (August 1973):120-7.

Van Gelder, Lindsy. "Gay Gothic" (two gay couples have a baby). *Ms.* 16 (July-August 1987):146-7+.

West, Cheryl. "Lesbian Daughter" (of a lesbian mother). *Sage,* "Mothers and Daughters II" 4:2 (Fall 1987):42-4.

"'Your Mum's a Lessy-bin!'" (Lesbian Mothers', Lovers', and Children's Weekend, New Zealand, April 1983; from *bitches, witches, and dykes,* New Zealand lesbian feminist quarterly, June 1982). *Connexions,* "Global Lesbianism 2" 10 (Fall 1983):12-13.

Zuckerman, Elizabeth. "Second Parent Adoption for Lesbian-Parented Families: Legal Recognition of the Other Mother." *U.C. Davis Law Review* 19:3 (Spring 1986):729-59.

Clark, Judy (political prisoner):
Moira, Fran. "Judy Clark: 75 to Life, but Life Goes On" (interview). *off our backs* 14:11 (December 1984):2-8.

Dobkin, Alix (musician):
Armstrong, Toni, Jr. "A Mother-Daughter Conversation: Alix Dobkin & Adrian Hood" (musician and her daughter). *Hot Wire* 5:2 (May 1989):36-9.

<u>Hopkins, Lea</u> (African-American activist, lesbian mother, and former Playboy bunny):
Ebert, Alan. "Lea Hopkins: Just Different." *Essence* 10:12 (April 1980):88-9+.

<u>Pratt, Minnie Bruce</u> (writer):
Zipter, Yvonne. "Minnie Bruce Pratt Wins Lamont Prize" (awarded by the Academy of American Poets, for *Crime Against Nature,* about losing custody of her two sons). *Hot Wire* 6:1 (January 1990):43.

<u>Reagon, Toshi</u> (musician):
Yount, Rena. "Each in Her Own Generation: Bernice & Toshi Reagon" (African-American singer/songwriters who are mother and daughter). *Hot Wire* 5:2 (May 1989):34-5+.

<u>Rich, Adrienne</u> (writer):
Armip, K. "Adrienne Rich Poet Mother Lesbian." *Atlantis* (Canada) 8:1 (Fall 1982):97-110.

Parents of Lesbians (see Families of Lesbians)

Passing Women (see Transvestism)

Peace Activism (see also: Nonviolence)

Smith, Barbara. "'Fractious, Kicking, Messy, Free': Feminist Writers Confront the Nuclear Abyss." *New England Review/Bread Loaf Quarterly* (Summer 1983):581-92.

<u>Deming, Barbara</u> (activist and writer, 1917-1984):
Fritz, Leah. "'We Are All Part of One Another' -- a Tribute to Barbara Deming." *Ms.* 13 (December 1984):41-2.

Glasgow, Joanne. "Barbara Deming, 1917-84." *New Directions for Women* 13:5 (September/October 1984):2.

Lindsey, Karen. "Barbara Deming: a Remembrance." *Woman of Power* 2 (Summer 1985):70+.

Pratt, Minnie Bruce. "'Dancing Toward Death' -- Barbara Deming, 1917-84." *off our backs* 14:9 (October 1984):28.

Robson, Ruthann. "An Interview with Barbara Deming." *Kalliope* 6:1 (1984):37-45.

Segrest, Mab. "Barbara Deming: 1917-84." *Southern Exposure* 13:2-3 (1985):72-5.

The Future Is Female Project:
Cheatham, Annie and Mary Clare Powell. "The Future Is Female Project." *Woman of Power* 2 (Summer 1985):43-7.

Graetz, Susan (activist and musician):
Reynolds, Cindy. "Profile: 'Woman as Warrior' -- 'To Know Somebody Worth the Strain': Susan Graetz" (peace activist involved in Women's Encampment for a Future of Peace and Justice in New York, and musician and founder of On Our Way Productions, who committed suicide in 1985). *Woman of Power* 3 (Winter/Spring 1986):63-5.

Greenham Common Womyn's Peace Encampment, England:
Emberley, Julia and Donna Landry. "Coverage of Greenham and Greenham as 'Coverage.'" *Feminist Studies* 15:3 (Fall 1989):485-98.

Grossholtz, Jean. "American Women on the Right Side of the Fence at Greenham." *Common Lives/Lesbian Lives* 13 (Autumn 1984):100-5.

Kalioaka. "Greenham Common Wimmin's Peace Camp." *Woman of Power,* "International Feminism" 7 (Summer 1987):57-9+.

Mansueto, Connie. "Peace Camp at Greenham Common." *off our backs* 13:2 (February 1983):2-3.

Romalis, Shelly. "Carrying Greenham Home: the London Women's Peace Support Network." *Atlantis* (Canada) 12 (Spring 1987):90-8.

International Lesbian Information Service Conference, Switzerland, 1986:

Haggard, Judith. (letter about vandalism of nuclear bunkers at International Lesbian Information Service conference in Geneva, Switzerland, March 1986). *Gossip* (Great Britain) 6 (1988):15-17.

"Notice to the Entire Lesbian Movement: Terrorism at the End of the 8th ILIS [International Lesbian Information Service] Conference ... " (and letters about incident). *Gossip* (Great Britain) 3 (no date):9-16.

Mygatt, Tracy (activist):

Manahan, Nancy. "Future Old Maids and Pacifist Agitators: the Story of Tracy Mygatt and Frances Witherspoon" (part of "Lesbian Survival Strategies, 1850-1950" panel at the National Women's Studies Association Convention in Storrs, Connecticut, 1981). *Women's Studies Quarterly* 10:1 (Spring 1982):10-13.

Near, Holly (activist and musician):

Landau, Deborah. "Near Journeys Far for World-Wide Peace." *New Directions for Women* 11 (November-December 1982):4+.

Philadelphia Women's Encampment:

Kulp, Denise. "The Philadelphia Women's Encampment" (discussion with several lesbian and bisexual women involved in the peace camp). *off our backs* 17:2 (February 1987):1-3+.

Seneca Women's Peace Camp:

Doremus, Andrea. "Women's Peace Camp, Seneca, New York." *Hysteria* 4 (July 1985):19-21.

Hayes, Lois. "Separatism and Disobedience: the Seneca Peace Encampment." *Radical America* 17:4 (1983):55-64.

McDaniel, Judith. "One Summer at Seneca: a Lesbian Feminist Looks Back in Anger." *Heresies #20,* 5:4 (1985):6-10.

Noll, Jane. "Seneca Peace Encampment." *off our backs* 13:7 (July 1983):15.

Witherspoon, Frances (activist):
Manahan, Nancy. "Future Old Maids and Pacifist Agitators: the Story of Tracy Mygatt and Frances Witherspoon" (part of "Lesbian Survival Strategies, 1850-1950" panel at the National Women's Studies Association Convention in Storrs, Connecticut, 1981). *Women's Studies Quarterly* 10:1 (Spring 1982):10-13.

Women's Pentagon Action, 1981:
Atatimur, Sara. "Untitled Piece" (blind woman's autobiographical narrative about The Women's Pentagon Action, November 1981, and coming out). *Common Lives/Lesbian Lives* 3 (Spring 1982):27+.

Women Take Liberty, 1986:
Curb, Rosemary. "Women Take Liberty in 1986" (women's music festival and political rally at Statue of Liberty, commemorating statue's 100th anniversary). *Hot Wire* 3:2 (March 1987):44-6.

Periodicals, Lesbian/Feminist/Gay (see also: Mass Media; Pornography)

Allen, Martha Leslie. "Women's Media: the Way to Revolution." *off our backs,* "20th Anniversary" 20:2 (February 1990):14-15+.

Faderman, Lillian. "Lesbian Magazine Fiction in the Early Twentieth Century." *Journal of Popular Culture* 11:4 (Spring 1978):800-17.

Herman, Ellen and Karen Kahn. "Exploring Our Sexual Fantasies: Women's Erotica -- Sex Magazine Publishing: a Roundtable Discussion" (with representatives of *Bad Attitude, Eidos* and *Outrageous Women*). *Sojourner* 14:2 (October 1988):30-1.

Horne, Larry and John Ramirez. "The UCLA Gay and Lesbian Media Conference." *Camera Obscura* 11 (Fall 1983):121-31.

Amazon Quarterly:

Biggs, Mary. "From Harriet Monroe to *AQ*: Selected Women's Literary Journals, 1912-1972." *13th Moon*, "Narrative Forms" 8:1/2 (1984):183-216.

Bad Attitude:

Herman, Ellen and Karen Kahn. "Exploring Our Sexual Fantasies: Women's Erotica -- Sex Magazine Publishing: a Roundtable Discussion" (with representatives of *Bad Attitude, Eidos* and *Outrageous Women*). *Sojourner* 14:2 (October 1988):30-1.

Bitch:

Cline, Cheryl. "'Bitch': the Women's Rock Mag with Bite." *Hot Wire* 3:3 (July 1987):44-5.

The Body Politic (Canada):

Bearchell, Chris. "Why I Am a Gay Liberationist: Thoughts on Sex, Freedom, the Family and the State" (gay liberation and lesbian-feminism, and Canada's gay/lesbian liberation journal, *The Body Politic*). *Resources for Feminist Research* (Canada), "The Lesbian Issue/Etre Lesbienne" 12:1(March 1983):57-60.

"*Body Politic* Acquitted" (Canadian gay newspaper acquitted of charges of "immorality"). *off our backs* 9:3 (March 1979):8.

CAD. "Gay Under the Crown" (legal attempts to censor Canadian gay liberation journal *The Body Politic*). *off our backs* 10:4 (April 1980):15.

------. "Lesbian/Gay Trips, Cruises & Marches" (U.S. and international news briefs; *The Body Politic*). *off our backs* 10:3 (March 1980):18-19+.

"Queer Bashing" (Canadian gay/lesbian newspaper *The Body Politic* charged with obscenity). *Broadside* 3:8 (1982):2.

470

Diva (The Netherlands):

"The Netherlands: Collective Chaos" (magazine moves from
collective to more hierarchical structure). _Connexions,_ "Women's
Movements: Thoughts Into Action" 19 (Winter 1986):28-9.

Eidos:

Herman, Ellen and Karen Kahn. "Exploring Our Sexual Fantasies:
Women's Erotica -- Sex Magazine Publishing: a Roundtable
Discussion" (with representatives of _Bad Attitude, Eidos_ and
Outrageous Women). _Sojourner_ 14:2 (October 1988):30-1.

Gaylife:

"_Gaylife_ Hostile to Women." _off our backs_ 13:7 (July 1983):16.

Gay News:

Parker, Jan and Suzanne Arnold. "_Gay News:_ Good News for
Lesbians?" (two _Spare Rib_ writers talk to Gillian Hanscombe
and Allison Hennigan, writers for _Gay News_). _Spare Rib_ (Great
Britain) 130 (May 1983):49-51.

Gossip (Great Britain):

"Editor's Introduction" (about publishing and political and ethical
issues in British lesbian-feminist community). _Gossip_ (Great
Britain) 1 (1986):5-7.

The Ladder:

Esterberg, Kristin Gay. "From Illness to Action: Conceptions of
Homosexuality in _The Ladder,_ 1956-1965" (magazine of the
Daughters of Bilitis). _Journal of Sex Research_ 27:1 (February
1990):65-80.

Smith, Elizabeth A. "Butches, Femmes, and Feminists: the Politics
of Lesbian Sexuality" (includes discussion of the Daughters of
Bilitis magazine _The Ladder_). _NWSA Journal_ 1:3 (Spring
1989):398-421.

Manushi (India):

Douglas, Carol Anne. "Feminism in India" (interview with Madhu
Kishwar, editor). _off our backs_ 10:5 (May 1980):2-4.

Nouvelle Question Féministe (France):

Cottingham, Laura. "Christine Delphy: French Feminist" (interview with activist, writer, and co-editor of *Nouvelle Question Féministe;* includes section on "Lesbianism in France"). *off our backs* 14:3 (March 1984):10-11+.

off our backs:

Cavin, Susan. "Two Decades and Counting." *off our backs,* "20th Anniversary" 20:2 (February 1990):19.

Dejanikus, Tacie, Carol Anne Douglas, and Susan R. Crites. "Marlene Wicks: Co-Founder of *oob*" (interview). *off our backs,* "Ten Years Growing!" 10:2 (February 1980):4+.

Douglas, Carol Anne. "Looking back on the Last 20 Years . . . " *off our backs,* "20th Anniversary" 20:2 (February 1990):15.

------. "1985-1989." *off our backs,* "20th Anniversary" 20:2 (February 1990):15-18.

Douglas, Carol Anne and Fran Moira. "*off our backs,* "Fifteenth Anniversary -- From Our Pages: the First Half of the 1980s." *off our backs* 15:2 (February 1985):8-10.

Moira, Fran. "Ten Years of *off our backs.*" *off our backs* 10:2 (February 1980):2-3+.

Ruby, Jennie. "What Is *off our backs?*" *off our backs,* "20th Anniversary" 20:2 (February 1990):1-3.

Seeger, Nancy and Rena Yount. "A Trip Through the Women's Communities of Washington, D.C." *Hot Wire* 6:1 (January 1990):40-4+.

Webb, Marilyn. "Marilyn Webb: Co-Founder of *oob.*" *off our backs,* "Ten Years Growing!" 10:2 (February 1980):5+.

On Our Backs:
Kulp, Denise. "Cruising *On Our Backs.*" *off our backs* 15:7 (July 1985):16-18.

The Other Face of the Moon (Peru):
"Peru: the Other Face of the Moon" (group publishes a magazine; compiled and trans. from articles in West German bimonthly *Tarantel,* January/February 1987 and Canadian monthly *Rites,* October 1985). *Connexions,* "Lesbian Activism" 29 (1989):16-17.

Outrageous Women:
Herman, Ellen and Karen Kahn. "Exploring Our Sexual Fantasies: Women's Erotica -- Sex Magazine Publishing: a Roundtable Discussion" (with representatives of *Bad Attitude, Eidos* and *Outrageous Women). Sojourner* 14:2 (October 1988):30-1.

Outwrite (Great Britain):
"England: a Working Collective." *Connexions,* "Media: Getting to Women" 16 (Spring 1985):3-4.

Sappho (Great Britain):
"Sappho Invaded" (British *Evening News* reporters trick lesbian newspaper into revealing names of lesbian mothers for a sensationalistic feature story). *off our backs* (February 1979):8.

Wilmer, Val. "A Salute to *Sappho*" (interview with Jackie Forster, editor of magazine that ceased publishing just short of its tenth anniversary). *Spare Rib* (Great Britain) 116 (March 1982):31-2.

Sinister Wisdom:
Dykewomon, Elana. "Notes for a Magazine: a Dyke Geography" (introduction to Dykewomon's first issue as editor). *Sinister Wisdom* 33 (Fall 1987):3-7.

Kaye/Kantrowitz, Melanie. "Notes from the Editor: a Letter to Elana" (from outgoing to incoming editor). *Sinister Wisdom* 32 (Summer 1987):126-8.

Tema (USSR):

Dorf, Julie. "On the Theme: Talking with the Editor of the Soviet Union's First Gay and Lesbian Newspaper" (editor uses pseudonym). *Out/Look #9,* 3:1 (Summer 1990):55-9.

Womanspirit:

Danab, Mint and Athame Mountainclimber. "An Interview with Ruth and Jean Mountaingrove" (editors). *Sinister Wisdom* 8 (Winter 1979):73-6.

Philosophy (see also: Political Theory; Religion; Separatism; Spirituality)

Catherine & Friends. "Notes on Deafness." *Sinister Wisdom* 8 (Winter 1979):63-6.

Cavin, Susan. "Lesbian Origins" (excerpt from book of the same title). *Lesbian Ethics* 1:2 (Spring 1985):3-28.

Cohen, Cheryl H. "The Feminist Sexuality Debate: Ethics and Politics." *Hypatia* 3 (Fall 1986):71-86.

Copper, Baba. "We Have to Ask the Question: What Is Happening?" (separatism and parenting). *Common Lives/Lesbian Lives* 9 (Fall 1983):22-32.

Daly, Mary. "On Lust and the Lusty" (excerpt from *Pure Lust: Elemental Feminist Philosophy*). *Trivia* 3 (Fall 1983):47-69.

------. "Spiraling Into the Nineties." *Woman of Power,* "Humor" 17 (Summer 1990):6-12.

Dellenbaugh, Anne G. "She Who Is and Is Not Yet: an Essay on Parthenogenesis." *Trivia* 1 (Fall 1982):43-63.

Douglas, Carol Anne. "Lesbian Ethics." *off our backs,* "National Women's Studies Association -- Feminist Education: Quality and Equality" 13:8 (August-September 1983):11.

------. "Toward a Feminist Ethic Based on Sex Class Consciousness." *off our backs* 15:11 (December 1985):14-15.

"Editor's Introduction." *Gossip* (Great Britain) 1 (1986):5-7.

Fite, Karen and Nikola Trumbo. "Betrayals Among Women: Barriers to a Common Language." *Lesbian Ethics* 1:1 (Fall 1984):70-89.

Frye, Marilyn. "History and Responsibility." *Women's Studies International Forum* 8:3 (1985):215-7.

------. "To Be and Be Seen: Metaphysical Misogyny." *Sinister Wisdom* 17 (1981):64-70.

Grimard-Leduc, Micheline. "The Mind-Drifting Islands" (excerpt from *L'île des Amantes;* discusses lesbians as an exiled island people because of Amazon heritage). *Trivia* 8 (Winter 1986):28-36.

Harris, Bertha. "The Lesbian: the Workmaker, the Leader" (includes "The Lesbian as Dionysus"). *Quest* 2:4 (Spring 1976):14-28.

Hoagland, Sarah Lucia. "Lesbian Ethics: Some Thoughts on Power in Our Interactions." *Lesbian Ethics* 2:1 (Spring 1986):5-32.

------. "Moral Agency Under Oppression" (first of series of excerpts from unpublished manuscript of *Lesbian Ethics: Toward New Value*). *Trivia* 9 (Fall 1986):73-90.

------. "Moral Agency Under Oppression: Beyond Praise and Blame" (excerpt from unpublished manuscript of *Lesbian Ethics: Toward New Value*). *Trivia* 10 (Spring 1987):24-39.

------. "Moral Agency Under Oppression: Playing Among Boundaries" (excerpt from unpublished manuscript, *Lesbian Ethics: Toward New Value*). *Trivia* 11 (Fall 1987):49-65.

------. "Vulnerability and Power" ("lesbian ethics"). *Sinister Wisdom* 19 (1982):13-23.

Kornegger, Peggy. "Cosmic Anarchism: Lesbians in the Sky with Diamonds." *Sinister Wisdom* 12 (Winter 1980):3-12.

Livia, Anna. "With Gossip Aforethought." *Gossip* (Great Britain) 1 (1986):60-7.

Meigs, Mary. "Some Thoughts About Lesbian Ethics" (in personal relationships). *Canadian Journal of Feminist Ethics* (Canada) 1:2 (Summer 1986):9-11.

Penelope, Julia. "The Mystery of Lesbians: III." *Lesbian Ethics* 1:3 (Fall 1985):3-15; also *Gossip* (Great Britain) 3 (no date):23-39.

Poppe, Terri. "Some Thoughts on the Concept of Full Communication" (response to "Notes on Deafness," same issue, pp.63-6). *Sinister Wisdom* 8 (Winter 1979):67-8.

Raymond, Janice. "A Genealogy of Female Friendship." *Trivia* 1 (Fall 1982):5-26.

Rich, Adrienne. "Women and Honor: Some Notes on Lying." *Heresies #1,* 1:1 (January 1977):23-6.

Saunders, Martha J. "Sexuality, Justice and Feminist Ethics." *Resources for Feminist Research* (Canada), "Confronting Heterosexuality/Confronter l'hétérosexualité" 19:3&4 (September/December 1990):33-9.

South, Cris. "The Deafness Syndrome" (response to "Notes on Deafness," same issue, pp.63-6). *Sinister Wisdom* 8 (Winter 1979):69-70.

Star, S.L. "Lesbian Feminism as an Altered State of Consciousness." *Sinister Wisdom* 5 (1978):83-102.

Trebilcot, Joyce. "Conceiving Women: Notes on the Logic of Feminism." *Sinister Wisdom* 11 (Fall 1979):43-50.

------. "Dyke Methods, or Principles for the Discovery/Creation of Withstanding" (of patriarchy by wimmin). *Hypatia* 3:2 (Summer 1988):1-13.

------. "More Dyke Methods" (response to Zita, "Lesbian Angels & Other Matters," this subject category). *Hypatia* 5:1 (Spring 1990):140-4.

------. "Notes on the Meaning of Life" (phallic images and ethics in everyday life). *Lesbian Ethics* 1:1 (Fall 1984):90-4.

Tremor. "The Hundredth Lezzie: Evolution by Design." *Trivia* 6 (Winter 1985):33-7.

Wittig, Monique. "*Homo Sum*" ("Man Am I"; lesbian as philosophically situated in society). *Feminist Issues* 10:1 (Spring 1990):3-11.

------. "One Is Not Born a Woman." *Feminist Issues* 1:2 (Winter 1981):47-54.

Zita, Jacquelyn N. "Female Bonding and Sexual Politics." *Sinister Wisdom* 14 (Summer 1980):8-16.

------. "Lesbian Angels & Other Matters" (response to Trebilcot, "Dyke Methods," this subject category). *Hypatia* 5:1 (Spring 1990):133-9.

Daly, Mary:
Cosstick, Vicky. "Mary Daly, Feminist Philosopher." *New Directions for Women* 8 (January 1979):1+.

Douglas, Carol Anne. "Mary Daly Speaks & Sparks." *off our backs* 9:5 (May 1979):22-3.

Heyward, Carter. "Ruether and Daly: Theologians Speaking and Sparking, Building and Burning." *Christianity and Crisis* 39 (April 2, 1979):66-72.

de Beauvoir, Simone:
Card, Claudia. "Lesbian Attitudes and the Second Sex." *Women's Studies International Forum* 8:3 (1985):209-14.

Culpepper, Emily Erwin. "Simone de Beauvoir and the Revolt of the Symbols" (includes discussion of Gloria Anzaldúa, Hélène Cixous, Michelle Cliff, Mary Daly, Judy Grahn, Susan Griffin, Julia Penelope (Stanley), and Monique Wittig). *Trivia* 6 (Winter 1985):6-32.

Dallery, Arleen B. "Sexual Embodiment: Beauvoir and French Feminism" (women's sexuality in Simone de Beauvoir, Hélène Cixous, Luce Irigaray and Julia Kristeva). *Women's Studies International Forum* 8:3 (1985):197-202.

Douglas, Carol Anne. "After the Second Sex: New Directions" (conference, including workshop on lesbian criticism of de Beauvoir's work, University of Pennsylvania, April 1984). *off our backs* 14:5 (May 1984):12.

Felstiner, Mary Lowenthal. "Seeing *The Second Sex* Through the Second Wave." *Feminist Studies* 6:2 (1980):247-76.

Ferguson, A. "Lesbian Identity: Beauvoir and History." *Women's Studies International Forum* 8:3 (1985):203-8.

Frye, Marilyn:
Card, Claudia. "Oppression and Resistance: Frye's Politics of Reality." *Hypatia* 1 (Spring 1986):149-66.

Hoagland, Sarah Lucia:
Frye, Marilyn, Maria Lugones, and Carol Van Kirk. "Review Symposium" (about Sarah Lucia Hoagland's *Lesbian Ethics*). *Hypatia* 5:3 (Fall 1990):132-52.

Plato:
Elliott, A. "Plato and Lesbianism." *Times Literary Supplement* 4263:1447 (1984) and (4256):1215 (1984).

Whitbeck, Caroline. "Love, Knowledge and Transformation" (love in Plato's Symposium and "lesbian feminist ontology"). *Women's Studies International Forum* (*Hypatia*) 7:5 (1984):393-405.

Rousseau, Jean-Jacques:
Wittig, Monique. "On the Social Contract" (as heterosexual). *Feminist Issues* 9:1 (Spring 1989):3-12.

Rich, Adrienne:
Murphy, Julien S. "The Look in Sartre and Rich." *Hypatia* 2 (Summer 1987):113-24.

Sartre, Jean-Paul:
Murphy, Julien S. "The Look in Sartre and Rich." *Hypatia* 2 (Summer 1987):113-24.

Photography (see also: Film and Video)

Parmar, Pratibha and Sunil Gupta. "Homosexualities Part Two: UK" (depiction of homosexuality in photography). *Ten.8* (Great Britain) 32 (Spring 1989):22-35.

Austen, Alice:
Novotny, Ann. "Alice Austen's World" (1866-1952). *Heresies #3*, "Lesbian Art and Artists" 1:3 (Fall 1977):27-33.

Biren, Joan E. (see JEB)

Brooke, Kaucyila:
Frueh, Joanna. "How Do You Play? The Deviant Narratives of Kaucyila Brooke." *Afterimage* 17:9 (April 1990):4-7.

Corinne, Tee:
CAD. "Gay . . . Communicating" (publication delay for performance arts quarterly *High Performance* because a printer refused to print Tee Corinne's erotic lesbian photograph). *off our backs* 10:5 (May 1980):9.

Corinne, Tee A. "Bodies: a Collage." *Woman of Power,* "Women's Bodies" 18 (Fall 1990):70-2.

Seajay, Carol. "Visual Conceptions: a Review of Two Slide Shows" (JEB's "Lesbian Images in Photography: 1850-1980" and Tee Corinne's "Erotic Images of Lesbians in the Fine Arts"). *off our backs* 10:3 (March 1980):18-19+.

"Tee Corinne" (the artist on her erotic photography/photomontage). *Gallerie: Women's Art* (1989 annual):34-8.

Hawarden, Clementina:

Corinne, Tee A. "Clementina Hawarden, Photographer" (b.1822). *Sinister Wisdom* 5 (Winter 1978):45-9.

JEB (Joan E. Biren):

"JEB" (by JEB, about her life and work). *Gallerie: Women's Art* (1989 annual):70-3.

Johnson, Angela. "JEB's Fabulous Multi-Image Slide Presentation: For Love and For Life" (about the March on Washington for Lesbian and Gay Rights, October 1987). *off our backs* 18:11 (December 1988):12-13.

Keaner, Martha. "Focus on Focus." *Broadside* (Canada) 2:8 (June 1981):15.

"Lesbian Photography: Neck and Neck." *Broadside* (Canada) 2:6 (April 1981):15.

Seajay, Carol. "Visual Conceptions: a Review of Two Slide Shows" (JEB's "Lesbian Images in Photography: 1850-1980" and Tee Corinne's "Erotic Images of Lesbians in the Fine Arts"). *off our backs* 10:3 (March 1980):18-19+.

Thomas, Joan. "Out of Bounds: a Lesbian Journey." *off our backs* 16:10 (November 1986):16.

Wallace, Jean. "JEB: Embracer of Lesbian Images." *Hot Wire* 4:1
(November 1987):20+.

Khurana, Rita:
Fraser, Jean. "Photography in Education: 'Someone to Talk to'"
(interview with Ritu Khurana and Mel Burns, who participated in
workshop involving young lesbian and gay photographers
producing educational materials). *Ten.8* (Great Britain) 32
(Spring 1989):50-6.

Kiss and Tell:
Kiss and Tell. "Drawing the Line: Where Do You Draw the Line on
Sexually Explicit Images?" (interactive photo exhibit by
Canadian art collective, San Francisco, California, June-July
1990). *Out/Look #10,* 3:2 (Fall 1990):6-11.

Vernée, Vada:
Armstrong, Toni, Jr., Lucy Diamond, and Kathy McKue. "Behind the
Scenes: Vada Vernée, Karen Hester, and Carrie Barton" (*Hot Wire*
photographer, women's music producer, and bassist,
respectively). *Hot Wire* 5:1 (January 1989):50-2.

Wilson, Susan:
Diamond, Lucy. "Behind the Scenes: Susan Wilson and Irene Young"
(photographers of prominent lesbian performers). *Hot Wire* 4:3
(July 1988):50-1.

Young, Irene:
Diamond, Lucy. "Behind the Scenes: Susan Wilson and Irene Young"
(photographers of prominent lesbian performers). *Hot Wire* 4:3
(July 1988):50-1.

Poetry (see also: Literary Critical Theory)

Aal, Katharyn Machan. "Judy Grahn on Women's Poetry Readings:
History and Performance (Part I)" (interview). *Sinister Wisdom*
25 (Winter 1984):67-76.

------. "Judy Grahn on Women's Poetry Readings: History and Performance (Part II)" (interview). *Sinister Wisdom* 27 (Fall 1984):54-61.

Alkalay-Gut, Karen. "The Lesbian Imperative in Poetry" (women choosing lesbianism as the only way they feel they can "write as women"). *Contemporary Review* (Great Britain) 242:1407 (April 1983):209-11.

Biggs, Mary. "From Harriet Monroe to *AQ* [*Amazon Quarterly*]: Selected Women's Literary Journals, 1912-1972." *13th Moon,* "Narrative Forms" 8:1/2 (1984):183-216.

Brannon, Rebecca. "Madison's Fourth Annual Lesbian Variety Show: I Got This Way from Kissing Girlz" (Madison, Wisconsin, November 1989). *Hot Wire* 6:2 (May 1990):36-8.

Brown, Rita Mae. "Gay Arts" (letter responding to Frances Lang, "Gay Arts Festival," *off our backs* 3:1 (September 1972):22; reply by Lang follows Brown's letter). *off our backs* 3:2 (October 1972):21.

Bulkin, Elly. "'Kissing/Against the Light': a Look at Lesbian Poetry." *Radical Teacher* 10 (1978):7-17.

------. "Teaching Lesbian Poetry." *Women's Studies Newsletter* 8:2 (Spring 1980):5-8.

------. "'A Whole New Poetry Beginning Here': Teaching Lesbian Poetry." *College English* 40 (1979):874-88.

Carruthers, Mary. "Imagining Women: Notes Towards a Feminist Poetic." *Massachusetts Review* 20:2 (1979):281-307.

Culpepper, Emily Erwin. "New Tools for Theology: Writings by Women of Color" (draws on works of Audre Lorde, Pat Parker, Beverly Smith, Gloria Anzaldúa, but never explicitly discusses lesbianism). *Journal of Feminist Studies in Religion* 4:2 (Fall 1988):39-50.

Grahn, Judy. "'Gay or Lesbian Writer': Hardly an Alienated Occupation" (keynote address at OUT Write '90, national lesbian and gay writers conference, San Francisco, California, March 1990). *Out/Look #9,* 3:1 (Summer 1990):38-41.

Gubar, Susan. "Sapphistries" (influence of Sappho on women poets, focusing on modernists and especially on Renée Vivien, H.D., Amy Lowell, and Marguerite Yourcenar). *Signs* 10:1 (Autumn 1984):43-62.

Koolish, Lynda. "Choosing Ourselves, Each Other, and This Life: Feminist Poetry and Transgenerational Affiliations." *Sinister Wisdom* 10 (Summer 1979):94-102.

Lang, Frances. "Gay Arts Festival" (Catholic University, August 1972; festival included reading and lecture by Rita Mae Brown and reading by Lee Lally; Brown responds to article in *off our backs* 3:2 (October 1972):21). *off our backs* 3:1 (September 1972):22.

"Lesbian Poets" (trans. from *CLIT 007,* Swiss lesbian quarterly). *Connexions,* "Global Lesbianism 2" 10 (Fall 1983):18.

Libertin, Mary. "Female Friendship in Women's Verse: Toward a New Theory of Female Poetics" (argues that the point in defining lesbian writing is not evidence of genital contact). *Women's Studies* 9:3 (1982):291-308.

Parker, Pat. "Poetry at Women's Music Festivals: Oil and Water." *Hot Wire* 3:1 (November 1986):52-3+.

Ruby, Jennie. "The Black Diaspora" (Michelle Parkerson, Audre Lorde, and Cheryl Clarke speaking on diversity of self-expression among African-American women, in a session at the 10th annual National Women's Studies Association conference, University of Minnesota in Minneapolis, June 1988, "African American Women and the Black Diaspora"). *off our backs* 18:8 (August-September 1988):10.

Segrest, Mab. "Lines I Dare to Write: Lesbian Writing in the South." *Southern Exposure,* "Festival: Celebrating Southern Literature" 9:2 (Summer 1981):53-62.

Sorrel, L. "Lesbian Poetry: Interview" (with Elly Bulkin, co-editor of *Lesbian Poetry*). *off our backs* 11:8 (August-September 1981):20.

Tether, D. "Lesbian Poets." *Booklegger* 2:7 (January 1975):25.

Wakeling, Louise Katherine, Margaret Bradstock, and Mary Fallon. "Poetry Doesn't Sell" (Australia). *Connexions,* "Women's Words" 13 (Summer 1984):26-7.

White, T. "Southern Lesbian Poets Workshop." *off our backs* 11:4 (April 1981):19.

Whitlock, Monica. "Naming the Waves" (interview with Christian McEwan, editor of lesbian poetry anthology, *Naming the Waves*). *Spare Rib* (Great Britain) 189 (April 1988):26-7.

Allen, Paula Gunn:

Caputi, Jane. "Interview with Paula Gunn Allen." *Trivia,* "Breaking Forms" 16/17 (1990):50-67.

Anzaldúa, Gloria:

Culpepper, Emily Erwin. "New Tools for Theology: Writings by Women of Color" (draws on works of Audre Lorde, Pat Parker, Beverly Smith, Gloria Anzaldúa, but never explicitly discusses lesbianism). *Journal of Feminist Studies in Religion* 4:2 (Fall 1988):39-50.

DeShazer, Mary K. "'Sisters in Arms' -- the Warrior Construct in Writings by Contemporary U.S. Women of Color" (including Gloria Anzaldúa and Audre Lorde). *NWSA Journal* 2:3 (Summer 1990):349-73.

Freedman, Diana P. "Living on the Borderland: The Poetic Prose of Gloria Anzaldúa and Susan Griffin." *Women and Language* 12:1 (Spring 1989):1-14.

Bates, Katharine Lee:
Schwarz, Judith. "*Yellow Clover:* Katharine Lee Bates and Katharine Coman" (two turn-of-the-century Wellesley College professors). *Frontiers* 4:1 (Spring 1979):59-67.

Baudelaire, Charles:
Shaw, Annette. "Baudelaire's *Femmes Damnées:* the Androgynous Space." *Centerpoint #11,* 3:3/4 (Fall-Spring 1980):57-65.

Bishop, Elizabeth:
Rich, Adrienne. "The Eye of the Outsider: the Poetry of Elizabeth Bishop." *Boston Review* 8:2 (April 1983):15-17.

Bogus, SDiane:
Birtha, Becky. "Celebrating Themselves: Four Self-Published Black Lesbian Authors" (part 2: III. Doris Davenport; IV. SDiane Bogus). *off our backs* 15:8 (August-September 1985):19-21.

Boye, Karin:
Garde, Pia. "How to Remember Her?" (Swedish poet, novelist and critic, b.1900). *Connexions,* "Global Lesbianism 2" 10 (Fall 1983):22-3.

Broumas, Olga:
Carruthers, Mary J. "The Re-Vision of the Muse: Adrienne Rich, Audre Lorde, Judy Grahn, Olga Broumas." *The Hudson Review* 36:2 (Summer 1983):293-322.

Brown, Linda:
Birtha, Becky. "Celebrating Themselves: Four Self-Published Black Lesbian Authors" (part 3: V. Linda Brown, and "Books by Self-Identified Black Lesbians"). *off our backs* 15:9 (October 1985):16-17.

<u>Brown, Rita Mae:</u>

Brown, Rita Mae. "Gay Arts" (letter responding to Frances Lang, "Gay Arts Festival," *off our backs* 3:1 (September 1972):22; reply by Lang follows Brown's letter). *off our backs* 3:2 (October 1972):21.

Lang, Frances. "Gay Arts Festival" (Catholic University, August 1972; festival included reading and lecture by Rita Mae Brown and reading by Lee Lally; Brown responds to article in *off our backs* 3:2 (October 1972):21). *off our backs* 3:1 (September 1972):22.

<u>Byrd, Stephanie:</u>

Birtha, Becky. "Celebrating Themselves: Four Self-Published Black Lesbian Authors" (part 1: I. Introduction; II. Stephanie Byrd). *off our backs* 15:7 (July 1985):22.

"A Conversation With Stephanie Byrd." *Visibilities* 3:2 (March/April 1989):7-10.

<u>Chrystos:</u>

Claudia, Karen and Lorraine Sorrel. "Chrystos: Not Vanishing -- & In Person" (interview and review of her book, *Not Vanishing*). *off our backs* 19:3 (March 1989):18-19.

<u>Clarke, Cheryl:</u>

Clarke, Cheryl. "Inspiration: Seven Stories of Creating Art -- Creating Sexual Poetry." *Hot Wire* 4:1 (November 1987):28-9.

Ruby, Jennie. "The Black Diaspora" (Michelle Parkerson, Audre Lorde, and Cheryl Clarke speaking on diversity of self-expression among African-American women, in a session at the 10th annual National Women's Studies Association conference, University of Minnesota in Minneapolis, June 1988, "African American Women and the Black Diaspora"). *off our backs* 18:8 (August-September 1988):10.

Cliff, Michelle:

Dejanikus, Tacie and Loie Hayes. "Claiming an Identity: an Interview with Michelle Cliff." *off our backs* 11:6 (June 1981):18-20.

Davenport, Doris:

Birtha, Becky. "Celebrating Themselves: Four Self-Published Black Lesbian Authors" (part 2: III. Doris Davenport; IV. SDiane Bogus). *off our backs* 15:8 (August-September 1985):19-21.

de la Cruz, Sor Juana Inez:

Harper, Jorjet. "Sor Juana: the Other Tenth Muse." *Hot Wire* 5:2 (May 1989):14-15+.

"Sor Juana: Trials and Triumphs in the Convent" (17th century poet and nun; trans. from Venezuelan bimonthly *La Mala Vida* (May/June 1988)). *Connexions,* "Feminism and Religion" 28 (1988-89):4-6.

Deken, Aagje:

Everard, Myriam. "Tribade of *Zielsvriendin*" (18th century Dutch poet). *Groniek* 77 (1982):16-20.

Dickinson, Emily:

Faderman, Lillian. "Emily Dickinson's Letters to Sue Gilbert." *The Massachusetts Review* 18 (September 1979):19-27.

Hart, Ellen Louise. "The Encoding of Homoerotic Desire: Emily Dickinson's Letters and Poems to Susan Dickinson, 1850-1886." *Tulsa Studies in Women's Literature* 9:2 (Fall 1990):251-72.

Homans, Margaret. "'Syllables of Velvet': Dickinson, Rossetti, and the Rhetorics of Sexuality." *Feminist Studies* 11:3 (Fall 1985):569-93.

Smith, Martha Nell. "'To Fill a Gap.'" *San Jose Studies* 13:3 (Fall 1987):3-25.

Doolittle, Hilda (see H.D.)

Dunbar Nelson, Alice:

Hart, Betty. "A Cry in the Wilderness: The Diary of Alice Dunbar Nelson." *Women's Studies Quarterly* 17:3&4 (Fall/Winter 1989):74-8.

Field, Michael:

White, Christine. "Poets and Lovers Evermore: Interpreting Female Love in the Poetry and Journals of Michael Field." *Textual Practice,* "Lesbian and Gay Cultures: Theories and Texts" 4:2 (1990):197-212.

Gidlow, Elsa:

Gidlow, Elsa. "Lesbianism as a Liberating Force." *Heresies #3,* "Lesbian Art and Artists" 1:3 (Fall 1977):94-5.

------. "Memoirs" (coming out in the early 20th century; introduction by Rayna Rapp). *Feminist Studies* 6:1 (Spring 1980):103-27.

Wells, Karen. "Elsa Gidlow." *Margins,* "Lesbian Feminist Writing and Publishing" 23 (August 1975):53-5.

West, Celeste. "Elsa Gidlow: In Memoriam." *Hot Wire* 3:1 (November 1986):58+.

Grahn, Judy:

Aal, Katharyn Machan. "Judy Grahn on Women's Poetry Readings: History and Performance (Part I)" (interview). *Sinister Wisdom* 25 (Winter 1984):67-76.

------. "Judy Grahn on Women's Poetry Readings: History and Performance (Part II)" (interview). *Sinister Wisdom* 27 (Fall 1984):54-61.

Abbott, S. "Judy Grahn: Creating a Gay and Lesbian Mythology." *Advocate* 4:2 (September 4, 1984):45.

Avi-Ram, Amitai. "The Politics of the Refrain in Judy Grahn's *A Woman Is Talking to Death.*" *Women and Language* 10:2 (Spring 1987):38-43.

Beckett, Judith. "Profile: 'Woman as Warrior -- Warrior/Dyke': Judy Grahn" (interview). *Woman of Power* 3 (Winter/Spring 1986):56-9.

Carruthers, Mary J. "The Re-Vision of the Muse: Adrienne Rich, Audre Lorde, Judy Grahn, Olga Broumas." *The Hudson Review* 36:2 (Summer 1983):293-322.

Constantine, Lynne and Suzanne Scott. "*Belles Lettres* Interview." *Belles Lettres* 2 (March-April 1987):7.

Grahn, Judy. "'Gay or Lesbian Writer': Hardly an Alienated Occupation" (keynote address at OUT Write '90, national lesbian and gay writers conference, San Francisco, California, March 1990). *Out/Look #9,* 3:1 (Summer 1990):38-41.

Martinez, Inez. "The Poetry of Judy Grahn." *Margins,* "Lesbian Feminist Writing and Publishing" 23 (August 1975):48-50.

Griffin, Susan:
Bulkin, Elly. "The Places We Have Been: the Poetry of Susan Griffin." *Margins,* "Lesbian Feminist Writing and Publishing" 23 (August 1975):31-4.

Freedman, Diana P. "Living on the Borderland: The Poetic Prose of Gloria Anzaldúa and Susan Griffin." *Women and Language* 12:1 (Spring 1989):1-14.

Pavel, Margaret. "Interview on 'Womanpower': Susan Griffin." *Woman of Power* 1 (Spring 1984):34-8.

H.D.:
Collecott, Diana. "What Is Not Said: a Study in Textual Inversion." *Textual Practice,* "Lesbian and Gay Cultures: Theories and Texts" 4:2 (1990):236-58.

Dunn, Margaret M. "Altered Patterns and New Endings: Reflections of Change in Stein's *Three Lives* and H.D.'s *Palimpsest.*" *Frontiers* 9:2 (1987):54-9.

DuPlessis, Rachel Blau and Susan Stanford Friedman. "'Woman Is Perfect': H.D.'s Debate with Freud." *Feminist Studies* 7:3 (Fall 1981):417-30.

Friedman, Susan Stanford. "'I Go Where I Love': an Intertextual Study of H.D. and Adrienne Rich." *Signs* 9:2 (Winter 1983):228-45.

------. "Reply to Rich" (refers to Adrienne Rich's "Comment on Friedman's '"I Go Where I Love": an Intertextual Study of H.D. and Adrienne Rich,'" *Signs*, "The Lesbian Issue" 9:4 (Summer 1984):733-8). *Signs*, "The Lesbian Issue" 9:4 (Summer 1984):738-40.

Gubar, Susan. "Sapphistries" (influence of Sappho on women poets, focusing on modernists and especially on Renée Vivien, H.D., Amy Lowell, and Marguerite Yourcenar). *Signs* 10:1 (Autumn 1984):43-62.

Laity, Cassandra. "H.D. and A.C. Swinburne: Decadence and Modernist Women's Writing." *Feminist Studies* 15:3 (Fall 1989):461-84.

Rich, Adrienne. "Comment on Friedman's '"I Go Where I Love": an Intertextual Study of H.D. and Adrienne Rich'" (Friedman's article appeared in *Signs* 9:2 (Winter 1983):228-45). *Signs*, "The Lesbian Issue" 9:4 (Summer 1984):733-8.

Shugar, Dana R. "Faustine Re-Membered: H.D.'s Use of Swinburne's Poetry in *Hermione*." *Sagetrieb* 9:1-2 (Spring-Fall 1990):79-94.

Hacker, Marilyn:
Hammond, Karla. "An Interview with Marilyn Hacker." *Frontiers* 5:3 (Fall 1980):22-7.

Hirazuka Raicho:
"Lesbian Poets" (Japanese Poets Miamoto Yuriko, Hirazuka Raicho, and Yoshia Nobuko; trans. from *CLIT 007,* Swiss lesbian-feminist quarterly, June 1983). *Connexions,* "Global Lesbianism 2" 10 (Fall 1983):18.

Jewell, Terri L.:
Jewell, Terri L. "Crawling Around Inside One Black Writer." *off our backs* 13:6 (June 1983):18.

Jewett, Sarah Orne:
Donovan, Josephine. "The Unpublished Love Poems of Sarah Orne Jewett." *Frontiers,* "Lesbian History" 4:3 (Fall 1979):26-31.

Klepfisz, Irena:
Beck, Evelyn Torton. "From Nightmare to Vision: an Introduction to the Essays of Irena Klepfisz" (abridged version of introduction to Klepfisz's 1990 book *Dreams of an Insomniac: Jewish Feminist Essays, Speeches and Diatribes*). *Belles Lettres* 6:1 (Fall 1990):2-5.

Johnson, Barbara. "*Belles Lettres* Interview" (about *The Tribe of Dina: a Jewish Women's Anthology,* which Klepfisz co-edited). *Belles Lettres* 2 (September-October 1987):5.

Kelly, Janis and Amy Stone. "Irena Klepfisz" (interview with the poet about *Keeper of Accounts,* dealing with her experience as a Holocaust survivor). *off our backs* 13:11 (December 1983):10-11.

Lally, Lee:
"In Memoriam: Lee Lally" (author of *In These Days*). *off our backs* 16:4 (April 1986):23.

Lorde, Audre:
Alexander-Fleurant, Maimouna Pausa. "'Audre Lorde Is Very Special To Me.'" *Sojourner* 13:1 (September 1987):18.

Carruthers, Mary J. "The Re-Vision of the Muse: Adrienne Rich, Audre Lorde, Judy Grahn, Olga Broumas." *The Hudson Review* 36:2 (Summer 1983):293-322.

Chiaramonte, Lee. "Letter From Berlin: Audre Lorde Answers Questions on Writing, Voice and Being a Woman Warrior." *Visibilities* 2:5 (September/October 1988):4-7.

Cornwell, Anita. "'So Who's Giving Guarantees?' An Interview with Audre Lorde." *Sinister Wisdom* 4 (Fall 1977):15-21.

Culpepper, Emily Erwin. "New Tools for Theology: Writings by Women of Color" (draws on works of Audre Lorde, Pat Parker, Beverly Smith, Gloria Anzaldúa, but never explicitly discusses lesbianism). *Journal of Feminist Studies in Religion* 4:2 (Fall 1988):39-50.

DeShazer, Mary K. "'Sisters in Arms' -- the Warrior Construct in Writings by Contemporary U.S. Women of Color" (including Gloria Anzaldúa and Audre Lorde). *NWSA Journal* 2:3 (Summer 1990):349-73.

Folayan, Ayofemi. "I Am Your Sister: a Tale of Two Conferences" (celebrating African-American writer/activist Audre Lorde, Boston, Massachusetts, October 1990; disabled women's access limited). *off our backs* 20:11 (December 1990):1-2.

Foster, Thomas. "'The Very House of Difference': Gender as 'Embattled' Standpoint" (bases postmodern discussion of coalition politics on Audre Lorde's poetry). *Genders* 8 (July 1990):17-37.

Harper, Jorjet and Toni L. Armstrong. "Audre Lorde" (interview). *Hot Wire* 5:1 (January 1989):2-6.

"An Interview: Audre Lorde and Adrienne Rich." *Signs* 6:4 (Summer 1981):713-36.

Larkin, Joan. "Nothing Safe: the Poetry of Audre Lorde." *Margins,* "Lesbian Feminist Writing and Publishing" 23 (August 1975):23-5.

Lewis, Gail. "Audre Lorde: Vignettes and Mental Conversations" (about Lorde's poetry). *Feminist Review* (Great Britain), "Perverse Politics: Lesbian Issues" 34 (Spring 1990):100-14.

Lorde, Audre. "No, We Never Go Out of Fashion . . . for Each Other" (discussion among three black feminists and Audre Lorde at International Feminist Bookfair, England, June 1984). *Spare Rib* 149 (December 1984):26-9.

------. "Poems Are Not Luxuries." *Chrysalis* 3 (1977):7-9.

------, Adrienne Rich, and Alice Walker. "In the Name of All Women: the National Book Award Speech" (read by Rich, who won the award; all three authors were nominated and agreed that whoever won would accept "in the name of all the women whose voices have gone and still go unheard in a patriarchal world"). *Margins,* "Lesbian Feminist Writing and Publishing" 23 (August 1975):23.

Moira, Fran and Lorraine Sorrel. "Audre Lorde: Lit from Within" (interview). *off our backs* 12:4 (April 1982):2-3.

Parmer, Pratibha and Jackie Kay. "Frontiers: Interview [with] Black Author and Activist, Audre Lorde." *Spare Rib* (Great Britain) 188 (March 1988):37-41.

Ruby, Jennie. "The Black Diaspora" (Michelle Parkerson, Audre Lorde, and Cheryl Clarke speaking on diversity of self-expression among African-American women, in a session at the 10th annual National Women's Studies Association conference, University of Minnesota in Minneapolis, June 1988, "African American Women and the Black Diaspora"). *off our backs* 18:8 (August-September 1988):10.

Stato, Joanne. "I Am Your Sister Celeconference: Tribute to Audre Lorde" (Boston, Massachusetts, October 1990). *off our backs* 20:11 (December 1990):1-5+.

Sturgis, Susanna J. "Audre Lorde: a Radio Profile." *Sojourner* 14:5 (January 1989):33.

Lowell, Amy:

Faderman, Lillian. "Warding Off the Watch and Ward Society: Amy Lowell's Treatment of the Lesbian Theme." *Gay Books Bulletin* 1:2 (Summer 1979):23-7.

Gubar, Susan. "Sapphistries" (influence of Sappho on women poets, focusing on modernists and especially on Renée Vivien, H.D., Amy Lowell, and Marguerite Yourcenar). *Signs* 10:1 (Autumn 1984):43-62.

Miamoto Yuriko:

"Lesbian Poets" (Japanese Poets Miamoto Yuriko, Hirazuka Raicho, and Yoshia Nobuko; trans. from *CLIT 007*, Swiss lesbian-feminist quarterly, June 1983). *Connexions,* "Global Lesbianism 2" 10 (Fall 1983):18.

Parker, Pat:

Beemyn, Brett. "Bibliography of Works By and About Pat Parker (1944-1989)." *Sage* 6:1 (Summer 1989):81-2.

Brimstone, Lyndie. "Pat Parker: a Tribute." *Feminist Review* (Great Britain), "Perverse Politics: Lesbian Issues" 34 (Spring 1990):4-7.

"Coming Together: the Benefit for Pat Parker" (fundraiser for poet to attend seminar at the Cancer Support and Education Center). *Hot Wire* 5:1 (January 1989):38.

Culpepper, Emily Erwin. "New Tools for Theology: Writings by Women of Color" (draws on works of Audre Lorde, Pat Parker, Beverly Smith, Gloria Anzaldúa, but never explicitly discusses lesbianism). *Journal of Feminist Studies in Religion* 4:2 (Fall 1988):39-50.

Parker, Pat. "Poetry at Women's Music Festivals: Oil and Water." *Hot Wire* 3:1 (November 1986):52-3+.

------. "1987 March on Washington: the Morning Rally." *Hot Wire* 5:1 (January 1989):16-17.

Smith, Barbara. "Naming the UnNameable: the Poetry of Pat Parker." *Conditions: three* 1:3 (Spring 1978):99-103.

Stato, Joanne. "Pat Parker, 1944-1989" (poet and activist). *off our backs* 19:8 (August-September 1989):1+.

Woodwoman, Libby. "Pat Parker Talks About Her Life and Her Work" (interview). *Margins,* "Lesbian Feminist Writing and Publishing" 23 (August 1975):60-1.

Philips, Katherine:
Andreadis, Harriette. "The Sapphic-Platonics of Katherine Philips, 1632-1664." *Signs* 15:1 (Autumn 1989):34-60.

Pratt, Minnie Bruce:
Zipter, Yvonne. "Minnie Bruce Pratt Wins Lamont Prize" (awarded by the Academy of American Poets, for *Crime Against Nature,* about losing custody of her two sons). *Hot Wire* 6:1 (January 1990):43.

Rich, Adrienne:
Arnup, Katherine. "Adrienne Rich: Poet, Mother, Lesbian Feminist, Visionary." *Atlantis* (Canada) 8 (Fall 1982):97-110.

Bulkin, Elly. "An Interview with Adrienne Rich, Part 1." *Conditions: one* 1:1 (April 1977):50-65.

------. "An Interview with Adrienne Rich, Part 2." *Conditions: two* 1:2 (October 1977):53-66.

Carruthers, Mary. "Adrienne Rich's 'Sources.'" *River Styx,* "Women's Issues" 15 (1984):69-74.

------. "The Re-Vision of the Muse: Adrienne Rich, Audre Lorde, Judy Grahn, Olga Broumas." *The Hudson Review* 36:2 (Summer 1983):293-322.

Farwell, Marilyn R. "Toward a Definition of the Lesbian Literary Imagination" (focuses on Adrienne Rich, Monique Wittig, and lesbian literary criticism). *Signs* 14:1 (Autumn 1988):100-18.

Friedman, Susan Stanford. "'I Go Where I Love': an Intertextual Study of H.D. and Adrienne Rich." *Signs* 9:2 (Winter 1983):228-45.

------. "Reply to Rich" (refers to Adrienne Rich's "Comment on Friedman's "'I Go Where I Love": an Intertextual Study of H.D. and Adrienne Rich'" *Signs,* "The Lesbian Issue" 9:4 (Summer 1984):733-8). *Signs,* "The Lesbian Issue" 9:4 (Summer 1984):738-40.

Gentile, Mary. "Adrienne Rich and Separatism: the Language of Multiple Realities." *Maenad,* "The Lesbian/Heterosexual Split" 2:2 (Winter 1982):136-46.

"An Interview: Audre Lorde and Adrienne Rich." *Signs* 6:4 (Summer 1981):713-36.

Lockey, Ottie. (interview). *Broadside* (Canada) 2:8 (June 1981):10-11.

Murphy, Julien S. "The Look in Sartre and Rich." *Hypatia* 2:2 (Summer 1987):113-24.

------, Audre Lorde, and Alice Walker. "In the Name of All Women: the National Book Award Speech" (read by Rich, who won the award; all three authors were nominated and agreed that whoever won would accept "in the name of all the women whose voices have gone and still go unheard in a patriarchal world"). *Margins,* "Lesbian Feminist Writing and Publishing" 23 (August 1975):23.

Packwood, Marilyn. "Adrienne Rich" (interview). *Spare Rib* (Great Britain) 103 (February 1981):14-16.

Runzo, Sandra. "Adrienne Rich's Voice of Treason." *Women's Studies* 18:2-3 (1990):135-51.

Stimpson, Catharine. "Adrienne Rich and Lesbian/Feminist Poetry." *Parnassus* 12:2/13:1 (Spring/Summer/Fall/Winter 1985):249-68.

Templeton, Alice. "The Dream and the Dialogue: Rich's Feminist Poetics and Gadamer's Hermeneutics." *Tulsa Studies in Women's Literature* 7:2 (Fall 1988):283-96.

Wilson, Jean. "Adrienne Rich: Journey Towards a Common Language." *Broadside* (Canada) 2:9 (July 1981):8-9.

Zaremba, Eve. "Adrienne Rich: the Taste and Smell of Life." *Broadside* (Canada) 3:7 (1982):20.

------. "Stand Fast and Move Forward." *Broadside* (Canada) 2:10 (August/September 1981):4.

Rossetti, Christina:
Homans, Margaret. "'Syllables of Velvet': Dickinson, Rossetti, and the Rhetorics of Sexuality." *Feminist Studies* 11:3 (Fall 1985):569-93.

Sappho:
Balmer, Josephine. "Sappho: Out at Last." *Spare Rib* (Great Britain) 125 (December 1982):36-9.

Gubar, Susan. "Sapphistries" (influence of Sappho on women poets, focusing on modernists and especially on Renée Vivien, H.D., Amy Lowell, and Marguerite Yourcenar). *Signs* 10:1 (Autumn 1984):43-62.

Hallett, Judith P. "Sappho and Her Social Context: Sense and Sensuality." *Signs* 4:3 (Spring 1979):447-64.

Harper, Jorjet. "Sappho: a Woman's Place." *Hot Wire* 4:3 (July 1988):14-15+.

------. "Sappho and Her Lesbian Lovers." *Hot Wire* 4:2 (March 1988):14-15+.

------. "Sappho and the Goddess Aphrodite -- Sappho's Religion: the Erotic Dimension of the Sacred." *Hot Wire* 3:1 (November 1986):16-18.

------. "Sappho: Image, Legend, and Reality." *Hot Wire* 3:3 (July 1987):16-17+.

------. "Sappho: Lost and Rediscovered." *Hot Wire* 3:2 (March 1987):14-16.

------. "Sappho of Lesbos." *Hot Wire* 2:2 (March 1986):16-17+.

------. "Sappho: Poet, Teacher, Priestess." *Hot Wire* 2:3 (July 1986):16-17+.

------. "Sappho's Musical Genius." *Hot Wire* 4:1 (November 1987):14-15+.

------. "The Tenth Muse -- Sappho: Rediscovering Lesbian Space." *Hot Wire* 6:3 (September 1990):48-9.

Moonwomon, Birch. "Psappha" (Sappho). *Women: a Journal of Liberation,* "Women Loving Women" 5:2 (1977):27-9.

Stehle, Eva. "Sappho's Gaze: Fantasies of a Goddess and a Young Man." *Differences*, "Sexuality in Greek and Roman Society" 2:1 (Spring 1990):88-125.

Stigers, Eva Stehle. "Romantic Sensuality, Poetic Sense: a Response to Hallett on Sappho" (Hallett, Judith P., "Sappho and Her Social Context: Sense and Sensuality," same issue, pp.447-64). *Signs* 4:3 (Spring 1979):465-71.

------. "Sappho's Private World." *Women's Studies*, "Women in Antiquity" 8:1/2 (1981):47-64.

Winkler, Jack. "Garden of Nymphs: Public and Private in Sappho's Lyrics." *Women's Studies*, "Women in Antiquity" 8:1/2 (1981):65-92.

Sarton, May:
Bakerman, Jane S. "'Work is My Rest': A Conversation with May Sarton." *Moving Out* 7:2 & 8:1 (1978):8-12+.

Carter, Nancy Corson. "An Interview with May Sarton." *Kalliope* 5:2 (1983):37-48.

Hershman, Marcie. "May Sarton at 70: 'a Viable Life Against the Odds.'" *Ms.* 11 (October 1982):23-6.

Shelley, D. "Conversation with May Sarton." *Women and Literature* 7:2 (Spring 1979):33-41.

Springer, Marlene. "As We Shall Be: May Sarton and Aging." *Frontiers* 5:3 (Fall 1980):46-9.

Woodward, K. "May Sarton and Fictions of Old Age." *Women and Literature* 1 (1980):108-27.

Sexton, Anne:
Fitzgerald, Margot. "Using Sexton to Read Freud: the Pre-Oedipal Phase and the Etiology of Lesbianism in Sexton's 'Rapunzel.'" *Journal of Homosexuality* 19:4 (1990):55-66.

Sherman, Susan:

Clausen, Jan. "That Question That Is Our Lives: the Poetry of Susan Sherman." *Conditions: one* 1:1 (April 1977):66-76.

Vivien, Renée:

Annas, Pamela J. "'Drunk with Chastity': the Poetry of Renée Vivien." *Women's Studies* 13:1/2 (1986):11-22.

Bourbonnais, Nicole. "Femme Métonymique, Femme Métaphorique: la Poésie d'Anne Hébert et de Renée Vivien." *Atlantis* (Canada) 11:2 (Spring 1986):108-14.

Gubar, Susan. "Sapphistries" (influence of Sappho on women poets, focusing on modernists and especially on Renée Vivien, H.D., Amy Lowell, and Marguerite Yourcenar). *Signs* 10:1 (Autumn 1984):43-62.

Walker, Alice:

Walker, Alice, Adrienne Rich, and Audre Lorde. "In the Name of All Women: the National Book Award Speech" (read by Rich, who won the award; all three authors were nominated and agreed that whoever won would accept "in the name of all the women whose voices have gone and still go unheard in a patriarchal world"). *Margins,* "Lesbian Feminist Writing and Publishing" 23 (August 1975):23.

Yoshia Nobuko:

"Lesbian Poets" (Japanese Poets Miamoto Yuriko, Hirazuka Raicho, and Yoshia Nobuko; trans. from *CLIT 007,* Swiss lesbian-feminist quarterly, June 1983). *Connexions,* "Global Lesbianism 2" 10 (Fall 1983):18.

<u>Political Organizing</u> (see also: Conferences; Equal Rights
Amendment; Gay Liberation Movement; Lesbians and the Right;
Lesbians of Color; National Organization for Women; Political
Protest; Political Theory; Politicians; Pornography; Separatism)

Baker, A.J. "The Problem of Authority in Radical Movement Groups: A
Case Study of Lesbian-Feminist Organization." *Journal of
Applied Behavioral Science* 13:3 (1982):323-41.

Black Scholar, "Black Women and Feminism," vol. 16, no. 2,
March/April 1985.

Brittingham, Midge Wood. "Shared Interest" (guidelines for setting up
lesbian/gay alumni groups, based on Oberlin College's alumni
association). *Currents* 16:4 (April 1990):42-3.

Brooke. "The State of Feminism" (lesbian and straight separatism as bad
for the movement). *off our backs,* "Ten Years Growing!" 10:2
(February 1980):8+.

CAD. "Gays Win Some" (gay issues in elections in California,
Washington, Florida, New York, and Washington D.C.;
tentative plans for a lesbian and gay march on Washington D.C.
in 1979). *off our backs* 8:11 (December 1978):11.

------. "New Gay Groups" (organized after the 1979 March for Lesbian and
Gay Rights in Washington, D.C.). *off our backs* 9:11 (December
1979):7.

Chapman, Frances. "Brooke" (interview with feminist activist in
Philadelphia and Boston; part of series on "women who are felt
to be important by the women in the women's movement, not
the male-dominated newsmedia"). *off our backs* 3:8 (May
1973):4-5.

"Chile" (excerpt from article in *Women's News,* Irish feminist bimonthly,
(December/January 1989)). *Connexions,* "Lesbian Activism" 29
(1989):15.

Cooper, Aaron. "No Longer Invisible: Gay and Lesbian Jews Build a Movement." *Journal of Homosexuality,* "Homosexuality and Religion" 18:3/4 (1989/1990):83-94.

Diedrichs, Gary. "Fun & Games in Our Newest City" (lesbian/gay community and the incorporation of the City of West Hollywood, California). *Los Angeles* 30 (October 1985):184-94.

Douglas, Carol Anne. "Radical Feminism Still Radical" (response to CLIT Statement #3, same issue, pp.10-11). *off our backs* 6:7 (October 1976):12.

Dykewomon, Elana. "Lesbian Theory and Social Organization: the Knots of Process." *Sinister Wisdom,* "With an Emphasis on Lesbian Theory" 37 (Spring 1989):29-34.

"East Germany: the Sunday Club" (only lesbian/gay group allowed to meet outside the Protestant Church or bars; trans. and excerpted from West German lesbian quarterly, *Lebenstich* (Spring 1988)). *Connexions,* "Lesbian Activism" 29 (1989):22.

Edelson, Carol and Evgenia B. "No Victory in a Vacuum" (response to CLIT Statement #3, same issue, pp.10-11). *off our backs* 6:7 (October 1976):12-13.

Ehrlich, Carol. "The Women's Liberation Movement in the 1970's." *off our backs,* "Ten Years Growing!" 10:2 (February 1980):24.

Gabriner, Vicki. "Coming out Slugging!" (lesbian softball teams as basis for activism). *Quest,* "Organizations and Strategies" 2:3 (Winter 1976):52-7.

Gevisser, Mark. "Legitimate or Liberate? Lesbian and Gay Students Choose" (college activism). *The Nation* 246:12 (March 26, 1988):413-14.

Gottlieb, Rhonda and Debra Kessler. "Where Are All the Militant Dykes?" (in the Women's Liberation Movement). *off our backs,* "Ten Years Growing!" 10:2 (February 1980):9+.

H., Mia. "Austria: Lesbians Organize" (Women's Section of Homosexuelle Initiative, Vienna). *off our backs* 20:3 (March 1990):11.

Hartwell, Shirley. "The Lie of the Feminist Right Wing Ethic" (the denial of existing hierarchies, "the tyranny of structurelessness"). *Trivia,* "Breaking Forms" 16/17 (1990):68-80.

Hayes, Janice. "Seattle Lesbian Center Thrives." *New Directions for Women* 16 (November-December 1987):9.

Henry, Alice. "Mexican Lesbian Speaks Out" (about her writing, homophobia, and political organizing in Mexico, remaining anonymous for fear of repression). *off our backs* 16:1 (January 1986):8.

Hobart Women's Action Group. "Sexism and the Women's Liberation Movement" (heterosexism of the movement). *Refractory Girl* (Australia), "Lesbian Issue" 5 (Summer 1974):30-3.

Irving, Kim. "Nicaragua: Lesbian Sandinista" (interview with young lesbian activist and Sandinista; reprint from Canadian monthly *Rites,* March 1987). *Connexions,* "Lesbian Activism" 29 (1989):10-11.

"Japan -- Regumi: a New Spelling of Our Name" (interview with Japanese lesbian activist). *Connexions,* "Lesbian Activism" 29 (1989):24-5.

Jennings, Paula. "Lesbian Liberation Later" (homophobia in the women's movement). *Gossip* (Great Britain) 3 (no date):77-81.

Kahn, Rabbi Yoel H. "Judaism and Homosexuality: the Traditionalist/ Progressive Debate." *Journal of Homosexuality,* "Homosexuality and Religion" 18:3/4 (1989/90):47-82.

Kaye/Kantrowitz, Melanie. "Observations: The Next Step." *NWSA Journal* 2:2 (Spring 1990):236-44.

Kelly, Janis, Carol Anne Douglas, and Alice Henry. "Women's Agenda" ("Beyond Suffrage, the U.S. National Agenda" conference, Washington D.C., October 1976; including talk by Charlotte Bunch of the National Gay Task Force and performance by singer Maxine Feldman). *off our backs* 6:8 (November 1976):8+.

Kokula, Ilse. "Poland: Going Public, Step-by-Step" (trans. and excerpted from West German lesbian quarterly, *Lebenstich* (Spring 1988)). *Connexions*, "Lesbian Activism" 29 (1989):11.

Kolasinska, Wiesia. "Lesbian Feminism and the Pro-Choice Movement." *Resources for Feminist Research* (Canada), "The Lesbian Issue/Etre Lesbienne" 12:1(March 1983):61-2.

Lorde, Audre. "I Am Your Sister: Black Women Organizing Across Sexualities." *Women & Therapy* 6 (Winter 1987):25-30.

McCoy, Renée. "NCBLG Is a Family" (National Coalition of Black Lesbians and Gays). *Black/Out*, "We Are Family" 2:2 (Summer 1989):3-4.

------. "Ten Years Ago: Ten Years Ahead" (tenth anniversary of the National Coalition for Black Lesbians and Gays). *Black/Out*, "Tenth Anniversary Edition: NCBLG Celebrates Homecoming" 2:1 (Fall 1988):3-4.

------. "The Truth of the Matter" (by new executive director of the National Coalition for Black Lesbians and Gays, about the organization). *Black/Out* 1:3/4 (1987):3.

McCoy, Sherry and Maureen Hicks. "A Psychological Retrospective on Power in the Contemporary Lesbian-Feminist Community" (based on study of Los Angeles, California community). *Frontiers*, "Lesbian History" 4:3 (Fall 1979):65-9.

Maenad, "The Lesbian/Heterosexual Split," vol. 2, no. 2, Winter 1982.

Meredith, Diana. "Lesbians and Abortion." *Broadside* (Canada) 4:2 (1982):7.

"Mexican Lesbian Group" (Grupo Lesbico Patlamali de Guadalajara). *off our backs* 18:9 (October 1988):11.

MNM. "Get It in Righting" (news briefs about activism on behalf of lesbian and gay rights bills in New York City, Wichita, Kansas, Boston, Massachusetts, and Woodstock, New York). *off our backs* 8:5 (May 1978):17.

Morganthau, Tom, et al. "Gay America in Transition; a Turning Point Has Been Reached, and AIDS May Mean the Party Is Over" (mostly about gay men). *Newsweek* 102 (August 8, 1983):30-8.

"Mythmaking in the Women's Movement" (the lesbian/heterosexual split). *Refractory Girl* (Australia), "Lesbian Issue" 5 (Summer 1974):34-8.

"OUTRAGE: New Lesbian and Gay Direct Action Group" (British group modeled after U.S. AIDS Coalition to Unleash Power (ACT-UP)). *Spare Rib* (Great Britain) 214 (July 1990):43.

"Peru: the Other Face of the Moon" (compiled and trans. from articles in West German bimonthly *Tarantel,* January/February 1987 and Canadian monthly *Rites,* October 1985). *Connexions,* "Lesbian Activism" 29 (1989):16-17.

Pitz, L.S. "Alliances Lesbians Make." *Common Lives/Lesbian Lives* 5 (Fall 1982):5-10.

Poppe, Terre. "Southeast Lesbian Network." *off our backs* 9:8 (August-September 1979):28-30.

Radical Lesbian Front. "Political Lesbianism -- the Battle Rages" (trans. from *Masques,* French gay theoretical journal, Fall 1981). *Connexions,* "Global Lesbianism" 3 (January 1982):28-9.

"Revolutionary People's Constitutional Convention: Lesbian Testimony" (homophobia in the New Left). *off our backs* 1:11 (September 30, 1970):4-5.

Ross, Becki. "The House that Jill Built: Lesbian Feminist Organizing in Toronto, 1976-1980" (Ontario). *Feminist Review* (Great Britain) 35 (Summer 1990):75-91.

Rupp, Leila J. "The Women's Community in the National Women's Party, 1945 to the 1960s." *Signs,* "Communities of Women" 10:4 (Summer 1985):715-40.

Ryskamp, John. "The Women's Movement and the Dialectic of Sex: the Failure of Positive Schism." *Journal of Thought* 10 (January 1975):46-57.

Silveira, Jeannette. "Strategy and Class" (letter to "A Readers' Forum -- Separatism: Beyond the Debate," about how to use resources of separatists of all classes to revolutionary ends, rather than accusing some of not being true separatists because of where and with whom they work). *Lesbian Ethics* 3:2 (Fall 1988):22-5.

Smartt, Dorothea and Val Mason-John. "Black Feminists Organising on Both Sides of the Atlantic." *Spare Rib* (Great Britain) 171 (October 1986):20-4.

"South Africa" (summarized from "Black Gays and Lesbians in South Africa" in Canadian monthly *Rites* (October 1987)). *Connexions,* "Lesbian Activism" 29 (1989):15.

Sternbach, Nancy Saporta. "Argentina 'In Democracy': Feminism 1985" (including section on "Women's Groups and Homophobia"). *off our backs* 16:1 (January 1986):6-8.

Tobin, Ann. "Lesbianism and the Labour Party: The GLC Experience" (Gay and Lesbian Center). *Feminist Review* (Great Britain), "Perverse Politics: Lesbian Issues" 34 (Spring 1990):56-66.

Vaid, Urvashi. "We Have a Blueprint; Now We Need Tools" (part of "Messages to the Movement . . . Where We Are Twenty Years After Stonewall"). *Out/Look #5,* 2:1 (Summer 1989):59-60.

Wallsgrove, Ruth. "A Guide to Lesbian Groups" (Sappho, Kenric, NOOL (National Organization of Lesbians), Lesbian Link, Lesbian Line, Gemma, Action for Lesbian Parents, Wages Due Lesbians, and Lesbian Left). *Spare Rib* (Great Britain) 74 (September 1978):26-9.

Willenborg, Erleen. "Organizing with Music: Blazing Star." *Heresies #9*, 3:1 (1980):32-3.

"Yugoslavia: We Love Women" (trans. and excerpted from West German lesbian quarterly, *Lebenstich,* Spring 1988). *Connexions,* "Lesbian Activism" 29 (1989):21.

Castelón, Alida (organizer of the first lesbian Encuentro, Cuernavaca, Mexico, October 1987):
"Mexico: the First Lesbian *Encuentro*" (from Canadian monthly, *Rites* 4:4 (September 1987)). *Connexions,* "Lesbian Activism" 29 (1989):26-7.

Johnson, Sonia (writer):
Bowen, Angela, Jacqui Alexander, Jennifer Abod, and Terri Ortiz. "Taking Issue with Sonia" (response to interview with Sonia Johnson in *Sojourner* 13:5 (January 1988)). *Sojourner* 13:6 (February 1988):14-15.

Jones, Heidi (straight leader of the New Jersey Lesbian and Gay Coalition):
Gilbert-Neiss, Connie. "Meet Heidi Jones: the Straight Gay Leader." *Out/Look #8*, 2:4 (Spring 1990):54-5.

Pérez, Lourdes (organizer of the first lesbian Encuentro, Cuernavaca, Mexico, October 1987):
"Mexico: the First Lesbian *Encuentro*" (from Canadian monthly, *Rites* 4:4 (September 1987)). *Connexions,* "Lesbian Activism" 29 (1989):26-7.

Tremblay, Lucie Blue (musician):
Armstrong Toni L. "Lucie Blue Tremblay." *Hot Wire* 3:1 (November 1986):2-5.

Political Prisoners

FM. "Control for 'New Breed'" (first Maximum Security Unit for women in the federal prison system, used for political prisoners, among others). *off our backs* 8:6 (June 1978):7.

Amnesty International:
"Amnesty Rejects Homosexuals." *off our backs* 13:2 (February 1983):16.

Brown, Rita:
BLW (from Judy Holmes' releases). "Rita D. Brown Harassed, Transferred." *off our backs* 10:8 (August-September 1980):29; note: cover reads 10:7.

Fridley, Mary. "Anarcha-Feminism: Growing Stronger" (first anarcha-feminist conference, Ithaca, New York, June 1978; includes discussion of political prisoner Rita Brown). *off our backs* 8:7 (July 1978):20.

Reid, Marian. "Is Anybody Listening?" *off our backs* 10:9 (June 1980):15.

Rita Brown Defense Committee. "25 Years for Rita Brown" (political prisoner). *off our backs* 8:5 (May 1978):8.

"Rita Brown Missing." *off our backs* 10:9 (June 1980):15.

Clark, Judy (white lesbian mother, incarcerated for her role in a Black Liberation Army Brinks truck robbery):
Kalman, Marilyn and Rachel Lederman. "Talking with Three Lesbian Political Prisoners" (Judy Clark, Linda Evans, and Laura Whitehorn interviewed by two activist lawyers). *Sinister Wisdom,* "With an Emphasis on Lesbian Theory" 37 (Spring 1989):100-10.

Moira, Fran. "Judy Clark: 75 to Life, but Life Goes On" (interview). *off our backs* 14:11 (December 1984):2-8.

Le Deaux, Joanna:

MJ. "Rules of the Game" (press conference calling for release of Jill
Raymond, Joanna Le Deaux, and Veronica Vigil). *off our backs*
6:3 (May 1976):6.

Raymond, Jill (detained for 14 months, during which she refused to
testify before a federal grand jury investigating the women's
movement and the gay liberation movement):
"Jill Raymond Statement on Leaving Jail." *off our backs* 6:4 (June
1976):8.

MJ. "Jill Expecting Release." *off our backs* 6:3 (May 1976):6.

------. "Rules of the Game" (press conference calling for release of Jill
Raymond, Joanna Le Deaux, and Veronica Vigil). *off our backs*
6:3 (May 1976):6.

"Raymond Remains in Jail." *off our backs* 5:11 (January-February
1976):6.

The Resistance Conspiracy Case (Laura Whitehorn, Marilyn Buck,
Susan Rosenberg, and Linda Evans indicted for "seeking to
influence, change, and protest policies and practices of the United
States government concerning various international and domestic
matters through the use of violent and illegal means"):
Ellsworth, Kelley. "Resistance Conspiracy Case." *off our backs* 19:5
(May 1989):20-1.

Greenspan, Judy. "Political Prisoners" (Susan Rosenberg, Alan
Berkman, Linda Evans, Laura Whitehorn, Tim Blunk, and
Marilyn Buck held in solitary confinement for activities with
women's, lesbian/gay, and Black Liberation groups). *off our
backs* 18:9 (October 1988):20.

Kalman, Marilyn and Rachel Lederman. "Talking with Three Lesbian
Political Prisoners" (Judy Clark, Linda Evans, and Laura
Whitehorn interviewed by two activist lawyers). *Sinister
Wisdom,* "With an Emphasis on Lesbian Theory" 37 (Spring
1989):100-10.

O'Malveny, Mary. "Writings of Women of the Resistance Conspiracy Case." *Phoebe,* "Women, Crime and Justice" 2:1 (Spring 1990):82-9.

<u>Saxe, Susan</u> (radical activist tried for armed robbery after living as a fugitive for five years):
AH and TD. "Saxe Trial" (update). *off our backs* 6:8 (November 1976):4.

Aronsen, Byrna. "Slight to Saxe: Frustrated Friends" (see Susan Saxe Defense Fund, *off our backs* 6:7 (October 1976):13). *off our backs* 6:5 (July-August 1976):21.

CAD. "Saxe Shuttled" (among prisons). *off our backs* 6:5 (July-August 1976):12.

------. "Saxe Trial Starts." *off our backs* 6:7 (October 1976):5.

Dejanikus, Tacie. "Political Prisoners" (150 women attend benefit for Susan Saxe and Assata Shakur, New York City, February 1976). *off our backs* 6:1 (March 1976):9+.

Kearns, Martha. "Susan Saxe to Stand Trial Again." *off our backs* 6:10 (January 1977):4.

Madeleine. "Saxe's Motions Denied." *off our backs* 6:3 (May 1976):7.

"Radical Lesbian/Woman" (news brief). *off our backs* 6:4 (June 1976):5.

"Saxe Denied Right of Self-Defense" (disallowed to act as her own co-counsel). *off our backs* 6:2 (April 1976):10.

Saxe, Susan. "A Letter to the Movement." *off our backs* 6:1 (March 1976):22.

------. "Susan Saxe Pleads Guilty." *off our backs* 7:2 (March 1977):5.

Susan Saxe Defense Fund. "Letter to the Leadership of the July 4th Coalition" (which didn't read Saxe's "Letter to the Movement" at a rally in Philadelphia, Pennsylvania). *off our backs* 6:7 (October 1976):13.

Vigil, Veronica:
MJ. "Rules of the Game" (press conference calling for release of Jill Raymond, Joanna Le Deaux, and Veronica Vigil). *off our backs* 6:3 (May 1976):6.

Weather Underground:
Gabriner, Vicki. "Bugged By the Past" (former Weather Underground and SDS member appeals passport fraud conviction related to anti-Vietnam War activities). *off our backs* 7:8 (October 1977):11.

Political Protest (see also: Acquired Immune Deficiency Syndrome; Equal Rights Amendment; Lesbians and the Right; Political Organizing)

Banks, Johnette. "March Plans Advance" (meeting of steering committee for March on Washington for Lesbian and Gay Rights, October 11, 1987). *off our backs* 17:4 (April 1987):4.

"Bedford Hills" (demonstration in support of prisoners' demands, Bedford Hills, New York). *off our backs* 8:10 (November 1978):4.

Beverley, Brooke, and Wendy Stevens. "Why Protest Windows?" (movie about a psychotic lesbian who hires a man to rape a straight woman). *off our backs* 10:4 (April 1980):9+.

Bowles, Sheila. "Active Lesbianism." *Lesbian Ethics* 2:1 (Spring 1986):87-8.

"Britain: Stop the Clause" (anti-gay Clause 28; excerpted from British Feminist monthly *Outwrite* 65 (May 1988)). *Connexions, Lesbian Activism*" 29 (1989):9.

CAD. "Dykes, Gays Marching" (meeting in Philadelphia, Pennsylvania, February 1979, to plan march on Washington D.C. for lesbian and gay rights). *off our backs* 9:4 (April 1979):11.

------. "Holiday Out" (boycott of Holiday Inn hotels after Memphis hotel tried to break contract with the planning committee for the fifth southeastern Conference for Lesbians and Gay Men). *off our backs* 10:10 (November 1980):9.

------. "Lesbian/Gay Trips, Cruises & Marches" (U.S. and international news briefs). *off our backs* 10:3 (March 1980):18-19+.

------. "Not CBS" (boycott of network in response to a documentary about gay politics that emphasized public sex and sadomasochism). *off our backs* 10:8 (August-September 1980):15; note: cover reads 10:7.

------. "To Speak Or Not to Speak" (controversy in San Francisco and New York over whether to have political speakers at lesbian/gay pride celebrations). *off our backs* 10:8 (August-September 1980):15+; cover reads 10:7.

------. "Walking Gay" (walk across Florida to Tallahassee to demonstrate for human rights). *off our backs* 10:6 (June 1980):9.

Chasin, Susan T. "Stonewall: For Once and All" (refers to the Stonewall Riots in New York City, which sparked the contemporary gay rights movement). *Visibilities* 3:4 (July/August 1989):4-8.

Douglas, Carol Anne. "Gay Resistance" (reaction to light sentence given to Dan White, who murdered gay San Francisco supervisor Harvey Milk). *off our backs* 9:7 (July 1979):15+.

------. "Gays March Locally . . . March on Washington; Transpersons Transcendent." *off our backs* 9:8 (August-September 1979):9.

Douglas, Carol Anne. "Spain: a Kiss is Just a Kiss" (lesbian kiss-in protesting arrest of two women for kissing in public). *off our backs* 17:5 (May 1987):18.

"Dyketactics" (lesbian-feminist collective sit-in at Philadelphia City
      Council). *off our backs* 5:11 (January-February 1976):9.

"Dyketactics" (Philadelphia group sits in at City Council chambers to
      protest Council's failure to act on gay rights bill). *off our backs*
      6:6 (September 1976):10.

Epstein, Barbara. "Direct Action: Lesbians Lead the Movement."
      Out/Look 1:2 (Summer 1988):26-32.

Flowing. "Lesbian Acts" (activist groups). *Lesbian Ethics* 2:1 (Spring
      1986):89-92.

"For a New Coalition" (National March for Lesbian and Gay Rights,
      October 11, 1987). *The Nation* 245:13(October 24, 1987):433.

"Gay Gala" (Christopher Street Gay Liberation Days commemorating the
      1969 Stonewall Riots, New York City, June 1970). *off our
      backs* 1:7 (June 26, 1970):14.

"Gays on the March" (unsympathetic cover story on the surge of gay
      pride/visibility). *Time* 106 (September 8, 1975):32-43.

"Greensboro" (lesbian and gay groups among crowd opposing the Ku
      Klux Klan on the twentieth anniversary of the Woolworth lunch
      counter sit-in, Greensboro, North Carolina, February 1980). *off
      our backs* 10:3 (March 1980):13.

"High School Dyketactics" (Philadelphia lesbian group, Dyketactics,
      demonstrate at high school where lesbian students and alumni
      were harassed). *off our backs* 6:5 (July-August 1976):13.

"Holland: Never Going Underground" (bus tour of Western Europe by Dutch lesbian/gay rights organization Labda, to benefit the movement against British anti-lesbian/gay Clause 28). *Connexions,* "Lesbian Activism" 29 (1989):7-8.

Hollibaugh, Amber. "Writers as Activists: Moving Working-Class Oral Protest Onto the Printed Page." *Out/Look #10,* 3:2 (Fall 1990):69-72.

Hughes, Janice. "Civil Disobedience: National March on Washington for Lesbian and Gay Rights" (and rally protesting Bowers v. Hardwick Supreme Court ruling, October 1987). *off our backs* 17:11 (December 1987):15+.

Johnson, Angela. "JEB's Fabulous Multi-Image Slide Presentation: For Love and For Life" (Joan E. Biren's slide show and video of the March on Washington for Lesbian and Gay Rights, October 1987). *off our backs* 18:11 (December 1988):12-13.

Johnston, Jill. "Lesbian/Feminism Reconsidered." *Salmagundi,* "Homosexuality: Sacrilege, Vision, Politics" 58-59 (Fall 1982-Winter 1983):76-88.

Kelly, Janis. "Relighting Feminist Fires: National Women's Independence Day." *off our backs* 11:8 (August-September 1981):18-19.

Kogan, Marcela. "Gays Will March to Promote Rights" (National March for Lesbian and Gay Rights, October 11, 1987, Washington, D.C.). *New Directions for Women* 16 (July-August 1987):6.

Kulp, Denise. "National March on Washington for Lesbian and Gay Rights" (October 1987). *off our backs* 17:10 (November 1987):1-2.

Kurs, Katherine and Robert S. Cathcart. "The Feminist Movement -- Lesbian-Feminism as Confrontation." *Women's Studies in Communication* 6 (Spring 1983):12-23.

McDonald, Tracy. "Gay Catholics Protest" (Cardinal John O'Connor's banning of special mass for gay Catholic group Dignity). *off our backs* 17:5 (May 1987):16.

MacLean, Judy. "The Untapped Lobby: Lesbian Daughters and Gay Sons of Politicians." *Out/Look #5,* 2:1 (Summer 1989):62-7.

Maran, Meredith. "October 11, 1987" (National March for Lesbian and Gay Rights, Washington, D.C., October 11, 1987). *Out/Look* 1:1 (Spring 1988):6+.

Melechen, Wendy. "Resistance Day -- Lesbians and Gays Rally" (Lesbian and Gay Day of Resistance, Washington, D.C., April 1982). *off our backs* 12:6 (June 1982):13.

Members of the Coalition of Black Gay Women and Men. "Gay Pride Day -- a Community Affair?" (controversy over lack of political protest message in Washington, D.C. Gay Pride Day, June 1978). *off our backs* 8:7 (July 1978):12+.

Meyers, Cheryl. "Lesbians Jailed" (for sit-in at marriage license bureau in Niles, Illinois, where they were denied a license; controversy in the gay/lesbian community, because some thought the protest jeopardized a pending "gay civil rights bill" in Congress). *off our backs* 5:9 (November 1975):11.

MNM. "Chalking One Up" (Bay Area Coalition Against the Briggs Initiative, which would prohibit gay school teachers, holds speakout, San Francisco, California, March 1978). *off our backs* 8:5 (May 1978):10.

"New York: Cathedral Demo" (St. Patrick's Cathedral, New York City, December 1989). *off our backs* 20:3 (March 1990):13.

"OUTRAGE: New Lesbian and Gay Direct Action Group" (British group modeled after U.S. AIDS Coalition to Unleash Power (ACT-UP)). *Spare Rib* (Great Britain) 214 (July 1990):43.

"OUTRAGE Protests Anti-Gay Murders" (in England; direct action group modeled after U.S. AIDS Coalition to Unleash Power (ACT-UP)). *Spare Rib* 216 (September 1990):44.

Parker, Pat. "1987 March on Washington: the Morning Rally." *Hot Wire* 5:1 (January 1989):16-17.

A Radicalesbian. "Sister Love" (lesbians in first annual Christopher Street Gay Liberation Day, commemorating 1969 Stonewall Riots, New York City, June 1970). *off our backs* 1:9&10 (July 31, 1970):3.

Rule, Jane. "Lesbian Leadership." *Resources for Feminist Research* (Canada), "The Lesbian Issue/Etre Lesbienne" 12:1(March 1983):56.

"Sappho Zaps Plato at Columbia" (banner with names of women writers hung over names of classical writers atop Butler Library at Columbia University, New York City). *New Directions for Women* 19:1 (January-February 1990):5.

Sargent, Margaret Lee. "Women Rising in Resistance." *Lesbian Ethics* 2:1 (Spring 1986):92-3.

"Sit-in" (at *London Evening News*, protesting articles opposing lesbian artificial insemination). *off our backs* 8:2 (February 1978):3.

Stevens, Lynne. "The Window: a Look Inside" (protest against "Windows," movie about a psychotic lesbian who hires a man to rape a straight woman). *off our backs* 10:3 (March 1980):16-17.

"Switzerland: What You Should Know About Lesbians" (pamphlet imitating the format and tone of official government educational materials, widely distributed in Switzerland; trans. from Swiss lesbian quarterly *CLIT 007* (1986)). *Connexions,* "Lesbian Activism" 29 (1989):14.

<u>Political Theory</u> (see also: Equal Rights Amendment; Gay Liberation Movement; Lesbians and the Right; Lesbians of Color; National Organization for Women; Philosophy; Political Organizing; Political Protest; Pornography; Separatism; S/M; Socialism)

Amazones d'hier, Lesbiennes d'aujourd'hui. "Radical Lesbianism" (excerpts, included in "A Readers' Forum -- Separatism: Beyond the Debate"). *Lesbian Ethics* 3:2 (Fall 1988):17-20.

Apuzzo, Virginia M. "Brand X: Why We Need to Be More Generic" ("Is this a movement for social change, or is it a movement to make it okay to be gay or lesbian?" -- part of "Messages to the Movement . . . Where We Are Twenty Years After Stonewall"). *Out/Look #5*, 2:1 (Summer 1980):60-1.

Arnup, Katherine. "Lesbian Feminist Theory." *Resources for Feminist Research* (Canada), "The Lesbian Issue/Etre Lesbienne" 12:1 (March 1983):53-5.

Brooke. "The State of Feminism" (lesbian and straight separatism as bad for the movement). *off our backs*, "Ten Years Growing!" 10:2 (February 1980):8+.

Brown, Rita Mae. "It's All Dixie Cups to Me" (lesbians in the Women's Liberation Movement). *Quest* 1:3 (Winter 1975):44-50.

Bunch, Charlotte. "Feminism and Education: Not by Degrees." *Quest* 5:1 (Summer 1979):7-18; also *New Directions for Women* 10:5 (September-October 1981):8-9 and 10:6 (November/December 1981):19.

------. "Lesbian Feminist Politics" (excerpt from speech delivered at the Sojourner Truth School, course on "Tactics and Strategies for the Women's Movement"). *off our backs* 3:7 (April 1973):17.

------. "Not for Lesbians Only." *Quest*, "Theories of Revolution" 2:2 (Fall 1975):50-6.

------. "Self Definition and Political Survival." *Quest* 1:3 (Winter 1975):2-15.

------. "Visions and Revisions: Women and the Power to Change" (part of final panel of the first National Women's Studies Association conference, Lawrence, Kansas, May 30-June 3, 1979). *Women's Studies Newsletter* 7:3 (Summer 1979):20-1.

Campbell, Beatrix. "A Feminist Sexual Politics: Now You See It, Now You Don't." *Feminist Review* (Great Britain) 5 (1980):1-18.

CLIT (Collective Lesbian International Terrors). "CLIT Statement #3" (militant feminism and separatism, with discussion of classism and racism). *off our backs* 6:7 (October 1976):10-11.

------. "CLIT Statement #4 - Necropolis, USA: a Dying Empire Fucks Itself (CLIT Reviews the Nineteen Seventies)." *off our backs* 10:8 (August-September 1980):16-18; note: cover reads 10:7.

Cohen, Cheryl H. "The Feminist Sexuality Debate: Ethics and Politics." *Hypatia* 3 (Fall 1986):71-86.

Le Colectif: Amazones d'Hier, Lesbiennes d'Aujourd'hui. "Lesbianisme Radical." *Resources for Feminist Research* (Canada) 15 (December 1986/January 1987):5-7.

------, trans. Denise Blais. "Radical Lesbianism." *Gossip* (Great Britain) 4 (no date):21-6.

Douglas, Carol Anne. "Feminist Theory: Notes From the Third Decade." *off our backs*, "20th Anniversary" 20:2 (February 1990):24.

------. "Radical Feminism Still Radical" (response to CLIT Statement #3, same issue, pp.10-11). *off our backs* 6:7 (October 1976):12.

------. "What the Hell Is a Radical Feminist." *off our backs*, "Ten Years Growing!" 10:2 (February 1980):15.

Etorre, Betsy. "Sappho Revisited: a New Look at Lesbianism" (links between feminism and lesbianism for some women). *Women's Studies International Quarterly* 3:4 (1980):415-28.

Fenwomyn, Carol. "Lesbian Ethics Workshop Reports: 'Love Your Enemy?': Political Lesbianism." *Gossip* (Great Britain) 6 (1988):110-16.

Fernbach, D. "Toward a Marxist Theory of Gay Oppression." *Socialist Revolution* 6:2 (1976):29-41.

Frances. "The Soul Selects: a New Separate Way" (radicalesbianism, feminism, and lesbianism). *off our backs*, "Women Loving: 2" 2:5 (January 1972):7.

Fridley, Mary. "Anarcha-Feminism: Growing Stronger" (first anarcha-feminist conference, Ithaca, New York, June 1978). *off our backs* 8:7 (July 1978):20.

Gomez, Jewelle. "We Haven't Come Such a Long Way, Baby" (part of "Messages to the Movement . . . Where We Are Twenty Years After Stonewall"). *Out/Look #5*, 2:1 (Summer 1989):55-6.

Haber, Barbara. "Is Personal Life Still a Political Issue?" (divisions between lesbian and heterosexual feminists). *Feminist Studies* 5:3 (1979):417-30.

Hillman, Terry. "Feminism and Lesbianism." *Moving Out* 1:2 (1971):75-7.

Hoagland, Sarah Lucia. "Coercive Consensus." *Sinister Wisdom* 6 (Summer 1978):86-92.

Hutchins, Lorraine. "Biatribe -- a Feminist Bisexual Politic for Change." *off our backs* 18:2 (February 1988):16-18.

Jaeckel, Monika. "Feminist Catch-as-Catch-Can" (German lesbian-feminist discusses need to overcome conflicts between feminists). *Women's Studies International Forum* 8:1 (1985):5-8.

Johnston, Jill. "Lesbian/Feminism Reconsidered." *Salmagundi,* "Homosexuality: Sacrilege, Vision, Politics" 58-59 (Fall 1982-Winter 1983):76-88.

Karlen, A. "The New Lesbian Politics and the Decline of Social-Science." *Salmagundi,* "Homosexuality: Sacrilege, Vision, Politics" 58-59 (Fall 1982-Winter 1983):300-7.

Kaye/Kantrowitz, Melanie. "Observations: The Next Step." *NWSA Journal* 2:2 (Spring 1990):236-44.

Kingston, Bev. "Lesbianism and Feminist Theory." *Refractory Girl* (Australia), "Lesbian Issue" 5 (Summer 1974):3-5.

Krebs, Paula M. "Lesbianism as a Political Strategy." *off our backs* 17:6 (June 1987):17.

Le Grenade, Carole. "La Gauche ou le Non-lieu du Lesbianisme." *Resources for Feminist Research* (Canada), "The Lesbian Issue/Etre Lesbienne" 12:1 (March 1983):67-8.

Man, Killa. "Trying Hard to Forget All I've Known" (social control of women and false consciousness of many lesbians; written by a member of Collective Lesbian International Terrors (CLIT)). *off our backs* 4:8 (July 1974):20-1.

Negrin, Su. "(Hetero)Sexual Politics" (except from *Begin at Start: Some Thoughts on Personal Liberation and World Change*). *Edcentric* 31-2 (November 1974):47-9.

O'Sullivan, Susan. "Passionate Beginnings: Ideological Politics 1969-72." *Feminist Review* (Great Britain), "Sexuality" 11 (Summer 1982):70-86.

Penelope, Julia. "The Mystery of Lesbians: I" (separatist lesbian-feminism as opposed to reformism of 1980s feminism). *Lesbian Ethics* 1:1 (Fall 1984):7-33; also *Gossip* (Great Britain) 1 (1986):9-45.

------. "The Mystery of Lesbians: II" (separatist political theory). *Lesbian Ethics* 1:2 (Spring 1985):29-67; also *Gossip* (Great Britain) 2 (1986):16-68.

------. "The Mystery of Lesbians: III." *Lesbian Ethics* 1:3 (Fall 1985):3-15; also *Gossip* (Great Britain) 3 (no date):23-39.

Raymond, Janice. "Putting the Politics Back Into Lesbianism" (lesbianism as a political movement vs. as a lifestyle). *Women's Studies International Forum* 12:2 (1989):149-56.

Rich, Adrienne. "Compulsory Heterosexuality and Lesbian Existence." *Signs* 5:4 (Summer 1980):631-60.

Rosemary. "Prodding the Wheels of Revolution." *Changes* (April 1980):3.

Ruby, Jennie. "Lesbian Theory" (workshop at National Women's Studies Association conference, Towson State University, Maryland, June 1989; reports on Betty Tallen, "A Lesbian-Feminist Critique of 12-Step Programs"; Jeffner Allen, "Passions in the Gardens of Delight"; and Sarah Lucia Hoagland on Lesbian Ethics). *off our backs* 19:8 (August-September 1989):8.

------. "Lesbian Theory: Pursuing Lesbian Meaning" (Lesbian Theory session of the National Women's Studies' Association conference in Minneapolis, Minnesota, June 1988; includes reports on the following papers: Betty Tallen, "Lesbian Feminist Theory: a View from the Political Theory Trenches"; Lee Evans, "Lesbians, Community, and Patriarchal Consumer Values"; Elana Dykewomon, "The Knots of Process"; Anna Lee, "New Age Spirituality Is the Invention of Heteropatriarchy"; Sarah Hoagland, "Lesbian Agency" and "Lesbian Space"; and Jeffner Allen on writing). *off our backs* 18:9 (October 1988):18-19.

Rule, Jane. "Rule Making." *Lesbian Ethics* 1:1 (Fall 1984):65-9.

Sarah, Elizabeth. "Re-Thinking Feminism: Some Thoughts on the Limitations of 'Basics'-Training." *Women's Studies International Forum* 8:1 (1985):9-13.

Silveira, Jeannette. "Strategy and Class" (letter to "A Readers' Forum -- Separatism: Beyond the Debate," about how to use resources of separatists of all classes to revolutionary ends, rather than accusing some of not being true separatists because of where and with whom they work). *Lesbian Ethics* 3:2 (Fall 1988):22-5.

------. "Why Men Oppress Women" (marxist-lesbian/feminist discussion of reproduction, misogyny, and a lesbian future). *Lesbian Ethics* 1:1 (Fall 1984):34-56.

Sinister Wisdom, "With an Emphasis on Lesbian Theory," no. 37, Spring 1989.

Stanley, Julia P. "Notes on the Edge" (lesbian revolution as *the* revolution; lesbians in relation to other world revolutions). *WIN: Peace and Freedom Through Nonviolent Action,* "Lesbian Culture" 11:22 (June 26, 1975):8-10.

Sturgis, Susanna J. "Is This the New Thing We're Going to Have to be Politically Correct About?" *Sinister Wisdom* 24 (Winter 1983):16-27.

Tallen, Betty. "Lesbian-Feminist Theory: a View from the Political Theory Trenches." *Sinister Wisdom,* "With an Emphasis on Lesbian Theory" 37 (Spring 1989):35-45.

Trebilcot, Joyce. "Dyke Methods, or Principles for the Discovery/Creation of Withstanding" (of patriarchy by wimmin). *Hypatia* 3:2 (Summer 1988):1-13.

------. "In Partial Response to those Who Worry That Separatism May Be a Political Cop-Out: an Expanded Definition of Activism." *Gossip* (Great Britain) 3 (no date):82-4; also, earlier version in *off our backs* 16:5 (May 1986):13.

Valverde, Mariana. "Heterosexism: a Challenge to the Left." *Canadian Dimension* (Canada) 17:1 (March 1983):36-8.

Wildeman, Marlene. "Theorizing Lesbian Existence: Reflections on Site" (focusing on "lesbian *locus,* as distinct from female heterosexual political and erotic locality," without being separatist). *Fireweed* (Canada) 29 (Summer 1989):55-65.

Wittig, Monique. "One Is Not Born a Woman." *Feminist Issues* 1:2 (Winter 1981):47-54.

Zimmerman, Bonnie. "The Politics of Transliteration: Lesbian Personal Narratives." *Signs,* "The Lesbian Issue" 9:4 (Summer 1984):663-82.

Zita, Jacquelyn N. "Female Bonding and Sexual Politics." *Sinister Wisdom* 14 (Summer 1980):8-16.

<u>Collective Lesbian International Terrors</u> (CLIT; activist group):
Edelson, Carol and Eugenia B. "No Victory in a Vacuum" (response to CLIT Statement #3, same issue, pp.10-11). *off our backs* 6:7 (October 1976):12-13.

<u>"Compulsory Heterosexuality and Lesbian Existence</u>" (essay by Adrienne Rich):
Cameron, Deborah. "Ten Years On: 'Compulsory Heterosexuality and Lesbian Existence.'" *Women: a Cultural Review* (Great Britain) 1:1 (April 1990):35-7.

Ferguson, Ann, Jacquelyn N. Zita, and Kathryn Pine Adelson. "On 'Compulsory Heterosexuality and Lesbian Existence': Defining the Issues" (three responses to Rich's essay in *Signs* 5:4 (Summer 1980):631-60). *Signs,* "French Feminism and Theory" 7:1 (Autumn 1981):158-99.

Thompson, Martha E. "Comment on Rich's 'Compulsory Heterosexuality and Lesbian Existence'" (Adrienne Rich's essay appears in *Signs,* 5:4 (Summer 1980):631-60). *Signs* 6:4 (Summer 1981):790-4.

Delphy, Christine (French activist, writer, and co-editor with Simone de Beauvoir of *Nouvelle Question Féministe*):
Cottingham, Laura. "Christine Delphy: French Feminist" (includes section on "Lesbianism in France"). *off our backs* 14:3 (March 1984):10-11+.

Dworkin, Andrea (activist and writer):
"Interview on 'Womanpower': Andrea Dworkin." *Woman of Power* 1 (Spring 1984):24-6+.

Wilson, Elizabeth. "Interview with Andrea Dworkin." *Feminist Review* (Great Britain), "Sexuality" 11 (Summer 1982):23+.

Frye, Marilyn (philosopher):
Card, Claudia. "Oppression and Resistance: Frye's Politics of Reality." *Hypatia* 1 (Spring 1986):149-66.

Griffin, Susan (writer):
Pavel, Margaret. "Interview on 'Womanpower': Susan Griffin." *Woman of Power* 1 (Spring 1984):34-8.

Johnson, Sonia (writer):
Armstrong, Toni Jr., Laura Post, and Sara Wolfersberger. "Sonia Johnson Speaks of Creating a 'Women's World.'" *Hot Wire* 6:3 (September 1990):37-9.

Bowen, Angela, Jacqui Alexander, Jennifer Abod, and Terri Ortiz. "Taking Issue with Sonia" (response to interview with Johnson in *Sojourner* 13:5 (January 1988)). *Sojourner* 13:6 (February 1988):14-15.

Salkind, Betsy and Vanessa Cruz. "Sonia Johnson: Breaking Free" (see response in *Sojourner* 13:6 (February 1988)). *Sojourner* 13:5 (January 1988):16-17.

Lorde, Audre (writer):
Foster, Thomas. "'The Very House of Difference': Gender as 'Embattled' Standpoint" (bases postmodern discussion of coalition politics on Audre Lorde's poetry). *Genders* 8 (July 1990):17-37.

Rich, Adrienne:
Cameron, Deborah. "Ten Years On: 'Compulsory Heterosexuality and Lesbian Existence.'" *Women: a Cultural Review* (Great Britain) 1:1 (April 1990):35-7.

Ferguson, Ann, Jacquelyn N. Zita, and Kathryn Pine Adelson. "On 'Compulsory Heterosexuality and Lesbian Existence': Defining the Issues" (three responses to Rich's essay in *Signs* 5:4 (Summer 1980):631-60). *Signs,* "French Feminism and Theory" 7:1 (Autumn 1981):158-99.

Thompson, Martha E. "Comment on Rich's 'Compulsory Heterosexuality and Lesbian Existence'" (Adrienne Rich's essay appears in *Signs,* 5:4 (Summer 1980):631-60). *Signs* 6:4 (Summer 1981):790-4.

The Second Sex (by philosopher Simone de Beauvoir):
Felstiner, Mary Lowenthal. "Seeing *The Second Sex* Through the Second Wave." *Feminist Studies* 6:2 (1980):247-76.

Politicians

"Congressional Closet." *off our backs* 13:2 (February 1983):16.

Achtenberg, Roberta (San Francisco Supervisor and State Assembly candidate):
Chasnoff, Debra. "Ms. Achtenberg (Almost) Goes to Sacramento: Campaigning for the California State Assembly." *Out/Look* 1:4 (Winter 1989):22-31.

Carter, Jimmy (U.S. President):

CAD. "Democrats Smile at Gays" (Carter administration and Democratic Party make "some moves toward opposing discrimination against lesbians and gays"). *off our backs* 10:8 (August-September 1980):15; note: cover reads 10:7.

Eshuis, Evelien (Dutch lesbian parliament member):

Rosalind. "Parliamentary Pink." *Connexions,* "Global Lesbianism 2" 10 (Fall 1983):28.

Glick, Deborah (lesbian running for New York State Legislature):

Chasin, Susan T. "Force for Political Change: Deborah Glick." *Visibilities* 4:4 (July/August 1990):4-8.

Ferguson, Rosemary F. "Deborah Glick: No Ordinary Pol." *New Directions for Women* (New York Metro Supplement) 19:6 (November/December 1990):1.

Johnson, Sonia (writer and 1984 U.S. Presidential candidate):

Johnson, Sonia. "Running to Win." *New Directions For Women* 13 (July-August 1984):3.

Kulp, Denise. "Sonia Johnson: The Answer is Feminism.'" *off our backs* 14:9 (October 1984):20-3.

Leonard, Vickie. "Presidential Politics x Two" (Vice-presidential candidate Geraldine Ferraro and Sonia Johnson). *off our backs* 14:9 (October 1984):23+.

"Sonia Johnson Seeks Legal Determination that Media Access to Voters Is Integral Part of Election Process." *Media Report to Women* 12 (November-December 1984):1+.

Meyer, Joyce (activist running for Champaign, Illinois City Council):

"Lesbian to Run for Illinois Seat." *off our backs* 20:9 (October 1990):4.

Noble, Elaine (Massachusetts legislator):
Nies, Judith. "Elaine Noble: Not Just Another Gay Legislator." *Ms.*
4 (August 1975):58-61.

Noonan, Liz (candidate in the Irish General Election):
"Lesbian's Stand." *Spare Rib* (Great Britain) 108 (July 1981):15.

Norman, Pat (director of the San Francisco Youth Environment
Studies Training Center and coordinator of the People of Color
Caucus for the 1987 March on Washington for Lesbian and Gay
Rights):
Bowen, Angela. "Pat Norman, the Y.E.S. Woman: an Interview."
Black/Out, "We Are Family" 2:2 (Summer 1989):41+.

Oesterle-Schwerin, Jutta (Green Party member of West German
Parliament):
"West Germany: Chaos in the Assembly" (trans. from West German
feminist monthly *Emma,* No.1 (January 1989)). *Connexions,*
"Lesbian Activism" 29 (1989):4-5.

Roosevelt, Eleanor (First Lady):
Beasley, M. "Lorena M. Hickok: Her Journalistic Influence on
Eleanor Roosevelt" (discusses the possible sexual nature of their
close relationship). *Journalism Quarterly* 57 (Summer
1980):281-6.

Terrigno, Valerie (mayor of West Hollywood, California):
Dixon, Edie. "Lesbian Mayor Investigated." *off our backs* 15:4 (April
1985):2.

Pornography (see also: Censorship; S/M)

Cohen, Cheryl H. "The Feminist Sexuality Debate: Ethics and Politics."
Hypatia 3 (Fall 1986):71-86.

Collis, Rose. "Pleasure Is a Risky Business" (erotica for women). *Spare
Rib* (Great Britain) 191 (June 1988):10-12.

Coveney, Lal and Leslie Kay. "A Symposium on Feminism, Sexuality, and Power" (Five College Women's Studies Committee and Faculty Seminar, Mt. Holyoke College). *off our backs* 17:1 (January 1987):12-13.

Coward, Rosalind. "Sexual Outlaws" (erotica in women's writing). *New Statesman and Society* (Great Britain) 2 (June 9, 1989):42-3.

DancingFire, Laura Rose. "On Lawyering, Passing and Pornography." *Sinister Wisdom,* "Passing" 35 (Summer/Fall 1988):72-4.

Dejanikus, Tacie. "Charges of Exclusion & McCarthyism at Barnard Conference" (Towards a Politics of Sexuality (Barnard College Sexuality Conference), New York City, April 1982). *off our backs* 12:6 (June 1982):5+.

Dunn, Sara. "Voyages of the Valkyries: Recent Lesbian Pornographic Writing." *Feminist Review* (Great Britain), "Perverse Politics: Lesbian Issues" 34 (Spring 1990):161-70.

Durrell, Anna. "Uproar Over Violent Images" (S/M debates in London's lesbian/gay movement). *New Statesman* (Great Britain) 109 (June 14, 1985):16-17.

Dworkin, Andrea. "Antifeminism." *Trivia* 2 (Spring 1983):6-35.

------. "Censorship, Pornography, and Equality." *Trivia* 7 (Summer 1985):11-32.

------. "The Lesbian in Pornography: a Tribute to Male Power." *Sinister Wisdom,* "Lesbianism: Sexuality and Power; The Patriarchy: Violence and Pornography" 15 (Fall 1980):73-4.

Desmoines, Harriet. "Notes for a Magazine II" (founding concepts for *Sinister Wisdom*; discusses politically left revolutionary politics, racism, and classism). *Sinister Wisdom* 1:1 (Summer 1976):27-34.

Douglas, Carol Anne. "Commentary: Hope for Feminism" (response to The Sexual Liberals and the Attack on Feminism conference, New York University Law School, April 1987). *off our backs* 17:5 (May 1987):21.

Elman, R. Amy. "Sexual Subordination and State Intervention: Lessons for Feminists from the Nazi State." *Trivia* 15 (Fall 1989):50-64.

Grover, Jan Zita. "Words to Lust By" (lesbian erotica and pornography). *Women's Review of Books* 8 (November 1990):21-3.

Horowitz, Gad. "Amazon Fantasy Trouble" (by woman whose lover fantasizes about dominance/submission during sex). *Canadian Dimension* (Canada) 22:3 (May 1988):40-2.

Kaufman, Gloria. "S/M and Porn Touchy Issues for the Movement." *New Directions for Women* 11 (September-October 1982):4.

Kulp, Denise. "Redefining Feminism and Excluding Women" (response to The Sexual Liberals and the Attack on Feminism conference, New York University Law School, April 1987). *off our backs* 17:5 (May 1987):22.

Lootens, Tricia. "Third Women in Print Conference" (Berkeley, California, May 1985; reports on workshops including classism, erotica, lesbian nuns, women of color, pornography, censorship, raid on British gay book store). *off our backs* 15:8 (August-September 1985):8-9+.

McCombs, Annie. "A Letter *Ms.* Didn't Print." *Lesbian Ethics* 1:3 (Fall 1985):85-8.

Marx, Sabine. "Desire Cannot Be Fragmented" (trans. and excerpted from West German feminist quarterly, *Tarantel,* 1988). *Connexions,* "Women and AIDS" 33 (1990):6-9.

off our backs, on the feminist pornography debates, vol. 15, no. 6, June 1985.

O'Sullivan, Sue. "The Sexual Schism: the British in Barcelona" (lesbian erotica and pornography attacked at panel meeting of the International Feminist Bookfair, Barcelona, Spain, Summer 1990). *off our backs* 20:9 (October 1990):9-11.

Penelope, Julia. "Mystery and Monster: the Lesbian in Heterosexual Fantasies." *Sinister Wisdom,* "Lesbianism: Sexuality and Power; The Patriarchy: Violence and Pornography" 15 (Fall 1980):76-91.

Russ, Joanna. "Being Against Pornography." *13th Moon* 6:1/2 (1982):55-61.

------. "Pornography and the Doubleness of Sex for Women." *13th Moon,* "Narrative Forms" 8:1/2 (1984):19-30.

Russo, Ann. "Conflicts and Contradictions Among Feminists Over Issues of Pornography and Sexual Freedom." *Women's Studies International Forum* 10:2 (1987):103-12.

Sinister Wisdom, "Lesbianism: Sexuality and Power; The Patriarchy: Violence and Pornography," no. 15, Fall 1980.

Smyth, Cherry. "The Pleasure Threshold: Looking at Lesbian Pornography on Film." *Feminist Review* (Great Britain), "Perverse Politics: Lesbian Issues" 34 (Spring 1990):152-9.

South, Chris. "Diary of a Woman/Wife/Queer." *Sinister Wisdom,* "Lesbianism: Sexuality and Power; The Patriarchy: Violence and Pornography" 15 (Fall 1980):65-9.

Steffensen, Jyanni. "Things Change . . . And About Time Too: a Critical Review of Women's Erotic Writing." *Hecate* (Australia) 15:2 (1989):26-33.

Swedborg, Deborah. "What Do We See When We See Woman/Woman Sex in Pornographic Movies?" *NWSA Journal* 1:4 (Summer 1989):602-616.

Bad Attitude (magazine):
Herman, Ellen and Karen Kahn. "Exploring Our Sexual Fantasies:
Women's Erotica -- Sex Magazine Publishing: a Roundtable
Discussion" (with representatives of _Bad Attitude, Eidos_ and
Outrageous Women). _Sojourner_ 14:2 (October 1988):30-1.

Bright, Susie (activist, sex magazine editor, and writer):
Gonsalves, Sharon. "Exploring Our Sexual Fantasies: Women's
Erotica -- Susie Bright: On the Line." _Sojourner_ 14:2 (October
1988):30-1.

Drawing the Line (interactive photography exhibit):
Kiss and Tell. "Drawing the Line: Where Do You Draw the Line on
Sexually Explicit Images?" (San Francisco, June-July 1990).
Out/Look #10, 3:2 (Fall 1990):6-11.

Dworkin, Andrea (activist and writer):
Anderson, Alison. "Cleaning Up the Cosmos: Women Write About
Pornography" (Andrea Dworkin, Beatrice Faust, and Susan
Griffin). _Hecate_ (Australia) 8:1 (1982):97-101.

Braeman, Elizabeth and Carol Cox. "Andrea Dworkin: From a War
Zone" (interview about Dworkin's book _Letters From a War
Zone: Writings 1976-1989). off our backs_ 20:1 (January
1990):8-9+.

Loach, Loretta. "Where Angels Fear to Tread" (interview with Andrea
Dworkin about her anti-pornography work). _Spare Rib_ (Great
Britain) 167 (June 1986):40-2.

Stoil, Julie-Maya. "Profile: 'Woman as Warrior' -- Radical Visionary
for Justice: Andrea Dworkin" (activist and writer). _Woman of
Power_ 3 (Winter/Spring 1986):26-9+.

Wilson, Elizabeth. "Interview with Andrea Dworkin" (activist and
writer). _Feminist Review_ (Great Britain), "Sexuality" 11
(Summer 1982):23+.

Eidos (magazine):

Herman, Ellen and Karen Kahn. "Exploring Our Sexual Fantasies: Women's Erotica -- Sex Magazine Publishing: a Roundtable Discussion" (with representatives of *Bad Attitude, Eidos* and *Outrageous Women*). *Sojourner* 14:2 (October 1988):30-1.

Griffin, Susan (writer):

Anderson, Alison. "Cleaning Up the Cosmos: Women Write About Pornography" (Andrea Dworkin, Beatrice Faust, and Susan Griffin). *Hecate* (Australia) 8:1 (1982):97-101.

Jeffreys, Sheila (British activist and historian):

Hunt, Margaret. "The De-Eroticization of Women's Liberation: Social Purity Movements and the Revolutionary Feminism of Sheila Jeffreys." *Feminist Review* (Great Britain), "Perverse Politics: Lesbian Issues" 34 (Spring 1990):23-46.

Nestle, Joan (co-founder of the Lesbian Herstory Archives and writer):

Ardill, Susan and Sue O'Sullivan. "Sex in the Summer of '88" (sex and pornography controversies, including anti-gay Clause 28; *A Restricted Country,* book by Joan Nestle; *She Must Be Seeing Things,* video by Sheila McLaughlin). *Feminist Review* (Great Britain), "The Past Before Us: Twenty Years of Feminism" 31 (Spring 1989):126-34.

On Our Backs (magazine):

Kulp, Denise. "Cruising *On Our Backs.*" *off our backs* (July 1985):16-18.

Outrageous Women (magazine):

Herman, Ellen and Karen Kahn. "Exploring Our Sexual Fantasies: Women's Erotica -- Sex Magazine Publishing: a Roundtable Discussion" (with representatives of *Bad Attitude, Eidos* and *Outrageous Women*). *Sojourner* 14:2 (October 1988):30-1.

Rich, Adrienne (writer):

MacKinnon, Catharine. "An Open Letter to Adrienne Rich" (about pornography laws and FACT). *off our backs* 15:9 (October 1985):18+.

She Must Be Seeing Things (film):

Ardill, Susan and Sue O'Sullivan. "Sex in the Summer of '88" (sex and pornography controversies, including anti-gay Clause 28; *A Restricted Country,* book by Joan Nestle; *She Must Be Seeing Things,* video by Sheila McLaughlin). *Feminist Review* (Great Britain), "The Past Before Us: Twenty Years of Feminism" 31 (Spring 1989):126-34.

"Whatever Happened at the Lesbian Archive?" (dispute in collective over showing of film with S/M content, *She Must Be Seeing Things,* and over alleged racism in hiring). *Spare Rib* (Great Britain) 199 (March 1989):17.

Prison (see also: Political Prisoners)

Anderson, Alice and Laura Galluci. "'We Won't Stop Until Something Is Done'" (authors are lovers writing about discrimination and harassment they face in New Jersey prison). *Common Lives/Lesbian Lives* 14 (Winter 1984):43-7.

Culver, Veronica VerLyn. "I Invite You Into Washington State Lesbian's Prison." *Common Lives/Lesbian Lives* 15/16 (Summer 1985):170-5.

Goddemaer, Nicky. "The 'She-Wolf'" (personal account of incarceration in Belgian juvenile hall). *Connexions,* "Lesbians Inside and Out" 14 (Fall 1984):18-19.

Hall, Kandis. "Prison: the 'Women's,' the 'Lesbian's' Experience." *Common Lives/Lesbian Lives* 3 (Spring 1982):5-10.

Innes, Charlotte. "Lesbians Get Pink-Tagged" (in Florida's Polk County Jail; also reports on discrimination in other prisons). *New Directions for Women* 19:2 (March-April 1990):6-7.

"Jock Shorts" (soccer team formed by lesbians in women's prison near Lima, Peru). *Connexions,* "Global Lesbianism 2" 10 (Fall 1983):11.

Johnson, Loretta. "In a Penal Colony" (friendship). *Sinister Wisdom,* "On Friendship" 40 (Spring 1990):15-16.

Kallenberg, Tracy. "Where Is the Justice?" (letter from lesbian imprisoned for murder, regarding judicial and prison systems, and lesbians in prison). *Connexions,* "Women Inside and Out" 14 (Fall 1984):29.

Klein, Mary. "Prisoners Fight Sex Rule" (forbidding sexual activity in the Oregon Women's Correctional Center). *off our backs* 10:5 (May 1980):7.

Leger, Robert G. "Lesbianism Among Women Prisoners; Participants and Nonparticipants." *Criminal Justice and Behavior* 14:4 (December 1987):448-67.

"Lesbians in Soviet Jails." *off our backs* 19:1 (January 1989):6; note: cover reads 18:11 (December 1988).

Propper, Alice M. "Lesbianism in Female and Coed Correctional Institutions." *Journal of Homosexuality* 3:3 (Spring 1978):265-74.

------. "Make Believe Families and Homosexuality Among Imprisoned Girls." *Criminology* 20 (May 1982):127-38.

Quinn, Kelli. "The Killing Ground: Police Powers and Psychiatry" (the demands of ex-psychiatric inpatients after someone was handed over to authorities for disruptive behavior at the Michigan Womyn's Music Festival). *Women & Therapy,* "Women and Mental Health: New Directions for Change" 3:3/4 (Fall/Winter 1984):71-7.

"Segregation" (of lesbians from heterosexual women in California prisons). *off our backs* 6:9 (December 1976):8.

Singer, Pat. "Love in Prison." *off our backs,* "Women in Prison" 2:8 (April 1972):8.

stomp, bruiser, fang, sparks . . . and footnote. "Womyn in the
Joint/Wimmin in the Joint." *Sinister Wisdom,* "With an
Emphasis on Lesbian Theory" 37 (Spring 1989):94-9.

Wald, Karen. "Women Join Forces Against Prisons." *off our backs* 7:11
(December 1977):2.

Ward, D.A. and G.G. Kassebaum. "Homosexuality: a Mode of Adoption
in a Prison for Women." *Social Problems* 12:2 (1974):159-77.

Bedford Hills Prison:
"Bedford Hills" (demonstration in support of prisoners' demands,
Bedford Hills, New York). *off our backs* 8:10 (November
1978):4.

Charoula. "Bedford Hills: a Lesbian Separatist View" (about New
York's only women-only prison). *off our backs* 8:4 (April
1978):14-15.

Solidarity with Sisters Committee. "Bedford Hills: Commentary" (11
women of color file suit to remove male prison guards whom
they accuse of sexual abuse; state accuses women of being anti-
male lesbians). *off our backs* 8:2 (February 1978):9-10.

Prostitution

Carol and Laura. "Hookers" (letter by two lesbian prostitutes, regarding
The First World Meeting of Prostitutes, Washington, D.C., June
1976; conference covered in *off our backs* 6:5, July-August
1976). *off our backs* 6:6 (September 1976):28.

"Gay for Gain: a Talk with a Lesbian Prostitute." *off our backs,* "Women
Loving: 2" 2:5 (January 1972):18-19.

"'I Don't Make Love, I Work'" (anonymous article by a Swiss lesbian
who works as a heterosexual prostitute; trans. from *CLIT 007,*
Swiss lesbian quarterly, September 1982). *Connexions,* "Women
and Prostitution" 12 (Spring 1984):28.

Summer, Toby. "Women, Lesbians and Prostitution: a Workingclass Dyke Speaks Out Against Buying Women for Sex." *Lesbian Ethics* 2:3 (Summer 1987):33-44.

Working Girls (film):
Bishop, Marla and Lucy O'Brien. "Working Girls" (interview with director Lizzie Borden about her film about a lesbian working as a heterosexual prostitute). *Spare Rib* (Great Britain) 175 (February 1987):37-9.

Psychology (see also: Adolescent Lesbians; Children of Lesbians; Homophobia/Heterosexism; Labels/Identity; Parenting; Psychotherapy; Relationships; Substance Abuse and Recovery; Violence Among Lesbians)

Adelman, Marcy R. "A Comparison of Professionally Employed Lesbians and Heterosexual Women on the MMPI." *Archives of Sexual Behavior* 6:3 (May 1977):193-202.

Albro, Joyce C. and Carol Tully. "A Study of Lesbian Lifestyles in the Homosexual Micro-culture and the Heterosexual Macro-culture." *Journal of Homosexuality* 4:4 (Summer 1979):331-54.

Anderson, Elizabeth A. "The Elusive Homosexual: a Reply to Stone and Schneider." *Journal of Personality Assessment* 39 (December 1975):580-2.

Barale, Michele Aina. "The Lesbian Academic: Negotiating New Boundaries." *Women & Therapy,* "Lesbianism: Affirming Nontraditional Roles" 8:1/2 (1989):183-94.

Belote, Deborah and Joan Jesting. "Demographic and Self-Report Characteristics of Lesbians." *Psychological Reports* 39 (October 1976):621-2.

Bernard, Jessie. "Homosociality and Female Depression" (concludes that raised consciousness is mentally healthy and that the modern decline of female homosociality leads to depression). *Journal of Social Issues* 32 (1976):213-38.

Boxer, Andrew M. and Bertram J. Cohler. "The Life Course of Gay and Lesbian Youth: an Immodest Proposal for the Study of Lives." *Journal of Homosexuality,* "Gay and Lesbian Youth: Part II" 17:3/4 (1989):315-44.

Brannock, Joanna C. and Benta E. Chapman. "Negative Sexual Experiences with Men Among Heterosexual Women and Lesbians" (no correlation found between negative experiences and lesbianism). *Journal of Homosexuality* 19:1 (1990):105-10.

Brown, Laura S. "New Voices, New Visions: Toward a Lesbian/Gay Paradigm for Psychology." *Psychology of Women Quarterly* 13:4 (December 1989):445-59.

Buhrich, Neil and Carlson Loke. "Homosexuality, Suicide, and Parasuicide in Australia." *Journal of Homosexuality,* "Psychopathology and Psychotherapy in Homosexuality" 15:1/2 (1988):113-30.

Bullough, Vern L. and Martha Voght. "Homosexuality and its Confusion with the Secret Sin in Pre-Freudian America." *Journal of the History of Medicine and Allied Sciences* 28 (April 1973):143-55.

Carlson, Helena M. and Leslie A. Baxter. "Androgyny, Depression and Self-Esteem in Irish Homosexual and Heterosexual Males and Females." *Sex Roles* 10 (March 1984):457-67.

Carne, Roz. "Homosexuality: Sexual 'Problem' or Political Problem?" (conference of gays and representatives of the medical profession/social counselling services to discuss medical and social attitudes toward homosexuality, Bradford University, Great Britain, April 1975). *Spare Rib* (Great Britain) 36 (June 1975):19.

Cartledge, Sue and Susan Hemmings. "How Did We Get This Way? Sue Cartledge and Susan Hemmings Look at Explanations of Lesbianism." *Spare Rib* (Great Britain) 86 (September 1979):43-7.

Cass, Vivienne C. "Homosexual Identity Formation: a Theoretical Model." *Journal of Homosexuality* 4:3 (Spring 1979):219-35.

Chafitz, Janet S., et al. "A Study of Homosexual Women" (early literature/interview study challenging the professional literature). *Social Work* 19 (November 1974):714-23.

Chambers, Jay L. and Mary Beth Surma. "Motivation Concepts and Sexual Identity." *Journal of Research in Personality* 10:2 (June 1976):228-36.

Chan, C.S. "Issues of Identity Development Among Asian-American Lesbians and Gay Men." *Journal of Counseling and Development*, "Lesbian, Gay and Bisexual Issues in Counseling" 68:1 (September-October 1989):16-20.

Chapman, Beata E. and JoAnn C. Brannock. "Proposed Model of Lesbian Identity Development: an Empirical Examination." *Journal of Homosexuality* 14:3/4 (1987):69-80.

Chauncey, George. "From Sexual Inversion to Homosexuality: Medicine and the Changing Conceptualization of Female Deviance." *Salmagundi*, "Homosexuality: Sacrilege, Vision, Politics" 58-59 (Fall 1982-Winter 1983):114-46.

Chesler, Phyllis. "Women and Madness: the Modern Paradox" (excerpts from book of same title; includes section on lesbians). *Spare Rib* (Great Britain) 12 (June 1973):29-30.

Cooper, Margaret. "Rejecting 'Femininity': Some Research Notes on Gender Identity Development in Lesbians." *Deviant Behavior* 11:4 (October-December 1990):371-80.

Cronin, Denise M. "Female Homosexuality: Behavior Following the Social Script Model of Sexuality." *NASPA (National Association of Student Personnel Administrators)* 13:4 (Spring 1976):57-61.

D'Augelli, A.R. "The Development of a Helping Community for Lesbians and Gay Men -- a Case-Study in Community Psychology." *Journal of Community Psychology* 17:1 (1989):18-29.

D'Augelli, Anthony R., et al. "Social Support Patterns of Lesbian Women in a Rural Helping Network." *Journal of Rural Community Psychology* 8:1 (1987):12-22.

DeFries, Zira. "A Comparison of Political and Apolitical Lesbians." *Journal of the American Academy of Psychoanalysis* 7 (January 1979):57-66.

------. "Political Lesbianism and Sexual Politics." *Journal of the American Academy of Psychoanalysis* 6 (1978):71-8.

Duckitt, John H. and Laetitia du Toit. "Personality Profiles of Homosexual Men and Women" (in South Africa). *The Journal of Psychology* 123:5 (September 1989):497-505.

Eisenbud, Ruth-Jean. "Early and Later Determinants of Lesbian Choice." *Psychoanalytic Review* 69:1 (Spring 1982):85-110.

Elliott, Phyllis E. "Theory and Research on Lesbian Identity Formation." *International Journal of Women's Studies* (Canada), "Feminist Psychology" 8:1 (January/February 1985):64-71.

Esterberg, Kristin Gay. "From Illness to Action: Conceptions of Homosexuality in *The Ladder,* 1956-1965" (magazine of the Daughters of Bilitis). *Journal of Sex Research* 27:1 (February 1990):65-80.

Ettorre, Betsy. "Compulsory Heterosexuality and Psych/Atrophy: Some Thoughts on Lesbian Feminist Theory." *Women's Studies International Forum* 8:5 (1985):421-8.

Falk, P.J. "Lesbian Mothers -- Psychosocial Assumptions in Family-Law." *American Psychologist* 44:6 (1989):941-7.

Ferguson, K.D. and D.C. Finkler. "An Involvement and Overtness Measure for Lesbians: Its Development and Relation to Anxiety and Social Zeitgeist." *Archives of Sexual Behavior* 7:3 (1978):211-27.

"Gays on the March" (unsympathetic cover story on the surge of gay pride/visibility). *Time* 106 (September 8, 1975):32-43.

Gonsiorek, John C. "Mental Health Issues of Gay and Lesbian Adolescents." *Journal of Adolescent Health Care* 9:2 (March 1988):114-22.

------. "The Use of Diagnostic Concepts in Working with Gay and Lesbian Populations." *Journal of Homosexuality,* "Homosexuality and Psychotherapy -- a Practitioner's Handbook of Affirmative Models" 7:2-3 (Winter-Spring 1982):9+.

Gottman, Julie Schwartz. "Children of Gay and Lesbian Parents" (a review of research literature). *Marriage and Family Review* 14:3-4 (1989):177-96.

Granero, M. "Differences Between Homosexuals and Heterosexuals (Males and Females) in Fears, Assertivity and Self-Sufficiency." *Revista Latinoamericana de Psychologia* 16:1 (1984):39-52.

Gundlach, Ralph H. "Birth Order Among Lesbians: New Light on an 'Only Child.'" *Psychological Reports* 40 (February 1977):250+.

Hamer, Diane. "Significant Others: Lesbians and Psychoanalytic Theory." *Feminist Review* (Great Britain), "Perverse Politics: Lesbian Issues" 34 (Spring 1990):134-51.

Harris, Craig. "Black Lesbians and Gays: Empirically Speaking" (report on "The Black Women's Relationship Project: a National Survey of Black Lesbians" (Mays, Cochran, Peplau, 1986) and "Influence of Assimilation on the Psychosocial Adjustment of Black Homosexual Men" (Johnson, 1981)). *Black/Out,* "Tenth Anniversary Edition: NCBLG Celebrates Homecoming" 2:1 (Fall 1988):9-11+.

Hassell, Julie and Edward W.L. Smith. "Female Homosexuals' Concepts of Self, Men, and Women" (concludes that lesbians are "strong," "independent," "sexually preoccupied," and "less well-adjusted" than heterosexual women). *Journal of Personality Assessment* 39 (April 1975):154-9.

Hedblom, Jack H. and John J. Hartman. "Research on Lesbianism: Selected Effects of Time, Geographic Location, and Data Collection Technique." *Archives of Sexual Behavior* 9 (June 1980):217-34.

Henderson, Ann Fleck. "College Age Lesbianism as a Developmental Phenomenon." *Journal of the American College Health Association* 28:3 (December 1979):176-8.

------. "Homosexuality in the College Years: Developmental Differences Between Men and Women." *Journal of American College Health* 32:4 (April 1984):216-19.

Hess, Elizabeth P. "Feminist and Lesbian Development: Parallels and Divergencies." *Journal of Humanistic Psychology* 23:1 (Winter 1983):67-78.

Hetrick, Emery S. and A. Damien Martin. "Developmental Issues and Their Resolution for Gay and Lesbian Adolescents." *Journal of Homosexuality,* "Psychotherapy with Homosexual Men and Women: Integrated Identity Approaches for Clinical Practice" 14:1/2 (1987):25-44.

Hogan, Robert A., N.A. Fox, and J.H. Kirchner. "Attitudes, Opinions and Sexual Development of 205 Homosexual Women." *Journal of Homosexuality* 3:1 (Autumn 1977):123-36.

Hooper, Judith. "Gay Origins" (Kinsey Institute Study, *Sexual Preference*). *Omni* 4 (March 1982):22+.

Janzen, William B. and William C. Coe. "Clinical and Sign Prediction: the Draw-A-Person and Female Homosexuality." *Journal of Clinical Psychology* 31 (October 1975):757-64.

Jensen, Mehri S. "Role Differentiation in Female Homosexual Quasi-Marital Unions." *Journal of Marriage and the Family* 36 (May 1974):360-7.

Journal of Social Issues, "Psychology and the Gay Community," vol. 34, no. 3, 1978.

Kimmel, D.C. "Adult Development and Aging: a Gay Perspective." *Journal of Social Issues* 34:3 (1978):113-30.

Kite, Mary E. and Kay Deaux. "Gender Belief Systems -- Homosexuality and the Implicit Inversion Theory." *Psychology of Women Quarterly* 11 (March 1987):83-96.

Kitzinger, Celia and Rex Stainton Rogers. "A Q-Methodological Study of Lesbian Identities." *European Journal of Social Psychology* 15:2 (1985):167-87.

LaTorre, Ronald A. and Kristina Wendenburg. "Psychological Characteristics of Bisexual, Heterosexual and Homosexual Women." *Journal of Homosexuality* 9:1 (Autumn 1983):87-98.

Leavy, Richard L. and Eve M. Adams. "Feminism as a Correlate of Self-Esteem, Self-Acceptance, and Social Support Among Lesbians." *Psychology of Women Quarterly* 10:4 (December 1986):321-6.

Levine, Martin P. "The Sociology of Male Homosexuality and
Lesbianism -- an Introductory Bibliography." *Journal of
Homosexuality* 5:3 (Spring 1980):249-76.

Lewis, L.A. "The Coming Out Process for Lesbians: Integrating a Stable
Identity." *Social Work* 29 (September-October 1984):464-9.

Loewenstein, Sophie Freud. "Understanding Lesbian Women." *Social
Casework* 61 (January 1980):29-38.

Loiacano, Darryl K. "Gay Identity Issues among Black Americans:
Racism, Homophobia, and the Need for Validation." *Journal of
Counseling and Development,* "Lesbian, Gay and Bisexual Issues
in Counseling" 68:1 (September-October 1989):21-5.

Loney, Jan. "Family Dynamics in Homosexual Women" (study of
upbringing). *Archives of Sexual Behavior* 2:4 (1973):343-50.

Lutz, J. "The Effect of Delay of [Lesbian] Labeling on Memory." *Journal
of General Psychology* 109 (October 1983):211-17.

McCoy, Sherry and Maureen Hicks. "A Psychological Retrospective on
Power in the Contemporary Lesbian-Feminist Community."
Frontiers, "Lesbian History" 4:3 (Fall 1979):65-9.

MacDonald, A.P. "A Little Bit of Lavender Goes a Long Way: a Critique
of Research on Sexual Orientation." *Journal of Sex Research* 19
(February 1983):94.

Miller, J.A. et al. "A Comparison of Family Relationships: Homosexual
versus Heterosexual Women." *Psychological Reports* 46pt2
(June 1980):1127-32.

Minton, Henry L. "Femininity in Men and Masculinity in Women:
American Psychiatry and Psychology Portray Homosexuality in
the 1930s." *Journal of Homosexuality* 13:1 (Fall 1986):1-22.

Miranda, J. and M. Storms. "Psychological Adjustment of Lesbians and Gay Men." *Journal of Counseling and Development,* "Lesbian, Gay and Bisexual Issues in Counseling" 68:1 (September-October 1989):41-5.

Moberly, Elizabeth. "Homosexuality: Restating the Conservative Case" (shaping of the debate over "the homosexual question"). *Salmagundi,* "Homosexuality: Sacrilege, Vision, Politics" 58-59 (Fall 1982-Winter 1983):281-99.

Morin, S.F. "Heterosexual Bias in Psychological Research on Lesbianism and Male Homosexuality." *American Psychologist* 32 (August 1977):629-37.

Nichols, Margaret and Sandra R. Leiblum. "Lesbianism as a Personal Identity and Social Role: a Model." *Affilia* 1:1 (Spring 1986):48-59.

Oberstone, Andrea and Harriet Suconeck. "Psychological Adjustment of Single Lesbians and Single Heterosexual Women." *Psychology of Women Quarterly* 1:2 (Winter 1976):172-88.

Oldham, Sue, Doug Farnill, and Ian Ball. "Sex-Role Identity of Female Homosexuals." *Journal of Homosexuality* 8:1 (Autumn 1982):41-86.

Parker, Richard. "Youth, Identity, and Homosexuality: the Changing Shape of Sexual Life in Contemporary Brazil." *Journal of Homosexuality,* "Gay and Lesbian Youth: Part II" 17:3/4 (1989):269-90.

Perkins, Muriel W. "On Birth Order Among Lesbians." *Psychological Reports* 43pt1 (December 1978):814-15.

Quinn, Alice. "Insanity and Control: a Class Trap." *Quest* 1:2 (Fall 1974):35-49.

Renik, O. "Analysis of a Woman's Homosexual Strivings By a Male Analyst." *Psychoanalytic Quarterly* 59:1 (1990):41-53.

Rich, Adrienne. "Compulsory Heterosexuality and Lesbian Existence."
Signs 5:4 (Summer 1980):631-60.

Ricketts, Mary. "Epistemological Values of Feminists in Psychology"
(includes comparison of heterosexual and lesbian feminists).
Psychology of Women Quarterly, "Theory and Method in
Feminist Psychology" 13:4 (December 1989):401-15.

Riess, Bernard F., Jeanne Safer, and William Yotive. "Psychological Test
Data on Female Homosexuality: a Review of the Literature."
Journal of Homosexuality 1:1 (Autumn 1974):71-85.

Robertiello, Richard C. "One Psychiatrist's View of Female
Homosexuality." *Journal of Sex Research* 9 (February 1973):30-
3.

Robinson, Bryan E. et al. "Gay Men's and Women's Perceptions of Early
Family Life and Their Relationships with Parents." *Family
Relations* 31 (January 1982):79-84.

Rose, Suzanna and Laurie Roades. "Feminism and Women's Friendships"
(friendships among lesbian, straight, feminist, and non-feminist
women). *Psychology of Women Quarterly* 11 (June 1987):243-
54.

Rothblum, Esther D. "Introduction: Lesbianism as a Model of a Positive
Lifestyle for Women." *Women & Therapy,* "Lesbianism:
Affirming Nontraditional Roles" 8:1/2 (1989):1-12.

Russell, Tanya G. "AIDS Education, Homosexuality, and the Counselor's
Role." *School Counselor* 36:5 (May 1989):333-7.

Sang, Barbara E. "New Directions in Lesbian Research, Theory, and
Education." *Journal of Counseling and Development,* "Lesbian,
Gay and Bisexual Issues in Counseling" 68:1 (September-
October 1989):92-6.

Savin-Williams, Ritch. "Parental Influences on the Self-Esteem of Gay and Lesbian Youths: a Reflected Appraisals Model." *Journal of Homosexuality,* "Gay and Lesbian Youth: Part I" 17:1/2 (1989):93-110.

Schafer, Siegrid. "Sexual and Social Problems Among Lesbians." *Journal of Sex Research* 12 (February 1975):50-69.

Schmeck, Harold M., Jr. "Psychiatrists Approve Change on Homosexuals: Association Backs Trustees on Deleting Condition From List of Mental Disorders." *New York Times* (April 9, 1974):12.

Shachar, Sandra A. and Lucia A. Gilbert. "Working Women: Role Conflicts and Coping Strategies." *Psychology of Women Quarterly* 7 (Spring 1983):244-56.

Siegelman, Marion. "Adjustment of Homosexual and Heterosexual Women" (lesbians higher on goal-directedness and self-acceptance, lower on depression). *British Journal of Psychiatry* (Great Britain) 120 (1972):477-81.

Siegelman, Marvin. "Parental Backgrounds of Homosexual and Heterosexual Women: a Cross-National Replication." *Archives of Sexual Behavior* 10 (August 1981):371-8.

Silverstein, C. "The Ethical and Moral Implications of Sexual Classification -- a Commentary" (removal of homosexuality as a mental illness from psychology DSM). *Journal of Homosexuality* 9:4 (Summer 1984):29-38.

Sophie, Joan. "A Critical Examination of Stage Theories of Lesbian Identity Development." *Journal of Homosexuality* 12:2 (Winter 1985/86):39-52.

------. "Internalized Homophobia and Lesbian Identity." *Journal of Homosexuality,* "Psychotherapy with Homosexual Men and Women: Integrated Identity Approaches for Clinical Practice" 14:1/2 (1987):53-66.

Swanson, D.W., S.D. Loomis, R. Lukesh, R. Cronin, and J. Smith. "Clinical Features of the Homosexual Patient: a Comparison with the Heterosexual Patient." *Journal of Nervous and Mental Disease* 155 (1972):119-24.

Terry, Jennifer. "Lesbians Under the Medical Gaze: Scientists Search for Remarkable Differences" (1930s). *Journal of Sex Research* 27:3 (1990):317-39.

Thomas, Paul K. "Marriage Annulments for Gay Men and Lesbian Women: New Canonical and Psychological Insight." *The Jurist* 43:2 (Spring 1983):318-42.

Thompson, Norman L., Boyd R. McCandless, and B.P. Strickland. "Personality Adjustment of Male and Female Homosexuals and Heterosexuals" (lesbians higher on self-confidence than heterosexual women; no difference on defensiveness, personal or psychological adjustment). *Journal of Abnormal Psychology* 78 (October 1971):237-40.

Vance, Brenda Kaye and Vicki Green. "Lesbian Identities: an Examination of Sexual Behavior and Sex Role Attribution as Related to Age of Initial Same-Sex Sexual Encounter." *Psychology of Women Quarterly* 8:3 (Spring 1984):293-307.

Watters, Alan T. "Heterosexual Bias in Psychological Research on Lesbianism and Male Homosexuality (1979-1983), Utilizing the Bibliographic and Taxonomic System of Morin." *Journal of Homosexuality* 13:1 (Fall 1986):35-58.

Weiss, C. and R. Dain. "Ego Development and Sexual Attitudes in Heterosexual and Homosexual Men and Women" (no significant differences found; heterosexual men more homophobic than heterosexual women). *Archives of Sexual Behavior* 8:4 (July 1979):341-56.

White, T.A. "Attitudes of Psychiatric Nurses Toward Same Sex Orientations." *Nursing Research* 28 (September-October 1979):276-81.

Wills, Sue. "The Psychologist and the Lesbian." *Refractory Girl* (Australia) 9 (Winter 1975):41-5.

Wilson, M. and R. Green. "Personality Characteristics of Female Homosexuals" (lesbians higher on competence measures, heterosexual women higher on neuroticism on Eyseneck and California Personality Inventories). *Psychological Reports* 28 (1971):407-12.

Wilson, M.L. "Female Homosexuals' Need for Dominance and Endurance." *Psychological Reports* 55 (August 1984):79-82.

Zacks, E., R.J. Green, and J. Marrow. "Comparing Lesbian and Heterosexual Couples on the Circumplex Model -- an Initial Investigation." *Family Process* 27:4 (1988):471-84.

Deutsch, Helene (psychoanalyst):
Silva, Jorge Garcia. "Two Cases of Female Homosexuality: a Critical Study of Sigmund Freud and Helene Deutsch." *Contemporary Psychoanalysis* 11 (July 1975):357-76.

Erikson, Erik (psychoanalyst trained by Freud):
Sohier, Raphella. "Homosexual Mutuality: Variation on a Theme by Erik Erikson." *Journal of Homosexuality* 12:2 (Winter 1985/86):25-38.

Freud, Sigmund (founder of psychoanalysis):
DuPlessis, Rachel Blau and Susan Stanford Friedman. "'Woman Is Perfect': H.D.'s Debate with Freud." *Feminist Studies* 7:3 (Fall 1981):417-30.

Fitzgerald, Margot. "Using Sexton to Read Freud: the Pre-Oedipal Phase and the Etiology of Lesbianism in Sexton's 'Rapunzel.'" *Journal of Homosexuality* 19:4 (1990):55-66.

Silva, Jorge Garcia. "Two Cases of Female Homosexuality: a Critical Study of Sigmund Freud and Helene Deutsch." *Contemporary Psychoanalysis* 11 (July 1975):357-76.

H.D. (writer, analyzed by Sigmund Freud):

DuPlessis, Rachel Blau and Susan Stanford Friedman. "'Woman Is Perfect': H.D.'s Debate with Freud." *Feminist Studies* 7:3 (Fall 1981):417-30.

Kristeva, Julia (psychoanalyst):

Butler, Judith. "The Body Politics of Julia Kristeva" (not exclusively about lesbians). *Hypatia* 3 (Winter 1989):104-18.

Rich, Adrienne (writer):

Cameron, Deborah. "Ten Years On: 'Compulsory Heterosexuality and Lesbian Existence'" (essay by Adrienne Rich, in *Signs* 5:4 (Summer 1980):631-60). *Women: a Cultural Review* (Great Britain) 1:1 (April 1990):35-7.

Sexton, Anne (poet):

Fitzgerald, Margot. "Using Sexton to Read Freud: the Pre-Oedipal Phase and the Etiology of Lesbianism in Sexton's 'Rapunzel.'" *Journal of Homosexuality* 19:4 (1990):55-66.

Wolff, Charlotte (psychiatrist and writer):

Steakley, James D. "Love Between Women and Love Between Men: an Interview with Charlotte Wolff." *New German Critique* 23 (Spring-Summer 1981):73-81.

Psychotherapy (see also: Adolescent Lesbians; Children of Lesbians; Homophobia/Heterosexism; Parenting; Psychology; Relationships; Substance Abuse and Recovery)

Anthony, Bronwyn D. "Lesbian Client-Lesbian Therapist: Opportunities and Challenges in Working Together." *Journal of Homosexuality*, "Homosexuality and Psychotherapy -- a Practitioner's Handbook of Affirmative Models" 7:2-3 (Winter-Spring 1982):45-70.

Arrow. "Women Against Psychiatric Assault." *off our backs* 12:3 (March 1982):26-7.

Baptiste, David A., Jr. "Psychotherapy with Gay/Lesbian Couples and Their Children in 'Stepfamilies': a Challenge for Marriage and Family Therapists." *Journal of Homosexuality,* "Psychotherapy with Homosexual Men and Women: Integrated Identity Approaches for Clinical Practice" 14:1/2 (1987):213-22.

Barnes, Rosemary. "Dykes in Search of Affection and Independence." *Resources for Feminist Research* (Canada), "The Lesbian Issue/Etre Lesbienne" 12:1(March 1983):46-7.

Berg-Cross, Linda. "Existential Issues in the Treatment of Lesbian Clients." *Women & Therapy,* "Therapeutic Issues with Lesbian Clients" 1:4 (Winter 1982):67-83; responses by Mariel R. Burch, Terry Gorfine and others, *Women & Therapy* 3 (Summer 1983):65-76.

Bertrand, Luce. "L'Homosexualité N'est Pas Une Maladie . . . Elle ne Peut Donc pas se Guérir" ("Homosexuality Is Not an Illness . . . It Therefore Cannot be Cured"). *Canadian Woman Studies* (Canada), "Sexuality and Symbol/Symbolisme et Sexualité" 3:2 (1981):57-8.

Blanchard, Margaret. "Off the Couch: Two Women's Experiences in Therapy." *Women: a Journal of Liberation,* "Women Loving Women" 5:2 (1977):17-21.

Borhek, Mary V. "Helping Gay and Lesbian Adolescents and Their Families" (with psychotherapy). *Journal of Adolescent Health Care* 9:2 (March 1988):123-8.

Brown, Laura S. "Beyond Thou Shalt Not: Thinking About Ethics in the Lesbian Therapy Community." *Women & Therapy,* "Lesbianism: Affirming Nontraditional Roles" 8:1/2 (1989):13-25.

------. "Confronting Internalized Oppression in Sex Therapy with Lesbians." *Journal of Homosexuality,* "Historical, Literary, and Erotic Aspects of Lesbianism" 12:3/4 (May 1986):99-108.

------. "How Is This Feminist Different From All Other Feminists? Or, My Journey from Pirke Avot to Feminist Therapy Ethics." *Women & Therapy* 10:4 (1990):41-55.

------. "Power, Responsibility, Boundaries: Ethical Concerns for the Lesbian Feminist Therapist." *Lesbian Ethics* 1:3 (Fall 1985):30-45.

Browning, Christine. "Therapeutic Issues and Intervention Strategies with Young Adult Lesbian Clients: a Developmental Approach." *Journal of Homosexuality,* "Psychotherapy with Homosexual Men and Women: Integrated Identity Approaches for Clinical Practice" 14:1/2 (1987):45-52.

Buhrke, R.A. "Female Student Perspectives on Training in Lesbian and Gay Issues." *Counseling Psychologist* 17:4 (October 1989):629-36.

------. "Incorporating Lesbian and Gay Issues into Counselor Training -- a Resource Guide." *Journal of Counseling and Development,* "Lesbian, Gay and Bisexual Issues in Counseling" 68:1 (September-October 1989):77-80.

Buhrke, Robin A. "Lesbian-Related Issues in Counseling Supervision." *Women & Therapy,* "Lesbianism: Affirming Nontraditional Roles" 8:1/2 (1989):195-206.

Burch, Beverly. "Psychological Merger in Lesbian Couples: a Joint Ego Psychological and Systems Approach." *Family Therapy* (Fall 1982):201+.

Burns, Jan. "The Translation of Knowledge Between Client and Therapist Concerning Lesbian Sexuality: All You Wanted to Know About Lesbian Sex and Were Scared to Ask." *Counselling Psychology Quarterly* 3:4 (1990):383-7.

Cardea, Caryatis. "The Lesbian Revolution and the 50-minute Hour: a Working Class Look at Therapy and the Movement." *Lesbian Ethics* 1:3 (Fall 1985):46-68.

Cayleff, Susan E. "Ethical Issues in Counselling Gender, Race, and Culturally Distinct Groups." *Journal of Counseling and Development* 64:5 (January 1986):345-7.

Cocke, Electra Shocka. "From the Stake to the Scalpel" (oppression of women in psychiatric hospitals; written by a member of Collective Lesbian International Terrors (CLIT)). *off our backs* 4:8 (July 1974):14.

Coleman, Eli. "The Married Lesbian." *Marriage and Family Review* 14:3-4 (1989):119-35.

Coleman, E. and G. Remafedi. "Gay, Lesbian, and Bisexual Adolescents -- a Critical Challenge to Counselors." *Journal of Counseling and Development,* "Lesbian, Gay and Bisexual Issues in Counseling" 68:1 (September-October 1989):36-40.

Crowden, John J. "The Love That Dares Now Speak Its Name" (bibliography on sexuality, history, gender identity, gay liberation, research, psychotherapy, social attitudes). *Choice* 11 (April 1974):209-27.

Dalsemer, Terry. "Counseling Lesbians." *Women: a Journal of Liberation,* "Women Loving Women" 5:2 (1977):22-6.

D'Augelli, Anthony R. "Lesbian Women in a Rural Helping Network: Exploring Informal Helping Resources." *Women & Therapy,* "Lesbianism: Affirming Nontraditional Roles" 8:1/2 (1989):119-30.

Decker, B. "Counseling Gay and Lesbian Couples." *Journal of Social Work and Human Sexuality* 2 (1983):39-52.

Dulaney, Diana D. and James Kelly. "Improving Services to Gay and Lesbian Clients." *Social Work* 27:2 (March 1982):78-83.

Dworkin, S.H. and F. Gutierrez. "Gay, Lesbian, and Bisexual Issues in Counseling." *Journal of Counseling and Development,* "Lesbian, Gay and Bisexual Issues in Counseling" 68:1 (September-October 1989):6-8.

Dworkin, Sari H. "Not in Man's Image: Lesbians and the Cultural Oppression of Body Image." *Women & Therapy,* "Lesbianism: Affirming Nontraditional Roles" 8:1/2 (1989):27-39.

Dykewomon, Elana. "Notes for a Magazine: Surviving Psychiatric Assault & Creating Emotional Well-Being in Our Communities." *Sinister Wisdom* 36 (Winter 1988/89):3-7.

Erlichman, Karen Lee. "Lesbian Mothers: Ethical Issues in Social Work Practice." *Women & Therapy,* "Lesbianism: Affirming Nontraditional Roles" 8:1/2 (1989):207-24.

Friend, Richard A. "The Individual and Social Psychology of Aging: Clinical Implications for Lesbians and Gay Men." *Journal of Homosexuality,* "Psychotherapy with Homosexual Men and Women: Integrating Identity Approaches for Clinical Practice" 14:1/2 (1987):307-32.

Gartrell, N. "Combatting Homophobia in the Psychotherapy of Lesbians." *Women & Therapy* 3:2 (Spring 1984):13-29.

------. "The Lesbian as a 'Single' Woman." *American Journal of Psychotherapy* 35:4 (October 1981):504+.

"Gay Couple Counseling -- Proceedings of a Conference: Panel of Female Couples" (sponsored by The Homosexual Community Counseling Center, New York City, May 1974; participants: Barbara Sang, David Balderston, Jo League, Dorothy Levinson, Arlene Louis, Susanne Schad-Somers). *Homosexual Counseling Journal* 1:3 (July 1974):125-38.

Girard, Judy and Cathy Collett. "Dykes & Psychs." *Resources for Feminist Research* (Canada), "The Lesbian Issue/Etre Lesbienne" 12:1(March 1983):47-50.

Glaus, Kathleen O'Halleran. "Alcoholism, Chemical Dependency, and the Lesbian Client." *Women & Therapy,* "Lesbianism: Affirming Nontraditional Roles" 8:1/2 (1989):131-44.

Glenn, Audrey A. and Richard K. Russell. "Heterosexual Bias Among Counselor Trainees." *Counselor Education and Supervision* 25:3 (March 1986):222-9.

Gonsiorek, John C. "Organizational and Staff Problems in Gay/Lesbian Mental Health Agencies." *Journal of Homosexuality,* "Homosexuality and Psychotherapy -- a Practitioner's Handbook of Affirmative Models" 7:2-3 (Winter-Spring 1982):193+.

------. "Present and Future Direction in Gay/Lesbian Mental Health." *Journal of Homosexuality,* "Homosexuality and Psychotherapy -- a Practitioner's Handbook of Affirmative Models" 7:2-3 (Winter-Spring 1982):5-8.

Greene, Beverly A. "When the Therapist Is White and the Patient Is Black: Considerations for Psychotherapy in the Feminist Heterosexual and Lesbian Communities." *Women & Therapy,* "The Dynamics of Feminist Therapy" 5:2/3 (Summer/Fall 1986):41-65.

Groves, Patricia A. "Coming Out: Issues for the Therapist Working with Lesbians in the Process of Lesbian Identity Formation." *Women & Therapy* 4:1 (Summer 1985):17-22.

Groves, Patricia A. and Lois A. Ventura. "The Lesbian Coming Out Process: Therapeutic Concerns." *Personnel and Guidance Journal* 62:3 (November 1983):146-9.

Hall, Marny. "Sex Therapy with Lesbian Couples: a Four Stage Approach." *Journal of Homosexuality,* "Psychotherapy with Homosexual Men and Women: Integrated Identity Approaches for Clinical Practice" 14:1/2 (1987):137-56.

Hamadock, Susan. "Lesbian Sexuality in the Framework of Psychotherapy: a Practical Model for the Lesbian Therapist." *Women & Therapy,* "Women and Sex Therapy" 7:2/3 (1989):207-20.

Hetherington, C. and A. Orzek. "Career Counseling and Life Planning with Lesbian Women." *Journal of Counseling and Development,* "Lesbian, Gay and Bisexual Issues in Counseling" 68:1 (September-October 1989):52-7.

Johnson, Susan R. and Susan M. Guenther. "The Role of 'Coming Out' by the Lesbians in the Physician-Patient Relationship." *Women & Therapy,* "Women, Power, and Therapy: Issues for Women" 6:1 (Spring-Summer 1987):231-8.

Journal of Counseling and Development, "Gay, Lesbian, and Bisexual Issues in Counseling," vol. 68, no. 1, September-October 1989.

Journal of Homosexuality, "Homosexuality and Psychotherapy -- a Practitioner's Handbook of Affirmative Models," vol. 7, nos. 2/3, Winter/Spring 1982.

------, "Psychotherapy with Homosexual Men and Women: Integrated Identity Approaches for Clinical Practice," vol. 14, nos. 1/2, 1987.

Kaye/Kantrowitz, Melanie. "The Issue is Power: Some Notes on Jewish Women in Therapy." *Women & Therapy,* "Jewish Women in Therapy: Seen But Not Heard" 10:4 (1990):7-18.

Kingdon, Margaret A. "Principles for [Counseling] Specific Subgroups of Women: Lesbians." *Counseling Psychologist* 8:1 (1979):44-5.

Kirkpatrick, Martha. "Clinical Implications of Lesbian Mother Studies." *Journal of Homosexuality,* "Psychotherapy with Homosexual Men and Women: Integrated Identity Approaches and Clinical Practice" 14:1/2 (1987):201-12.

Krestan, Jo-Ann. "Lesbian Daughters and Lesbian Mothers: the Crisis of Disclosure from a Family Systems Perspective." *Journal of Psychotherapy and the Family* 3:4 (1987):113-30.

Krysiak, Gloria J. "A Very Silent and Gay Minority" (adolescents). *School Counselor* 34:4 (March 1987):304-7.

Leeder, Elaine. "Enmeshed In Pain: Counselling the Lesbian Battering Couple." *Women & Therapy* 7:1 (1988):81-99.

Lenskyj, Helen. "Often Invisible: Conference on Counselling Gay and Lesbian Youth" (Toronto, Ontario, Canada, March 1989). *Resources for Feminist Research* (Canada) 18:2 (June 1989):37-8.

"Lesbian Therapy: a Reader's Forum -- Malpractice." *Lesbian Ethics* 1:3 (Fall 1985):20-2.

Loulan, JoAnn. "Research on Sex Practices on 1566 Lesbians and the Clinical Applications." *Women & Therapy*, "Women and Sex Therapy" 7:2/3 (1989):221-34.

McCandlish, Barbara M. "Therapeutic Issues with Lesbian Couples." *Journal of Homosexuality*, "Homosexuality and Psychotherapy -- a Practitioner's Handbook of Affirmative Models" 7:2-3 (Winter-Spring 1982):71-92.

McDermott, D., L. Tyndall, and J.W. Lichtenberg. "Factors Related to Counselor Preference Among Gays and Lesbians." *Journal of Counseling and Development*, "Lesbian, Gay and Bisexual Issues in Counseling" 68:1 (September-October 1989):31-5.

Martin, A. "Some Issues in the Treatment of Gay and Lesbian Patients." *Psychotherapy: Theory, Research and Practice* 19 (Autumn 1982):341-8.

Masterson, J. "Lesbian Consciousness-Raising Discussion Groups." *Journal for Specialists in Group Work* 8 (1983):24-30.

Mercier, Lucy R. and Raymond M. Berger. "Social Service Needs of Lesbian and Gay Adolescents: Telling It Their Way." *Journal of Social Work and Human Sexuality* 8:1 (1989):75-95.

Miller, Mev. "Lesbian Therapy: a Reader's Forum -- an Open Letter to an Abusive Therapist." *Lesbian Ethics* 1:3 (Fall 1985):16-20.

Mitchell, Valery. "Using Kohut's Self Psychology in Work with Lesbian Couples." *Women & Therapy,* "Lesbianism: Affirming Nontraditional Roles" 8:1/2 (1989):157-66.

Moberly, Elizabeth. "Homosexuality: Restating the Conservative Case" (shaping of the debate over "the homosexual question"). *Salmagundi,* "Homosexuality: Sacrilege, Vision, Politics," 58-59 (Fall 1982-Winter 1983):281-99.

Morris, Vicki. "Helping Lesbian Couples Cope with Jealousy." *Women & Therapy,* "Therapeutic Issues with Lesbian Clients" 1:4 (Winter 1982):27-34.

Morrow, S.L. and D.M. Hawxhurst. "Lesbian Partner Abuse -- Implications for Therapists." *Journal of Counseling and Development,* "Lesbian, Gay and Bisexual Issues in Counseling" 68:1 (September-October 1989):58-62.

Mountaingrove, Ruth. "Lesbian Therapy: a Reader's Forum -- Touch: the Ethics of Nourishment." *Lesbian Ethics* 1:3 (Fall 1985):26-9.

Mundy, Jean. "Feminist Therapy with Lesbians and Other Women." *Homosexual Counseling Journal* 1:4 (October 1974):154-9.

Murphy, Sheila. "Counseling Lesbian Women Religious." *Women & Therapy* 5:4 (Winter 1986):7-17.

Newman, Bernie S. "Including Curriculum Content on Lesbian and Gay Issues." *Journal of Social Work Education* 25:3 (Fall 1989):202-11.

Nichols, Margaret. "Bisexuality in Women: Myths, Realities, and Implications for Therapy." *Women & Therapy* 7:2/3 (1989):235-52.

------. "The Treatment of Inhibited Sexual Desire (ISD) in Lesbian Couples." *Women & Therapy,* "Therapeutic Issues with Lesbian Clients" 1:4 (Winter 1982):49-66.

Nittera, Dee Dee. "Money Changes Everything" (therapy as part of "the misery industry"). *Sinister Wisdom* 36 (Winter 1988/89):76-86.

Orzek, Ann M. "The Lesbian Victim of Sexual Assault: Special Considerations for the Mental Health Professional." *Women & Therapy,* "Lesbianism: Affirming Nontraditional Roles" 8:1/2 (1989):107-17.

Padesky, Christine A. "Attaining and Maintaining Positive Lesbian Self-Identity: a Cognitive Therapy Approach." *Women & Therapy,* "Lesbianism: Affirming Nontraditional Roles" 8:1/2 (1989):145-56.

Pendergrass, Virginia E. "Marriage Counseling with Lesbian Couples." *Psychotherapy: Theory, Research and Practice* 12 (Spring 1975):93-6.

Pies, Cheri. "Lesbians Choosing Children: the Use of Social Group Work in Maintaining and Strengthening the Primary Relationship" (between the two lesbian lovers). *Journal of Social Work and Human Sexuality* 5:2 (1987):79-88.

Poppe, Terri. "Professionalism: To What Degree?" (commentary on the first national gay health conference, Washington, D.C., May 1978). *off our backs* 8:7 (July 1978):22.

Potter, Sandra J. and Trudy E. Darty. "Social Work and the Invisible Minority: an Exploration of Lesbianism." *Social Work* 26 (May 1981):187-92.

Powell, Robert Earl. "Homosexual Behavior and the School Counselor." *School Counselor* 34:3 (January 1987):202-8.

Quinadoz, J.M. "Female Homosexual Patients in Psychoanalysis." *International Journal of Psychoanalysis* 70:1 (1989):55-63.

Quinn, Kelli. "The Killing Ground: Police Powers and Psychiatry" (the demands of ex-psychiatric inpatients after someone was handed over to authorities for disruptive behavior at the Michigan Womyn's Music Festival). *Women & Therapy,* "Woman and Mental Health: New Directions for Change" 3:3/4 (Fall/Winter 1984):71-7.

Rabin, Jack. "Enhancing Services for Sexual-Minority Clients: a Community Mental Health Approach." *Social Work* 31:4 (July-August 1986):294-8.

Raymond, Chris Anne. "Addressing Homosexuals' Mental Health Problems." *JAMA, the Journal of the American Medical Association* 259 (January 1, 1988):19.

Riddle, Dorothy and Barbara Sang. "Psychotherapy with Lesbians." *Journal of Social Issues,* "Psychology and the Gay Community" 34:3 (1978):84-100.

Ritter, Kathleen Y. and Craig. W. O'Neill. "Moving Through Loss: the Spiritual Journey of Gay Men and Lesbian Women" (transforming relationships with traditional religion and mental health professionals). *Journal of Counseling and Development,* "Gay, Lesbian, and Bisexual Issues in Counseling" 68:1 (September-October 1989):9-15.

Rochlin, Martin. "Sexual Orientation of the Therapist and Therapeutic Effectiveness with Gay Clients." *Journal of Homosexuality* 7:2/3 (Winter 1981/Spring 1982):21-9.

Rooney, Frances. "Lesbians in Therapy." *Healthsharing* (Canada), "Women and Therapy" 4:1 (Winter 1982):19-22.

Rosenthal, A. "Heterosexism and Clinical Assessment." *Smith College Studies in Social Work* 52 (March 1982):145-59.

Roth, Sallyann. "Psychotherapy with Lesbian Couples: Individual Issues, Female Socialization, and the Social Context." *Journal of Marital and Family Therapy* 11:3 (July 1985):273-86.

Rothberg, Barbara and Vivian Ubell. "The Co-Existence of System Theory and Feminism in Working with Heterosexual and Lesbian Couples." *Women & Therapy* 4:1 (Spring 1985):19-36.

Rothblum, Esther D. "Depression Among Lesbians: an Invisible and Unresearched Phenomenon." *Journal of Gay & Lesbian Psychotherapy* 1:3 (1990):67-87.

RT: a Journal of Radical Therapy, "Lesbians in Therapy," vol. 4, no. 8, 1974.

Russell, Tanya G. "AIDS Education, Homosexuality, and the Counselor's Role." *School Counselor* 36:5 (May 1989):333-7.

Schneider, Margaret and Bob Tremble. "Training Service Providers to Work with Gay or Lesbian Adolescents: a Workshop." *Journal of Counseling and Development* 65:2 (October 1986):98-9.

Schrag, Keith G. "Relationship Therapy with Same-Gender Couples." *Family Relations* 33 (April 1984):9-12.

Shernoff, Michael J. "Family Therapy for Lesbian and Gay Clients." *Social Work* 29:4 (July-August 1984):393-6.

Siegel, Rachel Josefowitz. "Beyond Homophobia: Learning to Work with Lesbian Clients." *Women & Therapy,* "Women, Power, and Therapy: Issues for Women" 6:1/2 (Spring/Summer 1987):125-33.

Silveira, Jeanette. "Lesbian Therapy: a Reader's Forum -- Lesbian Feminist Therapy: a Report and Some Thoughts." *Lesbian Ethics* 1:3 (Fall 1985):22-6.

Slater, B.R. "Essential Issues in Working with Lesbian and Gay Male Youths." *Professional Psychology -- Research and Practice* 19:2 (1988):226-35.

Smart, Corinna. "Counselling Practice: Counselling Homosexual/Bisexual People with Particular Reference to Young Lesbian Women." *International Journal of Adolescence and Youth* 1:4 (1989):379-93.

Smith, Adrienne J. "Reflections of a Jewish Lesbian-Feminist Activist-Therapist; Or, First of All I Am Jewish, the Rest Is Commentary." *Women & Therapy,* "Jewish Women in Therapy: Seen But Not Heard" 10:4 (1990):57-64.

Sobocinski, M.R. "Ethical Principles in the Counseling of Gay and Lesbian Adolescents: Issues of Autonomy, Competence, and Confidentiality." *Professional Psychology - Research and Practice* 21:4 (1990):240-7.

Sophie, Joan. "Counseling Lesbians." *Personnel and Guidance Journal* 60:6 (February 1982):341-5.

Stein, Terry S. "Theoretical Considerations in Psychotherapy with Gay Men and Lesbians." *Journal of Homosexuality,* "Psychopathology and Psychotherapy in Homosexuality" 15:1/2 (1988):75-96.

Steinhorn, Audrey I. "Lesbian Adolescents in Residential Treatment." *Social Casework* 60 (October 1979):494-504.

Thompson, George H. and William R. Fishburn. "Attitudes Toward Homosexuality Among Graduate Counseling Students." *Counselor Education and Supervision* 17:2 (December 1977):121-9.

Thundercloud R.D.O.C., Flying. "Voices" (incest and psychotherapy). *Common Lives/Lesbian Lives* 15/16 (Summer 1985):35-9.

Ward, Joan M. "Therapism and the Taming of the Lesbian Community."
    Sinister Wisdom 36 (Winter 1988/89):33-41.

Waterman, Caroline K., Lori J. Dawson, and Michael J. Bologna.
    "Sexual Coercion in Gay Male and Lesbian Relationships:
    Predictors and Implications for Support Services." *Journal of Sex
    Research* 26:1 (February 1989):118-24.

Way, Peggy. "Homosexual Counseling As a Learning Ministry."
    Christianity and Crisis, "Homosexuality" 37:9&10 (May 30 &
    June 13, 1977):123-31.

Wills, Sue. "The Psychologist and the Lesbian." *Refractory Girl*
    (Australia) 9 (Winter 1975):41-5.

Women & Therapy: a Feminist Quarterly, "Therapeutic Issues with
    Lesbian Clients," vol. 1, no. 4, Winter 1982.

------, "Lesbianism: Affirming Nontraditional Roles," vol. 8, nos. 1/2,
    1989; note: cover reads 1988.

Woodman, Natalie Jane. "Mental Health Issues of Relevance to Lesbian
    Women and Gay Men" (especially how people deal with loss).
    Journal of Gay & Lesbian Psychotherapy 1:1 (1989):53-63.

Publishing (see also: Censorship; Mass Media; Periodicals:
    Lesbian/Feminist/Gay)

Anonymous, with Kim Schive and Nancy Becker. "Alternatives to Print:
    On the Other Hand" (access to feminist education for deaf
    people). *Sinister Wisdom,* "Lesbian Writing and Publishing" 13
    (Spring 1980):97-8.

Bunch, Charlotte. "Feminist Publishing: an Antiquated Form? Notes for a
    Talk at the Old Wives' Tales Bookstore, San Francisco,
    California, February 27, 1977." *Heresies #3,* "Lesbian Art and
    Artists" 1:3 (Fall 1977):24-6.

Clardy, Andrea Fleck. "Best-Sellers from Crone's Own, Light Cleaning, Down There, and Dozens of Other Feminist Presses." *Ms.* 14:2 (August 1985):65-8.

Clausen, Jan. "The Politics of Publishing and the Lesbian Community." *Sinister Wisdom,* "Lesbian Writing and Publishing" 1:2 (Fall 1976):95-115.

Henry, Alice. "Workshop Reports" (from the second national Women in Print Conference, Washington, D.C., October 1981; includes reports on "Creating a Lesbian Literature: How Conscious Are We?" (of race, class, age, and disability; "Lesbian/Feminism and Radical Feminism in the 1980s"; and "Lesbian Feminists and Heterosexual Feminists"). *off our backs* 11:11 (December 1981):3+.

Jay, Karla. "A Look at Lesbian Magazines." *Margins,* "Lesbian Feminist Writing and Publishing" 23 (August 1975):19-21.

Keener, K.M. "Out of the Archives and into the Academy: Opportunities for Research and Publishing in Lesbian Literature." *College English* 44:3 (March 1982):301-13.

Lootens, Tricia. "Third Women in Print Conference" (Berkeley, California, May 1985; reports on workshops including classism, erotica, lesbian nuns, women of color, pornography, censorship, raid on British gay book store). *off our backs* 15:8 (August-September 1985):8-9+.

Margins, "Lesbian Feminist Writing and Publishing," no. 23, August 1975.

Melville, Joy. "I'm Not a Feminist, But . . . " (feminist publishing in Great Britain). *New Society* 68 (June 7, 1984):391-2.

Parmar, Pratibha and Sue O'Sullivan. "The Second International Feminist Bookfair" (Oslo, Norway, June 1986; includes section on "Global Day/Lesbian Day"). *Spare Rib* (Great Britain) 169 (August 1986):18-19.

Poore, Nancy (with Jorjet Harper). "The Women in Print Movement." *Hot Wire* 1:2 (March 1985):56-7.

Powell, Leslie. "The Gay Writer: 'This Will Hurt You With the Publishers.'" *Progressive* 45 (November 1981):46-7.

Sinister Wisdom, "Lesbian Writing and Publishing," vol. 1, no. 2, Fall 1976.

------, "Lesbian Writing and Publishing," no. 13, Spring 1980.

Thomas, June. "3rd International Feminist Book Fair: Promoting Lesbian Writing" (Montréal, Québec, Canada, June 1988). *off our backs* 18:10 (November 1988):3.

van Deurs, Kady and Eileen Pagan. "Catalogue for Women Who Are Blind" (list of "Womanbooks for Women Who Are Blind and/or Physically Challenged"). *Sinister Wisdom,* "Lesbian Writing and Publishing" 13 (Spring 1980):100.

"Views: Publishers, Readers, Writers, Editors" (short essays and quotations about lesbian writing and publishing). *Sinister Wisdom,* "Lesbian Writing and Publishing" 13 (Spring 1980):35-50.

Wakeling, Louise Katherine, Margaret Bradstock, Mary Fallon. "Poetry Doesn't Sell" (Australia). *Connexions,* "Women's Words" 13 (Summer 1984):26-7.

Wilson, Barbara. "European Feminist Publishing." *off our backs* 14:5 (May 1984):14-15.

"Women's Movement Publishers Meet in 70 Workshops to Plan Expanded Influence and Outreach" (Third National Women in Print Conference, Berkeley, California, May 1985). *Media Report to Women* 13 (July-August 1985):4.

Bunch, Charlotte:

Doughty, Frances. "Frances Doughty Talks to Charlotte Bunch About Women's Publishing." *Sinister Wisdom,* "Lesbian Writing and Publishing" 13 (Spring 1980):71-7.

Daughters, Inc.:

Desmoines, Harriet. "Retrieved from Silence: My Life and Times with Daughters, Inc." *Sinister Wisdom* 5 (Winter 1978):62-9.

Diamonds Are a Dyke's Best Friend (novel):

Zipter, Yvonne. "Re:Inking -- Diamonds in the Rough: The Making of a Book" (publication of her book *Diamonds Are a Dyke's Best Friend*). *Hot Wire* 5:2 (May 1989):46-7+.

Diana Press:

Conner, K. Patrick. "Diana Press: a Story of Survival" (office vandalized October 1977). *Small Press Review* No. 65, 10:6 (June 1978):8-9.

Nicholson, Catherine. "The Rape of Diana: Catherine Interviews Casey Czarnik and Coletta Reid" (founders). *Sinister Wisdom* 5 (Winter 1978):73-6.

Firebrand Books:

Gambill, Sue. "Firebrand Books: Making Available the Quality Works of Lesbian and Feminist Writers." *Hot Wire* 2:3 (July 1986):20-1.

Vine, Elynor. "Nancy Bereano: Feminist, Lesbian, Publisher." *Visibilities* 4:5 (September/October 1990):10-12.

Helaine Victoria Press:

Tilchen, Maida. "Helaine Victoria Press" (interview with Jocelyn Helaine Cohen, Nancy Taylor, and Victoria Poore of Helaine Victoria Press postcard company). *Sinister Wisdom,* "Lesbian Writing and Publishing" 13 (Spring 1980):87-90.

Iowa City Women's Press:

Barb and Joan. "The Invisible Lesbian-Feminist Printer." *Common Lives/Lesbian Lives* 5 (Fall 1982):42-5 and *off our backs* 12:8 (August-September 1982):16+.

The Common Lives/Lesbian Lives Collective. "Don't Let This Lesbian Press Stop" (Iowa City Women's Press). *Common Lives/Lesbian Lives* 15/16 (Summer 1985):4-6.

Kitchen Table Women of Color Press:

Jewell, Terri L. "Barbara Smith and Kitchen Table Women of Color Press." *Hot Wire* 6:2 (May 1990):20-2+.

Parkerson, Michelle. "Some Place That's Our Own -- an Interview with Barbara Smith." *off our backs* 14:4 (April 1984):10-12+.

Smith, Barbara. "A Press of Our Own: Kitchen Table: Women of Color Press." *Frontiers* 10:3 (1989):11-13.

Lesbian Nuns (anthology by Naiad Press; publisher allowed excerpts to be printed in *Penthouse Forum Magazine*):

Grier, Barbara. "Barbara Grier on *Lesbian Nuns.*" *off our backs* 15:8 (August-September 1985):29.

Krebs, Paula. "Breaking Silence About *Lesbian Nuns.*" *off our backs* 15:5 (May 1985):1-4.

O'Shea, Kathleen. "Lesbian Nun: Breaking Silence Again" (letter from contributor; related letters from Jan Raymond, Pat Hynes and Sister Mary Joan). *off our backs* 15:6 (June 1985):27+.

Stocker, Midge. "More Than a Controversy -- *Lesbian Nuns:* a Brief History." *Hot Wire* 2:2 (March 1986):52-3+.

Sturgis, Susanna J. "Breaking Silence, Breaking Faith: the Promotion of *Lesbian Nuns.*" *Lesbian Ethics* 1:3 (Fall 1985):89-107.

Livia, Anna:

Thomas, June. "Anna Livia: Lesbian Author, Publisher." *off our backs* 18:11 (December 1988):10+.

Metis Press:

"Metis Press" (interview with editors Chris Straayer, Chris Johnson, and Janet Soule). *Sinister Wisdom,* "Lesbian Writing and Publishing" 13 (Spring 1980):91-4.

Naiad Press:

Damon, Gene (Barbara Grier, current owner of Naiad Press). "The Naiad Press" (interview with Naiad co-founders, Anyda Marchant and Muriel Crawford). *Sinister Wisdom,* "Lesbian Writing and Publishing" 1:2 (Fall 1976):116-19.

Gambill, Sue. "The World's Oldest and Largest Lesbian-Feminist Publishing House." *Hot Wire* 3:2 (March 1987):18-19+.

"1950s Lesbian Novels Reissued by Naiad Press." *Publishers Weekly* 222 (February 11, 1983):44.

Onlywomen Press:

Fritz, Leah. "Publishing and Flourishing" (Sheba Press Limited, Onlywomen Press, and other British non-lesbian feminist presses). *Women's Review of Books* 3 (February 1986):16-17.

Out & Out Books:

Creighton, Jane, Joan Larkin, and Ellen Shapiro. "Self-Interview: Out & Out Books." *Sinister Wisdom* 14 (Summer 1980):106-9.

Persephone Press:

Rich, Cynthia. "Persephone Press" (interview with Gloria Greenfield, Pat McGloin, and Deborah Snow, editors of now-defunct feminist press). *Sinister Wisdom,* "Lesbian Writing and Publishing" 13 (Spring 1980):81-5.

"'Successful' Persephone Press Closes Up; Molly Lovelock Interview Asks Reasons." *Media Report to Women* 12:3 (May/June 1984):15-16.

Seal Press:

Herman, Ellen. "Seal Press: an Object Lesson." *Women's Review of Books* 2 (February 1985):13-14.

Leonard, Vickie and Denise Kulp. "An Interview with Barbara Wilson" (writer, and founder of Seal Press). *off our backs* 14:11 (December 1984):26-7+.

Thomas, June. "Barbara Wilson Talks About: Feminist Publishing, Crime and Punishment." *off our backs* 20:1 (January 1990):10-11.

Sheba Publisher (Great Britain):

Fritz, Leah. "Publishing and Flourishing" (Sheba Press Limited, Onlywomen Press, and other British non-lesbian feminist presses). *Women's Review of Books* 3 (February 1986):16-17.

Ross, Becki. "Black Women of Letters" (excerpt of interview with Michelle McKenzie and Araba Mercer, from Canadian monthly *Rites,* November 1988). *Connexions,* "Women on Work" 30 (1989):24-5.

Spinsters, Ink:

Klepfisz, Irena. "Spinsters, Ink: an Interview with Maureen Brady and Judith McDaniel." *Sinister Wisdom,* "Lesbian Writing and Publishing" 13 (Spring 1980):77-81.

Women's Press Collective:

"Women's Press Collective." *Sinister Wisdom,* "Lesbian Writing and Publishing" 1:2 (Fall 1976):120-1.

Violet Press:

Winant, Fran. "Lesbians Publish Lesbians: My Life and Times with Violet Press." *Margins,* "Lesbian Feminist Writing and Publishing" 23 (August 1975):62-6.

Pulp Novels

Benno, Susanna. "Sappho in Soft Cover: Notes on Lesbian Pulp."
Fireweed (Canada), "Popular Culture" 11 (1981):35-43.

Koski, Fran and Maida Tilchen. "Some Pulp Sappho." *Margins,* "Lesbian
Feminist Writing and Publishing" 23 (August 1975):41-5.

"Lesbian Identity and Pulp Novels" (report on paper given by Jane
Lindsay Miller at the National Women's Studies Association
conference, Towson State University, Maryland, June 1989). *off
our backs* 19:8 (August-September 1989):10.

"1950s Lesbian Novels Reissued by Naiad Press." *Publishers Weekly* 222
(February 11, 1983):44.

Ruthchild, Nancy M. "Lesbian Books: a Long and Painful Search."
Mother Jones 1 (April 1976):63-5.

Silk, Kay. "Lesbian Novels in the Fifties." *Focus* (August 1973):4-7.

Bannon, Ann:
Bannon, Ann. "Then and Now: Speaking to Women Through
Fiction." *Hot Wire* 4:2 (March 1988):48+.

Lootens, Tricia. "Ann Bannon: a Lesbian Audience Discovers Its
Lost Literature." *off our backs* 13:11 (December 1983):13.

------. "Ann Bannon: a Writer of Lost Lesbian Fiction Finds Herself
and Her Public" (interview). *off our backs* 13:11 (December
1983):14-15+.

Walters, Suzanna Danuta. "As Her Hand Crept Slowly Up Her
Thigh: Ann Bannon and the Politics of Pulp." *Social Text* 23
(Fall-Winter 1989):83-101.

<u>Taylor, Valerie</u>:

Corinne, Tee A. "Remembering as a Way of Life" (lesbian 'National Treasures', including June Arnold, Jeannete Foster, Valerie Taylor, Barbara Grier, Audre Lorde, Anita Cornwell, Sarah Aldridge, Sonny Wainwright). *Common Lives/Lesbian Lives* 19 (Spring 1986):15-18.

Corinne, Tee and Caroline Overman. "Valerie Taylor Interview." *Common Lives/Lesbian Lives* 25 (Winter 1988):61-72.

Racism (see also: African-American Lesbians; Anti-Semitism; Asian/Pacifica Lesbians; Chicana Lesbians; Latina/Chicana Lesbians; Lesbians of Color; Native American Lesbians; Violence Against Lesbians and Gay Men; Violence Against Women)

Armstrong, Toni L. "The Great White Folk Music Myth." *Hot Wire* 4:3 (July 1988):22.

Bravmann, Scott. "Telling (Hi)stories: Rethinking the Lesbian and Gay Historical Imagination" (problems of race, class, and gender in recovering lesbian and gay history). *Out/Look #8,* 2:4 (Spring 1990):68-74.

Brooke. "A Feminist Future?" ("The Women's Movement: Forum," conference sponsored by The Matriarchists, New York City, September 1978; speakers included Robin Morgan, Gloria Steinem, Dianne Feeley, Willamette Brown, Elizabeth Shanklin, Jean O'Leary, Judith Levy, Kate Millett, Arlie Scott, Midge Costanza, Marisa de Los Angeles, Flo Kennedy, and Ti-Grace Atkinson; picketed by group accusing forum of token inclusion of women of color). *off our backs* 8:10 (November 1978):10-12.

Brown, Fern. "As a Jewish Lesbian: Questions of Race and Anti-Racism." *Common Lives/Lesbian Lives* 3 (Spring 1982):42-6.

Bulkin, Elly. "An Interchange on Feminist Criticism on 'Dancing Through the Minefield'" (Judith Kegan Gardiner, Elly Bulkin, and Rena Grasso Patterson comment on Annette Kolodny's article, "Dancing Through the Minefield: Some Observations on the Theory, Practice, and Politics of a Feminist Literary Criticism"; Bulkin's contribution discusses heterosexism and racism in Kolodny's essay; Kolodny's response is on pp.665-75). *Feminist Studies* 8:3 (Fall 1982):635-54.

------. "Racism and Writing: Some Implications for White Lesbian Critics." *Sinister Wisdom,* "Lesbian Writing and Publishing" 13 (Spring 1980):3-22.

Carmen, Gail, Sheila, and Pratibha. "Becoming Visible: Black Lesbian Discussions." *Feminist Review* (Great Britain), "Many Voices, One Chant: Black Feminist Perspectives" 17 (Autumn 1984):53-72.

Carter, Colevia. "Classism, Racism . . . the Enemy is Closer to Home" (response to Burning Cloud (Consuelo Sison), Nisqually Nation. "Open Letter from Filipina/Indian Dyke," *off our backs* 8:11 (December 1978):8-9). *off our backs* 9:2 (February 1979):17.

Clark, Terri. "Denial of Possible Racism" (response to Burning Cloud (Consuelo Sison), Nisqually Nation. "Open Letter from Filipina/Indian Dyke," *off our backs* 8:11 (December 1978):8-9). *off our backs* 9:2 (February 1979):2.

CLIT (Collective Lesbian International Terrors). "CLIT Statement #3" (militant feminism and separatism, with discussion of classism and racism). *off our backs* 6:7 (October 1976):10-11.

Cohen, Sherrie. "White Wimmin Have Got to Educate Themselves" (about racism; response to Burning Cloud (Consuelo Sison), Nisqually Nation. "Open Letter from Filipina/Indian Dyke," *off our backs* 8:11 (December 1978):8-9). *off our backs* 9:2 (February 1979):2.

Davis, Rebecca. "Young Women Fight Movement Racism" (Feminist Futures: The First National Conference By, For and About Women in Their 20s, Washington, D.C., November 1989). *New Directions for Women* 19:1 (January/February 1990):5.

Demetreous and Sheila Brown. "The Personal Is Political" (response to Burning Cloud (Consuelo Sison), Nisqually Nation. "Open Letter from Filipina/Indian Dyke," *off our backs* 8:11 (December 1978):8-9). *off our backs* 9:2 (February 1979):2-3.

de Monteflores, Carmen. "Invisible Audiences: Writing Fiction as a Form of Coming Out" (written by author of *Singing Softly/Cantando Bajito*). *Out/Look #10,* 3:2 (Fall 1990):65-8.

Desmoines, Harriet. "Notes for a Magazine II" (founding concepts for *Sinister Wisdom* ; discusses politically left revolutionary politics, racism, and classism). *Sinister Wisdom* 1:1 (Summer 1976):27-34.

Dykewomon, Elana. "Notes for a Magazine: On Passing." *Sinister Wisdom,* "Passing" 35 (Summer/Fall 1988):3-6.

FE. "Williams-Sonoma Sued for Firing Lesbians of Color." *off our backs* 20:3 (March 1990):17.

Fite, Karen and Nikola Trumbo. "Betrayals Among Women: Barriers to a Common Language." *Lesbian Ethics* 1:1 (Fall 1984):70-89.

Fukaya, Michiyo. "Will the Real Me Please Stand Up?" *Common Lives/Lesbian Lives* 10 (Winter 1983):89-98.

Goldsby, Jackie. "What It Means to Be Colored Me." *Out/Look #9,* 3:1 (Summer 1990):9-17.

Gomez, Jewelle. "Imagine a Lesbian . . . a Black Lesbian . . . " *Trivia* 12 (Spring 1988):45-60.

------. "Repeat After Me: We Are Different, We Are the Same." *New York University Review of Law & Social Change* 14:4 (Fall 1986):935-41.

Greene, Beverly A. "When the Therapist Is White and the Patient Is Black: Considerations for Psychotherapy in the Feminist Heterosexual and Lesbian Communities." *Women and Therapy* 5 (Summer/Fall 1986):41-65.

"Greensboro" (lesbian and gay groups among crowd opposing the Ku Klux Klan on the twentieth anniversary of the Woolworth lunch counter sit-in, Greensboro, North Carolina, February 1980). *off our backs* 10:3 (March 1980):13.

Henry, Alice. "Separatism, Racism, Lesbianism." *off our backs* 11:7 (July 1981):5-6+.

------. "Workshop Reports" (from the second national Women in Print Conference, Washington, D.C., October 1981; includes reports on "Creating a Lesbian Literature: How Conscious Are We?" of race, class, age, and disability; "Lesbian/Feminism and Radical Feminism in the 1980s"; and "Lesbian Feminists and Heterosexual Feminists"). *off our backs* 11:11 (December 1981):3+.

Hollibaugh, Amber and Cherríe Moraga. "What We're Rollin' Around in Bed With -- Sexual Silences in Feminism: a Conversation Toward Ending Them." *Heresies #12,* "The Sex Issue" 3:4 (1981):58-62.

Jewell, Terri L. "A Call to Black Lesbian Sisters" (racism and skin-color prejudice among African-American lesbians). *Sinister Wisdom,* "Passing" 35 (Summer/Fall 1988):12-4; also *Black/Out,* "Tenth Anniversary Edition: NCBLG Celebrates Homecoming" 2:1 (Fall 1988):53.

Karp, Mitchell. "The Challenge of Symbolism" (written by white member of Men of All Colors Together, an anti-racist, anti-sexist organization). *New York University Review of Law & Social Change* 14:4 (Fall 1986):943-7.

Lee, Anna. "Interstices of Race and Class: Creating Intimacy" (building community). *Lesbian Ethics* 4:1 (Spring 1990):77-83.

Lewis, Barbara L. "Lack of Sensitivity" (about racism; response to Burning Cloud (Consuelo Sison), Nisqually Nation. "Open Letter from Filipina/Indian Dyke," *off our backs* 8:11 (December 1978):8-9). *off our backs* 9:2 (February 1979):17.

Loiacano, Darryl K. "Gay Identity Issues among Black Americans: Racism, Homophobia, and the Need for Validation." *Journal of Counseling and Development,* "Lesbian, Gay and Bisexual Issues in Counseling" 68:1 (September-October 1989):21-5.

Lorde, Audre. "The Role of Difference" (presentation on "The Personal is Political" panel of The Second Sex -- Thirty Years Later: a Commemorative Conference on Feminist Theory, September 1979; Lorde responds to lack of presence and discussion of lesbians/women of color). *off our backs* 9:12 (December 1979):5+.

------. "The Uses of Anger" (keynote speech to the 3rd National Women's Studies Association conference, "Women Respond to Racism," Storrs, Connecticut, 1981). *Women's Studies Quarterly* 9:3 (Fall 1981):7-10.

------. "Women, Power, and Difference" (talk delivered at the Women in America: Legacies of Race and Ethnicity conference, Georgetown University, Washington, D.C., April 1988; Lorde discusses living in St. Croix, the U.S. Virgin Islands). *Sojourner* 15:3 (November 1989):18-19.

Louise, Vivienne. "Genuine Desire" (letter to "A Readers' Forum --
    Separatism: Beyond the Debate," asking "Why don't white
    lesbians have a genuine desire to learn from lesbians of African
    descent?"). *Lesbian Ethics* 3:2 (Fall 1988):5-8.

Mays, Vickie M. "I Hear Voices But See No Faces: Reflections on
    Racism and Women-Identified Relationships of Afro-American
    Women." *Heresies #12,* "The Sex Issue" 3:4 (1981):74-6.

Minkowitz, D. "Racism: Blacks Shut Out of Lesbian Event." *Guardian*
    29:19 (February 11, 1987):4.

------. "Racism Exists in Lesbian Community." *New Directions for
    Women* 16 (July 1987):6.

Moirai, Catherine Risingflame, with Merril Mushroom. "White Lies and
    Common Language: Notes for Lesbian Writers and Readers."
    Common Lives/Lesbian Lives 5 (Fall 1982):46-58.

Moira, Fran. "Combatting Racism in the Women's Movement" (forum
    sponsored by the D.C. Area Feminist Alliance, Washington,
    D.C., May 1980). *off our backs* 10:6 (June 1980):4-5.

Moore, Tracy and Terry Wolverton. "Including Ourselves in the Future:
    White Lesbian Anti-Racism." *Common Lives/Lesbian Lives* 1
    (Fall 1981):42-50.

Moraga, Cherríe and Barbara Smith. "Lesbian Literature: a Third World
    Perspective." *Radical Teacher,* "Gay and Lesbian Studies" 24 (no
    date; c. 1983):12-14.

The *off our backs* Collective. "OOB Statement" (response to Burning
    Cloud (Consuelo Sison), Nisqually Nation. "Open Letter from
    Filipina/Indian Dyke," *off our backs* 8:11 (December 1978):8-9).
    off our backs 9:2 (February 1979):3.

Palladino, Diane and Yanela Stephenson. "Perceptions of the Sexual Self: Their Impact on Relationships Between Lesbian and Heterosexual Women." *Women & Therapy,* "Diversity and Complexity in Feminist Therapy: Part II" 9:3 (1990):231-53.

Paz, Juana Maria. "Statement to the Racism Workshop" (March 1980, Fayeteville, Arkansas). *Common Lives/Lesbian Lives* 4 (Summer 1982):11-17.

Peeples, Edward, Jr., Walter W. Tunstall, and Everett Eberhardt. "The Veil of Hurt" (survey of 508 gay, lesbian, and bisexual African-Americans and European-Americans in Richmond and Alexandria, Virginia, regarding discrimination in the business and private sectors). *Southern Exposure* 13:5 (1985):24-7.

Penelope, Julia. "The Mystery of Lesbians: II" (separatist political theory). *Lesbian Ethics* 1:2 (Spring 1985):29-67; also *Gossip* (Great Britain) 2 (1986):16-68.

"Questionnaire: What Misunderstandings or Cross-purposes Have Arisen in Your Group Due to Racial, Sexual, Class, Religious, or Age Differences?" *Heresies #20,* "Activists" 5:4 (1985):82-5.

"Racism and Homophobia: Letters to *Plexus* and *off our backs." off our backs* 9:10 (November 1979):12-13.

"Racism: Lesbian Artists Have Their Say" (the Dynamics of Color Art Exhibition, part of the Dynamics of Color Conference, San Francisco, California, October 1989). *Out/Look #8,* 2:4 (Spring 1990):38-43.

Rich, Adrienne. "'Disloyal to Civilization': Feminism, Racism, and Gynophobia." *Chrysalis* 7 (1979):9-27.

------. "Disobedience Is What NWSA Is Potentially About" (keynote speech to the 3rd National Women's Studies Association conference, "Women Respond to Racism," Storrs, Connecticut, 1981). *Women's Studies Quarterly* 9:3 (Fall 1981):4-6.

------. "Notes for a Magazine: What Does Separatism Mean?" *Sinister Wisdom* 18 (1981):83-91.

------. "Resisting Amnesia" (the importance of reporting all of history). *Ms.* 15:9 (March 1987):66-7.

Sears, James T. "The Impact of Gender and Race on Growing Up Lesbian and Gay in the South." *NWSA Journal* 1:3 (Spring 1989):422-57.

Smith, Barbara. "The NEA Is the Least of It" (silencing through overt censorship, as the National Endowment for the Arts, and through internalized oppression). *Ms.: The World of Women* 1:3 (November/December 1990):65-7.

------. "Visions and Revisions: Women and Power to Change" (part of final panel at First National Women's Studies Association Conference, Lawrence, Kansas, May 30-June 3, 1979). *Women's Studies Newsletter* 7:3 (Summer 1979):19-20.

"South Africa" (summarized from "Black Gays and Lesbians in South Africa" in Canadian monthly *Rites* (October 1987)). *Connexions*, "Lesbian Activism" 29 (1989):15.

Stato, Joanne. "14th Michigan Womyn's Music Festival" (the politics of the event -- who attended, what was discussed, including lesbians of color, racism, S/M, disability, and music). *off our backs* 19:9 (October 1989):20-1.

"Three Black Women Talk About Sexuality and Racism." *Spare Rib* (Great Britain) 135 (October 1983):6-8.

Tiik. "Needed Change Is at Birth" (about racism; response to Burning Cloud (Consuelo Sison), Nisqually Nation. "Open Letter from Filipina/Indian Dyke," *off our backs* 8:11 (December 1978):8-9). *off our backs* 9:2 (February 1979):17.

Towey, Shawn. "Reproductive Rights National Network Meets: Racism and Heterosexism Discussed" (Reproductive Rights National Network Conference, Philadelphia, Pennsylvania, April 1983). *off our backs* 13:7 (July 1983):15.

"Whatever Happened at the Lesbian Archive?" (dispute in collective over showing of film with S/M content, "She Must Be Seeing Things," and over alleged racism in hiring). *Spare Rib* (Great Britain) 199 (March 1989):17.

White, Judy. "Women Divided?" (racism, classism, lesbian-heterosexual split in the women's liberation movement; and the Congress to Unite Women, New York City, May 1970). *off our backs* 1:5 (May 1970):5.

Brady, Maureen (white writer):
Brady, Maureen. "An Exploration of Class and Race Dynamics in the Writing of *Folly*" (by the novel's author). *13th Moon*, "Working Class Experience" 7:1/2 (1983):145-51.

Deming, Barbara (white civil rights and peace activist):
Fritz, Leah. "'We Are All Part of One Another' -- a Tribute to Barbara Deming." *Ms.* 13 (December 1984):41-2.

Glasgow, Joanne. "Barbara Deming, 1917-84." *New Directions for Women* 13:5 (September/October 1984):2.

Pratt, Minnie Bruce. "'Dancing Toward Death' -- Barbara Deming: 1917-84." *off our backs* 14 (October 1984):28.

Segrest, Mab. "Barbara Deming: 1917-84." *Southern Exposure* 13:2-3 (1985):72-5.

Ifateyo, Ajowa (African socialist journalist)
Douglas, Carol Anne. "Ajowa Ifateyo: Speaking Up Front" (interview with one of the founders of *Upfront*, national black women's quarterly, and former editor of *The Running Spear*, African People's Socialist Party newspaper). *off our backs* 14:10 (November 1984):10-12.

Lorde, Audre (African-American writer):

Parmer, Pratibha and Jackie Kay. "Frontiers: Interview [with] Black Author and Activist, Audre Lorde." *Spare Rib* (Great Britain) 188 (March 1988):37-41.

Stato, Joanne. "I Am Your Sister Celeconference: Tribute to Audre Lorde" (Boston, Massachusetts, October 1990). *off our backs* 20:11 (December 1990):1-5+.

Rich, Adrienne (white writer):

Packwood, Marilyn. "Adrienne Rich" (interview with poet and essayist). *Spare Rib* (Great Britain) 103 (February 1981):14-16.

Roberts, Roxanne E.B. (African-American writer):

Ottey, Shan. "Black Lesbian: Alienation and Aloneness" (interview; includes discussion of being African-American in a lesbian bar). *off our backs* 5:5 (May-June 1975):15.

Shockley, Ann Allen (African-American writer):

White, Evelyn C. "Comprehensive Oppression: Lesbians and Race in the Work of Ann Allen Shockley." *Backbone* 3 (1981):38-40.

Smith, Lillian (southern white anti-racist activist and writer):

Murray, Hugh. "Lillian Smith: a Neglected Southern Heroine." *Journal of Ethnic Studies* 17:1 (Spring 1989):136-40.

The Washington Sisters (African-American musicians):

Armstrong, Toni L. "The Washington Sisters" (musicians Sondra and Sharon Washington). *Hot Wire* 4:1 (November 1987):2-4+.

Radio (see also: Mass Media)

Gardner, Kay. "How to Get Airplay on Non-Commercial Radio." *Hot Wire* 6:3 (September 1990):50-1.

Laner, Mary Liege. "Media Mating II: Personals Advertising of Lesbian Women." *Journal of Homosexuality* 4:1 (Autumn 1978):41-62.

Lumsden, Andrew. "IBA Gets an Overdue Earful from Lesbians and Gays" (Independent Broadcasting Authority). *New Statesman* (Great Britain) 111 (February 21, 1986):6.

Seeger, Nancy. "'Sophie's Parlor': On the Air" (feminist radio show on WPFW, Washington, D.C.). *Hot Wire* 3:3 (July 1987):18-19+.

Stamps, Wickie. "They Say It Sister, On the Air" ("Say It, Sister," Boston radio show on women's public affairs, produced by Kate Rushin, Jennifer Abod, Madge Kaplan, Tatiana Schreiber, and Donna Kerner). *New Directions for Women* 18:5 (September/October 1989):7.

Rape (see Violence Against Lesbians and Gay Men; Violence Against Women)

Recovery (see Substance Abuse and Recovery)

Relationships (see also: Butch/Femme; Children of Lesbians; Domestic Partnership; Families of Lesbians; Friendship; Monogamy; Parenting; Sexuality; S/M; Violence Among Lesbians)

Alicen, Debbie. "Intertextuality: the Language of Lesbian Relationships." *Trivia* 3 (Fall 1983):6-26.

Baptiste, David A., Jr. "Psychotherapy with Gay/Lesbian Couples and Their Children in 'Stepfamilies': a Challenge for Marriage and Family Therapists." *Journal of Homosexuality,* "Psychotherapy with Homosexual Men and Women: Integrated Identity Approaches for Clinical Practice" 14:1/2 (1987):213-22.

Bennett, Linda. "Lesbian Family Registry" (lesbian/gay couples register with National Family Registry of the Human Rights Campaign Fund to increase visibility). *off our backs,* "20th Anniversary" 20:2 (February 1990):8.

Berger, Raymond M. "Passing: Impact on the Quality of Same-Sex Couple Relationships." *Social Work* 35:4 (July 1990):328-32.

Bristow, Ann R. and Pearn, Pam Langford. "Comment on Krieger's 'Lesbian Identity and Community: Recent Social Science Literature'" (in *Signs*, 8:1 (Autumn 1982):91-108). *Signs*, "The Lesbian Issue" 9:4 (Summer 1984):729-32.

Burch, Beverly. "Psychological Merger in Lesbian Couples: a Joint Ego Psychological and Systems Approach." *Family Therapy* (Fall 1982):201+.

Cabaj, R.P. "Gay and Lesbian Couples -- Lessons on Human Intimacy." *Psychiatric Annals* 18:1 (1988):21-5.

CAD. "Lesbian Relationships" (workshop at National Women's Studies Association Conference, Towson State University, Maryland, June 1989). *off our backs* 19:9 (October 1989):23.

Caldwell, M.A. and Letitia A. Peplau. "The Balance of Power in Lesbian Relationships." *Sex Roles* 10:7-8 (April 1984):587-99.

Clare, Elizabeth. "Friends, Lovers and Passion." *Sinister Wisdom,* "On Friendship" 40 (Spring 1990):96-8.

Colton, Wayne L. "Social and Sexual Relationships of Lesbians" (concludes that lesbians are as likely as heterosexual women to form long-lasting relationships). *Journal of Sex Research* 11:2 (May 1975):139-48.

Decker, B. "Counseling Gay and Lesbian Couples." *Journal of Social Work and Human Sexuality* 2 (1983):39-52.

Dixon, Joan. "Sexuality and Relationship Changes in Married Females Following the Commencement of Bisexual Activity." *Journal of Homosexuality,* "Bisexualities: Theory and Research" 11:1/2 (Spring 1985):115-34.

Douglas, Carol Anne. "Lesbian-Feminism: Love & Struggle." *off our backs* (November 1976):16.

------. "Love & Feminism: She Is Not What You Bargained For." *off our backs* 8:2 (February 1978):14-15.

Duffy, Sally M. and Caryl E. Rusbult. "Satisfaction and Commitment in Homosexual and Heterosexual Relationships." *Journal of Homosexuality* 12:2 (Winter 1985/86):1-24.

Dykewomon, Elana. "Notes for a Magazine: Did You Say Love?" (about the problematic concept of "romantic love"). *Sinister Wisdom,* "With an Emphasis on Lesbian Relationships" 38 (Summer/Fall 1989):3-5.

Eldridge, Natalie S. and Lucia A. Gilbert. "Correlates of Relationship Satisfaction in Lesbian Couples." *Psychology of Women Quarterly* 14:1 (1990):43-62.

Ettelbrick, Paula L. "Gay Marriage: a Must or a Bust? -- Since When Was Marriage the Path to Liberation?" (published before the San Francisco Domestic Partners ballot initiative was defeated inNovember 1989). *Out/Look #6,* 2:2 (Fall 1989):9+.

------. "Under the Law -- Protecting Relationships." *Visibilities* 2:1 (January/February 1988):18-20.

------. "Under the Law -- Who Comes First When There Is No Marriage?" *Visibilities* 3:5 (September/October 1989):18-19.

"Gay Couple Counseling -- Proceedings of a Conference: Panel of Female Couples" (sponsored by The Homosexual Community Counseling Center, New York City, May 1974; participants: Barbara Sang, David Balderston, Jo League, Dorothy Levinson, Arlene Louis, Susanne Schad-Somers). *Homosexual Counseling Journal* 1:3 (July 1974):125-38.

Hall, Marny. "Sex Therapy with Lesbian Couples: a Four Stage Approach." *Journal of Homosexuality,* "Psychotherapy with Homosexual Men and Women: Integrated Identity Approaches for Clinical Practice" 14:1/2 (1987):137-56.

Hamer, Diane. "Significant Others: Lesbians and Psychoanalytic Theory." *Feminist Review* (Great Britain), "Perverse Politics: Lesbian Issues" 34 (Spring 1990):134-51.

Harris, Craig. "Black Lesbians and Gays: Empirically Speaking" (report on "The Black Women's Relationship Project: a National Survey of Black Lesbians" (Mays, Cochran, Peplau, 1986) and "Influence of Assimilation on the Psychosocial Adjustment of Black Homosexual Men" (Johnson, 1981)). *Black/Out,* "Tenth Anniversary Edition: NCBLG Celebrates Homecoming" 2:1 (Fall 1988):9-11+.

Kaufman, P.A., E. Harrison, and M.L. Hyde. "Distancing for Intimacy in Lesbian Relationships." *American Journal of Psychiatry* 141 (April 1984):530-3.

Kaye, H.E. "Lesbian Relationships." *Sexual Behavior* 1:1 (April 1971):80-7.

Kreston, J. and Claudia Bepko. "The Problem of Fusion in the Lesbian Relationship." *Family Process* 19:3 (September 1980):277-89.

Krieger, Susan. "Reply to Sandoval and Bristow and Pearn" (*Signs,* "The Lesbian Issue" 9:4 (Summer 1984):725-31, response to Krieger's "Lesbian Identity and Community: Recent Social Science Literature," *Signs* 8:1 (Autumn 1982):91-108). *Signs,* "The Lesbian Issue" 9:4 (Summer 1984):732-3.

Kulp, Denise. "One Woman's Search for the Woman of My Dreams." *off our backs* 14:2 (February 1984):12.

Kurdek, Lawrence A. "Relationship Quality of Gay and Lesbian Cohabiting Couples." *Journal of Homosexuality* 15:3/4 (1988):93-118.

------. "Relationship Quality of Gay and Lesbian Cohabiting Couples: a One-Year Follow-Up Study." *Journal of Social and Personal Relationships* 6:1 (1989):39-59.

Laner, Mary Riege. "Permanent Partner Priorities: Gay and Straight." *Journal of Homosexuality* 3:1 (Autumn 1977):21-40.

Lee, Julie. "The Lesbian Household" (part of series titled "Alternate Lifestyles"). *New Directions for Women* 4:3 (Autumn 1975):8.

"Letter from a Lover Who Didn't Make Love." *off our backs* 14:2 (February 1984):9-10.

Lindenbaum, Joyce P. "The Shattering of an Illusion: the Problem of Competition in Lesbian Relationships." *Feminist Studies* 11:1 (Spring 1985):85-104.

Lootens, Tricia. "Lovers Who Don't Make Love" (special section, "Love/Sex"). *off our backs* 14:2 (February 1984):6-8.

McCandlish, Barbara M. "Therapeutic Issues with Lesbian Couples." *Journal of Homosexuality,* "Homosexuality and Psychotherapy-- a Practitioner's Handbook of Affirmative Models" 7:2-3 (Winter-Spring 1982):71-92.

Marecek, Jeanne, Stephen E. Finn, and Mona Cardell. "Gender Roles in the Relationships of Lesbians and Gay Men." *Journal of Homosexuality* 8:2 (Winter 1982):45-50.

Martin, Del and Phyllis Lyon. "Lesbian Love and Sexuality" (excerpt from the book *Lesbian/Woman*). *Ms.* 1:1 (July 1972):74-7+.

Max, J. "A Remedy for Frustration." *Lesbian Ethics* 2:2 (Fall 1986):83.

Mays, Vickie M. "Black Women Working Together: Diversity in Same Sex Relationships." *Women's Studies International Forum* 8:1 (1985):67-71.

Meigs, Mary. "Some Thoughts About Lesbian Ethics" (in personal relationships). *Canadian Journal of Feminist Ethics* (Canada) 1:2 (Summer 1986):9-11.

Mitchell, Valery. "Using Kohut's Self Psychology in Work with Lesbian Couples." *Women & Therapy,* "Lesbianism: Affirming Nontraditional Roles" 8:1/2 (1989):157-66.

Morris, V. "Helping Lesbian Couples Cope with Jealousy." *Women & Therapy* 1 (1982):27-34.

Mountaingrove, Ruth. "A Question of Jealousy." *Common Lives/Lesbian Lives* 15/16 (Summer 1985):74-7.

Murphy, B.C. "Lesbian Couples and Their Parents -- The Effects of Perceived Parental Attitudes on the Couple." *Journal of Counseling and Development* 68:1 (1989):46-51.

Nichols, Margaret. "The Treatment of Inhibited Sexual Desire (ISD) in Lesbian Couples." *Women & Therapy,* "Therapeutic Issues with Lesbian Clients" 1:4 (Winter 1982):49-66.

Pearlman, Sarah F. "Distancing and Connectedness: Impact on Couple Formation in Lesbian Relationships." *Women & Therapy,* "Lesbianism: Affirming Nontraditional Roles" 8:1/2 (1989):77-88.

Peplau, Letitia Anne. "Research on Homosexual Couples: an Overview." *Journal of Homosexuality* 8:1 (Autumn 1983):3-8.

------. "What Homosexuals Want in a Relationship." *Psychology Today* 15:3 (March 1981):28-38.

Peplau, Letitia Anne., S. Cochran, K. Rook, and Christine Padesky. "Loving Women: Attachment and Autonomy in Lesbian Relationships." *Journal of Social Issues,* "Psychology and the Gay Community" 34:3 (1978):7-27.

Peplau, Letitia Anne, Christine Padesky, and Mykol Hamilton. "Satisfaction in Lesbian Relationships." *Journal of Homosexuality* 8:2 (Winter 1982):23-36.

Pies, Cheri. "Lesbians Choosing Children: the Use of Social Group Work in Maintaining and Strengthening the Primary Relationship" (between the two lesbian lovers). *Journal of Social Work and Human Sexuality* 5:2 (1987):79-88.

Post, Dianne. "Interindependence: a New Concept in Relationships" (opposed to codependence). *Lesbian Ethics* 4:1 (Spring 1990):88-92.

Quinlan, Judith. "Lesbian Relationships." *Resources for Feminist Research* (Canada), "The Lesbian Issue/Etre Lesbienne" 12:1(March 1983):50-1.

Reilly, Mary Ellen and Jean M. Lynch. "Power-Sharing in Lesbian Partnerships." *Journal of Homosexuality* 19:3 (1990):1-30.

Rotenberg, Lorie. "Impact of Homophobia, Heterosexism and Closetedness on Intimacy Dynamics in Lesbian Relationships." *Resources for Feminist Research* (Canada) 18:2 (June 1989):1-2.

Roth, Sallyann. "Psychotherapy with Lesbian Couples: Individual Issues, Female Socialization, and the Social Context." *Journal of Marital and Family Therapy* 11:3 (July 1985):273-86.

Rule, Jane. "Rule Making." *Lesbian Ethics* 1:1 (Fall 1984):65-9.

Sargent, Mary Lee. "Loving and Leaving Lesbians: Breaking Up and Starting Over." *off our backs* 18:4 (April 1988):18-19.

------. "Loving and Leaving Lesbians: Why We Break Up." *Women & Language* 11:1 (Winter 1987):8-11.

Schneider, Margaret S. "The Office Affair: Myth and Reality for Heterosexual and Lesbian Women Workers." *Sociological Perspectives* 27:4 (1984):443-64.

------. "The Relationships of Cohabiting Lesbian and Heterosexual Couples: a Comparison." *Psychology of Women Quarterly* 10:3 (September 1986):234-9.

Schrag, Keith G. "Relationship Therapy with Same-Gender Couples." *Family Relations* 33 (April 1984):9-12.

Schwartz, Patricia Roth. "Lesbian Love in Limbo" (discusses child abuse and incest). *off our backs* 20:6 (June 1990):18-20.

Shachar, Sandra A. and Lucia A. Gilbert. "Working Women: Role Conflicts and Coping Strategies." *Psychology of Women Quarterly* 7 (Spring 1983):244-56.

Smalley, Sondra. "Dependency Issues in Lesbian Relationships." *Journal of Homosexuality,* "Psychotherapy with Homosexual Men and Women: Integrated Identity Approaches for Clinical Practice" 14:1/2 (1987):125-36.

Stanleigh, Judy. "What Is This Thing Called Love?" *Broadside* (Canada) 3:6 (1982):7.

Stiglitz, Eloise. "Caught Between Two Worlds: the Impact of a Child on a Lesbian Couple's Relationship." *Women & Therapy,* "Motherhood: a Feminist Perspective" 10:1/2 (1990):99-116.

Vetere, V.A. "The Role of Friendship in the Development and Maintenance of Lesbian Love Relationships." *Journal of Homosexuality* 8:2 (Winter 1982):51-66.

Wallsgrove, Ruth. "Loving and Leaving Lesbians: a Response" (to May Lee Sargent, "Loving and Leaving Lesbians: Breaking Up and Starting Over," *off our backs* 18:4 (April 1988)). *off our backs* 18:7 (July 1988):14-15.

Yates, Dicey. "Mystical Unioning" ("during Lesbian sexlove"). *Lesbian Ethics* 2:3 (Summer 1987):3-32.

Zacks, E., R.J. Green, and J. Marrow. "Comparing Lesbian and Heterosexual Couples on the Circumplex Model -- an Initial Investigation." *Family Process* 27:4 (1988):471-84.

Erikson, Erik (psychoanalyst trained by Sigmund Freud):
Sohier, Raphella. "Homosexual Mutuality: Variation on a Theme by Erik Erikson." *Journal of Homosexuality* 12:2 (Winter 1985/86):25-38.

Green, G. Dorsey (co-author of *Lesbian Couples*):
Douglas, Carol Anne. "Lesbian Couples" (interview). *off our backs* 18:7 (July 1988):12-13.

Religion (see also: Jewish Lesbians; Nuns; Spirituality)

Berry, Delores. "Come Out, Come Out . . . " (African-American lesbian minister). *Women: a Journal of Liberation* 5:2 (1977):47-9.

Boyd, Malcolm and Virginia Ramey Mollenkott. "Homosexual Love: an Explanation/an Exploration." *Insight: a Quarterly of Lesbian/Gay Christian Opinion* 3:4 (Fall 1979):5-8.

Christianity and Crisis, "Homosexuality," vol. 37, nos. 9&10, May 30 & June 13, 1977.

Clark, J. Michael, Joanne Carlson Brown, and Lorna M. Hochstein. "Institutional Religion and Gay/Lesbian Oppression." *Marriage and Family Review* 14:3-4 (1989):265-84.

Comstock, Gary David. "Aliens in the Promised Land?: Keynote Address for the 1986 National Gathering of the United Church of Christ's Coalition for Lesbian/Gay Concerns." *Journal of Homosexuality,* "Homosexuality and Religion" 18:3/4 (1989/1990):133-44.

D'Angelo, Mary Rose. "Women Partners in the New Testament" (as belonging to "lesbian continuum"; e.g., Tryphaena and Tryphosa, Evodia and Syntyche, Martha and Mary). *Journal of Feminist Studies in Religion* 6:1 (Spring 1990):65-86.

"Deacons Suspended" (lesbians in the Anglican Church of Canada). *Christian Century* 103 (April 2, 1986):322.

"East Germany: Lesbians Take Refuge in the Church" (lesbians legally allowed to meet under the auspices of the Protestant Church; trans. and excerpted from Swiss feminist quarterly, *Frauenzitig* 23 (Fall 1987)). *Connexions,* "Feminism and Religion" 28 (1988-89):28.

Fischer, Clare B. "A Bonding of Choice: Values and Identity Among Lesbian and Gay Religious Leaders." *Journal of Homosexuality,* "Homosexuality and Religion" 18:3/4 (1989/90):145-74.

Foloyan, Ayofemi. "National Black Gay and Lesbian Leadership Forum: a Conference Report" (Atlanta, Georgia, February 1990). *off our backs* 20:4 (April 1990):2-3.

"Gays on the March" (unsympathetic cover story on the surge of gay pride/visibility). *Time* 106 (September 8, 1975):32-43.

Gearhart, Sally. "The Lesbian and God-the-Father." *Radical Religion* 1:2 (Spring 1974):19-21.

"God, Gays, & the Media." *off our backs* 13:2 (February 1983):16.

Heyward, Carter. "Heterosexist Theology: Being Above It All." *Journal of Feminist Studies in Religion* 3:1 (Spring 1987):29-38.

Heyward, Carter, Mary Hunt, Bernadette J. Brooten, Claire B. Fischer, Delores Williams, and Evelyn Torton Beck. "Roundtable Discussion: Lesbianism and Feminist Theology." *Journal of Feminist Studies in Religion* 2:2 (Fall 1986):95-106.

Hiltner, Seward. "Neglected Phenomenon of Female Homosexuality" (review of recent literature, and argument for tolerance and to remember that there are female as well as male homosexuals). *Christian Century* 91:21 (May 29, 1974):591-3.

Hunt, Mary. "Toward a Gay Christian Ethic" (one of several short articles on this topic). *Insight: a Quarterly of Lesbian/Gay Christian Opinion* 3:2 (Spring-Summer 1979):5-12.

Journal of Homosexuality, "Homosexuality and Religion," vol. 18, nos. 3/4, 1989/1990.

JT. "Bishop Bars Dignity" (Catholic lesbian and gay group, in Brooklyn, New York). *off our backs* 17:4 (April 1987):4.

Kahn, Rabbi Yoel H. "Judaism and Homosexuality: The Traditionalist/Progressive Debate." *Journal of Homosexuality,* "Homosexuality and Religion" 18:3/4 (1989/90):47-82.

Kratt, Mary. "The Church: 'Always Resistant to Change'" (lesbian priest). *Christian Century* 97 (February 27, 1980):237-8.

Krody, Nancy E. "An Open Lesbian Looks at the Church" (why she stays in the church, which she finds oppressive). *Foundations: Baptist Journal of History and Theology* 20:2 (April-June 1977):148-62.

------. "Woman, Lesbian, Feminist, Christian." *Christianity and Crisis,* "Homosexuality" 37:9&10 (May 30 & June 13, 1977):131-5.

"The Lesbian Priest." *Time* 109 (January 24, 1977):58.

McCoy, Renée. "Church for a Different Community" (African-American lesbian/gay alternative churches, and homophobia of the traditional African-American church). *Black/Out,* "We Are Family" 2:2 (Summer 1989):60-1.

McDonald, Tracy. "Gay Catholics Protest" (Cardinal John O'Connor's banning of special mass for gay Catholic group Dignity). *off our backs* 17:5 (May 1987):16.

Matter, E. Ann. "Discourses of Desire: Sexuality and Christian Women's Visionary Narratives." *Journal of Homosexuality,* "Homosexuality and Religion" 18:3/4 (1989/1990):119-32.

------. "My Sister, My Spouse: Woman-Identified Women in Medieval Christianity." *Journal of Feminist Studies in Religion* 2:2 (Fall 1986):81-93.

Maynard, Rona. "Does a Lesbian Belong in the Pulpit?" *Chatelaine* 62:5 (May 1989):125+.

Meier, Peg. "Opening the Door." *MPLS-St. Paul Magazine* 13 (January 1985):102-4.

Mendola, Mary. "Catholic Lesbian Visible, Vocal." *National Catholic Reporter* 19 (May 13, 1983):15.

Naheed, Kishwar (trans. *Diva* editorial board). "Of Lesbianism" (in relation to Pakistan and Muslim religious texts). *Diva: a Quarterly of South Asian Women* 1:2 (1988):24-9.

"New York: Cathedral Demo" (St. Patrick's Cathedral, New York City, December 1989). *off our backs* 20:3 (March 1990):13.

Nugent, Robert and Jeannine Grammick. "Homosexuality: Protestant, Catholic, and Jewish Issues; a Fishbone Tale." *Journal of Homosexuality,* "Homosexuality and Religion" 18:3/4 (1989/1990):7-46.

"Ordination of Gays" (news briefs about various U.S. Christian and Jewish organizations). *off our backs* 20:8 (August/September 1990):6.

Ritter, Kathleen Y. and Craig W. O'Neill. "Moving Through Loss: the Spiritual Journey of Gay Men and Lesbian Women" (transforming relationships with traditional religion and mental health professionals). *Journal of Counseling and Development,* "Gay, Lesbian, and Bisexual Issues in Counseling" 68:1 (September-October 1989):9-15.

Rumscheidt, Barbara. "Institutionalizing Christian Heterosexism in
    Maritime Conference of the United Church of Canada."
    Resources for Feminist Research (Canada), "Confronting
    Heterosexuality/Confronter l'hétérosexualité" 19:3&4
    (September/December 1990):75-80.

Ryan. "O'Connor-Gay Meeting a First" (Archbishop John J. O'Connor).
    National Catholic Reporter 20 (September 28, 1984):9.

Saunders, Martha J. "Sexuality, Justice and Feminist Ethics." *Resources
    for Feminist Research* (Canada), "Confronting
    Heterosexuality/Confronter l'hétérosexualité" 19:3&4
    (September/December 1990):33-9.

Shulman, Sheila. "Some Thoughts on Biblical Prophecy and Feminist
    Vision." *Gossip* (Great Britain) 6 (1988):68-79.

Smith, Andy. "Journeys in Peacemaking: the Eighth Evangelical
    Women's Caucus Conference" (lesbian participation in Christian
    conference, Chicago, July 1988). *off our backs* 19:1 (January
    1989):8; note: cover reads 18:11 (December 1988).

Thomas, Paul K. "Marriage Annulments for Gay Men and Lesbian
    Women: New Canonical and Psychological Insight." *The Jurist*
    43:2 (Spring 1983):318-42.

"UUA Endorses Gay Rites" (Unitarian Universalist Association approves
    unions in place of heterosexual marriages). *Christian Century*
    101:25 (August 15-22, 1984):768-9.

Way, Peggy. "Homosexual Counseling As a Learning Ministry."
    Christianity and Crisis, "Homosexuality" 37:9&10 (May 30 &
    June 13, 1977):123-31.

Anzaldúa, Gloria (Chicana writer):
Culpepper, Emily Erwin. "New Tools for Theology: Writings by
    Women of Color" (Audre Lorde, Pat Parker, Beverly Smith,
    Gloria Anzaldúa; never explicitly discusses lesbianism). *Journal
    of Feminist Studies in Religion* 4:2 (Fall 1988):39-50.

<u>Armstrong amendment</u> (exempts religious institutions from anti-
discrimination laws):
"Congress Undermines Gay Rights." *off our backs* 18:10 (November
1988):7.

DAR. "Senate Threatens DC" (Washington, D.C.). *off our backs*
18:8 (August-September 1988):5.

<u>Brin, Deborah</u> (rabbi):
"Lesbian Rabbi Resigns" (after coming out and feeling "oppressive"
working environment develop; Downsview, Ontario, Canada).
off our backs 20:10 (November 1990):9.

<u>A Challenge to Love: Gay and Lesbian Catholics in the Church</u>:
"Another Book Ban" (by the Vatican). *Christian Century* 101:19
(May 30, 1984):568.

Day, Mark R. "How Critics Rated *Challenge to Love.*" *National
Catholic Reporter* 20 (May 18, 1984):23.

<u>Clark, Joan</u> (fired from the Board of Global Ministries of the United
Methodist Church, for lesbianism):
Bunch, Charlotte. "A Tradition of Human Rights in the Balance."
Ms. 8:4 (October 1984):29.

Clark, Joan L. "Coming Out: the Process and Its Price." *Christianity
and Crisis* 39:10 (June 11, 1979):149-53.

Clark, Joan L. and Madge Rinehardt. "Silencing of Gay Issues in the
Christian Churches." *Insight: a Quarterly of Lesbian/Gay
Christian Opinion* 3:3 (Summer 1979):5-13.

"In the Matter of Joan L. Clark." *Christianity and Crisis* 39:10 (June
11, 1979):146-8.

<u>Curran, Charles</u> (priest):

Bader, Eleanor. "Church Wages War on Dissenters" (including Archbishop Raymond Hunthausen, for allowing gay rights group to hold Mass; Father Charles Curran, for not strongly condemning homosexuality). *New Directions for Women* 15 (November-December 1986):1+.

<u>Daly, Mary</u> (philosopher and theologian):

Cosstick, Vicky. "Mary Daly, Feminist Philosopher." *New Directions for Women* 8:1 (Anniversary 1979):1+.

Heyward, Carter. "Ruether and Daly: Theologians Speaking and Sparking, Building and Burning." *Christianity and Crisis* 39 (April 2, 1979):66-72.

<u>de la Cruz, Sor Juana Inez</u> (17th century Mexican nun and poet):

"Sor Juana: Trials and Triumphs in the Convent" (trans. from Venezuelan bimonthly *La Mala Vida* (May/June 1988)). *Connexions,* "Feminism and Religion" 28 (1988-89):4-6.

<u>Denman, Rose Mary</u> (United Methodist minister):

"Lesbian on Suspension." *Christianity Today* 31 (October 2, 1987):58.

Starr, Mark. "A Methodist on Trial: the Bishop and a Lesbian." *Newsweek* 110 (September 7, 1987):62.

<u>Eyega, Zeinab</u> (Sudanese feminist living in exile):

Salomyn, Shay. "Black Women in Sudan." *off our backs* 20:3 (March 1990):8.

<u>Heyward, Carter</u> (Episcopalian priest):

Saz, Marnette. "Pioneer Priest Assesses Last 20 Years." *New Directions for Women* 13:4 (July/August 1984):5.

Hunthausen, Raymond (archbishop):
Bader, Eleanor. "Church Wages War on Dissenters" (including
    Archbishop Raymond Hunthausen, for allowing gay rights group
    to hold Mass; Father Charles Curran, for not strongly
    condemning homosexuality). *New Directions for Women* 15
    (November-December 1986):1+.

Johnson, Sonia (ex-Mormon and writer):
Bowen, Angela, Jacqui Alexander, Jennifer Abod, and Terri Ortiz.
    "Taking Issue with Sonia" (response to interview with Sonia
    Johnson in *Sojourner* 13:5 (January 1988)). *Sojourner* 13:6
    (February 1988):14-15.

Lorde, Audre (African-American writer):
Culpepper, Emily Erwin. "New Tools for Theology: Writings by
    Women of Color" (draws on works of Audre Lorde, Pat Parker,
    Beverly Smith, Gloria Anzaldúa, but never explicitly discusses
    lesbianism). *Journal of Feminist Studies in Religion* 4:2 (Fall
    1988):39-50.

Parker, Pat (African-American poet):
Culpepper, Emily Erwin. "New Tools for Theology: Writings by
    Women of Color" (draws on works of Audre Lorde, Pat Parker,
    Beverly Smith, Gloria Anzaldúa, but never explicitly discusses
    lesbianism). *Journal of Feminist Studies in Religion* 4:2 (Fall
    1988):39-50.

Ruether, Rosemary Radford (theologian):
Heyward, Carter. "Ruether and Daly: Theologians Speaking and
    Sparking, Building and Burning." *Christianity and Crisis* 39
    (April 2, 1979):66-72.

Smith, Beverly (African-American activist and writer):
Culpepper, Emily Erwin. "New Tools for Theology: Writings by
    Women of Color" (draws on works of Audre Lorde, Pat Parker,
    Beverly Smith, Gloria Anzaldúa, but never explicitly discusses
    lesbianism). *Journal of Feminist Studies in Religion* 4:2 (Fall
    1988):39-50.

<u>Ziegler, Karen</u> (minister):

Chasin, Susan T. "Karen Ziegler: the Journey of a Lesbian Pastor."
Visibilities 4:3 (May/June 1990):8-11.

Reproduction (see also: Adoption; Child Custody; Children of
Lesbians; Foster Care; Parenting)

Breeze, Nancy. "Who's Going to Rock the Petri Dish? For Feminists
Who Have Considered Parthenogenesis When the Movement Is
Not Enough." *Trivia* 4 (Spring 1984):43-8.

CAD. "Dr. Strange Love" (news briefs about anti-lesbian/gay
discrimination in U.S. and Great Britain). *off our backs* 8:3
(March 1978):10.

Coffey, Mary Anne. "Of Father Born: a Lesbian Feminist Critique of the
Ontario Law Reform Commission Recommendations on
Artificial Insemination." *Canadian Journal of Women and the
Law* (Canada) 1:2 (1986):424-33.

------. "Seizing the Means of Reproduction: Proposal for an Exploratory
Study of Alternative Fertilization and Parenting Strategies
Among Lesbian Women." *Resources for Feminist Research*
(Canada) 18:3 (September 1989):76-9.

Cougar, Jesse. "The Selfish Sperm Theory." *Lesbian Ethics* 4:1 (Spring
1990):28-43.

Dellenbaugh, Anne G. "She Who Is and Is Not Yet: an Essay on
Parthenogenesis." *Trivia* 1 (Fall 1982):43-63.

Edwards, Ryn. "The Choreographing of Reproductive DNA"
(parthenogenesis). *Lesbian Ethics* 4:1 (Spring 1990):44-51.

Eskenazi, B., C. Pies, A. Newstetter, C. Shepard, and K. Pearson. "HIV
Serology in Artificially Inseminated Lesbians." *Journal of
Acquired Immune Deficiency Syndromes* 2:2 (1989):187-93.

Ettelbrick, Paula L. "Under the Law -- Does a Sperm Donor Have Parental Rights to a Lesbian Couple's Child?" *Visibilities* 2:2 (March/April 1988):17.

------. "Under the Law -- How Can We Create a Lesbian Family?" *Visibilities* 2:3 (May/June 1988):16-17.

------. "Under the Law -- Reproductive Choice." *Visibilities* 3:3 (May/June 1989):16-17.

Golombok, Susan and John Rust. "The Warnok Report and Single Women: What About the Children?" (criticism of decision to not sanction artificial insemination for single heterosexual women and lesbians). *Journal of Medical Ethics* 12 (December 1986):182-6.

Herman, Ellen. "The Romance of Lesbian Motherhood." *Sojourner* 13:7 (March 1988):12-13.

Higgs, Roger, et al. "Lesbian Couples: Should Help Extend to Aid?" *Journal of Medical Ethics* 4 (June 1978):91-5.

"Lesbian Births Stir Parliament Debate" (donor insemination). *Medical World News* 19 (February 6, 1978):7-8.

"Lesbian Couple Are Parents by Artificial Insemination." *Jet* 55 (February 15, 1979):40-1.

Liljesfraund, Petra. "Children without Fathers: Handling the Anonymous Donor Question." *Out/Look* 1:3 (Fall 1988):24-9.

Meredith, Diana. "Lesbians and Abortion." *Broadside* (Canada) 4:2 (1982):7.

Moira, Fran. "Lesbian Self-Insemination: Life Without Father." *off our backs* 12:1 (January 1982):12-13.

"Ova Easy" (response by Women's Reproductive Rights Information Campaign to the Warnock Report, British government commission on reproductive technologies). *Connexions,* "Changing Technology" 15 (Winter 1985):8.

Pies, Cheri and Francine Hornstein. "Baby M and the Gay Family." *Out/Look* 1:1 (Spring 1988):79-85.

Raymond, Chris Anne. "'Ticking Clocks' and Changing Mores" (artificial insemination). *JAMA, The Journal of the American Medical Association* 258 (October 16, 1987):2025.

Rosser, Sue V. "Multiple Perspectives: Teaching About Sexuality and Reproduction." *Women's Studies Quarterly* 12:4 (Winter 1984):31-3.

Shapiro, E. Donald and Lisa Schultz. "Single-Sex Families: the Impact of Birth Innovations Upon Traditional Family Notions." *Journal of Family Law* 24:2 (January 1986):271-81.

Shulman, Sheila. "Lesbian Feminists and the Great Baby Con." *Gossip* (Great Britain) 1 (1986):68-90; also *Spinster* (Great Britain) 4 (1980).

Silveira, Jeanette. "Why Men Oppress Women" (marxist-lesbian/feminist discussion of reproduction, misogyny and a lesbian future). *Lesbian Ethics* 1:1 (Fall 1984):34-56.

"Sit-in" (at *London Evening News,* protesting articles opposing lesbian artificial insemination). *off our backs* 8:2 (February 1978):3.

Sitka, Chris. "Lesbian Rebirth" (ancient matriarchy, contemporary technology, and parthenogenesis). *Lesbian Ethics* 4:1 (Spring 1990):4-27.

"Sperm Smorgasbord: Switzerland" (trans. from *Frauenzitig,* Swiss bimonthly, November 1988). *Connexions,* "Reproductive Technologies" 32 (1990):21.

Stern, Susan. "Lesbian Insemination." *Coevolution Quarterly* (Summer 1980):108-16.

Sutton, Stuart A. "The Lesbian Family: Rights in Conflict Under the Uniform Parentage Act." *Golden Gate University Law Review* 10:1 (1980):1007-41.

Towey, Shawn. "Reproductive Rights National Network Meets: Racism and Heterosexism Discussed" (Reproductive Rights National Network Conference, Philadelphia, Pennsylvania, April 1983). *off our backs* 13:7 (July 1983):15.

Tremor. "The Hundredth Lezzie: Evolution by Design." *Trivia* 6 (Winter 1985):33-7.

Rural Lesbians

Amana, Rue. "Becoming a 'Real' Dyke: Employment and Housing" (moving out of cities as the lesbian dream; returning to cities to work with People With AIDS). *Canadian Woman Studies* (Canada), "Women & Housing" 11:2 (Fall 1990):43+.

Copper, Baba, with Peggy Cleveland. "Country Women Talking." *Common Lives/Lesbian Lives* 2 (Winter 1981):17-25.

D'Augelli, Anthony R. "Social Support Patterns of Lesbian Women in a Rural Helping Network." *Journal of Rural Community Psychology* 8:1 (1987):12-22.

------. "Lesbian Women in a Rural Helping Network: Exploring Informal Helping Resources." *Women & Therapy,* "Lesbianism: Affirming Nontraditional Roles" 8:1/2 (1989):119-30.

Pas, Faux. "Lesbian Separatism: What Do We Mean?" (letter to "A Readers' Forum -- Separatism: Beyond the Debate," questioning how "radical" different varieties of separatism are). *Lesbian Ethics* 3:2 (Fall 1988):10-11.

Poppe, Terri. "Women on the Land." *off our backs* 7:2 (March 1977):2+.

White, Toni. "Casa Nuestra: Oasis for Desert Dykes" (Tucson, Arizona). *off our backs* 11:2 (February 1981):24.

Sadomasochism (see S/M)

Science and Technology

Hooper, Judith. "Gay Origins" (Kinsey Institute Study, *Sexual Preference*). *Omni* 4 (March 1982):22+.

Segerberg, Marsha. "Re/de/e/volving: Feminist Theories of Science" (symposia sponsored by the Association for Women in Science, Houston, Texas, January 1979). *off our backs* 9:3 (March 1979):12.

Terry, Jennifer. "Lesbians Under the Medical Gaze: Scientists Search for Remarkable Differences" (1930s). *Journal of Sex Research* 27:3 (1990):317-39.

Hughes, Holly (performance artist):
Schneider, Rebecca. "Holly Hughes: Polymorphous Perversity and the Lesbian Scientist" (interview with performance artist). *Drama Review* 33 (Spring 1989):171+.

Science Fiction/Fantasy

Dykewomon, Elana. "Notes for a Magazine: Lesbian Visions, Fantasy, Science Fiction." *Sinister Wisdom,* "Lesbian Visions, Fantasy, Science Fiction" 34 (Spring 1988):3-5.

Garber, Eric. "Uranian Worlds: the Best of Gay Sci-Fi and Fantasies." *Out/Look* 1:4 (Winter 1989):83-5.

Hollerith, J.P. "Reading, Raging and Writing: Some Thoughts on Speculative Fiction and Radical Feminism." *Gossip* (Great Britain) 4 (no date):51-8.

Sinister Wisdom, "Lesbian Visions, Fantasy, Science Fiction," no. 34, Spring 1988.

Yount, Rena. "Women in Utopia." *Hot Wire* 2:3 (July 1986):36-8+.

<u>Bradley, Marion Zimmer</u> (writer):
Kimpel, Richard. "The Mists of Avalon?/Die Nebel von Avalon: Marion Zimmer Bradley's German Bestseller." *Journal of American Culture* 9 (Fall 1986):25-8.

<u>Elgin, Suzette Haden</u> (linguist and writer):
Murphy, Patrick D. "Feminism Faces the Fantastic" (Suzette Haden Elgin's *Native Tongue,* Mary Mackey's *The Last Warrior,* Joanna Russ' *Extraordinary People*). *Women's Studies* 14:2 (1987):91-9.

<u>Forrest, Katherine V.</u> (writer):
Zaki, Hoda M. "Utopia and Ideology in *Daughters of a Coral Dawn* [by Katherine V. Forrest] and Contemporary Feminist Utopia." *Women's Studies* 14:2 (1987):119-33.

Levin, Jenifer. "Aboard the *Scorpio IV* -- and Other Places -- with Katherine V. Forrest." *Visibilities* 2:4 (July/August 1988):4-7.

<u>Gearhart, Sally</u> (writer):
Sturgis, Susanna J. "Discovering the Underground: an Interview with Sally Gearhart." *off our backs* 10:1 (January 1980):24-5+.

<u>Mackey, Mary</u> (writer):
Murphy, Patrick D. "Feminism Faces the Fantastic" (Suzette Haden Elgin's *Native Tongue,* Mary Mackey's *The Last Warrior,* Joanna Russ' *Extraordinary People*). *Women's Studies* 14:2 (1987):91-9.

<u>Russ, Joanna</u> (writer):
Murphy, Patrick D. "Feminism Faces the Fantastic" (Suzette Haden Elgin's *Native Tongue,* Mary Mackey's *The Last Warrior,* Joanna Russ' *Extraordinary People*). *Women's Studies* 14:2 (1987):91-9.

<u>Wittig, Monique</u> (French critic and writer):
Rosenfeld, Marthe. "Language and the Vision of a Lesbian-Feminist Utopia in Wittig's *Les Guérillères.*" *Frontiers* 6:1-2 (Spring-Summer 1981):6-9.

<u>Separatism</u> (see also: Rural Lesbians)

Addison, Lois Anne. "Separatism Revisited" (response to Adrienne Rich, *Sinister Wisdom* 18). *Sinister Wisdom* 21 (1982):29-34.

Anderson, Jacqueline. "Separation in Black: a Personal Journey" (African-American lesbian separatism). *Lesbian Ethics* 3:2 (Fall 1988):78-81.

Anne, Sheila. "Womyn or Children First? Lesbian Space Elusive at East Coast Fest: Separatist Positive Perspective" (controversy over baby boys attending and lack of wheelchair accessibility at the 1st annual East Coast Lesbian Festival in West Stockbridge, Massachusetts, September 1989). *off our backs* 19:9 (October 1989):27-8.

Ayres, Tara, and Lori Saxe. "Politics, Vision and Play: Some Thoughts on the Lesbian Separatist Conference" (First Annual Lesbian Separatist Conference and Gathering in southeastern Wisconsin, June 1988). *Lesbian Ethics* 3:2 (Fall 1988):106-15.

Boucher, Sandy. "Men: Living Without Them -- Three Who've Tried It and Liked It." *Ms.* 4:4 (October 1975):69-70.

Bowles, Sheila. "Lesbian Separatism *for* Ourselves" (letter to "A Readers' Forum -- Separatism: Beyond the Debate," about separatist/non-separatist split among lesbians). *Lesbian Ethics* 3:2 (Fall 1988):20-1.

Braeman, Elizabeth. "Womyn or Children First? The Debate Continues: In Defense of Separatists" (regarding controversy over interracial lesbian couple who took their young son to the East Coast Lesbian Festival, West Stockbridge, Massachusetts, September 1989). *off our backs* 19:10 (November 1989):20.

Brooke. "The State of Feminism" (lesbian and straight separatism as bad for the movement). *off our backs*, "Ten Years Growing!" 10:2 (February 1980):8+.

Brunet, Ariane and Louise Turcotte. "Separatism and Radicalism: an Analysis of the Differences and Similarities" (U.S. separatism and French Canadian radical lesbianism). *Lesbian Ethics* 2:1 (Spring 1986):41-9.

Bunch, Charlotte. "Forum: Learning from Lesbian Separatism." *Ms.* 5:5 (November 1976):60-1+.

Chamberlain, Pia. "/Separatism/ Another Look." *Common Lives/Lesbian Lives* 15/16 (Summer 1985):69-73.

Charoula. "Bedford Hills: a Lesbian Separatist View" (New York's only women-only prison). *off our backs* 8:4 (April 1978):14-15.

Chrystos. "Nidishenok (Sisters)." *Maenad*, "The Lesbian/Heterosexual Split" 2:2 (Winter 1982):23-32.

Claire, Roxanne. "Compulsory Heterosexuality and Separatism." *ISIS International Bulletin* 21 (1981):24-5.

Claudia. "about class" (letter to "A Readers' Forum -- Separatism: Beyond the Debate," calling for all lesbians to acknowledge class background and bias). *Lesbian Ethics* 3:2 (Fall 1988):12.

CLIT (Collective Lesbian International Terrors). "CLIT Statement #3" (militant feminism and separatism, with discussion of classism and racism). *off our backs* 6:7 (October 1976):10-11.

Copper, Baba. "We Have to Ask the Question: What Is Happening?" (separatism and parenting). *Common Lives/Lesbian Lives* 9 (Fall 1983):22-32.

DancingFire, Laura Rose. "On Lawyering, Passing and Pornography." *Sinister Wisdom,* "Passing" 35 (Summer/Fall 1988):72-4.

Dervin, Dan. "Making Utopia Out of Dystopia: the Role of Men as Poison Containers in Radical Feminism." *Journal of Psychohistory* 16:4 (1989):427-43.

Desmoines, Harriet. "Notes for a Magazine II" (founding concepts for *Sinister Wisdom*; discusses politically left revolutionary politics, racism, and classism). *Sinister Wisdom* 1:1 (Summer 1976):27-34.

Dixon, Janet. "Separatism" (excerpt from *Radical Records: Thirty Years of Lesbian and Gay History*). *Spare Rib* (Great Britain) 192 (June 1988):6-11.

Dominy, Michèle D. "Lesbian-Feminist Gender Conceptions: Separatism in Christchurch, New Zealand." *Signs* 11:2 (Winter 1986):274-89.

Douglas, Carol Anne. "Toward a Feminist Ethic Based on Sex Class Consciousness." *off our backs* 15:11 (December 1985):14-15.

Dworkin, Andrea. "Biological Superiority: the World's Most Dangerous and Deadly Idea." *Heresies #6,* 2:2 (Summer 1978):46-51.

Dykewomon, Elana. "Notes for a Magazine: a Dyke Geography" (introduction to Dykewomon's first issue as editor of *Sinister Wisdom*). *Sinister Wisdom* 33 (Fall 1987):3-7.

Edelson, Carol and Eugenia B. "No Victory in a Vacuum" (response to CLIT Statement #3, same issue, pp.10-11). *off our backs* 6:7 (October 1976):12-13.

Frances. "The Soul Selects: a New Separate Way" (radicalesbianism, feminism, and lesbianism). *off our backs*, "Women Loving: 2" 2:5 (January 1972):7.

Frye, Marilyn. "Some Reflections on Separatism and Power." *Sinister Wisdom* 6 (Summer 1978):30-9.

------. "The Possibility of Community." *Lesbian Ethics* 4:1 (Spring 1990):84-7.

Gilfillan, Caroline. "Lesbian Summer Camp" (Danish women's liberation movement group, "The Redstockings," hold annual camp on the island of Femø; article about first year of lesbian separatist camp simultaneous with camp open to heterosexuals). *Spare Rib* (Great Britain) 64 (November 1977):14-15.

Harper, Jorjet. "Accessibility, Male Children an Issue at Lesbian Fest (First Annual East Coast Lesbian Festival, West Stockbridge, Massachusetts, Summer 1989). *Hot Wire* 6:1 (January 1990):29+.

Hayes, Lois. "Separatism and Disobedience: the Seneca Peace Encampment." *Radical America* 17:4 (1983):55-64.

Henry, Alice. "Separatism, Racism, Lesbianism" (discussed by Barbara Smith, Minnie Bruce Pratt, Elly Bulkin, and Barbara Cameron at the National Women's Studies Association Conference, Storrs, Connecticut, May 31-June 4, 1981). *off our backs* 11:6 (July 1981):5-6+.

Hoagland, Sarah Lucia. "Lesbian Separatism: an Empowering Reality." *Gossip* (Great Britain) 6 (1988):24-36; also *Sinister Wisdom*, "Lesbian Visions, Fantasy, Science Fiction" 34 (Spring 1988):23-33.

Japenga, Ann. "Refusing to Smile at/Cook for/Kowtow to Men: the Separatist Revival." *Out/Look #8*, 2:4 (Spring 1990):78-83.

Johnson, Angela. "Womyn or Children First? The Debate Continues: There Must Be a Better Way" (regarding controversy over interracial lesbian couple who took their young son to the East Coast Lesbian Festival, West Stockbridge, Massachusetts, September 1989). *off our backs* 19:10 (November 1989):20.

Johnson, Dotty. "Womyn or Children First? Lesbian Space Elusive at East Coast Fest" (regarding controversy over presence of male workers and an interracial lesbian couple who took their young son to the East Coast Lesbian Festival, West Stockbridge, Massachusetts, September 1989). *off our backs* 19:9 (October 1989):27.

Lee, Anna. "For the Love of Separatism" (African-American lesbian separatism). *Lesbian Ethics* 3:2 (Fall 1988):54-63.

------. "The Tired Old Question of Male Children." *Lesbian Ethics* 1:2 (Spring 1985):106-8.

Leonard, Vicki. "I'm OK . . . You're Not" (treatment of heterosexuals at New York Sexuality Conference, 1987). *off our backs* 17:7 (July 1987):12+.

Lesbian, Amber. "Made in Amazon Nation." *Lesbian Ethics* 2:2 (Fall 1986):84-5.

Lettice. "Lesbian Ethics Workshop: Separatism." *Gossip* (Great Britain) 6 (1988):107-10.

Louise, Vivienne. "Genuine Desire" (letter to "A Readers' Forum -- Separatism: Beyond the Debate," asking "Why don't white lesbians have a genuine desire to learn from lesbians of African descent?"). *Lesbian Ethics* 3:2 (Fall 1988):5-8.

Maenad, "The Lesbian/Heterosexual Split," vol. 2, no. 2, Winter 1982.

Man, Killa. "Trying Hard to Forget All I've Known" (social control of women and false consciousness of many lesbians; written by a member of Collective Lesbian International Terrors (CLIT)). *off our backs* 4:8 (July 1974):20-1.

Mara, Jane. "A Lesbian Perspective." *Women & Therapy,* "Women Changing Therapy: New Assessments, Values and Strategies in Feminist Therapy" 2:2/3 (Summer/Fall 1983):145-55.

Maria, C. "Separatism Is Not a Luxury: Some Thoughts on Separatism and Class." *Lesbian Ethics* 4:1 (Spring 1990):66-76.

Marsha. "Cabbages and Kings" (response to responses to CLIT Statement #3, *off our backs* 6:7 (October 1976):10-13). *off our backs* 6:8 (November 1976):17-18.

Mudd, Karen. "Lesbian Separatism: Herstory and Theory." *off our backs,* "National Women's Studies Association -- Feminist Education: Quality and Equality" 13:8 (August-September 1983):10.

Parks, Adrienne. "Great Southeastern Lesbians" (conference, Atlanta, Georgia, May 1975). *off our backs* 5:6 (July 1975):25.

Pas, Faux. "Lesbian Separatism: What Do We Mean?" (letter to "A Readers' Forum -- Separatism: Beyond the Debate," questioning how "radical" (root) different varieties of separatism are). *Lesbian Ethics* 3:2 (Fall 1988):10-11.

Penelope, Julia. "The Mystery of Lesbians: I." *Lesbian Ethics* 1:1 (Fall 1984):7-33; also *Gossip* (Great Britain) 1 (1986):9-45.

------. "The Mystery of Lesbians: II." *Lesbian Ethics* 1:2 (Spring 1985):29-67; also *Gossip* (Great Britain) 2 (1986):16-68.

------. "The Mystery of Lesbians: III." *Lesbian Ethics* 1:3 (Fall 1985):3-15; also *Gossip* (Great Britain) 3 (no date):23-39.

------. "Women - and Lesbian - Only Spaces: Thought Into Action." *off our backs* 20:5 (May 1990):14-16.

Poppe, Terri. "Women on the Land." *off our backs* 7:2 (March 1977):2+.

Rich, Adrienne. "Notes for a Magazine: What Does Separatism Mean?" *Sinister Wisdom* 18 (1981):83-91.

sardyke, lahl. "joyous separatism" (letter to "A Readers' Forum -- Separatism: Beyond the Debate" about whom one upsets by having short or long hair). *Lesbian Ethics* 3:2 (Fall 1988):8-10.

Shinell, Grace. "In These Pregnant Times: Lesbian Parturition." *Maenad,* "The Lesbian/Heterosexual Split" 2:2 (Winter 1982):108-11.

Silveira, Jeannette. "Strategy and Class" (letter to "A Readers' Forum -- Separatism: Beyond the Debate," about how to use resources of separatists of all classes to revolutionary ends, rather than accusing some of not being true separatists because of where and with whom they work). *Lesbian Ethics* 3:2 (Fall 1988):22-5.

Smith, Barbara. (letter responding to Adrienne Rich, *Sinister Wisdom* 18). *Sinister Wisdom* 20 (1982):100-4.

Smith, Margaret 'Chase'. "Crookery" (theft as a way to make a living and challenge the heteropatriarchy). *Lesbian Ethics* 3:2 (Fall 1988):48-53.

Spinster, Sidney. "Biophilic Lesbian Separatism: Lesbian Freedom in Our Lifetimes." *Lesbian Ethics* 2:2 (Fall 1986):3-21.

------. (letter responding to Adrienne Rich, *Sinister Wisdom* 18). *Sinister Wisdom* 20 (1982):104-5.

Stanley, Julia P. "Notes on the Edge" (lesbian revolution as *the* revolution; lesbians in relation to other world revolutions). *WIN: Peace and Freedom Through Nonviolent Action,* "Lesbian Culture" 11:22 (June 26, 1975):8-10.

Stato, Joanne. "14th Michigan Womyn's Music Festival" (who attended, what was discussed: including lesbians of color, racism, S/M, disability, and music). *off our backs* 19:9 (October 1989):20-1.

------. "On Women's Space" (at Michigan Womyn's Music Festival and elsewhere). *off our backs* 20:9 (October 1990):14.

T., Geraldine. "Practicing Separatism" (letter to "A Readers' Forum -- Separatism: Beyond the Debate"). *Lesbian Ethics* 3:2 (Fall 1988):3-5.

Trebilcot, Joyce. "In Partial Response to Those Who Worry That Separatism May be a Political Cop-Out: an Expanded Definition of Activism." *Gossip* (Great Britain) 3 (no date):82-4; also, an earlier version in *off our backs* 16:5 (May 1986):13.

Valeska, Lucia. "The Future of Female Separatism." *Quest*, "Theories of Revolution" 2:2 (Fall 1975):2-16.

Yates, Dicey. "Dear Dyke Separatist Strangers" (posits that only dyke separatist community can save the Earth from destruction by men). *Lesbian Ethics* 3:2 (Fall 1988):26-47.

Dobkin, Alix (musician):
Claudia, Karen. "Alix Dobkin as Separatist/Symbol/Songwriter." *off our backs* 18:2 (February 1988):14-15.

Hoagland, Sarah (philosopher):
Collis, Rose. "For Lesbians Only -- an Interview with Sarah Hoagland." *Spare Rib* (Great Britain) 197 (December 1988/January 1989):31.

Picard, Jane (filmmaker):
Willer, Marilyn. "An Interview with Jane Picard." *Maenad*, "The Lesbian/Heterosexual Split" 2:2 (Winter 1982):87-97.

Rich, Adrienne (writer):
Gentile, Mary. "Adrienne Rich and Separatism: the Language of Multiple Realities." *Maenad*, The Lesbian/Heterosexual Split" 2:2 (Winter 1982):136-46.

Sexual Harassment

Schneider, Beth E. "Consciousness About Sexual Harassment Among Heterosexual and Lesbian Women Workers." *Journal of Social Issues* 28:4 (1982):75-97.

stomp, bruiser, fang, sparks . . . and footnote. "Womyn in the Joint/Wimmin in the Joint." *Sinister Wisdom,* "With an Emphasis on Lesbian Theory" 37 (Spring 1989):94-9.

Sexuality (see also: Bisexuality; Butch/Femme; Celibacy; Labels/Identity; Monogamy; Pornography; Prostitution; Relationships; S/M)

Ardill, Susan and Sue O'Sullivan. "Upsetting an Applecart: Difference, Desire and Lesbian Sadomasochism." *Feminist Review* (Great Britain), "Socialist Feminism: Out of the Blue" 23 (Summer 1986):31-57.

Beckett, Judith E. "Recollections of a Sexual Life, Revelations of a Celibate Time." *Lesbian Ethics* 3:1 (Spring 1988):23-36.

Bell, Rudolph and Judith Butler. "Renaissance Sexuality and the Florentine Archives: an Exchange." *Renaissance Quarterly* 40:3 (Autumn 1987):485-511.

Bird, Jenny. "Young People and Sex." *Healthright* 2 (February 1983):45-6+.

Bogus, SDiane. "Dyke Hands." *Common Lives/Lesbian Lives* 5 (Fall 1982):72-7.

Brannock, Joanna C. and Benta E. Chapman. "Negative Sexual Experiences with Men Among Heterosexual Women and Lesbians" (no correlation found between negative experiences and lesbianism). *Journal of Homosexuality* 19:1 (1990):105-10.

"Breaking the Links of Lies" (Lesbian Sexuality Conference). *Resources for Feminist Research* (Canada) 14 (March 1985):9-10.

Bressler, Lauren C. and Abraham D. Lavender. "Sexual Fulfillment of Heterosexual, Bisexual, and Homosexual Women." *Journal of Homosexuality,* "Historical, Literary, and Erotic Aspects of Lesbianism" 12:3/4 (May 1986):109-22.

"Britain: a New Intimacy" (bisexual women write about AIDS and sexual practices, from *Bisexual Lives* (Great Britain) (1988)). *Connexions,* Women and AIDS" 33 (1990):26.

Brock, Deborah R. "The Sex Debates: Toward a Feminist Epistemology and Ontology?" (not exclusively about lesbians). *Atlantis* (Canada) 13:1 (Fall 1987):98-110.

Brodsky, Marla B. "Music and Sexuality." *Hot Wire* 4:3 (July 1988):42-3.

Brody, Rachel. "Butch/Femme: Knowing Myself and Trusting in Desire." *Common Lives/Lesbian Lives* 11 (Spring 1984):56-60.

Brown, Jan. "Sex, Lies, and Penetration: a Butch Finally 'Fesses Up." *Out/Look #7,* 2:3 (Winter 1990):30-4.

Burns, Jan. "The Translation of Knowledge Between Client and Therapist Concerning Lesbian Sexuality: All You Wanted to Know About Lesbian Sex and Were Scared to Ask." *Counselling Psychology Quarterly* 3:4 (1990):383-7.

CAD. "Lesbian Plenary: Combatting Heterosexism" (at 10th annual National Women's Studies Association convention, University of Minnesota in Minneapolis, June 1988; panel members Beth Brant, Michelle Parkerson, Joan Nestle, Gloria Anzaldúa). *off our backs* 18:8 (August-September 1988):3+.

------. "Not CBS" (boycott of network in response to a documentary about gay politics emphasizing public sex and sadomasochism). *off our backs* 10:8 (August-September 1980):15; note: cover reads 10:7.

------. "Theories of Sexuality Forum" (at the National Women's Studies Association Conference, Akron, Ohio, June 1990). *off our backs* 20:8 (August/September 1990):17.

Califia, Pat. "Lesbian Sexuality." *Journal of Homosexuality* 4:3 (Spring 1979):255-66.

------. "We Know What We Want: Lesbian Literature Meets the Sexual Revolution" (lesbian sexuality in books). *Sinister Wisdom,* "Lesbian Writing and Publishing" 1:2 (Fall 1976):67-72.

Campbell, Beatrix. "A Feminist Sexual Politics: Now You See It, Now You Don't" (not exclusively lesbian). *Feminist Review* (Great Britain) 5 (1980):1-18.

Canadian Woman Studies/Les Cahiers de la Femme, Canada, "Sexuality and Symbol/*Symbolisme et Sexualité,*" vol. 3, no. 2, 1981.

Chapman, Frances. "Talking It Out in New York City: Is the Sexual Political?" ("Lesbian/Feminist Dialogue," conference at Columbia University, New York City, December 1972). *off our backs* 3:5 (January 1973):6.

Chitty, Elizabeth. "You Can't Rock the Boat with Cold Fact" (feminist response to lesbian-feminist sexual imagery). *Fuse* (Canada) 4:2 (January 1980):117+.

Clare, Elizabeth. "Friends, Lovers and Passion." *Sinister Wisdom,* "On Friendship" 40 (Spring 1990):96-8.

Clark, Wendy. "The Dyke, The Feminist, and The Devil." *Feminist Review* (Great Britain), "Sexuality" 11 (Summer 1982):30-9.

Clarke, Cheryl. "Inspiration: Seven Stories of Creating Art -- Creating Sexual Poetry." *Hot Wire* 4:1 (November 1987):28-9.

Clausen, Jan. "My Interesting Condition: What Does It Mean When a Lesbian Falls in Love with a Man?" *Out/Look #7,* 2:3 (Winter 1990):10-21.

Cohen, Cheryl H. "The Feminist Sexuality Debate: Ethics and Politics." *Hypatia*, "Motherhood and Sexuality" 1:2 (Fall 1986):71-86.

Collis, Rose. "Pleasure Is a Risky Business" (erotica for women). *Spare Rib* (Great Britain) 191 (June 1988):10-12.

Corinne, Tee A. "Bodies: a Collage" (essay and photographs). *Woman of Power*, "Women's Bodies" 18 (Fall 1990):70-2.

Coveney, Lal and Leslie Kay. "A Symposium on Feminism, Sexuality, and Power" (Five College Women's Studies Committee and Faculty Seminar, Mt. Holyoke College). *off our backs* 17:1 (January 1987):12-13.

Crowden, John J. "The Love That Dares Now Speak Its Name" (bibliography on sexuality, history, gender identity, gay liberation, research, psychotherapy, social attitudes). *Choice* 11 (April 1974):209-27.

Dejanikus, Tacie and Fran Moira. "At Home: With Sexuality" (lesbian open house/"kitchen klatsch" in Arlington, Virginia). *off our backs* 4:3 (February 1974):10-11.

de Veaux, Alexis. "Sister Love" (personal narrative of an African-American lesbian-feminist). *Essence* 14 (October 1983):82-4+.

Diamond, Irene and Lee Quinby. "The Feminist Sexuality Debates: American Feminism in the Age of the Body." *Signs* 10:1 (Autumn 1984):119-25.

Dixon, Joan. "Sexuality and Relationship Changes in Married Females Following the Commencement of Bisexual Activity." *Journal of Homosexuality*, "Bisexualities: Theory and Research" 11:1/2 (Spring 1985):115-34.

Donahoe, Betsy. "Ms. Continental" (interview with Pinky and Cheryl, who run New York's only bath house for women). *off our backs* 3:6 (February-March 1973):10-11.

Doucette, Joan. "Breaking the Links of Lies" (disability; lesbian sexuality conference). *Resources for Feminist Research* (Canada) 14 (March 1985):9-10.

Douglas, Carol Anne. "Commentary: Hope for Feminism" (response to The Sexual Liberals and the Attack on Feminism conference, New York University Law School, April 1987). *off our backs* 17:5 (May 1987):21.

------. "Lesbian Sex: Whirlpools in the Waterfall." *off our backs* 14:2 (February 1984):20-1.

English, Deirdre, Amber Hollibaugh, and Gayle Rubin. "Talking Sex: a Conversation on Sexuality and Feminism." *Socialist Review* 2:4 (July-August 1981):43-62.

Fassler, Barbara. "Theories of Homosexuality as Sources of Bloomsbury's Androgyny" (Virginia Woolf's circle of literary/artist friends). *Signs* 5:2 (Winter 1979):237-51.

Feminist Review, Great Britain, "Sexuality," no. 11, Summer 1982.

FM. "Intercourse & Cervical Cancer" (includes section on "Virgins & Lesbians"). *off our backs* 10:8 (August-September 1980):4-5; note: cover reads 10:7.

Frye, Marilyn. "Lesbian 'Sex.'" *Sinister Wisdom,* "Passing" 35 (Summer/Fall 1988):46-54.

Goode, Erich. "Sexual Correlates of Homosexual Experiences Among College Women." *Journal of Sex Research* 13 (February 1977):12-21.

Hall, Marny. "Sex Therapy with Lesbian Couples: a Four Stage Approach." *Journal of Homosexuality,* "Psychotherapy with Homosexual Men and Women: Integrated Identity Approaches for Clinical Practice" 14:1/2 (1987):137-56.

Hamadock, Susan. "Lesbian Sexuality in the Framework of Psychotherapy: a Practical Model for the Lesbian Therapist." *Women & Therapy,* "Women and Sex Therapy" 7:2/3 (1989):207-20.

Harrison, Barbara Grizzuti. "Sexual Chic, Sexual Fascism, and Sexual Confusion." *New York* 7:13 (April 1, 1974):25-30.

Hedblom, Jack H. "Dimensions of Lesbian Sexual Experience." *Archives of Sexual Behavior* 2 (December 1973):329-41.

Hemmings, Susan and Manny. "Lesbians National . . . and International" (National Lesbian Conference on Sex and Sexual Practice, London, England, April 1983, and International Lesbian Service Conference, Paris, France, April 1983). *Spare Rib* (Great Britain) 131 (June 1983):12-13.

Heresies: a Feminist Publication on Art and Politics #12 , "The Sex Issue," vol. 3, no. 4, 1981.

Hollibaugh, Amber and Cherríe Moraga. "What We're Rollin' Around in Bed With -- Sexual Silences in Feminism: a Conversation Toward Ending Them." *Heresies #12,* "The Sex Issue" 3:4 (1981):58-62.

Horowitz, Gad. "Amazon Fantasy Trouble" (by woman whose lover fantasizes about dominance/submission during sex). *Canadian Dimension* (Canada) 22:3 (May 1988):40-2.

Kaplan, Gisela T. and Lesley T. Rogers. "Breaking Out of the Dominant Paradigm: a New Look at Sexual Attraction." *Journal of Homosexuality,* "Controversy Over the Bisexual and Homosexual Identities: Commentaries and Reactions" 10:3/4 (Winter 1984):71-5.

Kaye, Melanie. "Sexual Power." *Sinister Wisdom,* "Lesbianism: Sexuality and Power; The Patriarchy: Violence and Pornography" 15 (Fall 1980):45-50.

Kelly, Janis. "Into the Eighties" (predicts that "sex . . . will become less important as a way of defining ourselves" and "lesbians will still feel free to mess around with men"). *off our backs,* "Ten Years Growing!" 10:2 (February 1980):6.

------. "Supreme Court, Sodomy, and Me" (U.S. Supreme Court affirms states' rights to outlaw certain sexual acts). *off our backs* 6:3 (May 1976):10.

Kerr, Barbara T. and Mirtha N. Quintales. "The Complexity of Desire: Conversations on Sexuality and Difference." *Conditions: eight* 3:2 (Spring 1982):52-71.

Kiss and Tell. "Drawing the Line: Where Do You Draw the Line on Sexually Explicit Images?" (interactive photo exhibit by Canadian art collective, San Francisco, June-July 1990). *Out/Look #10,* 3:2 (Fall 1990):6-11.

Kulp, Denise. "Cruising *On Our Backs." off our backs* 15:7 (July 1985):16-18.

------. "Redefining Feminism and Excluding Women" (response to The Sexual Liberals and the Attack on Feminism conference, New York University Law School, April 1987). *off our backs* 17:5 (May 1987):22.

Kurdek, Lawrence A. "Relationship Quality of Gay and Lesbian Cohabiting Couples." *Journal of Homosexuality* 15:3/4 (1988):93-118.

Lehman, J. Lee. "Lust Is Just a Four-Letter Word." *Heresies #12,* "The Sex Issue" 3:4 (1981):80-1.

Livia, Anna. (letter about S/M, and lesbian sexuality in literature). *Lesbian Ethics* 2:2 (Fall 1986):105-6.

Lootens, Tricia. "Third Women in Print Conference" (Berkeley, California, May 1985; reports on workshops including classism, erotica, lesbian nuns, women of color, pornography, censorship, raid on British gay book store). *off our backs* 15:8 (August-September 1985):8-9+.

Lorde, Audre. "The Erotic as Power." *Chrysalis* 9 (Fall 1979):29-31.

Loulan, JoAnn. "Good News About Lesbian Sex." *Out/Look* 1:1 (Spring 1988):90-93.

------. "Research on Sex Practices on 1566 Lesbians and the Clinical Applications." *Women & Therapy,* "Women and Sex Therapy" 7:2/3 (1989):221-34.

MacDonald, Ingrid. "Customary Bias: Canada Customs Is Preventing Positive Images of Lesbian Sex." *Broadside* (Canada) 8 (July 1987):4.

Malinovich, Myriam Miedzian. "Opinion: on Lesbianism and Peer Group Pressure." *Mademoiselle* 82 (April 1976):84-6.

Mara, Jane. "A Lesbian Perspective." *Women and Therapy,* "Women Changing Therapy: New Assessments, Values and Strategies in Feminist Therapy" 2:2/3 (Summer/Fall 1983):145-55.

Marmor, Judd. "'Normal' and 'Deviant' Sexual Behavior." *American Medical Association Journal* 217 (January 12, 1971):165-70.

Martin, Del and Phyllis Lyon. "Lesbian Love and Sexuality" (excerpt from the book *Lesbian/Woman*). *Ms.* 1:1 (July 1972):74-7+.

Matter, E. Ann. "Discourses of Desire: Sexuality and Christian Women's Visionary Narratives." *Journal of Homosexuality,* "Homosexuality and Religion" 18:3/4 (1989/1990):119-32.

Meulenbett, Anja. "Women and Women" (excerpt from *For Ourselves: Our Bodies and Sexuality from Women's Point of View,* Great Britain). *ISIS International Bulletin* 25 (December 1982):12-13.

Michaele. "Notes on an Artist in Search of an Erotic Image." *Sinister Wisdom* 15 (Fall 1980):51-5.

Moraga, Cherríe and Amber Hollibaugh. "What We're Rollin' Around in Bed With -- Sexual Silences in Feminism: a Conversation Toward Ending Them." *Heresies #12,* "The Sex Issue" 3:4 (1981):58-62.

Nappi, Maureen. "Clit Tapes" (video installation of women masturbating, with transcript of dialog between artist and one of her models). *Heresies #16,* "Film and Video" 4:4 (1983):24-5.

New York University Review of Law & Social Change, "Symposium: Sex, Politics and the Law; Lesbians and Gay Men Take the Offensive," vol. 14, no. 4, Fall 1986.

Nichols, Margaret. "What Feminists Can Learn from the Lesbian Sex Radicals." *Conditions: fourteen* 5:2 (1987):152-63.

Nyberg, Kenneth L. "Sexual Aspirations and Sexual Behaviors Among Homosexually Behaving Males and Females: the Impact of the Gay Community."*Journal of Homosexuality* 2:1 (Autumn 1976):29-37.

Patton, Cindy. "The Cum Shot: 3 Takes on Lesbian and Gay Sexuality" (in film). *Out/Look* 1:3 (Fall 1988):72-7.

Radecki, Susanna. "Agreeing to Differ? Lesbian Sadomasochism" (argues for new thinking about lesbian sexuality). *Spare Rib* (Great Britain) 170 (September 1986):41.

Raymond, Janice. "Putting the Politics Back Into Lesbianism" (lesbianism as a political movement vs. as a lifestyle). *Women's Studies International Forum* 12:2 (1989):149-56.

"Readers' Forum: Sex" (letters by Minny Seva, D.A. Clarke, Bonnie Sullivan, Kris Drumm, Joyce Trebilcot, Terri Jewell, and three anonymous writers). *Lesbian Ethics* 2:3 (Summer 1987):45-63.

Rich, B. Ruby. "Feminism and Sexuality in the 1980s" (review essay of periodicals/books on female sexuality). *Feminist Studies* 12 (Fall 1986):525-61.

Ross, Becki. "Launching Lesbian Cultural Offensives" (a response to interception of lesbian books by Canadian customs officials). *Resources for Feminist Research* (Canada) 17:2 (June 1988):12-15.

Rosser, Sue V. "Multiple Perspectives: Teaching About Sexuality and Reproduction." *Women's Studies Quarterly* 12:4 (Winter 1984):31-3.

Ruby, Jennie. "The Black Diaspora" (Michelle Parkerson, Audre Lorde, and Cheryl Clarke speaking on diversity of self-expression among African-American women, in a session at the 10th annual National Women's Studies Association conference, University of Minnesota in Minneapolis, June 1988, "African American Women and the Black Diaspora"). *off our backs* 18:8 (August-September 1988):10.

Rule, Jane. "Sexuality in Literature." *Fireweed* (Canada), "Women and Language" 5&6 (Winter 1979-80 & Spring 1980):22-7.

Schafer, Siegrid. "Sexual and Social Problems Among Lesbians." *Journal of Sex Research* 12 (February 1975):50-69.

------. "Sociosexual Behavior in Male and Female Homosexuals: a Study in Sex Differences" (West Germany). *Archives of Sexual Behavior* 6 (1977):355+.

Schwartz, Patricia Roth. "Lesbian Love in Limbo" (discusses child abuse and incest). *off our backs* 20:6 (June 1990):18-20.

Signs, "Women -- Sex and Sexuality," vol. 5, no. 4, Summer 1980.

Sinister Wisdom, "Lesbianism: Sexuality and Power; The Patriarchy: Violence and Pornography," no. 15, Fall 1980.

Smith, Barbara. "Agreeing to Differ? Lesbian Sadomasochism" (definitions of sexuality). *Spare Rib* (Great Britain) 170 (September 1986):38-9.

Spalter-Roth, Bobbie. "Health Festival" (section on "Women Loving Women" in article about "Becoming a Whole Woman: a Women's Health Festival," Washington, D.C., June 1974). *off our backs* 4:8 (July 1974):6+.

Steffensen, Jyanni. "Things Change . . . And About Time Too: a Critical Review of Women's Erotic Writing." *Hecate* (Australia) 15:2 (1989):26-33.

Sturgis, Susanna J. "Homage to Discord." *Common Lives/Lesbian Lives* 6 (Winter 1982):48-52.

"Three Black Women Talk About Sexuality and Racism." *Spare Rib* (Great Britain) 135 (October 1983):6-8.

Vance, Brenda Kaye and Vicki Green. "Lesbian Identities: an Examination of Sexual Behavior and Sex Role Attribution as Related to Age of Initial Same-Sex Sexual Encounter." *Psychology of Women Quarterly* 8:3 (Spring 1984):293-307.

Wells, Joel W. "Sexual Language Usage in Different Interpersonal Contexts: a Comparison of Gender and Sexual Orientation." *Archives of Sexual Behavior* 18:2 (April 1989):127-43.

------. "The Sexual Vocabularies of Heterosexual and Homosexual Males and Females for Communicating Erotically with a Sexual Partner." *Archives of Sexual Behavior* 19:2 (April 1990):139-47.

"When the Flirtin's Said and Done: Lesbian Sexuality Interview." *Women: a Journal of Liberation,* "Women Loving Women" 5:2 (1977):5-8.

Yates, Dicey. "Mystical Unioning" ("during Lesbian sexlove"). *Lesbian Ethics* 2:3 (Summer 1987):3-32.

Zaremba, Eve. "Voicing the Unspeakable." *Broadside* (Canada) 2:9 (July 1981):19.

Bad Attitude (magazine):
Herman, Ellen and Karen Kahn. "Exploring Our Sexual Fantasies: Women's Erotica -- Sex Magazine Publishing: a Roundtable Discussion" (with representatives of *Bad Attitude, Eidos* and *Outrageous Women*). *Sojourner* 14:2 (October 1988):30-1.

Barnard College Sexuality Conference, "Towards a Politics of Sexuality," 1982:
Charbonneau, Claudette. "Sexual Confusion at Barnard." *off our backs* 12:6 (June 1982):25+.

Dejanikus, Tacie. "Charges of Exclusion & McCarthyism at Barnard Conference." *off our backs* 12:6 (June 1982):5+.

Douglas, Carol Anne. "Towards a Politics of Sexuality." New York City, April 1982). *off our backs* 12:6 (June 1982):2-4+.

Moira, Fran. "Barnard Finale." *off our backs* 12:6 (June 1982):24.

------. "Politically Correct, Politically Incorrect Sexuality." *off our backs* 12:6 (June 1982):22-3.

Bright, Susie (sex magazine editor and writer):
Gonsalves, Sharon. "Exploring Our Sexual Fantasies: Women's Erotica -- Susie Bright: On the Line." *Sojourner* 14:2 (October 1988):30-1.

Cixous, Hélène (French psychoanalytic critic and writer):
Dallery, Arleen B. "Sexual Embodiment: Beauvoir and French Feminism" (women's sexuality in Simone de Beauvoir, Hélène Cixous, Luce Irigaray and Julia Kristeva). *Women's Studies International Forum* 8:3 (1985):197-202.

Corinne, Tee (erotic photographer and writer):
Henry, Alice. "Images of Lesbian Sexuality" (interview). *off our backs* 13:4 (April 1983):10-12.

Seajay, Carol. "Visual Conceptions: a Review of Two Slide Shows" (JEB's "Lesbian Images in Photography: 1850-1980" and Tee Corinne's "Erotic Images of Lesbians in the Fine Arts"). *off our backs* 10:3 (March 1980):18-19+.

de Beauvoir, Simone (French philosopher):

Dallery, Arleen B. "Sexual Embodiment: Beauvoir and French Feminism" (women's sexuality in Simone de Beauvoir, Hélène Cixous, Luce Irigaray and Julia Kristeva). *Women's Studies International Forum* 8:3 (1985):197-202.

de Lauretis, Teresa (critic):

Marshall, Pam. "Desire Makes the Difference: Representation of Sexuality in the Structures of Narrative" (discusses the work of theorist Teresa de Lauretis, and Jane Rule's *Desert of the Heart*). *Phoebe* 1:2 (October 1989):82-5.

Desert of the Heart (novel):

Marshall, Pam. "Desire Makes the Difference: Representation of Sexuality in the Structures of Narrative" (discusses the work of theorist Teresa de Lauretis, and Jane Rule's *Desert of the Heart*). *Phoebe* 1:2 (October 1989):82-5.

Eidos (magazine):

Herman, Ellen and Karen Kahn. "Exploring Our Sexual Fantasies: Women's Erotica -- Sex Magazine Publishing: a Roundtable Discussion" (with representatives of *Bad Attitude, Eidos* and *Outrageous Women*). *Sojourner* 14:2 (October 1988):30-1.

Irigaray, Luce (French psychoanalyst and critic):

Dallery, Arleen B. "Sexual Embodiment: Beauvoir and French Feminism" (women's sexuality in Simone de Beauvoir, Hélène Cixous, Luce Irigaray and Julia Kristeva). *Women's Studies International Forum* 8:3 (1985):197-202.

JEB (photographer):
Seajay, Carol. "Visual Conceptions: a Review of Two Slide Shows"
    (JEB's "Lesbian Images in Photography: 1850-1980" and Tee
    Corinne's "Erotic Images of Lesbians in the Fine Arts"). *off our
    backs* 10:3 (March 1980):18-19+.

Jeffreys, Sheila (British activist and historian):
Hunt, Margaret. "The De-Eroticization of Women's Liberation:
    Social Purity Movements and the Revolutionary Feminism of
    Sheila Jeffreys." *Feminist Review* (Great Britain), "Perverse
    Politics: Lesbian Issues" 34 (Spring 1990):23-46.

Kristeva, Julia (French psychoanalyst):
Dallery, Arleen B. "Sexual Embodiment: Beauvoir and French
    Feminism" (women's sexuality in Simone de Beauvoir, Hélène
    Cixous, Luce Irigaray and Julia Kristeva). *Women's Studies
    International Forum* 8:3 (1985):197-202.

Loulan, JoAnn (sex/relationship writer and therapist)
Armstrong, Toni Jr. "Education as Entertainment: Lesbian Sexpert
    JoAnn Loulan." *Hot Wire* 6:1 (January 1990):2-5.

Wallsgrove, Ruth and Alice Henry. "JoAnn Loulan Interview . . . and
    Workshop." *off our backs* 15:10 (November 1985):18-20.

Moraga, Cherríe (Chicana writer):
Yarbro-Bejarano, Yvonne. "Cherríe Moraga's *Giving Up the Ghost:
    the* Representation of Female Desire." *Third Woman* 3:1-2
    (1986):113-20.

Nestle, Joan (co-founder of the Lesbian Herstory Archives):
Ardill, Susan and Sue O'Sullivan. "Sex in the Summer of '88" (sex
    and pornography controversies, including anti-gay Clause 28; *A
    Restricted Country,* book by Joan Nestle; *She Must Be Seeing
    Things,* video by Sheila McLaughlin). *Feminist Review* (Great
    Britain), "The Past Before Us: Twenty Years of Feminism" 31
    (Spring 1989):126-34.

Forster, Jackie. "A Restricted Country" (interview). *Spare Rib* (Great Britain) 195 (October 1988):10-12.

National Organization for Women:

Moira, Fran. "NOW: It'll Be a Long Time Coming" (report on lesbian workshop at mostly heterosexual National Organization for Women "Conference on Sexuality," October 1974). *off our backs* 4:11 (November 1974):3.

Outrageous Women (magazine):

Herman, Ellen and Karen Kahn. "Exploring Our Sexual Fantasies: Women's Erotica -- Sex Magazine Publishing: a Roundtable Discussion" (with representatives of *Bad Attitude, Eidos* and *Outrageous Women*). *Sojourner* 14:2 (October 1988):30-1.

She Must Be Seeing Things (film):

Ardill, Susan and Sue O'Sullivan. "Sex in the Summer of '88" (sex and pornography controversies, including anti-gay Clause 28; *A Restricted Country,* book by Joan Nestle; *She Must Be Seeing Things,* video by Sheila McLaughlin). *Feminist Review* (Great Britain), "The Past Before Us: Twenty Years of Feminism" 31 (Spring 1989):126-34.

S/M (see also: Butch/Femme; Fashion; Pornography; Relationships; Sexuality)

Alicen, Debbie. "Intertextuality: the Language of Lesbian Relationships." *Trivia* 3 (Fall 1983):6-26.

Ardill, Susan and Sue O'Sullivan. "Sex in the Summer of '88" (sex and pornography controversies, including anti-gay Clause 28; *A Restricted Country,* book by Joan Nestle; *She Must Be Seeing Things,* video by Sheila McLaughlin). *Feminist Review* (Great Britain), "The Past Before Us: Twenty Years of Feminism" 31 (Spring 1989):126-34.

------. "Upsetting an Applecart: Difference, Desire and Lesbian Sadomasochism." *Feminist Review* (Great Britain), "Socialist Feminism: Out of the Blue" 23 (Summer 1986):31-57.

Barker, Donna. "S&M Is an Adventure." *Fireweed* (Canada), "Lesbiantics" 28 (Spring 1989):115-21.

Barry, Kathleen. "'Sadomasochism': the Backlash to Feminism." *Trivia* 1 (Fall 1982):77-92.

Blackman, Inge and Kathryn Perry. "Skirting the Issue: Lesbian Fashion for the 1990s." *Feminist Review* (Great Britain), "Perverse Politics: Lesbian Issues" 34 (Spring 1990):67-78.

CAD. "Theories of Sexuality Forum" (at the National Women's Studies Association Conference, Akron, Ohio, June 1990). *off our backs* 20:8 (August/September 1990):17.

Califia, Pat. "Feminism and Sadomasochism." *Heresies #12,* "The Sex Issue" 3:4 (1981):30-4.

Carola, Elizabeth. "Agreeing to Differ? Lesbian Sadomasochism" (by member of Lesbians Against Sadomasochism, London, England). *Spare Rib* (Great Britain) 170 (September 1986):39-40.

Cohen, Cheryl H. "The Feminist Sexuality Debate: Ethics and Politics." *Hypatia,* "Motherhood and Sexuality" 3 (Fall 1986):71-86.

Cole, Susan G. "From Ms. to S/M." *Fireweed* (Canada), "Lesbiantics" 13 (1982):118-23.

Collis, Rose. "Pleasure Is a Risky Business" (erotica for women). *Spare Rib* (Great Britain) 191 (June 1988):10-12.

Cottingham, Laura. "Feminism and Lesbian S/M." *off our backs* 13:5 (May 1983):23-4.

Coveney, Lal and Leslie Kay. "A Symposium on Feminism, Sexuality, and Power" (Five College Women's Studies Committee and Faculty Seminar, Mt. Holyoke College). *off our backs* 17:1 (January 1987):12-13.

Dejanikus, Tacie. "Our Legacy" (response to letter by Pat Califia in *off our backs* 10:9 (October 1980):25). *off our backs* 10:10 (November 1980):17+.

Desmoines, Harriet. "Notes for a Magazine II" (founding concepts for *Sinister Wisdom;* discusses politically left revolutionary politics, racism, and classism). *Sinister Wisdom* 1:1 (Summer 1976):27-34.

Diamond, Irene and Lee Quinby. "The Feminist Sexuality Debates: American Feminism in the Age of the Body." *Signs* 10:1 (Autumn 1984):119-25.

Douglas, Carol Anne. "Commentary: Hope for Feminism" (response to The Sexual Liberals and the Attack on Feminism conference, New York University Law School, April 1987). *off our backs* 17:5 (May 1987):21.

------. "Sex and Violence: Titillating or Depressing?" (response to letter by Pat Califia in *off our backs* 10:9 (October 1980):25). *off our backs* 10:10 (November 1980):17.

------. "S&M -- Sensuality or Machismo?" (anti-S/M) *off our backs* 6:4 (June 1976):14.

Durrell, Anna. "Uproar Over Violent Images" (S/M debates in London's lesbian/gay movement). *New Statesman* 109 (June 14, 1985):16-17.

France, Marie. "Sadomasochism and Feminism." *Feminist Review* (Great Britain) 16 (Summer 1984):35-42.

Griffith, Nicola. "Agreeing to Differ? Lesbian Sadomasochism" (argues that S/M disempowers women). *Spare Rib* (Great Britain) 170 (September 1986):36-7.

Hollibaugh, Amber and Cherríe Moraga. "What We're Rollin' Around in Bed With -- Sexual Silences in Feminism: a Conversation Toward Ending Them." *Heresies #12*, "The Sex Issue" 3:4 (1981):58-62.

Horowitz, Gad. "Amazon Fantasy Trouble" (by woman whose lover fantasizes about dominance/submission during sex). *Canadian Dimension* (Canada) 22:3 (May 1988):40-2.

Jeffreys, Sheila. "Sado-Masochism: The Erotic Cult of Fascism." *Lesbian Ethics* 2:1 (Spring 1986):65-82.

Jennings, Paula. "The Hunt Saboteurs in Fox Furs." *Gossip* (Great Britain) 6 (1988):80-91.

Katz, Sue. "The Vanilla Tourist" (the S/M debate in Israel's "underground" lesbian community). *Common Lives/Lesbian Lives* 30 (Spring 1989):31-8.

Kaufman, Gloria. "S/M and Porn Touchy Issues for the Movement." *New Directions for Women* 11:5 (September/October 1982):4.

Kelly, Janis. "Another View" (response to Douglas, "S&M -- Sensuality or Machismo?," *off our backs* 6:4 (June 1976):14; both articles anti-S/M). *off our backs* 6:4 (June 1976):14.

Klein, Yvonne M. "Illusions of Power." *Fireweed* (Canada) 14 (Fall 1982):71-7.

Kulp, Denise. "Redefining Feminism and Excluding Women" (response to The Sexual Liberals and the Attack on Feminism conference, New York University Law School, April 1987). *off our backs* 17:5 (May 1987):22.

Le Masters, Carol. "S/M and the Violence of Desire" (pro-S/M). *Trivia* 15 (Fall 1989):17-30.

Livia, Anna. (letter about S/M, and lesbian sexuality in literature). *Lesbian Ethics* 2:2 (Fall 1986):105-6.

Moraga, Cherríe and Amber Hollibaugh. "What We're Rollin' Around in Bed With -- Sexual Silences in Feminism: a Conversation Toward Ending Them." *Heresies #12*, "The Sex Issue" 3:4 (1981):58-62.

Neath, Jeanne F. "Let's Discuss Dyke S/M and Quit the Name Calling: a Response to Sheila Jeffreys" (Jeffreys' article "Sado-Masochism: the Erotic Cult of Fascism" appears in *Lesbian Ethics* 2:1 (Spring 1986):65-82). *Lesbian Ethics* 2:3 (Summer 1987):95-9.

Nichols, Margaret. "What Feminists Can Learn from the Lesbian Sex Radicals." *Conditions: fourteen* 5:2 (1987):152-63.

Penelope, Julia. "The Illusion of Control: Sado-Masochism and the Sexual Metaphors of Childhood." *Lesbian Ethics* 2:3 (Summer 1987):84-94.

------. "Women - and Lesbian - Only Spaces: Though Into Action." *off our backs* 20:5 (May 1990):14-16.

Radecki, Susanna. "Agreeing to Differ? Lesbian Sadomasochism" (argues for new thinking about lesbian sexuality). *Spare Rib* (Great Britain) 170 (September 1986):41.

Raymond, Janice. "Putting the Politics Back Into Lesbianism" (lesbianism as a political movement vs. as a lifestyle). *Women's Studies International Forum* 12:2 (1989):149-56.

"Readers' Forum: Sex" (letters by Minny Seva, D.A. Clarke, Bonnie Sullivan, Kris Drumm, Joyce Trebilcot, Terri Jewell, and three anonymous writers). *Lesbian Ethics* 2:3 (Summer 1987):45-63.

Rich, B. Ruby. "Feminism and Sexuality in the 1980s" (review essay of periodicals/books on female sexuality). *Feminist Studies* 12 (Fall 1986):525-61.

Russo, Ann. "Conflicts and Contradictions Among Feminists Over Issues of Pornography and Sexual Freedom." *Women's Studies International Forum* 10:2 (1987):103-12.

"S/M Aesthetic." *Out/Look* 1:4 (Winter 1989):42-3.

Smith, Barbara. "Agreeing to Differ? Lesbian Sadomasochism" (definitions of sexuality). *Spare Rib* (Great Britain) 170 (September 1986):38-9.

Sturgis, Susanna J. "Homage to Discord." *Common Lives/Lesbian Lives* 6 (Winter 1982):48-52.

"Whatever Happened at the Lesbian Archive?" (dispute in collective over showing of film with S/M content, *She Must Be Seeing Things,* and over alleged racism in hiring). *Spare Rib* (Great Britain) 199 (March 1989):17.

Bad Attitude (magazine):
Herman, Ellen and Karen Kahn. "Exploring Our Sexual Fantasies: Women's Erotica -- Sex Magazine Publishing: a Roundtable Discussion" (with representatives of *Bad Attitude, Eidos* and *Outrageous Women*). *Sojourner* 14:2 (October 1988):30-1.

Barnard College Sexuality Conference, "Towards a Politics of Sexuality," 1982:
Bonovoglia, Angela. "Tempers Flare Over Sexuality Conference" (includes official statement by the Coalition for a Feminist Sexuality and Against Sadomasochism, and a petition responding to the statement). *New Directions for Women* 11:4 (July/August 1982):15.

Charbonneau, Claudette. "Sexual Confusion at Barnard." *off our backs* 12:6 (June 1982):25+.

Dejanikus, Tacie. "Charges of Exclusion & McCarthyism at Barnard Conference." *off our backs* 12:6 (June 1982):5+.

Moira, Fran. "Lesbian Sex Mafia ('I S/M') Speakout" *off our backs* 12:6 (June 1982):23-4.

------. "Politically Correct, Politically Incorrect Sexuality." *off our backs* 12:6 (June 1982):22-3.

Califia, Pat (writer):
"Califia's Attackers Plead Guilty" (to misdemeanor aggravated assault, in response to alleged battery of one of them by Califia during an S/M encounter). *off our backs* 13:2 (February 1983):14.

CBS (television network):
CAD. "Not CBS" (boycott of network in response to a documentary about gay politics that emphasized public sex and sadomasochism). *off our backs* 10:8 (August-September 1980):15; note: cover reads 10:7.

Eidos (magazine):
Herman, Ellen and Karen Kahn. "Exploring Our Sexual Fantasies: Women's Erotica -- Sex Magazine Publishing: a Roundtable Discussion" (with representatives of *Bad Attitude, Eidos* and *Outrageous Women*). *Sojourner* 14:2 (October 1988):30-1.

Jeffreys, Sheila (British activist and historian):
Hunt, Margaret. "The De-Eroticization of Women's Liberation: Social Purity Movements and the Revolutionary Feminism of Sheila Jeffreys." *Feminist Review* (Great Britain), "Perverse Politics: Lesbian Issues" 34 (Spring 1990):23-46.

Michigan Womyn's Music Festival:
Kaufman, Gloria. "A Time for Intolerance: Letter from the Front Lines" (on report of S/M at the Michigan Womyn's Music Festival, with answer on behalf of the Festival by Barbara Price and Lisa Vogel). *off our backs* 5:5 (May 1985):27.

Stato, Joanne. "14th Michigan Womyn's Music Festival" (the politics of the event -- who attended, what was discussed, including lesbians of color, racism, S/M, disability, and music). *off our backs* 19:9 (October 1989):20-1.

<u>Nestle, Joan</u> (writer):

Ardill, Susan and Sue O'Sullivan. "Sex in the Summer of '88" (sex and pornography controversies, including anti-gay Clause 28; *A Restricted Country,* book by Joan Nestle; *She Must Be Seeing Things,* video by Sheila McLaughlin). *Feminist Review* (Great Britain), "The Past Before Us: Twenty Years of Feminism" 31 (Spring 1989):126-34.

Forster, Jackie. "A Restricted Country" (interview with author Joan Nestle). *Spare Rib* (Great Britain) 195 (October 1988):10-12.

<u>On Our Backs</u> (magazine):
Kulp, Denise. "Cruising *On Our Backs.*" *off our backs* (July 1985):16-18.

<u>Outrageous Women</u> (magazine):
Herman, Ellen and Karen Kahn. "Exploring Our Sexual Fantasies: Women's Erotica -- Sex Magazine Publishing: a Roundtable Discussion" (with representatives of *Bad Attitude, Eidos* and *Outrageous Women*). *Sojourner* 14:2 (October 1988):30-1.

<u>She Must Be Seeing Things</u> (film):
"Whatever Happened at the Lesbian Archive?" (dispute in collective over showing of film with S/M content, *She Must Be Seeing Things,* and over alleged racism in hiring). *Spare Rib* (Great Britain) 199 (March 1989):17.

Ardill, Susan and Sue O'Sullivan. "Sex in the Summer of '88" (sex and pornography controversies, including anti-gay Clause 28; *A Restricted Country,* book by Joan Nestle; *She Must Be Seeing Things,* video by Sheila McLaughlin). *Feminist Review* (Great Britain), "The Past Before Us: Twenty Years of Feminism" 31 (Spring 1989):126-34.

Socialism

Hindin, Roanne. "Radical Women National Conference: the Third Wave of Feminism" (Santa Monica, California, February 1990). *off our backs* 20:6 (June 1990):9.

"Lesbianism and Socialist Feminism" (statement delivered at the First National Conference on Socialist Feminism, Yellow Springs, Ohio, July 1975; addresses racism, classism, ageism, lesbian parenting, and homophobia in the socialist feminist movement). *off our backs* 5:8 (September-October 1975):19.

Moira, Fran. "Focus on Criticism and Women's Place" (at the First National Conference on Socialist Feminism, Yellow Springs, Ohio, July 1975; article includes "Lesbian Overview"). *off our backs* 5:7 (August 1975):3-4.

Post, Dianne. "Radical Women National Conference: a Cold Shower" (Santa Monica, California, February 1990). *off our backs* 20:6 (June 1990):10-11.

Sociology (see also: Community; Identity)

Bristow, Ann R. and Pearn, Pam Langford. "Comment on Krieger's 'Lesbian Identity and Community: Recent Social Science Literature'" (in *Signs* 8:1 (Autumn 1982):91-108). *Signs,* "The Lesbian Issue" 9:4 (Summer 1984):729-32.

Cavin, Susan. "Lesbian Origins Sex Ratio Theory" (challenges heterosexism in the social sciences). *Sinister Wisdom* 9 (Spring 1979):14-19.

Gerstel, Camille J., Andrew J. Feraios, and Gilbert Herdt. "Widening Circles: an Ethnographic Profile of a Youth Group" (Chicago Gay and Lesbian Youth Project). *Journal of Homosexuality,* "Gay and Lesbian Youth: Part I" 17:1/2 (1989):75-92.

Kamano, Saori. "Cross-National Analysis of the Social Construction of
     Homosexuality and Gender." *NWSA Journal* 2 (Autumn
     1990):696-8.

Kitzinger, Celia and Rex Stainton Rogers. "A Q-Methodological Study of
     Lesbian Identities." *European Journal of Social Psychology*
     15:2 (1985):167-87.

Krieger, Susan. "Lesbian Identity and Community: Recent Social Science
     Literature." *Signs* 8:1 (Autumn 1982):91-108.

------. "Reply to Sandoval and Bristow and Pearn" (*Signs*, "The Lesbian
     Issue" 9:4 (Summer 1984):725-31, response to Krieger's
     "Lesbian Identity and Community: Recent Social Science
     Literature," *Signs* 8:1 (Autumn 1982):91-108). *Signs*, "The
     Lesbian Issue" 9:4 (Summer 1984):732-3.

Levine, Martin P. "The Sociology of Male Homosexuality and
     Lesbianism -- an Introductory Bibliography." *Journal of
     Homosexuality* 5:3 (Spring 1980):249-76.

Parker, Richard. "Youth, Identity, and Homosexuality: the Changing
     Shape of Sexual Life in Contemporary Brazil." *Journal of
     Homosexuality,* "Gay and Lesbian Youth: Part II" 17:3/4
     (1989):269-90.

Risman, Barbara J. and Pepper Schwartz. "Sociological Research on Male
     and Female Homosexuality." *Annual Review of Sociology* 14
     (1988):125-47.

Sandoval, Chela. "Comment on Krieger's 'Lesbian Identity and
     Community: Recent Social Science Literature'" (in *Signs* 8:1
     (Autumn 1982):91-108). *Signs*, "The Lesbian Issue" 9:4
     (Summer 1984):725-9.

Schneider, Margaret S. "The Office Affair: Myth and Reality for
     Heterosexual and Lesbian Women Workers." *Sociological
     Perspectives* 27:4 (1984):443-64.

Tremble, Bob, Margaret Schneider, and Carol Appathurai. "Growing Up Gay or Lesbian in a Multicultural Context" (study based on Toronto, Ontario, Canada). *Journal of Homosexuality,* "Gay and Lesbian Youth: Part II" 17:3/4 (1989):253-68.

Tuddé, Oedipussy. "The Agent Within" (how divisions within lesbian community help patriarchy co-opt the movement; written by a sociologist, member of the Collective Lesbian International Terrors (CLIT collective)). *off our backs* 4:8 (July 1974):15-16.

Southern Lesbians

Calla. "Southeast Meets to Plan for the National Lesbian Conference." *off our backs* 19:4 (April 1989):8.

Harper, Jorjet. "Southern: the 'Live and Let Live' Festival" (Southern Women's Music and Comedy Festival, Georgia, Summer 1990). *Hot Wire* 6:3 (September 1990):40-2.

Henson, Brenda. "Women's Music in the Deep South at the First Annual Gulf Coast Women's Festival" (Mississippi, Summer 1989). *Hot Wire* 6:1 (January 1990):38-9.

Landau, Penny M. "First Southern [Women's Music] Festival." *Hot Wire* 1:1 (November 1984):30.

McVey, Judy. "The Southern [Women's Music and Comedy] Festival and Disability." *Hot Wire* 3:1 (November 1986):30-1+.

MacKay, Karen. "A Matter of Tradition" (banjo playing singer/songwriter; learning from "Aunt Jennie" Wilson). *Hot Wire* 1:3 (July 1985):14-16.

Parks, Adrienne. "Great Southeastern Lesbians" (conference, Atlanta, Georgia, May 1975). *off our backs* 5:6 (July 1975):25.

Poppe, Terre. "Southeast Lesbian Network." *off our backs* 9:8 (August-September 1979):28-30.

Sears, James T. "The Impact of Gender and Race on Growing Up Lesbian and Gay in the South." *NWSA Journal* 1:3 (Spring 1989):422-57.

Segrest, Mab. "Lines I Dare to Write: Lesbian Writing in the South." *Southern Exposure,* "Festival: Celebrating Southern Literature" 9:2 (Summer 1981):53-62.

------. "Southern Reflections: Nothing Can Stop Us Now! But From What?" (keynote address to 12th annual Southeastern Lesbian and Gay Conference, Atlanta, Georgia, 1988). *Out/Look* 1:4 (Winter 1989):10-15.

<u>Brown, Rita Mae</u> (writer):
Chew, Martha. "Rita Mae Brown: Feminist Theorist and Southern Novelist." *Southern Quarterly* 22:1 (Fall 1983):61-80.

<u>Davidson, Dianne</u> (musician):
Hanrahan, Noelle. "Dianne Davidson: Southern, Feminist, and Proud." *Sojourner* 14:8 (April 1989):34-5.

<u>Smith, Lillian</u> (Civil Rights activist and writer):
Murray, Hugh. "Lillian Smith: a Neglected Southern Heroine." *Journal of Ethnic Studies* 17:1 (Spring 1989):136-40.

Spirituality (see also: Religion)

Daly, Mary. "The Qualitative Leap Beyond Patriarchal Religion." *Quest,* "Women and Spirituality" 1:4 (Spring 1975):20-40.

Desertdyke, Sage. "Reader's Forum: Healing with a Hex." *Lesbian Ethics* 3:1 (Spring 1988):72-5.

Dirzhud-Rashid, Shani. "New Age Rage: Spiritual Path a Choice" (response to Angela Johnson, "Pre-packaged Spiritualism," *off our backs* 19:1 (January 1989):10; note: cover reads 18:11 (December 1988)). *off our backs* 19:2 (February 1989):19.

Downing, Christine. "Same-Sex Love Among the Greek Goddesses." *Woman of Power,* "Faces of the Goddess" 15 (Fall/Winter 1990):50-3.

Gidlow, Elsa. "The Spiritual Significance of the Self-Identified Women" (edited version of essay by the same title which appeared in *Maenad* 1:3 (Spring 1981):73-9). *Woman of Power,* "Women's Experience of The Sacred" 12 (Winter 1989):16-17.

Grace, Cindee. "Women's Music, Magic, and Matrism." *Hot Wire* 1:1 (November 1984):22.

Grey, Morgan and Julia Penelope. "Found Goddesses" (excerpt from forthcoming book, *The Book of Found Goddesses, from Asphalta to Vulva*). *Lesbian Ethics* 2:2 (Fall 1986):42-9.

Hardy, Jan. "New Age Rage: 'Zucchini of My Being?'" (supportive response to Angela Johnson, "Prepackaged Spiritualism," *off our backs* 19:1 (January 1989); note: front cover reads 18:11 (December 1988)). *off our backs* 19:2 (February 1989):19.

Harris, Bertha. "The Lesbian: the Workmaker, the Leader." *Quest,* "Leadership" 2:4 (Spring 1976):14-28.

Hart, Nett. "Radical Lesbian Spirituality." *Lesbian Ethics* 3:1 (Spring 1988):64-73.

Haught, Linda. "First Conference on Gay Spirituality" (Berkeley, California, January 1986). *off our backs* 16:8 (August-September 1986):22-4.

Healy, Eloise Klein. "Looking for the Amazons" ("amazon" warriors/spiritual figures in history, prehistory and mythology). *Lesbian Ethics* 2:1 (Spring 1986):50-64.

Iami. "Readers' Forum: Playing Indian." *Lesbian Ethics* 3:1 (Spring 1988):80-2.

Jeter, Kris. "The Shaman: the Gay and Lesbian Ancestor of Humankind." *Marriage and Family Review* 14:3-4 (1989):317-34.

Johnson, Angela. "Pre-packaged Spiritualism" (criticism of New Age spirituality). *off our backs* 19:1 (January 1989):10; note: cover reads 18:11 (December 1988).

Johnson, Flowing Margaret. "I'm a Material Dyke." *Lesbian Ethics* 3:1 (Spring 1988):55-63.

Kaye/Kantrowitz, Melanie. "Elements." *Common Lives/Lesbian Lives* 25 (Winter 1988):29-32.

Lee, Anna. "New Age Spirituality Is the Invention of Heteropatriarchy." *Sinister Wisdom,* "With an Emphasis on Lesbian Theory" 37 (Spring 1989):20-8.

Moon, K. "Reader's Forum: Playing Indian." *Lesbian Ethics* 3:1 (Spring 1988):82.

Mountaingrove, Jean. "The Presence in the Grove" (by founding editor of *WomanSpirit* magazine). *Woman of Power,* "Faces of the Goddess" 15 (Fall/Winter 1990):80-1.

------. "Reader's Forum: a Lavender Tithe." *Lesbian Ethics* 3:1 (Spring 1988):82-4.

Nadeau, Denise. "Lesbian Spirituality." *Resources for Feminist Research* (Canada), "The Lesbian Issue/Etre Lesbienne" 12:1 (March 1983):37-9.

Ritter, K.Y. and C.W. O'Neill. "Moving Through Loss -- The Spiritual Journey of Gay Men and Lesbian Women." *Journal of Counseling and Development* 68:1 (1989):9-15.

Rose, Reba. "Reader's Forum: Sweet Mother, She's Alive!" *Lesbian Ethics* 3:1 (Spring 1988):77-80.

Ruby, Jennie. "Lesbian Theory: Pursuing Lesbian Meaning" (Lesbian Theory session of the National Women's Studies' Association conference in Minneapolis, Minnesota, June 1988; includes reports on the following papers: Betty Tallen, "Lesbian Feminist Theory: a View from the Political Theory Trenches"; Lee Evans, "Lesbians, Community, and Patriarchal Consumer Values"; Elana Dykewomon, "The Knots of Process"; Anna Lee, "New Age Spirituality Is the Invention of Heteropatriarchy"; Sarah Hoagland, "Lesbian Agency" and "Lesbian Space"; and Jeffner Allen on writing). *off our backs* 18:9 (October 1988):18-19.

Silveira, Jeanette. "Reader's Forum: Dyke Magic." *Lesbian Ethics* 3:1 (Spring 1988):75-7.

Springer, Judy. "Goddesses Unite: the Making of a Mural." *Canadian Woman Studies* (Canada), "Feminism & Visual Art/Le féminisme et l'art visuel" 11:1 (Spring 1990):97-8.

Star, Leigh. "The Politics of Wholeness: Feminism and the New Spirituality." *Sinister Wisdom* 3 (Spring 1977):36-44.

Stein, Diane. "Writing the 'Kwan Yin Book of Changes'" (lesbian-feminist revision of the I-Ching). *Hot Wire* 3:3 (July 1987):52-3+.

Sturgis, Susanna J. "New Age Rage: New Age Fills a Need" (response to Angela Johnson, "Prepackaged Spiritualism," *off our backs* 19:1 (January 1989); note: cover reads 18:11 (December 1988)). *off our backs* 19:2 (February 1989):17.

Winston, Rachel. "New Age Rage: Crystal Mining Depletes Environment" (supportive response to Angela Johnson, "Prepackaged Spiritualism," *off our backs* 19:1 (January 1989):10; note: cover reads 18:11 (December 1988)). *off our backs* 19:2 (February 1989):20.

Yates, Dicey. "Mystical Unioning" ("during Lesbian sexlove"). *Lesbian Ethics* 2:3 (Summer 1987):3-32.

Zana/Raven. "Two Pieces on Dis-Ability: And What of Those Who
Remain Unhealed?; The Perfect Matriarchal Future." *Lesbian
Ethics* 3:1 (Spring 1988):97-101.

Allen, Paula Gunn (Native American writer):
Caputi, Jane. "Interview with Paula Gunn Allen." *Trivia*, "Breaking
Forms" 16/17 (1990):50-67.

Wynne, Patrice. "Recovering Spiritual Reality in Native American
Traditions: an Interview with Paula Gunn Allen." *Woman of
Power*, "ReVisioning the Dark" 8 (Winter 1988):68-70.

Deming, Barbara (white civil rights and peace activist):
Lindsey, Karen. "Barbara Deming: a Remembrance" (of writer and
civil rights and peace activist). *Woman of Power* 2 (Summer
1985):70+.

The Future Is Female Project:
Cheatham, Annie and Mary Clare Powell. "The Future Is Female
Project." *Woman of Power* 2 (Summer 1985):43-7.

Gardner, Kay (musician):
Armstrong, Toni L. "Kay Gardner." *Hot Wire* 2:2 (March 1986):2-6.

Mountaingrove, Jean and Ruth Mountaingrove (founders of
WomanSpirit magazine):
Danab, Mint and Athame Mountainclimber. "An Interview with Ruth
and Jean Mountaingrove." *Sinister Wisdom* 8 (Winter 1979):73-
6.

Sappho (ancient Lesbian poet):
Harper, Jorjet. "Sappho and the Goddess Aphrodite -- Sappho's
Religion: the Erotic Dimension of the Sacred." *Hot Wire* 3:1
(November 1986):16-18.

Sports and Games

Chapman, Frances and Bernice. "A Conference Is Bringing Together" (Midwest Gay Pride Conference, Iowa City, Iowa, and Lesbian Extravaganza, East Lansing, Michigan; topics covered include building community, athletics, parenting, publications, gay art and politics (talk by Rita Mae Brown), music, and theater). *off our backs* 5:5 (May-June 1975):4-5+.

Gabriner, Vicki. "Coming Out Slugging!" (lesbian softball teams as basis for activism). *Quest,* "Organizations and Strategies" 2:3 (Winter 1976):52-7.

Gennino, Angela. "Keeping the Path Straight" (Sierra Club refusal to officially recognize "Gay/Lesbian Sierrans"). *Mother Jones* 10:8 (October 1985):14.

Kidd, Dorothy. "Getting Physical: Compulsory Heterosexuality and Sport" (discusses the film *Personal Best*). *Canadian Woman Studies* (Canada), "Sport" 4:3 (Spring/May 1983):62-5.

Krebs, Paula. "At the Starting Blocks: Women Athletes' New Agenda" (New Agenda: A Blueprint for the Future of Women's Sports, conference, Washington, D.C., November 1983). *off our backs* 14:1 (January 1984):1-3.

Lenskyj, Helen. "Combatting Homophobia in Sports." *off our backs* 20:6 (June 1990):2-3.

------. "Female Sexuality and Women's Sports." *Women's Studies International Forum* 10:4 (1987):381-6.

Levin, Jenifer. "Sports: the 7th Annual Gay Pride Run." *Visibilities* 2:6 (November/December 1988):4-7.

Palzkill, Birit. "Between Gymshoes and High-Heels: the Development of a Lesbian Identity and Existence in Top Class Sport." *International Review for the Sociology of Sport* 25:3 (1990):221-34.

Penelope, Julia. "The Mystery of Lesbians: II" (separatist political theory). *Lesbian Ethics* 1:2 (Spring 1985):29-67; also *Gossip* (Great Britain) 2 (1986):16-68.

Pitts, Brenda G. "Beyond the Bars: the Development of Leisure-Activity Management in the Lesbian and Gay Population in America." *Leisure Information Quarterly* 15:3 (1989):4-7.

Post, Laura. "The Story behind the Products: Two Lesbian Games" (DYKE and Dyke Dilemma). *Hot Wire* 6:2 (May 1990):24-6+.

"Slow Curve on the Outside Corner" (interview with three players on a championship women's amateur softball team). *Woman: a Journal of Liberation,* "Women Loving Women" 5:2 (1977):10-13.

Zipter, Yvonne. "The All-American Girls' Baseball League." *Hot Wire* 3:3 (July 1987):20-2+.

------. "The Double Play, or, Love on the Softball Field." *Out/Look* 1:3 (Fall 1988):32-5.

------. "Re:Inking -- Diamonds in the Rough: The Making of a Book" (publication of her book *Diamonds Are a Dyke's Best Friend*). *Hot Wire* 5:2 (May 1989):46-7+.

King, Billie Jean (tennis player sued for palimony by a woman):
Axthelm, Pete. "The Case of Billie Jean King." *Newsweek* 97 (May 18, 1981):133.

Beach, Bennet H. "A Disputed Love Match." *Time* 117 (May 11, 1981):77.

Kirshenbaum, Jerry. "Facing Up to Billie Jean's Revelations." *Sports Illustrated* 54 (May 11, 1981):13-14.

Manning, Janet Earley. "Tennis King Past and Jean Queen Present Make News." *New Directions for Women* 10:4 (July/August 1981):8.

Nobile, Philip. "King's Difficult Climb from the Closet." *National Catholic Reporter* 17 (May 22, 1981):16.

Roberts, Shelly. "Bad Form, Billie Jean" (reproaches King for publicly denouncing her admitted lesbian relationship). *Newsweek* 97:21 (May 25, 1981):19.

Navratilova, Martina (tennis player):
Morris, Bonnie. "How I (Almost) Met Martina Navratilova." *Hot Wire* 6:3 (September 1990):22.

"Navratilova Called 'Unfit Role Model'" (because of her sexuality, by former tennis champion Margaret Court). *off our backs* 20:9 (October 1990):4.

Parsons, Pam (University of South Carolina women's basketball coach who quit amid charges of lesbianism and drug abuse, then sued *Sports Illustrated* for libeling her):
Lieber, Jill and Jerry Kirshenbaum. "Stormy Weather at South Carolina." *Sports Illustrated* 56 (February 8, 1982):30-7.

Vance, N. Scott. "Former Basketball Coach Settles Lawsuit Against University of South Carolina." *Chronicle of Higher Education* 26 (August 3, 1983):15+.

Pumping Iron II -- The Women (film):
Millar, Ruth. "Pumping Iron: a Feminist Response." *Gossip* (Great Britain) 2 (1986):76-9.

------. (response to Lynnette Mitchell's "Skinny Lizzie Strikes Back: an Apologia for Thin Women's Liberation," *Gossip* (Great Britain) 3 (no date); see also, related letters in *Gossip* 4 (no date)). *Gossip* 4 (no date):10-11.

Mitchell, Lynnette. "Skinny Lizzie Strikes Back: an Apologia for Thin Women's Liberation" (response to Ruth Millar, "Pumping Iron: a Feminist Response," *Gossip* (Great Britain) 2 (1986)). *Gossip* 3 (no date):40-4.

Substance Abuse and Recovery

Anderson, Sandra C. and Donna C. Henderson. "Working with Lesbian Alcoholics." *Social Work* 30:6 (November-December 1985):518-25.

Diamond, Deborah L. and Sharon C. Wilsnack. "Alcohol Abuse Among Lesbians: a Descriptive Study." *Journal of Homosexuality* 4:2 (Winter 1978):123-42.

Diamond-Friedman, Cassandra. "A Multivariant Model of Alcoholism Specific to Gay-Lesbian Populations." *Alcoholism Treatment Quarterly* 7:2 (1990):111-17.

Freeman, Beth. "Twelve Steps Anonymous" (the problem of virtual addiction to 12-step recovery programs). *off our backs* 19:3 (March 1989):20-1.

Fridley, Mary. "The Health Closet: Opening the Door on Gay Health Issues" (first national gay health conference, Washington, D.C., May 1978). *off our backs* 8:7 (July 1978):14+.

Germain, Robin. "Internal Trap" (co-dependence). *Common Lives/Lesbian Lives* 3 (Spring 1982):86-9.

Glaus, Kathleen O'Halleran. "Alcoholism, Chemical Dependency, and the Lesbian Client." *Women & Therapy,* "Lesbianism: Affirming Nontraditional Roles" 8:1/2 (1989):131-44.

Hall, Joanne M. "Alcoholism in Lesbians: Developmental, Symbolic Interactionist, and Critical Perspectives." *Health Care for Women International* 11:1 (Winter 1990):89-107.

Herman, Ellen. "Getting to Serenity: Do Addiction Programs Sap Our Political Vitality?" *Out/Look* 1:2 (Summer 1988):10-21.

Hugs, Diane. "Where Have All the Lesbians Gone?" (difference between caring and "co-ing," and between alcoholism and disability). *Sinister Wisdom,* "On Disability" 39 (Winter 1989-90):73-5.

Israelstam, S. "Knowledge and Opinions of Alcohol Intervention Workers in Ontario, Canada, Regarding Issues Affecting Male Gays and Lesbians." *International Journal of the Addictions* 23:3 (1988):227-52.

Israelstam, Stephen and Sylvia Lambert. "Homosexuals Who Indulge in Excessive Use of Alcohol and Drugs: Psychosocial Factors to be Taken into Account by Community and Intervention Workers." *Journal of Alcohol and Drug Education* 34:3 (Spring 1989):54-69.

Johnson, Sandie. "Helping Lesbian Alcoholics." *off our backs* 10:6 (June 1980):7.

Lewis, Collins E., Marcel T. Saghir, and Eli Robins. "Drinking Patterns in Homosexual and Heterosexual Women." *Journal of Clinical Psychiatry* 43 (December 1982):277-9.

McKirnan, D.J. and P.L. Peterson. "Alcohol and Drug-Use Among Homosexual Men and Women: Epidemiology and Population Characteristics." *Addictive Behaviors* 14:5 (1989):545-53.

Martin, Marcelina. "The Isolation of the Lesbian Alcoholic." *Frontiers,* "Equal Opportunity Addiction: Women, Alcohol, and Drugs" 4:2 (Summer 1979):32-3.

Mosbacher, D. "Lesbian Alcohol and Substance Abuse." *Psychiatric Annals* 18:1 (1988):47-50.

Nardi, Peter M. "Alcohol Treatment and the Non-Traditional 'Family' Structures of Gays and Lesbians." *Journal of Alcohol and Drug Education* 27 (Winter 1982):83-9.

Post, Dianne. "Interindependence: a New Concept in Relationships" (opposed to codependence). *Lesbian Ethics* 4:1 (Spring 1990):88-92.

Rothblum, Esther D. "Depression Among Lesbians: an Invisible and Unresearched Phenomenon." *Journal of Gay & Lesbian Psychotherapy* 1:3 (1990):67-87.

Ruby, Jennie. "Lesbian Theory" (workshop at National Women's Studies Association conference, Towson State University, Maryland, June 1989; reports on Betty Tallen, "A Lesbian-Feminist Critique of 12-Step Programs"; Jeffner Allen, "Passions in the Gardens of Delight"; and Sarah Lucia Hoagland on Lesbian Ethics). *off our backs* 19:8 (August-September 1989):8.

Schilit, Rebecca, Mark W. Clark, and Elizabeth Ann Shallenberger. "Social Supports and Lesbian Alcoholics." *Affilia* 3:2 (Summer 1988):27-40.

Schilit, Rebecca, Gwat-Yong Lie, and Marilyn Montagne. "Substance Use as a Correlate of Violence in Intimate Lesbian Relationships." *Journal of Homosexuality* 19:3 (1990):51-66.

Swallow, Jean E. "What Is Calistoga?" (alcoholism). *Common Lives/Lesbian Lives* 4 (Summer 1982):38-49.

Tallen, Bette S. "Twelve Step Programs: a Lesbian Feminist Critique." *NWSA Journal* 2:3 (Summer 1990):390-407.

Yarrow. "Chemical Free Space" (in the lesbian community). *off our backs* 14:5 (May 1984):21.

Christian, Meg (musician):
Pollock, Mary. "Recovery and Integrity: the Music of Meg Christian." *Frontiers* 9:2 (1987):29-34.

Suicide

Buhrich, Neil and Carlson Loke. "Homosexuality, Suicide, and Parasuicide in Australia." *Journal of Homosexuality,* "Psychopathology and Psychotherapy in Homosexuality" 15:1/2 (1988):113-30.

CAD. "Indian Women Fight Possession, Violence" (includes section on "Lesbian Suicides"). *off our backs* 10:10 (November 1980):2.

Hunter, Joyce. "Violence Against Lesbian and Gay Male Youths" (especially people of color, and related suicide attempts). *Journal of Interpersonal Violence* 5:3 (1990):295-300.

Kourany, Ronald F.C. "Suicide Among Homosexual Adolescents." *Journal of Homosexuality* 13:4 (Summer 1987):111-18.

Rothblum, Esther D. "Depression Among Lesbians: an Invisible and Unresearched Phenomenon." *Journal of Gay & Lesbian Psychotherapy* 1:3 (1990):67-87.

Saunders, J.M. "Suicide Risk Among Gay Men and Lesbians: a Bibliographical Review." *Death Studies* 11:1 (1987):1-23.

Television (see also: Mass Media)

"Gay TV" (show featuring a lesbian couple censored in Seattle, Washington). *off our backs* 9:2 (February 1979):8.

"Netherlands: Gay News on TV." *off our backs* 17:3 (March 1987):9.

Whitaker, Judy. "Hollywood Transformed" (interviews with lesbians who grew up in the environment of film and television). *Jump Cut,* "Lesbians and Film" 24/5 (March 1981):33-5.

Heartbeat:

Toepfer, Susan. "Is Prime Time Ready for Its First Lesbian? Gail Strickland Hopes So -- and She's About to Find Out." *People Weekly* 29 (April 25, 1988):95.

My Two Loves:

Kulp, Denise. "Whatever's For Us: Lesbians in Popular Culture" (television show *My Two Loves;* film *Desert Hearts;* play, Lily Tomlin's *The Search for Intelligent Life in the Universe*). *off our backs* 16:6 (June 1986):24-5.

Out on Tuesdays (Great Britain):

Collis, Rose. "Out on Tuesdays: Not for Beginners" (lesbian/gay magazine-format series on British television channel 4). *Spare Rib* (Great Britain) 198 (February 1989):33.

"Lesbians Hit Prime Time" (interview with Mandy Merck, editor). *Spare Rib* (Great Britain) 213 (June 1990):39-42.

Police Woman:

Douglas, Carol Anne and Janis Kelly. "NBC: Network of Evil" ("Flowers of Evil" episode of "Police Woman" portraying lesbians as murderers running an old age home; lesbian protest with a 24-hour sit-in). *off our backs* 4:12 (December 1974):2+.

"T.V. Lesbians" ("Police Woman" episode about "a trio of Lesbians who run an old folks home with a view to murder" and protest by lesbians/gays). *off our backs* 4:11 (November 1974):5.

Two in Twenty (soap opera):

DeLuca, Nancy and Debra Granik. "Lesbian Soap Opera on Cable TV: 'Two in Twenty.'" *Hot Wire* 3:3 (July 1987):24-5+.

Lindsey, Karen. "As the (Lesbian) World Turns" (cable-t.v. soap opera, "Two in Twenty"). *Sojourner* 13:6 (February 1988):13.

Veronica4Rose (Great Britain):

"Veronica4Rose." *Connexions,* "Global Lesbianism 2" 10 (Fall 1983):10.

<u>Winfrey, Oprah</u> (talk show host):

Knapp, Lucretia. "Oprah Winfrey Presents: The Lesbian As Spectacle." *Feminisms* 2:2 (Spring 1988):4-6.

<u>Winterson, Jeanette</u> (writer):

Kay, Jackie. "Unnatural Passions" (interview conducted shortly after the movie version of her novel *Oranges Are Not the Only Fruit* was televised in England). *Spare Rib* (Great Britain) 209 (February 1990):26-9.

Theater

Bell, Gay. "From a Resistance to Lesbian Theatre to a Lesbian Theatre of Resistance." *Resources for Feminist Research* (Canada), "The Lesbian Issue/Etre Lesbienne" 12:1 (March 1983):30-4.

Brannon, Rebecca. "Madison's Fourth Annual Lesbian Variety Show: I Got This Way from Kissing Girlz" (Madison, Wisconsin, November 1989). *Hot Wire* 6:2 (May 1990):36-8.

CAD. "Lesbian/Gay Trips, Cruises & Marches" (U.S. and international news briefs; first lesbian play performed in Ulster, Northern Ireland). *off our backs* 10:3 (March 1980):18-19+.

Canadian Theatre Review, Canada, "Homosexuality and the Theatre" (not specifically about lesbians; written by gay men), no. 12, Fall 1976.

Chapman, Frances and Bernice. "A Conference Is Bringing Together" (Midwest Gay Pride Conference, Iowa City, Iowa, and Lesbian Extravaganza, East Lansing, Michigan; topics covered include building community, athletics, parenting, publications, gay art and politics (talk by Rita Mae Brown), music, and theater). *off our backs* 5:5 (May-June 1975):4-5+.

Case, Sue-Ellen. "Towards a Butch-Femme Aesthetic" (the problem of a female subject position). *Discourse: Journal for Theoretical Studies in Media and Culture* 11:1 (Fall-Winter 1988-89):55-73.

"CLIT Statement #2" (Collective Lesbian International Terrors, group
    formed "to counterattack recent media insults against lesbians").
    off our backs 4:8 (July 1974):10-11.

Damon, Betsey. "The 7,000 Year Old Woman" (street performance).
    Heresies #3, "Lesbian Art and Artists" 1:3 (Fall 1977):10-13.

Davy, Kate. "Constructing the Spectator, Reception, Context, and
    Address in Lesbian Performance." *Performing Arts Journal* 10:2
    (1986):43-52.

de Lauretis, Teresa. "Sexual Indifference and Lesbian Representation"
    (discusses novels *The Well of Loneliness, Nightwood,* and *The
    Lesbian Body,* and the film *She Must Be Seeing Things*).
    Theatre Journal 40:2 (May 1988):155-77.

Dickler, Gloria. "Towards a Woman's Theatre." *Visibilities* 2:4
    (July/August 1988):8-11.

Dolan, Jill. "Breaking the Code: Musings on Lesbian Sexuality and the
    Performer." *Modern Drama* 32:1 (March 1989):146-58.

Ellenberger, Harriet. "The Dream Is the Bridge: In Search of Lesbian
    Theatre." *Trivia* 5 (Fall 1984):17-59.

Kendall, Kathryn. "From Heroine to Devoted Wife: Or, What the Stage
    Would Allow" (lesbian plot in two plays by women, in the 17th
    and 19th centuries). *Journal of Homosexuality,* "Historical,
    Literary, and Erotic Aspects of Lesbianism" 12:3/4 (May
    1986):9-22.

"Lesbian Thespians: Gay Sweatshop." *Broadside* (Canada) 7 (December
    1985/January 1986):13.

Moore, Honor. "Theater Will Never Be the Same" (feminist theater
    groups, including some lesbian projects). *Ms.* 6:6 (December
    1977):36-9+.

Rea, Charlotte. "Women for Women" (women-only performances) *The Drama Review*, "Indigenous Theatre Issue" 18:4 [T-64] (December 1974):77-87.

Sisley, Emily L. "Notes on Lesbian Theater." *Drama Review*, "The Sex and Performance Issue" 25:1 [T-89] (March 1981):47-56.

Sloan, Judy. "Reclaiming a Past: a Search Into Jewish Identity" (actress discusses reintegrating "Sophie" into performance for lesbian-feminist audiences). *Hot Wire* 3:3 (July 1987):46-8+.

Solomon, Alisa. "Gay Rights and Revels: New York's Lesbian/Gay Pride Day" (street theater). *Theater* 19:1 (Fall-Winter 1987):19-23.

Zeig, Sande. "The Actor as Activator: Deconstructing Gender Through Gesture" (lesbians in political theater). *Feminist Issues* 5:1 (1985):21-5.

Allen, Beth:

Bowstead, Lisa Morgan. "Remembrances of Jane Chambers and Beth Allen." *Visibilities* 4:2 (March/April 1990):12-14.

Allen, Claudia (playwright):

Allen, Claudia. "As You Like It: Lesbian Plays" (short descriptions of plays by Jane Chambers, Sarah Dreher, Claudia Allen, Patricia Montley, Cherríe Moraga, Eve Powell, Terry Baum, Carolyn Myers, Lesléa Newman, Amy Rubin, Adele Prandini/Sue Zemel/Jan Cole, Cappy Kotz/Phrin Prickett, Holly Hughes, Judy Grahn, Yvonne Zipter, and Sandra Dettelen/Kate Kasten). *Hot Wire* 5:3 (September 1989):38-9+.

Baum, Terry (actor and playwright):

Allen, Claudia. "As You Like It: Lesbian Plays" (short descriptions of plays by Jane Chambers, Sarah Dreher, Claudia Allen, Patricia Montley, Cherríe Moraga, Eve Powell, Terry Baum, Carolyn Myers, Lesléa Newman, Amy Rubin, Adele Prandini/Sue Zemel/Jan Cole, Cappy Kotz/Phrin Prickett, Holly Hughes, Judy Grahn, Yvonne Zipter, and Sandra Dettelen/Kate Kasten). *Hot Wire* 5:3 (September 1989):38-9+.

Chambers, Jane (playwright):
Allen, Claudia. "As You Like It: Lesbian Plays" (short descriptions
    of plays by Jane Chambers, Sarah Dreher, Claudia Allen,
    Patricia Montley, Cherríe Moraga, Eve Powell, Terry Baum,
    Carolyn Myers, Lesléa Newman, Amy Rubin, Adele
    Prandini/Sue Zemel/Jan Cole, Cappy Kotz/Phrin Pickett, Holly
    Hughes, Judy Grahn, Yvonne Zipter, and Sandra Dettelen/Kate
    Kasten). *Hot Wire* 5:3 (September 1989):38-9+.

Bowstead, Lisa Morgan. "Remembrances of Jane Chambers and Beth
    Allen." *Visibilities* 4:2 (March/April 1990):12-14.

Landau, Peggy M. "Jane Chambers: In Memoriam" (playwright of
    "Last Summer at Bluefish Cove" and "My Blue Heaven").
    Women & Performance 1:2 (Winter 1984):55-7.

Coventry Lesbian Theatre Group (England):
Mohin, Lilian. "Herstory interview with members of the Coventry
    Lesbian Theatre Group: Lou Hart, Jane Skeates, Vicki Ryder,
    and Suzanne Ciechomski." *Gossip* (Great Britain) 4 (no date):59-
    85.

Dettelen, Sandra and Kate Kasten (playwrights):
Allen, Claudia. "As You Like It: Lesbian Plays" (short descriptions
    of plays by Jane Chambers, Sarah Dreher, Claudia Allen,
    Patricia Montley, Cherríe Moraga, Eve Powell, Terry Baum,
    Carolyn Myers, Lesléa Newman, Amy Rubin, Adele
    Prandini/Sue Zemel/Jan Cole, Cappy Kotz/Phrin Pickett, Holly
    Hughes, Judy Grahn, Yvonne Zipter, and Sandra Dettelen/Kate
    Kasten). *Hot Wire* 5:3 (September 1989):38-9+.

Dreher, Sarah (playwright):
Allen, Claudia. "As You Like It: Lesbian Plays" (short descriptions
    of plays by Jane Chambers, Sarah Dreher, Claudia Allen,
    Patricia Montley, Cherríe Moraga, Eve Powell, Terry Baum,
    Carolyn Myers, Lesléa Newman, Amy Rubin, Adele
    Prandini/Sue Zemel/Jan Cole, Cappy Kotz/Phrin Pickett, Holly
    Hughes, Judy Grahn, Yvonne Zipter, and Sandra Dettelen/Kate
    Kasten). *Hot Wire* 5:3 (September 1989):38-9+.

FAT LIP Readers' Theatre:
Bock, Laura. "FAT LIP Readers' Theatre." *Woman of Power,*
"Humor" 17 (Summer 1990):32-3.

Giving Up the Ghost:
Yarbro-Bejarano, Yvonne. "Cherríe Moraga's *Giving Up the Ghost:*
the Representation of Female Desire." *Third Woman* 3:1-2
(1986):113-20.

The God of Vengeance:
Curtin, Kaier. "Roaring Twenties Scandal: Yiddish Lesbian Play
Rocks Broadway" ("The God of Vengeance" by Sholom Asch;
written 1907; performed on Broadway 1922; cast arrested). *Lilith*
19 (Spring 1988/5748):13-14.

Grahn, Judy (poet):
Allen, Claudia. "As You Like It: Lesbian Plays" (short descriptions
of plays by Jane Chambers, Sarah Dreher, Claudia Allen,
Patricia Montley, Cherríe Moraga, Eve Powell, Terry Baum,
Carolyn Myers, Lesléa Newman, Amy Rubin, Adele
Prandini/Sue Zemel/Jan Cole, Cappy Kotz/Phrin Pickett, Holly
Hughes, Judy Grahn, Yvonne Zipter, and Sandra Dettelen/Kate
Kasten). *Hot Wire* 5:3 (September 1989):38-9+.

Grosberg, Carol:
Jay, Karla. "Carol Grosberg on Lesbian Theater." *Margins,* "Lesbian
Feminist Writing and Publishing" 23 (August 1975):55-7; also
WIN: Peace and Freedom Through Nonviolent Action, "Lesbian
Culture" 11:22 (June 26, 1975):15-17.

Hair:
Chasin, Susan. "A Special Event: '*Hair* . . . For the Next
Generation.'" *Visibilities* 2:5 (September/October 1988):12-13.

Hansson, Eva (actor):
"Sweden: Speaking the Truth in Schools" (one-woman play about
teenage lesbian love; trans. and excerpted from Swedish feminist
bimonthly *Kvinnobulletinen,* January/February 1988).
Connexions, "Girls Speak Out!" 27 (1988):23.

<u>Hughes, Holly</u> (performance artist):
Allen, Claudia. "As You Like It: Lesbian Plays" (short descriptions
    of plays by Jane Chambers, Sarah Dreher, Claudia Allen,
    Patricia Montley, Cherríe Moraga, Eve Powell, Terry Baum,
    Carolyn Myers, Lesléa Newman, Amy Rubin, Adele
    Prandini/Sue Zemel/Jan Cole, Cappy Kotz/Phrin Pickett, Holly
    Hughes, Judy Grahn, Yvonne Zipter, and Sandra Dettelen/Kate
    Kasten). *Hot Wire* 5:3 (September 1989):38-9+.

Sawyer, Robin. "Censorship: NEA Denies Grants to Lesbians &
    Gays" (Holly Hughes, John Fleck, and Tim Miller, plus pro-gay
    straight feminist Karen Finley). *off our backs* 20:8
    (August/September 1990):5.

Hornaday, Ann. "Holly Hughes, Playing the Ironies" (performance
    artist). *Ms.: The World of Women* 1:3 (November/December
    1990):64.

<u>Johnson, Eva</u> (Aboriginal black Playwright):
Poggi, Stephanie, Jennifer Abod, Jacqui Alexander, and Evelynn
    Hammonds. "Claiming My Mothers, Exposing Aboriginal
    Consciousness to the World: an Interview with Aboriginal,
    Black Lesbian Playwright Eva Johnson." *Black/Out,* "We Are
    Family" 2:2 (Summer 1989):48-53.

<u>Katz, Judy</u> (playwright):
Spalter-Roth, Bobbie. "Waft Comes Out: the Franny Chicago Play"
    (production of Judy Katz's play about three lesbians, by
    Washington Area Feminist Theatre). *off our backs* 4:10 (October
    1974):22-3.

<u>Marchessault, Jovette</u> (Canadian playwright):
Bell, Gay. "Where Nest the Wet Hens: Interviews of Michelle
    Rossignol and Jovette Marchessault" (director and playwright of
    "The Saga of the Wet Hens"). *Broadside* (Canada) 3:4 (1982):12-
    13.

<u>Montley, Patricia</u> (playwright):

Allen, Claudia. "As You Like It: Lesbian Plays" (short descriptions
of plays by Jane Chambers, Sarah Dreher, Claudia Allen,
Patricia Montley, Cherríe Moraga, Eve Powell, Terry Baum,
Carolyn Myers, Lesléa Newman, Amy Rubin, Adele
Prandini/Sue Zemel/Jan Cole, Cappy Kotz/Phrin Pickett, Holly
Hughes, Judy Grahn, Yvonne Zipter, and Sandra Dettelen/Kate
Kasten). *Hot Wire* 5:3 (September 1989):38-9+.

<u>Moraga, Cherríe</u> (playwright):

Allen, Claudia. "As You Like It: Lesbian Plays" (short descriptions
of plays by Jane Chambers, Sarah Dreher, Claudia Allen,
Patricia Montley, Cherríe Moraga, Eve Powell, Terry Baum,
Carolyn Myers, Lesléa Newman, Amy Rubin, Adele
Prandini/Sue Zemel/Jan Cole, Cappy Kotz/Phrin Pickett, Holly
Hughes, Judy Grahn, Yvonne Zipter, and Sandra Dettelen/Kate
Kasten). *Hot Wire* 5:3 (September 1989):38-9+.

Allison, Dorothy, Tomás Almaguer, and Jackie Goldsby. "'Writing Is
the Measure of My Life . . . ': an Interview with Cherríe
Moraga" (activist, essayist, and playwright). *Out/Look* 1:4
(Winter 1989):53-7.

Yarbro-Bejarano, Yvonne. "Cherríe Moraga's *Giving Up the Ghost:*
the Representation of Female Desire." *Third Woman* 3:1-2
(1986):113-20.

<u>Mothertongue Readers' Theater</u>:

Brandt, Kate. "'What a Revelation . . . ' Ten Years of Mothertongue
Readers' Theater." *Hot Wire* 2:3 (July 1986):18-19+.

<u>Myers, Carolyn</u> (playwright):

Allen, Claudia. "As You Like It: Lesbian Plays" (short descriptions
of plays by Jane Chambers, Sarah Dreher, Claudia Allen,
Patricia Montley, Cherríe Moraga, Eve Powell, Terry Baum,
Carolyn Myers, Lesléa Newman, Amy Rubin, Adele
Prandini/Sue Zemel/Jan Cole, Cappy Kotz/Phrin Pickett, Holly
Hughes, Judy Grahn, Yvonne Zipter, and Sandra Dettelen/Kate
Kasten). *Hot Wire* 5:3 (September 1989):38-9+.

Newman, Lesléa (Jewish playwright):

Allen, Claudia. "As You Like It: Lesbian Plays" (short descriptions of plays by Jane Chambers, Sarah Dreher, Claudia Allen, Patricia Montley, Cherríe Moraga, Eve Powell, Terry Baum, Carolyn Myers, Lesléa Newman, Amy Rubin, Adele Prandini/Sue Zemel/Jan Cole, Cappy Kotz/Phrin Pickett, Holly Hughes, Judy Grahn, Yvonne Zipter, and Sandra Dettelen/Kate Kasten). *Hot Wire* 5:3 (September 1989):38-9+.

An Oral Herstory of Lesbianism:

Wolverton, Terry. "An Oral Herstory of Lesbianism" (experimental theater piece). *Frontiers,* "Lesbian History" 4:3 (Fall 1979):52-3.

The Paris Project:

Sherman, Deborah. "The Paris Project and the Art of Lesbian Relationship" (theater group which performed about Natalie Barney and her circle). *Heresies #22,* 6:2 (1987):9-13.

Powell, Eve (playwright):

Allen, Claudia. "As You Like It: Lesbian Plays" (short descriptions of plays by Jane Chambers, Sarah Dreher, Claudia Allen, Patricia Montley, Cherríe Moraga, Eve Powell, Terry Baum, Carolyn Myers, Lesléa Newman, Amy Rubin, Adele Prandini/Sue Zemel/Jan Cole, Cappy Kotz/Phrin Pickett, Holly Hughes, Judy Grahn, Yvonne Zipter, and Sandra Dettelen/Kate Kasten). *Hot Wire* 5:3 (September 1989):38-9+.

Prandini, Adele, Sue Zemel, Jan Cole, Cappy Kotz, and Phrin Pickett (playwrights):

Allen, Claudia. "As You Like It: Lesbian Plays" (short descriptions of plays by Jane Chambers, Sarah Dreher, Claudia Allen, Patricia Montley, Cherríe Moraga, Eve Powell, Terry Baum, Carolyn Myers, Lesléa Newman, Amy Rubin, Adele Prandini/Sue Zemel/Jan Cole, Cappy Kotz/Phrin Prickett, Holly Hughes, Judy Grahn, Yvonne Zipter, and Sandra Dettelen/Kate Kasten). *Hot Wire* 5:3 (September 1989):38-9+.

The Return of the Hammer:

Friends of the Hammer (Fabiola Rodriguez, Cappy Kotz, and Phrin Prickett). "*The Return of the Hammer* and Its Sequel: Lesbian Musical Theater." *Hot Wire* 5:2 (May 1989):30-1.

Rossignol, Michelle (director):

Bell, Gay. "Where Nest the Wet Hens: Interviews of Michelle Rossignol and Jovette Marchessault" (director and playwright of "The Saga of the Wet Hens"). *Broadside* (Canada) 3:4 (1982):12-13.

Rubin, Amy (playwright):

Allen, Claudia. "As You Like It: Lesbian Plays" (short descriptions of plays by Jane Chambers, Sarah Dreher, Claudia Allen, Patricia Montley, Cherríe Moraga, Eve Powell, Terry Baum, Carolyn Myers, Lesléa Newman, Amy Rubin, Adele Prandini/Sue Zemel/Jan Cole, Cappy Kotz/Phrin Pickett, Holly Hughes, Judy Grahn, Yvonne Zipter, and Sandra Dettelen/Kate Kasten). *Hot Wire* 5:3 (September 1989):38-9+.

Takarazuka Revue (Japan):

Robertson, Jennifer. "Gender-Bending in Paradise: Doing 'Female' and 'Male' in Japan" (Takarazuka Revue, all-female theater founded in 1914). *Genders* 5 (July 1989):50-69.

Tomlin, Lily (comic actor):

Kulp, Denise. "Whatever's For Us: Lesbians in Popular Culture" (television show, "My Two Loves"; film, "Desert Hearts"; theatre, Lily Tomlin's "The Search For Signs of Intelligent Life in the Universe"). *off our backs* 16:6 (June 1986):24-5.

Zipter, Yvonne (playwright):

Allen, Claudia. "As You Like It: Lesbian Plays" (short descriptions of plays by Jane Chambers, Sarah Dreher, Claudia Allen, Patricia Montley, Cherríe Moraga, Eve Powell, Terry Baum, Carolyn Myers, Lesléa Newman, Amy Rubin, Adele Prandini/Sue Zemel/Jan Cole, Cappy Kotz/Phrin Pickett, Holly Hughes, Judy Grahn, Yvonne Zipter, and Sandra Dettelen/Kate Kasten). *Hot Wire* 5:3 (September 1989):38-9+.

<u>Transsexualism</u> (see also: Androgyny; Transvestism)

Feinbloom, Deborah Heller, et al. "Lesbian/Feminist Orientation Among
Male-to-Female Transsexuals." *Journal of Homosexuality* 2:1
(Fall 1976):59-71.

Hyánková, Karla. (letter from lesbian activist about female to male
transsexuals and their relationship to the status of violence
against women in Czechoslovakia). *Connexions,* "Defy
Violence" 34 (1990):2-3.

McCauley, Elizabeth A. and Anke A. Erhardt. "Role Expectations and
Definitions: a Comparison of Female Transsexuals and
Lesbians." *Journal of Homosexuality* (Winter 1977):137-47.

<u>Transvestism</u> (see also: Androgyny; Transsexualism)

Bardsley, Barney. "The Impersonators . . . Women Who Were Musical
Halls' 'Men.'" *Spare Rib* (Great Britain) 126 (January 1983):49.

Blackwood, Evelyn. "Sexuality and Gender in Certain North American
Tribes: the Case of Cross-Gender Females." *Signs* 10:1 (Autumn
1984):27-42.

Gubar, Susan. "Blessings in Disguise: Cross-dressing as Re-dressing for
Female Modernists." *Massachusetts Review* 22:3 (Autumn
1981):477-508.

Shapiro, Susan C. "Amazons, Hermaphrodites, and Plain Monsters: the
'Masculine' Woman in English Satire and Social Criticism from
1580-1640." *Atlantis* (Canada) 13 (Fall 1987):65-76.

Zeig, Sande. "The Actor as Activator: Deconstructing Gender Through
Gesture" (lesbians in political theater). *Feminist Issues* 5:1
(1985):21-5.

Craft, Ellen (escaped slave):

Archer, Koree. "This Great Drama" (Ellen Craft, escaped slave from Georgia, and Sarah Edmonds, Canadian passing woman who spied for the Union Army). *Sinister Wisdom,* "Passing" 35 (Summer/Fall 1988):86-94.

DeLarvie, Miss Stormé (male impersonator):

Parkerson, Michelle. "Beyond Chiffon" (1950s drag show at The Jewel Box, including male impersonator Miss Stormé DeLarvie, about whom Parkerson made the film "Stormé). *Black/Out* 1:3/4 (1987):21-2.

Edmonds, Sarah (Canadian passing woman):

Archer, Koree. "This Great Drama" (Ellen Craft, escaped slave from Georgia, and Sarah Edmonds, Canadian passing woman who spied for the Union Army). *Sinister Wisdom,* "Passing" 35 (Summer/Fall 1988):86-94.

Edwards, Marion/Bill (passing woman):

Summers, Anne. "Marion/Bill Edwards" (born 1881). *Refractory Girl* (Australia), "Lesbian Issue" 5 (Summer 1974):21-2.

Evans, Edward de Lacy (Australian passing woman):

"Out in the Outback" (discovered in 1879 after three marriages to women). *Connexions,* "Global Lesbianism 2" 10 (Fall 1983):20.

Hall, Radclyffe (British writer):

Newton, Esther. "The Mythic Mannish Lesbian: Radclyffe Hall and the New Woman." *Signs,* "The Lesbian Issue" 9:4 (Summer 1984):557-75.

Vampires

Gomez, Jewelle. "Re-Casting the Mythology: Writing Vampire Fiction." *Hot Wire* 4:1 (November 1987):42-3+.

Williamson, Judith. "In the Pink" (gay and lesbian films at London's Tyneside Festival, including *The Lesbian Vampire on Film, Underground Canada,* and *Novembermoon* about two lesbians during the Nazi occupation of France). *New Statesman* 114 (October 9, 1987):22-3.

Daughters of Darkness (film):
Zimmerman, Bonnie. "*Daughters of Darkness:* Lesbian Vampires." *Jump Cut* 24-5 (March 1981):23-4.

Nightwood (novel):
Levine, Nancy J. "'I've Always Suffered from Sirens': the Cinema and Djuna Barnes' *Nightwood.*" *Women's Studies: an Interdisciplinary Journal* 16:3-4 (1989):271-81.

Weiss, Andrea (filmmaker):
Collis, Rose. "Blood Sisters" (interview with Andrea Weiss about her film *Blood and Roses: Under the Spell of the Lesbian Vampire*). *Spare Rib* (Great Britain) 183 (October 1987):40-1.

Video (see Film and Video; Television)

Violence Against Lesbians and Gay Men (see also: The Holocaust; Homophobia/Heterosexism; Sexual Harassment; Violence Against Women; Violence Among Lesbians)

Comstock, Gary David. "Victims of Anti-Gay/Lesbian Violence." *Journal of Interpersonal Violence* 4:1 (March 1989):101-6.

DancingFire, Laura Rose. "The Love That Dared Not Speak Its Name" (speech delivered at the 1988 March for Justice, Louisville, Kentucky). *Common Lives/Lesbian Lives* 34 (Spring 1990):87-90.

"D.C. to Form Pink Panthers" (lesbian/gay street patrol, Washington D.C.). *off our backs* 20:9 (October 1990):5.

Herek, G.M. "Hate Crimes Against Lesbians and Gays -- Issues for Research and Policy." *American Psychologist* 44:6 (1989):948-55.

Hunter, Joyce. "Violence Against Lesbian and Gay Male Youths" (especially people of color, and related suicide attempts). *Journal of Interpersonal Violence* 5:3 (1990):295-300.

Lamson, Carrie. "Lesbian Bashing" (news brief about incident in Lynn, Massachusetts). *off our backs* 16:1 (January 1986):14.

McDonald, Tracy. "Gay Bashing an Attack on Civil Rights" (Massachusetts State Attorney General's office brief). *off our backs* 17:5 (May 1987):16.

McKnight, J. "Lesbian Murder." *off our backs* 15:4 (April 1985):7.

MacAuley, Donna, Laurie Chesley, and Janice Ristock. "Coming Out About Violence." *Broadside* (Canada) 10:5 (August/September 1989):14+.

Martin, A. Damien and Emery S. Hetrick. "The Stigmatization of the Gay and Lesbian Adolescent." *Journal of Homosexuality,* "Psychopathology and Psychotherapy in Homosexuality" 15:1/2 (1988):163-84.

"Mexican Gays Attacked" (at rally held by the Comité de Lesbianas y Homosexuales en Apoyo a Rosario Ibarra in Mexico City, March 1982). *off our backs* 12:6 (June 1982):10.

"NGLTF Violence Report" (National Gay and Lesbian Task Force report on 42% increase in reports on anti-gay/lesbian violence between 1986 and 1987). *off our backs* 18:7 (July 1988):5.

Oliver, Maureen. "Lesbians Attacked in Stockholm" (European bus Tour Against British Section (Clause) 28). *Spare Rib* (Great Britain) 198 (February 1989):45-6.

"OUTRAGE Protests Anti-Gay Murders" (in England; direct action group modeled after U.S. AIDS Coalition to Unleash Power (ACT-UP)). *Spare Rib* (Great Britain) 216 (September 1990):44.

Ratterman, Debra. "Lesbians Beaten" (by ex-boyfriend of one of the two). *off our backs* 18:11 (December 1988):3.

Rothblum, Esther D. "Depression Among Lesbians: an Invisible and Unresearched Phenomenon." *Journal of Gay & Lesbian Psychotherapy* 1:3 (1990):67-87.

Stevens, Wendy. "Lady, What You Need is a Good PoliceMAN" (meeting between lesbian and gay community members and Washington, D.C. police officials about anti-gay violence). *off our backs* 8:10 (November 1978):3.

------. "That's the Way the Bar Bounces" (lesbians assaulted outside of Washington D.C. lesbian bar). *off our backs* 8:7 (July 1978):8.

Tallmer, Abby. "Violence Against Lesbians." *Sojourner* 9:6 (February 1984):11+.

"Violence Vs. Gays" (in Washington, D.C.). *off our backs* 9:2 (February 1979):8.

Wertheimer, David M. "Treatment and Service Interventions for Lesbian and Gay Male Crime Victims." *Journal of Interpersonal Violence* 5:3 (1990):384-400.

Zia, Helen. "Double Jeopardy, Double Courage: Fighting Straight Hate." *Ms.,* "Everyday Violence Against Women" 1:2 (September/October 1990):47.

Brenner, Claudia (injured while camping with her lover, Rebecca Wight, who was murdered):
"Homophobe Gets Life in Prison." *New Directions for Women* 18:2 (March/April 1989):6.

DAR. "Lesbian Murdered." *off our backs* 18:8 (August-September 1988):5.

<u>Hate Crimes Statistics Act</u>:
AM. "Anti-Gay Violence Bill." *off our backs* 17:10 (November 1987):3; note: cover reads 17:9.

DAR. "Hate Crimes Bill." *off our backs* 18:8 (August-September 1988):5.

Maguire, Amanda. "Anti-Gay Violence Bill." *off our backs* 17:10 (May 1987):3.

<u>Milk, Harvey</u> (assassinated San Francisco Supervisor):
CAD. "Blows Struck -- Gay Struggle Continues." *off our backs* 9:1 (January 1979):10.

Kornegger, Peggy. "The Meaning of Milk's Murder for Women." *off our backs* 9:1 (January 1979):10.

<u>Riethmiller, Stephanie</u> (kidnapped and raped, allegedly with her family's knowledge, in an attempt to "deprogram" her lesbianism):
CAD. "Lesbian 'Deprogrammed.'" *off our backs* 11:11 (December 1981):9.

"Love with an Improper Stranger." *Time* 119 (May 3, 1982):22.

Raskin, Richard. "The 'Deprogramming' of Stephanie Riethmiller." *Ms.* 11:3 (September 1982):19.

<u>Wight, Rebecca</u> (lesbian murdered while camping with her lover, Claudia Brenner, who was injured):
"Homophobe Gets Life in Prison." *New Directions for Women* 18:2 (March/April 1989):6.

DAR. "Lesbian Murdered." *off our backs* 18:8 (August-September 1988):5.

<u>Violence Against Women</u> (see also: Child Abuse; Incest;
Homophobia/Heterosexism; Sexual Harassment; Violence
Against Lesbians and Gay Men; Violence Among Lesbians)

Allen, Jeffner. "Looking at Our Blood: a Lesbian Response to Men's
Terrorization of Women" ("lesbian violence" (Monique Wittig)
as pro-freedom, anti-destruction). *Trivia* 4 (Spring 1984):11-30.

Dejanikus, Tacie. "NY Tribunal: Crimes Versus Women" (The New York
Tribunal on Crimes Against Women, February 1976;
simultaneous tribunals held around the U.S., to coincide with the
International Tribunal on Crimes Against Women in Europe).
off our backs 6:2 (April 1976):8.

Desmoines, Harriet. "Notes for a Magazine II" (founding concepts for
Sinister Wisdom; discusses politically left revolutionary politics,
racism, and classism). *Sinister Wisdom* 1:1 (Summer 1976):27-
34.

Garthwaite, Al. "English WAVAW [Women Against Violence Against
Women] Conference: Pressure to Be Straight" (London). *off our
backs* 12:2 (February 1982):2-3.

Grazia. "The Tribunal of Crimes Against Women" (International Tribunal
of Crimes Against Women, Brussels, Belgium, March 1976;
including official and unofficial lesbian workshops). *off our
backs* 6:3 (May 1976):9.

Gundlach, Ralph H. "Sexual Molestation and Rape Reported by
Homosexual and Heterosexual Women." *Journal of
Homosexuality* 2:4 (Summer 1977):367-84.

Hyánková, Karla. (letter from lesbian activist about female to male
transsexuals and their relationship to the status of violence
against women in Czechoslovakia). *Connexions,* "Defy
Violence" 34 (1990):2-3.

Kaye(/Kantrowitz), Melanie. "Women and Violence" (implications of
fighting back). *Sinister Wisdom* 9 (Spring 1979):75-9.

Linden, Robin Ruth. "Notes on Age, Rage and Language." *Sinister Wisdom,* "On Being Old and Age" 10 (Summer 1979):29-30.

Lootens, Tricia. "Homophobia: Thin End of Antifeminist Wedge" (Lesbian Caucus meeting of the Pulling Together: Being with Children in Shelter Conference, Washington, D.C., December 1981). *off our backs* 12:3 (March 1982):30.

------. "Lesbian-Baiting in the Women's Movement" (statement by lesbians in the battered women's shelter movement, at the Pulling Together: Being with Children in Shelter Conference, Washington, D.C., December 1981). *off our backs* 12:3 (March 1982):17.

McNeil, Sarah. "English WAVAW [Women Against Violence Against Women] Conference: Female Sexuality." (London). *off our backs* 12:2 (February 1982):2-3.

Max, J. "A Remedy for Frustration." *Lesbian Ethics* 2:2 (Fall 1986):83.

"NCADV Meets" (National Coalition Against Domestic Violence, Seattle, Washington, July 1988; includes section on lesbian battering). *off our backs* 18:9 (October 1988):1-3+.

Nicarthy, Ginny. "NCADV Meets [part 2]" (National Coalition Against Domestic Violence, July 1988, Seattle; includes section on lesbian battering). *off our backs* 18:10 (November 1988):16-17.

Orzek, Ann M. "The Lesbian Victim of Sexual Assault: Special Considerations for the Mental Health Professional." *Women & Therapy,* "Lesbianism: Affirming Nontraditional Roles" 8:1/2 (1989):107-17.

Salik, Peggy. "Just a Woman" (personal narrative of a police officer). *Common Lives/Lesbian Lives* 11 (Spring 1984):72-9.

André, Marie (activist and gang rape survivor):
"France: To Recognize Rape as a Political Crime" (trans. from *Elles Voient Rouge,* French feminist periodical, No.3, May 1980). *Connexions,* "Women Organizing Against Violence" 1 (Summer 1981):26-7.

Culver, Casse (musician):
Moira, Fran. "Casse Culver: 'Integrated Separatism'" (interview, including conversation about violence against women). *off our backs* 4:11 (November 1974):12-13.

Shame (Australian film):
Harper, Jorjet. "The Women's Action/Adventure Film: 'Shame.' *Hot Wire* 5:2 (May 1989):24-5.

Windows (film):
Beverley, Brooke, and Wendy Stevens. "Why Protest Windows?" (movie about a psychotic lesbian who hires a man to rape a straight woman). *off our backs* 10:4 (April 1980):9+.

CAD. "Gays and Media" (*Windows, Cruising, A Comedy in Six Unnatural Acts*). *off our backs* 10:6 (June 1980):9.

Stevens, Lynne. "The Window: a Look Inside" (protest against "Windows," movie about a psychotic lesbian who hires a man to rape a straight woman). *off our backs* 10:3 (March 1980):16-17.

Violence Among Lesbians

Bell, Ellen. "Britain: Women Abusing Women" (from *Trouble & Strife,* British feminist quarterly, 1989). *Connexions,* "Defy Violence" 34 (1990):28-30.

Brand, P. and A. Kidd. "Frequency of Physical Aggression in Heterosexual and Female Homosexual Dyads." *Psychological Reports* 59 (1986):1307-13.

Card, Claudia. "Defusing the Bomb: Lesbian Ethics and Horizontal Violence" (builds on ideas of "attending" and "community" in Sarah Lucia Hoagland's book *Lesbian Ethics,* to discuss lesbian battering). *Lesbian Ethics* 3:3 (Summer 1989):91-100.

Davis, Karen. "Violence Against Women by Women." *off our backs* 14:6 (June 1984):4.

Edgington, Amy. "Lesbian Battering Conference" (June 1988, Little Rock, Arkansas). *off our backs* 18:10 (November 1988):8-9+.

Evans, Lee and Shelley Bannister. "Lesbian Violence, Lesbian Victims: How to Identify Battering in Relationships." *Lesbian Ethics* 4:1 (Spring 1990):52-65.

Hammond, Nancy. "Lesbian Victims of Relationship Violence." *Women & Therapy,* "Lesbianism: Affirming Nontraditional Roles" 8:1/2 (1989):89-105.

Hirshorn, H. "The Tip of the Iceberg: Lesbian Battering." *Womanews* (June 1984):5.

Hurley, Kate. "Love as Addiction: a Story of Battering." *Common Lives/Lesbian Lives* 8 (Summer 1983):83-7.

Kanuha, Valli. "Compounding the Triple Jeopardy: Battering in Lesbian of Color Relationships." *Women & Therapy,* "Diversity and Complexity in Feminist Therapy: Part I" 9:1/2 (1990):169-84.

LAW. "Battered Women's Conference" (National Coalition Against Domestic Violence Conference, Washington, D.C., February 1980; including section on battered lesbians). *off our backs* 10:4 (April 1980):4.

Leeder, Elaine. "Enmeshed In Pain: Counselling the Lesbian Battering Couple." *Women & Therapy* 7:1 (1988):81-99.

MacAuley, Donna, Laurie Chesley, and Janice Ristock. "Coming Out
     About Violence." *Broadside* (Canada) 10:5 (August/September
     1989):14+.

Marie, Susan. "Lesbian Battering: an Inside View" (letter). *Victimology*
     9:1 (Winter 1984):16.

Morrow, S.L. and D.M. Hawxhurst. "Lesbian Partner Abuse --
     Implications for Therapists." *Journal of Counseling and
     Development,* "Gay, Lesbian, and Bisexual Issues in
     Counseling" 68:1 (September-October 1989):58-62.

"NCADV Meets" (National Coalition Against Domestic Violence, July
     1988, Seattle; includes section on lesbian battering). *off our
     backs* 18:9 (October 1988):1-3+.

Nicarthy, Ginny. "NCADV Meets [part 2]" (National Coalition Against
     Domestic Violence, Seattle, Washington, July 1988; includes
     section on lesbian battering). *off our backs* 18:10 (November
     1988):16-17.

Renzetti, C.M. "Building a Second Closet: Third Party Responses to
     Victims of Lesbian Partner Abuse." *Family Relations* 38:2
     (April 1989):157-63.

Renzetti, Claire M. "Violence in Lesbian Relationships: a Preliminary
     Analysis of Causal Factors." *Journal of Interpersonal Violence*
     3:4 (1988):381-99.

Schilit, Rebecca, Gwat-Yong Lie, and Marilyn Montagne. "Substance
     Use as a Correlate of Violence in Intimate Lesbian
     Relationships." *Journal of Homosexuality* 19:3 (1990):51-66.

Shadle, V. "Women Hurting Women." *Ithaca Times* (August 14-20,
     1986):6.

Silver, Quick. "They Call It Battery -- (or -- Baby It Hurts Too Much to
     Talk About With You)." *Common Lives/Lesbian Lives* 18
     (Winter 1985):51-8.

"Statement on Lesbian Battering and Sexual Violence: To the Lesbian Nation" (statement distributed by the lesbian caucus of the National Coalition Against Domestic Violence, developed by the caucus at the NCADV conference in Washington, D.C., September 1983). *off our backs* 14:1 (January 1984):15.

Waterman, Caroline K., Lori J. Dawson, and Michael J. Bologna. "Sexual Coercion in Gay Male and Lesbian Relationships: Predictors and Implications for Support Services." *Journal of Sex Research* 26:1 (February 1989):118-24.

Work (see also: Class and Classism; Economics; Education: Lesbians in Academe/Lesbians in the Classroom; Legal Issues; Prostitution; Sexual Harassment)

Agger, Ellen and Francie Wyland. "Lesbian Mothers Fight Back: Wages Due Lesbians." *Quest* 5:1 (Spring 1979):57-62.

Alibrando, Julie. "Up Lambda" (lesbian files sex discrimination complaint against gay bookstore in Washington, D.C. after she was fired and her job was given to a man). *off our backs* 6:9 (December 1976):12.

Allen, Jeffner. "Lesbian Economics." *Trivia* 8 (Winter 1986):37-53.

Batchelder, Eleanor Olds and Linda Nathan Marks. "Creating Alternatives: a Survey of Women's Projects." *Heresies #7,* "Women Working Together" 2:3 (Spring 1979):97-127.

Beaven, Betsey, Selma Miriam, Pat Shea, and Samn Stockwell. "Bloodroot: Four Views of One Women's Business" (restaurant and bookstore, Bridgeport, Connecticut). *Heresies #7,* "Women Working Together" 2:3 (Spring 1979):64-9.

Bennett, Linda. "Greensboro Quits Discriminating" (against lesbians and gay men in the work place; North Carolina). *off our backs* 20:1 (January 1990):6.

Benton, Sarah. "Gay Workers Acknowledge Debt to Women's Movement" (first national Gay Workers' Conference, Leeds, England, May 1974). *Spare Rib* (Great Britain) 37 (July 1975):22.

The Bloodroot Collective. "Bloodroot: Brewing Visions" (restaurant and bookstore in Bridgeport, Connecticut). *Lesbian Ethics* 3:1 (Spring 1988):3-22.

CAD. "Gay . . . Antichrists" (news briefs; lesbian police officer fired in Washington, D.C.). *off our backs* 10:5 (May 1980):9.

Crow, Margie, Margaret DeVoe, and Fran Moira. "Revolution Over a Cup of Coffee" (interview with lesbians planning to open a women-only coffeehouse in Washington, D.C.). *off our backs* 5:2 (February 1975):2-3.

DancingFire, Laura Rose. "On Lawyering, Passing and Pornography." *Sinister Wisdom,* "Passing" 35 (Summer/Fall 1988):72-4.

FE. "Williams-Sonoma Sued for Firing Lesbians of Color." *off our backs* 20:3 (March 1990):17.

Freespirit, Judy. "Lament of the Unemployed Lesbian: a (Bad) Mood Piece." *Common Lives/Lesbian Lives* 11 (Spring 1984):61-4.

"Gays on the Job" (alliances formed between San Francisco Bay Area Gay Liberation Labor Committee and local unions). *off our backs* 6:10 (January 1977):5.

Gelwick, Beverly Prosser, et al. "Life-Styles of 6 Professional Women Engaged in College Student Development Careers: the Lesbian Professional." *Journal of College Student Personnel* 25:5 (September 1984):419-21.

Genge, Susan. "Sexual Orientation and Union Protection." *Resources for Feminist Research* (Canada), "Women and Trade Unions" 10:2 (July 1981):28-9.

Guse, C.W. "The Music Industry Conference: Third Annual Gathering at NWMF" (National Women's Music Festival, Bloomington, Indiana). *Hot Wire* 2:1 (November 1985):38-9.

Hall, Marny. "The Lesbian Corporate Experience." *Journal of Homosexuality,* "Historical, Literary, and Erotic Aspects of Lesbianism" 12:3/4 (May 1986):59-76.

Heatherly, Gail E. "Gay and Lesbian Rights: Employment Discrimination." *Annual Survey of American Law* (1985):901-2.

Hedgpeth, Judith M. "Employment Discrimination Law and the Rights of Gay Persons." *Journal of Homosexuality,* "Homosexuality and the Law" 5:1-2 (Fall 1979-Winter 1980):67-78.

Hetherington, C. and A. Orzek. "Career Counseling and Life Planning with Lesbian Women." *Journal of Counseling and Development,* "Gay, Lesbian, and Bisexual Issues in Counseling" 68:1 (September-October 1989):52-7.

"'I Don't Make Love, I Work'" (anonymous article by a Swiss lesbian who works as a heterosexual prostitute; trans. from *CLIT 007,* Swiss lesbian quarterly, September 1982). *Connexions,* "Women and Prostitution" 12 (Spring 1984):28.

"India: Lesbian Police" (fired and reinstated due to public protest). *off our backs* 18:9 (October 1988):10.

"Insurance for Lover Denied" (to a lesbian employed by the State of Wisconsin). *off our backs* 18:9 (October 1988):11.

Journal of Homosexuality, "Lesbians Over 60 Speak for Themselves," vol. 16, nos. 3/4, 1988.

Kelly, Janis. "Nearly Everybody Loses" (sex discrimination complaint against Lambda Rising gay bookstore in Washington, D.C.). *off our backs* 6:10 (January 1977):18.

Krebs, Paula. "Gay Workers Unionize" (staff of the Gay and Lesbian
    Community Services Center, Los Angeles, California). *off our
    backs* 14:3 (March 1984):19.

Leonard, A.S. "Watkins v. United-States Army and the Employment
    Rights of Lesbians and Gay Men." *Labor Law Journal* 40:7
    (1989):438-45.

Leonard, Robin and Martin P. Levine. "Discrimination Against Lesbians
    in the Workforce." *Signs,* "The Lesbian Issue" 9:4 (Summer
    1984):700-10.

"Lesbian Self-Disclosure in the Workplace" (report on paper given by
    Sharon Dewey at the National Women's Studies Association
    conference, June 1989, Towson State University, Maryland). *off
    our backs* 19:8 (August-September 1989):10.

"Lesbians Sue Boss" (for being forced to quit because of a hostile work
    environment). *off our backs* 6:7 (October 1976):5.

Lynn (told to Judith McDaniel). "Lesbian Cop: One Woman's Story."
    Common Lives/Lesbian Lives 9 (Fall 1983):90-103.

Miller, Rosalie J. "'Women's' Professions: the Journey of a
    Lesbian/Feminist." *Visibilities* 4:2 (March/April 1990):4-8.

"NGTF Attacks Gov't Order" (National Gay Task Force calls for end to
    executive order restricting government employment of lesbians
    and gays). *off our backs* 13:6 (June 1983):15.

Poliakoff, Phaye. "The Pebble Lounge: Oral Histories of Go-Go
    Dancers." *Frontiers* 7:1 (1983):56-60.

Poppe, Terri. "Professionalism: To What Degree?" (commentary on the
    first National Gay Health Conference, Washington, D.C., May
    1978). *off our backs* 8:7 (July 1978):22.

Ratterman, Debbie. "Gay Rights Order" (state employment anti-discrimination law in Oregon). *off our backs* 17:10 (November 1987):3.

Rich, Adrienne. "Conditions for Work: the Common World of Women." *Heresies #3,* "Lesbian Art and Artists" 1:3 (Fall 1977):52-6.

Rickgarn, Ralph L. "Developing Support Systems for Gay and Lesbian Staff Members." *Journal of College and University Student Housing* 14:1 (Summer 1984):32-6.

Rosenblatt, Joy and Toni L. Armstrong. "Women's Coffeehouses: Operating Your Local Goldmine." *Hot Wire* 1:3 (July 1985):44-7.

Ross, Becki. "Heterosexuals Only Need Apply: the Secretary of State's Regulation of Lesbian Existence." *Resources for Feminist Research* (Canada), "Feminist Perspectives on the Canadian State/Perspectives Féministes sur l'État Canadien" 17:3 (September 1988):35-8.

Salik, Peggy. "Just a Woman" (personal narrative of a police officer). *Common Lives/Lesbian Lives* 11 (Spring 1984):72-9.

Schmitz, T.J. "Career Counseling Implications with the Gay and Lesbian Community." *Journal of Employment Counseling* 25:2 (1988):51-6.

Schneider, Margaret S. "The Office Affair: Myth and Reality for Heterosexual and Lesbian Women Workers." *Sociological Perspectives* 27:4 (1984):443-64.

Shachar, Sandra A. and Lucia A. Gilbert. "Working Lesbians: Role Conflicts and Coping Strategies." *Psychology of Women Quarterly* 7 (Spring 1983):244-56.

Valeska, Lucia. "Double Trouble for Lesbians in the Workforce" (testimony to the New York City Commission on the Status of Women, given by the co-executive director of the National Gay Task Force). *New Directions for Women* 10:1 (January/February 1981):11.

Weston, Kathleen M. and Lisa B. Rofel. "Sexuality, Class, and Conflict in a Lesbian Workplace." *Signs,* "The Lesbian Issue" 9:4 (Summer 1984):623-46.

Wise, Donna L. "Challenging Sexual Preference Discrimination in Private Employment." *Ohio State Law Journal* 41:2 (Fall 1980):501-31.

Wolverton, Terry. "Lesbian Art Project" (Natalie Barney Art Collective, Los Angeles, California). *Heresies #7,* "Women Working Together" 2:3 (Spring 1979):14-19.

Zalsberg, Kitty. "Hairdressing" (in London's East End; interview with Trisha Ziff). *Spare Rib* (Great Britain) 93 (April 1980):6-8.

Andrews, Karen (librarian fighting for employee spousal benefits in Canada):
"Canada: I Will Not Be Shelved" (interview; from Canadian monthly *Rites,* March 1988). *Connexions,* "Lesbian Activism" 29 (1989):18-20.

Butcher, Linda (welder):
Tabor, Martha. "Linda Butcher: Striking While the Iron's Hot." *off our backs* (February 1979):14-15+.

Canaan, Andrea Ruth (African-American lesbian, fired for coming out):
Robins, Becky. "Coming Out at Work." *off our backs* 10:8 (August-September 1980):20; note: cover reads 10:7.

Fier, Debbie (musician):
Armstrong, Toni L. "Making Our Dreams Our Jobs: Making Ends
    Meet Through Music" (Teresa Trull, Robin Flower, Ruth
    Pelham, Debbie Fier, Betty MacDonald, Musica Femina,
    Rhiannon, Jean Fineberg). *Hot Wire* 3:2 (March 1987):34-9.

Fineberg, Jean (musician):
Armstrong, Toni L. "Making Our Dreams Our Jobs: Making Ends
    Meet Through Music" (Teresa Trull, Robin Flower, Ruth
    Pelham, Debbie Fier, Betty MacDonald, Musica Femina,
    Rhiannon, Jean Fineberg). *Hot Wire* 3:2 (March 1987):34-9.

Flower, Robin (musician):
Armstrong, Toni L. "Making Our Dreams Our Jobs: Making Ends
    Meet Through Music" (Teresa Trull, Robin Flower, Ruth
    Pelham, Debbie Fier, Betty MacDonald, Musica Femina,
    Rhiannon, Jean Fineberg). *Hot Wire* 3:2 (March 1987):34-9.

Hopkins, Lea (African American activist and former Playboy bunny):
Ebert, Alan. "Lea Hopkins: Just Different." *Essence* 10:12 (April
    1980):88-9+.

MacDonald, Betty (musician):
Armstrong, Toni L. "Making Our Dreams Our Jobs: Making Ends
    Meet Through Music" (Teresa Trull, Robin Flower, Ruth
    Pelham, Debbie Fier, Betty MacDonald, Musica Femina,
    Rhiannon, Jean Fineberg). *Hot Wire* 3:2 (March 1987):34-9.

Musica Femina (music group):
Armstrong, Toni L. "Making Our Dreams Our Jobs: Making Ends
    Meet Through Music" (Teresa Trull, Robin Flower, Ruth
    Pelham, Debbie Fier, Betty MacDonald, Musica Femina,
    Rhiannon, Jean Fineberg). *Hot Wire* 3:2 (March 1987):34-9.

Pelham, Ruth (musician):
Armstrong, Toni L. "Making Our Dreams Our Jobs: Making Ends
    Meet Through Music" (Teresa Trull, Robin Flower, Ruth
    Pelham, Debbie Fier, Betty MacDonald, Musica Femina,
    Rhiannon, Jean Fineberg). *Hot Wire* 3:2 (March 1987):34-9.

<u>Rhiannon</u> (musician):
Armstrong, Toni L. "Making Our Dreams Our Jobs: Making Ends
Meet Through Music" (Teresa Trull, Robin Flower, Ruth
Pelham, Debbie Fier, Betty MacDonald, Musica Femina,
Rhiannon, Jean Fineberg). *Hot Wire* 3:2 (March 1987):34-9.

<u>Shaw, Anna Howard</u> (equal work opportunity activist and suffragist):
Finn, Barbara R. "Anna Howard Shaw and Women's Work" (her
relationship, not necessarily sexual, with Lucy Anthony).
Frontiers, "Lesbian History" 4:3 (Fall 1979):21-5.

<u>Trull, Teresa</u> (musician):
Armstrong, Toni L. "Making Our Dreams Our Jobs: Making Ends
Meet Through Music" (Teresa Trull, Robin Flower, Ruth
Pelham, Debbie Fier, Betty MacDonald, Musica Femina,
Rhiannon, Jean Fineberg). *Hot Wire* 3:2 (March 1987):34-9.

<u>Youth</u> (see Adolescent Lesbians; Child Abuse; Children of Lesbians;
Incest)

Special Issues of Journals

Belles Lettres: a Review of Books, "Lesbian Writers," vol. 2, no. 4,
March/April 1987.

Black Scholar, "Black Women and Feminism," vol. 16, no. 2,
March/April 1985.

Black/Out, "Tenth Anniversary Edition: NCBLG Celebrates
Homecoming" (National Coalition of Black Lesbians and Gays),
vol. 2, no. 1, Fall 1988.

Canadian Fiction Magazine, Canada, on Jane Rule, no. 23, 1976.

Canadian Theatre Review, Canada, "Homosexuality and the Theatre"
(not specifically about lesbians; written by gay men), no. 12,
Fall 1976.

Canadian Woman Studies/Les Cahiers de la Femme, Canada, "Sexuality and Symbol/*Symbolisme et Sexualité*," vol. 3, no. 2, 1981.

Christianity and Crisis, "Homosexuality," vol. 37, nos. 9 & 10, May 30 & June 13, 1977.

Connexions: an International Women's Quarterly, "Global Lesbianism," no. 3, January 1982.

------, "Global Lesbianism 2," no. 10, Fall 1983.

------, "Lesbian Activism," no. 29, 1989.

Differences, "Sexuality in Greek and Roman Society," vol. 2, no. 1, Spring 1990.

Feminist Review, Great Britain, "Sexuality," no. 11, Summer 1982.

------, "Perverse Politics: Lesbian Issues," no. 34, Spring 1990.

Fireweed: a Feminist Quarterly, Canada, "Lesbiantics," no. 13, 1982.

------, "Lesbiantics," no. 28, Spring 1989.

Frontiers: a Journal of Women's Studies, "Lesbian History," vol. 4, no. 3, Fall 1979.

Heresies: a Feminist Publication on Art and Politics #3, "Lesbian Art and Artists," vol. 1, no. 3, Fall 1977.

------, *#12* "The Sex Issue," vol. 3, no. 4, 1981.

Interracial Books for Children Bulletin, "Homophobia and Education: How to Deal with Name-Calling," vol. 14, nos. 3/4, 1983.

Journal of Counseling and Development, "Gay, Lesbian, and Bisexual Issues in Counseling," vol. 68, no. 1, September-October 1989.

Journal of Homosexuality, "Research on the Violations of Civil Liberties of Homosexual Men and Women," vol. 2, no. 4, Summer 1977.

------, "Homosexuality and the Law," vol. 5, nos. 1-2, Fall 1979-Winter 1980.

------, "Homosexuality and Psychotherapy -- a Practitioner's Handbook of Affirmative Models," vol. 7, nos. 2/3, Winter/Spring 1982.

------, "Bisexual and Homosexual Identities: Critical Theoretical Issues," vol. 9, nos. 2/3, Winter 1983/Spring 1984.

------, "Homophobia: an Overview," vol. 10, nos. 1/2, Fall 1984.

------, "Controversy Over the Bisexual and Homosexual Identities: Commentaries and Reactions," vol. 10, nos. 3/4, Winter 1984.

------, "Bisexualities: Theory and Research," vol. 11, nos. 1/2, Spring 1985.

------, "Anthropology and Homosexual Behavior," vol. 11, nos. 3/4, Summer 1985.

------, "Interdisciplinary Research on Homosexuality in the Netherlands," vol. 13, nos. 2/3, Winter 1986/Spring 1987.

------, "Psychotherapy with Homosexual Men and Women: Integrated Identity Approaches for Clinical Practice," vol. 14, nos. 1/2, 1987.

------, "Lesbians Over 60 Speak for Themselves," vol. 16, nos. 3/4, 1988.

------, "Gay and Lesbian Youth: Part I," vol. 17, nos. 1/2, 1989.

------, "Gay and Lesbian Youth: Part II," vol. 17, nos. 3/4, 1989.

------, "Homosexuality and the Family," vol. 18, nos. 1/2, 1989.

------, "Homosexuality and Religion," vol. 18, nos. 3/4, 1989/1990.

Journal of Social Issues, "Psychology and the Gay Community," vol. 34, no. 3, 1978.

Jump Cut, "Lesbians and Film," nos. 24/5, March 1981.

Maenad, "The Lesbian/Heterosexual Split," vol. 2, no. 2, Winter 1982.

Margins, "Lesbian Feminist Writing and Publishing," no. 23, August 1975.

New York University Review of Law & Social Change, "Symposium: Sex, Politics and the Law; Lesbians and Gay Men Take the Offensive," vol. 14, no. 4, Fall 1986.

off our backs, "Women and Loving: 1," vol. 2, no. 4, December 1971.

------, "Women and Loving: 2," vol. 2, no. 5, January 1972.

------, on the feminist pornography debates, vol. 15, no. 6, June 1985.

Phi Delta Kappan, "The Homosexual Teacher," vol. 59, no. 2, October 1977.

Quest, "Organizers' Dialogue: Lesbian Mothers Fight Back," vol. 5, Summer 1979.

Radical Teacher, on African-American women, no. 17, November 1980.

------, "Gay and Lesbian Studies," no. 24, no date: c.1983.

Refractory Girl, Australia, "Lesbian Issue" (includes extensive bibliography of pre-1970s fiction/nonfiction books and artwork), no. 5, Summer 1974.

RFR/DRF -- Resources for Feminist Research/Documentation sur le Recherche Féministe (cited throughout as *Resources for Feminist Research*), Canada, "The Lesbian Issue/Etre Lesbienne," vol. 12, no. 1, March/mars 1983.

------, "Confronting Heterosexuality/Confronter l'hétérosexualité," vol. 19, nos. 3&4, September/December 1990.

RT: a Journal of Radical Therapy, "Lesbians in Therapy," vol. 4, no. 8, 1974.

Salmagundi: a Quarterly of the Humanities and Social Sciences, "Homosexuality: Sacrilege, Vision, Politics," nos. 58-59, Fall 1982-Winter 1983.

Shmate: a Journal of Progressive Jewish Thought, "Lesbian and Gay Jews," vol. 1, no. 2, June/July 1982.

Signs, "Women -- Sex and Sexuality," vol. 5, no. 4, Summer 1980.

------, "The Lesbian Issue," vol. 9, no. 4, Summer 1984.

Sinister Wisdom, Berkeley, California, "Lesbian Writing and Publishing," vol. 1, no. 2, Fall 1976.

------, "On Being Old & Age," no. 10, Summer 1979.

------, "Lesbian Writing and Publishing," no. 13, Spring 1980.

------, "Lesbianism: Sexuality and Power; The Patriarchy: Violence and Pornography," no. 15, Fall 1980.

------, "A Gathering of Spirit" (Native American women), nos. 22/3, 1983.

------, "The Tribe of Dina: a Jewish Women's Anthology," nos. 29/30, 1986/5746.

------, "Lesbian Visions, Fantasy, Science Fiction," no. 34, Spring 1988.

------, "Passing," no. 35, Summer/Fall 1988.

------, "With an Emphasis on Lesbian Theory," no. 37, Spring 1989.

------, "On Disability," no. 39, Winter 1989-90.

------, "On Friendship," no. 40, Spring 1990.

------, "il viaggio delle donne" (Italian-American Issue), no. 41, Summer/Fall 1990.

------, "Lesbian Voices," no. 42, Winter 1990/1991.

Textual Practice, "Lesbian and Gay Cultures: Theories and Texts," vol. 4, no. 2, Summer 1990.

VLASTA: Révue des Fictions Utopies Amazoniennes, France, "Spécial: Monique Wittig," no. 4.

WIN: Peace and Freedom Through Nonviolent Action, "Lesbian Culture," vol. 11, no. 22, June 26, 1975.

Women: a Journal of Liberation, "Women Loving Women," vol. 5, no. 2, 1977.

Women & Therapy: a Feminist Quarterly, "Therapeutic Issues with Lesbian Clients," vol. 1, no. 4, Winter 1982.

------, "Lesbianism: Affirming Nontraditional Roles," vol. 8, nos. 1/2, 1989; (note: cover reads 1988).

Women's Annual, "Lesbians" (overview of publications on lesbians in 1983-84, with bibliography, by historian Judith Schwarz), no. 4, 1983-84.

Women's Studies, on Willa Cather, vol. 11, no. 3, 1984.